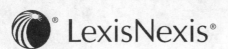

FEDERAL RULES OF COURT

2015 EDITION

(Includes amendments through January 26, 2015)

Prepared by the Editorial Staff of the Publisher

QUESTIONS ABOUT THIS PUBLICATION?

For CUSTOMER SERVICE ASSISTANCE concerning replacement pages, shipments, billing, reprint permission, or other matters,

please call Customer Service Department at 800-833-9844
email *customer.support@lexisnexis.com*
or visit our interactive customer service website at *www.lexisnexis.com/printcdsc*

For EDITORIAL **content questions** concerning this publication,

please email: *LLP.CLP@lexisnexis.com*

For **information on other LEXISNEXIS MATTHEW BENDER publications,**

please call us at 800-223-1940
or visit our online bookstore at *www.lexisnexis.com/bookstore*

ISBN: 978-1-63282-389-2

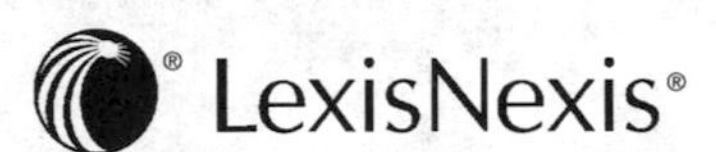

Matthew Bender & Company, Inc.
Editorial Offices
701 E. Water Street
Charlottesville, VA 22902
800-446-3410
www.lexisnexis.com

Product Number 4115029

(Pub. 41150)

PREFACE

RULES

Federal Rules of Court contains national rules of practice and procedure, with official forms. These rules and forms have been updated with amendments received by the publisher through January 26, 2015.

UPDATES

Federal Rules of Court will be replaced annually and supplemented in the interim when necessary.

INDEXES

Indexes to the various sets of rules appear at the end of the volume. These indexes are arranged in alphabetical sequence, based on the key word in the title of the rules set.

USER INFORMATION

We are committed to providing legal professionals with the most comprehensive, current and useful publications possible. If you have comments and suggestions, please write to Federal Rules Editor, LexisNexis, 701 E. Water Street, Charlottesville, Virginia, 22902; call us toll-free at 1-800-833-9844; fax toll-free at 1-800-643-1280; E-mail us at llp.clp@lexisnexis.com; or visit our Internet website at http://www.lexisnexis.com. By providing us with your informed comments, you will be assured of having available a working tool which increases in value each year.

Visit LexisNexis's Internet home page at http://www.lexisnexis.com for an online bookstore, technical support, customer service, and other company information.

March 2015

TABLE OF CONTENTS

Page

CONSTITUTION OF THE UNITED STATES OF AMERICA

FEDERAL RULES OF COURT

CONSTITUTION
OF THE
UNITED STATES OF AMERICA

PREAMBLE

We the People of the United States, in Order to form a more perfect Union, establish Justice, insure domestic Tranquility, provide for the common defence, promote the general Welfare, and secure the Blessings of Liberty to ourselves and our Posterity, do ordain and establish this Constitution for the United States of America.

ARTICLE I. — LEGISLATIVE DEPARTMENT

Section 1. Legislative powers vested in Congress.

All legislative Powers herein granted shall be vested in a Congress of the United States, which shall consist of a Senate and House of Representatives.

Sec. 2, Clause 1. House of Representatives—Composition—Electors.

The House of Representatives shall be composed of Members chosen every second Year by the People of the several States, and the Electors in each State shall have the Qualifications requisite for Electors of the most numerous Branch of the State Legislature.

Sec. 2, Cl. 2. Qualifications of Representatives.

No person shall be a Representative who shall not have attained to the Age of twenty five Years, and been seven Years a Citizen of the United States, and who shall not, when elected, be an Inhabitant of that State in which he shall be chosen.

Sec. 2, Cl. 3. Apportionment of Representatives and direct taxes.

[Representatives and direct Taxes shall be apportioned among the several States which may be included within this Union, according to their respective Numbers, which shall be determined by adding to the whole Number of free Persons, including those bound to Service for a Term of Years, and excluding Indians not taxed, three fifths of all other Persons.] The actual Enumeration shall be made within three Years after the first Meeting of the Congress of the United States, and within every subsequent Term of ten Years, in such Manner as they shall by Law direct. The Number of Representatives shall not exceed one for every thirty Thousand, but each State shall have at Least one Representative; and until such enumeration shall be made, the State of New Hampshire shall be entitled to chuse three, Massachusetts eight, Rhode-Island and Providence Plantations one, Connecticut five, New-York six, New Jersey four, Pennsylvania eight, Delaware one, Maryland six, Virginia ten, North Carolina five, South Carolina five, and Georgia three.

Sec. 2, Cl. 4. Vacancies.

When vacancies happen in the Representation from any State, the Executive Authority thereof shall issue Writs of Election to fill such Vacancies.

Sec. 2, Cl. 5. Officers and impeachment.

The House of Representatives shall chuse their Speaker and other Officers; and shall have the sole Power of Impeachment.

Section 3, Clause 1. Senate—Composition.

[The Senate of the United States shall be composed of two Senators from each State, chosen by the Legislature thereof, for six Years; and each Senator shall have one Vote.]

Sec. 3, Cl. 2. Classification of Senators.

Immediately after they shall be assembled in Consequence of the first Election, they shall be divided as equally as may be into three Classes. The Seats of the Senators of the first Class shall be vacated at the Expiration of the second Year, of the second Class at the Expiration of the fourth Year, and of the third Class at the Expiration of the sixth Year, so that one third may be chosen every second Year; [and if Vacancies happen by Resignation, or otherwise, during the Recess of the Legislature of any State, the Executive thereof may make temporary Appointments until the next Meeting of the Legislature, which shall then fill such Vacancies].

Sec. 3, Cl. 3. Qualifications of Senators.

No Person shall be a Senator who shall not have attained to the Age of thirty Years, and been nine Years a Citizen of the United States, and who shall not, when elected, be an Inhabitant of that State for which he shall be chosen.

Sec. 3, Cl. 4. President of the Senate.

The Vice President of the United States shall be President of the Senate, but shall have no Vote, unless they be equally divided.

Sec. 3, Cl. 5. Officers of the Senate.

The Senate shall chuse their other Officers, and also a President pro tempore, in the Absence of the

Vice President, or when he shall exercise the Office of President of the United States.

Sec. 3, Cl. 6. Trial of impeachments.

The Senate shall have the sole Power to try all Impeachments. When sitting for that Purpose, they shall be on Oath or Affirmation. When the President of the United States is tried, the Chief Justice shall preside: And no Person shall be convicted without the Concurrence of two thirds of the Members present.

Sec. 3, Cl. 7. Judgment in cases of impeachment.

Judgment in Cases of Impeachment shall not extend further than to removal from Office, and disqualification to hold and enjoy any Office of honor, Trust or Profit under the United States: but the Party convicted shall nevertheless be liable and subject to Indictment, Trial, Judgment and Punishment, according to Law.

Section 4, Clause 1. Elections.

The Times, Places and Manner of holding Elections for Senators and Representatives, shall be prescribed in each State by the Legislature thereof; but the Congress may at any time by Law make or alter such Regulations, except as to the Places of chusing Senators.

Sec. 4, Cl. 2. Meetings.

The Congress shall assemble at least once in every Year, and such Meeting shall be on the [first Monday in December], unless they shall by Law appoint a different Day.

Section 5, Clause 1. Organization of Congress.

Each House shall be the Judge of the Elections, Returns and Qualifications of its own Members, and a Majority of each shall constitute a Quorum to do Business; but a smaller Number may adjourn from day to day, and may be authorized to compel the Attendance of absent Members, in such Manner, and under such Penalties as each House may provide.

Sec. 5, Cl. 2. Rules of proceedings—Punishment of members.

Each House may determine the Rules of its Proceedings, punish its Members for disorderly Behaviour, and, with the Concurrence of two thirds, expel a Member.

Sec. 5, Cl. 3. Journal of proceedings.

Each House shall keep a Journal of its Proceedings, and from time to time publish the same, excepting such Parts as may in their Judgment require Secrecy; and the Yeas and Nays of the Members of either House on any question shall, at the Desire of one fifth of those Present, be entered on the Journal.

Sec. 5, Cl. 4. Adjournment.

Neither House, during the Session of Congress, shall, without the Consent of the other, adjourn for more than three days, nor to any other Place than that in which the two Houses shall be sitting.

Section 6, Clause 1. Compensation and privileges of members.

The Senators and Representatives shall receive a Compensation for their Services, to be ascertained by Law, and paid out of the Treasury of the United States. They shall in all Cases, except Treason, Felony and Breach of the Peace, be privileged from Arrest during their Attendance at the Session of their respective Houses, and in going to and returning from the same; and for any Speech or Debate in either House, they shall not be questioned in any other Place.

Sec. 6, Cl. 2. Holding other offices.

No Senator or Representative shall, during the Time for which he was elected, be appointed to any civil Office under the Authority of the United States, which shall have been created, or the Emoluments whereof shall have been encreased during such time; and no Person holding any Office under the United States, shall be a Member of either House during his Continuance in Office.

Section 7, Clause 1. Bills and Resolutions—Revenue bills

All Bills for raising Revenue shall originate in the House of Representatives; but the Senate may propose or concur with Amendments as on other Bills.

Sec. 7, Cl. 2. Approval or veto of bills—Passage over veto.

Every Bill which shall have passed the House of Representatives and the Senate, shall, before it become a Law, be presented to the President of the United States; If he approve he shall sign it, but if not he shall return it, with his Objections to that House in which it shall have originated, who shall enter the Objections at large on their Journal, and proceed to reconsider it. If after such Reconsideration two thirds of that House shall agree to pass the Bill, it shall be sent, together with the Objections, to the other House, by which it shall likewise be reconsidered, and if approved by two thirds of that House, it shall become a Law. But in all such Cases the Votes of both Houses shall be determined by yeas and Nays, and the Names of the Persons voting for and against the Bill shall be entered on the Journal of each House respectively. If any Bill shall not be returned by the President within ten Days (Sundays excepted) after it shall have been presented to him, the Same shall be a Law, in like Manner as if he had signed it, unless the Congress by their Adjournment prevent its Return, in which Case it shall not be a Law.

Sec. 7, Cl. 3. Approval or veto of Resolutions, orders, or votes—Passage over veto.

Every Order, Resolution, or Vote to which the Concurrence of the Senate and House of Representatives may be necessary (except on a question of Adjournment) shall be presented to the President of the United States; and before the Same shall take Effect, shall be approved by him, or being disapproved by him, shall be repassed by two thirds of the Senate and House of Representatives, according to the Rules and Limitations prescribed in the Case of a Bill.

Section 8, Cl. 1. Powers of Congress—Taxation.

The Congress shall have Power To lay and collect Taxes, Duties, Imposts and Excises, to pay the Debts and provide for the common Defence and general Welfare of the United States; but all Duties, Imposts and Excises shall be uniform throughout the United States;

Sec. 8, Cl. 2. Power of Congress to borrow money.

To borrow Money on the credit of the United States;

Sec. 8, Cl. 3. Power of Congress to regulate commerce.

To regulate Commerce with foreign Nations, and among the several States, and with the Indian Tribes;

Sec. 8, Cl. 4. Naturalization—Bankruptcy.

To establish an uniform Rule of Naturalization, and uniform Laws on the subject of Bankruptcies throughout the United States;

Sec. 8, Cl. 5. Coinage, weights and measures.

To coin Money, regulate the Value thereof, and of foreign Coin, and fix the Standard of Weights and Measures;

Sec. 8, Cl. 6. Counterfeiting.

To provide for the Punishment of counterfeiting the Securities and current Coin of the United States;

Sec. 8, Cl. 7. Post offices and post roads.

To establish Post Offices and post Roads;

Sec. 8, Cl. 8. Patents and copyrights.

To promote the Progress of Science and useful Arts, by securing for limited Times to Authors and Inventors the exclusive Right to their respective Writings and Discoveries;

Sec. 8, Cl. 9. Inferior tribunals.

To constitute Tribunals inferior to the supreme Court;

Sec. 8, Cl. 10. Offenses.

To define and punish Piracies and Felonies committed on the high Seas, and Offences against the Law of Nations;

Sec. 8, Cl. 11. Declare War.

To declare War, grant Letters of Marque and Reprisal, and make Rules concerning Captures on Land and Water;

Sec. 8, Cl. 12. Raise and support armies.

To raise and support Armies, but no Appropriation of Money to that Use shall be for a longer Term than two Years;

Sec. 8, Cl. 13. Navy.

To provide and maintain a Navy;

Sec. 8, Cl. 14. Government and regulation of land and naval forces.

To make Rules for the Government and Regulation of the land and naval Forces;

Sec. 8, Cl. 15. Calling forth militia.

To provide for calling forth the Militia to execute the Laws of the Union, suppress Insurrections and repel Invasions;

Sec. 8, Cl. 16. Organizing militia.

To provide for organizing, arming, and disciplining, the Militia, and for governing such Part of them as may be employed in the Service of the United States, reserving to the States respectively, the Appointment of the Officers, and the Authority of training the Militia according to the discipline prescribed by Congress;

Sec. 8, Cl. 17. Authority over places purchased or ceded.

To exercise exclusive Legislation in all Cases whatsoever, over such District (not exceeding ten Miles square) as may, by Cession of particular States, and the Acceptance of Congress, become the Seat of the Government of the United States, and to exercise like Authority over all Places purchased by the Consent of the Legislature of the State in which the Same shall be, for the Erection of Forts, Magazines, Arsenals, dock-Yards, and other needful Buildings;—And

Sec. 8, Cl. 18. All necessary and proper laws.

To make all Laws which shall be necessary and proper for carrying into Execution the foregoing Powers, and all other Powers vested by this Constitution in the Government of the United States, or in any Department or Officer thereof.

Section 9, Clause 1. Prohibited powers—Migration or importation of persons.

The Migration or Importation of such Persons as any of the States now existing shall think proper to admit, shall not be prohibited by the Congress prior to the Year one thousand eight hundred and eight, but a Tax or duty may be imposed on such Importation, not exceeding ten dollars for each Person.

Sec. 9, Cl. 2. Habeas corpus.

The Privilege of the Writ of Habeas Corpus shall not be suspended, unless when in Cases of Rebellion or Invasion the public Safety may require it.

Sec. 9, Cl. 3. Bill of attainder—Ex post facto laws.

No Bill of Attainder or ex post facto Law shall be passed.

Sec. 9, Cl. 4. Capitation or direct taxes.

No Capitation, or other direct, Tax shall be laid, unless in Proportion to the Census or Enumeration herein before directed to be taken.

Sec. 9, Cl. 5. Tax on exports from state.

No Tax or Duty shall be laid on Articles exported from any State.

Sec. 9, Cl. 6. Preference of ports.

No Preference shall be given by any Regulation of Commerce or Revenue to the Ports of one State over those of another: nor shall Vessels bound to, or from, one State, be obliged to enter, clear, or pay Duties in another.

Sec. 9, Cl. 7. Expenditures of public money.

No Money shall be drawn from the Treasury, but in Consequence of Appropriations made by Law; and a regular Statement and Account of the Receipts and Expenditures of all public Money shall be published from time to time.

Sec. 9, Cl. 8. Titles of nobility—Presents from foreign state.

No Title of Nobility shall be granted by the United States: And no Person holding any Office of Profit or Trust under them, shall, without the Consent of the Congress, accept of any present, Emolument, Office, or Title, of any kind whatever, from any King, Prince, or foreign State.

Section 10, Clause 1. Powers denied states—Treaties—Money—Ex post facto laws—Obligation of contracts.

No State shall enter into any Treaty, Alliance, or Confederation; grant Letters of Marque and Reprisal; coin Money; emit Bills of Credit; make any Thing but gold and silver Coin a Tender in Payment of Debts; pass any Bill of Attainder, ex post facto Law, or Law impairing the Obligation of Contracts, or grant any Title of Nobility.

Sec. 10, Cl. 2. Imposts or duties.

No State shall, without the Consent of the Congress, lay any Imposts or Duties on Imports or Exports, except what may be absolutely necessary for executing it's inspection Laws: and the net Produce of all Duties and Imposts, laid by any State on Imports or Exports, shall be for the Use of the Treasury of the United States; and all such Laws shall be subject to the Revision and Controul of the Congress.

Sec. 10, Cl. 3. Tonnage—State compacts—War.

No State shall, without the Consent of Congress, lay any Duty of Tonnage, keep Troops, or Ships of War in time of Peace, enter into any Agreement or Compact with another State, or with a foreign Power, or engage in War, unless actually invaded, or in such imminent Danger as will not admit of delay.

ARTICLE II. — EXECUTIVE POWER

Section 1, Clause 1. President—Tenure.

The executive Power shall be vested in a President of the United States of America. He shall hold his Office during the Term of four Years, and, together with the Vice President, chosen for the same Term, be elected, as follows:

Sec. 1, Cl. 2. Presidential electors.

Each State shall appoint, in such Manner as the Legislature thereof may direct, a Number of Electors, equal to the whole Number of Senators and Representatives to which the State may be entitled in the Congress: but no Senator or Representative, or Person holding an Office of Trust or Profit under the United States, shall be appointed an Elector.

Sec. 1, Cl. 3. Election of President and Vice President.

[The Electors shall meet in their respective States, and vote by Ballot for two Persons, of whom one at least shall not be an Inhabitant of the same State with themselves. And they shall make a List of all the Persons voted for, and of the Number of Votes for each; which List they shall sign and certify, and transmit sealed to the Seat of the Government of the United States, directed to the President of the Senate. The President of the Senate shall, in the Presence of the Senate and House of Representatives, open all the Certificates, and the Votes shall then be counted. The Person having the greatest Number of Votes shall be the President, if such Number be a Majority of the whole Number of Electors appointed; and if there be more than one who have such Majority, and have an equal Number of Votes, then the House of Representatives shall immediately chuse by Ballot one of them for President; and if no Person have a Majority, then from the five highest on the List the said House shall in like Manner chuse the President. But in chusing the President, the Votes shall be taken by States, the Representation from each State having one Vote; A quorum for this Purpose shall consist of a Member or Members from two thirds of the States, and a Majority of all the States shall be necessary to a Choice. In every Case, after the Choice of the President, the Person having the greatest Number of Votes of the Electors shall be the Vice President. But if there should remain two or more who have equal Votes, the Senate shall chuse from them by Ballot the Vice President.]

Sec. 1, Cl. 4. Election day.

The Congress may determine the Time of chusing the Electors, and the Day on which they shall give their Votes; which Day shall be the same throughout the United States.

Sec. 1, Cl. 5. Eligibility for office of President.

No Person except a natural born Citizen, or a Citizen of the United States, at the time of the Adoption of this Constitution, shall be eligible to the Office of President; neither shall any Person be eligible to that Office who shall not have attained to the Age of thirty five Years, and been fourteen Years a Resident within the United States.

Sec. 1, Cl. 6. Succession to office of President.

In Case of the Removal of the President from Office, or of his Death, Resignation, or Inability to discharge the Powers and Duties of the said Office, the Same shall devolve on the Vice President, and the Congress may by Law provide for the Case of Removal, Death, Resignation, or Inability, both of the President and Vice President, declaring what Officer shall then act as President, and such Officer shall act accordingly, until the Disability be removed, or a President shall be elected.

Sec. 1, Cl. 7. Compensation of President.

The President shall, at stated Times, receive for his Services, a Compensation, which shall neither be encreased nor diminished during the Period for which he shall have been elected, and he shall not receive within that Period any other Emolument from the United States, or any of them.

Sec. 1, Cl. 8. Oath of office.

Before he enter on the Execution of His Office, he shall take the following Oath or Affirmation:—"I do solemnly swear (or affirm) that I will faithfully execute the Office of President of the United States, and will to the best of my Ability, preserve, protect and defend the Constitution of the United States."

Section 2, Clause 1. Commander in Chief—Opinions of department heads—Reprieves and pardons.

The President shall be Commander in Chief of the Army and Navy of the United States, and of the Militia of the several States, when called into the actual Service of the United States; he may require the Opinion, in writing, of the principal Officer in each of the executive Departments, upon any Subject relating to the Duties of their respective Offices, and he shall have Power to grant Reprieves and Pardons for Offences against the United States, except in Cases of Impeachment.

Sec. 2, Cl. 2. Treaties—Appointment of officers.

He shall have Power, by and with the Advice and Consent of the Senate, to make Treaties, provided two thirds of the Senators present concur; and he shall nominate, and by and with the Advice and Consent of the Senate, shall appoint Ambassadors, other public Ministers and Consuls, Judges of the supreme Court, and all other Officers of the United States, whose Appointments are not herein otherwise provided for, and which shall be established by Law: but the Congress may by Law vest the Appointment of such inferior Officers, as they think proper, in the President alone, in the Courts of Law, or in the Heads of Departments.

Sec. 2, Cl. 3. Appointments during recess of Senate.

The President shall have Power to fill up all Vacancies that may happen during the Recess of the Senate, by granting Commissions which shall expire at the End of their next Session.

Section 3. Recommendations to Congress—Convene and adjourn Congress—Receive ambassadors—Execute laws—Commission officers.

He shall from time to time give to the Congress Information of the State of the Union, and recommend to their Consideration such Measures as he shall judge necessary and expedient; he may, on extraordinary Occasions, convene both Houses, or either of them, and in Case of Disagreement between them, with Respect to the Time of Adjournment, he may adjourn them to such Time as he shall think proper; he shall receive Ambassadors and other public Ministers; he shall take Care that the Laws be faithfully executed, and shall Commission all the Officers of the United States.

Section 4. Removal from office.

The President, Vice President and all civil Officers of the United States, shall be removed from Office on Impeachment for, and Conviction of, Treason, Bribery, or other high Crimes and Misdemeanors.

ARTICLE III. — JUDICIAL POWER

Sec. 1. Supreme Court and inferior courts—Judges and compensation.

The judicial Power of the United States, shall be vested in one supreme Court, and in such inferior Courts as the Congress may from time to time ordain and establish. The Judges, both of the supreme and inferior Courts, shall hold their Offices during good Behaviour, and shall, at stated Times, receive for their Services, a Compensation, which shall not be diminished during their Continuance in Office.

Section 2, Clause 1. Subjects of jurisdiction.

The judicial Power shall extend to all Cases, in Law and Equity, arising under this Constitution, the Laws of the United States, and Treaties made, or which shall be made, under their Authority;—to all Cases affecting Ambassadors, other public Ministers and Consuls;—to all Cases of admiralty and maritime Jurisdiction;—to Controversies to which the United States shall be a Party;—to Controversies between two or more States;—between a State and Citizens of another State;—between Citizens of different States,—between Citizens of the same State claiming Lands under Grants of different States, and between a State, or the Citizens thereof, and foreign States, Citizens or Subjects.

Sec. 2, Cl. 2. Jurisdiction of Supreme Court

In all Cases affecting Ambassadors, other public Ministers and Consuls, and those in which a State shall be Party, the supreme Court shall have original Jurisdiction. In all the other Cases before mentioned, the supreme Court shall have appellate

Jurisdiction, both as to Law and Fact, with such Exceptions, and under such Regulations as the Congress shall make.

Sec. 2, Cl. 3. Trial by jury.

The Trial of all Crimes, except in Cases of Impeachment, shall be by Jury; and such Trial shall be held in the State where the said Crimes shall have been committed; but when not committed within any State, the Trial shall be at such Place or Places as the Congress may by Law have directed.

Section 3, Clause 1. Treason.

Treason against the United States, shall consist only in levying War against them, or in adhering to their Enemies, giving them Aid and Comfort. No Person shall be convicted of Treason unless on the Testimony of two Witnesses to the same overt Act, or on Confession in open Court.

Sec. 3, Cl. 2. Punishment of Treason

The Congress shall have Power to declare the Punishment of Treason, but no Attainder of Treason shall work Corruption of Blood, or Forfeiture except during the Life of the Person attainted.

ARTICLE IV. — RELATIONS BETWEEN STATES

Sec. 1. Full Faith and Credit.

Full Faith and Credit shall be given in each State to the public Acts, Records, and judicial Proceedings of every other State. And the Congress may by general Laws prescribe the Manner in which such Acts, Records and Proceedings shall be proved, and the Effect thereof.

Sec. 2, Cl. 1. Privileges and immunities of citizens.

The Citizens of each State shall be entitled to all Privileges and Immunities of Citizens in the several States.

Sec. 2, Cl. 2. Delivery of fugitives.

A Person charged in any State with Treason, Felony, or other Crime, who shall flee from Justice, and be found in another State, shall on Demand of the executive Authority of the State from which he fled, be delivered up, to be removed to the State having Jurisdiction of the Crime.

Sec. 2, Cl. 3. Runaway slaves.

No Person held to Service or Labour in one State, under the Laws thereof, escaping into another, shall, in Consequence of any Law or Regulation therein, be discharged from such Service or Labour, but shall be delivered up on Claim of the Party to whom such Service or Labour may be due.

Section 3, Clause 1. Admission of new states.

New States may be admitted by the Congress into this Union; but no new State shall be formed or erected within the Jurisdiction of any other State; nor any State be formed by the Junction of two or more States, or Parts of States, without the Consent of the Legislatures of the States concerned as well as of the Congress.

Sec. 3, Cl. 2. Territory or property of United States.

The Congress shall have Power to dispose of and make all needful Rules and Regulations respecting the Territory or other Property belonging to the United States; and nothing in this Constitution shall be so construed as to Prejudice any Claims of the United States, or of any particular State.

Sec. 4. Form of State governments—Protection.

The United States shall guarantee to every State in this Union a Republican Form of Government, and shall protect each of them against Invasion; and on Application of the Legislature, or of the Executive (when the Legislature cannot be convened) against domestic Violence.

ARTICLE V. — AMENDMENT OF CONSTITUTION

Amendment of Constitution.

The Congress, whenever two thirds of both Houses shall deem it necessary, shall propose Amendments to this Constitution, or, on the Application of the Legislatures of two thirds of the several States, shall call a Convention for proposing Amendments, which, in either Case, shall be valid to all Intents and Purposes, as Part of this Constitution, when ratified by the Legislatures of three fourths of the several States, or by Conventions in three fourths thereof, as the one or the other Mode of Ratification may be proposed by the Congress; Provided that no Amendment which may be made prior to the Year One thousand eight hundred and eight shall in any Manner affect the first and fourth Clauses in the Ninth Section of the first Article; and that no State, without its Consent, shall be deprived of its equal Suffrage in the Senate.

ARTICLE VI. — MISCELLANEOUS PROVISIONS

Clause 1. Prior debts valid under Constitution.

All Debts contracted and Engagements entered into, before the Adoption of this Constitution, shall be as valid against the United States under this Constitution, as under the Confederation.

Clause 2. Supreme law.

This Constitution, and the Laws of the United States which shall be made in Pursuance thereof; and all Treaties made, or which shall be made, under the Authority of the United States, shall be the supreme Law of the Land; and the Judges in every State shall be bound thereby, any Thing in the Constitution or Laws of any State to the Contrary notwithstanding.

Clause 3. Oath of office

The Senators and Representatives before mentioned, and the Members of the several State Legislatures, and all executive and judicial Officers, both of the United States and of the several States, shall be bound by Oath or Affirmation, to support this Constitution; but no religious Test shall ever be required as a Qualification to any Office or public Trust under the United States.

ARTICLE VII. — RATIFICATION

Ratification.

The Ratification of the Conventions of nine States, shall be sufficient for the Establishment of this Constitution between the States so ratifying the Same.

AMENDMENTS

AMENDMENT 1

Religious and political freedom.

Congress shall make no law respecting an establishment of religion, or prohibiting the free exercise thereof; or abridging the freedom of speech, or of the press; or the right of the people peaceably to assemble, and to petition the Government for a redress of grievances.

AMENDMENT 2

Right to bear arms.

A well regulated Militia, being necessary to the security of a free State, the right of the people to keep and bear Arms, shall not be infringed.

AMENDMENT 3

Quartering soldiers.

No Soldier shall, in time of peace be quartered in any house, without the consent of the Owner, nor in time of war, but in a manner to be prescribed by law.

AMENDMENT 4

Unreasonable searches and seizures.

The right of the people to be secure in their persons, houses, papers, and effects, against unreasonable searches and seizures, shall not be violated, and no Warrants shall issue, but upon probable cause, supported by Oath or affirmation, and particularly describing the place to be searched, and the persons or things to be seized.

AMENDMENT 5

Criminal actions—Provisions concerning—Due process of law and just compensation clauses.

No person shall be held to answer for a capital, or otherwise infamous crime, unless on a presentment or indictment of a Grand Jury, except in cases arising in the land or naval forces, or in the Militia, when in actual service in time of War or public danger; nor shall any person be subject for the same offence to be twice put in jeopardy of life or limb; nor shall be compelled in any criminal case to be a witness against himself, nor be deprived of life, liberty, or property, without due process of law; nor shall private property be taken for public use, without just compensation.

AMENDMENT 6

Rights of the accused.

In all criminal prosecutions, the accused shall enjoy the right to a speedy and public trial, by an impartial jury of the State and district wherein the crime shall have been committed, which district shall have been previously ascertained by law, and to be informed of the nature and cause of the accusation; to be confronted with the witnesses against him; to have compulsory process for obtaining witnesses in his favor, and to have the Assistance of Counsel for his defence.

AMENDMENT 7

Trial by jury in civil cases.

In Suits at common law, where the value in controversy shall exceed twenty dollars, the right of trial by jury shall be preserved, and no fact tried by a jury, shall be otherwise re-examined in any Court of the United States, than according to the rules of the common law.

AMENDMENT 8

Bail—Punishment.

Excessive bail shall not be required, nor excessive fines imposed, nor cruel and unusual punishments inflicted.

AMENDMENT 9

Rights retained by people.

The enumeration in the Constitution, of certain rights, shall not be construed to deny or disparage others retained by the people.

AMENDMENT 10

Powers reserved to states or people.

The powers not delegated to the United States by the Constitution, nor prohibited by it to the States, are reserved to the States respectively, or to the people.

AMENDMENT 11

Suits against states—Restriction of judicial power.

The Judicial power of the United States shall not be construed to extend to any suit in law or equity, commenced or prosecuted against one of the United States by Citizens of another State, or by Citizens or Subjects of any Foreign State.

AMENDMENT 12

Election of President and Vice-President.

The Electors shall meet in their respective states and vote by ballot for President and Vice-President, one of whom, at least, shall not be an inhabitant of the same state with themselves; they shall name in their ballots the person voted for as President, and in distinct ballots the person voted for as Vice-President, and they shall make distinct lists of all persons voted for as President, and of all persons voted for as Vice-President, and of the number of votes for each, which lists they shall sign and certify, and transmit sealed to the seat of the government of the United States, directed to the President of the Senate; — the President of the Senate shall, in the presence of the Senate and House of Representatives, open all the certificates and the votes shall then be counted; — The person having the greatest number of votes for President, shall be the President, if such number be a majority of the whole number of Electors appointed; and if no person have such majority, then from the persons having the highest numbers not exceeding three on the list of those voted for as President, the House of Representatives shall choose immediately, by ballot, the President. But in choosing the President, the votes shall be taken by states, the representation from each state having one vote; a quorum for this purpose shall consist of a member or members from two-thirds of the states, and a majority of all the states shall be necessary to a choice. And if the House of Representatives shall not choose a President whenever the right of choice shall devolve upon them, before the fourth day of March next following, then the Vice-President shall act as President, as in case of the death or other constitutional disability of the President. — The person having the greatest number of votes as Vice-President, shall be the Vice-President, if such number be a majority of the whole number of Electors appointed, and if no person have a majority, then from the two highest numbers on the list, the Senate shall choose the Vice-President; a quorum for the purpose shall consist of two-thirds of the whole number of Senators, and a majority of the whole number shall be necessary to a choice. But no person constitutionally ineligible to the office of President shall be eligible to that of Vice-President of the United States.

AMENDMENT 13

Sec. 1. [Slavery prohibited.]

Neither slavery nor involuntary servitude, except as a punishment for crime whereof the party shall have been duly convicted, shall exist within the United States, or any place subject to their jurisdiction.

Sec. 2. [Power to enforce amendment.]

Congress shall have power to enforce this article by appropriate legislation.

AMENDMENT 14

Sec. 1. [Citizens of the United States.]

All persons born or naturalized in the United States, and subject to the jurisdiction thereof, are citizens of the United States and of the State wherein they reside. No State shall make or enforce any law which shall abridge the privileges or immunities of citizens of the United States; nor shall any State deprive any person of life, liberty, or property, without due process of law; nor deny to any person within its jurisdiction the equal protection of the laws.

Sec. 2. [Representatives—Power to reduce apportionment.]

Representatives shall be apportioned among the several States according to their respective numbers, counting the whole number of persons in each State, excluding Indians not taxed. But when the right to vote at any election for the choice of electors for President and Vice-President of the United States, Representatives in Congress, the Executive and Judicial officers of a State, or the members of the Legislature thereof, is denied to any of the male inhabitants of such State, being twenty-one years of age, and citizens of the United States, or in any way abridged, except for participation in rebellion, or other crime, the basis of representation therein shall be reduced in the proportion which the number of such male citizens shall bear to the whole number of male citizens twenty-one years of age in such State.

Sec. 3. [Disqualification to hold office.]

No person shall be a Senator or Representative in Congress, or elector of President and Vice-President, or hold any office, civil or military, under the United States, or under any State, who, having previously taken an oath, as a member of Congress, or as an officer of the United States, or as a member of any State legislature, or as an executive or judicial officer of any State, to support the Constitution of the United States, shall have engaged in insurrection or rebellion against the same, or given aid or comfort to the enemies thereof. But Congress may by a vote of two-thirds of each House, remove such disability.

Sec. 4. [Public debt not to be questioned—Debts of the Confederacy and claims not to be paid.]

The validity of the public debt of the United States, authorized by law, including debts incurred for payment of pensions and bounties for services in suppressing insurrection or rebellion, shall not be questioned. But neither the United States nor any State shall assume or pay any debt or obligation incurred in aid of insurrection or rebellion against the United States, or any claim for the loss or emancipation of any slave; but all such debts, obligations and claims shall be held illegal and void.

Sec. 5. [Power to enforce amendment.]

The Congress shall have the power to enforce, by appropriate legislation, the provisions of this article.

AMENDMENT 15

Sec. 1. [Right of citizens to vote—Race or color not to disqualify.]

The right of citizens of the United States to vote shall not be denied or abridged by the United States or by any State on account of race, color, or previous condition of servitude—

Sec. 2. [Power to enforce amendment.]

The Congress shall have power to enforce this article by appropriate legislation.

AMENDMENT 16

[Income tax.]

The Congress shall have power to lay and collect taxes on incomes, from whatever source derived, without apportionment among the several States, and without regard to any census or enumeration.

AMENDMENT 17

Election of Senators.

The Senate of the United States shall be composed of two Senators from each State, elected by the people thereof, for six years; and each Senator shall have one vote. The electors in each State shall have the qualifications requisite for electors of the most numerous branch of the State legislatures. When vacancies happen in the representation of any State in the Senate, the executive authority of such State shall issue writs of election to fill such vacancies: *Provided*, That the legislature of any State may empower the executive thereof to make temporary appointments until the people fill the vacancies by election as the legislature may direct. This amendment shall not be so construed as to affect the election or term of any Senator chosen before it becomes valid as part of the Constitution.

AMENDMENT 18

Sec. 1. [National prohibition—Intoxicating liquors.]

After one year from the ratification of this article the manufacture, sale, or transportation of intoxicating liquors within, the importation thereof into, or the exportation thereof from the United States and all territory subject to the jurisdiction thereof for beverage purposes is hereby prohibited.

Sec. 2. [Concurrent power to enforce amendment.]

The Congress and the several States shall have concurrent power to enforce this article by appropriate legislation.

Sec. 3. [Time limit for adoption.]

This article shall be inoperative unless it shall have been ratified as an amendment to the Constitution by the legislatures of the several States, as provided in the Constitution, within seven years from the date of the submission hereof to the States by the Congress.

AMENDMENT 19

Sec. 1. [Woman suffrage.]

The right of citizens of the United States to vote shall not be denied or abridged by the United States or by any State on account of sex.

Sec. 2. [Power to enforce amendment.]

Congress shall have power to enforce this article by appropriate legislation.

AMENDMENT 20

Sec. 1. [Executive and legislative departments—Terms of elective officers]

The terms of the President and Vice President shall end at noon on the 20th day of January, and the terms of Senators and Representatives at noon on the 3d day of January, of the years in which such terms would have ended if this article had not been ratified; and the terms of their successors shall then begin.

Sec. 2. [Annual meeting of Congress—Date.]

The Congress shall assemble at least once in every year, and such meeting shall begin at noon on the 3d day of January, unless they shall by law appoint a different day.

Sec. 3. [Succession to office of President or Vice-President.]

If, at the time fixed for the beginning of the term of the President, the President elect shall have died, the Vice President elect shall become President. If a President shall not have been chosen before the time fixed for the beginning of his term, or if the President elect shall have failed to qualify, then the Vice President elect shall act as President until a President shall have qualified; and the Congress may by law provide for the case wherein neither a President elect nor a Vice President elect shall have qualified, declaring who shall then act as President, or the manner in which one who is to act shall be selected, and such person shall act accordingly until a President or Vice President shall have qualified.

Sec. 4. [Death of President or Vice-President—Selection of successor—Choice devolving on either house.]

The Congress may by law provide for the case of the death of any of the persons from whom the House of Representatives may choose a President whenever the right of choice shall have devolved upon them, and for the case of the death of any of the persons from whom the Senate may choose a Vice President whenever the right of choice shall have devolved upon them.

Sec. 5. [Effective date of amendment.]

Sections 1 and 2 shall take effect on the 15th day of October following the ratification of this article.

Sec. 6. [Time for ratification.]

This article shall be inoperative unless it shall have been ratified as an amendment to the Constitution by the legislatures of three-fourths of the several States within seven years from the date of its submission.

AMENDMENT 21

Sec. 1. [Repeal of Eighteenth Amendment.]

The eighteenth article of amendment to the Constitution of the United States is hereby repealed.

Sec. 2. [Intoxicating liquors, shipment into dry territory prohibited.]

The transportation or importation into any State, Territory, or Possession of the United States for delivery or use therein of intoxicating liquors, in violation of the laws thereof, is hereby prohibited.

Sec. 3. [Ratification, time limit.]

This article shall be inoperative unless it shall have been ratified as an amendment to the Constitution by conventions in the several States, as provided in the Constitution, within seven years from the date of the submission hereof to the States by the Congress.

AMENDMENT 22

Sec. 1. [Terms of Office of the President.]

No person shall be elected to the office of the President more than twice, and no person who has held the office of President, or acted as President, for more than two years of a term to which some other person was elected President shall be elected to the office of President more than once. But this Article shall not apply to any person holding the office of President when this Article was proposed by Congress, and shall not prevent any person who may be holding the office of President, or acting as President, during the term within which this Article becomes operative from holding the office of President or acting as President during the remainder of such term.

Sec. 2. [Ratification.]

This article shall be inoperative unless it shall have been ratified as an amendment to the Constitution by the legislatures of three-fourths of the several States within seven years from the date of its submission to the States by the Congress.

AMENDMENT 23

Sec. 1. [Representation in the electoral college to the District of Columbia.]

The District constituting the seat of Government of the United States shall appoint in such manner as Congress may direct: A number of electors of President and Vice President equal to the whole number of Senators and Representatives in Congress to which the District would be entitled if it were a State, but in no event more than the least populous State; they shall be in addition to those appointed by the States, but they shall be considered, for the purposes of the election of President and Vice President, to be electors appointed by a State; and they shall meet in the District and perform such duties as provided by the twelfth article of amendment.

Sec. 2. [Enforcement.]

The Congress shall have power to enforce this article by appropriate legislation.

AMENDMENT 24

Sec. 1. [Qualification of electors.]

The right of citizens of the United States to vote in any primary or other election for President or Vice President, for electors for President or Vice President, or for Senator or Representative in Congress, shall not be denied or abridged by the United States or any State by reason of failure to pay poll tax or other tax.

Sec. 2. [Enforcement.]

The Congress shall have power to enforce this article by appropriate legislation.

AMENDMENT 25

Sec. 1. [Succession to office of President.]

In case of the removal of the President from office or of his death or resignation, the Vice President shall become President.

Sec. 2. [Succession to office of Vice President.]

Whenever there is a vacancy in the office of the Vice President, the President shall nominate a Vice President who shall take office upon confirmation by a majority vote of both Houses of Congress.

Sec. 3. [Declaration by President of inability to serve.]

Whenever the President transmits to the President pro tempore of the Senate and the Speaker of the House of Representatives his written declaration that he is unable to discharge the powers and duties of his office, and until he transmits to them a written declaration to the contrary, such powers and duties shall be discharged by the Vice President as Acting President.

Sec. 4. [Declaration by others of President's inability to serve.]

Whenever the Vice President and a majority of either the principal officers of the executive departments or of such other body as Congress may by law provide, transmit to the President pro tempore of the Senate and the Speaker of the House of Representatives their written declaration that the President is unable to discharge the powers and duties of his office, the Vice President shall immediately assume the powers and duties of the office as Acting President. Thereafter, when the President transmits to the President pro tempore of the Senate and the Speaker of the House of Representatives his written declaration that no inability exists, he shall resume the powers and duties of his office unless the Vice President and a majority of either the principal officers of the executive department [departments] or of such other body as Congress may by law provide, transmit within four days to the President pro tempore of the Senate and the Speaker of the House of Representatives their written declaration that the President is unable to discharge the powers and duties of his office. Thereupon Congress shall decide the issue, assembling within forty-eight hours for that purpose if not in session. If the Congress, within twenty-one days after receipt of the latter written declaration, or, if Congress is not in session, within twenty-one days after Congress is required to assemble, determines by two-thirds vote of both Houses that the President is unable to discharge the powers and duties of his office, the Vice President shall continue to discharge the same as Acting President; otherwise, the President shall resume the powers and duties of his office.

AMENDMENT 26

Sec. 1. [Eighteen year old voting rights.]

The right of citizens of the United States, who are eighteen years of age or older, to vote shall not be denied or abridged by the United States or by any State on account of age.

Sec. 2. [Enforcement.]

The Congress shall have power to enforce this article by appropriate legislation.

AMENDMENT 27

[Compensation of Members of Congress.]

No law, varying the compensation for the services of the Senators and Representatives, shall take effect, until an election of Representatives shall have intervened.

FEDERAL RULES OF CIVIL PROCEDURE

TITLE I. SCOPE OF RULES; FORM OF ACTION

Rule 1. Scope and Purpose

These rules govern the procedure in all civil actions and proceedings in the United States district courts, except as stated in Rule 81. They should be construed and administered to secure the just, speedy, and inexpensive determination of every action and proceeding.

(As amended Dec. 29, 1948, eff. Oct. 20, 1949; Feb. 28, 1966, eff. July 1, 1966; April 22, 1993, eff. Dec. 1, 1993; April 30, 2007, eff. Dec. 1, 2007.)

Rule 2. One Form of Action

There is one form of action—the civil action.

(As amended April 30, 2007, eff. Dec. 1, 2007.)

TITLE II. COMMENCING AN ACTION; SERVICE OF PROCESS, PLEADINGS, MOTIONS, AND ORDERS

Rule 3. Commencing an Action

A civil action is commenced by filing a complaint with the court.

(As amended April 30, 2007, eff. Dec. 1, 2007.)

Rule 4. Summons

(a) Contents; Amendments. (1) *Contents.* A summons must:

(A) name the court and the parties;

(B) be directed to the defendant;

(C) state the name and address of the plaintiff's attorney or—if unrepresented—of the plaintiff;

(D) state the time within which the defendant must appear and defend;

(E) notify the defendant that a failure to appear and defend will result in a default judgment against the defendant for the relief demanded in the complaint;

(F) be signed by the clerk; and

(G) bear the court's seal.

(2) *Amendments.* The court may permit a summons to be amended.

(b) Issuance. On or after filing the complaint, the plaintiff may present a summons to the clerk for signature and seal. If the summons is properly completed, the clerk must sign, seal, and issue it to the plaintiff for service on the defendant. A summons—or a copy of a summons that is addressed to multiple defendants—must be issued for each defendant to be served.

(c) Service. (1) *In General.* A summons must be served with a copy of the complaint. The plaintiff is responsible for having the summons and complaint served within the time allowed by Rule 4(m) and must furnish the necessary copies to the person who makes service.

(2) *By Whom.* Any person who is at least 18 years old and not a party may serve a summons and complaint.

(3) *By a Marshal or Someone Specially Appointed.* At the plaintiff's request, the court may order that service be made by a United States marshal or deputy marshal or by a person specially appointed by the court. The court must so order if the plaintiff is authorized to proceed in forma pauperis under 28 U.S.C. § 1915 or as a seaman under 28 U.S.C. § 1916.

(d) Waiving Service. (1) *Requesting a Waiver.* An individual, corporation, or association that is subject to service under Rule 4(e), (f), or (h) has a duty to avoid unnecessary expenses of serving the summons. The plaintiff may notify such a defendant that an action has been commenced and request that the defendant waive service of a summons. The notice and request must:

(A) be in writing and be addressed:

(i) to the individual defendant; or

(ii) for a defendant subject to service under Rule 4(h), to an officer, a managing or general agent, or any other agent authorized by appointment or by law to receive service of process;

(B) name the court where the complaint was filed;

(C) be accompanied by a copy of the complaint, two copies of a waiver form, and a prepaid means for returning the form;

(D) inform the defendant, using text prescribed in Form 5, of the consequences of waiving and not waiving service;

(E) state the date when the request is sent;

(F) give the defendant a reasonable time of at least 30 days after the request was sent—or at least 60 days if sent to the defendant outside any judicial district of the United States—to return the waiver; and

(G) be sent by first-class mail or other reliable means.

(2) *Failure to Waive.* If a defendant located within the United States fails, without good cause, to sign and return a waiver requested by a plaintiff located within the United States, the court must impose on the defendant:

(A) the expenses later incurred in making service; and

(B) the reasonable expenses, including attorney's fees, of any motion required to collect those service expenses.

(3) *Time to Answer After a Waiver.* A defendant who, before being served with process, timely returns a waiver need not serve an answer to the complaint until 60 days after the request was sent—or until 90 days after it was sent to the defendant outside any judicial district of the United States.

(4) *Results of Filing a Waiver.* When the plaintiff files a waiver, proof of service is not required and these rules apply as if a summons and complaint had been served at the time of filing the waiver.

(5) *Jurisdiction and Venue Not Waived.* Waiving service of a summons does not waive any objection to personal jurisdiction or to venue.

(e) Serving an Individual Within a Judicial District of the United States. Unless federal law provides otherwise, an individual—other than a minor, an incompetent person, or a person whose waiver has been filed—may be served in a judicial district of the United States by:

(1) following state law for serving a summons in an action brought in courts of general jurisdiction in the state where the district court is located or where service is made; or

(2) doing any of the following:

(A) delivering a copy of the summons and of the complaint to the individual personally;

(B) leaving a copy of each at the individual's dwelling or usual place of abode with someone of suitable age and discretion who resides there; or

(C) delivering a copy of each to an agent authorized by appointment or by law to receive service of process.

(f) Serving an Individual in a Foreign Country. Unless federal law provides otherwise, an individual—other than a minor, an incompetent person, or a person whose waiver has been filed—may be served at a place not within any judicial district of the United States:

(1) by any internationally agreed means of service that is reasonably calculated to give notice, such as those authorized by the Hague Convention on the Service Abroad of Judicial and Extrajudicial Documents;

(2) if there is no internationally agreed means, or if an international agreement allows but does not specify other means, by a method that is reasonably calculated to give notice:

(A) as prescribed by the foreign country's law for service in that country in an action in its courts of general jurisdiction;

(B) as the foreign authority directs in response to a letter rogatory or letter of request; or

(C) unless prohibited by the foreign country's law, by:

(i) delivering a copy of the summons and of the complaint to the individual personally; or

(ii) using any form of mail that the clerk addresses and sends to the individual and that requires a signed receipt; or

(3) by other means not prohibited by international agreement, as the court orders.

(g) Serving a Minor or an Incompetent Person. A minor or an incompetent person in a judicial district of the United States must be served by following state law for serving a summons or like process on such a defendant in an action brought in the courts of general jurisdiction of the state where service is made. A minor or an incompetent person who is not within any judicial district of the United States must be served in the manner prescribed by Rule 4(f)(2)(A), (f)(2)(B), or (f)(3).

(h) Serving a Corporation, Partnership, or Association. Unless federal law provides otherwise or the defendant's waiver has been filed, a domestic or foreign corporation, or a partnership or other unincorporated association that is subject to suit under a common name, must be served:

(1) in a judicial district of the United States:

(A) in the manner prescribed by Rule 4(e)(1) for serving an individual; or

(B) by delivering a copy of the summons and of the complaint to an officer, a managing or general agent, or any other agent authorized by appointment or by law to receive service of process and—if the agent is one authorized by statute and the statute so requires—by also mailing a copy of each to the defendant; or

(2) at a place not within any judicial district of the

United States, in any manner prescribed by Rule 4(f) for serving an individual, except personal delivery under (f)(2)(C)(i).

(i) Serving the United States and Its Agencies, Corporations, Officers, or Employees. (1) *United States.* To serve the United States, a party must:

(A) (i) deliver a copy of the summons and of the complaint to the United States attorney for the district where the action is brought—or to an assistant United States attorney or clerical employee whom the United States attorney designates in a writing filed with the court clerk—or

(ii) send a copy of each by registered or certified mail to the civil-process clerk at the United States attorney's office;

(B) send a copy of each by registered or certified mail to the Attorney General of the United States at Washington, D.C.; and

(C) if the action challenges an order of a nonparty agency or officer of the United States, send a copy of each by registered or certified mail to the agency or officer.

(2) *Agency; Corporation; Officer or Employee Sued in an Official Capacity.* To serve a United States agency or corporation, or a United States officer or employee sued only in an official capacity, a party must serve the United States and also send a copy of the summons and of the complaint by registered or certified mail to the agency, corporation, officer, or employee.

(3) *Officer or Employee Sued Individually.* To serve a United States officer or employee sued in an individual capacity for an act or omission occurring in connection with duties performed on the United States' behalf (whether or not the officer or employee is also sued in an official capacity), a party must serve the United States and also serve the officer or employee under Rule 4(e), (f), or (g).

(4) *Extending Time.* The court must allow a party a reasonable time to cure its failure to:

(A) serve a person required to be served under Rule 4(i)(2), if the party has served either the United States attorney or the Attorney General of the United States; or

(B) serve the United States under Rule 4(i)(3), if the party has served the United States officer or employee.

(j) Serving a Foreign, State, or Local Government. (1) *Foreign State.* A foreign state or its political subdivision, agency, or instrumentality must be served in accordance with 28 U.S.C. § 1608.

(2) *State or Local Government.* A state, a municipal corporation, or any other state-created governmental organization that is subject to suit must be served by:

(A) delivering a copy of the summons and of the complaint to its chief executive officer; or

(B) serving a copy of each in the manner prescribed by that state's law for serving a summons or like process on such a defendant.

(k) Territorial Limits of Effective Service. (1) *In General.* Serving a summons or filing a waiver of service establishes personal jurisdiction over a defendant:

(A) who is subject to the jurisdiction of a court of general jurisdiction in the state where the district court is located;

(B) who is a party joined under Rule 14 or 19 and is served within a judicial district of the United States and not more than 100 miles from where the summons was issued; or

(C) when authorized by a federal statute.

(2) *Federal Claim Outside State-Court Jurisdiction.* For a claim that arises under federal law, serving a summons or filing a waiver of service establishes personal jurisdiction over a defendant if:

(A) the defendant is not subject to jurisdiction in any state's courts of general jurisdiction; and

(B) exercising jurisdiction is consistent with the United States Constitution and laws.

(l) Proving Service. (1) *Affidavit Required.* Unless service is waived, proof of service must be made to the court. Except for service by a United States marshal or deputy marshal, proof must be by the server's affidavit.

(2) *Service Outside the United States.* Service not within any judicial district of the United States must be proved as follows:

(A) if made under Rule 4(f)(1), as provided in the applicable treaty or convention; or

(B) if made under Rule 4(f)(2) or (f)(3), by a receipt signed by the addressee, or by other evidence satisfying the court that the summons and complaint were delivered to the addressee.

(3) *Validity of Service; Amending Proof.* Failure to prove service does not affect the validity of service. The court may permit proof of service to be amended.

(m) Time Limit for Service. If a defendant is not served within 120 days after the complaint is filed, the court—on motion or on its own after notice to the plaintiff—must dismiss the action without prejudice against that defendant or order that service be made within a specified time. But if the plaintiff shows good cause for the failure, the court must extend the time for service for an appropriate period. This subdivision (m) does not apply to service in a foreign country under Rule 4(f) or 4(j)(1).

(n) Asserting Jurisdiction over Property or Assets. (1) *Federal Law.* The court may assert jurisdiction over property if authorized by a federal statute. Notice to claimants of the property must be given as provided in the statute or by serving a summons under this rule.

(2) *State Law.* On a showing that personal jurisdiction over a defendant cannot be obtained in the district where the action is brought by reasonable efforts to serve a summons under this rule, the court may assert jurisdiction over the defendant's assets found in the district. Jurisdiction is acquired by seizing the assets under the circumstances and in

the manner provided by state law in that district.

(As amended Jan. 21, 1963, eff. July 1, 1963; Feb. 28, 1966, eff. July 1, 1966; April 29, 1980, eff. Aug. 1, 1980; Jan. 12, 1983, P. L. 97-462, § 2, 96 Stat. 2527, eff. Feb. 26, 1983; March 2, 1987, eff. Aug. 1, 1987; April 22, 1993, eff. Dec. 1, 1993; April 17, 2000, eff. Dec. 1, 2000; April 30, 2007, eff. Dec. 1, 2007.)

Rule 4.1. Serving Other Process

(a) In General. Process—other than a summons under Rule 4 or a subpoena under Rule 45—must be served by a United States marshal or deputy marshal or by a person specially appointed for that purpose. It may be served anywhere within the territorial limits of the state where the district court is located and, if authorized by a federal statute, beyond those limits. Proof of service must be made under Rule 4(l).

(b) Enforcing Orders: Committing for Civil Contempt. An order committing a person for civil contempt of a decree or injunction issued to enforce federal law may be served and enforced in any district. Any other order in a civil-contempt proceeding may be served only in the state where the issuing court is located or elsewhere in the United States within 100 miles from where the order was issued.

(As added April 22, 1993, eff. Dec. 1, 1993; amended April 30, 2007, eff. Dec. 1, 2007.)

Rule 5. Serving and Filing Pleadings and Other Papers

(a) Service: When Required. (1) *In General.* Unless these rules provide otherwise, each of the following papers must be served on every party:

(A) an order stating that service is required;

(B) a pleading filed after the original complaint, unless the court orders otherwise under Rule 5(c) because there are numerous defendants;

(C) a discovery paper required to be served on a party, unless the court orders otherwise;

(D) a written motion, except one that may be heard ex parte; and

(E) a written notice, appearance, demand, or offer of judgment, or any similar paper.

(2) *If a Party Fails to Appear.* No service is required on a party who is in default for failing to appear. But a pleading that asserts a new claim for relief against such a party must be served on that party under Rule 4.

(3) *Seizing Property.* If an action is begun by seizing property and no person is or need be named as a defendant, any service required before the filing of an appearance, answer, or claim must be made on the person who had custody or possession of the property when it was seized.

(b) Service: How Made. (1) *Serving an Attorney.* If a party is represented by an attorney, service under this rule must be made on the attorney unless the court orders service on the party.

(2) *Service in General.* A paper is served under this rule by:

(A) handing it to the person;

(B) leaving it:

(i) at the person's office with a clerk or other person in charge or, if no one is in charge, in a conspicuous place in the office; or

(ii) if the person has no office or the office is closed, at the person's dwelling or usual place of abode with someone of suitable age and discretion who resides there;

(C) mailing it to the person's last known address—in which event service is complete upon mailing;

(D) leaving it with the court clerk if the person has no known address;

(E) sending it by electronic means if the person consented in writing—in which event service is complete upon transmission, but is not effective if the serving party learns that it did not reach the person to be served; or

(F) delivering it by any other means that the person consented to in writing—in which event service is complete when the person making service delivers it to the agency designated to make delivery.

(3) *Using Court Facilities.* If a local rule so authorizes, a party may use the court's transmission facilities to make service under Rule 5(b)(2)(E).

(c) Serving Numerous Defendants. (1) *In General.* If an action involves an unusually large number of defendants, the court may, on motion or on its own, order that:

(A) defendants' pleadings and replies to them need not be served on other defendants;

(B) any crossclaim, counterclaim, avoidance, or affirmative defense in those pleadings and replies to them will be treated as denied or avoided by all other parties; and

(C) filing any such pleading and serving it on the plaintiff constitutes notice of the pleading to all parties.

(2) *Notifying Parties.* A copy of every such order must be served on the parties as the court directs.

(d) Filing. (1) *Required Filings; Certificate of Service.* Any paper after the complaint that is required to be served—together with a certificate of service—must be filed within a reasonable time after service. But disclosures under Rule 26(a)(1) or (2) and the following discovery requests and responses must not be filed until they are used in the proceeding or the court orders filing: depositions, interrogatories, requests for documents or tangible things or to permit entry onto land, and requests for admission.

(2) *How Filing Is Made—In General.* A paper is filed by delivering it:

(A) to the clerk; or

(B) to a judge who agrees to accept it for filing, and who must then note the filing date on the paper and promptly send it to the clerk.

(3) *Electronic Filing, Signing, or Verification.* A

court may, by local rule, allow papers to be filed, signed, or verified by electronic means that are consistent with any technical standards established by the Judicial Conference of the United States. A local rule may require electronic filing only if reasonable exceptions are allowed. A paper filed electronically in compliance with a local rule is a written paper for purposes of these rules.

(4) *Acceptance by the Clerk.* The clerk must not refuse to file a paper solely because it is not in the form prescribed by these rules or by a local rule or practice.

(As amended Jan. 21, 1963, eff. July 1, 1963; March 30, 1970, eff. July 1, 1970; April 29, 1980, eff. Aug. 1, 1980; March 2, 1987, eff. Aug. 1, 1987; April 30, 1991, eff. Dec. 1, 1991; April 22, 1993, eff. Dec. 1, 1993; April 23, 1996, eff. Dec. 1, 1996; Apr. 17, 2000, eff. Dec. 1, 2000; Apr. 23, 2001, eff. Dec. 1, 2001; Apr. 12, 2006, eff. Dec. 1, 2006; Apr. 30, 2007, eff. Dec. 1, 2007.)

Rule 5.1. Constitutional Challenge to a Statute—Notice, Certification, and Intervention

(a) Notice by a Party. A party that files a pleading, written motion, or other paper drawing into question the constitutionality of a federal or state statute must promptly:

(1) file a notice of constitutional question stating the question and identifying the paper that raises it, if:

(A) a federal statute is questioned and the parties do not include the United States, one of its agencies, or one of its officers or employees in an official capacity; or

(B) a state statute is questioned and the parties do not include the state, one of its agencies, or one of its officers or employees in an official capacity; and

(2) serve the notice and paper on the Attorney General of the United States if a federal statute is questioned—or on the state attorney general if a state statute is questioned—either by certified or registered mail or by sending it to an electronic address designated by the attorney general for this purpose.

(b) Certification by the Court. The court must, under 28 U.S.C. § 2403, certify to the appropriate attorney general that a statute has been questioned.

(c) Intervention; Final Decision on the Merits. Unless the court sets a later time, the attorney general may intervene within 60 days after the notice is filed or after the court certifies the challenge, whichever is earlier. Before the time to intervene expires, the court may reject the constitutional challenge, but may not enter a final judgment holding the statute unconstitutional.

(d) No Forfeiture. A party's failure to file and serve the notice, or the court's failure to certify, does not forfeit a constitutional claim or defense that is otherwise timely asserted.

(As added April 12, 2006, eff. Dec. 1, 2006; amended April 30, 2007, eff. Dec. 1, 2007.)

Rule 5.2. Privacy Protection For Filings Made with the Court

(a) Redacted Filings. Unless the court orders otherwise, in an electronic or paper filing with the court that contains an individual's social-security number, taxpayer-identification number, or birth date, the name of an individual known to be a minor, or a financial-account number, a party or nonparty making the filing may include only:

(1) the last four digits of the social-security number and taxpayer-identification number;

(2) the year of the individual's birth;

(3) the minor's initials; and

(4) the last four digits of the financial-account number.

(b) Exemptions from the Redaction Requirement. The redaction requirement does not apply to the following:

(1) a financial-account number that identifies the property allegedly subject to forfeiture in a forfeiture proceeding;

(2) the record of an administrative or agency proceeding;

(3) the official record of a state-court proceeding;

(4) the record of a court or tribunal, if that record was not subject to the redaction requirement when originally filed;

(5) a filing covered by Rule 5.2(c) or (d); and

(6) a pro se filing in an action brought under 28 U.S.C. §§ 2241, 2254, or 2255.

(c) Limitations on Remote Access to Electronic Files; Social-Security Appeals and Immigration Cases. Unless the court orders otherwise, in an action for benefits under the Social Security Act, and in an action or proceeding relating to an order of removal, to relief from removal, or to immigration benefits or detention, access to an electronic file is authorized as follows:

(1) the parties and their attorneys may have remote electronic access to any part of the case file, including the administrative record;

(2) any other person may have electronic access to the full record at the courthouse, but may have remote electronic access only to:

(A) the docket maintained by the court; and

(B) an opinion, order, judgment, or other disposition of the court, but not any other part of the case file or the administrative record.

(d) Filings Made Under Seal. The court may order that a filing be made under seal without redaction. The court may later unseal the filing or order the person who made the filing to file a redacted version for the public record.

(e) Protective Orders. For good cause, the court may by order in a case:

(1) require redaction of additional information; or

(2) limit or prohibit a nonparty's remote electronic access to a document filed with the court.

(f) Option for Additional Unredacted Filing Under Seal. A person making a redacted filing may also file an unredacted copy under seal. The court must retain the unredacted copy as part of the record.

(g) Option for Filing a Reference List. A filing that contains redacted information may be filed together with a reference list that identifies each item of redacted information and specifies an appropriate identifier that uniquely corresponds to each item listed. The list must be filed under seal and may be amended as of right. Any reference in the case to a listed identifier will be construed to refer to the corresponding item of information.

(h) Waiver of Protection of Identifiers. A person waives the protection of Rule 5.2(a) as to the person's own information by filing it without redaction and not under seal.

(As added April 30, 2007, eff. Dec. 1, 2007.)

Rule 6. Computing and Extending Time; Time for Motion Papers

(a) Computing Time. The following rules apply in computing any time period specified in these rules, in any local rule or court order, or in any statute that does not specify a method of computing time.

(1) *Period Stated in Days or a Longer Unit.* When the period is stated in days or a longer unit of time:

(A) exclude the day of the event that triggers the period;

(B) count every day, including intermediate Saturdays, Sundays, and legal holidays; and

(C) include the last day of the period, but if the last day is a Saturday, Sunday, or legal holiday, the period continues to run until the end of the next day that is not a Saturday, Sunday, or legal holiday.

(2) *Period Stated in Hours.* When the period is stated in hours:

(A) begin counting immediately on the occurrence of the event that triggers the period;

(B) count every hour, including hours during intermediate Saturdays, Sundays, and legal holidays; and

(C) if the period would end on a Saturday, Sunday, or legal holiday, the period continues to run until the same time on the next day that is not a Saturday, Sunday, or legal holiday.

(3) *Inaccessibility of the Clerk's Office.* Unless the court orders otherwise, if the clerk's office is inaccessible:

(A) on the last day for filing under Rule 6(a)(1), then the time for filing is extended to the first accessible day that is not a Saturday, Sunday, or legal holiday; or

(B) during the last hour for filing under Rule 6(a)(2), then the time for filing is extended to the same time on the first accessible day that is not a Saturday, Sunday, or legal holiday.

(4) *"Last Day" Defined.* Unless a different time is set by a statute, local rule, or court order, the last day ends:

(A) for electronic filing, at midnight in the court's time zone; and

(B) for filing by other means, when the clerk's office is scheduled to close.

(5) *"Next Day" Defined.* The "next day" is determined by continuing to count forward when the period is measured after an event and backward when measured before an event.

(6) *"Legal Holiday" Defined.* "Legal holiday" means:

(A) the day set aside by statute for observing New Year's Day, Martin Luther King Jr.'s Birthday, Washington's Birthday, Memorial Day, Independence Day, Labor Day, Columbus Day, Veterans' Day, Thanksgiving Day, or Christmas Day;

(B) any day declared a holiday by the President or Congress; and

(C) for periods that are measured after an event, any other day declared a holiday by the state where the district court is located.

(b) Extending Time. (1) *In General.* When an act may or must be done within a specified time, the court may, for good cause, extend the time:

(A) with or without motion or notice if the court acts, or if a request is made, before the original time or its extension expires; or

(B) on motion made after the time has expired if the party failed to act because of excusable neglect.

(2) *Exceptions.* A court must not extend the time to act under Rules 50(b) and (d), 52(b), 59(b), (d), and (e), and 60(b).

(c) Motions, Notices of Hearing, and Affidavits. (1) *In General.* A written motion and notice of the hearing must be served at least 14 days before the time specified for the hearing, with the following exceptions:

(A) when the motion may be heard ex parte;

(B) when these rules set a different time; or

(C) when a court order—which a party may, for good cause, apply for ex parte—sets a different time.

(2) *Supporting Affidavit.* Any affidavit supporting a motion must be served with the motion. Except as Rule 59(c) provides otherwise, any opposing affidavit must be served at least 7 days before the hearing, unless the court permits service at another time.

(d) Additional Time After Certain Kinds of Service. When a party may or must act within a specified time after service and service is made under Rule 5(b)(2)(C), (D), (E), or (F), 3 days are added after the period would otherwise expire under Rule 6(a).

(As amended Dec. 27, 1946, eff. March 19, 1948; Jan. 21, 1963, eff. July 1, 1963; Feb. 28, 1966, eff. July 1, 1966; Dec. 4, 1967, eff. July 1, 1968; March 1, 1971, eff. July 1, 1971; April 28, 1983, eff. Aug. 1, 1983; April 29, 1985, eff. August 1, 1985; March 2, 1987, eff. August 1, 1987; April 26, 1999, eff. Dec. 1, 1999; April 23, 2001, eff. Dec. 1, 2001; April 25, 2005, eff. Dec. 1, 2005; April 30, 2007, eff. Dec. 1, 2007; March 26, 2009, eff. Dec. 1, 2009.)

TITLE III. PLEADINGS AND MOTIONS

Rule 7. Pleadings Allowed; Form of Motions and Other Papers

(a) Pleadings. Only these pleadings are allowed:

(1) a complaint;

(2) an answer to a complaint;

(3) an answer to a counterclaim designated as a counterclaim;

(4) an answer to a crossclaim;

(5) a third-party complaint;

(6) an answer to a third-party complaint; and

(7) if the court orders one, a reply to an answer.

(b) Motions and Other Papers. (1) *In General.* A request for a court order must be made by motion. The motion must:

(A) be in writing unless made during a hearing or trial;

(B) state with particularity the grounds for seeking the order; and

(C) state the relief sought.

(2) *Form.* The rules governing captions and other matters of form in pleadings apply to motions and other papers.

(As amended Dec. 27, 1946, eff. March 19, 1948; Jan. 21, 1963, eff. July 1, 1963; April 28, 1983, eff. Aug. 1, 1983; April 30, 2007, eff Dec. 1, 2007.)

Civil Procedure
Rule 7

Rule 7.1. Disclosure Statement

(a) Who Must File; Contents. A nongovernmental corporate party must file two copies of a disclosure statement that:

(1) identifies any parent corporation and any publicly held corporation owning 10% or more of its stock; or

(2) states that there is no such corporation.

(b) Time to File; Supplemental Filing. A party must:

(1) file the disclosure statement with its first appearance, pleading, petition, motion, response, or other request addressed to the court; and

(2) promptly file a supplemental statement if any required information changes.

(As added April 29, 2002, eff. Dec. 1, 2002; amended April 30, 2007, eff. Dec. 1, 2007.)

Rule 8. General Rules of Pleading

(a) Claim for Relief. A pleading that states a claim for relief must contain:

(1) a short and plain statement of the grounds for the court's jurisdiction, unless the court already has jurisdiction and the claim needs no new jurisdictional support;

(2) a short and plain statement of the claim showing that the pleader is entitled to relief; and

(3) a demand for the relief sought, which may include relief in the alternative or different types of relief.

(b) Defenses; Admissions and Denials. (1) *In General.* In responding to a pleading, a party must:

(A) state in short and plain terms its defenses to each claim asserted against it; and

(B) admit or deny the allegations asserted against it by an opposing party.

(2) *Denials—Responding to the Substance.* A denial must fairly respond to the substance of the allegation.

(3) *General and Specific Denials.* A party that intends in good faith to deny all the allegations of a pleading—including the jurisdictional grounds—may do so by a general denial. A party that does not intend to deny all the allegations must either specifically deny designated allegations or generally deny all except those specifically admitted.

(4) *Denying Part of an Allegation.* A party that intends in good faith to deny only part of an allegation must admit the part that is true and deny the rest.

(5) *Lacking Knowledge or Information.* A party that lacks knowledge or information sufficient to form a belief about the truth of an allegation must so state, and the statement has the effect of a denial.

(6) *Effect of Failing to Deny.* An allegation—other than one relating to the amount of damages—is admitted if a responsive pleading is required and the allegation is not denied. If a responsive pleading is not required, an allegation is considered denied or avoided.

(c) Affirmative Defenses. (1) *In General.* In responding to a pleading, a party must affirmatively state any avoidance or affirmative defense, including:

- accord and satisfaction;
- arbitration and award;
- assumption of risk;
- contributory negligence;
- duress;
- estoppel;
- failure of consideration;
- fraud;
- illegality;
- injury by fellow servant;
- laches;
- license;
- payment;
- release;
- res judicata;
- statute of frauds;
- statute of limitations; and
- waiver.

(2) *Mistaken Designation.* If a party mistakenly designates a defense as a counterclaim, or a counterclaim as a defense, the court must, if justice requires, treat the pleading as though it were correctly designated, and may impose terms for doing so.

(d) Pleading to Be Concise and Direct; Alternative Statements; Inconsistency. (1) *In General.* Each allegation must be simple, concise, and direct. No technical form is required.

(2) *Alternative Statements of a Claim or Defense.* A party may set out two or more statements of a claim or defense alternatively or hypothetically, either in a single count or defense or in separate ones.

If a party makes alternative statements, the pleading is sufficient if any one of them is sufficient.

(3) *Inconsistent Claims or Defenses.* A party may state as many separate claims or defenses as it has, regardless of consistency.

(e) Construing Pleadings. Pleadings must be construed so as to do justice.

(As amended Feb. 28, 1966, eff. July 1, 1966; March 2, 1987, eff. Aug. 1, 1987; April 30, 2007, eff. Dec. 1, 2007; April 28, 2010, eff. Dec. 1, 2010.)

Rule 9. Pleading Special Matters

(a) Capacity or Authority to Sue; Legal Existence. (1) *In General.* Except when required to show that the court has jurisdiction, a pleading need not allege:

(A) a party's capacity to sue or be sued;

(B) a party's authority to sue or be sued in a representative capacity; or

(C) the legal existence of an organized association of persons that is made a party.

(2) *Raising Those Issues.* To raise any of those issues, a party must do so by a specific denial, which must state any supporting facts that are peculiarly within the party's knowledge.

(b) Fraud or Mistake; Conditions of Mind. In alleging fraud or mistake, a party must state with particularity the circumstances constituting fraud or mistake. Malice, intent, knowledge, and other conditions of a person's mind may be alleged generally.

(c) Conditions Precedent. In pleading conditions precedent, it suffices to allege generally that all conditions precedent have occurred or been performed. But when denying that a condition precedent has occurred or been performed, a party must do so with particularity.

(d) Official Document or Act. In pleading an official document or official act, it suffices to allege that the document was legally issued or the act legally done.

(e) Judgment. In pleading a judgment or decision of a domestic or foreign court, a judicial or quasi-judicial tribunal, or a board or officer, it suffices to plead the judgment or decision without showing jurisdiction to render it.

(f) Time and Place. An allegation of time or place is material when testing the sufficiency of a pleading.

(g) Special Damages. If an item of special damage is claimed, it must be specifically stated.

(h) Admiralty or Maritime Claim. (1) *How Designated.* If a claim for relief is within the admiralty or maritime jurisdiction and also within the court's subject-matter jurisdiction on some other ground, the pleading may designate the claim as an admiralty or maritime claim for purposes of Rules 14(c), 38(e), and 82 and the Supplemental Rules for Admiralty or Maritime Claims and Asset Forfeiture Actions. A claim cognizable only in the admiralty or maritime jurisdiction is an admiralty or maritime claim for those purposes, whether or not so designated.

(2) *Designation for Appeal.* A case that includes an admiralty or maritime claim within this subdivision (h) is an admiralty case within 28 U.S.C. § 1292(a)(3).

(As amended Feb. 28, 1966, eff. July 1, 1966; Dec. 4, 1967, eff. July 1, 1968; March 30, 1970, eff. July 1, 1970; March 2, 1987, eff. Aug. 1, 1987; April 11, 1997, eff. Dec. 1, 1997; April 12, 2006, eff. Dec. 1, 2006; April 30, 2007, eff. Dec. 1, 2007.)

Rule 10. Form of Pleadings

(a) Caption; Names of Parties. Every pleading must have a caption with the court's name, a title, a file number, and a Rule 7(a) designation. The title of the complaint must name all the parties; the title of other pleadings, after naming the first party on each side, may refer generally to other parties.

(b) Paragraphs; Separate Statements. A party must state its claims or defenses in numbered paragraphs, each limited as far as practicable to a single set of circumstances. A later pleading may refer by number to a paragraph in an earlier pleading. If doing so would promote clarity, each claim founded on a separate transaction or occurrence—and each defense other than a denial—must be stated in a separate count or defense.

(c) Adoption by Reference; Exhibits. A statement in a pleading may be adopted by reference elsewhere in the same plAs amended Apr. 30, 2007, eff. eading or in any other pleading or motion. A copy of a written instrument that is an exhibit to a pleading is a part of the pleading for all purposes.

(As amended Apr. 30, 2007, eff. Dec. 1, 2007.)

Rule 11. Signing Pleadings, Motions, and Other Papers; Representations to the Court; Sanctions

(a) Signature. Every pleading, written motion, and other paper must be signed by at least one attorney of record in the attorney's name—or by a party personally if the party is unrepresented. The paper must state the signer's address, e-mail address, and telephone number. Unless a rule or statute specifically states otherwise, a pleading need not be verified or accompanied by an affidavit. The court must strike an unsigned paper unless the omission is promptly corrected after being called to the attorney's or party's attention.

(b) Representations to the Court. By presenting to the court a pleading, written motion, or other paper—whether by signing, filing, submitting, or later advocating it—an attorney or unrepresented party certifies that to the best of the person's knowledge, information, and belief, formed after an inquiry reasonable under the circumstances:

(1) it is not being presented for any improper purpose, such as to harass, cause unnecessary delay, or needlessly increase the cost of litigation;

(2) the claims, defenses, and other legal conten-

tions are warranted by existing law or by a nonfrivolous argument for extending, modifying, or reversing existing law or for establishing new law;

(3) the factual contentions have evidentiary support or, if specifically so identified, will likely have evidentiary support after a reasonable opportunity for further investigation or discovery; and

(4) the denials of factual contentions are warranted on the evidence or, if specifically so identified, are reasonably based on belief or a lack of information.

(c) Sanctions. (1) *In General.* If, after notice and a reasonable opportunity to respond, the court determines that Rule 11(b) has been violated, the court may impose an appropriate sanction on any attorney, law firm, or party that violated the rule or is responsible for the violation. Absent exceptional circumstances, a law firm must be held jointly responsible for a violation committed by its partner, associate, or employee.

(2) *Motion for Sanctions.* A motion for sanctions must be made separately from any other motion and must describe the specific conduct that allegedly violates Rule 11(b). The motion must be served under Rule 5, but it must not be filed or be presented to the court if the challenged paper, claim, defense, contention, or denial is withdrawn or appropriately corrected within 21 days after service or within another time the court sets. If warranted, the court may award to the prevailing party the reasonable expenses, including attorney's fees, incurred for the motion.

(3) *On the Court's Initiative.* On its own, the court may order an attorney, law firm, or party to show cause why conduct specifically described in the order has not violated Rule 11(b).

(4) *Nature of a Sanction.* A sanction imposed under this rule must be limited to what suffices to deter repetition of the conduct or comparable conduct by others similarly situated. The sanction may include nonmonetary directives; an order to pay a penalty into court; or, if imposed on motion and warranted for effective deterrence, an order directing payment to the movant of part or all of the reasonable attorney's fees and other expenses directly resulting from the violation.

(5) *Limitations on Monetary Sanctions.* The court must not impose a monetary sanction:

(A) against a represented party for violating Rule 11(b)(2); or

(B) on its own, unless it issued the show-cause order under Rule 11(c)(3) before voluntary dismissal or settlement of the claims made by or against the party that is, or whose attorneys are, to be sanctioned.

(6) *Requirements for an Order.* An order imposing a sanction must describe the sanctioned conduct and explain the basis for the sanction.

(d) Inapplicability to Discovery. This rule does not apply to disclosures and discovery requests, responses, objections, and motions under Rules 26 through 37.

(As amended April 28, 1983, eff. Aug. 1, 1983; March 2, 1987, eff. Aug. 1, 1987; April 22, 1993, eff. Dec. 1, 1993; April 30, 2007, eff. Dec. 1, 2007.)

Rule 12. Defenses and Objections: When and How Presented; Motion for Judgment on the Pleadings; Consolidating Motions; Waiving Defenses; Pretrial Hearing

(a) Time to Serve a Responsive Pleading. (1) *In General.* Unless another time is specified by this rule or a federal statute, the time for serving a responsive pleading is as follows:

(A) A defendant must serve an answer:

(i) within 21 days after being served with the summons and complaint; or

(ii) if it has timely waived service under Rule 4(d), within 60 days after the request for a waiver was sent, or within 90 days after it was sent to the defendant outside any judicial district of the United States.

(B) A party must serve an answer to a counterclaim or crossclaim within 21 days after being served with the pleading that states the counterclaim or crossclaim.

(C) A party must serve a reply to an answer within 21 days after being served with an order to reply, unless the order specifies a different time.

(2) *United States and Its Agencies, Officers, or Employees Sued in an Official Capacity.* The United States, a United States agency, or a United States officer or employee sued only in an official capacity must serve an answer to a complaint, counterclaim, or crossclaim within 60 days after service on the United States attorney.

(3) *United States Officers or Employees Sued in an Individual Capacity.* A United States officer or employee sued in an individual capacity for an act or omission occurring in connection with duties performed on the United States' behalf must serve an answer to a complaint, counterclaim, or crossclaim within 60 days after service on the officer or employee or service on the United States attorney, whichever is later.

(4) *Effect of a Motion.* Unless the court sets a different time, serving a motion under this rule alters these periods as follows:

(A) if the court denies the motion or postpones its disposition until trial, the responsive pleading must be served within 14 days after notice of the court's action; or

(B) if the court grants a motion for a more definite statement, the responsive pleading must be served within 14 days after the more definite statement is served.

(b) How to Present Defenses. Every defense to a claim for relief in any pleading must be asserted in the responsive pleading if one is required. But a party may assert the following defenses by motion:

(1) lack of subject-matter jurisdiction;

(2) lack of personal jurisdiction;

(3) improper venue;

(4) insufficient process;

(5) insufficient service of process;

(6) failure to state a claim upon which relief can be granted; and

(7) failure to join a party under Rule 19.

A motion asserting any of these defenses must be made before pleading if a responsive pleading is allowed. If a pleading sets out a claim for relief that does not require a responsive pleading, an opposing party may assert at trial any defense to that claim. No defense or objection is waived by joining it with one or more other defenses or objections in a responsive pleading or in a motion.

(c) Motion for Judgment on the Pleadings. After the pleadings are closed—but early enough not to delay trial—a party may move for judgment on the pleadings.

(d) Result of Presenting Matters Outside the Pleadings. If, on a motion under Rule 12(b)(6) or 12(c), matters outside the pleadings are presented to and not excluded by the court, the motion must be treated as one for summary judgment under Rule 56. All parties must be given a reasonable opportunity to present all the material that is pertinent to the motion.

(e) Motion for a More Definite Statement. A party may move for a more definite statement of a pleading to which a responsive pleading is allowed but which is so vague or ambiguous that the party cannot reasonably prepare a response. The motion must be made before filing a responsive pleading and must point out the defects complained of and the details desired. If the court orders a more definite statement and the order is not obeyed within 14 days after notice of the order or within the time the court sets, the court may strike the pleading or issue any other appropriate order.

(f) Motion to Strike. The court may strike from a pleading an insufficient defense or any redundant, immaterial, impertinent, or scandalous matter. The court may act:

(1) on its own; or

(2) on motion made by a party either before responding to the pleading or, if a response is not allowed, within 21 days after being served with the pleading.

(g) Joining Motions. (1) *Right to Join.* A motion under this rule may be joined with any other motion allowed by this rule.

(2) *Limitation on Further Motions.* Except as provided in Rule 12(h)(2) or (3), a party that makes a motion under this rule must not make another motion under this rule raising a defense or objection that was available to the party but omitted from its earlier motion.

(h) Waiving and Preserving Certain Defenses. (1) *When Some Are Waived.* A party waives any defense listed in Rule 12(b)(2)–(5) by:

(A) omitting it from a motion in the circumstances described in Rule 12(g)(2); or

(B) failing to either:

(i) make it by motion under this rule; or

(ii) include it in a responsive pleading or in an amendment allowed by Rule 15(a)(1) as a matter of course.

(2) *When to Raise Others.* Failure to state a claim upon which relief can be granted, to join a person required by Rule 19(b), or to state a legal defense to a claim may be raised:

(A) in any pleading allowed or ordered under Rule 7(a);

(B) by a motion under Rule 12(c); or

(C) at trial.

(3) *Lack of Subject-Matter Jurisdiction.* If the court determines at any time that it lacks subject-matter jurisdiction, the court must dismiss the action.

(i) Hearing Before Trial. If a party so moves, any defense listed in Rule 12(b)(1)–(7)—whether made in a pleading or by motion—and a motion under Rule 12(c) must be heard and decided before trial unless the court orders a deferral until trial.

(Amended March 19, 1948; July 1, 1963; July 1, 1966; Aug. 1, 1987; Dec. 1, 1993; Dec. 1, 2000; Dec. 1, 2007; Dec. 1, 2009.)

Rule 13. Counterclaim and Crossclaim

(a) Compulsory Counterclaim. (1) *In General.* A pleading must state as a counterclaim any claim that—at the time of its service—the pleader has against an opposing party if the claim:

(A) arises out of the transaction or occurrence that is the subject matter of the opposing party's claim; and

(B) does not require adding another party over whom the court cannot acquire jurisdiction.

(2) *Exceptions.* The pleader need not state the claim if:

(A) when the action was commenced, the claim was the subject of another pending action; or

(B) the opposing party sued on its claim by attachment or other process that did not establish personal jurisdiction over the pleader on that claim, and the pleader does not assert any counterclaim under this rule.

(b) Permissive Counterclaim. A pleading may state as a counterclaim against an opposing party any claim that is not compulsory.

(c) Relief Sought in a Counterclaim. A counterclaim need not diminish or defeat the recovery sought by the opposing party. It may request relief that exceeds in amount or differs in kind from the relief sought by the opposing party.

(d) Counterclaim Against the United States. These rules do not expand the right to assert a counterclaim—or to claim a credit—against the United States or a United States officer or agency.

(e) Counterclaim Maturing or Acquired After Pleading. The court may permit a party to file a supplemental pleading asserting a counterclaim that matured or was acquired by the party after serving an earlier pleading.

(f) [Abrogated]

(g) Crossclaim Against a Coparty. A pleading may state as a crossclaim any claim by one party against a coparty if the claim arises out of the transaction or occurrence that is the subject matter of the original action or of a counterclaim, or if the claim relates to any property that is the subject matter of the original action. The crossclaim may include a claim that the coparty is or may be liable to the crossclaimant for all or part of a claim asserted in the action against the crossclaimant.

(h) Joining Additional Parties. Rules 19 and 20 govern the addition of a person as a party to a counterclaim or crossclaim.

(i) Separate Trials; Separate Judgments. If the court orders separate trials under Rule 42(b), it may enter judgment on a counterclaim or crossclaim under Rule 54(b) when it has jurisdiction to do so, even if the opposing party's claims have been dismissed or otherwise resolved.

(Amended March 19, 1948; July 1, 1963; July 1, 1966; Aug. 1, 1987; Dec. 1, 2007; Dec. 1, 2009.)

Rule 14. Third-Party Practice

(a) When a Defending Party May Bring in a Third Party. (1) *Timing of the Summons and Complaint.* A defending party may, as third-party plaintiff, serve a summons and complaint on a nonparty who is or may be liable to it for all or part of the claim against it. But the third-party plaintiff must, by motion, obtain the court's leave if it files the third-party complaint more than 14 days after serving its original answer.

(2) *Third-Party Defendant's Claims and Defenses.* The person served with the summons and third-party complaint—the "third-party defendant":

(A) must assert any defense against the third-party plaintiff's claim under Rule 12;

(B) must assert any counterclaim against the third-party plaintiff under Rule 13(a), and may assert any counterclaim against the third-party plaintiff under Rule 13(b) or any crossclaim against another third-party defendant under Rule 13(g);

(C) may assert against the plaintiff any defense that the third-party plaintiff has to the plaintiff's claim; and

(D) may also assert against the plaintiff any claim arising out of the transaction or occurrence that is the subject matter of the plaintiff's claim against the third-party plaintiff.

(3) *Plaintiff's Claims Against a Third-Party Defendant.* The plaintiff may assert against the third-party defendant any claim arising out of the transaction or occurrence that is the subject matter of the plaintiff's claim against the third-party plaintiff. The third-party defendant must then assert any defense under Rule 12 and any counterclaim under Rule 13(a), and may assert any counterclaim under Rule 13(b) or any crossclaim under Rule 13(g).

(4) *Motion to Strike, Sever, or Try Separately.* Any party may move to strike the third-party claim, to sever it, or to try it separately.

(5) *Third-Party Defendant's Claim Against a Nonparty.* A third-party defendant may proceed under this rule against a nonparty who is or may be liable to the third-party defendant for all or part of any claim against it.

(6) *Third-Party Complaint In Rem.* If it is within the admiralty or maritime jurisdiction, a third-party complaint may be in rem. In that event, a reference in this rule to the "summons" includes the warrant of arrest, and a reference to the defendant or third-party plaintiff includes, when appropriate, a person who asserts a right under Supplemental Rule C(6)(a)(i) in the property arrested.

(b) When a Plaintiff May Bring in a Third Party. When a claim is asserted against a plaintiff, the plaintiff may bring in a third party if this rule would allow a defendant to do so.

(c) Admiralty or Maritime Claim. (1) *Scope of Impleader.* If a plaintiff asserts an admiralty or maritime claim under Rule 9(h), the defendant or a person who asserts a right under Supplemental Rule C(6)(a)(i) may, as a third-party plaintiff, bring in a third-party defendant who may be wholly or partly liable—either to the plaintiff or to the third-party plaintiff—for remedy over, contribution, or otherwise on account of the same transaction, occurrence, or series of transactions or occurrences.

(2) *Defending Against a Demand for Judgment for the Plaintiff.* The third-party plaintiff may demand judgment in the plaintiff's favor against the third-party defendant. In that event, the third-party defendant must defend under Rule 12 against the plaintiff's claim as well as the third-party plaintiff's claim; and the action proceeds as if the plaintiff had sued both the third-party defendant and the third-party plaintiff.

(Amended March 19, 1948; July 1, 1963; July 1, 1966; Aug. 1, 1987; Dec. 1, 2000; Dec. 1, 2006; Dec. 1, 2007; Dec. 1, 2009.)

Rule 15. Amended and Supplemental Pleadings

(a) Amendments Before Trial. (1) *Amending as a Matter of Course.* A party may amend its pleading once as a matter of course within:

(A) 21 days after serving it, or

(B) if the pleading is one to which a responsive pleading is required, 21 days after service of a responsive pleading or 21 days after service of a motion under Rule 12(b), (e), or (f), whichever is earlier.

(2) *Other Amendments.* In all other cases, a party may amend its pleading only with the opposing party's written consent or the court's leave. The court should freely give leave when justice so requires.

(3) *Time to Respond.* Unless the court orders otherwise, any required response to an amended pleading must be made within the time remaining to

respond to the original pleading or within 14 days after service of the amended pleading, whichever is later.

(b) Amendments During and After Trial. (1) *Based on an Objection at Trial.* If, at trial, a party objects that evidence is not within the issues raised in the pleadings, the court may permit the pleadings to be amended. The court should freely permit an amendment when doing so will aid in presenting the merits and the objecting party fails to satisfy the court that the evidence would prejudice that party's action or defense on the merits. The court may grant a continuance to enable the objecting party to meet the evidence.

(2) *For Issues Tried by Consent.* When an issue not raised by the pleadings is tried by the parties' express or implied consent, it must be treated in all respects as if raised in the pleadings. A party may move—at any time, even after judgment—to amend the pleadings to conform them to the evidence and to raise an unpleaded issue. But failure to amend does not affect the result of the trial of that issue.

(c) Relation Back of Amendments. (1) *When an Amendment Relates Back.* An amendment to a pleading relates back to the date of the original pleading when:

(A) the law that provides the applicable statute of limitations allows relation back;

(B) the amendment asserts a claim or defense that arose out of the conduct, transaction, or occurrence set out—or attempted to be set out—in the original pleading; or

(C) the amendment changes the party or the naming of the party against whom a claim is asserted, if Rule 15(c)(1)(B) is satisfied and if, within the period provided by Rule 4(m) for serving the summons and complaint, the party to be brought in by amendment:

(i) received such notice of the action that it will not be prejudiced in defending on the merits; and

(ii) knew or should have known that the action would have been brought against it, but for a mistake concerning the proper party's identity.

(2) *Notice to the United States.* When the United States or a United States officer or agency is added as a defendant by amendment, the notice requirements of Rule 15(c)(1)(C)(i) and (ii) are satisfied if, during the stated period, process was delivered or mailed to the United States attorney or the United States attorney's designee, to the Attorney General of the United States, or to the officer or agency.

(d) Supplemental Pleadings. On motion and reasonable notice, the court may, on just terms, permit a party to serve a supplemental pleading setting out any transaction, occurrence, or event that happened after the date of the pleading to be supplemented. The court may permit supplementation even though the original pleading is defective in stating a claim or defense. The court may order that the opposing party plead to the supplemental pleading within a specified time.

(Amended July 1, 1963; July 1, 1966, Aug. 1, 1987; Dec. 1, 1991; Dec. 9, 1991, P. L. 102-198, § 11(a), 105 Stat. 1626; Dec. 1, 1993; Dec. 1, 2007; Dec. 1, 2009.)

Rule 16. Pretrial Conferences; Scheduling; Management

(a) Purposes of a Pretrial Conference. In any action, the court may order the attorneys and any unrepresented parties to appear for one or more pretrial conferences for such purposes as:

(1) expediting disposition of the action;

(2) establishing early and continuing control so that the case will not be protracted because of lack of management;

(3) discouraging wasteful pretrial activities;

(4) improving the quality of the trial through more thorough preparation; and

(5) facilitating settlement.

(b) Scheduling. (1) *Scheduling Order.* Except in categories of actions exempted by local rule, the district judge—or a magistrate judge when authorized by local rule—must issue a scheduling order:

(A) after receiving the parties' report under Rule 26(f); or

(B) after consulting with the parties' attorneys and any unrepresented parties at a scheduling conference or by telephone, mail, or other means.

(2) *Time to Issue.* The judge must issue the scheduling order as soon as practicable, but in any event within the earlier of 120 days after any defendant has been served with the complaint or 90 days after any defendant has appeared.

(3) *Contents of the Order.* (A) Required Contents. The scheduling order must limit the time to join other parties, amend the pleadings, complete discovery, and file motions.

(B) Permitted Contents. The scheduling order may:

(i) modify the timing of disclosures under Rules 26(a) and 26(e)(1);

(ii) modify the extent of discovery;

(iii) provide for disclosure or discovery of electronically stored information;

(iv) include any agreements the parties reach for asserting claims of privilege or of protection as trial-preparation material after information is produced;

(v) set dates for pretrial conferences and for trial; and

(vi) include other appropriate matters.

(4) *Modifying a Schedule.* A schedule may be modified only for good cause and with the judge's consent.

(c) Attendance and Matters for Consideration at a Pretrial Conference. (1) *Attendance.* A represented party must authorize at least one of its attorneys to make stipulations and admissions about all matters that can reasonably be anticipated for discussion at a pretrial conference. If appropriate, the court may require that a party or its representative be present or reasonably available by other means to consider possible settlement.

(2) *Matters for Consideration.* At any pretrial conference, the court may consider and take appropriate action on the following matters:

(A) formulating and simplifying the issues, and eliminating frivolous claims or defenses;

(B) amending the pleadings if necessary or desirable;

(C) obtaining admissions and stipulations about facts and documents to avoid unnecessary proof, and ruling in advance on the admissibility of evidence;

(D) avoiding unnecessary proof and cumulative evidence, and limiting the use of testimony under Federal Rule of Evidence 702;

(E) determining the appropriateness and timing of summary adjudication under Rule 56;

(F) controlling and scheduling discovery, including orders affecting disclosures and discovery under Rule 26 and Rules 29 through 37;

(G) identifying witnesses and documents, scheduling the filing and exchange of any pretrial briefs, and setting dates for further conferences and for trial;

(H) referring matters to a magistrate judge or a master;

(I) settling the case and using special procedures to assist in resolving the dispute when authorized by statute or local rule;

(J) determining the form and content of the pretrial order;

(K) disposing of pending motions;

(L) adopting special procedures for managing potentially difficult or protracted actions that may involve complex issues, multiple parties, difficult legal questions, or unusual proof problems;

(M) ordering a separate trial under Rule 42(b) of a claim, counterclaim, crossclaim, third-party claim, or particular issue;

(N) ordering the presentation of evidence early in the trial on a manageable issue that might, on the evidence, be the basis for a judgment as a matter of law under Rule 50(a) or a judgment on partial findings under Rule 52(c);

(O) establishing a reasonable limit on the time allowed to present evidence; and

(P) facilitating in other ways the just, speedy, and inexpensive disposition of the action.

(d) Pretrial Orders. After any conference under this rule, the court should issue an order reciting the action taken. This order controls the course of the action unless the court modifies it.

(e) Final Pretrial Conference and Orders. The court may hold a final pretrial conference to formulate a trial plan, including a plan to facilitate the admission of evidence. The conference must be held as close to the start of trial as is reasonable, and must be attended by at least one attorney who will conduct the trial for each party and by any unrepresented party. The court may modify an order issued after a final pretrial conference only to prevent manifest injustice.

(f) Sanctions. (1) *In General.* On motion or on its own, the court may issue any just orders, including those authorized by Rule 37(b)(2)(A)(ii)–(vii), if a party or its attorney:

(A) fails to appear at a scheduling or other pretrial conference;

(B) is substantially unprepared to participate—or does not participate in good faith—in the conference; or

(C) fails to obey a scheduling or other pretrial order.

(2) *Imposing Fees and Costs.* Instead of or in addition to any other sanction, the court must order the party, its attorney, or both to pay the reasonable expenses—including attorney's fees—incurred because of any noncompliance with this rule, unless the noncompliance was substantially justified or other circumstances make an award of expenses unjust.

(Amended Aug. 1, 1983; Aug. 1, 1987; Dec. 1, 1993; Dec. 1, 2006; Dec. 1, 2007.)

TITLE IV. PARTIES

Rule 17. Plaintiff and Defendant; Capacity; Public Officers

(a) Real Party in Interest. (1) *Designation in General.* An action must be prosecuted in the name of the real party in interest. The following may sue in their own names without joining the person for whose benefit the action is brought:

(A) an executor;

(B) an administrator;

(C) a guardian;

(D) a bailee;

(E) a trustee of an express trust;

(F) a party with whom or in whose name a contract has been made for another's benefit; and

(G) a party authorized by statute.

(2) *Action in the Name of the United States for Another's Use or Benefit.* When a federal statute so provides, an action for another's use or benefit must be brought in the name of the United States.

(3) *Joinder of the Real Party in Interest.* The court may not dismiss an action for failure to prosecute in the name of the real party in interest until, after an objection, a reasonable time has been allowed for the real party in interest to ratify, join, or be substituted into the action. After ratification, joinder, or substitution, the action proceeds as if it had been originally commenced by the real party in interest.

(b) Capacity to Sue or Be Sued. Capacity to sue or be sued is determined as follows:

(1) for an individual who is not acting in a representative capacity, by the law of the individual's domicile;

(2) for a corporation, by the law under which it was organized; and

(3) for all other parties, by the law of the state where the court is located, except that:

(A) a partnership or other unincorporated association with no such capacity under that state's law may sue or be sued in its common name to enforce a substantive right existing under the United States Constitution or laws; and

(B) 28 U.S.C. §§ 754 and 959(a) govern the capacity of a receiver appointed by a United States court to sue or be sued in a United States court.

(c) Minor or Incompetent Person. (1) *With a Representative.* The following representatives may sue or defend on behalf of a minor or an incompetent person:

(A) a general guardian;

(B) a committee;

(C) a conservator; or

(D) a like fiduciary.

(2) *Without a Representative.* A minor or an incompetent person who does not have a duly appointed representative may sue by a next friend or by a guardian ad litem. The court must appoint a guardian ad litem—or issue another appropriate order—to protect a minor or incompetent person who is unrepresented in an action.

(d) Public Officer's Title and Name. A public officer who sues or is sued in an official capacity may be designated by official title rather than by name, but the court may order that the officer's name be added.

(Amended March 19, 1948; Oct. 20, 1949; July 1, 1966; Aug. 1, 1987; Aug. 1, 1988; Nov. 18, 1988, P. L. 100-690, Title VII, Subtitle B, § 7049, 102 Stat. 4401; Dec. 1, 2007.)

Rule 18. Joinder of Claims

(a) In General. A party asserting a claim, counterclaim, crossclaim, or third-party claim may join, as independent or alternative claims, as many claims as it has against an opposing party.

(b) Joinder of Contingent Claims. A party may join two claims even though one of them is contingent on the disposition of the other; but the court may grant relief only in accordance with the parties' relative substantive rights. In particular, a plaintiff may state a claim for money and a claim to set aside a conveyance that is fraudulent as to that plaintiff, without first obtaining a judgment for the money.

(Amended July 1, 1966; Aug. 1, 1987; Dec. 1, 2007.)

Rule 19. Required Joinder of Parties

(a) Persons Required to Be Joined if Feasible. (1) *Required Party.* A person who is subject to service of process and whose joinder will not deprive the court of subject-matter jurisdiction must be joined as a party if:

(A) in that person's absence, the court cannot accord complete relief among existing parties; or

(B) that person claims an interest relating to the subject of the action and is so situated that disposing of the action in the person's absence may:

(i) as a practical matter impair or impede the person's ability to protect the interest; or

(ii) leave an existing party subject to a substantial risk of incurring double, multiple, or otherwise inconsistent obligations because of the interest.

(2) *Joinder by Court Order.* If a person has not been joined as required, the court must order that the person be made a party. A person who refuses to join as a plaintiff may be made either a defendant or, in a proper case, an involuntary plaintiff.

(3) *Venue.* If a joined party objects to venue and the joinder would make venue improper, the court must dismiss that party.

(b) When Joinder Is Not Feasible. If a person who is required to be joined if feasible cannot be joined, the court must determine whether, in equity and good conscience, the action should proceed among the existing parties or should be dismissed. The factors for the court to consider include:

(1) the extent to which a judgment rendered in the person's absence might prejudice that person or the existing parties;

(2) the extent to which any prejudice could be lessened or avoided by:

(A) protective provisions in the judgment;

(B) shaping the relief; or

(C) other measures;

(3) whether a judgment rendered in the person's absence would be adequate; and

(4) whether the plaintiff would have an adequate remedy if the action were dismissed for nonjoinder.

(c) Pleading the Reasons for Nonjoinder. When asserting a claim for relief, a party must state:

(1) the name, if known, of any person who is required to be joined if feasible but is not joined; and

(2) the reasons for not joining that person.

(d) Exception for Class Actions. This rule is subject to Rule 23.

(Amended July 1, 1966; Aug. 1, 1987; Dec. 1, 2007.)

Rule 20. Permissive Joinder of Parties

(a) Persons Who May Join or Be Joined. (1) *Plaintiffs.* Persons may join in one action as plaintiffs if:

(A) they assert any right to relief jointly, severally, or in the alternative with respect to or arising out of the same transaction, occurrence, or series of transactions or occurrences; and

(B) any question of law or fact common to all plaintiffs will arise in the action.

(2) *Defendants.* Persons—as well as a vessel, cargo, or other property subject to admiralty process in rem—may be joined in one action as defendants if:

(A) any right to relief is asserted against them jointly, severally, or in the alternative with respect to or arising out of the same transaction, occurrence, or series of transactions or occurrences; and

(B) any question of law or fact common to all defendants will arise in the action.

(3) *Extent of Relief.* Neither a plaintiff nor a defendant need be interested in obtaining or defending against all the relief demanded. The court may

grant judgment to one or more plaintiffs according to their rights, and against one or more defendants according to their liabilities.

(b) Protective Measures. The court may issue orders—including an order for separate trials—to protect a party against embarrassment, delay, expense, or other prejudice that arises from including a person against whom the party asserts no claim and who asserts no claim against the party.

(Amended July 1, 1966; Aug. 1, 1987; Dec. 1, 2007.)

Rule 21. Misjoinder and Nonjoinder of Parties

Misjoinder of parties is not a ground for dismissing an action. On motion or on its own, the court may at any time, on just terms, add or drop a party. The court may also sever any claim against a party.

(Amended Dec. 1, 2007.)

Rule 22. Interpleader

(a) Grounds. (1) *By a Plaintiff.* Persons with claims that may expose a plaintiff to double or multiple liability may be joined as defendants and required to interplead. Joinder for interpleader is proper even though:

(A) the claims of the several claimants, or the titles on which their claims depend, lack a common origin or are adverse and independent rather than identical; or

(B) the plaintiff denies liability in whole or in part to any or all of the claimants.

(2) *By a Defendant.* A defendant exposed to similar liability may seek interpleader through a crossclaim or counterclaim.

(b) Relation to Other Rules and Statutes. This rule supplements—and does not limit—the joinder of parties allowed by Rule 20. The remedy it provides is in addition to—and does not supersede or limit—the remedy provided by 28 U.S.C. §§ 1335, 1397, and 2361. An action under those statutes must be conducted under these rules.

(Amended Oct. 20, 1949; Aug. 1, 1987; Dec. 1, 2007.)

Rule 23. Class Actions

(a) Prerequisites. One or more members of a class may sue or be sued as representative parties on behalf of all members only if:

(1) the class is so numerous that joinder of all members is impracticable;

(2) there are questions of law or fact common to the class;

(3) the claims or defenses of the representative parties are typical of the claims or defenses of the class; and

(4) the representative parties will fairly and adequately protect the interests of the class.

(b) Types of Class Actions. A class action may be maintained if Rule 23(a) is satisfied and if:

(1) prosecuting separate actions by or against individual class members would create a risk of:

(A) inconsistent or varying adjudications with respect to individual class members that would establish incompatible standards of conduct for the party opposing the class; or

(B) adjudications with respect to individual class members that, as a practical matter, would be dispositive of the interests of the other members not parties to the individual adjudications or would substantially impair or impede their ability to protect their interests;

(2) the party opposing the class has acted or refused to act on grounds that apply generally to the class, so that final injunctive relief or corresponding declaratory relief is appropriate respecting the class as a whole; or

(3) the court finds that the questions of law or fact common to class members predominate over any questions affecting only individual members, and that a class action is superior to other available methods for fairly and efficiently adjudicating the controversy. The matters pertinent to these findings include:

(A) the class members' interests in individually controlling the prosecution or defense of separate actions;

(B) the extent and nature of any litigation concerning the controversy already begun by or against class members;

(C) the desirability or undesirability of concentrating the litigation of the claims in the particular forum; and

(D) the likely difficulties in managing a class action.

(c) Certification Order; Notice to Class Members; Judgment; Issues Classes; Subclasses. (1) *Certification Order.* (A) Time to Issue. At an early practicable time after a person sues or is sued as a class representative, the court must determine by order whether to certify the action as a class action.

(B) Defining the Class; Appointing Class Counsel. An order that certifies a class action must define the class and the class claims, issues, or defenses, and must appoint class counsel under Rule 23(g).

(C) Altering or Amending the Order. An order that grants or denies class certification may be altered or amended before final judgment.

(2) *Notice.* (A) For (b)(1) or (b)(2) Classes. For any class certified under Rule 23(b)(1) or (b)(2), the court may direct appropriate notice to the class.

(B) For (b)(3) Classes. For any class certified under Rule 23(b)(3), the court must direct to class members the best notice that is practicable under the circumstances, including individual notice to all members who can be identified through reasonable effort. The notice must clearly and concisely state in plain, easily understood language:

(i) the nature of the action;

(ii) the definition of the class certified;

(iii) the class claims, issues, or defenses;

(iv) that a class member may enter an appearance

through an attorney if the member so desires;

(v) that the court will exclude from the class any member who requests exclusion;

(vi) the time and manner for requesting exclusion; and

(vii) the binding effect of a class judgment on members under Rule 23(c)(3).

(3) *Judgment.* Whether or not favorable to the class, the judgment in a class action must:

(A) for any class certified under Rule 23(b)(1) or (b)(2), include and describe those whom the court finds to be class members; and

(B) for any class certified under Rule 23(b)(3), include and specify or describe those to whom the Rule 23(c)(2) notice was directed, who have not requested exclusion, and whom the court finds to be class members.

(4) *Particular Issues.* When appropriate, an action may be maintained as a class action with respect to particular issues.

(5) *Subclasses.* When appropriate, a class may be divided into subclasses that are each treated as a class under this rule.

(d) Conducting the Action. (1) *In General.* In conducting an action under this rule, the court may issue orders that:

(A) determine the course of proceedings or prescribe measures to prevent undue repetition or complication in presenting evidence or argument;

(B) require—to protect class members and fairly conduct the action—giving appropriate notice to some or all class members of:

(i) any step in the action;

(ii) the proposed extent of the judgment; or

(iii) the members' opportunity to signify whether they consider the representation fair and adequate, to intervene and present claims or defenses, or to otherwise come into the action;

(C) impose conditions on the representative parties or on intervenors;

(D) require that the pleadings be amended to eliminate allegations about representation of absent persons and that the action proceed accordingly; or

(E) deal with similar procedural matters.

(2) *Combining and Amending Orders.* An order under Rule 23(d)(1) may be altered or amended from time to time and may be combined with an order under Rule 16.

(e) Settlement, Voluntary Dismissal, or Compromise. The claims, issues, or defenses of a certified class may be settled, voluntarily dismissed, or compromised only with the court's approval. The following procedures apply to a proposed settlement, voluntary dismissal, or compromise:

(1) The court must direct notice in a reasonable manner to all class members who would be bound by the proposal.

(2) If the proposal would bind class members, the court may approve it only after a hearing and on finding that it is fair, reasonable, and adequate.

(3) The parties seeking approval must file a statement identifying any agreement made in connection with the proposal.

(4) If the class action was previously certified under Rule 23(b)(3), the court may refuse to approve a settlement unless it affords a new opportunity to request exclusion to individual class members who had an earlier opportunity to request exclusion but did not do so.

(5) Any class member may object to the proposal if it requires court approval under this subdivision (e); the objection may be withdrawn only with the court's approval.

(f) Appeals. A court of appeals may permit an appeal from an order granting or denying class-action certification under this rule if a petition for permission to appeal is filed with the circuit clerk within 14 days after the order is entered. An appeal does not stay proceedings in the district court unless the district judge or the court of appeals so orders.

(g) Class Counsel. (1) *Appointing Class Counsel.* Unless a statute provides otherwise, a court that certifies a class must appoint class counsel. In appointing class counsel, the court:

(A) must consider:

(i) the work counsel has done in identifying or investigating potential claims in the action;

(ii) counsel's experience in handling class actions, other complex litigation, and the types of claims asserted in the action;

(iii) counsel's knowledge of the applicable law; and

(iv) the resources that counsel will commit to representing the class;

(B) may consider any other matter pertinent to counsel's ability to fairly and adequately represent the interests of the class;

(C) may order potential class counsel to provide information on any subject pertinent to the appointment and to propose terms for attorney's fees and nontaxable costs;

(D) may include in the appointing order provisions about the award of attorney's fees or nontaxable costs under Rule 23(h); and

(E) may make further orders in connection with the appointment.

(2) *Standard for Appointing Class Counsel.* When one applicant seeks appointment as class counsel, the court may appoint that applicant only if the applicant is adequate under Rule 23(g)(1) and (4). If more than one adequate applicant seeks appointment, the court must appoint the applicant best able to represent the interests of the class.

(3) *Interim Counsel.* The court may designate interim counsel to act on behalf of a putative class before determining whether to certify the action as a class action.

(4) *Duty of Class Counsel.* Class counsel must fairly and adequately represent the interests of the class.

(h) Attorney's Fees and Nontaxable Costs. In a certified class action, the court may award reasonable attorney's fees and nontaxable costs that are authorized by law or by the parties' agreement. The following procedures apply:

(1) A claim for an award must be made by motion under Rule 54(d)(2), subject to the provisions of this subdivision (h), at a time the court sets. Notice of the motion must be served on all parties and, for motions by class counsel, directed to class members in a reasonable manner.

(2) A class member, or a party from whom payment is sought, may object to the motion.

(3) The court may hold a hearing and must find the facts and state its legal conclusions under Rule 52(a).

(4) The court may refer issues related to the amount of the award to a special master or a magistrate judge, as provided in Rule 54(d)(2)(D).

(Amended July 1, 1966; Aug. 1, 1987; Dec. 1, 1998; Dec. 1, 2003; Dec. 1, 2007; Dec. 1, 2009.)

Rule 23.1. Derivative Actions

(a) Prerequisites. This rule applies when one or more shareholders or members of a corporation or an unincorporated association bring a derivative action to enforce a right that the corporation or association may properly assert but has failed to enforce. The derivative action may not be maintained if it appears that the plaintiff does not fairly and adequately represent the interests of shareholders or members who are similarly situated in enforcing the right of the corporation or association.

(b) Pleading Requirements. The complaint must be verified and must:

(1) allege that the plaintiff was a shareholder or member at the time of the transaction complained of, or that the plaintiff's share or membership later devolved on it by operation of law;

(2) allege that the action is not a collusive one to confer jurisdiction that the court would otherwise lack; and

(3) state with particularity:

(A) any effort by the plaintiff to obtain the desired action from the directors or comparable authority and, if necessary, from the shareholders or members; and

(B) the reasons for not obtaining the action or not making the effort.

(c) Settlement, Dismissal, and Compromise. A derivative action may be settled, voluntarily dismissed, or compromised only with the court's approval. Notice of a proposed settlement, voluntary dismissal, or compromise must be given to shareholders or members in the manner that the court orders.

(Added Feb. 28, 1966, eff. July 1, 1966; March 2, 1987, eff. Aug. 1, 1987; April 30, 2007, eff. Dec. 1, 2007.)

Rule 23.2. Actions Relating to Unincorporated Associations

This rule applies to an action brought by or against the members of an unincorporated association as a class by naming certain members as representative parties. The action may be maintained only if it appears that those parties will fairly and adequately protect the interests of the association and its members. In conducting the action, the court may issue any appropriate orders corresponding with those in Rule 23(d), and the procedure for settlement, voluntary dismissal, or compromise must correspond with the procedure in Rule 23(e).

(Added Feb. 28, 1966, eff. July 1, 1966; April 30, 2007, eff. Dec. 1, 2007.)

Rule 24. Intervention

(a) Intervention of Right. On timely motion, the court must permit anyone to intervene who:

(1) is given an unconditional right to intervene by a federal statute; or

(2) claims an interest relating to the property or transaction that is the subject of the action, and is so situated that disposing of the action may as a practical matter impair or impede the movant's ability to protect its interest, unless existing parties adequately represent that interest.

(b) Permissive Intervention. (1) *In General.* On timely motion, the court may permit anyone to intervene who:

(A) is given a conditional right to intervene by a federal statute; or

(B) has a claim or defense that shares with the main action a common question of law or fact.

(2) *By a Government Officer or Agency.* On timely motion, the court may permit a federal or state governmental officer or agency to intervene if a party's claim or defense is based on:

(A) a statute or executive order administered by the officer or agency; or

(B) any regulation, order, requirement, or agreement issued or made under the statute or executive order.

(3) *Delay or Prejudice.* In exercising its discretion, the court must consider whether the intervention will unduly delay or prejudice the adjudication of the original parties' rights.

(c) Notice and Pleading Required. A motion to intervene must be served on the parties as provided in Rule 5. The motion must state the grounds for intervention and be accompanied by a pleading that sets out the claim or defense for which intervention is sought.

(Amended Dec. 27, 1946, eff. March 19, 1948; Dec. 29, 1948, eff. Oct. 20, 1949; Jan. 21, 1963, eff. July 1, 1963; Feb. 28, 1966, eff. July 1, 1966; March 2, 1987, eff. Aug. 1, 1987; April 30, 1991, eff. Dec. 1, 1991; April 12, 2006, eff. Dec. 1, 2006; April 30, 2007, eff. Dec. 1, 2007.)

Rule 25. Substitution of Parties

(a) Death. (1) *Substitution if the Claim Is Not Extinguished.* If a party dies and the claim is not extinguished, the court may order substitution of the proper party. A motion for substitution may be made by any party or by the decedent's successor or representative. If the motion is not made within 90 days after service of a statement noting the death, the action by or against the decedent must be dismissed.

(2) *Continuation Among the Remaining Parties.* After a party's death, if the right sought to be enforced survives only to or against the remaining parties, the action does not abate, but proceeds in favor of or against the remaining parties. The death should be noted on the record.

(3) *Service.* A motion to substitute, together with a notice of hearing, must be served on the parties as provided in Rule 5 and on nonparties as provided in Rule 4. A statement noting death must be served in the same manner. Service may be made in any judicial district.

(b) Incompetency. If a party becomes incompetent, the court may, on motion, permit the action to be continued by or against the party's representative. The motion must be served as provided in Rule 25(a)(3).

(c) Transfer of Interest. If an interest is transferred, the action may be continued by or against the original party unless the court, on motion, orders the transferee to be substituted in the action or joined with the original party. The motion must be served as provided in Rule 25(a)(3).

(d) Public Officers; Death or Separation from Office. An action does not abate when a public officer who is a party in an official capacity dies, resigns, or otherwise ceases to hold office while the action is pending. The officer's successor is automatically substituted as a party. Later proceedings should be in the substituted party's name, but any misnomer not affecting the parties' substantial rights must be disregarded. The court may order substitution at any time, but the absence of such an order does not affect the substitution.

(Amended Dec. 29, 1948, eff. Oct. 20, 1949; April 17, 1961, eff. July 19, 1961; Jan. 21, 1963, eff. July 1, 1963; March 2, 1987, eff. Aug. 1, 1987; April 30, 2007, eff. Dec. 1, 2007.)

TITLE V. DISCLOSURES AND DISCOVERY

Rule 26. Duty to Disclose; General Provisions Governing Discovery

(a) Required Disclosures. (1) *Initial Disclosure.* (A) In General. Except as exempted by Rule 26(a)(1)(B) or as otherwise stipulated or ordered by the court, a party must, without awaiting a discovery request, provide to the other parties:

(i) the name and, if known, the address and telephone number of each individual likely to have discoverable information—along with the subjects of that information—that the disclosing party may use to support its claims or defenses, unless the use would be solely for impeachment;

(ii) a copy—or a description by category and location—of all documents, electronically stored information, and tangible things that the disclosing party has in its possession, custody, or control and may use to support its claims or defenses, unless the use would be solely for impeachment;

(iii) a computation of each category of damages claimed by the disclosing party—who must also make available for inspection and copying as under Rule 34 the documents or other evidentiary material, unless privileged or protected from disclosure, on which each computation is based, including materials bearing on the nature and extent of injuries suffered; and

(iv) for inspection and copying as under Rule 34, any insurance agreement under which an insurance business may be liable to satisfy all or part of a possible judgment in the action or to indemnify or reimburse for payments made to satisfy the judgment.

(B) Proceedings Exempt from Initial Disclosure. The following proceedings are exempt from initial disclosure:

(i) an action for review on an administrative record;

(ii) a forfeiture action in rem arising from a federal statute;

(iii) a petition for habeas corpus or any other proceeding to challenge a criminal conviction or sentence;

(iv) an action brought without an attorney by a person in the custody of the United States, a state, or a state subdivision;

(v) an action to enforce or quash an administrative summons or subpoena;

(vi) an action by the United States to recover benefit payments;

(vii) an action by the United States to collect on a student loan guaranteed by the United States;

(viii) a proceeding ancillary to a proceeding in another court; and

(ix) an action to enforce an arbitration award.

(C) Time for Initial Disclosures—In General. A party must make the initial disclosures at or within 14 days after the parties' Rule 26(f) conference unless a different time is set by stipulation or court order, or unless a party objects during the conference that initial disclosures are not appropriate in this action and states the objection in the proposed discovery plan. In ruling on the objection, the court must determine what disclosures, if any, are to be made and must set the time for disclosure.

(D) Time for Initial Disclosures—For Parties Served or Joined Later. A party that is first served or otherwise joined after the Rule 26(f) conference must make the initial disclosures within 30 days after being served or joined, unless a different time is set by stipulation or court order.

(E) Basis for Initial Disclosure; Unacceptable Excuses. A party must make its initial disclosures based on the information then reasonably available to it. A party is not excused from making its disclosures because it has not fully investigated the case or because it challenges the sufficiency of another party's disclosures or because another party has not made its disclosures.

(2) *Disclosure of Expert Testimony.* (A) In General. In addition to the disclosures required by Rule 26(a)(1), a party must disclose to the other parties the identity of any witness it may use at trial to present evidence under Federal Rule of Evidence 702, 703, or 705.

(B) Witnesses Who Must Provide a Written Report. Unless otherwise stipulated or ordered by the court, this disclosure must be accompanied by a written report—prepared and signed by the witness—if the witness is one retained or specially employed to provide expert testimony in the case or one whose duties as the party's employee regularly involve giving expert testimony. The report must contain:

(i) a complete statement of all opinions the witness will express and the basis and reasons for them;

(ii) the facts or data considered by the witness in forming them;

(iii) any exhibits that will be used to summarize or support them;

(iv) the witness's qualifications, including a list of all publications authored in the previous 10 years;

(v) a list of all other cases in which, during the previous 4 years, the witness testified as an expert at trial or by deposition; and

(vi) a statement of the compensation to be paid for the study and testimony in the case.

(C) Witnesses Who Do Not Provide a Written Report. Unless otherwise stipulated or ordered by the court, if the witness is not required to provide a written report, this disclosure must state:

(i) the subject matter on which the witness is expected to present evidence under Federal Rule of Evidence 702, 703, or 705; and

(ii) a summary of the facts and opinions to which the witness is expected to testify.

(D) Time to Disclose Expert Testimony. A party must make these disclosures at the times and in the sequence that the court orders. Absent a stipulation or a court order, the disclosures must be made:

(i) at least 90 days before the date set for trial or for the case to be ready for trial; or

(ii) if the evidence is intended solely to contradict or rebut evidence on the same subject matter identified by another party under Rule 26(a)(2)(B) or (C), within 30 days after the other party's disclosure.

(E) Supplementing the Disclosure. The parties must supplement these disclosures when required under Rule 26(e).

(3) *Pretrial Disclosures.* (A) In General. In addition to the disclosures required by Rule 26(a)(1) and (2), a party must provide to the other parties and promptly file the following information about the evidence that it may present at trial other than solely for impeachment:

(i) the name and, if not previously provided, the address and telephone number of each witness—separately identifying those the party expects to present and those it may call if the need arises;

(ii) the designation of those witnesses whose testimony the party expects to present by deposition and, if not taken stenographically, a transcript of the pertinent parts of the deposition; and

(iii) an identification of each document or other exhibit, including summaries of other evidence—separately identifying those items the party expects to offer and those it may offer if the need arises.

(B) Time for Pretrial Disclosures; Objections. Unless the court orders otherwise, these disclosures must be made at least 30 days before trial. Within 14 days after they are made, unless the court sets a different time, a party may serve and promptly file a list of the following objections: any objections to the use under Rule 32(a) of a deposition designated by another party under Rule 26(a)(3)(A)(ii); and any objection, together with the grounds for it, that may be made to the admissibility of materials identified under Rule 26(a)(3)(A)(iii). An objection not so made—except for one under Federal Rule of Evidence 402 or 403—is waived unless excused by the court for good cause.

(4) *Form of Disclosures.* Unless the court orders otherwise, all disclosures under Rule 26(a) must be in writing, signed, and served.

(b) Discovery Scope and Limits. (1) *Scope in General.* Unless otherwise limited by court order, the scope of discovery is as follows: Parties may obtain discovery regarding any nonprivileged matter that is relevant to any party's claim or defense—including the existence, description, nature, custody, condition, and location of any documents or other tangible things and the identity and location of persons who know of any discoverable matter. For good cause, the court may order discovery of any matter relevant to the subject matter involved in the action. Relevant information need not be admissible at the trial if the discovery appears reasonably calculated to lead to the discovery of admissible evidence. All discovery is subject to the limitations imposed by Rule 26(b)(2)(C).

(2) *Limitations on Frequency and Extent.* (A) When Permitted. By order, the court may alter the limits in these rules on the number of depositions and interrogatories or on the length of depositions under Rule 30. By order or local rule, the court may also limit the number of requests under Rule 36.

(B) Specific Limitations on Electronically Stored Information. A party need not provide discovery of electronically stored information from sources that the party identifies as not reasonably accessible because of undue burden or cost. On motion to compel discovery or for a protective order, the party from whom discovery is sought must show that the information is not reasonably accessible because of undue burden or cost. If that showing is made, the court may nonetheless order discovery from such sources if the requesting party shows good cause, considering the limitations of Rule 26(b)(2)(C). The court may specify conditions for the discovery.

(C) When Required. On motion or on its own, the court must limit the frequency or extent of discovery otherwise allowed by these rules or by local rule if it determines that:

(i) the discovery sought is unreasonably cumulative or duplicative, or can be obtained from some other source that is more convenient, less burdensome, or less expensive;

(ii) the party seeking discovery has had ample opportunity to obtain the information by discovery in the action; or

(iii) the burden or expense of the proposed discovery outweighs its likely benefit, considering the needs of the case, the amount in controversy, the parties' resources, the importance of the issues at stake in the action, and the importance of the discovery in resolving the issues.

(3) *Trial Preparation: Materials.* (A) Documents and Tangible Things. Ordinarily, a party may not discover documents and tangible things that are prepared in anticipation of litigation or for trial by or for another party or its representative (including the other party's attorney, consultant, surety, indemnitor, insurer, or agent). But, subject to Rule 26(b)(4), those materials may be discovered if:

(i) they are otherwise discoverable under Rule 26(b)(1); and

(ii) the party shows that it has substantial need for the materials to prepare its case and cannot, without undue hardship, obtain their substantial equivalent by other means.

(B) Protection Against Disclosure. If the court orders discovery of those materials, it must protect against disclosure of the mental impressions, conclusions, opinions, or legal theories of a party's attorney or other representative concerning the litigation.

(C) Previous Statement. Any party or other person may, on request and without the required showing, obtain the person's own previous statement about the action or its subject matter. If the request is refused, the person may move for a court order, and Rule 37(a)(5) applies to the award of expenses. A previous statement is either:

(i) a written statement that the person has signed or otherwise adopted or approved; or

(ii) a contemporaneous stenographic, mechanical, electrical, or other recording—or a transcription of it—that recites substantially verbatim the person's oral statement.

(4) *Trial Preparation: Experts.* (A) Deposition of an Expert Who May Testify. A party may depose any person who has been identified as an expert whose opinions may be presented at trial. If Rule 26(a)(2)(B) requires a report from the expert, the deposition may be conducted only after the report is provided.

(B) Trial-Preparation Protection for Draft Reports or Disclosures. Rules 26(b)(3)(A) and (B) protect drafts of any report or disclosure required under Rule 26(a)(2), regardless of the form in which the draft is recorded.

(C) Trial-Preparation Protection for Communications Between a Party's Attorney and Expert Witnesses. Rules 26(b)(3)(A) and (B) protect communications between the party's attorney and any witness required to provide a report under Rule 26(a)(2)(B), regardless of the form of the communications, except to the extent that the communications:

(i) relate to compensation for the expert's study or testimony;

(ii) identify facts or data that the party's attorney provided and that the expert considered in forming the opinions to be expressed; or

(iii) identify assumptions that the party's attorney provided and that the expert relied on in forming the opinions to be expressed.

(D) Expert Employed Only for Trial Preparation. Ordinarily, a party may not, by interrogatories or deposition, discover facts known or opinions held by an expert who has been retained or specially employed by another party in anticipation of litigation or to prepare for trial and who is not expected to be called as a witness at trial. But a party may do so only:

(i) as provided in Rule 35(b); or

(ii) on showing exceptional circumstances under which it is impracticable for the party to obtain facts or opinions on the same subject by other means.

(E) Payment. Unless manifest injustice would result, the court must require that the party seeking discovery:

(i) pay the expert a reasonable fee for time spent in responding to discovery under Rule 26(b)(4)(A) or (D); and

(ii) for discovery under (D), also pay the other party a fair portion of the fees and expenses it reasonably incurred in obtaining the expert's facts and opinions.

(5) *Claiming Privilege or Protecting Trial-Preparation Materials.* (A) Information Withheld. When a party withholds information otherwise discoverable by claiming that the information is privileged or subject to protection as trial-preparation material, the party must:

(i) expressly make the claim; and

(ii) describe the nature of the documents, communications, or tangible things not produced or disclosed—and do so in a manner that, without revealing information itself privileged or protected, will enable other parties to assess the claim.

(B) Information Produced. If information produced in discovery is subject to a claim of privilege or of protection as trial-preparation material, the party making the claim may notify any party that received the information of the claim and the basis for it. After being notified, a party must promptly return, sequester, or destroy the specified information and any copies it has; must not use or disclose the information until the claim is resolved; must take reasonable steps to retrieve the information if the party disclosed it before being notified; and may promptly present the information to the court under seal for a determination of the claim. The producing party must preserve the information until the claim is resolved.

(c) Protective Orders. (1) *In General.* A party or any person from whom discovery is sought may move for a protective order in the court where the action is pending—or as an alternative on matters relating to a deposition, in the court for the district where the deposition will be taken. The motion must include a certification that the movant has in good faith conferred or attempted to confer with other affected parties in an effort to resolve the dispute without court action. The court may, for good cause, issue an order to protect a party or person from annoyance, embarrassment, oppression, or undue burden or expense, including one or more of the following:

(A) forbidding the disclosure or discovery;

(B) specifying terms, including time and place, for the disclosure or discovery;

(C) prescribing a discovery method other than the one selected by the party seeking discovery;

(D) forbidding inquiry into certain matters, or limiting the scope of disclosure or discovery to certain matters;

(E) designating the persons who may be present while the discovery is conducted;

(F) requiring that a deposition be sealed and opened only on court order;

(G) requiring that a trade secret or other confidential research, development, or commercial information not be revealed or be revealed only in a specified way; and

(H) requiring that the parties simultaneously file specified documents or information in sealed envelopes, to be opened as the court directs.

(2) *Ordering Discovery.* If a motion for a protective order is wholly or partly denied, the court may, on just terms, order that any party or person provide or permit discovery.

(3) *Awarding Expenses.* Rule 37(a)(5) applies to the award of expenses.

(d) Timing and Sequence of Discovery. (1) *Timing.* A party may not seek discovery from any source before the parties have conferred as required by Rule 26(f), except in a proceeding exempted from initial disclosure under Rule 26(a)(1)(B), or when authorized by these rules, by stipulation, or by court order.

(2) *Sequence.* Unless, on motion, the court orders otherwise for the parties' and witnesses' convenience and in the interests of justice:

(A) methods of discovery may be used in any sequence; and

(B) discovery by one party does not require any other party to delay its discovery.

(e) Supplementing Disclosures and Responses. (1) *In General.* A party who has made a disclosure under Rule 26(a)—or who has responded to an interrogatory, request for production, or request for admission—must supplement or correct its disclosure or response:

(A) in a timely manner if the party learns that in some material respect the disclosure or response is incomplete or incorrect, and if the additional or corrective information has not otherwise been made known to the other parties during the discovery process or in writing; or

(B) as ordered by the court.

(2) *Expert Witness.* For an expert whose report must be disclosed under Rule 26(a)(2)(B), the party's duty to supplement extends both to information included in the report and to information given during the expert's deposition. Any additions or changes to this information must be disclosed by the time the party's pretrial disclosures under Rule 26(a)(3) are due.

(f) Conference of the Parties; Planning for Discovery. (1) *Conference Timing.* Except in a proceeding exempted from initial disclosure under Rule 26(a)(1)(B) or when the court orders otherwise, the parties must confer as soon as practicable—and in any event at least 21 days before a scheduling conference is held or a scheduling order is due under Rule 16(b).

(2) *Conference Content; Parties' Responsibilities.* In conferring, the parties must consider the nature and basis of their claims and defenses and the possibilities for promptly settling or resolving the case; make or arrange for the disclosures required by Rule 26(a)(1); discuss any issues about preserving discoverable information; and develop a proposed discovery plan. The attorneys of record and all unrepresented parties that have appeared in the case are jointly responsible for arranging the conference, for attempting in good faith to agree on the proposed discovery plan, and for submitting to the court within 14 days after the conference a written report outlining the plan. The court may order the parties or attorneys to attend the conference in person.

(3) *Discovery Plan.* A discovery plan must state the parties' views and proposals on:

(A) what changes should be made in the timing, form, or requirement for disclosures under Rule 26(a), including a statement of when initial disclosures were made or will be made;

(B) the subjects on which discovery may be needed, when discovery should be completed, and whether discovery should be conducted in phases or be limited to or focused on particular issues;

(C) any issues about disclosure or discovery of electronically stored information, including the form or forms in which it should be produced;

(D) any issues about claims of privilege or of protection as trial-preparation materials, including—if the parties agree on a procedure to assert these claims after production—whether to ask the court to include their agreement in an order;

(E) what changes should be made in the limitations on discovery imposed under these rules or by local rule, and what other limitations should be imposed; and

(F) any other orders that the court should issue under Rule 26(c) or under Rule 16(b) and (c).

(4) *Expedited Schedule.* If necessary to comply with its expedited schedule for Rule 16(b) conferences, a court may by local rule:

(A) require the parties' conference to occur less than 21 days before the scheduling conference is held or a scheduling order is due under Rule 16(b); and

(B) require the written report outlining the discovery plan to be filed less than 14 days after the parties' conference, or excuse the parties from submitting a written report and permit them to report orally on their discovery plan at the Rule 16(b) conference.

(g) Signing Disclosures and Discovery Requests, Responses, and Objections. (1) *Signature Required; Effect of Signature.* Every disclosure under Rule 26(a)(1) or (a)(3) and every discovery request, response, or objection must be signed by at least one attorney of record in the attorney's own name—or by the party personally, if unrepresented—and must state the signer's address, e-mail address, and telephone number. By signing, an attorney or party certifies that to the best of the person's knowledge, information, and belief formed after a reasonable inquiry:

(A) with respect to a disclosure, it is complete and correct as of the time it is made; and

(B) with respect to a discovery request, response, or objection, it is:

(i) consistent with these rules and warranted by existing law or by a nonfrivolous argument for extending, modifying, or reversing existing law, or for establishing new law;

(ii) not interposed for any improper purpose, such as to harass, cause unnecessary delay, or needlessly increase the cost of litigation; and

(iii) neither unreasonable nor unduly burdensome or expensive, considering the needs of the case, prior discovery in the case, the amount in controversy, and the importance of the issues at stake in the action.

(2) *Failure to Sign.* Other parties have no duty to act on an unsigned disclosure, request, response, or objection until it is signed, and the court must strike it unless a signature is promptly supplied after the omission is called to the attorney's or party's attention.

(3) *Sanction for Improper Certification.* If a certification violates this rule without substantial justification, the court, on motion or on its own, must impose an appropriate sanction on the signer, the party on whose behalf the signer was acting, or both. The sanction may include an order to pay the reasonable expenses, including attorney's fees, caused by the violation.

(Amended Dec. 27, 1946, eff. March 19, 1948; Jan. 21, 1963, eff. July 1, 1963; Feb. 28, 1966, eff. July 1, 1966; March 30, 1970, eff. July 1, 1970; Apr. 29, 1980, eff. Aug. 1, 1980; Apr. 28, 1983, eff. Aug. 1, 1983; March 2, 1987, eff. Aug. 1, 1987; Dec. 1, 1993; Dec. 1, 2000; Dec. 1, 2006; Dec. 1, 2007; Dec. 1, 2010.)

Rule 27. Depositions to Perpetuate Testimony

(a) Before an Action Is Filed. (1) *Petition.* A person who wants to perpetuate testimony about any matter cognizable in a United States court may file a verified petition in the district court for the district where any expected adverse party resides. The petition must ask for an order authorizing the petitioner to depose the named persons in order to perpetuate their testimony. The petition must be titled in the petitioner's name and must show:

(A) that the petitioner expects to be a party to an action cognizable in a United States court but cannot presently bring it or cause it to be brought;

(B) the subject matter of the expected action and the petitioner's interest;

(C) the facts that the petitioner wants to establish by the proposed testimony and the reasons to perpetuate it;

(D) the names or a description of the persons whom the petitioner expects to be adverse parties and their addresses, so far as known; and

(E) the name, address, and expected substance of the testimony of each deponent.

(2) *Notice and Service.* At least 21 days before the hearing date, the petitioner must serve each expected adverse party with a copy of the petition and a notice stating the time and place of the hearing. The notice may be served either inside or outside the district or state in the manner provided in Rule 4. If that service cannot be made with reasonable diligence on an expected adverse party, the court may order service by publication or otherwise. The court must appoint an attorney to represent persons not served in the manner provided in Rule 4 and to cross-examine the deponent if an unserved person is not otherwise represented. If any expected adverse party is a minor or is incompetent, Rule 17(c) applies.

(3) *Order and Examination.* If satisfied that perpetuating the testimony may prevent a failure or delay of justice, the court must issue an order that designates or describes the persons whose depositions may be taken, specifies the subject matter of the examinations, and states whether the depositions will be taken orally or by written interrogatories. The depositions may then be taken under these rules, and the court may issue orders like those authorized by Rules 34 and 35. A reference in these rules to the court where an action is pending means, for purposes of this rule, the court where the petition for the deposition was filed.

(4) *Using the Deposition.* A deposition to perpetu-

ate testimony may be used under Rule 32(a) in any later-filed district-court action involving the same subject matter if the deposition either was taken under these rules or, although not so taken, would be admissible in evidence in the courts of the state where it was taken.

(b) Pending Appeal. (1) *In General.* The court where a judgment has been rendered may, if an appeal has been taken or may still be taken, permit a party to depose witnesses to perpetuate their testimony for use in the event of further proceedings in that court.

(2) *Motion.* The party who wants to perpetuate testimony may move for leave to take the depositions, on the same notice and service as if the action were pending in the district court. The motion must show:

(A) the name, address, and expected substance of the testimony of each deponent; and

(B) the reasons for perpetuating the testimony.

(3) *Court Order.* If the court finds that perpetuating the testimony may prevent a failure or delay of justice, the court may permit the depositions to be taken and may issue orders like those authorized by Rules 34 and 35. The depositions may be taken and used as any other deposition taken in a pending district-court action.

(c) Perpetuation by an Action. This rule does not limit a court's power to entertain an action to perpetuate testimony.

(Amended Dec. 27, 1946, eff. March 19, 1948; Dec. 29, 1948, eff. Oct. 20, 1949; March 1, 1971, eff. July 1, 1971; March 2, 1987, eff. Aug. 1, 1987; April 25, 2005, eff. Dec. 1, 2005; April 30, 2007, eff. Dec. 1, 2007; March 26, 2009, eff. Dec. 1, 2009.)

Rule 28. Persons Before Whom Depositions May Be Taken

(a) Within the United States. (1) *In General.* Within the United States or a territory or insular possession subject to United States jurisdiction, a deposition must be taken before:

(A) an officer authorized to administer oaths either by federal law or by the law in the place of examination; or

(B) a person appointed by the court where the action is pending to administer oaths and take testimony.

(2) *Definition of "Officer."* The term "officer" in Rules 30, 31, and 32 includes a person appointed by the court under this rule or designated by the parties under Rule 29(a).

(b) In a Foreign Country. (1) *In General.* A deposition may be taken in a foreign country:

(A) under an applicable treaty or convention;

(B) under a letter of request, whether or not captioned a "letter rogatory";

(C) on notice, before a person authorized to administer oaths either by federal law or by the law in the place of examination; or

(D) before a person commissioned by the court to administer any necessary oath and take testimony.

(2) *Issuing a Letter of Request or a Commission.* A letter of request, a commission, or both may be issued:

(A) on appropriate terms after an application and notice of it; and

(B) without a showing that taking the deposition in another manner is impracticable or inconvenient.

(3) *Form of a Request, Notice, or Commission.* When a letter of request or any other device is used according to a treaty or convention, it must be captioned in the form prescribed by that treaty or convention. A letter of request may be addressed "To the Appropriate Authority in [name of country]." A deposition notice or a commission must designate by name or descriptive title the person before whom the deposition is to be taken.

(4) *Letter of Request—Admitting Evidence.* Evidence obtained in response to a letter of request need not be excluded merely because it is not a verbatim transcript, because the testimony was not taken under oath, or because of any similar departure from the requirements for depositions taken within the United States.

(c) Disqualification. A deposition must not be taken before a person who is any party's relative, employee, or attorney; who is related to or employed by any party's attorney; or who is financially interested in the action.

(Amended Dec. 27, 1946, eff. March 19, 1948; Jan. 21, 1963, eff. July 1, 1963; Apr. 29, 1980, eff. Aug. 1, 1980; March 2, 1987, eff. Aug. 1, 1987; Apr. 22, 1993, eff. Dec. 1, 1993; Apr. 1, 2007, eff. Dec. 1, 2007.)

Rule 29. Stipulations About Discovery Procedure

Unless the court orders otherwise, the parties may stipulate that:

(a) a deposition may be taken before any person, at any time or place, on any notice, and in the manner specified—in which event it may be used in the same way as any other deposition; and

(b) other procedures governing or limiting discovery be modified—but a stipulation extending the time for any form of discovery must have court approval if it would interfere with the time set for completing discovery, for hearing a motion, or for trial.

(Amended March 30, 1970, eff. July 1, 1970; April 22, 1993, eff. Dec. 1, 1993; April 30, 2007, eff. Dec. 1, 2007.)

Rule 30. Depositions by Oral Examination

(a) When a Deposition May Be Taken. (1) *Without Leave.* A party may, by oral questions, depose any person, including a party, without leave of court except as provided in Rule 30(a)(2). The deponent's attendance may be compelled by subpoena under Rule 45.

(2) *With Leave.* A party must obtain leave of court, and the court must grant leave to the extent consis-

tent with Rule 26(b)(2):

(A) if the parties have not stipulated to the deposition and:

(i) the deposition would result in more than 10 depositions being taken under this rule or Rule 31 by the plaintiffs, or by the defendants, or by the third-party defendants;

(ii) the deponent has already been deposed in the case; or

(iii) the party seeks to take the deposition before the time specified in Rule 26(d), unless the party certifies in the notice, with supporting facts, that the deponent is expected to leave the United States and be unavailable for examination in this country after that time; or

(B) if the deponent is confined in prison.

(b) Notice of the Deposition; Other Formal Requirements. (1) *Notice in General.* A party who wants to depose a person by oral questions must give reasonable written notice to every other party. The notice must state the time and place of the deposition and, if known, the deponent's name and address. If the name is unknown, the notice must provide a general description sufficient to identify the person or the particular class or group to which the person belongs.

(2) *Producing Documents.* If a subpoena duces tecum is to be served on the deponent, the materials designated for production, as set out in the subpoena, must be listed in the notice or in an attachment. The notice to a party deponent may be accompanied by a request complying with Rule 34 to produce documents and tangible things at the deposition.

(3) *Method of Recording.* (A) Method Stated in the Notice. The party who notices the deposition must state in the notice the method for recording the testimony. Unless the court orders otherwise, testimony may be recorded by audio, audiovisual, or stenographic means. The noticing party bears the recording costs. Any party may arrange to transcribe a deposition.

(B) Additional Method. With prior notice to the deponent and other parties, any party may designate another method for recording the testimony in addition to that specified in the original notice. That party bears the expense of the additional record or transcript unless the court orders otherwise.

(4) *By Remote Means.* The parties may stipulate—or the court may on motion order—that a deposition be taken by telephone or other remote means. For the purpose of this rule and Rules 28(a), 37(a)(2), and 37(b)(1), the deposition takes place where the deponent answers the questions.

(5) *Officer's Duties.* (A) Before the Deposition. Unless the parties stipulate otherwise, a deposition must be conducted before an officer appointed or designated under Rule 28. The officer must begin the deposition with an on-the-record statement that includes:

(i) the officer's name and business address;

(ii) the date, time, and place of the deposition;

(iii) the deponent's name;

(iv) the officer's administration of the oath or affirmation to the deponent; and

(v) the identity of all persons present.

(B) Conducting the Deposition; Avoiding Distortion. If the deposition is recorded nonstenographically, the officer must repeat the items in Rule 30(b)(5)(A)(i)–(iii) at the beginning of each unit of the recording medium. The deponent's and attorneys' appearance or demeanor must not be distorted through recording techniques.

(C) After the Deposition. At the end of a deposition, the officer must state on the record that the deposition is complete and must set out any stipulations made by the attorneys about custody of the transcript or recording and of the exhibits, or about any other pertinent matters.

(6) *Notice or Subpoena Directed to an Organization.* In its notice or subpoena, a party may name as the deponent a public or private corporation, a partnership, an association, a governmental agency, or other entity and must describe with reasonable particularity the matters for examination. The named organization must then designate one or more officers, directors, or managing agents, or designate other persons who consent to testify on its behalf; and it may set out the matters on which each person designated will testify. A subpoena must advise a nonparty organization of its duty to make this designation. The persons designated must testify about information known or reasonably available to the organization. This paragraph (6) does not preclude a deposition by any other procedure allowed by these rules.

(c) Examination and Cross-Examination; Record of the Examination; Objections; Written Questions. (1) *Examination and Cross-Examination.* The examination and cross-examination of a deponent proceed as they would at trial under the Federal Rules of Evidence, except Rules 103 and 615. After putting the deponent under oath or affirmation, the officer must record the testimony by the method designated under Rule 30(b)(3)(A). The testimony must be recorded by the officer personally or by a person acting in the presence and under the direction of the officer.

(2) *Objections.* An objection at the time of the examination—whether to evidence, to a party's conduct, to the officer's qualifications, to the manner of taking the deposition, or to any other aspect of the deposition—must be noted on the record, but the examination still proceeds; the testimony is taken subject to any objection. An objection must be stated concisely in a nonargumentative and nonsuggestive manner. A person may instruct a deponent not to answer only when necessary to preserve a privilege, to enforce a limitation ordered by the court, or to present a motion under Rule 30(d)(3).

(3) *Participating Through Written Questions.* Instead of participating in the oral examination, a

party may serve written questions in a sealed envelope on the party noticing the deposition, who must deliver them to the officer. The officer must ask the deponent those questions and record the answers verbatim.

(d) Duration; Sanction; Motion to Terminate or Limit. (1) *Duration.* Unless otherwise stipulated or ordered by the court, a deposition is limited to 1 day of 7 hours. The court must allow additional time consistent with Rule 26(b)(2) if needed to fairly examine the deponent or if the deponent, another person, or any other circumstance impedes or delays the examination.

(2) *Sanction.* The court may impose an appropriate sanction—including the reasonable expenses and attorney's fees incurred by any party—on a person who impedes, delays, or frustrates the fair examination of the deponent.

(3) *Motion to Terminate or Limit.* (A) Grounds. At any time during a deposition, the deponent or a party may move to terminate or limit it on the ground that it is being conducted in bad faith or in a manner that unreasonably annoys, embarrasses, or oppresses the deponent or party. The motion may be filed in the court where the action is pending or the deposition is being taken. If the objecting deponent or party so demands, the deposition must be suspended for the time necessary to obtain an order.

(B) Order. The court may order that the deposition be terminated or may limit its scope and manner as provided in Rule 26(c). If terminated, the deposition may be resumed only by order of the court where the action is pending.

(C) Award of Expenses. Rule 37(a)(5) applies to the award of expenses.

(e) Review by the Witness; Changes. (1) *Review; Statement of Changes.* On request by the deponent or a party before the deposition is completed, the deponent must be allowed 30 days after being notified by the officer that the transcript or recording is available in which:

(A) to review the transcript or recording; and

(B) if there are changes in form or substance, to sign a statement listing the changes and the reasons for making them.

(2) *Changes Indicated in the Officer's Certificate.* The officer must note in the certificate prescribed by Rule 30(f)(1) whether a review was requested and, if so, must attach any changes the deponent makes during the 30-day period.

(f) Certification and Delivery; Exhibits; Copies of the Transcript or Recording; Filing. (1) *Certification and Delivery.* The officer must certify in writing that the witness was duly sworn and that the deposition accurately records the witness's testimony. The certificate must accompany the record of the deposition. Unless the court orders otherwise, the officer must seal the deposition in an envelope or package bearing the title of the action and marked "Deposition of [witness's name]" and must promptly send it to the attorney who arranged for the transcript or recording. The attorney must store it under conditions that will protect it against loss, destruction, tampering, or deterioration.

(2) *Documents and Tangible Things.* (A) Originals and Copies. Documents and tangible things produced for inspection during a deposition must, on a party's request, be marked for identification and attached to the deposition. Any party may inspect and copy them. But if the person who produced them wants to keep the originals, the person may:

(i) offer copies to be marked, attached to the deposition, and then used as originals—after giving all parties a fair opportunity to verify the copies by comparing them with the originals; or

(ii) give all parties a fair opportunity to inspect and copy the originals after they are marked—in which event the originals may be used as if attached to the deposition.

(B) Order Regarding the Originals. Any party may move for an order that the originals be attached to the deposition pending final disposition of the case.

(3) *Copies of the Transcript or Recording.* Unless otherwise stipulated or ordered by the court, the officer must retain the stenographic notes of a deposition taken stenographically or a copy of the recording of a deposition taken by another method. When paid reasonable charges, the officer must furnish a copy of the transcript or recording to any party or the deponent.

(4) *Notice of Filing.* A party who files the deposition must promptly notify all other parties of the filing.

(g) Failure to Attend a Deposition or Serve a Subpoena; Expenses. A party who, expecting a deposition to be taken, attends in person or by an attorney may recover reasonable expenses for attending, including attorney's fees, if the noticing party failed to:

(1) attend and proceed with the deposition; or

(2) serve a subpoena on a nonparty deponent, who consequently did not attend.

(Amended Jan. 21, 1963, eff. July 1, 1963; March 30, 1970, eff. July 1, 1970; March 1, 1971, eff. July 1, 1971; Nov. 20, 1972, eff. July 1, 1975; April 29, 1980, eff. Aug. 1, 1980; March 2, 1987, eff. Aug. 1, 1987; April 22, 1993, eff. Dec. 1, 1993; April 17, 2000, eff. Dec. 1, 2000; April 30, 2007, eff. Dec. 1, 2007.)

Rule 31. Depositions by Written Questions

(a) When a Deposition May Be Taken. (1) *Without Leave.* A party may, by written questions, depose any person, including a party, without leave of court except as provided in Rule 31(a)(2). The deponent's attendance may be compelled by subpoena under Rule 45.

(2) *With Leave.* A party must obtain leave of court, and the court must grant leave to the extent consistent with Rule 26(b)(2):

(A) if the parties have not stipulated to the deposition and:

(i) the deposition would result in more than 10

depositions being taken under this rule or Rule 30 by the plaintiffs, or by the defendants, or by the third-party defendants;

(ii) the deponent has already been deposed in the case; or

(iii) the party seeks to take a deposition before the time specified in Rule 26(d); or

(B) if the deponent is confined in prison.

(3) *Service; Required Notice.* A party who wants to depose a person by written questions must serve them on every other party, with a notice stating, if known, the deponent's name and address. If the name is unknown, the notice must provide a general description sufficient to identify the person or the particular class or group to which the person belongs. The notice must also state the name or descriptive title and the address of the officer before whom the deposition will be taken.

(4) *Questions Directed to an Organization.* A public or private corporation, a partnership, an association, or a governmental agency may be deposed by written questions in accordance with Rule 30(b)(6).

(5) *Questions from Other Parties.* Any questions to the deponent from other parties must be served on all parties as follows: cross-questions, within 14 days after being served with the notice and direct questions; redirect questions, within 7 days after being served with cross-questions; and recross-questions, within 7 days after being served with redirect questions. The court may, for good cause, extend or shorten these times.

(b) Delivery to the Officer; Officer's Duties. The party who noticed the deposition must deliver to the officer a copy of all the questions served and of the notice. The officer must promptly proceed in the manner provided in Rule 30(c), (e), and (f) to:

(1) take the deponent's testimony in response to the questions;

(2) prepare and certify the deposition; and

(3) send it to the party, attaching a copy of the questions and of the notice.

(c) Notice of Completion or Filing. (1) *Completion.*The party who noticed the deposition must notify all other parties when it is completed.

(2) *Filing.* A party who files the deposition must promptly notify all other parties of the filing.

(Amended March 30, 1970, eff. July 1, 1970; March 2, 1987, eff. Aug. 1, 1987; April 22, 1993, eff. Dec. 1, 1993; April 30, 2007, eff. Dec. 1, 2007.)

Rule 32. Using Depositions in Court Proceedings

(a) Using Depositions. (1) *In General.* At a hearing or trial, all or part of a deposition may be used against a party on these conditions:

(A) the party was present or represented at the taking of the deposition or had reasonable notice of it;

(B) it is used to the extent it would be admissible under the Federal Rules of Evidence if the deponent were present and testifying; and

(C) the use is allowed by Rule 32(a)(2) through (8).

(2) *Impeachment and Other Uses.* Any party may use a deposition to contradict or impeach the testimony given by the deponent as a witness, or for any other purpose allowed by the Federal Rules of Evidence.

(3) *Deposition of Party, Agent, or Designee.* An adverse party may use for any purpose the deposition of a party or anyone who, when deposed, was the party's officer, director, managing agent, or designee under Rule 30(b)(6) or 31(a)(4).

(4) *Unavailable Witness.* A party may use for any purpose the deposition of a witness, whether or not a party, if the court finds:

(A) that the witness is dead;

(B) that the witness is more than 100 miles from the place of hearing or trial or is outside the United States, unless it appears that the witness's absence was procured by the party offering the deposition;

(C) that the witness cannot attend or testify because of age, illness, infirmity, or imprisonment;

(D) that the party offering the deposition could not procure the witness's attendance by subpoena; or

(E) on motion and notice, that exceptional circumstances make it desirable—in the interest of justice and with due regard to the importance of live testimony in open court—to permit the deposition to be used.

(5) *Limitations on Use.* (A) Deposition Taken on Short Notice. A deposition must not be used against a party who, having received less than 14 days' notice of the deposition, promptly moved for a protective order under Rule 26(c)(1)(B) requesting that it not be taken or be taken at a different time or place—and this motion was still pending when the deposition was taken.

(B) Unavailable Deponent; Party Could Not Obtain an Attorney. A deposition taken without leave of court under the unavailability provision of Rule 30(a)(2)(A)(iii) must not be used against a party who shows that, when served with the notice, it could not, despite diligent efforts, obtain an attorney to represent it at the deposition.

(6) *Using Part of a Deposition.* If a party offers in evidence only part of a deposition, an adverse party may require the offeror to introduce other parts that in fairness should be considered with the part introduced, and any party may itself introduce any other parts.

(7) *Substituting a Party.* Substituting a party under Rule 25 does not affect the right to use a deposition previously taken.

(8) *Deposition Taken in an Earlier Action.* A deposition lawfully taken and, if required, filed in any federal- or state-court action may be used in a later action involving the same subject matter between the same parties, or their representatives or successors in interest, to the same extent as if taken in the later action. A deposition previously taken may also be used as allowed by the Federal Rules of Evidence.

(b) Objections to Admissibility. Subject to

Rules 28(b) and 32(d)(3), an objection may be made at a hearing or trial to the admission of any deposition testimony that would be inadmissible if the witness were present and testifying.

(c) Form of Presentation. Unless the court orders otherwise, a party must provide a transcript of any deposition testimony the party offers, but may provide the court with the testimony in nontranscript form as well. On any party's request, deposition testimony offered in a jury trial for any purpose other than impeachment must be presented in nontranscript form, if available, unless the court for good cause orders otherwise.

(d) Waiver of Objections. (1) *To the Notice.* An objection to an error or irregularity in a deposition notice is waived unless promptly served in writing on the party giving the notice.

(2) *To the Officer's Qualification.* An objection based on disqualification of the officer before whom a deposition is to be taken is waived if not made:

(A) before the deposition begins; or

(B) promptly after the basis for disqualification becomes known or, with reasonable diligence, could have been known.

(3) *To the Taking of the Deposition.* (A) Objection to Competence, Relevance, or Materiality. An objection to a deponent's competence—or to the competence, relevance, or materiality of testimony—is not waived by a failure to make the objection before or during the deposition, unless the ground for it might have been corrected at that time.

(B) Objection to an Error or Irregularity. An objection to an error or irregularity at an oral examination is waived if:

(i) it relates to the manner of taking the deposition, the form of a question or answer, the oath or affirmation, a party's conduct, or other matters that might have been corrected at that time; and

(ii) it is not timely made during the deposition.

(C) Objection to a Written Question. An objection to the form of a written question under Rule 31 is waived if not served in writing on the party submitting the question within the time for serving responsive questions or, if the question is a recross-question, within 7 days after being served with it.

(4) *To Completing and Returning the Deposition.* An objection to how the officer transcribed the testimony—or prepared, signed, certified, sealed, endorsed, sent, or otherwise dealt with the deposition—is waived unless a motion to suppress is made promptly after the error or irregularity becomes known or, with reasonable diligence, could have been known.

(Amended March 30, 1970, eff. July 1, 1970; Nov. 20, 1972, eff. July 1, 1975; April 29, 1980, eff. Aug. 1, 1980; March 2, 1987, eff. Aug. 1, 1987; April 22, 1993, eff. Dec. 1, 1993; April 30, 2007, eff. Dec. 1, 2007; March 26, 2009, eff. Dec. 1, 2009.)

Rule 33. Interrogatories to Parties

(a) In General. (1) *Number.* Unless otherwise stipulated or ordered by the court, a party may serve on any other party no more than 25 written interrogatories, including all discrete subparts. Leave to serve additional interrogatories may be granted to the extent consistent with Rule 26(b)(2).

(2) *Scope.* An interrogatory may relate to any matter that may be inquired into under Rule 26(b). An interrogatory is not objectionable merely because it asks for an opinion or contention that relates to fact or the application of law to fact, but the court may order that the interrogatory need not be answered until designated discovery is complete, or until a pretrial conference or some other time.

(b) Answers and Objections. (1) *Responding Party.* The interrogatories must be answered:

(A) by the party to whom they are directed; or

(B) if that party is a public or private corporation, a partnership, an association, or a governmental agency, by any officer or agent, who must furnish the information available to the party.

(2) *Time to Respond.* The responding party must serve its answers and any objections within 30 days after being served with the interrogatories. A shorter or longer time may be stipulated to under Rule 29 or be ordered by the court.

(3) *Answering Each Interrogatory.* Each interrogatory must, to the extent it is not objected to, be answered separately and fully in writing under oath.

(4) *Objections.* The grounds for objecting to an interrogatory must be stated with specificity. Any ground not stated in a timely objection is waived unless the court, for good cause, excuses the failure.

(5) *Signature.* The person who makes the answers must sign them, and the attorney who objects must sign any objections.

(c) Use. An answer to an interrogatory may be used to the extent allowed by the Federal Rules of Evidence.

(d) Option to Produce Business Records. If the answer to an interrogatory may be determined by examining, auditing, compiling, abstracting, or summarizing a party's business records (including electronically stored information), and if the burden of deriving or ascertaining the answer will be substantially the same for either party, the responding party may answer by:

(1) specifying the records that must be reviewed, in sufficient detail to enable the interrogating party to locate and identify them as readily as the responding party could; and

(2) giving the interrogating party a reasonable opportunity to examine and audit the records and to make copies, compilations, abstracts, or summaries.

(Amended Dec. 27, 1946, eff. March 19, 1948; March 30, 1970, eff. July 1, 1970; April 29, 1980, eff. Aug. 1, 1980; April 22, 1993, eff. Dec. 1, 1993; April 12, 2006, eff. Dec. 1, 2006; April 30, 2007, eff. Dec. 1, 2007.)

Rule 34. Producing Documents, Electronically Stored Information, and Tangible Things, or Entering onto Land, for Inspection and Other Purposes

(a) In General. A party may serve on any other party a request within the scope of Rule 26(b):

(1) to produce and permit the requesting party or its representative to inspect, copy, test, or sample the following items in the responding party's possession, custody, or control:

(A) any designated documents or electronically stored information—including writings, drawings, graphs, charts, photographs, sound recordings, images, and other data or data compilations—stored in any medium from which information can be obtained either directly or, if necessary, after translation by the responding party into a reasonably usable form; or

(B) any designated tangible things; or

(2) to permit entry onto designated land or other property possessed or controlled by the responding party, so that the requesting party may inspect, measure, survey, photograph, test, or sample the property or any designated object or operation on it.

(b) Procedure. (1) *Contents of the Request.* The request:

(A) must describe with reasonable particularity each item or category of items to be inspected;

(B) must specify a reasonable time, place, and manner for the inspection and for performing the related acts; and

(C) may specify the form or forms in which electronically stored information is to be produced.

(2) *Responses and Objections.* (A) Time to Respond. The party to whom the request is directed must respond in writing within 30 days after being served. A shorter or longer time may be stipulated to under Rule 29 or be ordered by the court.

(B) Responding to Each Item. For each item or category, the response must either state that inspection and related activities will be permitted as requested or state an objection to the request, including the reasons.

(C) Objections. An objection to part of a request must specify the part and permit inspection of the rest.

(D) Responding to a Request for Production of Electronically Stored Information. The response may state an objection to a requested form for producing electronically stored information. If the responding party objects to a requested form—or if no form was specified in the request—the party must state the form or forms it intends to use.

(E) Producing the Documents or Electronically Stored Information. Unless otherwise stipulated or ordered by the court, these procedures apply to producing documents or electronically stored information:

(i) A party must produce documents as they are kept in the usual course of business or must organize and label them to correspond to the categories in the request;

(ii) If a request does not specify a form for producing electronically stored information, a party must produce it in a form or forms in which it is ordinarily maintained or in a reasonably usable form or forms; and

(iii) A party need not produce the same electronically stored information in more than one form.

(c) Nonparties. As provided in Rule 45, a nonparty may be compelled to produce documents and tangible things or to permit an inspection.

(Amended March 19, 1948; July 1, 1970; Aug. 1, 1980; Aug. 1, 1987; Dec. 1, 1991; Dec. 1, 1993; Dec. 1, 2006; Dec. 1, 2007.)

Rule 35. Physical and Mental Examinations

(a) Order for an Examination. (1) *In General.* The court where the action is pending may order a party whose mental or physical condition—including blood group—is in controversy to submit to a physical or mental examination by a suitably licensed or certified examiner. The court has the same authority to order a party to produce for examination a person who is in its custody or under its legal control.

(2) *Motion and Notice; Contents of the Order.* The order:

(A) may be made only on motion for good cause and on notice to all parties and the person to be examined; and

(B) must specify the time, place, manner, conditions, and scope of the examination, as well as the person or persons who will perform it.

(b) Examiner's Report. (1) *Request by the Party or Person Examined.* The party who moved for the examination must, on request, deliver to the requester a copy of the examiner's report, together with like reports of all earlier examinations of the same condition. The request may be made by the party against whom the examination order was issued or by the person examined.

(2) *Contents.* The examiner's report must be in writing and must set out in detail the examiner's findings, including diagnoses, conclusions, and the results of any tests.

(3) *Request by the Moving Party.* After delivering the reports, the party who moved for the examination may request—and is entitled to receive—from the party against whom the examination order was issued like reports of all earlier or later examinations of the same condition. But those reports need not be delivered by the party with custody or control of the person examined if the party shows that it could not obtain them.

(4) *Waiver of Privilege.* By requesting and obtaining the examiner's report, or by deposing the examiner, the party examined waives any privilege it may have—in that action or any other action involving the same controversy—concerning testimony about all examinations of the same condition.

(5) *Failure to Deliver a Report.* The court on

motion may order—on just terms—that a party deliver the report of an examination. If the report is not provided, the court may exclude the examiner's testimony at trial.

(6) *Scope.* This subdivision (b) applies also to an examination made by the parties' agreement, unless the agreement states otherwise. This subdivision does not preclude obtaining an examiner's report or deposing an examiner under other rules.

(Amended July 1, 1970; Aug. 1, 1987; Nov. 18, 1988; Dec. 1, 1991; Dec. 1, 2007.)

Rule 36. Requests for Admission

(a) Scope and Procedure. (1) *Scope.* A party may serve on any other party a written request to admit, for purposes of the pending action only, the truth of any matters within the scope of Rule 26(b)(1) relating to:

(A) facts, the application of law to fact, or opinions about either; and

(B) the genuineness of any described documents.

(2) *Form; Copy of a Document.* Each matter must be separately stated. A request to admit the genuineness of a document must be accompanied by a copy of the document unless it is, or has been, otherwise furnished or made available for inspection and copying.

(3) *Time to Respond; Effect of Not Responding.* A matter is admitted unless, within 30 days after being served, the party to whom the request is directed serves on the requesting party a written answer or objection addressed to the matter and signed by the party or its attorney. A shorter or longer time for responding may be stipulated to under Rule 29 or be ordered by the court.

(4) *Answer.* If a matter is not admitted, the answer must specifically deny it or state in detail why the answering party cannot truthfully admit or deny it. A denial must fairly respond to the substance of the matter; and when good faith requires that a party qualify an answer or deny only a part of a matter, the answer must specify the part admitted and qualify or deny the rest. The answering party may assert lack of knowledge or information as a reason for failing to admit or deny only if the party states that it has made reasonable inquiry and that the information it knows or can readily obtain is insufficient to enable it to admit or deny.

(5) *Objections.* The grounds for objecting to a request must be stated. A party must not object solely on the ground that it presents a genuine issue for trial.

(6) *Motion Regarding the Sufficiency of an Answer or Objection.* The requesting party may move to determine the sufficiency of an answer or objection. Unless the court finds an objection justified, it must order that an answer be served. On finding that an answer does not comply with this rule, the court may order either that the matter is admitted or that an amended answer be served. The court may defer its final decision until a pretrial conference or a specified time before trial. Rule 37(a)(5) applies to an award of expenses.

(b) Effect of an Admission; Withdrawing or Amending It. A matter admitted under this rule is conclusively established unless the court, on motion, permits the admission to be withdrawn or amended. Subject to Rule 16(e), the court may permit withdrawal or amendment if it would promote the presentation of the merits of the action and if the court is not persuaded that it would prejudice the requesting party in maintaining or defending the action on the merits. An admission under this rule is not an admission for any other purpose and cannot be used against the party in any other proceeding.

(Amended March 19, 1948; July 1, 1970; Aug. 1, 1987; Dec. 1, 1993; Dec. 1, 2007.)

Rule 37. Failure to Make Disclosures or to Cooperate in Discovery; Sanctions

(a) Motion for an Order Compelling Disclosure or Discovery. (1) *In General.* On notice to other parties and all affected persons, a party may move for an order compelling disclosure or discovery. The motion must include a certification that the movant has in good faith conferred or attempted to confer with the person or party failing to make disclosure or discovery in an effort to obtain it without court action.

(2) *Appropriate Court.* A motion for an order to a party must be made in the court where the action is pending. A motion for an order to a nonparty must be made in the court where the discovery is or will be taken.

(3) *Specific Motions.* (A) To Compel Disclosure. If a party fails to make a disclosure required by Rule 26(a), any other party may move to compel disclosure and for appropriate sanctions.

(B) To Compel a Discovery Response. A party seeking discovery may move for an order compelling an answer, designation, production, or inspection. This motion may be made if:

(i) a deponent fails to answer a question asked under Rule 30 or 31;

(ii) a corporation or other entity fails to make a designation under Rule 30(b)(6) or 31(a)(4);

(iii) a party fails to answer an interrogatory submitted under Rule 33; or

(iv) a party fails to respond that inspection will be permitted—or fails to permit inspection—as requested under Rule 34.

(C) Related to a Deposition. When taking an oral deposition, the party asking a question may complete or adjourn the examination before moving for an order.

(4) *Evasive or Incomplete Disclosure, Answer, or Response.* For purposes of this subdivision (a), an evasive or incomplete disclosure, answer, or response must be treated as a failure to disclose, answer, or respond.

(5) *Payment of Expenses; Protective Orders.* (A) If the Motion Is Granted (or Disclosure or Discovery Is Provided After Filing). If the motion is granted—or if

the disclosure or requested discovery is provided after the motion was filed—the court must, after giving an opportunity to be heard, require the party or deponent whose conduct necessitated the motion, the party or attorney advising that conduct, or both to pay the movant's reasonable expenses incurred in making the motion, including attorney's fees. But the court must not order this payment if:

(i) the movant filed the motion before attempting in good faith to obtain the disclosure or discovery without court action;

(ii) the opposing party's nondisclosure, response, or objection was substantially justified; or

(iii) other circumstances make an award of expenses unjust.

(B) If the Motion Is Denied. If the motion is denied, the court may issue any protective order authorized under Rule 26(c) and must, after giving an opportunity to be heard, require the movant, the attorney filing the motion, or both to pay the party or deponent who opposed the motion its reasonable expenses incurred in opposing the motion, including attorney's fees. But the court must not order this payment if the motion was substantially justified or other circumstances make an award of expenses unjust.

(C) If the Motion Is Granted in Part and Denied in Part. If the motion is granted in part and denied in part, the court may issue any protective order authorized under Rule 26(c) and may, after giving an opportunity to be heard, apportion the reasonable expenses for the motion.

(b) Failure to Comply with a Court Order. (1) *Sanctions Sought in the District Where the Deposition Is Taken.*If the court where the discovery is taken orders a deponent to be sworn or to answer a question and the deponent fails to obey, the failure may be treated as contempt of court. If a deposition-related motion is transferred to the court where the action is pending, and that court orders a deponent to be sworn or to answer a question and the deponent fails to obey, the failure may be treated as contempt of either the court where the discovery is taken or the court where the action is pending.

(2) *Sanctions Sought in the District Where the Action Is Pending.* (A) For Not Obeying a Discovery Order. If a party or a party's officer, director, or managing agent—or a witness designated under Rule 30(b)(6) or 31(a)(4)—fails to obey an order to provide or permit discovery, including an order under Rule 26(f), 35, or 37(a), the court where the action is pending may issue further just orders. They may include the following:

(i) directing that the matters embraced in the order or other designated facts be taken as established for purposes of the action, as the prevailing party claims;

(ii) prohibiting the disobedient party from supporting or opposing designated claims or defenses, or from introducing designated matters in evidence;

(iii) striking pleadings in whole or in part;

(iv) staying further proceedings until the order is obeyed;

(v) dismissing the action or proceeding in whole or in part;

(vi) rendering a default judgment against the disobedient party; or

(vii) treating as contempt of court the failure to obey any order except an order to submit to a physical or mental examination.

(B) For Not Producing a Person for Examination. If a party fails to comply with an order under Rule 35(a) requiring it to produce another person for examination, the court may issue any of the orders listed in Rule 37(b)(2)(A)(i)–(vi), unless the disobedient party shows that it cannot produce the other person.

(C) Payment of Expenses. Instead of or in addition to the orders above, the court must order the disobedient party, the attorney advising that party, or both to pay the reasonable expenses, including attorney's fees, caused by the failure, unless the failure was substantially justified or other circumstances make an award of expenses unjust.

(c) Failure to Disclose, to Supplement an Earlier Response, or to Admit. (1) *Failure to Disclose or Supplement.* If a party fails to provide information or identify a witness as required by Rule 26(a) or (e), the party is not allowed to use that information or witness to supply evidence on a motion, at a hearing, or at a trial, unless the failure was substantially justified or is harmless. In addition to or instead of this sanction, the court, on motion and after giving an opportunity to be heard:

(A) may order payment of the reasonable expenses, including attorney's fees, caused by the failure;

(B) may inform the jury of the party's failure; and

(C) may impose other appropriate sanctions, including any of the orders listed in Rule 37(b)(2)(A)(i)–(vi).

(2) *Failure to Admit.* If a party fails to admit what is requested under Rule 36 and if the requesting party later proves a document to be genuine or the matter true, the requesting party may move that the party who failed to admit pay the reasonable expenses, including attorney's fees, incurred in making that proof. The court must so order unless:

(A) the request was held objectionable under Rule 36(a);

(B) the admission sought was of no substantial importance;

(C) the party failing to admit had a reasonable ground to believe that it might prevail on the matter; or

(D) there was other good reason for the failure to admit.

(d) Party's Failure to Attend Its Own Deposition, Serve Answers to Interrogatories, or Respond to a Request for Inspection. (1) *In General.* (A) Motion; Grounds for Sanctions. The court where the action is pending may, on motion, order sanctions if:

(i) a party or a party's officer, director, or managing agent—or a person designated under Rule 30(b)(6) or 31(a)(4)—fails, after being served with proper notice, to appear for that person's deposition; or

(ii) a party, after being properly served with interrogatories under Rule 33 or a request for inspection under Rule 34, fails to serve its answers, objections, or written response.

(B) Certification. A motion for sanctions for failing to answer or respond must include a certification that the movant has in good faith conferred or attempted to confer with the party failing to act in an effort to obtain the answer or response without court action.

(2) *Unacceptable Excuse for Failing to Act.* A failure described in Rule 37(d)(1)(A) is not excused on the ground that the discovery sought was objectionable, unless the party failing to act has a pending motion for a protective order under Rule 26(c).

(3) *Types of Sanctions.* Sanctions may include any of the orders listed in Rule 37(b)(2)(A)(i)–(vi). Instead of or in addition to these sanctions, the court must require the party failing to act, the attorney advising that party, or both to pay the reasonable expenses, including attorney's fees, caused by the failure, unless the failure was substantially justified or other circumstances make an award of expenses unjust.

(e) Failure to Provide Electronically Stored Information. Absent exceptional circumstances, a court may not impose sanctions under these rules on a party for failing to provide electronically stored information lost as a result of the routine, good-faith operation of an electronic information system.

(f) Failure to Participate in Framing a Discovery Plan. If a party or its attorney fails to participate in good faith in developing and submitting a proposed discovery plan as required by Rule 26(f), the court may, after giving an opportunity to be heard, require that party or attorney to pay to any other party the reasonable expenses, including attorney's fees, caused by the failure.

(Amended Oct. 20, 1949; July 1, 1970; Aug. 1, 1980; Oct. 1, 1981; Aug. 1, 1987; Dec. 1, 1993; Dec. 1, 2000; Dec. 1, 2006; Dec. 1, 2007; Dec. 1, 2013.)

TITLE VI. TRIALS

Rule 38. Right to a Jury Trial; Demand

(a) Right Preserved. The right of trial by jury as declared by the Seventh Amendment to the Constitution—or as provided by a federal statute—is preserved to the parties inviolate.

(b) Demand. On any issue triable of right by a jury, a party may demand a jury trial by:

(1) serving the other parties with a written demand—which may be included in a pleading—no later than 14 days after the last pleading directed to the issue is served; and

(2) filing the demand in accordance with Rule 5(d).

(c) Specifying Issues. In its demand, a party may specify the issues that it wishes to have tried by a jury; otherwise, it is considered to have demanded a jury trial on all the issues so triable. If the party has demanded a jury trial on only some issues, any other party may—within 14 days after being served with the demand or within a shorter time ordered by the court—serve a demand for a jury trial on any other or all factual issues triable by jury.

(d) Waiver; Withdrawal. A party waives a jury trial unless its demand is properly served and filed. A proper demand may be withdrawn only if the parties consent.

(e) Admiralty and Maritime Claims. These rules do not create a right to a jury trial on issues in a claim designated as an admiralty or maritime claim under Rule 9(h).

(Amended July 1, 1966; Aug. 1, 1987; Dec. 1, 1993; Dec. 1, 2007; Dec. 1, 2009.)

Rule 39. Trial by Jury or by the Court

(a) When a Demand Is Made. When a jury trial has been demanded under Rule 38, the action must be designated on the docket as a jury action. The trial on all issues so demanded must be by jury unless:

(1) the parties or their attorneys file a stipulation to a nonjury trial or so stipulate on the record; or

(2) the court, on motion or on its own, finds that on some or all of those issues there is no federal right to a jury trial.

(b) When No Demand Is Made. Issues on which a jury trial is not properly demanded are to be tried by the court. But the court may, on motion, order a jury trial on any issue for which a jury might have been demanded.

(c) Advisory Jury; Jury Trial by Consent. In an action not triable of right by a jury, the court, on motion or on its own:

(1) may try any issue with an advisory jury; or

(2) may, with the parties' consent, try any issue by a jury whose verdict has the same effect as if a jury trial had been a matter of right, unless the action is against the United States and a federal statute provides for a nonjury trial.

(Amended Dec. 1, 2007.)

Rule 40. Scheduling Cases for Trial

Each court must provide by rule for scheduling trials. The court must give priority to actions entitled to priority by a federal statute.

(As amended Dec. 1, 2007.)

Rule 41. Dismissal of Actions

(a) Voluntary Dismissal. (1) *By the Plaintiff.* (A) Without a Court Order. Subject to Rules 23(e), 23.1(c), 23.2, and 66 and any applicable federal statute, the plaintiff may dismiss an action without a court order by filing:

(i) a notice of dismissal before the opposing party serves either an answer or a motion for summary judgment; or

(ii) a stipulation of dismissal signed by all parties who have appeared.

(B) Effect. Unless the notice or stipulation states otherwise, the dismissal is without prejudice. But if the plaintiff previously dismissed any federal- or state-court action based on or including the same claim, a notice of dismissal operates as an adjudication on the merits.

(2) *By Court Order; Effect.* Except as provided in Rule 41(a)(1), an action may be dismissed at the plaintiff's request only by court order, on terms that the court considers proper. If a defendant has pleaded a counterclaim before being served with the plaintiff's motion to dismiss, the action may be dismissed over the defendant's objection only if the counterclaim can remain pending for independent adjudication. Unless the order states otherwise, a dismissal under this paragraph (2) is without prejudice.

(b) Involuntary Dismissal; Effect. If the plaintiff fails to prosecute or to comply with these rules or a court order, a defendant may move to dismiss the action or any claim against it. Unless the dismissal order states otherwise, a dismissal under this subdivision (b) and any dismissal not under this rule—except one for lack of jurisdiction, improper venue, or failure to join a party under Rule 19—operates as an adjudication on the merits.

(c) Dismissing a Counterclaim, Crossclaim, or Third-Party Claim. This rule applies to a dismissal of any counterclaim, crossclaim, or third-party claim. A claimant's voluntary dismissal under Rule 41(a)(1)(A)(i) must be made:

(1) before a responsive pleading is served; or

(2) if there is no responsive pleading, before evidence is introduced at a hearing or trial.

(d) Costs of a Previously Dismissed Action. If a plaintiff who previously dismissed an action in any court files an action based on or including the same claim against the same defendant, the court:

(1) may order the plaintiff to pay all or part of the costs of that previous action; and

(2) may stay the proceedings until the plaintiff has complied.

(Amended March 19, 1948; July 1, 1963; July 1, 1966; July 1, 1968; Aug. 1, 1987; Dec. 1, 1991; Dec. 1, 2007.)

Rule 42. Consolidation; Separate Trials

(a) Consolidation. If actions before the court involve a common question of law or fact, the court may:

(1) join for hearing or trial any or all matters at issue in the actions;

(2) consolidate the actions; or

(3) issue any other orders to avoid unnecessary cost or delay.

(b) Separate Trials. For convenience, to avoid prejudice, or to expedite and economize, the court may order a separate trial of one or more separate issues, claims, crossclaims, counterclaims, or third-party claims. When ordering a separate trial, the court must preserve any federal right to a jury trial.

(Amended July 1, 1966; Dec. 1, 2007.)

Rule 43. Taking Testimony

(a) In Open Court. At trial, the witnesses' testimony must be taken in open court unless a federal statute, the Federal Rules of Evidence, these rules, or other rules adopted by the Supreme Court provide otherwise. For good cause in compelling circumstances and with appropriate safeguards, the court may permit testimony in open court by contemporaneous transmission from a different location.

(b) Affirmation Instead of an Oath. When these rules require an oath, a solemn affirmation suffices.

(c) Evidence on a Motion. When a motion relies on facts outside the record, the court may hear the matter on affidavits or may hear it wholly or partly on oral testimony or on depositions.

(d) Interpreter. The court may appoint an interpreter of its choosing; fix reasonable compensation to be paid from funds provided by law or by one or more parties; and tax the compensation as costs.

(Amended July 1, 1966; July 1, 1975; Aug. 1, 1987; Dec. 1, 1996; Dec. 1, 2007.)

Rule 44. Proving an Official Record

(a) Means of Proving. (1) *Domestic Record.* Each of the following evidences an official record—or an entry in it—that is otherwise admissible and is kept within the United States, any state, district, or commonwealth, or any territory subject to the administrative or judicial jurisdiction of the United States:

(A) an official publication of the record; or

(B) a copy attested by the officer with legal custody of the record—or by the officer's deputy—and accompanied by a certificate that the officer has custody. The certificate must be made under seal:

(i) by a judge of a court of record in the district or political subdivision where the record is kept; or

(ii) by any public officer with a seal of office and with official duties in the district or political subdivision where the record is kept.

(2) *Foreign Record.* (A) In General. Each of the following evidences a foreign official record—or an entry in it—that is otherwise admissible:

(i) an official publication of the record; or

(ii) the record—or a copy—that is attested by an authorized person and is accompanied either by a final certification of genuineness or by a certification under a treaty or convention to which the United States and the country where the record is located are parties.

(B) Final Certification of Genuineness. A final certification must certify the genuineness of the signature and official position of the attester or of any foreign official whose certificate of genuineness relates to the attestation or is in a chain of certificates of genuineness relating to the attestation. A final certification may be made by a secretary of a United States embassy or legation; by a consul general, vice consul, or consular agent of the United States; or by a diplomatic or consular official of the foreign country assigned or accredited to the United States.

(C) Other Means of Proof. If all parties have had a reasonable opportunity to investigate a foreign record's authenticity and accuracy, the court may, for good cause, either:

(i) admit an attested copy without final certification; or

(ii) permit the record to be evidenced by an attested summary with or without a final certification.

(b) Lack of a Record. A written statement that a diligent search of designated records revealed no record or entry of a specified tenor is admissible as evidence that the records contain no such record or entry. For domestic records, the statement must be authenticated under Rule 44(a)(1). For foreign records, the statement must comply with (a)(2)(C)(ii).

(c) Other Proof. A party may prove an official record—or an entry or lack of an entry in it—by any other method authorized by law.

(Amended July 1, 1966; Aug. 1, 1987; Dec. 1, 1991; Dec. 1, 2007.)

Rule 44.1. Determining Foreign Law

A party who intends to raise an issue about a foreign country's law must give notice by a pleading or other writing. In determining foreign law, the court may consider any relevant material or source, including testimony, whether or not submitted by a party or admissible under the Federal Rules of Evidence. The court's determination must be treated as a ruling on a question of law.

(Amended July 1, 1966; July 1, 1975; Aug. 1, 1987; Dec. 1, 2007.)

Rule 45. Subpoena

(a) In General. (1) *Form and Contents.* (A) Requirements—In General. Every subpoena must:

(i) state the court from which it issued;

(ii) state the title of the action and its civil-action number;

(iii) command each person to whom it is directed to do the following at a specified time and place: attend and testify; produce designated documents, electronically stored information, or tangible things in that person's possession, custody, or control; or permit the inspection of premises; and

(iv) set out the text of Rule 45(d) and (e).

(B) Command to Attend a Deposition—Notice of the Recording Method. A subpoena commanding attendance at a deposition must state the method for recording the testimony.

(C) Combining or Separating a Command to Produce or to Permit Inspection; Specifying the Form for Electronically Stored Information. A command to produce documents, electronically stored information, or tangible things or to permit the inspection of premises may be included in a subpoena commanding attendance at a deposition, hearing, or trial, or may be set out in a separate subpoena. A subpoena may specify the form or forms in which electronically stored information is to be produced.

(D) Command to Produce; Included Obligations. A command in a subpoena to produce documents, electronically stored information, or tangible things requires the responding party to permit inspection, copying, testing, or sampling of the materials.

(2) *Issuing Court.* A subpoena must issue from the court where the action is pending.

(3) *Issued by Whom.* The clerk must issue a subpoena, signed but otherwise in blank, to a party who requests it. That party must complete it before service. An attorney also may issue and sign a subpoena if the attorney is authorized to practice in the issuing court.

(4) *Notice to Other Parties Before Service.* If the subpoena commands the production of documents, electronically stored information, or tangible things or the inspection of premises before trial, then before it is served on the person to whom it is directed, a notice and a copy of the subpoena must be served on each party.

(b) Service. (1) *By Whom and How; Tendering Fees.* Any person who is at least 18 years old and not a party may serve a subpoena. Serving a subpoena requires delivering a copy to the named person and, if the subpoena requires that person's attendance, tendering the fees for 1 day's attendance and the mileage allowed by law. Fees and mileage need not be tendered when the subpoena issues on behalf of the United States or any of its officers or agencies.

(2) *Service in the United States.* A subpoena may be served at any place within the United States.

(3) *Service in a Foreign Country.* 28 U.S.C. § 1783 governs issuing and serving a subpoena directed to a United States national or resident who is in a foreign country.

(4) *Proof of Service.* Proving service, when necessary, requires filing with the issuing court a statement showing the date and manner of service and the names of the persons served. The statement must be certified by the server.

(c) Place of Compliance. (1) *For a Trial, Hearing, or Deposition.* A subpoena may command a person to attend a trial, hearing, or deposition only as follows:

(A) within 100 miles of where the person resides, is employed, or regularly transacts business in person; or

(B) within the state where the person resides, is employed, or regularly transacts business in person, if the person

(i) is a party or a party's officer; or

(ii) is commanded to attend a trial and would not incur substantial expense. (2) *For Other Discovery.*

A subpoena may command:

(A) production of documents, electronically stored information, or tangible things at a place within 100 miles of where the person resides, is employed, or regularly transacts business in person; and

(B) inspection of premises at the premises to be inspected.

(d) Protecting a Person Subject to a Subpoena; Enforcement. (1) *Avoiding Undue Burden or Expense; Sanctions.* A party or attorney responsible for issuing and serving a subpoena must take reasonable steps to avoid imposing undue burden or expense on a person subject to the subpoena. The court for the district where compliance is required must enforce this duty and impose an appropriate sanction—which may include lost earnings and reasonable attorney's fees—on a party or attorney who fails to comply.

(2) *Command to Produce Materials or Permit Inspection.*

(A) Appearance Not Required. A person commanded to produce documents, electronically stored information, or tangible things, or to permit the inspection of premises, need not appear in person at the place of production or inspection unless also commanded to appear for a deposition, hearing, or trial.

(B) Objections. A person commanded to produce documents or tangible things or to permit inspection may serve on the party or attorney designated in the subpoena a written objection to inspecting, copying, testing, or sampling any or all of the materials or to inspecting the premises—or to producing electronically stored information in the form or forms requested. The objection must be served before the earlier of the time specified for compliance or 14 days after the subpoena is served. If an objection is made, the following rules apply:

(i) At any time, on notice to the commanded person, the serving party may move the court for the district where compliance is required for an order compelling production or inspection.

(ii) These acts may be required only as directed in the order, and the order must protect a person who is neither a party nor a party's officer from significant expense resulting from compliance.

(3) *Quashing or Modifying a Subpoena.*

(A) When Required. On timely motion, the court for the district where compliance is required must quash or modify a subpoena that:

(i) fails to allow a reasonable time to comply;

(ii) requires a person to comply beyond the geographical limits specified in Rule 45(c);

(iii) requires disclosure of privileged or other protected matter, if no exception or waiver applies; or

(iv) subjects a person to undue burden.

(B) When Permitted. To protect a person subject to or affected by a subpoena, the court for the district where compliance is required may, on motion, quash or modify the subpoena if it requires:

(i) disclosing a trade secret or other confidential research, development, or commercial information; or

(ii) disclosing an unretained expert's opinion or information that does not describe specific occurrences in dispute and results from the expert's study that was not requested by a party.

(C) Specifying Conditions as an Alternative. In the circumstances described in Rule 45(d)(3)(B), the court may, instead of quashing or modifying a subpoena, order appearance or production under specified conditions if the serving party:

(i) shows a substantial need for the testimony or material that cannot be otherwise met without undue hardship; and

(ii) ensures that the subpoenaed person will be reasonably compensated.

(e) Duties in Responding to a Subpoena. (1) *Producing Documents or Electronically Stored Information.* These procedures apply to producing documents or electronically stored information:

(A) Documents. A person responding to a subpoena to produce documents must produce them as they are kept in the ordinary course of business or must organize and label them to correspond to the categories in the demand.

(B) Form for Producing Electronically Stored Information Not Specified. If a subpoena does not specify a form for producing electronically stored information, the person responding must produce it in a form or forms in which it is ordinarily maintained or in a reasonably usable form or forms.

(C) Electronically Stored Information Produced in Only One Form. The person responding need not produce the same electronically stored information in more than one form.

(D) Inaccessible Electronically Stored Information. The person responding need not provide discovery of electronically stored information from sources that the person identifies as not reasonably accessible because of undue burden or cost. On motion to compel discovery or for a protective order, the person responding must show that the information is not reasonably accessible because of undue burden or cost. If that showing is made, the court may nonetheless order discovery from such sources if the requesting party shows good cause, considering the limitations of Rule 26(b)(2)(C). The court may specify conditions for the discovery. (2) *Claiming Privilege or Protection.*

(A) Information Withheld. A person withholding subpoenaed information under a claim that it is privileged or subject to protection as trial-preparation material must:

(i) expressly make the claim; and

(ii) describe the nature of the withheld documents, communications, or tangible things in a manner that, without revealing information itself privileged or protected, will enable the parties to assess the claim.

(B) Information Produced. If information produced in response to a subpoena is subject to a claim of privilege or of protection as trial-preparation material, the person making the claim may notify any party that received the information of the claim and the basis for it. After being notified, a party must promptly return, sequester, or destroy the specified information and any copies it has; must not use or disclose the information until the claim is resolved; must take reasonable steps to retrieve the information if the party disclosed it before being notified; and may promptly present the information under seal to the court for the district where compliance is required for a determination of the claim. The person who produced the information must preserve the information until the claim is resolved.

(f) Transferring a Subpoena-Related Motion. When the court where compliance is required did not issue the subpoena, it may transfer a motion under this rule to the issuing court if the person subject to the subpoena consents or if the court finds exceptional circumstances. Then, if the attorney for a person subject to a subpoena is authorized to practice in the court where the motion was made, the attorney may file papers and appear on the motion as an officer of the issuing court. To enforce its order, the issuing court may transfer the order to the court where the motion was made.

(g) Contempt. The court for the district where compliance is required—and also, after a motion is transferred, the issuing court—may hold in contempt a person who, having been served, fails without adequate excuse to obey the subpoena or an order related to it.

(Amended March 19, 1948; Oct. 20, 1949; July 1, 1970; Aug. 1, 1980; Aug. 1, 1985; Aug. 1, 1987; Dec. 1, 1991; Dec. 1, 2005; Dec. 1, 2006; Dec. 1, 2007; Dec. 1, 2013.)

Rule 46. Objecting to a Ruling or Order

A formal exception to a ruling or order is unnecessary. When the ruling or order is requested or made, a party need only state the action that it wants the court to take or objects to, along with the grounds for the request or objection. Failing to object does not prejudice a party who had no opportunity to do so when the ruling or order was made.

(Amended Aug. 1, 1987; Dec. 1, 2007.)

Rule 47. Selecting Jurors

(a) Examining Jurors. The court may permit the parties or their attorneys to examine prospective jurors or may itself do so. If the court examines the jurors, it must permit the parties or their attorneys to make any further inquiry it considers proper, or must itself ask any of their additional questions it considers proper.

(b) Peremptory Challenges. The court must allow the number of peremptory challenges provided by 28 U.S.C. § 1870.

(c) Excusing a Juror. During trial or deliberation, the court may excuse a juror for good cause.

(Amended July 1, 1966; Dec. 1, 1991; Dec. 1, 2007.)

Rule 48. Number of Jurors; Verdict

(a) Number of Jurors. A jury must begin with at least 6 and no more than 12 members, and each juror must participate in the verdict unless excused under Rule 47(c).

(b) Verdict. Unless the parties stipulate otherwise, the verdict must be unanimous and must be returned by a jury of at least 6 members.

(c) Polling. After a verdict is returned but before the jury is discharged, the court must on a party's request, or may on its own, poll the jurors individually. If the poll reveals a lack of unanimity or lack of assent by the number of jurors that the parties stipulated to, the court may direct the jury to deliberate further or may order a new trial.

(Amended Dec. 1, 1991; Dec. 1, 2007; Dec. 1, 2009.)

Rule 49. Special Verdict; General Verdict and Questions

(a) Special Verdict. (1) *In General.* The court may require a jury to return only a special verdict in the form of a special written finding on each issue of fact. The court may do so by:

(A) submitting written questions susceptible of a categorical or other brief answer;

(B) submitting written forms of the special findings that might properly be made under the pleadings and evidence; or

(C) using any other method that the court considers appropriate.

(2) *Instructions.* The court must give the instructions and explanations necessary to enable the jury to make its findings on each submitted issue.

(3) *Issues Not Submitted.* A party waives the right to a jury trial on any issue of fact raised by the pleadings or evidence but not submitted to the jury unless, before the jury retires, the party demands its submission to the jury. If the party does not demand submission, the court may make a finding on the issue. If the court makes no finding, it is considered to have made a finding consistent with its judgment on the special verdict.

(b) General Verdict with Answers to Written Questions. (1) *In General.* The court may submit to the jury forms for a general verdict, together with written questions on one or more issues of fact that the jury must decide. The court must give the instructions and explanations necessary to enable the jury to render a general verdict and answer the questions in writing, and must direct the jury to do both.

(2) *Verdict and Answers Consistent.* When the general verdict and the answers are consistent, the court must approve, for entry under Rule 58, an appropriate judgment on the verdict and answers.

(3) *Answers Inconsistent with the Verdict.* When the answers are consistent with each other but one or more is inconsistent with the general verdict, the

court may:

(A) approve, for entry under Rule 58, an appropriate judgment according to the answers, notwithstanding the general verdict;

(B) direct the jury to further consider its answers and verdict; or

(C) order a new trial.

(4) *Answers Inconsistent with Each Other and the Verdict.* When the answers are inconsistent with each other and one or more is also inconsistent with the general verdict, judgment must not be entered; instead, the court must direct the jury to further consider its answers and verdict, or must order a new trial.

(Amended July 1, 1963; Aug. 1, 1987; Dec. 1, 2007.)

Rule 50. Judgment as a Matter of Law in a Jury Trial; Related Motion for a New Trial; Conditional Ruling

(a) Judgment as a Matter of Law. (1) *In General.* If a party has been fully heard on an issue during a jury trial and the court finds that a reasonable jury would not have a legally sufficient evidentiary basis to find for the party on that issue, the court may:

(A) resolve the issue against the party; and

(B) grant a motion for judgment as a matter of law against the party on a claim or defense that, under the controlling law, can be maintained or defeated only with a favorable finding on that issue.

(2) *Motion.* A motion for judgment as a matter of law may be made at any time before the case is submitted to the jury. The motion must specify the judgment sought and the law and facts that entitle the movant to the judgment.

(b) Renewing the Motion After Trial; Alternative Motion for a New Trial. If the court does not grant a motion for judgment as a matter of law made under Rule 50(a), the court is considered to have submitted the action to the jury subject to the court's later deciding the legal questions raised by the motion. No later than 28 days after the entry of judgment—or if the motion addresses a jury issue not decided by a verdict, no later than 28 days after the jury was discharged—the movant may file a renewed motion for judgment as a matter of law and may include an alternative or joint request for a new trial under Rule 59. In ruling on the renewed motion, the court may:

(1) allow judgment on the verdict, if the jury returned a verdict;

(2) order a new trial; or

(3) direct the entry of judgment as a matter of law.

(c) Granting the Renewed Motion; Conditional Ruling on a Motion for a New Trial. (1) *In General.* If the court grants a renewed motion for judgment as a matter of law, it must also conditionally rule on any motion for a new trial by determining whether a new trial should be granted if the judgment is later vacated or reversed. The court must state the grounds for conditionally granting or denying the motion for a new trial.

(2) *Effect of a Conditional Ruling.* Conditionally granting the motion for a new trial does not affect the judgment's finality; if the judgment is reversed, the new trial must proceed unless the appellate court orders otherwise. If the motion for a new trial is conditionally denied, the appellee may assert error in that denial; if the judgment is reversed, the case must proceed as the appellate court orders.

(d) Time for a Losing Party's New-Trial Motion. Any motion for a new trial under Rule 59 by a party against whom judgment as a matter of law is rendered must be filed no later than 28 days after the entry of the judgment.

(e) Denying the Motion for Judgment as a Matter of Law; Reversal on Appeal. If the court denies the motion for judgment as a matter of law, the prevailing party may, as appellee, assert grounds entitling it to a new trial should the appellate court conclude that the trial court erred in denying the motion. If the appellate court reverses the judgment, it may order a new trial, direct the trial court to determine whether a new trial should be granted, or direct the entry of judgment.

(Amended July 1, 1963; Aug. 1, 1987; Dec. 1, 1991; Dec. 1, 1993; Dec. 1, 1995; Dec. 1, 2007; Dec. 1, 2009.)

Rule 51. Instructions to the Jury; Objections; Preserving a Claim of Error

(a) Requests. (1) *Before or at the Close of the Evidence.* At the close of the evidence or at any earlier reasonable time that the court orders, a party may file and furnish to every other party written requests for the jury instructions it wants the court to give.

(2) *After the Close of the Evidence.* After the close of the evidence, a party may:

(A) file requests for instructions on issues that could not reasonably have been anticipated by an earlier time that the court set for requests; and

(B) with the court's permission, file untimely requests for instructions on any issue.

(b) Instructions. The court:

(1) must inform the parties of its proposed instructions and proposed action on the requests before instructing the jury and before final jury arguments;

(2) must give the parties an opportunity to object on the record and out of the jury's hearing before the instructions and arguments are delivered; and

(3) may instruct the jury at any time before the jury is discharged.

(c) Objections. (1) *How to Make.* A party who objects to an instruction or the failure to give an instruction must do so on the record, stating distinctly the matter objected to and the grounds for the objection.

(2) *When to Make.* An objection is timely if:

(A) a party objects at the opportunity provided

under Rule 51(b)(2); or

(B) a party was not informed of an instruction or action on a request before that opportunity to object, and the party objects promptly after learning that the instruction or request will be, or has been, given or refused.

(d) Assigning Error; Plain Error. (1) *Assigning Error.* A party may assign as error:

(A) an error in an instruction actually given, if that party properly objected; or

(B) a failure to give an instruction, if that party properly requested it and—unless the court rejected the request in a definitive ruling on the record—also properly objected.

(2) *Plain Error.* A court may consider a plain error in the instructions that has not been preserved as required by Rule 51(d)(1) if the error affects substantial rights.

(Amended Aug. 1, 1987; Dec. 1, 2003; Dec. 1, 2007.)

Rule 52. Findings and Conclusions by the Court; Judgment on Partial Findings

(a) Findings and Conclusions. (1) *In General.* In an action tried on the facts without a jury or with an advisory jury, the court must find the facts specially and state its conclusions of law separately. The findings and conclusions may be stated on the record after the close of the evidence or may appear in an opinion or a memorandum of decision filed by the court. Judgment must be entered under Rule 58.

(2) *For an Interlocutory Injunction.* In granting or refusing an interlocutory injunction, the court must similarly state the findings and conclusions that support its action.

(3) *For a Motion.* The court is not required to state findings or conclusions when ruling on a motion under Rule 12 or 56 or, unless these rules provide otherwise, on any other motion.

(4) *Effect of a Master's Findings.* A master's findings, to the extent adopted by the court, must be considered the court's findings.

(5) *Questioning the Evidentiary Support.* A party may later question the sufficiency of the evidence supporting the findings, whether or not the party requested findings, objected to them, moved to amend them, or moved for partial findings.

(6) *Setting Aside the Findings.* Findings of fact, whether based on oral or other evidence, must not be set aside unless clearly erroneous, and the reviewing court must give due regard to the trial court's opportunity to judge the witnesses' credibility.

(b) Amended or Additional Findings. On a party's motion filed no later than 28 days after the entry of judgment, the court may amend its findings—or make additional findings—and may amend the judgment accordingly. The motion may accompany a motion for a new trial under Rule 59.

(c) Judgment on Partial Findings. If a party has been fully heard on an issue during a nonjury trial and the court finds against the party on that issue, the court may enter judgment against the party on a claim or defense that, under the controlling law, can be maintained or defeated only with a favorable finding on that issue. The court may, however, decline to render any judgment until the close of the evidence. A judgment on partial findings must be supported by findings of fact and conclusions of law as required by Rule 52(a).

(Amended March 19, 1948; Aug. 1, 1983; Aug. 1, 1985; Dec. 1, 1991; Dec. 1, 1993; Dec. 1, 1995; Dec. 1, 2007; Dec. 1, 2009.)

Rule 53. Masters

(a) Appointment. (1) *Scope.* Unless a statute provides otherwise, a court may appoint a master only to:

(A) perform duties consented to by the parties;

(B) hold trial proceedings and make or recommend findings of fact on issues to be decided without a jury if appointment is warranted by:

(i) some exceptional condition; or

(ii) the need to perform an accounting or resolve a difficult computation of damages; or

(C) address pretrial and posttrial matters that cannot be effectively and timely addressed by an available district judge or magistrate judge of the district.

(2) *Disqualification.* A master must not have a relationship to the parties, attorneys, action, or court that would require disqualification of a judge under 28 U.S.C. § 455, unless the parties, with the court's approval, consent to the appointment after the master discloses any potential grounds for disqualification.

(3) *Possible Expense or Delay.* In appointing a master, the court must consider the fairness of imposing the likely expenses on the parties and must protect against unreasonable expense or delay.

(b) Order Appointing a Master. (1) *Notice.* Before appointing a master, the court must give the parties notice and an opportunity to be heard. Any party may suggest candidates for appointment.

(2) *Contents.* The appointing order must direct the master to proceed with all reasonable diligence and must state:

(A) the master's duties, including any investigation or enforcement duties, and any limits on the master's authority under Rule 53(c);

(B) the circumstances, if any, in which the master may communicate ex parte with the court or a party;

(C) the nature of the materials to be preserved and filed as the record of the master's activities;

(D) the time limits, method of filing the record, other procedures, and standards for reviewing the master's orders, findings, and recommendations; and

(E) the basis, terms, and procedure for fixing the master's compensation under Rule 53(g).

(3) *Issuing.* The court may issue the order only after:

(A) the master files an affidavit disclosing whether

there is any ground for disqualification under 28 U.S.C. § 455; and

(B) if a ground is disclosed, the parties, with the court's approval, waive the disqualification.

(4) *Amending.* The order may be amended at any time after notice to the parties and an opportunity to be heard.

(c) Master's Authority. (1) *In General.* Unless the appointing order directs otherwise, a master may:

(A) regulate all proceedings;

(B) take all appropriate measures to perform the assigned duties fairly and efficiently; and

(C) if conducting an evidentiary hearing, exercise the appointing court's power to compel, take, and record evidence.

(2) *Sanctions.* The master may by order impose on a party any noncontempt sanction provided by Rule 37 or 45, and may recommend a contempt sanction against a party and sanctions against a nonparty.

(d) Master's Orders. A master who issues an order must file it and promptly serve a copy on each party. The clerk must enter the order on the docket.

(e) Master's Reports. A master must report to the court as required by the appointing order. The master must file the report and promptly serve a copy on each party, unless the court orders otherwise.

(f) Action on the Master's Order, Report, or Recommendations. (1) *Opportunity for a Hearing; Action in General.* In acting on a master's order, report, or recommendations, the court must give the parties notice and an opportunity to be heard; may receive evidence; and may adopt or affirm, modify, wholly or partly reject or reverse, or resubmit to the master with instructions.

(2) *Time to Object or Move to Adopt or Modify.* A party may file objections to—or a motion to adopt or modify—the master's order, report, or recommendations no later than 21 days after a copy is served, unless the court sets a different time.

(3) *Reviewing Factual Findings.* The court must decide de novo all objections to findings of fact made or recommended by a master, unless the parties, with the court's approval, stipulate that:

(A) the findings will be reviewed for clear error; or

(B) the findings of a master appointed under Rule 53(a)(1)(A) or (C) will be final.

(4) *Reviewing Legal Conclusions.* The court must decide de novo all objections to conclusions of law made or recommended by a master.

(5) *Reviewing Procedural Matters.* Unless the appointing order establishes a different standard of review, the court may set aside a master's ruling on a procedural matter only for an abuse of discretion.

(g) Compensation. (1) *Fixing Compensation.* Before or after judgment, the court must fix the master's compensation on the basis and terms stated in the appointing order, but the court may set a new basis and terms after giving notice and an opportunity to be heard.

(2) *Payment.* The compensation must be paid either:

(A) by a party or parties; or

(B) from a fund or subject matter of the action within the court's control.

(3) *Allocating Payment.* The court must allocate payment among the parties after considering the nature and amount of the controversy, the parties' means, and the extent to which any party is more responsible than other parties for the reference to a master. An interim allocation may be amended to reflect a decision on the merits.

(h) Appointing a Magistrate Judge. A magistrate judge is subject to this rule only when the order referring a matter to the magistrate judge states that the reference is made under this rule.

(Amended July 1, 1966; Aug. 1, 1983; Aug. 1, 1987; Dec. 1, 1991; Dec. 1, 1993; Dec. 1, 2003; Dec. 1, 2007; Dec. 1, 2009.)

TITLE VII. JUDGMENT

Rule 54. Judgments; Costs

(a) Definition; Form. "Judgment" as used in these rules includes a decree and any order from which an appeal lies. A judgment must not include recitals of pleadings, a master's report, or a record of prior proceedings.

(b) Judgment on Multiple Claims or Involving Multiple Parties. When an action presents more than one claim for relief—whether as a claim, counterclaim, crossclaim, or third-party claim—or when multiple parties are involved, the court may direct entry of a final judgment as to one or more, but fewer than all, claims or parties only if the court expressly determines that there is no just reason for delay. Otherwise, any order or other decision, however designated, that adjudicates fewer than all the claims or the rights and liabilities of fewer than all the parties does not end the action as to any of the claims or parties and may be revised at any time before the entry of a judgment adjudicating all the claims and all the parties' rights and liabilities.

(c) Demand for Judgment; Relief to Be Granted. A default judgment must not differ in kind from, or exceed in amount, what is demanded in the pleadings. Every other final judgment should grant the relief to which each party is entitled, even if the party has not demanded that relief in its pleadings.

(d) Costs; Attorney's Fees. (1) *Costs Other Than Attorney's Fees.* Unless a federal statute, these rules, or a court order provides otherwise, costs—other than attorney's fees—should be allowed to the prevailing party. But costs against the United States, its officers, and its agencies may be imposed only to the extent allowed by law. The clerk may tax costs on 14 days' notice. On motion served within the next 7 days, the court may review the clerk's action.

(2) *Attorney's Fees.* (A) Claim to Be by Motion. A claim for attorney's fees and related nontaxable

expenses must be made by motion unless the substantive law requires those fees to be proved at trial as an element of damages.

(B) Timing and Contents of the Motion. Unless a statute or a court order provides otherwise, the motion must:

(i) be filed no later than 14 days after the entry of judgment;

(ii) specify the judgment and the statute, rule, or other grounds entitling the movant to the award;

(iii) state the amount sought or provide a fair estimate of it; and

(iv) disclose, if the court so orders, the terms of any agreement about fees for the services for which the claim is made.

(C) Proceedings. Subject to Rule 23(h), the court must, on a party's request, give an opportunity for adversary submissions on the motion in accordance with Rule 43(c) or 78. The court may decide issues of liability for fees before receiving submissions on the value of services. The court must find the facts and state its conclusions of law as provided in Rule 52(a).

(D) Special Procedures by Local Rule; Reference to a Master or a Magistrate Judge. By local rule, the court may establish special procedures to resolve fee-related issues without extensive evidentiary hearings. Also, the court may refer issues concerning the value of services to a special master under Rule 53 without regard to the limitations of Rule 53(a)(1), and may refer a motion for attorney's fees to a magistrate judge under Rule 72(b) as if it were a dispositive pretrial matter.

(E) Exceptions. Subparagraphs (A)–(D) do not apply to claims for fees and expenses as sanctions for violating these rules or as sanctions under 28 U.S.C. § 1927.

(Amended March 19, 1948; July 19, 1961; Aug. 1, 1987; Dec. 1, 1993; Dec. 1, 2002; Dec. 1, 2003; Dec. 1, 2007; Dec. 1, 2009.)

Rule 55. Default; Default Judgment

(a) Entering a Default. When a party against whom a judgment for affirmative relief is sought has failed to plead or otherwise defend, and that failure is shown by affidavit or otherwise, the clerk must enter the party's default.

(b) Entering a Default Judgment. (1) *By the Clerk.* If the plaintiff's claim is for a sum certain or a sum that can be made certain by computation, the clerk—on the plaintiff's request, with an affidavit showing the amount due—must enter judgment for that amount and costs against a defendant who has been defaulted for not appearing and who is neither a minor nor an incompetent person.

(2) *By the Court.* In all other cases, the party must apply to the court for a default judgment. A default judgment may be entered against a minor or incompetent person only if represented by a general guardian, conservator, or other like fiduciary who has appeared. If the party against whom a default judgment is sought has appeared personally or by a representative, that party or its representative must be served with written notice of the application at least 7 days before the hearing. The court may conduct hearings or make referrals—preserving any federal statutory right to a jury trial—when, to enter or effectuate judgment, it needs to:

(A) conduct an accounting;

(B) determine the amount of damages;

(C) establish the truth of any allegation by evidence; or

(D) investigate any other matter.

(c) Setting Aside a Default or a Default Judgment. The court may set aside an entry of default for good cause, and it may set aside a default judgment under Rule 60(b).

(d) Judgment Against the United States. A default judgment may be entered against the United States, its officers, or its agencies only if the claimant establishes a claim or right to relief by evidence that satisfies the court.

(Amended Aug. 1, 1987; Dec. 1, 2007; Dec. 1, 2009.)

Rule 56. Summary Judgment

(a) Motion for Summary Judgment or Partial Summary Judgment. A party may move for summary judgment, identifying each claim or defense - or the part of each claim or defense—on which summary judgment is sought. The court shall grant summary judgment if the movant shows that there is no genuine dispute as to any material fact and the movant is entitled to judgment as a matter of law. The court should state on the record the reasons for granting or denying the motion.

(b) Time to File a Motion. Unless a different time is set by local rule or the court orders otherwise, a party may file a motion for summary judgment at any time until 30 days after the close of all discovery.

(c) Procedures. (1) *Supporting Factual Positions.* A party asserting that a fact cannot be or is genuinely disputed must support the assertion by:

(A) citing to particular parts of materials in the record, including depositions, documents, electronically stored information, affidavits or declarations, stipulations (including those made for purposes of the motion only), admissions, interrogatory answers, or other materials; or

(B) showing that the materials cited do not establish the absence or presence of a genuine dispute, or that an adverse party cannot produce admissible evidence to support the fact.

(2) *Objection That a Fact Is Not Supported by Admissible Evidence.* A party may object that the material cited to support or dispute a fact cannot be presented in a form that would be admissible in evidence.

(3) *Materials Not Cited.* The court need consider only the cited materials, but it may consider other materials in the record.

(4) *Affidavits or Declarations.* An affidavit or dec-

laration used to support or oppose a motion must be made on personal knowledge, set out facts that would be admissible in evidence, and show that the affiant or declarant is competent to testify on the matters stated.

(d) When Facts Are Unavailable to the Nonmovant. If a nonmovant shows by affidavit or declaration that, for specified reasons, it cannot present facts essential to justify its opposition, the court may:

(1) defer considering the motion or deny it;

(2) allow time to obtain affidavits or declarations or to take discovery; or

(3) issue any other appropriate order.

(e) Failing to Properly Support or Address a Fact. If a party fails to properly support an assertion of fact or fails to properly address another party's assertion of fact as required by Rule 56(c), the court may:

(1) give an opportunity to properly support or address the fact;

(2) consider the fact undisputed for purposes of the motion;

(3) grant summary judgment if the motion and supporting materials—including the facts considered undisputed—show that the movant is entitled to it; or

(4) issue any other appropriate order.

(f) Judgment Independent of the Motion. After giving notice and a reasonable time to respond, the court may:

(1) grant summary judgment for a nonmovant;

(2) grant the motion on grounds not raised by a party; or

(3) consider summary judgment on its own after identifying for the parties material facts that may not be genuinely in dispute.

(g) Failing to Grant All the Requested Relief. If the court does not grant all the relief requested by the motion, it may enter an order stating any material fact—including an item of damages or other relief—that is not genuinely in dispute and treating the fact as established in the case.

(h) Affidavit or Declaration Submitted in Bad Faith. If satisfied that an affidavit or declaration under this rule is submitted in bad faith or solely for delay, the court—after notice and a reasonable time to respond—may order the submitting party to pay the other party the reasonable expenses, including attorney's fees, it incurred as a result. An offending party or attorney may also be held in contempt or subjected to other appropriate sanctions.

(Amended March 19, 1948; July 1, 1963; Aug. 1, 1987; Dec. 1, 2007; Dec. 1, 2009; Dec. 1, 2010.)

Rule 57. Declaratory Judgment

These rules govern the procedure for obtaining a declaratory judgment under 28 U.S.C. § 2201. Rules 38 and 39 govern a demand for a jury trial. The existence of another adequate remedy does not preclude a declaratory judgment that is otherwise appropriate. The court may order a speedy hearing of a declaratory-judgment action.

(Amended Oct. 20, 1949; Dec. 1, 2007.)

Rule 58. Entering Judgment

(a) Separate Document. Every judgment and amended judgment must be set out in a separate document, but a separate document is not required for an order disposing of a motion:

(1) for judgment under Rule 50(b);

(2) to amend or make additional findings of fact under Rule 52(b);

(3) for attorney's fees under Rule 54;

(4) for a new trial, or to alter or amend the judgment, under Rule 59; or

(5) for relief under Rule 60.

(b) Entering Judgment. (1) *Without the Court's Direction.* Subject to Rule 54(b) and unless the court orders otherwise, the clerk must, without awaiting the court's direction, promptly prepare, sign, and enter the judgment when:

(A) the jury returns a general verdict;

(B) the court awards only costs or a sum certain; or

(C) the court denies all relief.

(2) *Court's Approval Required.* Subject to Rule 54(b), the court must promptly approve the form of the judgment, which the clerk must promptly enter, when:

(A) the jury returns a special verdict or a general verdict with answers to written questions; or

(B) the court grants other relief not described in this subdivision (b).

(c) Time of Entry. For purposes of these rules, judgment is entered at the following times:

(1) if a separate document is not required, when the judgment is entered in the civil docket under Rule 79(a); or

(2) if a separate document is required, when the judgment is entered in the civil docket under Rule 79(a) and the earlier of these events occurs:

(A) it is set out in a separate document; or

(B) 150 days have run from the entry in the civil docket.

(d) Request for Entry. A party may request that judgment be set out in a separate document as required by Rule 58(a).

(e) Cost or Fee Awards. Ordinarily, the entry of judgment may not be delayed, nor the time for appeal extended, in order to tax costs or award fees. But if a timely motion for attorney's fees is made under Rule 54(d)(2), the court may act before a notice of appeal has been filed and become effective to order that the motion have the same effect under Federal Rule of Appellate Procedure 4(a)(4) as a timely motion under Rule 59.

(Amended March 19, 1948; July 1, 1963; Dec. 1, 1993; Dec. 1, 2002; Dec. 1, 2007.)

Rule 59. New Trial; Altering or Amending a Judgment

(a) In General. (1) *Grounds for New Trial.* The court may, on motion, grant a new trial on all or some of the issues—and to any party—as follows:

(A) after a jury trial, for any reason for which a new trial has heretofore been granted in an action at law in federal court; or

(B) after a nonjury trial, for any reason for which a rehearing has heretofore been granted in a suit in equity in federal court.

(2) *Further Action After a Nonjury Trial.* After a nonjury trial, the court may, on motion for a new trial, open the judgment if one has been entered, take additional testimony, amend findings of fact and conclusions of law or make new ones, and direct the entry of a new judgment.

(b) Time to File a Motion for a New Trial. A motion for a new trial must be filed no later than 28 days after the entry of judgment.

(c) Time to Serve Affidavits. When a motion for a new trial is based on affidavits, they must be filed with the motion. The opposing party has 14 days after being served to file opposing affidavits. The court may permit reply affidavits.

(d) New Trial on the Court's Initiative or for Reasons Not in the Motion. No later than 28 days after the entry of judgment, the court, on its own, may order a new trial for any reason that would justify granting one on a party's motion. After giving the parties notice and an opportunity to be heard, the court may grant a timely motion for a new trial for a reason not stated in the motion. In either event, the court must specify the reasons in its order.

(e) Motion to Alter or Amend a Judgment. A motion to alter or amend a judgment must be filed no later than 28 days after the entry of the judgment.

(Amended March 19, 1948; July 1, 1966; Dec. 1, 1995; Dec. 1, 2007; Dec. 1, 2009.)

Rule 60. Relief from a Judgment or Order

(a) Corrections Based on Clerical Mistakes; Oversights and Omissions. The court may correct a clerical mistake or a mistake arising from oversight or omission whenever one is found in a judgment, order, or other part of the record. The court may do so on motion or on its own, with or without notice. But after an appeal has been docketed in the appellate court and while it is pending, such a mistake may be corrected only with the appellate court's leave.

(b) Grounds for Relief from a Final Judgment, Order, or Proceeding. On motion and just terms, the court may relieve a party or its legal representative from a final judgment, order, or proceeding for the following reasons:

(1) mistake, inadvertence, surprise, or excusable neglect;

(2) newly discovered evidence that, with reasonable diligence, could not have been discovered in time to move for a new trial under Rule 59(b);

(3) fraud (whether previously called intrinsic or extrinsic), misrepresentation, or misconduct by an opposing party;

(4) the judgment is void;

(5) the judgment has been satisfied, released, or discharged; it is based on an earlier judgment that has been reversed or vacated; or applying it prospectively is no longer equitable; or

(6) any other reason that justifies relief.

(c) Timing and Effect of the Motion. (1) *Timing.* A motion under Rule 60(b) must be made within a reasonable time—and for reasons (1), (2), and (3) no more than a year after the entry of the judgment or order or the date of the proceeding.

(2) *Effect on Finality.* The motion does not affect the judgment's finality or suspend its operation.

(d) Other Powers to Grant Relief. This rule does not limit a court's power to:

(1) entertain an independent action to relieve a party from a judgment, order, or proceeding;

(2) grant relief under 28 U.S.C. § 1655 to a defendant who was not personally notified of the action; or

(3) set aside a judgment for fraud on the court.

(e) Bills and Writs Abolished. The following are abolished: bills of review, bills in the nature of bills of review, and writs of coram nobis, coram vobis, and audita querela.

(Amended March 19, 1948; Oct. 20, 1949; Aug. 1, 1987; Dec. 1, 2007.)

Rule 61. Harmless Error

Unless justice requires otherwise, no error in admitting or excluding evidence—or any other error by the court or a party—is ground for granting a new trial, for setting aside a verdict, or for vacating, modifying, or otherwise disturbing a judgment or order. At every stage of the proceeding, the court must disregard all errors and defects that do not affect any party's substantial rights.

(As amended Dec. 1, 2007.)

Rule 62. Stay of Proceedings to Enforce a Judgment

(a) Automatic Stay; Exceptions for Injunctions, Receiverships, and Patent Accountings. Except as stated in this rule, no execution may issue on a judgment, nor may proceedings be taken to enforce it, until 14 days have passed after its entry. But unless the court orders otherwise, the following are not stayed after being entered, even if an appeal is taken:

(1) an interlocutory or final judgment in an action for an injunction or a receivership; or

(2) a judgment or order that directs an accounting in an action for patent infringement.

(b) Stay Pending the Disposition of a Motion. On appropriate terms for the opposing party's security, the court may stay the execution of a judgment—or any proceedings to enforce it—pending disposition of any of the following motions:

(1) under Rule 50, for judgment as a matter of law;

(2) under Rule 52(b), to amend the findings or for additional findings;

(3) under Rule 59, for a new trial or to alter or amend a judgment; or

(4) under Rule 60, for relief from a judgment or order.

(c) Injunction Pending an Appeal. While an appeal is pending from an interlocutory order or final judgment that grants, dissolves, or denies an injunction, the court may suspend, modify, restore, or grant an injunction on terms for bond or other terms that secure the opposing party's rights. If the judgment appealed from is rendered by a statutory three-judge district court, the order must be made either:

(1) by that court sitting in open session; or

(2) by the assent of all its judges, as evidenced by their signatures.

(d) Stay with Bond on Appeal. If an appeal is taken, the appellant may obtain a stay by supersedeas bond, except in an action described in Rule 62(a)(1) or (2). The bond may be given upon or after filing the notice of appeal or after obtaining the order allowing the appeal. The stay takes effect when the court approves the bond.

(e) Stay Without Bond on an Appeal by the United States, Its Officers, or Its Agencies. The court must not require a bond, obligation, or other security from the appellant when granting a stay on an appeal by the United States, its officers, or its agencies or on an appeal directed by a department of the federal government.

(f) Stay in Favor of a Judgment Debtor Under State Law. If a judgment is a lien on the judgment debtor's property under the law of the state where the court is located, the judgment debtor is entitled to the same stay of execution the state court would give.

(g) Appellate Court's Power Not Limited. This rule does not limit the power of the appellate court or one of its judges or justices:

(1) to stay proceedings—or suspend, modify, restore, or grant an injunction—while an appeal is pending; or

(2) to issue an order to preserve the status quo or the effectiveness of the judgment to be entered.

(h) Stay with Multiple Claims or Parties. A court may stay the enforcement of a final judgment entered under Rule 54(b) until it enters a later judgment or judgments, and may prescribe terms necessary to secure the benefit of the stayed judgment for the party in whose favor it was entered.

(Amended March 19, 1948; Oct. 20, 1949; July 19, 1961; Aug. 1, 1987; Dec. 1, 2007; Dec. 1, 2009.)

Rule 62.1. Indicative Ruling on a Motion for Relief That is Barred by a Pending Appeal

(a) Relief Pending Appeal. If a timely motion is made for relief that the court lacks authority to grant because of an appeal that has been docketed and is pending, the court may:

(1) defer considering the motion;

(2) deny the motion; or

(3) state either that it would grant the motion if the court of appeals remands for that purpose or that the motion raises a substantial issue.

(b) Notice to the Court of Appeals. The movant must promptly notify the circuit clerk under Federal Rule of Appellate Procedure 12.1 if the district court states that it would grant the motion or that the motion raises a substantial issue.

(c) Remand. The district court may decide the motion if the court of appeals remands for that purpose.

(As added Dec. 1, 2009.)

Rule 63. Judge's Inability to Proceed

If a judge conducting a hearing or trial is unable to proceed, any other judge may proceed upon certifying familiarity with the record and determining that the case may be completed without prejudice to the parties. In a hearing or a nonjury trial, the successor judge must, at a party's request, recall any witness whose testimony is material and disputed and who is available to testify again without undue burden. The successor judge may also recall any other witness.

(Amended Aug. 1, 1987; Dec. 1, 1991; Dec. 1, 2007.)

TITLE VIII. PROVISIONAL AND FINAL REMEDIES

Rule 64. Seizing a Person or Property

(a) Remedies Under State Law—In General. At the commencement of and throughout an action, every remedy is available that, under the law of the state where the court is located, provides for seizing a person or property to secure satisfaction of the potential judgment. But a federal statute governs to the extent it applies.

(b) Specific Kinds of Remedies. The remedies available under this rule include the following—however designated and regardless of whether state procedure requires an independent action:

- arrest;
- attachment;
- garnishment;
- replevin;
- sequestration; and
- other corresponding or equivalent remedies.

(Amended Dec. 1, 2007.)

Rule 65. Injunctions and Restraining Orders

(a) Preliminary Injunction. (1) *Notice.* The court may issue a preliminary injunction only on notice to the adverse party.

(2) *Consolidating the Hearing with the Trial on the Merits.* Before or after beginning a hearing on a

motion for a preliminary injunction, the court may advance the trial on the merits and consolidate it with the hearing. Even when consolidation is not ordered, evidence that is received on the motion and that would be admissible at trial becomes part of the trial record and need not be repeated at trial. But the court must preserve any party's right to a jury trial.

(b) Temporary Restraining Order. (1) *Issuing Without Notice.* The court may issue a temporary restraining order without written or oral notice to the adverse party or its attorney only if:

(A) specific facts in an affidavit or a verified complaint clearly show that immediate and irreparable injury, loss, or damage will result to the movant before the adverse party can be heard in opposition; and

(B) the movant's attorney certifies in writing any efforts made to give notice and the reasons why it should not be required.

(2) *Contents; Expiration.* Every temporary restraining order issued without notice must state the date and hour it was issued; describe the injury and state why it is irreparable; state why the order was issued without notice; and be promptly filed in the clerk's office and entered in the record. The order expires at the time after entry—not to exceed 14 days—that the court sets, unless before that time the court, for good cause, extends it for a like period or the adverse party consents to a longer extension. The reasons for an extension must be entered in the record.

(3) *Expediting the Preliminary-Injunction Hearing.* If the order is issued without notice, the motion for a preliminary injunction must be set for hearing at the earliest possible time, taking precedence over all other matters except hearings on older matters of the same character. At the hearing, the party who obtained the order must proceed with the motion; if the party does not, the court must dissolve the order.

(4) *Motion to Dissolve.* On 2 days' notice to the party who obtained the order without notice—or on shorter notice set by the court—the adverse party may appear and move to dissolve or modify the order. The court must then hear and decide the motion as promptly as justice requires.

(c) Security. The court may issue a preliminary injunction or a temporary restraining order only if the movant gives security in an amount that the court considers proper to pay the costs and damages sustained by any party found to have been wrongfully enjoined or restrained. The United States, its officers, and its agencies are not required to give security.

(d) Contents and Scope of Every Injunction and Restraining Order. (1) *Contents.* Every order granting an injunction and every restraining order must:

(A) state the reasons why it issued;

(B) state its terms specifically; and

(C) describe in reasonable detail—and not by referring to the complaint or other document—the act or acts restrained or required.

(2) *Persons Bound.* The order binds only the following who receive actual notice of it by personal service or otherwise:

(A) the parties;

(B) the parties' officers, agents, servants, employees, and attorneys; and

(C) other persons who are in active concert or participation with anyone described in Rule 65(d)(2)(A) or (B).

(e) Other Laws Not Modified. These rules do not modify the following:

(1) any federal statute relating to temporary restraining orders or preliminary injunctions in actions affecting employer and employee;

(2) 28 U.S.C. § 2361, which relates to preliminary injunctions in actions of interpleader or in the nature of interpleader; or

(3) 28 U.S.C. § 2284, which relates to actions that must be heard and decided by a three-judge district court.

(f) Copyright Impoundment. This rule applies to copyright-impoundment proceedings.

(Amended March 19, 1948; Oct. 20, 1949; July 1, 1966; Aug. 1, 1987; Dec. 1, 2001; Dec. 1, 2007; Dec. 1, 2009.)

Rule 65.1. Proceedings Against a Surety

Whenever these rules (including the Supplemental Rules for Admiralty or Maritime Claims and Asset Forfeiture Actions) require or allow a party to give security, and security is given through a bond or other undertaking with one or more sureties, each surety submits to the court's jurisdiction and irrevocably appoints the court clerk as its agent for receiving service of any papers that affect its liability on the bond or undertaking. The surety's liability may be enforced on motion without an independent action. The motion and any notice that the court orders may be served on the court clerk, who must promptly mail a copy of each to every surety whose address is known.

(Added July 1, 1966; amended Aug. 1, 1987; Dec. 1, 2006; Dec. 1, 2007.)

Rule 66. Receivers

These rules govern an action in which the appointment of a receiver is sought or a receiver sues or is sued. But the practice in administering an estate by a receiver or a similar court-appointed officer must accord with the historical practice in federal courts or with a local rule. An action in which a receiver has been appointed may be dismissed only by court order.

(Amended March 19, 1948; Oct. 20, 1949; Dec. 1, 2007.)

Rule 67. Deposit into Court

(a) Depositing Property. If any part of the relief sought is a money judgment or the disposition of a sum of money or some other deliverable thing, a party—on notice to every other party and by leave of court—may deposit with the court all or part of the money or thing, whether or not that party claims any of it. The depositing party must deliver to the clerk a copy of the order permitting deposit.

(b) Investing and Withdrawing Funds. Money paid into court under this rule must be deposited and withdrawn in accordance with 28 U.S.C. §§ 2041 and 2042 and any like statute. The money must be deposited in an interest-bearing account or invested in a court-approved, interest-bearing instrument.

(Amended Oct. 20, 1949; Aug. 1, 1983; Dec. 1, 2007.)

Rule 68. Offer of Judgment

(a) Making an Offer; Judgment on an Accepted Offer. At least 14 days before the date set for trial, a party defending against a claim may serve on an opposing party an offer to allow judgment on specified terms, with the costs then accrued. If, within 14 days after being served, the opposing party serves written notice accepting the offer, either party may then file the offer and notice of acceptance, plus proof of service. The clerk must then enter judgment.

(b) Unaccepted Offer. An unaccepted offer is considered withdrawn, but it does not preclude a later offer. Evidence of an unaccepted offer is not admissible except in a proceeding to determine costs.

(c) Offer After Liability Is Determined. When one party's liability to another has been determined but the extent of liability remains to be determined by further proceedings, the party held liable may make an offer of judgment. It must be served within a reasonable time—but at least 14 days—before the date set for a hearing to determine the extent of liability.

(d) Paying Costs After an Unaccepted Offer. If the judgment that the offeree finally obtains is not more favorable than the unaccepted offer, the offeree must pay the costs incurred after the offer was made.

(Amended March 19, 1948; July 1, 1966; Aug. 1, 1987; Dec. 1, 2007; Dec. 1, 2009.)

Rule 69. Execution

(a) In General. (1) *Money Judgment; Applicable Procedure.* A money judgment is enforced by a writ of execution, unless the court directs otherwise. The procedure on execution—and in proceedings supplementary to and in aid of judgment or execution—must accord with the procedure of the state where the court is located, but a federal statute governs to the extent it applies.

(2) *Obtaining Discovery.* In aid of the judgment or execution, the judgment creditor or a successor in interest whose interest appears of record may obtain discovery from any person—including the judgment debtor—as provided in these rules or by the procedure of the state where the court is located.

(b) Against Certain Public Officers. When a judgment has been entered against a revenue officer in the circumstances stated in 28 U.S.C. § 2006, or against an officer of Congress in the circumstances stated in 2 U.S.C. § 118, the judgment must be satisfied as those statutes provide.

(Amended Oct. 20, 1949; July 1, 1970; Aug. 1, 1987; Dec. 1, 2007.)

Rule 70. Enforcing a Judgment for a Specific Act

(a) Party's Failure to Act; Ordering Another to Act. If a judgment requires a party to convey land, to deliver a deed or other document, or to perform any other specific act and the party fails to comply within the time specified, the court may order the act to be done—at the disobedient party's expense—by another person appointed by the court. When done, the act has the same effect as if done by the party.

(b) Vesting Title. If the real or personal property is within the district, the court—instead of ordering a conveyance—may enter a judgment divesting any party's title and vesting it in others. That judgment has the effect of a legally executed conveyance.

(c) Obtaining a Writ of Attachment or Sequestration. On application by a party entitled to performance of an act, the clerk must issue a writ of attachment or sequestration against the disobedient party's property to compel obedience.

(d) Obtaining a Writ of Execution or Assistance. On application by a party who obtains a judgment or order for possession, the clerk must issue a writ of execution or assistance.

(e) Holding in Contempt. The court may also hold the disobedient party in contempt.

(As amended Dec. 1, 2007.)

Rule 71. Enforcing Relief For or Against a Nonparty

When an order grants relief for a nonparty or may be enforced against a nonparty, the procedure for enforcing the order is the same as for a party.

(Amended Aug. 1, 1987; Dec. 1, 2007.)

TITLE IX. SPECIAL PROCEEDINGS

Rule 71.1. Condemning Real or Personal Property

(a) Applicability of Other Rules. These rules govern proceedings to condemn real and personal property by eminent domain, except as this rule provides otherwise.

(b) Joinder of Properties. The plaintiff may join separate pieces of property in a single action, no matter whether they are owned by the same persons or sought for the same use.

(c) Complaint. (1) *Caption.* The complaint must

contain a caption as provided in Rule 10(a). The plaintiff must, however, name as defendants both the property—designated generally by kind, quantity, and location—and at least one owner of some part of or interest in the property.

(2) *Contents.* The complaint must contain a short and plain statement of the following:

(A) the authority for the taking;

(B) the uses for which the property is to be taken;

(C) a description sufficient to identify the property;

(D) the interests to be acquired; and

(E) for each piece of property, a designation of each defendant who has been joined as an owner or owner of an interest in it.

(3) *Parties.* When the action commences, the plaintiff need join as defendants only those persons who have or claim an interest in the property and whose names are then known. But before any hearing on compensation, the plaintiff must add as defendants all those persons who have or claim an interest and whose names have become known or can be found by a reasonably diligent search of the records, considering both the property's character and value and the interests to be acquired. All others may be made defendants under the designation "Unknown Owners."

(4) *Procedure.* Notice must be served on all defendants as provided in Rule 71.1(d), whether they were named as defendants when the action commenced or were added later. A defendant may answer as provided in Rule 71.1(e). The court, meanwhile, may order any distribution of a deposit that the facts warrant.

(5) *Filing; Additional Copies.* In addition to filing the complaint, the plaintiff must give the clerk at least one copy for the defendants' use and additional copies at the request of the clerk or a defendant.

(d) Process. (1) *Delivering Notice to the Clerk.* On filing a complaint, the plaintiff must promptly deliver to the clerk joint or several notices directed to the named defendants. When adding defendants, the plaintiff must deliver to the clerk additional notices directed to the new defendants.

(2) *Contents of the Notice.* (A) Main Contents. Each notice must name the court, the title of the action, and the defendant to whom it is directed. It must describe the property sufficiently to identify it, but need not describe any property other than that to be taken from the named defendant. The notice must also state:

(i) that the action is to condemn property;

(ii) the interest to be taken;

(iii) the authority for the taking;

(iv) the uses for which the property is to be taken;

(v) that the defendant may serve an answer on the plaintiffs attorney within 21 days after being served with the notice;

(vi) that the failure to so serve an answer constitutes consent to the taking and to the court's authority to proceed with the action and fix the compensation; and

(vii) that a defendant who does not serve an answer may file a notice of appearance.

(B) Conclusion. The notice must conclude with the name, telephone number, and e-mail address of the plaintiff's attorney and an address within the district in which the action is brought where the attorney may be served.

(3) *Serving the Notice.* (A) Personal Service. When a defendant whose address is known resides within the United States or a territory subject to the administrative or judicial jurisdiction of the United States, personal service of the notice (without a copy of the complaint) must be made in accordance with Rule 4.

(B) Service by Publication.

(i) A defendant may be served by publication only when the plaintiff's attorney files a certificate stating that the attorney believes the defendant cannot be personally served, because after diligent inquiry within the state where the complaint is filed, the defendant's place of residence is still unknown or, if known, that it is beyond the territorial limits of personal service. Service is then made by publishing the notice—once a week for at least three successive weeks—in a newspaper published in the county where the property is located or, if there is no such newspaper, in a newspaper with general circulation where the property is located. Before the last publication, a copy of the notice must also be mailed to every defendant who cannot be personally served but whose place of residence is then known. Unknown owners may be served by publication in the same manner by a notice addressed to "Unknown Owners."

(ii) Service by publication is complete on the date of the last publication. The plaintiff's attorney must prove publication and mailing by a certificate, attach a printed copy of the published notice, and mark on the copy the newspaper's name and the dates of publication.

(4) *Effect of Delivery and Service.* Delivering the notice to the clerk and serving it have the same effect as serving a summons under Rule 4.

(5) *Amending the Notice; Proof of Service and Amending the Proof.* Rule 4(a)(2) governs amending the notice. Rule 4(l) governs proof of service and amending it.

(e) Appearance or Answer. (1) *Notice of Appearance.* A defendant that has no objection or defense to the taking of its property may serve a notice of appearance designating the property in which it claims an interest. The defendant must then be given notice of all later proceedings affecting the defendant.

(2) *Answer.* A defendant that has an objection or defense to the taking must serve an answer within 21 days after being served with the notice. The answer must:

(A) identify the property in which the defendant claims an interest;

(B) state the nature and extent of the interest; and

(C) state all the defendant's objections and defenses to the taking.

(3) *Waiver of Other Objections and Defenses; Evidence on Compensation.* A defendant waives all objections and defenses not stated in its answer. No other pleading or motion asserting an additional objection or defense is allowed. But at the trial on compensation, a defendant—whether or not it has previously appeared or answered—may present evidence on the amount of compensation to be paid and may share in the award.

(f) Amending Pleadings. Without leave of court, the plaintiff may—as often as it wants—amend the complaint at any time before the trial on compensation. But no amendment may be made if it would result in a dismissal inconsistent with Rule 71.1(i)(1) or (2). The plaintiff need not serve a copy of an amendment, but must serve notice of the filing, as provided in Rule 5(b), on every affected party who has appeared and, as provided in Rule 71.1(d), on every affected party who has not appeared. In addition, the plaintiff must give the clerk at least one copy of each amendment for the defendants' use, and additional copies at the request of the clerk or a defendant. A defendant may appear or answer in the time and manner and with the same effect as provided in Rule 71.1(e).

(g) Substituting Parties. If a defendant dies, becomes incompetent, or transfers an interest after being joined, the court may, on motion and notice of hearing, order that the proper party be substituted. Service of the motion and notice on a nonparty must be made as provided in Rule 71.1(d)(3).

(h) Trial of the Issues. (1) *Issues Other Than Compensation; Compensation.* In an action involving eminent domain under federal law, the court tries all issues, including compensation, except when compensation must be determined:

(A) by any tribunal specially constituted by a federal statute to determine compensation; or

(B) if there is no such tribunal, by a jury when a party demands one within the time to answer or within any additional time the court sets, unless the court appoints a commission.

(2) *Appointing a Commission; Commission's Powers and Report.* (A) Reasons for Appointing. If a party has demanded a jury, the court may instead appoint a three-person commission to determine compensation because of the character, location, or quantity of the property to be condemned or for other just reasons.

(B) Alternate Commissioners. The court may appoint up to two additional persons to serve as alternate commissioners to hear the case and replace commissioners who, before a decision is filed, the court finds unable or disqualified to perform their duties. Once the commission renders its final decision, the court must discharge any alternate who has not replaced a commissioner.

(C) Examining the Prospective Commissioners. Before making its appointments, the court must advise the parties of the identity and qualifications of each prospective commissioner and alternate, and may permit the parties to examine them. The parties may not suggest appointees, but for good cause may object to a prospective commissioner or alternate.

(D) Commission's Powers and Report. A commission has the powers of a master under Rule 53(c). Its action and report are determined by a majority. Rule 53(d), (e), and (f) apply to its action and report.

(i) Dismissal of the Action or a Defendant. (1) *Dismissing the Action.* (A) By the Plaintiff. If no compensation hearing on a piece of property has begun, and if the plaintiff has not acquired title or a lesser interest or taken possession, the plaintiff may, without a court order, dismiss the action as to that property by filing a notice of dismissal briefly describing the property.

(B) By Stipulation. Before a judgment is entered vesting the plaintiff with title or a lesser interest in or possession of property, the plaintiff and affected defendants may, without a court order, dismiss the action in whole or in part by filing a stipulation of dismissal. And if the parties so stipulate, the court may vacate a judgment already entered.

(C) By Court Order. At any time before compensation has been determined and paid, the court may, after a motion and hearing, dismiss the action as to a piece of property. But if the plaintiff has already taken title, a lesser interest, or possession as to any part of it, the court must award compensation for the title, lesser interest, or possession taken.

(2) *Dismissing a Defendant.* The court may at any time dismiss a defendant who was unnecessarily or improperly joined.

(3) *Effect.* A dismissal is without prejudice unless otherwise stated in the notice, stipulation, or court order.

(j) Deposit and Its Distribution. (1) *Deposit.* The plaintiff must deposit with the court any money required by law as a condition to the exercise of eminent domain and may make a deposit when allowed by statute.

(2) *Distribution; Adjusting Distribution.* After a deposit, the court and attorneys must expedite the proceedings so as to distribute the deposit and to determine and pay compensation. If the compensation finally awarded to a defendant exceeds the amount distributed to that defendant, the court must enter judgment against the plaintiff for the deficiency. If the compensation awarded to a defendant is less than the amount distributed to that defendant, the court must enter judgment against that defendant for the overpayment.

(k) Condemnation Under a State's Power of Eminent Domain. This rule governs an action involving eminent domain under state law. But if state law provides for trying an issue by jury—or for trying the issue of compensation by jury or commission or both—that law governs.

(l) Costs. Costs are not subject to Rule 54(d).

(Added Aug. 1, 1951; July 1, 1963; Aug. 1, 1985; Aug. 1, 1987; Aug. 1, 1988; Nov. 18, 1988, P. L. 100-690, Title VII, Subtitle B, § 7050, 102 Stat. 4401; Dec. 1, 1993; Dec. 1, 2003; Dec. 1, 2007; Dec. 1, 2009.)

Rule 71A. [Transferred]

(Amended Dec. 1, 2007.)

Rule 72. Magistrate Judges: Pretrial Order

(a) Nondispositive Matters. When a pretrial matter not dispositive of a party's claim or defense is referred to a magistrate judge to hear and decide, the magistrate judge must promptly conduct the required proceedings and, when appropriate, issue a written order stating the decision. A party may serve and file objections to the order within 14 days after being served with a copy. A party may not assign as error a defect in the order not timely objected to. The district judge in the case must consider timely objections and modify or set aside any part of the order that is clearly erroneous or is contrary to law.

(b) Dispositive Motions and Prisoner Petitions. (1) *Findings and Recommendations.* A magistrate judge must promptly conduct the required proceedings when assigned, without the parties' consent, to hear a pretrial matter dispositive of a claim or defense or a prisoner petition challenging the conditions of confinement. A record must be made of all evidentiary proceedings and may, at the magistrate judge's discretion, be made of any other proceedings. The magistrate judge must enter a recommended disposition, including, if appropriate, proposed findings of fact. The clerk must promptly mail a copy to each party.

(2) *Objections.* Within 14 days after being served with a copy of the recommended disposition, a party may serve and file specific written objections to the proposed findings and recommendations. A party may respond to another party's objections within 14 days after being served with a copy. Unless the district judge orders otherwise, the objecting party must promptly arrange for transcribing the record, or whatever portions of it the parties agree to or the magistrate judge considers sufficient.

(3) *Resolving Objections.* The district judge must determine de novo any part of the magistrate judge's disposition that has been properly objected to. The district judge may accept, reject, or modify the recommended disposition; receive further evidence; or return the matter to the magistrate judge with instructions.

(Added Aug. 1, 1983; Dec. 1, 1991; Dec. 1, 1993; Dec. 1, 2007; Dec. 1, 2009.)

Rule 73. Magistrate Judges: Trial by Consent; Appeal

(a) Trial by Consent. When authorized under 28 U.S.C. § 636(c), a magistrate judge may, if all parties consent, conduct a civil action or proceeding, including a jury or nonjury trial. A record must be made in accordance with 28 U.S.C. § 636(c)(5).

(b) Consent Procedure. (1) *In General.* When a magistrate judge has been designated to conduct civil actions or proceedings, the clerk must give the parties written notice of their opportunity to consent under 28 U.S.C. § 636(c). To signify their consent, the parties must jointly or separately file a statement consenting to the referral. A district judge or magistrate judge may be informed of a party's response to the clerk's notice only if all parties have consented to the referral.

(2) *Reminding the Parties About Consenting.* A district judge, magistrate judge, or other court official may remind the parties of the magistrate judge's availability, but must also advise them that they are free to withhold consent without adverse substantive consequences.

(3) *Vacating a Referral.* On its own for good cause—or when a party shows extraordinary circumstances—the district judge may vacate a referral to a magistrate judge under this rule.

(c) Appealing a Judgment. In accordance with 28 U.S.C. § 636(c)(3), an appeal from a judgment entered at a magistrate judge's direction may be taken to the court of appeals as would any other appeal from a district-court judgment.

(Added Aug. 1, 1983; Aug. 1, 1987; Dec. 1, 1993; Dec. 1, 1997; Dec. 1, 2007.)

Rule 74. [Abrogated]

Rule 75. [Abrogated]

Rule 76. [Abrogated]

TITLE X. DISTRICT COURTS AND CLERKS: CONDUCTING BUSINESS; ISSUING ORDERS

Rule 77. Conducting Business; Clerk's Authority; Notice of an Order or Judgment

(a) When Court Is Open. Every district court is considered always open for filing any paper, issuing and returning process, making a motion, or entering an order.

(b) Place for Trial and Other Proceedings. Every trial on the merits must be conducted in open court and, so far as convenient, in a regular courtroom. Any other act or proceeding may be done or conducted by a judge in chambers, without the attendance of the clerk or other court official, and anywhere inside or outside the district. But no hearing—other than one ex parte—may be conducted outside the district unless all the affected parties consent.

(c) Clerk's Office Hours; Clerk's Orders. (1) *Hours.* The clerk's office—with a clerk or deputy on duty—must be open during business hours every day except Saturdays, Sundays, and legal holidays.

But a court may, by local rule or order, require that the office be open for specified hours on Saturday or a particular legal holiday other than one listed in Rule 6(a)(6)(A).

(2) *Orders.* Subject to the court's power to suspend, alter, or rescind the clerk's action for good cause, the clerk may:

(A) issue process;

(B) enter a default;

(C) enter a default judgment under Rule 55(b)(1); and

(D) act on any other matter that does not require the court's action.

(d) Serving Notice of an Order or Judgment. (1) *Service.* Immediately after entering an order or judgment, the clerk must serve notice of the entry, as provided in Rule 5(b), on each party who is not in default for failing to appear. The clerk must record the service on the docket. A party also may serve notice of the entry as provided in Rule 5(b).

(2) *Time to Appeal Not Affected by Lack of Notice.* Lack of notice of the entry does not affect the time for appeal or relieve—or authorize the court to relieve—a party for failing to appeal within the time allowed, except as allowed by Federal Rule of Appellate Procedure (4)(a).

(Amended March 19, 1948; July 1, 1963; July 1, 1968; July 1, 1971; Aug. 1, 1987; Dec. 1, 1991; Dec. 1, 2001; Dec. 1, 2007; April 25, 2014, eff. Dec. 1, 2014.)

Rule 78. Hearing Motions; Submission on Briefs

(a) Providing a Regular Schedule for Oral Hearings. A court may establish regular times and places for oral hearings on motions.

(b) Providing for Submission on Briefs. By rule or order, the court may provide for submitting and determining motions on briefs, without oral hearings.

(Amended Aug. 1, 1987; Dec. 1, 2007.)

Rule 79. Records Kept by the Clerk

(a) Civil Docket. (1) *In General.* The clerk must keep a record known as the "civil docket" in the form and manner prescribed by the Director of the Administrative Office of the United States Courts with the approval of the Judicial Conference of the United States. The clerk must enter each civil action in the docket. Actions must be assigned consecutive file numbers, which must be noted in the docket where the first entry of the action is made.

(2) *Items to be Entered.* The following items must be marked with the file number and entered chronologically in the docket:

(A) papers filed with the clerk;

(B) process issued, and proofs of service or other returns showing execution; and

(C) appearances, orders, verdicts, and judgments.

(3) *Contents of Entries; Jury Trial Demanded.* Each entry must briefly show the nature of the paper filed or writ issued, the substance of each proof of service or other return, and the substance and date of entry of each order and judgment. When a jury trial has been properly demanded or ordered, the clerk must enter the word "jury" in the docket.

(b) Civil Judgments and Orders. The clerk must keep a copy of every final judgment and appealable order; of every order affecting title to or a lien on real or personal property; and of any other order that the court directs to be kept. The clerk must keep these in the form and manner prescribed by the Director of the Administrative Office of the United States Courts with the approval of the Judicial Conference of the United States.

(c) Indexes; Calendars. Under the court's direction, the clerk must:

(1) keep indexes of the docket and of the judgments and orders described in Rule 79(b); and

(2) prepare calendars of all actions ready for trial, distinguishing jury trials from nonjury trials.

(d) Other Records. The clerk must keep any other records required by the Director of the Administrative Office of the United States Courts with the approval of the Judicial Conference of the United States.

(Amended March 19, 1948; Oct. 20, 1949; July 1, 1963; Dec. 1, 2007.)

Rule 80. Stenographic Transcript as Evidence

If stenographically reported testimony at a hearing or trial is admissible in evidence at a later trial, the testimony may be proved by a transcript certified by the person who recorded it.

(Amended March 19, 1948; Dec. 1, 2007.)

TITLE XI. GENERAL PROVISIONS

Rule 81. Applicability of the Rules in General; Removed Actions

(a) Applicability to Particular Proceedings. (1) *Prize Proceedings.* These rules do not apply to prize proceedings in admiralty governed by 10 U.S.C. §§ 7651–7681.

(2) *Bankruptcy.* These rules apply to bankruptcy proceedings to the extent provided by the Federal Rules of Bankruptcy Procedure.

(3) *Citizenship.* These rules apply to proceedings for admission to citizenship to the extent that the practice in those proceedings is not specified in federal statutes and has previously conformed to the practice in civil actions. The provisions of 8 U.S.C. § 1451 for service by publication and for answer apply in proceedings to cancel citizenship certificates.

(4) *Special Writs.* These rules apply to proceedings for habeas corpus and for quo warranto to the extent that the practice in those proceedings:

(A) is not specified in a federal statute, the Rules Governing Section 2254 Cases, or the Rules Governing Section 2255 Cases; and

(B) has previously conformed to the practice in

civil actions.

(5) *Proceedings Involving a Subpoena.* These rules apply to proceedings to compel testimony or the production of documents through a subpoena issued by a United States officer or agency under a federal statute, except as otherwise provided by statute, by local rule, or by court order in the proceedings.

(6) *Other Proceedings.* These rules, to the extent applicable, govern proceedings under the following laws, except as these laws provide other procedures:

(A) 7 U.S.C. §§ 292, 499g(c), for reviewing an order of the Secretary of Agriculture;

(B) 9 U.S.C., relating to arbitration;

(C) 15 U.S.C. § 522, for reviewing an order of the Secretary of the Interior;

(D) 15 U.S.C. § 715d(c), for reviewing an order denying a certificate of clearance;

(E) 29 U.S.C. §§ 159, 160, for enforcing an order of the National Labor Relations Board;

(F) 33 U.S.C. §§ 918, 921, for enforcing or reviewing a compensation order under the Longshore and Harbor Workers' Compensation Act; and

(G) 45 U.S.C. § 159, for reviewing an arbitration award in a railway-labor dispute.

(b) Scire Facias and Mandamus. The writs of scire facias and mandamus are abolished. Relief previously available through them may be obtained by appropriate action or motion under these rules.

(c) Removed Actions. (1) *Applicability.* These rules apply to a civil action after it is removed from a state court.

(2) *Further Pleading.* After removal, repleading is unnecessary unless the court orders it. A defendant who did not answer before removal must answer or present other defenses or objections under these rules within the longest of these periods:

(A) 21 days after receiving—through service or otherwise—a copy of the initial pleading stating the claim for relief;

(B) 21 days after being served with the summons for an initial pleading on file at the time of service; or

(C) 7 days after the notice of removal is filed.

(3) *Demand for a Jury Trial.* (A) *As Affected by State Law.* A party who, before removal, expressly demanded a jury trial in accordance with state law need not renew the demand after removal. If the state law did not require an express demand for a jury trial, a party need not make one after removal unless the court orders the parties to do so within a specified time. The court must so order at a party's request and may so order on its own. A party who fails to make a demand when so ordered waives a jury trial.

(B) *Under Rule 38.* If all necessary pleadings have been served at the time of removal, a party entitled to a jury trial under Rule 38 must be given one if the party serves a demand within 14 days after:

(i) it files a notice of removal; or

(ii) it is served with a notice of removal filed by another party.

(d) Law Applicable. (1) *"State Law" Defined.* When these rules refer to state law, the term "law" includes the state's statutes and the state's judicial decisions.

(2) *"State" Defined.* The term "state" includes, where appropriate, the District of Columbia and any United States commonwealth or territory.

(3) *"Federal Statute" Defined in the District of Columbia.* In the United States District Court for the District of Columbia, the term "federal statute" includes any Act of Congress that applies locally to the District.

(Amended April 3, 1941; March 19, 1948; Oct. 20, 1949; Aug. 1, 1951; July 1, 1963; July 1, 1966; July 1, 1968; July 1, 1971; Aug. 1, 1987; Dec. 1, 2001; Dec. 1, 2002; Dec. 1, 2007; Dec. 1, 2009.)

Rule 82. Jurisdiction and Venue Unaffected

These rules do not extend or limit the jurisdiction of the district courts or the venue of actions in those courts. An admiralty or maritime claim under Rule 9(h) is not a civil action for purposes of 28 U.S.C. §§ 1391–1392.

(Amended Oct. 20, 1949; July 1, 1966; Dec. 1, 2001; Dec. 1, 2007.)

Rule 83. Rules by District Courts; Judge's Directives

(a) Local Rules. (1) *In General.* After giving public notice and an opportunity for comment, a district court, acting by a majority of its district judges, may adopt and amend rules governing its practice. A local rule must be consistent with—but not duplicate—federal statutes and rules adopted under 28 U.S.C. §§ 2072 and 2075, and must conform to any uniform numbering system prescribed by the Judicial Conference of the United States. A local rule takes effect on the date specified by the district court and remains in effect unless amended by the court or abrogated by the judicial council of the circuit. Copies of rules and amendments must, on their adoption, be furnished to the judicial council and the Administrative Office of the United States Courts and be made available to the public.

(2) *Requirement of Form.* A local rule imposing a requirement of form must not be enforced in a way that causes a party to lose any right because of a nonwillful failure to comply.

(b) Procedures When There is No Controlling Law. A judge may regulate practice in any manner consistent with federal law, rules adopted under 28 U.S.C. §§ 2072 and 2075, and the district's local rules. No sanction or other disadvantage may be imposed for noncompliance with any requirement not in federal law, federal rules, or the local rules unless the alleged violator has been furnished in the particular case with actual notice of the requirement.

(Amended Aug. 1, 1985; Dec. 1, 1995; Dec. 1, 2007.)

Rule 84. Forms

The forms in the Appendix suffice under these rules and illustrate the simplicity and brevity that these rules contemplate.

(Amended March 19, 1948; Dec. 1, 2007.)

Rule 85. Title

These rules may be cited as the Federal Rules of Civil Procedure.

(Amended Dec. 1, 2007.)

Rule 86. Effective Dates

(a) In General. These rules and any amendments take effect at the time specified by the Supreme Court, subject to 28 U.S.C. § 2074. They govern:

(1) proceedings in an action commenced after their effective date; and

(2) proceedings after that date in an action then pending unless:

(A) the Supreme Court specifies otherwise; or

(B) the court determines that applying them in a particular action would be infeasible or work an injustice.

(b) December 1, 2007 Amendments. If any provision in Rules 1–5.1, 6–73, or 77–86 conflicts with another law, priority in time for the purpose of 28 U.S.C. § 2072(b) is not affected by the amendments taking effect on December 1, 2007.

(Amended March 19, 1948; Oct. 20, 1949; July 19, 1961; July 1, 1963; Dec. 1, 2007.)

APPENDICES

APPENDIX OF FORMS

Form No. 1. Caption.

(Use on every summons, complaint, answer, motion, or other document.)

United States District Court
for the
______________ District of ______________

A B, Plaintiff)
)
v.)
)
C D, Defendant) **Civil Action No.__**
)
v.)
)
E F, Third-Party Defendant)
(Use if needed.))

(Name of Document)

Form No. 2. Date, Signature, Address, E-mail Address, and Telephone Number.

(Use at the conclusion of pleadings and other papers that require a signature.)

Date __________ ______________________

(Signature of the attorney or unrepresented party)

____

(Printed name)

____

(Address)

____

(E-mail address)

____

(Telephone number)

Form No. 3. Summons.

(Caption — See Form 1.)

To __*name the defendant:*__

A lawsuit has been filed against you.

Within 21 days after service of this summons on you (not counting the day you received it), you must serve on the plaintiff an answer to the attached complaint or a motion under Rule 12 of the Federal Rules of Civil Procedure. The answer or motion must be served on the plaintiff's attorney, __________, whose address is __________. If you fail to do so, judgment by default will be entered against you for the relief demanded in the complaint. You also must file your answer or motion with the court.

Date __________ ________________

Clerk of Court

(Court Seal)

(Use 60 days if the defendant is the United States or a United States agency, or is an officer or employee of the United States allowed 60 days by Rule 12(a)(3).)

(As amended Dec. 1, 2009.)

Form No. 4. Summons on a Third-Party Complaint.

(Caption — See Form 1.)

To __*name the third-party defendant:*__

A lawsuit has been filed against defendant ____, who as third-party plaintiff is making this claim against you to pay part or all of what [he] may owe to the plaintiff __________.

Within 21 days after service of this summons on you (not counting the day you received it), you must serve on the plaintiff and on the defendant an answer to the attached third-party complaint or a motion under Rule 12 of the Federal Rules of Civil Procedure. The answer or motion must be served on the defendant's attorney, __________, whose address is, __________, and also on the plaintiff's attorney, __________, whose address is, . If you fail to do so, judgment by default will be entered against you for the relief demanded in the third-party complaint. You also must file the answer or motion with the court and serve it on any other parties.

A copy of the plaintiff's complaint is also attached. You may—but are not required to—respond to it.

Date____________ ______________________
Clerk of Court
(Court Seal)
(As amended Dec. 1, 2009.)

Form No. 5. Notice of a Lawsuit and Request to Waive Service of a Summons.

(Caption — See Form 1.)

To *(name the defendant—or if the defendant is a corporation, partnership, or association name an officer or agent authorized to receive service):*

Why are you getting this?

A lawsuit has been filed against you, or the entity you represent, in this court under the number shown above. A copy of the complaint is attached.

This is not a summons, or an official notice from the court. It is a request that, to avoid expenses, you waive formal service of a summons by signing and returning the enclosed waiver. To avoid these expenses, you must return the signed waiver within (give at least 30 days or at least 60 days if the defendant is outside any judicial district of the United States) from the date shown below, which is the date this notice was sent. Two copies of the waiver form are enclosed, along with a stamped, self-addressed envelope or other prepaid means for returning one copy. You may keep the other copy.

What happens next?

If you return the signed waiver, I will file it with the court. The action will then proceed as if you had been served on the date the waiver is filed, but no summons will be served on you and you will have 60 days from the date this notice is sent (see the date below) to answer the complaint (or 90 days if this notice is sent to you outside any judicial district of the United States).

If you do not return the signed waiver within the time indicated, I will arrange to have the summons and complaint served on you. And I will ask the court to require you, or the entity you represent, to pay the expenses of making service.

Please read the enclosed statement about the duty to avoid unnecessary expenses.

I certify that this request is being sent to you on the date below.

(Date and sign — See Form 2.)

Form No. 6. Waiver of the Service of Summons.

(Caption — See Form 1.)

To *__name the plaintiff's attorney or the unrepresented plaintiff__:*

I have received your request to waive service of a summons in this action along with a copy of the complaint, two copies of this waiver form, and a prepaid means of returning one signed copy of the form to you.

I, or the entity I represent, agree to save the expense of serving a summons and complaint in this case.

I understand that I, or the entity I represent, will keep all defenses or objections to the lawsuit, the court's jurisdiction, and the venue of the action, but that I waive any objections to the absence of a summons or of service.

I also understand that I, or the entity I represent, must file and serve an answer or a motion under Rule 12 within 60 days from ________, the date when this request was sent (or 90 days if it was sent outside the United States). If I fail to do so, a default judgment will be entered against me or the entity I represent.

(Date and sign — See Form 2.)

(Attach the following to Form 6.)

Duty to Avoid Unnecessary Expenses of Serving a Summons

Rule 4 of the Federal Rules of Civil Procedure requires certain defendants to cooperate in saving unnecessary expenses of serving a summons and complaint. A defendant who is located in the United States and who fails to return a signed waiver of service requested by a plaintiff located in the United States will be required to pay the expenses of service, unless the defendant shows good cause for the failure.

"Good cause" does *not* include a belief that the lawsuit is groundless, or that it has been brought in an improper venue, or that the court has no jurisdiction over this matter or over the defendant or the defendant's property.

If the waiver is signed and returned, you can still make these and all other defenses and objections, but you cannot object to the absence of a summons or of service.

If you waive service, then you must, within the time specified on the waiver form, serve an answer or a motion under Rule 12 on the plaintiff and file a copy with the court. By signing and returning the waiver form, you are allowed more time to respond than if a summons had been served.

Form No. 7. Statement of Jurisdiction.

a. *(For diversity-of-citizenship jurisdiction.)* The plaintiff is [a citizen of *__Michigan__*] [a corporation incorporated under the laws of *__Michigan__* with its principal place of business in *__Michigan__*]. The defendant is [a citizen of *__New York__*] [a corporation incorporated under the laws of *__New York__* with its principal place of business in *__New York__*]. The amount in controversy, without interest and costs, exceeds the sum or value specified by 28 U.S.C. § 1332.

b. *(For federal-question jurisdiction.)* This action arises under [the United States Constitution, *specify the article or amendment and the section*] [a United States treaty, *specify*] [a federal statute,

__ U.S.C. § __].

c. *(For a claim in the admiralty or maritime jurisdiction.)* This is a case of admiralty or maritime jurisdiction. *(To invoke admiralty status under Rule 9(h) use the following:* This is an admiralty or maritime claim within the meaning of Rule 9(h).)

Form No. 8. Statement of Reasons for Omitting a Party.

(If a person who ought to be made a party under Rule 19(a) is not named, include this statement in accordance with Rule 19(c).)

This complaint does not join as a party __*name*__ who [is not subject to this court's personal jurisdiction] [cannot be made a party without depriving this court of subject-matter jurisdiction] because __*state the reason*__.

Form No. 9. Statement Noting a Party's Death.

(Caption — See Form 1.)

In accordance with Rule 25(a), __*name the person*__, who is [a party to this action] [a representative of or successor to the deceased party] notes the death during the pendency of this action of __*name*, [*describe as party* in this action].

(Date and sign — See Form 2.)

Form No. 10. Complaint to Recover a Sum Certain.

(Caption — See Form 1.)

1. (Statement of Jurisdiction — See Form 7.)

(Use one or more of the following as appropriate and include a demand for judgment.)

(a) On a Promissory Note

2. On __*date*__, the defendant executed and delivered a note promising to pay the plaintiff on __*date*__ the sum of $______ with interest at the rate of ____ percent. A copy of the note [is attached as Exhibit A] [is summarized as follows: ______________.]

3. The defendant has not paid the amount owed.

(b) On an Account

2. The defendant owes the plaintiff $______ according to the account set out in Exhibit A.

(c) For Goods Sold and Delivered

2. The defendant owes the plaintiff $______ for goods sold and delivered by the plaintiff to the defendant from __*date*__ to __*date*__.

(d) For Money Lent

2. The defendant owes the plaintiff $______ for money lent by the plaintiff to the defendant on __*date*__.

(e) For Money Paid by Mistake

2. The defendant owes the plaintiff $______ for money paid by mistake to the defendant on __*date*__ under these circumstances: __*describe with particularity in accordance with Rule 9(b)*__.

(f) For Money Had and Received

2. The defendant owes the plaintiff $______ for money that was received from __*name*__ on __*date*__ to be paid by the defendant to the plaintiff.

Demand for Judgment

Therefore, the plaintiff demands judgment against the defendant for $______, plus interest and costs.

(Date and sign — See Form 2.)

Form No. 11. Complaint for Negligence.

(Caption — See Form 1.)

1. (Statement of Jurisdiction — See Form 7.)

2. On __*date*__, at __*place*__, the defendant negligently drove a motor vehicle against the plaintiff.

3. As a result, the plaintiff was physically injured, lost wages or income, suffered physical and mental pain, and incurred medical expenses of $__.

Therefore, the plaintiff demands judgment against the defendant for $______, plus costs.

(Date and sign — See Form 2.)

Form No. 12. Complaint for Negligence When the Plaintiff Does Not Know Who Is Responsible.

(Caption — See Form 1.)

1. (Statement of Jurisdiction — See Form 7.)

2. On __*date*__, at __*place*__, defendant __*name*__ or defendant __*name*__ or both of them willfully or recklessly or negligently drove, or caused to be driven, a motor vehicle against the plaintiff.

3. As a result, the plaintiff was physically injured, lost wages or income, suffered mental and physical pain, and incurred medical expenses of $__.

Therefore, the plaintiff demands judgment against one or both defendants for $______, plus costs.

(Date and sign — See Form 2.)

Form No. 13. Complaint for Negligence Under the Federal Employers' Liability Act.

(Caption — See Form 1.)

1. (Statement of Jurisdiction — See Form 7.)

2. At the times below, the defendant owned and operated in interstate commerce a railroad line that passed through a tunnel located at __________.

3. On __*date*__, the plaintiff was working to repair and enlarge the tunnel to make it convenient and safe for use in interstate commerce.

4. During this work, the defendant, as the employer, negligently put the plaintiff to work in a section of the tunnel that the defendant had left unprotected and unsupported.

5. The defendant's negligence caused the plaintiff to be injured by a rock that fell from an unsupported portion of the tunnel.

6. As a result, the plaintiff was physically injured, lost wages or income, suffered mental and physical pain, and incurred medical expenses of $__.

Therefore, the plaintiff demands judgment against the defendant for $______, and costs.

(Date and sign — See Form 2.)

Form No. 14. Complaint for Damages Under the Merchant Marine Act.

(Caption — See Form 1.)

1. (Statement of Jurisdiction — See Form 7.)

2. At the times below, the defendant owned and operated the vessel __*name*__ and used it to transport cargo for hire by water in interstate and foreign commerce.

3. On __*date*__, at __*place*__, the defendant hired the plaintiff under seamen's articles of customary form for a voyage from __________ to __________ and return at a wage of $______ a month and found, which is equal to a shore worker's wage of $______ a month.

4. On __*date*__, the vessel was at sea on the return voyage. *(Describe the weather and the condition of the vessel.)*

5. *(Describe as in Form 11 the defendant's negligent conduct.)*

6. As a result of the defendant's negligent conduct and the unseaworthiness of the vessel, the plaintiff was physically injured, has been incapable of any gainful activity, suffered mental and physical pain, and has incurred medical expenses of $______.

Therefore, the plaintiff demands judgment against the defendant for $______, plus costs.

(Date and sign — See Form 2.)

Form No. 15. Complaint for the Conversion of Property.

(Caption — See Form 1.)

1. (Statement of Jurisdiction — See Form 7.)

2. On __*date*__, at __*place*__, the defendant converted to the defendant's own use property owned by the plaintiff. The property converted consists of __*describe*__.

3. The property is worth $______.

Therefore, the plaintiff demands judgment against the defendant for $______, plus costs.

(Date and sign — See Form 2.)

Form No. 16. Third-Party Complaint.

(Caption — See Form 1.)

1. Plaintiff __*name*__ has filed against defendant __*name*__ a complaint, a copy of which is attached.

2. *(State grounds entitling __defendant's name__ to recover from __third-party defendant's name__ for (all or an identified share) of any judgment for __plaintiff's name__ against __defendant's name__.)*

Therefore, the defendant demands judgment against __*third-party defendant's name*__ for __*all or an identified share*__ of sums that may be adjudged against the defendant in the plaintiff's favor.

(Date and sign — See Form 2.)

Form No. 17. Complaint for Specific Performance of a Contract to Convey Land.

(Caption — See Form 1.)

1. (Statement of Jurisdiction — See Form 7.)

2. On __*date*__, the parties agreed to the contract [attached as Exhibit A] [summarize the contract].

3. As agreed, the plaintiff tendered the purchase price and requested a conveyance of the land, but the defendant refused to accept the money or make a conveyance.

4. The plaintiff now offers to pay the purchase price.

Therefore, the plaintiff demands that:

(a) the defendant be required to specifically perform the agreement and pay damages of $______, plus interest and costs, or

(b) if specific performance is not ordered, the defendant be required to pay damages of $______, plus interest and costs.

(Date and sign — See Form 2.)

Form No. 18. Complaint for Patent Infringement.

(Caption — See Form 1.)

1. (Statement of Jurisdiction — See Form 7.)

2. On __*date*__, United States Letters Patent No. ______ were issued to the plaintiff for an invention in an __*electric motor*__. The plaintiff owned the patent throughout the period of the defendant's infringing acts and still owns the patent.

3. The defendant has infringed and is still infringing the Letters Patent by making, selling, and using __*electric motors*__ that embody the patented invention, and the defendant will continue to do so unless enjoined by this court.

4. The plaintiff has complied with the statutory requirement of placing a notice of the Letters Patent

on all *electric motors* it manufactures and sells and has given the defendant written notice of the infringement.

Therefore, the plaintiff demands:

(a) a preliminary and final injunction against the continuing infringement;

(b) an accounting for damages; and

(c) interest and costs.

(Date and sign — See Form 2.)

Form No. 19. Complaint for Copyright Infringement and Unfair Competition.

(Caption — See Form 1.)

1. (Statement of Jurisdiction — See Form 7.)

2. Before *date*, the plaintiff, a United States citizen, wrote a book entitled ____________.

3. The book is an original work that may be copyrighted under United States law. A copy of the book is attached as Exhibit A.

4. Between *date* and *date*, the plaintiff applied to the copyright office and received a certificate of registration dated ________ and identified as *date, class, number*.

5. Since *date*, the plaintiff has either published or licensed for publication all copies of the book in compliance with the copyright laws and has remained the sole owner of the copyright.

6. After the copyright was issued, the defendant infringed the copyright by publishing and selling a book entitled __________________, which was copied largely from the plaintiff's book. A copy of the defendant's book is attached as Exhibit B.

7. The plaintiff has notified the defendant in writing of the infringement.

8. The defendant continues to infringe the copyright by continuing to publish and sell the infringing book in violation of the copyright, and further has engaged in unfair trade practices and unfair competition in connection with its publication and sale of the infringing book, thus causing irreparable damage.

Therefore, the plaintiff demands that:

(a) until this case is decided the defendant and the defendant's agents be enjoined from disposing of any copies of the defendant's book by sale or otherwise;

(b) the defendant account for and pay as damages to the plaintiff all profits and advantages gained from unfair trade practices and unfair competition in selling the defendant's book, and all profits and advantages gained from infringing the plaintiff's copyright (but no less than the statutory minimum);

(c) the defendant deliver for impoundment all copies of the book in the defendant's possession or control and deliver for destruction all infringing copies and all plates, molds, and other materials for making infringing copies;

(d) the defendant pay the plaintiff interest, costs, and reasonable attorney's fees; and

(e) the plaintiff be awarded any other just relief.

(Date and sign — See Form 2.)

Form No. 20. Complaint for Interpleader and Declaratory Relief.

(Caption — See Form 1.)

1. (Statement of Jurisdiction — See Form 7.)

2. On *date*, the plaintiff issued a life insurance policy on the life of *name* with *name* as the named beneficiary.

3. As a condition for keeping the policy in force, the policy required payment of a premium during the first year and then annually.

4. The premium due on *date* was never paid, and the policy lapsed after that date.

5. On *date*, after the policy had lapsed, both the insured and the named beneficiary died in an automobile collision.

6. Defendant *name* claims to be the beneficiary in place of *name* and has filed a claim to be paid the policy's full amount.

7. The other two defendants are representatives of the deceased persons' estates. Each defendant has filed a claim on behalf of each estate to receive payment of the policy's full amount.

8. If the policy was in force at the time of death, the plaintiff is in doubt about who should be paid.

Therefore, the plaintiff demands that:

(a) each defendant be restrained from commencing any action against the plaintiff on the policy;

(b) a judgment be entered that no defendant is entitled to the proceeds of the policy or any part of it, but if the court determines that the policy was in effect at the time of the insured's death, that the defendants be required to interplead and settle among themselves their rights to the proceeds, and that the plaintiff be discharged from all liability except to the defendant determined to be entitled to the proceeds; and

(c) the plaintiff recover its costs.

(Date and sign — See Form 2.)

Form No. 21. Complaint on a Claim for a Debt and to Set Aside a Fraudulent Conveyance Under Rule 18(b).

(Caption — See Form 1.)

1. (Statement of Jurisdiction — See Form 7.)

2. On *date*, defendant *name* signed a note promising to pay to the plaintiff on *date* the sum of $______ with interest at the rate of ____ percent. [The pleader may, but need not, attach a copy or plead the note verbatim.]

3. Defendant *name* owes the plaintiff the amount of the note and interest.

4. On _date_, defendant _name_ conveyed all defendant's real and personal property _*if less than all, describe it fully*_ to defendant _name_ for the purpose of defrauding the plaintiff and hindering or delaying the collection of the debt.

Therefore, the plaintiff demands that:

(a) judgment for $_______, plus costs, be entered against defendant(s) _name(s)_; and

(b) the conveyance to defendant _name_ be declared void and any judgment granted be made a lien on the property.

(Date and sign — See Form 2.)

Form No. 30. Answer Presenting Defenses Under Rule 12(b).

(Caption — See Form 1.)

Responding to Allegations in the Complaint

1. Defendant admits the allegations in paragraphs _______.

2. Defendant lacks knowledge or information sufficient to form a belief about the truth of the allegations in paragraphs _______.

3. Defendant admits _*identify part of the allegation*_ in paragraph _______ and denies or lacks knowledge or information sufficient to form a belief about the truth of the rest of the paragraph.

Failure to State a Claim

4. The complaint fails to state a claim upon which relief can be granted.

Failure to Join a Required Party

5. If there is a debt, it is owed jointly by the defendant and _name_, who is a citizen of _______. This person can be made a party without depriving this court of jurisdiction over the existing parties.

Affirmative Defense—Statute of Limitations

6. The plaintiff's claim is barred by the statute of limitations because it arose more than _______ years before this action was commenced.

Counterclaim

7. *(Set forth any counterclaim in the same way a claim is pleaded in a complaint. Include a further statement of jurisdiction if needed.)*

Crossclaim

8. *(Set forth a crossclaim against a coparty in the same way a claim is pleaded in a complaint. Include a further statement of jurisdiction if needed.)*

(Date and sign — See Form 2.)

Form No. 31. Answer to a Complaint for Money Had and Received with a Counterclaim for Interpleader.

(Caption — See Form 1.)

Response to the Allegations in the Complaint

(See Form 30.)

Counterclaim for Interpleader

1. The defendant received from _name_ a deposit of $_______.

2. The plaintiff demands payment of the deposit because of a purported assignment from _name_, who has notified the defendant that the assignment is not valid and who continues to hold the defendant responsible for the deposit.

Therefore, the defendant demands that:

(a) _name_ be made a party to this action;

(b) the plaintiff and _name_ be required to interplead their respective claims;

(c) the court decide whether the plaintiff or _name_ or either of them is entitled to the deposit and discharge the defendant of any liability except to the person entitled to the deposit; and

(d) the defendant recover costs and attorney's fees.

(Date and sign — See Form 2.)

Form No. 40. Motion to Dismiss Under Rule 12(b) for Lack of Jurisdiction, Improper Venue, Insufficient Service of Process, or Failure to State a Claim.

(Caption — See Form 1.)

The defendant moves to dismiss the action because:

1. the amount in controversy is less than the sum or value specified by 28 U.S.C. § 1332;

2. the defendant is not subject to the personal jurisdiction of this court;

3. venue is improper (this defendant does not reside in this district and no part of the events or omissions giving rise to the claim occurred in the district);

4. the defendant has not been properly served, as shown by the attached affidavits of ____________; or

5. the complaint fails to state a claim upon which relief can be granted.

(Date and sign — See Form 2.)

Form No. 41. Motion to Bring in a Third-Party Defendant.

(Caption — See Form 1.)

The defendant, as third-party plaintiff, moves for

leave to serve on __name__ a summons and third-party complaint, copies of which are attached.

(Date and sign — See Form 2.)

Form No. 42. Motion to Intervene as a Defendant Under Rule 24.

(Caption — See Form 1.)

1. __name__ moves for leave to intervene as a defendant in this action and to file the attached answer.

(State grounds under Rule 24(a) or (b).)

2. The plaintiff alleges patent infringement. We manufacture and sell to the defendant the articles involved, and we have a defense to the plaintiff's claim.

3. Our defense presents questions of law and fact that are common to this action.

(Date and sign — See Form 2.)

[An Intervener's Answer must be attached. See Form 30.]

Form No. 50. Request to Produce Documents and Tangible Things, or to Enter onto Land Under Rule 34.

(Caption — See Form 1.)

The plaintiff __name__ requests that the defendant __name__ respond within ______ days to the following requests:

1. To produce and permit the plaintiff to inspect and copy and to test or sample the following documents, including electronically stored information:

(Describe each document and the electronically stored information, either individually or by category.)

(State the time, place, and manner of the inspection and any related acts.)

2. To produce and permit the plaintiff to inspect and copy—and to test or sample—the following tangible things:

(Describe each thing, either individually or by category.)

(State the time, place, and manner of the inspection and any related acts.)

3. To permit the plaintiff to enter onto the following land to inspect, photograph, test, or sample the property or an object or operation on the property.

(Describe the property and each object or operation.)

(State the time and manner of the inspection and any related acts.)

(Date and sign — See Form 2.)

Form No. 51. Request for Admissions Under Rule 36.

(Caption — See Form 1.)

The plaintiff __name__ asks the defendant __name__ to respond within 30 days to these requests by admitting, for purposes of this action only and subject to objections to admissibility at trial:

1. The genuineness of the following documents, copies of which [are attached] [are or have been furnished or made available for inspection and copying].

(List each document.)

2. The truth of each of the following statements:

(List each statement.)

(Date and sign — See Form 2.)

Form No. 52. Report of the Parties' Planning Meeting.

(Caption — See Form 1.)

1. The following persons participated in a Rule 26(f) conference on __date__ by __*state the method of conferring*__:

2. Initial Disclosures. The parties [have completed] [will complete by __date__] the initial disclosures required by Rule 26(a)(1).

3. Discovery Plan. The parties propose this discovery plan:

(Use separate paragraphs or subparagraphs if the parties disagree.)

(a) Discovery will be needed on these subjects: (*describe*)

(b) Disclosure or discovery of electronically stored information should be handled as follows: (*briefly describe the parties' proposals, including the form or forms for production.*)

(c) The parties have agreed to an order regarding claims of privilege or of protection as trial-preparation material asserted after production, as follows: (*briefly describe the provisions of the proposed order.*)

(d) (Dates for commencing and completing discovery, including discovery to be commenced or completed before other discovery.)

(e) (Maximum number of interrogatories by each party to another party, along with dates the answers are due.)

(f) (Maximum number of requests for admission, along with the dates responses are due.)

(g) (Maximum number of depositions for each party.)

(h) (Limits on the length of depositions, in hours.)

(i) (Dates for exchanging reports of expert witnesses.)

(j) (Dates for supplementations under Rule 26(e).)

4. Other Items:

(a) (A date if the parties ask to meet with the court before a scheduling order.)

(b) (Requested dates for pretrial conferences.)

(c) (Final dates for the plaintiff to amend pleadings or to join parties.)

(d) (Final dates for the defendant to amend pleadings or to join parties.)

(e) (Final dates to file dispositive motions.)

(f) (State the prospects for settlement.)

(g) (Identify any alternative dispute resolution procedure that may enhance settlement prospects.)

(h) (Final dates for submitting Rule 26(a)(3) witness lists, designations of witnesses whose testimony will be presented by deposition, and exhibit lists.)

(i) Final dates to file objections under Rule 26(a)(3).)

(j) Suggested trial date and estimate of trial length.)

(k) (Other matters.)

(Date and sign — See Form 2.)

(As amended Dec. 1, 2010.)

Form No. 60. Notice of Condemnation.

(Caption — See Form 1.)

To _*name the defendant*_.

1. A complaint in condemnation has been filed in the United States District Court for the ________ District of ________, to take property to use for _*purpose*_. The interest to be taken is _*describe*_. The court is located in the United States courthouse at this address: ____________.

2. The property to be taken is described below. You have or claim an interest in it.

(Describe the property.)

3. The authority for taking this property is _*cite*_.

4. If you want to object or present any defense to the taking you must serve an answer on the plaintiff's attorney within 21 days [after being served with this notice] [from _*insert the date of the last publication of notice*_]. Send your answer to this address: ____________.

5. Your answer must identify the property in which you claim an interest, state the nature and extent of that interest, and state all your objections and defenses to the taking. Objections and defenses not presented are waived.

6. If you fail to answer you consent to the taking and the court will enter a judgment that takes your described property interest.

7. Instead of answering, you may serve on the plaintiff's attorney a notice of appearance that designates the property in which you claim an interest. After you do that, you will receive a notice of any proceedings that affect you. Whether or not you have previously appeared or answered, you may present evidence at a trial to determine compensation for the property and share in the overall award.

(Date and sign — See Form 2.)

(As amended Dec. 1, 2009.)

Form No. 61. Complaint for Condemnation.

(Caption — See Form 1.)

1. (Statement of Jurisdiction — See Form 7.)

2. This is an action to take property under the power of eminent domain and to determine just compensation to be paid to the owners and parties in interest.

3. The authority for the taking is __________.

4. The property is to be used for __________.

5. The property to be taken is (*describe in enough detail for identification—or attach the description and state "is described in Exhibit A, attached"*).

6. The interest to be acquired is __________.

7. The persons known to the plaintiff to have or claim an interest in the property are: __________. (*For each person include the interest claimed.*)

8. There may be other persons who have or claim an interest in the property and whose names could not be found after a reasonably diligent search. They are made parties under the designation "Unknown Owners."

Therefore, the plaintiff demands judgment:

(a) condemning the property;

(b) determining and awarding just compensation; and

(c) granting any other lawful and proper relief.

(Date and sign — See Form 2.)

Form No. 70. Judgment on a Jury Verdict.

(Caption — See Form 1.)

This action was tried by a jury with Judge __________ presiding, and the jury has rendered a verdict.

It is ordered that:

[the plaintiff _*name*_ recover from the defendant _*name*_ the amount of $________ with interest at the rate of ____%, along with costs.]

[the plaintiff recover nothing, the action be dismissed on the merits, and the defendant __*name*__ recover costs from the plaintiff __*name*__.]

Date ____________ ______________________
Clerk of Court

Form No. 71. Judgment by the Court without a Jury.

(Caption — See Form 1.)

This action was tried by Judge __________ without a jury and the following decision was reached:

It is ordered that [the plaintiff __*name*__ recover from the defendant __*name*__ the amount of $____, with prejudgment interest at the rate of ____%, postjudgment interest at the rate of ____%, along with costs.] [the plaintiff recover nothing, the action be dismissed on the merits, and the defendant __*name*__ recover costs from the plaintiff __*name*__.]

Date ____________ ______________________
Clerk of Court

Form No. 80. Notice of a Magistrate Judge's Availability.

1. A magistrate judge is available under title 28 U.S.C. § 636(c) to conduct the proceedings in this case, including a jury or nonjury trial and the entry of final judgment. But a magistrate judge can be assigned only if all parties voluntarily consent.

2. You may withhold your consent without adverse substantive consequences. The identity of any party consenting or withholding consent will not be disclosed to the judge to whom the case is assigned or to any magistrate judge.

3. If a magistrate judge does hear your case, you may appeal directly to a United States court of appeals as you would if a district judge heard it.

A form called *Consent to an Assignment to a United States Magistrate Judge* is available from the court clerk's office.

Form No. 81. Consent to an Assignment to a Magistrate Judge.

(Caption — See Form 1.)

I voluntarily consent to have a United States magistrate judge conduct all further proceedings in this case, including a trial, and order the entry of final judgment. (Return this form to the court clerk—not to a judge or magistrate judge.)

Date ____________ ______________________
Signature of the Party

Form No. 82. Order of Assignment to a Magistrate Judge.

(Caption — See Form 1.)

With the parties' consent, it is ordered that this case be assigned to United States Magistrate Judge __________ of this district to conduct all proceedings and enter final judgment in accordance with 28 U.S.C. § 636(c).

Date ____________ ______________________
United States District Judge

SUPPLEMENTAL RULES FOR ADMIRALTY OR MARITIME CLAIMS AND ASSET FORFEITURE ACTIONS

Rule A. Scope of Rules.

(1) These Supplemental Rules apply to:

(A) the procedure in admiralty and maritime claims within the meaning of Rule 9(h) with respect to the following remedies:

(i) maritime attachment and garnishment,

(ii) actions in rem,

(iii) possessory, petitory, and partition actions, and

(iv) actions for exoneration from or limitation of liability;

(B) forfeiture actions in rem arising from a federal statute; and

(C) the procedure in statutory condemnation proceedings analogous to maritime actions in rem, whether within the admiralty and maritime jurisdiction or not. Except as otherwise provided, references in these Supplemental Rules to actions in rem include such analogous statutory condemnation proceedings.

(2) The Federal Rules of Civil Procedure also apply to the foregoing proceedings except to the extent that they are inconsistent with these Supplemental Rules.

(As amended Dec. 1, 2006.)

Rule B. In Personam Actions: Attachment and Garnishment

(1) When Available; Complaint, Affidavit, Judicial Authorization, and Process. In an in personam action:

(a) If a defendant is not found within the district when a verified complaint praying for attachment and the affidavit required by Rule B(1)(b) are filed, a verified complaint may contain a prayer for process to attach the defendant's tangible or intangible personal property—up to the amount sued for—in the hands of garnishees named in the process.

(b) The plaintiff or the plaintiff's attorney must sign and file with the complaint an affidavit stating that, to the affiant's knowledge, or on information and belief, the defendant cannot be found within the district. The court must review the complaint and affidavit and, if the conditions of this Rule B appear to exist, enter an order so stating and authorizing process of attachment and garnishment. The clerk may issue supplemental process enforcing the court's order upon application without further court order.

(c) If the plaintiff or the plaintiff's attorney certifies that exigent circumstances make court review impracticable, the clerk must issue the summons and process of attachment and garnishment. The plaintiff has the burden in any post-attachment hearing under Rule E(4)(f) to show that exigent circumstances existed.

(d) (i) If the property is a vessel or tangible property on board a vessel, the summons, process, and any supplemental process must be delivered to the marshal for service.

(ii) If the property is other tangible or intangible property, the summons, process, and any supplemental process must be delivered to a person or organization authorized to serve it, who may be (A) a marshal; (B) someone under contract with the United States; (C) someone specially appointed by the court for that purpose; or, (D) in an action brought by the United States, any officer or employee of the United States.

(e) The plaintiff may invoke state-law remedies under Rule 64 for seizure of person or property for the purpose of securing satisfaction of the judgment.

(2) Notice to Defendant. No default judgment may be entered except upon proof—which may be by affidavit—that:

(a) the complaint, summons, and process of attachment or garnishment have been served on the defendant in a manner authorized by Rule 4;

(b) the plaintiff or the garnishee has mailed to the defendant the complaint, summons, and process of attachment or garnishment, using any form of mail requiring a return receipt; or

(c) the plaintiff or the garnishee has tried diligently to give notice of the action to the defendant but could not do so.

(3) Answer. (a) *By Garnishee.* The garnishee shall serve an answer, together with answers to any interrogatories served with the complaint, within 21 days after service of process upon the garnishee. Interrogatories to the garnishee may be served with the complaint without leave of court. If the garnishee refuses or neglects to answer on oath as to the debts, credits, or effects of the defendant in the garnishee's hands, or any interrogatories concerning such debts, credits, and effects that may be propounded by the plaintiff, the court may award compulsory process against the garnishee. If the garnishee admits any debts, credits, or effects, they shall be held in the garnishee's hands or paid into the registry of the court, and shall be held in either case subject to the further order of the court.

(b) *By Defendant.* The defendant shall serve an answer within 30 days after process has been executed, whether by attachment of property or service on the garnishee.

(Amended effective Aug. 1, 1987; Dec. 1, 2000; Dec. 1, 2005; Dec. 1, 2009.)

Rule C. In Rem Actions: Special Provisions

(1) When Available. An action in rem may be brought:

(a) To enforce any maritime lien;

(b) Whenever a statute of the United States provides for a maritime action in rem or a proceeding analogous thereto.

Except as otherwise provided by law a party who may proceed in rem may also, or in the alternative, proceed in personam against any person who may be liable.

Statutory provisions exempting vessels or other property owned or possessed by or operated by or for the United States from arrest or seizure are not affected by this rule. When a statute so provides, an action against the United States or an instrumentality thereof may proceed on in rem principles.

(2) Complaint. In an action in rem the complaint must:

(a) be verified;

(b) describe with reasonable particularity the property that is the subject of the action; and

(c) state that the property is within the district or will be within the district while the action is pending;

(3) Judicial Authorization and Process. (a) *Arrest Warrant.* (i) The court must review the complaint and any supporting papers. If the conditions for an in rem action appear to exist, the court must issue an order directing the clerk to issue a warrant for the arrest of the vessel or other property that is the subject of the action.

(ii) If the plaintiff or the plaintiff's attorney certifies that exigent circumstances make court review impracticable, the clerk must promptly issue a summons and a warrant for the arrest of the vessel or other property that is the subject of the action. The plaintiff has the burden in any post-arrest hearing under Rule E(4)(f) to show that exigent circumstances existed.

(b) *Service.* (i) If the property that is the subject of the action is a vessel or tangible property on board a vessel, the warrant and any supplemental process must be delivered to the marshal for service.

(ii) If the property that is the subject of the action is other property, tangible or intangible, the warrant and any supplemental process must be delivered to a person or organization authorized to enforce it, who may be: (A) a marshal; (B) someone under contract with the United States; (C) someone specially appointed by the court for that purpose; or, (D) in an action brought by the United States, any officer or employee of the United States.

(c) *Deposit in Court.* If the property that is the subject of the action consists in whole or in part of freight, the proceeds of property sold, or other intangible property, the clerk must issue—in addition to the warrant—a summons directing any person controlling the property to show cause why it should not be deposited in court to abide the judgment.

(d) *Supplemental Process.* The clerk may upon application issue supplemental process to enforce the court's order without further court order.

(4) Notice. No notice other than execution of process is required when the property that is the subject of the action has been released under Rule E(5). If the property is not released within 14 days after execution, the plaintiff must promptly—or within the time that the court allows—give public notice of the action and arrest in a newspaper designated by court order and having general circulation in the district, but publication may be terminated if the property is released before publication is completed. The notice must specify the time under Rule C(6) to file a statement of interest in or right against the seized property and to answer. This rule does not affect the notice requirements in an action to foreclose a preferred ship mortgage under 46 U.S.C. §§ 31301 et seq., as amended.

(5) Ancillary process. In any action in rem in which process has been served as provided by this rule, if any part of the property that is the subject of the action has not been brought within the control of the court because it has been removed or sold, or because it is intangible property in the hands of a person who has not been served with process, the court may, on motion, order any person having possession or control of such property or its proceeds to show cause why it should not be delivered into the custody of the marshal or other person or organization having a warrant for the arrest of the property, or paid into court to abide the judgment; and, after hearing, the court may enter such judgment as law and justice may require.

(6) Responsive Pleading; Interrogatories. (a) *Statement of Interest; Answer.* In an action in rem:

(i) a person who asserts a right of possession or any ownership interest in the property that is the subject of the action must file a verified statement of right or interest:

(A) within 14 days after the execution of process, or

(B) within the time that the court allows;

(ii) the statement of right or interest must describe the interest in the property that supports the person's demand for its restitution or right to defend the action;

(iii) an agent, bailee, or attorney must state the authority to file a statement of right or interest on behalf of another; and

(iv) a person who asserts a right of possession or any ownership interest must serve an answer within 21 days after filing the statement of interest or right.

(b) *Interrogatories.* Interrogatories may be served with the complaint in an in rem action without leave of court. Answers to the interrogatories must be served with the answer to the complaint.

(Amended effective Aug. 1, 1987; Dec. 1, 1991; Dec. 1, 2000; Dec. 1, 2002; Dec. 1, 2005; Dec. 1, 2006; Dec. 1, 2008; Dec. 1, 2009.)

Rule D. Possessory, Petitory, and Partition Actions

In all actions for possession, partition, and to try title maintainable according to the course of the admiralty practice with respect to a vessel, in all actions so maintainable with respect to the possession of cargo or other maritime property, and in all actions by one or more part owners against the others to obtain security for the return of the vessel from any voyage undertaken without their consent, or by one or more part owners against the others to obtain possession of the vessel for any voyage on giving security for its safe return, the process shall be by a warrant of arrest of the vessel, cargo, or other property, and by notice in the manner provided by Rule B(2) to the adverse party or parties.

Rule E. Actions in Rem and Quasi in Rem: General Provisions

(1) Applicability. Except as otherwise provided, this rule applies to actions in personam with process of maritime attachment and garnishment, actions in rem, and petitory, possessory, and partition actions, supplementing Rules B, C, and D.

(2) Complaint; Security. (a) *Complaint.* In actions to which this rule is applicable the complaint shall state the circumstances from which the claim arises with such particularity that the defendant or claimant will be able, without moving for a more definite statement, to commence an investigation of the facts and to frame a responsive pleading.

(b) *Security for Costs.* Subject to the provisions of Rule 54(d) and of relevant statutes, the court may, on the filing of the complaint or on the appearance of any defendant, claimant, or any other party, or at any later time, require the plaintiff, defendant, claimant, or other party to give security, or additional security, in such sum as the court shall direct to pay all costs and expenses that shall be awarded against the party by any interlocutory order or by the final judgment, or on appeal by any appellate court.

(3) Process. (a) In admiralty and maritime proceedings process in rem or of maritime attachment and garnishment may be served only within the district.

(b) *Issuance and Delivery.* In forfeiture cases process in rem may be served within the district or outside the district when authorized by statute.

(c) *Issuance and Delivery.* Issuance and delivery of process in rem, or of maritime attachment and garnishment, shall be held in abeyance if the plaintiff so requests.

(4) Execution of Process; Marshal's Return; Custody of Property; Procedures for Release. (a) *In General.* Upon issuance and delivery of the process, or, in the case of summons with process of attachment and garnishment, when it appears that the defendant cannot be found within the district, the marshal or other person or organization having a warrant shall forthwith execute the process in accordance with this subdivision (4), making due and prompt return.

(b) *Tangible Property.* If tangible property is to be attached or arrested, the marshal or other person or organization having the warrant shall take it into the marshal's possession for safe custody. If the character or situation of the property is such that the taking of actual possession is impracticable, the marshal or other person executing the process shall affix a copy thereof to the property in a conspicuous place and leave a copy of the complaint and process with the person having possession or the person's agent. In furtherance of the marshal's custody of any vessel the marshal is authorized to make a written request to the collector of customs not to grant clearance to such vessel until notified by the marshal or deputy marshal or by the clerk that the vessel has been released in accordance with these rules.

(c) *Intangible Property.* If intangible property is to be attached or arrested the marshal or other person or organization having the warrant shall execute the process by leaving with the garnishee or other obligor a copy of the complaint and process requiring the garnishee or other obligor to answer as provided in Rules B(3)(a) and C(6); or the marshal may accept for payment into the registry of the court the amount owed to the extent of the amount claimed by the plaintiff with interest and costs, in which event the garnishee or other obligor shall not be required to answer unless alias process shall be served.

(d) *Directions With Respect to Property in Custody.* The marshal or other person or organization having the warrant may at any time apply to the court for directions with respect to property that has been attached or arrested, and shall give notice of such application to any or all of the parties as the court may direct.

(e) *Expenses of Seizing and Keeping Property; Deposit.* These rules do not alter the provisions of Title 28, USC, § 1921, as amended, relative to the expenses of seizing and keeping property attached or arrested and to the requirement of deposits to cover such expenses.

(f) *Procedure for Release from Arrest or Attachment.* Whenever property is arrested or attached, any person claiming an interest in it shall be entitled to a prompt hearing at which the plaintiff shall be required to show why the arrest or attachment should not be vacated or other relief granted consistent with these rules. This subdivision shall have no application to suits for seamen's wages when process is issued upon a certification of sufficient cause filed pursuant to Title 46, U.S.C. §§ 603 and 604 or to actions by the United States for forfeitures for violation of any statute of the United States.

(5) Release of Property. (a) *Special Bond.*

Whenever process of maritime attachment and garnishment or process in rem is issued the execution of such process shall be stayed, or the property released, on the giving of security, to be approved by the court or clerk, or by stipulation of the parties, conditioned to answer the judgment of the court or of any appellate court. The parties may stipulate the amount and nature of such security. In the event of the inability or refusal of the parties so to stipulate the court shall fix the principal sum of the bond or stipulation at an amount sufficient to cover the amount of the plaintiff's claim fairly stated with accrued interest and costs; but the principal sum shall in no event exceed (i) twice the amount of the plaintiff's claim or (ii) the value of the property on due appraisement, whichever is smaller. The bond or stipulation shall be conditioned for the payment of the principal sum and interest thereon at 6 per cent per annum.

(b) *General Bond.* The owner of any vessel may file a general bond or stipulation, with sufficient surety, to be approved by the court, conditioned to answer the judgment of such court in all or any actions that may be brought thereafter in such court in which the vessel is attached or arrested. Thereupon the execution of all such process against such vessel shall be stayed so long as the amount secured by such bond or stipulation is at least double the aggregate amount claimed by plaintiffs in all actions begun and pending in which such vessel has been attached or arrested. Judgments and remedies may be had on such bond or stipulation as if a special bond or stipulation had been filed in each of such actions. The district court may make necessary orders to carry this rule into effect, particularly as to the giving of proper notice of any action against or attachment of a vessel for which a general bond has been filed. Such bond or stipulation shall be indorsed by the clerk with a minute of the actions wherein process is so stayed. Further security may be required by the court at any time.

If a special bond or stipulation is given in a particular case, the liability on the general bond or stipulation shall cease as to that case.

(c) *Release by Consent or Stipulation; Order of Court or Clerk; Costs.* Any vessel, cargo, or other property in the custody of the marshal or other person or organization having the warrant may be released forthwith upon the marshal's acceptance and approval of a stipulation, bond, or other security, signed by the party on whose behalf the property is detained or the party's attorney and expressly authorizing such release, if all costs and charges of the court and its officers shall have first been paid. Otherwise no property in the custody of the marshal, other person or organization having the warrant, or other officer of the court shall be released without an order of the court; but such order may be entered as of course by the clerk, upon the giving of approved security as provided by law and these rules, or upon the dismissal or discontinuance of the action; but the marshal or other person or organization having the warrant shall not deliver any property so released until the costs and charges of the officers of the court shall first have been paid.

(d) *Possessory, Petitory, and Partition Actions.* The foregoing provisions of this subdivision (5) do not apply to petitory, possessory, and partition actions. In such cases the property arrested shall be released only by order of the court, on such terms and conditions and on the giving of such security as the court may require.

(6) Reduction or Impairment of Security. Whenever security is taken the court may, on motion and hearing, for good cause shown, reduce the amount of security given; and if the surety shall be or become insufficient, new or additional securities may be required on motion and hearing.

(7) Security on Counterclaim. (a) When a person who has given security for damages in the original action asserts a counterclaim that arises from the transaction or occurrence that is the subject of the original action, a plaintiff for whose benefit the security has been given must give security for damages demanded in the counterclaim unless the court, for cause shown, directs otherwise. Proceedings on the original claim must be stayed until this security is given, unless the court directs otherwise.

(b) The plaintiff is required to give security under Rule E(7)(a) when the United States or its corporate instrumentality counterclaims and would have been required to give security to respond in damages if a private party but is relieved by law from giving security.

(8) Restricted Appearance. An appearance to defend against an admiralty and maritime claim with respect to which there has issued process in rem, or process of attachment and garnishment, may be expressly restricted to the defense of such claim, and in that event is not an appearance for the purposes of any other claim with respect to which such process is not available or has not been served.

(9) Disposition of Property; Sales. (a) *Interlocutory Sales; Delivery.* [(i)] In any action in rem to enforce a forfeiture for violation of a statute of the United States the property shall be disposed of as provided by statute.

(ii) In the circumstances described in Rule E(9)(a)(i), the court, on motion by a defendant or a person filing a statement of interest or right under Rule C(6), may order that the property, rather than being sold, be delivered to the movant upon giving security under these rules.

(b) *Sales, Proceeds.* (i) On application of a party, the marshal, or other person having custody of the property, the court may order all or part of the property sold—with the sales proceeds, or as much of them as will satisfy the judgment, paid into court to await further orders of the court—if:

(A) the attached or arrested property is perishable, or liable to deterioration, decay, or injury by being detained in custody pending the action;

(B) the expense of keeping the property is excessive or disproportionate; or

(C) there is an unreasonable delay in securing release of the property.

(ii) In the circumstances described in Rule E(9)(b)(i), the court, on motion by a defendant or a person filing a statement of interest or right under Rule C(6), may order that the property, rather than being sold, be delivered to the movant upon giving security under these rules.

(c) *Sales, Proceeds.* All sales of property shall be made by the marshal or a deputy marshal, or by other person or organization having the warrant, or by any other person assigned by the court where the marshal or other person or organization having the warrant is a party in interest; and the proceeds of sale shall be forthwith paid into the registry of the court to be disposed of according to law.

(10) Preservation of Property. When the owner or another person remains in possession of property attached or arrested under the provisions of Rule E(4)(b) that permit execution of process without taking actual possession, the court, on a party's motion or on its own, may enter any order necessary to preserve the property and to prevent its removal.

(Amended effective Aug. 1, 1987; Dec. 1, 1991; Dec. 1, 2000; Dec. 1, 2006.)

Rule F. Limitation of Liability

(1) Time for Filing Complaint; Security. Not later than six months after receipt of a claim in writing, any vessel owner may file a complaint in the appropriate district court, as provided in subdivision (9) of this rule, for limitation of liability pursuant to statute. The owner (a) shall deposit with the court, for the benefit of claimants, a sum equal to the amount or value of the owner's interest in the vessel and pending freight, or approved security therefor, and in addition such sums, or approved security therefor, as the court may from time to time fix as necessary to carry out the provisions of the statutes as amended; or (b) at the owner's option shall transfer to a trustee to be appointed by the court, for the benefit of claimants, the owner's interest in the vessel and pending freight, together with such sums, or approved security therefor, as the court may from time to time fix as necessary to carry out the provisions of the statutes as amended. The plaintiff shall also give security for costs and, if the plaintiff elects to give security, for interest at the rate of 6 percent per annum from the date of the security.

(2) Complaint. The complaint shall set forth the facts on the basis of which the right to limit liability is asserted and all facts necessary to enable the court to determine the amount to which the owner's liability shall be limited. The complaint may demand exoneration from as well as limitation of liability. It shall state the voyage if any, on which the demands sought to be limited arose, with the date and place of its termination; the amount of all demands including all unsatisfied liens or claims of lien, in contract or in tort or otherwise, arising on that voyage, so far as known to the plaintiff, and what actions and proceedings, if any, are pending thereon; whether the vessel was damaged, lost, or abandoned, and, if so, when and where; the value of the vessel at the close of the voyage or, in case of wreck, the value of her wreckage, strippings, or proceeds, if any, and where and in whose possession they are; and the amount of any pending freight recovered or recoverable. If the plaintiff elects to transfer the plaintiff's interest in the vessel to a trustee, the complaint must further show any prior paramount liens thereon, and what voyages or trips, if any, she has made since the voyage or trip on which the claims sought to be limited arose, and any existing liens arising upon any such subsequent voyage or trip, with the amounts and causes thereof, and the names and addresses of the lienors, so far as known; and whether the vessel sustained any injury upon or by reason of such subsequent voyage or trip.

(3) Claims Against Owner; Injunction. Upon compliance by the owner with the requirements of subdivision (1) of this rule all claims and proceedings against the owner or the owner's property with respect to the matter in question shall cease. On application of the plaintiff the court shall enjoin the further prosecution of any action or proceeding against the plaintiff or the plaintiff's property with respect to any claim subject to limitation in the action.

(4) Notice to Claimants. Upon the owner's compliance with subdivision (1) of this rule the court shall issue a notice to all persons asserting claims with respect to which the complaint seeks limitation, admonishing them to file their respective claims with the clerk of the court and to serve on the attorneys for the plaintiff a copy thereof on or before a date to be named in the notice. The date so fixed shall not be less than 30 days after issuance of the notice. For cause shown, the court may enlarge the time within which claims may be filed. The notice shall be published in such newspaper or newspapers as the court may direct once a week for four successive weeks prior to the date fixed for the filing of claims. The plaintiff not later than the day of second publication shall also mail a copy of the notice to every person known to have made any claim against the vessel or the plaintiff arising out of the voyage or trip on which the claims sought to be limited arose. In cases involving death a copy of such notice shall be mailed to the decedent at the decedent's last known address, and also to any person who shall be known to have made any claim on account of such death.

(5) Claims and Answer. Claims shall be filed and served on or before the date specified in the notice provided for in subdivision (4) of this rule. Each claim shall specify the facts upon which the claimant relies in support of the claim, the items thereof, and the dates on which the same accrued. If a claimant desires to contest either the right to exoneration from or the right to limitation of liability the claimant shall file and serve an answer to the complaint unless the claim has included an answer.

(6) Information to be Given Claimants. Within 30 days after the date specified in the notice for filing claims, or within such time as the court thereafter may allow, the plaintiff shall mail to the attorney for each claimant (or if the claimant has no attorney to the claimant) a list setting forth (a) the name of each claimant, (b) the name and address of the claimant's attorney (if the claimant is known to have one), (c) the nature of the claim, i.e., whether property loss, property damage, death, personal injury etc., and (d) the amount thereof.

(7) Insufficiency of Fund or Security. Any claimant may by motion demand that the funds deposited in court or the security given by the plaintiff be increased on the ground that they are less than the value of the plaintiff's interest in the vessel and pending freight. Thereupon the court shall cause due appraisement to be made of the value of the plaintiff's interest in the vessel and pending freight; and if the court finds that the deposit or security is either insufficient or excessive it shall order its increase or reduction. In like manner any claimant may demand that the deposit or security be increased on the ground that it is insufficient to carry out the provisions of the statutes relating to claims in respect of loss of life or bodily injury; and, after notice and hearing, the court may similarly order that the deposit or security be increased or reduced.

(8) Objections to Claims: Distribution of Fund. Any interested party may question or controvert any claim without filing an objection thereto. Upon determination of liability the fund deposited or secured, or the proceeds of the vessel and pending freight, shall be divided pro rata, subject to all relevant provisions of law, among the several claimants in proportion to the amounts of their respective claims, duly proved, saving, however, to all parties any priority to which they may be legally entitled.

(9) Venue; Transfer. The complaint shall be filed in any district in which the vessel has been attached or arrested to answer for any claim with respect to which the plaintiff seeks to limit liability; or, if the vessel has not been attached or arrested, then in any district in which the owner has been sued with respect to any such claim. When the vessel has not been attached or arrested to answer the matters aforesaid, and suit has not been commenced against the owner, the proceedings may be had in the district in which the vessel may be, but if the vessel is not within any district and no suit has been commenced in any district, then the complaint may be filed in any district. For the convenience of parties and witnesses, in the interest of justice, the court may transfer the action to any district; if venue is wrongly laid the court shall dismiss or, if it be in the interest of justice, transfer the action to any district in which it could have been brought. If the vessel shall have been sold, the proceeds shall represent the vessel for the purposes of these rules.

(Amended effective Aug. 1, 1987)

Rule G. Forfeiture Actions In Rem

(1) Scope. This rule governs a forfeiture action in rem arising from a federal statute. To the extent that this rule does not address an issue, Supplemental Rules C and E and the Federal Rules of Civil Procedure also apply.

(2) Complaint. The complaint must:

(a) be verified;

(b) state the grounds for subject-matter jurisdiction, in rem jurisdiction over the defendant property, and venue;

(c) describe the property with reasonable particularity;

(d) if the property is tangible, state its location when any seizure occurred and—if different—its location when the action is filed;

(e) identify the statute under which the forfeiture action is brought; and

(f) state sufficiently detailed facts to support a reasonable belief that the government will be able to meet its burden of proof at trial.

(3) Judicial Authorization and Process. (a) *Real Property.* If the defendant is real property, the government must proceed under 18 U.S.C. § 985.

(b) *Other Property; Arrest Warrant.* If the defendant is not real property:

(i) the clerk must issue a warrant to arrest the property if it is in the government's possession, custody, or control;

(ii) the court—on finding probable cause—must issue a warrant to arrest the property if it is not in the government's possession, custody, or control and is not subject to a judicial restraining order; and

(iii) a warrant is not necessary if the property is subject to a judicial restraining order.

(c) *Execution of Process.* (i) The warrant and any supplemental process must be delivered to a person or organization authorized to execute it, who may be: (A) a marshal or any other United States officer or employee; (B) someone under contract with the United States; or (C) someone specially appointed by the court for that purpose.

(ii) The authorized person or organization must execute the warrant and any supplemental process on property in the United States as soon as practicable unless:

(A) the property is in the government's possession, custody, or control; or

(B) the court orders a different time when the complaint is under seal, the action is stayed before the warrant and supplemental process are executed, or the court finds other good cause.

(iii) The warrant and any supplemental process may be executed within the district or, when authorized by statute, outside the district.

(iv) If executing a warrant on property outside the

United States is required, the warrant may be transmitted to an appropriate authority for serving process where the property is located.

(4) Notice. (a) *Notice by Publication.* (i) When Publication Is Required. A judgment of forfeiture may be entered only if the government has published notice of the action within a reasonable time after filing the complaint or at a time the court orders. But notice need not be published if:

(A) the defendant property is worth less than $1,000 and direct notice is sent under Rule G(4)(b) to every person the government can reasonably identify as a potential claimant; or

(B) the court finds that the cost of publication exceeds the property's value and that other means of notice would satisfy due process.

(ii) Content of the Notice. Unless the court orders otherwise, the notice must:

(A) describe the property with reasonable particularity;

(B) state the times under Rule G(5) to file a claim and to answer; and

(C) name the government attorney to be served with the claim and answer.

(iii) Frequency of Publication. Published notice must appear:

(A) once a week for three consecutive weeks; or

(B) only once if, before the action was filed, notice of nonjudicial forfeiture of the same property was published on an official internet government forfeiture site for at least 30 consecutive days, or in a newspaper of general circulation for three consecutive weeks in a district where publication is authorized under Rule G(4)(a)(iv).

(iv) Means of Publication. The government should select from the following options a means of publication reasonably calculated to notify potential claimants of the action:

(A) if the property is in the United States, publication in a newspaper generally circulated in the district where the action is filed, where the property was seized, or where property that was not seized is located;

(B) if the property is outside the United States, publication in a newspaper generally circulated in a district where the action is filed, in a newspaper generally circulated in the country where the property is located, or in legal notices published and generally circulated in the country where the property is located; or

(C) instead of (A) or (B), posting a notice on an official internet government forfeiture site for at least 30 consecutive days.

(b) *Notice to Known Potential Claimants.* (i) Direct Notice Required. The government must send notice of the action and a copy of the complaint to any person who reasonably appears to be a potential claimant on the facts known to the government before the end of the time for filing a claim under Rule G(5)(a)(ii)(B).

(ii) Content of the Notice. The notice must state:

(A) the date when the notice is sent;

(B) a deadline for filing a claim, at least 35 days after the notice is sent;

(C) that an answer or a motion under Rule 12 must be filed no later than 21 days after filing the claim; and

(D) the name of the government attorney to be served with the claim and answer.

(iii) Sending Notice.

(A) The notice must be sent by means reasonably calculated to reach the potential claimant.

(B) Notice may be sent to the potential claimant or to the attorney representing the potential claimant with respect to the seizure of the property or in a related investigation, administrative forfeiture proceeding, or criminal case.

(C) Notice sent to a potential claimant who is incarcerated must be sent to the place of incarceration.

(D) Notice to a person arrested in connection with an offense giving rise to the forfeiture who is not incarcerated when notice is sent may be sent to the address that person last gave to the agency that arrested or released the person.

(E) Notice to a person from whom the property was seized who is not incarcerated when notice is sent may be sent to the last address that person gave to the agency that seized the property.

(iv) When Notice Is Sent. Notice by the following means is sent on the date when it is placed in the mail, delivered to a commercial carrier, or sent by electronic mail.

(v) Actual Notice. A potential claimant who had actual notice of a forfeiture action may not oppose or seek relief from forfeiture because of the government's failure to send the required notice.

(5) Responsive Pleadings. (a) *Filing a Claim.* (i) A person who asserts an interest in the defendant property may contest the forfeiture by filing a claim in the court where the action is pending. The claim must:

(A) identify the specific property claimed;

(B) identify the claimant and state the claimant's interest in the property;

(C) be signed by the claimant under penalty of perjury; and

(D) be served on the government attorney designated under Rule G(4)(a)(ii)(C) or (b)(ii)(D).

(ii) Unless the court for good cause sets a different time, the claim must be filed:

(A) by the time stated in a direct notice sent under Rule G(4)(b);

(B) if notice was published but direct notice was not sent to the claimant or the claimant's attorney, no later than 30 days after final publication of newspaper notice or legal notice under Rule G(4)(a) or no later than 60 days after the first day of publication on an official internet government forfeiture site; or

(C) if notice was not published and direct notice was not sent to the claimant or the claimant's attorney:

(1) if the property was in the government's possession, custody, or control when the complaint was filed, no later than 60 days after the filing, not counting any time when the complaint was under seal or when the action was stayed before execution of a warrant issued under Rule G(3)(b); or

(2) if the property was not in the government's possession, custody, or control when the complaint was filed, no later than 60 days after the government complied with 18 U.S.C. § 985(c) as to real property, or 60 days after process was executed on the property under Rule G(3).

(iii) A claim filed by a person asserting an interest as a bailee must identify the bailor, and if filed on the bailor's behalf must state the authority to do so.

(b) *Answer.* A claimant must serve and file an answer to the complaint or a motion under Rule 12 within 21 days after filing the claim. A claimant waives an objection to in rem jurisdiction or to venue if the objection is not made by motion or stated in the answer.

(6) Special Interrogatories. (a) *Time and Scope.* The government may serve special interrogatories limited to the claimant's identity and relationship to the defendant property without the court's leave at any time after the claim is filed and before discovery is closed. But if the claimant serves a motion to dismiss the action, the government must serve the interrogatories within 21 days after the motion is served.

(b) *Answers or Objections.* Answers or objections to these interrogatories must be served within 21 days after the interrogatories are served.

(c) *Government's Response Deferred.* The government need not respond to a claimant's motion to dismiss the action under Rule G(8)(b) until 21 days after the claimant has answered these interrogatories.

(7) Preserving, Preventing Criminal Use, and Disposing of Property; Sales. (a) *Preserving and Preventing Criminal Use of Property.* When the government does not have actual possession of the defendant property the court, on motion or on its own, may enter any order necessary to preserve the property, to prevent its removal or encumbrance, or to prevent its use in a criminal offense.

(b) *Interlocutory Sale or Delivery.* (i) Order to Sell. On motion by a party or a person having custody of the property, the court may order all or part of the property sold if:

(A) the property is perishable or at risk of deterioration, decay, or injury by being detained in custody pending the action;

(B) the expense of keeping the property is excessive or is disproportionate to its fair market value;

(C) the property is subject to a mortgage or to taxes on which the owner is in default; or

(D) the court finds other good cause.

(ii) Who Makes the Sale. A sale must be made by a United States agency that has authority to sell the property, by the agency's contractor, or by any person the court designates.

(iii) Sale Procedures. The sale is governed by 28 U.S.C. §§ 2001, 2002, and 2004, unless all parties, with the court's approval, agree to the sale, aspects of the sale, or different procedures.

(iv) Sale Proceeds. Sale proceeds are a substitute res subject to forfeiture in place of the property that was sold. The proceeds must be held in an interest-bearing account maintained by the United States pending the conclusion of the forfeiture action.

(v) Delivery on a Claimant's Motion. The court may order that the property be delivered to the claimant pending the conclusion of the action if the claimant shows circumstances that would permit sale under Rule G(7)(b)(i) and gives security under these rules.

(c) *Disposing of Forfeited Property.* Upon entry of a forfeiture judgment, the property or proceeds from selling the property must be disposed of as provided by law.

(8) Motions. (a) *Motion To Suppress Use of the Property as Evidence.* If the defendant property was seized, a party with standing to contest the lawfulness of the seizure may move to suppress use of the property as evidence. Suppression does not affect forfeiture of the property based on independently derived evidence.

(b) *Motion To Dismiss the Action.* (i) A claimant who establishes standing to contest forfeiture may move to dismiss the action under Rule 12(b).

(ii) In an action governed by 18 U.S.C. § 983(a)(3)(D) the complaint may not be dismissed on the ground that the government did not have adequate evidence at the time the complaint was filed to establish the forfeitability of the property. The sufficiency of the complaint is governed by Rule G(2).

(c) *Motion To Strike a Claim or Answer.* (i) At any time before trial, the government may move to strike a claim or answer:

(A) for failing to comply with Rule G(5) or (6), or

(B) because the claimant lacks standing.

(ii) The motion:

(A) must be decided before any motion by the claimant to dismiss the action; and

(B) may be presented as a motion for judgment on the pleadings or as a motion to determine after a hearing or by summary judgment whether the claimant can carry the burden of establishing standing by a preponderance of the evidence.

(d) *Petition To Release Property.* (i) If a United States agency or an agency's contractor holds property for judicial or nonjudicial forfeiture under a statute governed by 18 U.S.C. § 983(f), a person who has filed a claim to the property may petition for its release under § 983(f).

(ii) If a petition for release is filed before a judicial forfeiture action is filed against the property, the petition may be filed either in the district where the property was seized or in the district where a warrant to seize the property issued. If a judicial forfeiture action against the property is later filed in another district—or if the government shows that the action will be filed in another district—the petition may be transferred to that district under 28 U.S.C. § 1404.

(e) *Excessive Fines.* A claimant may seek to mitigate a forfeiture under the Excessive Fines Clause of the Eighth Amendment by motion for summary judgment or by motion made after entry of a forfeiture judgment if:

(i) the claimant has pleaded the defense under Rule 8; and

(ii) the parties have had the opportunity to conduct civil discovery on the defense.

(9) Trial. Trial is to the court unless any party demands trial by jury under Rule 38.

(As added Dec. 1, 2006; Dec. 1, 2009.)

RULES OF PROCEDURE OF THE JUDICIAL PANEL ON MULTIDISTRICT LITIGATION

I. RULES FOR MULTIDISTRICT LITIGATION UNDER 28 U.S.C. § 1407

II. RULES FOR MULTICIRCUIT PETITIONS FOR REVIEW UNDER 28 U.S.C. § 2112(a)(3)

I. RULES FOR MULTIDISTRICT LITIGATION UNDER 28 U.S.C. § 1407

The United States Judicial Panel on Multidistrict Litigation promulgates these Rules pursuant to its authority under 28 U.S.C. § 1407(f).

Rule 1.1. Definitions

(a) "Panel" means the members of the United States Judicial Panel on Multidistrict Litigation appointed by the Chief Justice of the United States pursuant to 28 U.S.C. § 1407.

(b) "Chair" means the Chair of the Panel appointed by the Chief Justice of the United States pursuant to Section 1407, or the member of the Panel properly designated to act as Chair.

(c) "Clerk of the Panel" means the official that the Panel appoints to that position. The Clerk of the Panel shall perform such duties that the Panel or the Panel Executive delegates.

(d) "Electronic Case Filing (ECF)" refers to the Panel's automated system that receives and stores documents filed in electronic form. All attorneys filing pleadings with the Panel must do so using ECF. All pro se individuals are non-ECF users, unless the Panel orders otherwise.

(e) "MDL" means a multidistrict litigation docket which the Panel is either considering or has created by transferring cases to a transferee district for coordinated or consolidated pretrial proceedings pursuant to Section 1407.

(f) "Panel Executive" means the official appointed to act as the Panel's Chief Executive and Legal Officer. The Panel Executive may appoint, with the approval of the Panel, necessary deputies, clerical assistants and other employees to perform or assist in the performance of the duties of the Panel Executive. The Panel Executive, with the approval of the Panel, may make such delegations of authority as are necessary for the Panel's efficient operation.

(g) "Pleadings" means all papers, motions, responses, or replies of any kind filed with the Panel, including exhibits attached thereto, as well as all orders and notices that the Panel issues.

(h) "Tag-along action" refers to a civil action pending in a district court which involves common questions of fact with either (1) actions on a pending motion to transfer to create an MDL or (2) actions previously transferred to an existing MDL, and which the Panel would consider transferring under Section 1407.

(i) "Transferee district" is the federal district court to which the Panel transfers an action pursuant to Section 1407, for inclusion in an MDL.

(j) "Transferor district" is the federal district court where an action was pending prior to its transfer pursuant to Section 1407, for inclusion in an MDL, and where the Panel may remand that action at or before the conclusion of pretrial proceedings.

Rule 2.1. Rules and Practice

(a) Customary Practice. The Panel's customary practice shall govern, unless otherwise fixed by statute or these Rules.

(b) Failure to Comply with Rules. When a pleading does not comply with these Rules, the Clerk of the Panel may advise counsel of the deficiencies and set a date for full compliance. If counsel does not fully comply within the established time, the Clerk of the Panel shall file the non-complying pleading, but the Chair may thereafter order it stricken.

(c) Admission to Practice before the Panel. Every member in good standing of the Bar of any district court of the United States is entitled to practice before the Panel, provided, however, that he or she has established and maintains a CM/ECF account with any United States federal court. Any attorney of record in any action transferred under Section 1407 may continue to represent his or her client in any district court of the United States to which such action is transferred. Parties are not required to obtain local counsel.

(d) Pendency of Motion or Conditional Order. The pendency of a motion, order to show cause, conditional transfer order or conditional remand order before the Panel pursuant to 28 U.S.C. § 1407 does not affect or suspend orders and pretrial proceedings in any pending federal district court action and does not limit the pretrial jurisdiction of that court. An order to transfer or remand pursuant to 28 U.S.C. § 1407 shall be effective only upon its filing with the clerk of the transferee district court.

(e) Reassignment. If for any reason the transferee judge is unable to continue those responsibilities, the Panel shall make the reassignment of a new transferee judge.

Rule 3.1. Electronic Records and Files; Copy Fees

(a) Electronic Record. Effective October 4, 2010, the official Panel record shall be the electronic file maintained on the Panel's servers. This record includes, but is not limited to, Panel pleadings, documents filed in paper and then scanned and made part of the electronic record, and Panel orders and notices filed. The official record also includes any documents or exhibits that may be impractical to scan. These documents and exhibits shall be kept in the Panel offices.

(b) Maintaining Records. Records and files generated prior to October 4, 2010, may be (i) maintained at the Panel offices, (ii) temporarily or permanently removed to such places at such times as the Clerk of the Panel or the Chair shall direct, or (iii) transferred whenever appropriate to the Federal Records Center.

(c) Fees. The Clerk of the Panel may charge fees for duplicating records and files, as prescribed by the Judicial Conference of the United States.

Rule 3.2. ECF Users: Filing Requirements

(a) Form of Pleadings. This Rule applies to pleadings that ECF users file with the Panel.

(i) Each pleading shall bear the heading "Before the United States Judicial Panel on Multidistrict Litigation," the identification "MDL No.______" and the descriptive title designated by the Panel. If the Panel has not yet designated a title, counsel shall use an appropriate description.

(ii) The final page of each pleading shall contain the name, address, telephone number, fax number and email address of the attorney or party designated to receive service of pleadings in the case, and the name of each party represented.

(iii) Each brief submitted with a motion and any response to it shall not exceed 20 pages, exclusive of exhibits. Each reply shall not exceed 10 pages and shall address arguments raised in the response(s). Absent exceptional circumstances and those set forth in Rule 6.1(d), the Panel will not grant motions to exceed page limits.

(iv) Each pleading shall be typed in size 12 point font (for both text and footnotes), double spaced (text only), in a letter size document (8 ½ × 11 inch) with sequentially numbered pages.

(v) Each exhibit shall be separately numbered and clearly identified.

(vi) Proposed Panel orders shall not be submitted.

(b) Place of Filing. Counsel shall sign and verify all pleadings electronically in accordance with these Rules and the Panel's Administrative Policies and Procedures for Electronic Case Filing found at www.jpml.uscourts.gov. A pleading filed electronically constitutes a written document for the purpose of these Rules and the Federal Rules of Civil Procedure and is deemed the electronically signed original thereof. All pleadings, except by pro se litigants, shall conform with this Rule beginning on October 4, 2010.

(i) Pleadings shall not be transmitted directly to any Panel member.

(c) Attorney Registration. Only attorneys identified, or to be identified, pursuant to Rule 4.1, shall file pleadings. Each of these attorneys must register as a Panel CM/ECF user through www.jpml.uscourts.gov. Registration/possession of a CM/ECF account with any United States federal court shall be deemed consent to receive electronic service of all Panel orders and notices as well as electronic service of pleadings from other parties before the Panel.

(d) Courtesy Copy of Specified Pleadings. Counsel shall serve the Clerk of the Panel, for delivery within 1 business day of filing, with a courtesy paper copy of any of the following pleadings: (i) a motion to transfer and its supporting brief; (ii) a response to a show cause order; (iii) a motion to vacate a conditional transfer order or a conditional remand order; (iv) any response, reply, supplemental information or interested party response related to the pleadings listed in (i), (ii) and (iii); and (v) a corporate disclosure statement. No courtesy copies of any other pleadings are required. Courtesy copies of pleadings totaling 10 pages or less (including any attachments) may be faxed to the Panel. The courtesy copy shall include all exhibits, shall be clearly marked "Courtesy Copy-Do Not File," shall contain the CM/ECF pleading number (if known), and shall be mailed or delivered to:

Clerk of the Panel
United States Judicial Panel on Multidistrict Litigation
Thurgood Marshall Federal Judiciary Building
One Columbus Circle, NE, Room G-255, North Lobby
Washington, DC 20002-8041

(e) Privacy Protections. The privacy protections contained in Rule 5.2 of the Federal Rules of Civil Procedure shall apply to all Panel filings.

(Amended July 6, 2011)

Rule 3.3. Non-ECF Users: Filing Requirements

(a) Definition of Non-ECF Users. Non-ECF

users are all pro se individuals, unless the Panel orders otherwise. This Rule shall apply to all motions, responses and replies that non-ECF users file with the Panel.

(b) Form of Pleadings. Unless otherwise set forth in this Rule, the provisions of Rule 3.2 shall apply to non-ECF users.

(i) Each pleading shall be flat and unfolded; plainly written or typed in size 12 point font (for both text and footnotes), double spaced (text only), and printed single-sided on letter size (8 ½ × 11 inch) white paper with sequentially numbered pages; and fastened at the top-left corner without side binding or front or back covers.

(ii) Each exhibit shall be separately numbered and clearly identified. Any exhibits exceeding a cumulative total of 50 pages shall be bound separately.

(c) Place of Filing. File an original and one copy of all pleadings with the Clerk of the Panel by mailing or delivering to:

Clerk of the Panel
United States Judicial Panel on Multidistrict Litigation
Thurgood Marshall Federal Judiciary Building
One Columbus Circle, NE, Room G-255, North Lobby
Washington, DC 20002-8041

(i) Pleadings not exceeding a total of 10 pages, including exhibits, may be faxed to the Panel office.

(ii) The Clerk of the Panel shall endorse the date for filing on all pleadings submitted for filing.

Rule 4.1. Service of Pleadings

(a) Proof of Service. The Panel's notice of electronic filing shall constitute service of pleadings. Registration/possession by counsel of a CM/ECF account with any United States federal court shall be deemed consent to receive electronic service of all pleadings. All pleadings shall contain a proof of service on all other parties in all involved actions. The proof of service shall indicate the name and manner of service. If a party is not represented by counsel, the proof of service shall indicate the name of the party and the party's last known address. The proof of service shall indicate why any person named as a party in a constituent complaint was not served with the Section 1407 pleading.

(b) Service Upon Transferor Court. The proof of service pertaining to motions for a transfer or remand pursuant to 28 U.S.C. § 1407 shall certify that counsel has transmitted a copy of the motion for filing to the clerk of each district court where an affected action is pending.

(c) Notice of Appearance. Within 14 days after the issuance of a (i) notice of filing of a motion to initiate transfer under Rule 6.2, (ii) notice of filed opposition to a CTO under Rule 7.1, (iii) a show cause order under Rules 8.1, (iv) notice of filed opposition to a CRO under Rule 10.2, or (v) notice of filing of a motion to remand under Rule 10.3, each party or designated attorney as required hereinafter shall file a Notice of Appearance notifying the Clerk of the Panel of the name, address and email address of the attorney designated to file and receive service of all pleadings. Each party shall designate only one attorney. Any party not represented by counsel shall be served by mailing such pleadings to the party's last known address. Except in extraordinary circumstances, the Panel will not grant requests for an extension of time to file the Notice of Appearance.

(d) Liaison Counsel. If the transferee district court appoints liaison counsel, this Rule shall be satisfied by serving each party in each affected action and all liaison counsel. Liaison counsel shall receive copies of all Panel orders concerning their particular litigation and shall be responsible for distribution to the parties for whom he or she serves as liaison counsel.

(Amended July 6, 2011)

Rule 5.1. Corporate Disclosure Statement

(a) Requirements. A nongovernmental corporate party must file a disclosure statement that: (1) identifies any parent corporation and any publicly held corporation owning 10% or more of its stock; or (2) states that there is no such corporation.

(b) Deadline. A party shall file the corporate disclosure statement within 14 days after issuance of a notice of the filing of a motion to transfer or remand, an order to show cause, or a motion to vacate a conditional transfer order or a conditional remand order.

(c) Updating. Each party must update its corporate disclosure statement to reflect any change in the information therein (i) until the matter before the Panel is decided, and (ii) within 14 days after issuance of a notice of the filing of any subsequent motion to transfer or remand, order to show cause, or motion to vacate a conditional transfer order or a conditional remand order in that docket.

(Amended July 6, 2011)

Rule 6.1. Motion Practice

(a) Application. This Rule governs all motions requesting Panel action generally. More specific provisions may apply to motions to transfer (Rule 6.2), miscellaneous motions (Rule 6.3), conditional transfer orders (Rule 7.1), show cause orders (Rule 8.1), conditional remand orders (Rule 10.2) and motions to remand (Rule 10.3).

(b) Form of Motions. All motions shall briefly describe the action or relief sought and shall include:

(i) a brief which concisely states the background of the litigation and movant's factual and legal contentions;

(ii) a numbered schedule providing

(A) the complete name of each action involved, listing the full name of each party included as such on the district court's docket sheet, not shortened by the use of references such as "et al." or "etc.";

(B) the district court and division where each action is pending;

(C) the civil action number of each action; and

(D) the name of the judge assigned each action, if known;

(iii) a proof of service providing

(A) a service list listing the full name of each party included on the district court's docket sheet and the complaint, including opt-in plaintiffs not listed on the docket sheet; and

(B) in actions where there are 25 or more plaintiffs listed on the docket sheet, list the first named plaintiff with the reference "et al." if all the plaintiffs are represented by the same attorney(s);

(iv) a copy of all complaints and docket sheets for all actions listed on the Schedule; and

(v) exhibits, if any, identified by number or letter and a descriptive title.

(c) Responses and Joinders. Any other party may file a response within 21 days after filing of a motion. Failure to respond to a motion shall be treated as that party's acquiescence to it. A joinder in a motion shall not add any action to that motion.

(d) Replies. The movant may file a reply within 7 days after the lapse of the time period for filing a response. Where a movant is replying to more than one response in opposition, the movant may file a consolidated reply with a limit of 20 pages.

(e) Alteration of Time Periods. The Clerk of the Panel has the discretion to shorten or enlarge the time periods set forth in this Rule as necessary.

(f) Notification of Developments. Counsel shall promptly notify the Clerk of the Panel of any development that would partially or completely moot any Panel matter.

Rule 6.2. Motions to Transfer for Coordinated or Consolidated Pretrial Proceedings

(a) Initiation of Transfer. A party to an action may initiate proceedings to transfer under Section 1407 by filing a motion in accordance with these Rules. A copy of the motion shall be filed in each district court where the motion affects a pending action.

(b) Notice of Filing of Motion to Transfer. Upon receipt of a motion, the Clerk of the Panel shall issue a "Notice of Filing of Motion to Transfer" to the service list recipients. The Notice shall contain the following: the filing date of the motion, caption, MDL docket number, briefing schedule and pertinent Panel policies. After a motion is filed, the Clerk of the Panel shall consider any other pleading to be a response unless the pleading adds an action. The Clerk of the Panel may designate such a pleading as a motion, and distribute a briefing schedule applicable to all or some of the parties, as appropriate.

(c) Notice of Appearance. Within 14 days of issuance of a "Notice of the Filing of a Motion to Transfer," each party or designated attorney shall file a Notice of Appearance in accordance with Rule 4.1(c).

(d) Notice of Potential Tag-along Actions. Any party or counsel in a new group of actions under consideration for transfer under Section 1407 shall promptly notify the Clerk of the Panel of any potential tag-along actions in which that party is also named or in which that counsel appears.

(e) Interested Party Responses. Any party or counsel in one or more potential tag-along actions as well as amicus curiae may file a response to a pending motion to transfer. Such a pleading shall be deemed an Interested Party Response.

(f) Amendment to a Motion. Before amending a motion to transfer, a party shall first contact the Clerk of the Panel to ascertain whether such amendment is feasible and permissible considering the Panel's hearing schedule. Any such amendment shall be entitled "Amendment to Motion for Transfer," and shall clearly and specifically identify and describe the nature of the amendment.

(i) Where the amended motion includes new civil actions, the amending party shall file a "Schedule of Additional Actions" and a revised Proof of Service.

(ii) The Proof of Service shall state (A) that all new counsel have been served with a copy of the amendment and all previously-filed motion papers, and (B) that all counsel previously served with the original motion have been served with a copy of the amendment.

(iii) The Clerk of the Panel may designate the amendment with a different denomination (e.g., a notice of potential tag-along action(s)) and treatment.

[(g)](h) Oral Argument. The Panel shall schedule oral arguments as needed and as set forth in Rule 11.1.

(Amended July 6, 2011)

Rule 6.3. Motions for Miscellaneous Relief

(a) Definition. Motions for miscellaneous relief include, but are not limited to, requests for extensions of time, exemption from ECF requirements, page limit extensions, or expedited consideration of any motion.

(b) Panel Action. The Panel, through the Clerk, may act upon any motion for miscellaneous relief, at any time, without waiting for a response. A motion for extension of time to file a pleading or perform an act under these Rules must state specifically the revised date sought and must be filed before the deadline for filing the pleading or performing the act. Any party aggrieved by the Clerk of the Panel's action may file objections for consideration. Absent exceptional circumstances, the Panel will not grant any extensions of time to file a notice of opposition to either a conditional transfer order or a conditional remand order.

Rule 7.1. Conditional Transfer Orders (CTO) for Tag-Along Actions

(a) Notification of Potential Tag-along Ac-

tions. Any party or counsel in actions previously transferred under Section 1407 shall promptly notify the Clerk of the Panel of any potential tag-along actions in which that party is also named or in which that counsel appears. The Panel has several options: (i) filing a CTO under Rule 7.1, (ii) filing a show cause order under Rule 8.1, or (iii) declining to act (Rule 7.1(b)(i)).

(b) Initiation of CTO. Upon learning of the pendency of a potential tag-along action, the Clerk of the Panel may enter a conditional order transferring that action to the previously designated transferee district court for the reasons expressed in the Panel's previous opinions and orders. The Clerk of the Panel shall serve this order on each party to the litigation but shall not send the order to the clerk of the transferee district court until 7 days after its entry.

(i) If the Clerk of the Panel determines that a potential tag-along action is not appropriate for inclusion in an MDL proceeding and does not enter a CTO, an involved party may move for its transfer pursuant to Rule 6.1.

(c) Notice of Opposition to CTO. Any party opposing the transfer shall file a notice of opposition with the Clerk of the Panel within the 7-day period. In such event, the Clerk of the Panel shall not transmit the transfer order to the clerk of the transferee district court, but shall notify the parties of the briefing schedule.

(d) Failure to Respond. Failure to respond to a CTO shall be treated as that party's acquiescence to it.

(e) Notice of Appearance. Within 14 days after the issuance of a "Notice of Filed Opposition" to a CTO, each opposing party or designated attorney shall file a Notice of Appearance in accordance with Rule 4.1(c).

(f) Motion to Vacate CTO. Within 14 days of the filing of its notice of opposition, the party opposing transfer shall file a motion to vacate the CTO and brief in support thereof. The Clerk of the Panel shall set the motion for the next appropriate hearing session. Failure to file and serve a motion and brief shall be treated as withdrawal of the opposition and the Clerk of the Panel shall forthwith transmit the order to the clerk of the transferee district court.

(g) Notification of Developments. Parties to an action subject to a CTO shall notify the Clerk of the Panel if that action is no longer pending in its transferor district court.

(h) Effective Date of CTO. CTOs are effective when filed with the clerk of the transferee district court.

(Amended July 6, 2011)

Rule 7.2. Miscellaneous Provisions Concerning Tag-along Actions

(a) Potential Tag-alongs in Transferee Court. Potential tag-along actions filed in the transferee district do not require Panel action. A party should request assignment of such actions to the Section 1407 transferee judge in accordance with applicable local rules.

(b) Failure to Serve. Failure to serve one or more of the defendants in a potential tag-along action with the complaint and summons as required by Rule 4 of the Federal Rules of Civil Procedure does not preclude transfer of such action under Section 1407. Such failure, however, may constitute grounds for denying the proposed transfer where prejudice can be shown. The failure of the Clerk of the Panel to serve a CTO on all plaintiffs or defendants or their counsel may constitute grounds for the Clerk to reinstate the CTO or for the aggrieved party to seek § 1407(c) remand.

(Amended July 6, 2011)

Rule 8.1. Show Cause Orders

(a) Entry of Show Cause Order. When transfer of multidistrict litigation is being considered on the initiative of the Panel pursuant to 28 U.S.C. § 1407(c)(i), the Clerk of the Panel may enter an order directing the parties to show cause why a certain civil action or actions should not be transferred for coordinated or consolidated pretrial proceedings. Any party shall also promptly notify the Clerk of the Panel whenever they learn of any other federal district court actions which are similar to those which the show cause order encompasses.

(b) Notice of Appearance. Within 14 days of the issuance of an order to show cause, each party or designated attorney shall file a Notice of Appearance in accordance with Rule 4.1(c).

(c) Responses. Unless otherwise provided by order, any party may file a response within 21 days of the filing of the show cause order. Failure to respond to a show cause order shall be treated as that party's acquiescence to the Panel action.

(d) Replies. Within 7 days after the lapse of the time period for filing a response, any party may file a reply.

(e) Notification of Developments. Counsel shall promptly notify the Clerk of the Panel of any development that would partially or completely moot any matter subject to a show cause order.

Rule 9.1. Transfer of Files; Notification Requirements

(a) Notice to Transferee Court Clerk. The Clerk of the Panel, via a notice of electronic filing, will notify the clerk of the transferee district whenever a Panel transfer order should be filed in the transferee district court. Upon receipt of an electronically certified copy of a Panel transfer order from the clerk of the transferee district, the clerk of the transferor district shall transmit the record of each transferred action to the transferee district and then, unless Rule 9.1(b) applies, close the transferred action in the transferor district.

(b) Retention of Claims. If the transfer order provides for the separation and simultaneous remand of any claim, cross-claim, counterclaim, or third-party claim, the clerk of the transferor district shall retain jurisdiction over any such claim and shall not close the action.

(c) Notice to Clerk of Panel. The clerk of the transferee district shall promptly provide the Clerk of the Panel with the civil action numbers assigned to all transferred actions and the identity of liaison counsel, if or when designated. The clerk of the transferee district shall also promptly notify the Clerk of the Panel of any dispositive ruling that terminates a transferred action.

Rule 10.1. Termination and Remand

(a) Termination. Where the transferee district court terminates an action by valid order, including but not limited to summary judgment, judgment of dismissal and judgment upon stipulation, the transferee district court clerk shall transmit a copy of that order to the Clerk of the Panel. The terminated action shall not be remanded to the transferor court and the transferee court shall retain the original files and records unless the transferee judge or the Panel directs otherwise.

(b) Initiation of Remand. Typically, the transferee judge recommends remand of an action, or a part of it, to the transferor court at any time by filing a suggestion of remand with the Panel. However, the Panel may remand an action or any separable claim, cross-claim, counterclaim or third-party claim within it, upon

(i) the transferee court's suggestion of remand,

(ii) the Panel's own initiative by entry of an order to show cause, a conditional remand order or other appropriate order, or

(iii) motion of any party.

Rule 10.2. Conditional Remand Orders (CRO)

(a) Entering a CRO. Upon the suggestion of the transferee judge or the Panel's own initiative, the Clerk of the Panel shall enter a conditional order remanding the action or actions to the transferor district court. The Clerk of the Panel shall serve this order on each party to the litigation but shall not send the order to the clerk of the transferee district court for 7 days from the entry thereof.

(i) The Panel may, on its own initiative, also enter an order that the parties show cause why a matter should not be remanded. Rule 8.1 applies to responses and replies with respect to such a show cause order.

(b) Notice of Opposition. Any party opposing the CRO shall file a notice of opposition with the Clerk of the Panel within the 7-day period. In such event, the Clerk of the Panel shall not transmit the remand order to the clerk of the transferee district court and shall notify the parties of the briefing schedule.

(c) Failure to Respond. Failure to respond to a CRO shall be treated as that party's acquiescence to it.

(d) Notice of Appearance. Within 14 days after the issuance of a "Notice of Filed Opposition" to a CRO, each opposing party or designated attorney shall file a Notice of Appearance in accordance with Rule 4.1(c).

(e) Motion to Vacate CRO. Within 14 days of the filing of its notice of opposition, the party opposing remand shall file a motion to vacate the CRO and brief in support thereof. The Clerk of the Panel shall set the motion for the next appropriate Panel hearing session. Failure to file and serve a motion and brief shall be treated as a withdrawal of the opposition and the Clerk of the Panel shall forthwith transmit the order to the clerk of the transferee district court.

(f) Effective Date of CRO. CROs are not effective until filed with the clerk of the transferee district court.

(Amended July 6, 2011)

Rule 10.3. Motion to Remand

(a) Requirements of the Motion. If the Clerk of the Panel does not enter a CRO, a party may file a motion to remand to the transferor court pursuant to these Rules. Because the Panel is reluctant to order a remand absent the suggestion of the transferee judge, the motion must include:

(i) An affidavit reciting whether the movant has requested a suggestion of remand and the judge's response, whether the parties have completed common discovery and other pretrial proceedings, and whether the parties have complied with all transferee court orders.

(ii) A copy of the transferee district court's final pretrial order, if entered.

(b) Filing Copy of Motion. Counsel shall file a copy of the motion to remand in the affected transferee district court.

(c) Notice of Appearance. Within 14 days of the issuance of a "Notice of Filing" of a motion to remand, each party or designated attorney shall file a Notice of Appearance in accordance with Rule 4.1(c).

(Amended July 6, 2011)

Rule 10.4. Transfer of Files on Remand

(a) Designating the Record. Upon receipt of an order to remand from the Clerk of the Panel, the parties shall furnish forthwith to the transferee district clerk a stipulation or designation of the contents of the record or part thereof to be remanded.

(b) Transfer of Files. Upon receipt of an order to remand from the Clerk of the Panel, the transferee district shall transmit to the clerk of the transferor district the following concerning each remanded action:

(i) a copy of the individual docket sheet for each action remanded;

(ii) a copy of the master docket sheet, if applicable;

(iii) the entire file for each action remanded, as originally received from the transferor district and augmented as set out in this Rule;

(iv) a copy of the final pretrial order, if applicable; and

(v) a "record on remand" as designated by the parties in accordance with 10.4(a).

Rule 11.1. Hearing Sessions and Oral Argument

(a) Schedule. The Panel shall schedule sessions for oral argument and consideration of other matters as desirable or necessary. The Chair shall determine the time, place and agenda for each hearing session. The Clerk of the Panel shall give appropriate notice to counsel for all parties. The Panel may continue its consideration of any scheduled matters.

(b) Oral Argument Statement. Any party affected by a motion may file a separate statement setting forth reasons why oral argument should, or need not, be heard. Such statements shall be captioned "Reasons Why Oral Argument Should [Need Not] Be Heard" and shall be limited to 2 pages.

(i) The parties affected by a motion to transfer may agree to waive oral argument. The Panel will take this into consideration in determining the need for oral argument.

(c) Hearing Session. The Panel shall not consider transfer or remand of any action pending in a federal district court when any party timely opposes such transfer or remand without first holding a hearing session for the presentation of oral argument. The Panel may dispense with oral argument if it determines that:

(i) the dispositive issue(s) have been authoritatively decided; or

(ii) the facts and legal arguments are adequately presented and oral argument would not significantly aid the decisional process.

Unless otherwise ordered, the Panel shall consider all other matters, such as a motion for reconsideration, upon the basis of the pleadings.

(d) Notification of Oral Argument. The Panel shall promptly notify counsel of those matters in which oral argument is scheduled, as well as those matters that the Panel will consider on the pleadings. The Clerk of the Panel shall require counsel to file and serve notice of their intent to either make or waive oral argument. Failure to do so shall be deemed a waiver of oral argument. If counsel does not attend oral argument, the matter shall not be rescheduled and that party's position shall be treated as submitted for decision on the basis of the pleadings filed.

(i) Absent Panel approval and for good cause shown, only those parties to actions who have filed a motion or written response to a motion or order shall be permitted to present oral argument.

(ii) The Panel will not receive oral testimony except upon notice, motion and an order expressly providing for it.

(e) Duty to Confer. Counsel in an action set for oral argument shall confer separately prior to that argument for the purpose of organizing their arguments and selecting representatives to present all views without duplication. Oral argument is a means for counsel to emphasize the key points of their arguments, and to update the Panel on any events since the conclusion of briefing.

(f) Time Limit for Oral Argument. Barring exceptional circumstances, the Panel shall allot a maximum of 20 minutes for oral argument in each matter. The time shall be divided among those with varying viewpoints. Counsel for the moving party or parties shall generally be heard first. [Reserved]

II. RULES FOR MULTICIRCUIT PETITIONS FOR REVIEW UNDER 28 U.S.C. § 2112(a)(3)

Rule 25.1 Definitions

The Panel promulgates these Rules pursuant to its authority under 28 U.S.C. § 2112(a)(3) to provide a means for the random selection of one circuit court of appeals to hear consolidated petitions for review of agency decisions.

An "Agency" means an agency, board, commission or officer of the United States government, that has received two or more petitions for review in a circuit court of appeals to enjoin, set aside, suspend, modify or otherwise review or enforce an action.

Rule 25.2. Filing of Notices

(a) Submitting Notice. An affected agency shall submit a notice of multicircuit petitions for review pursuant to 28 U.S.C. § 2112(a)(3) to the Clerk of the Panel by electronic means in the manner these Rules require and in accordance with the Panel's Administrative Policies and Procedures for Electronic Case Filing, except that the portion of Rule 3.2(d) requiring a courtesy copy is suspended in its entirety.

(b) Accompaniments to Notices. All notices of multicircuit petitions for review shall include:

(i) a copy of each involved petition for review as the petition for review is defined in 28 U.S.C. § 2112(a)(2);

(ii) a schedule giving

(A) the date of the relevant agency order;

(B) the case name of each petition for review involved;

(C) the circuit court of appeals in which each petition for review is pending;

(D) the appellate docket number of each petition for review;

(E) the date of filing by the court of appeals of each petition for review; and

(F) the date of receipt by the agency of each petition for review; and

(iii) proof of service (see Rule 25.3).

(c) Scope of Notice. All notices of multicircuit petitions for review shall embrace exclusively petitions for review filed in the courts of appeals within 10 days after issuance of an agency order and received by the affected agency from the petitioners within that 10-day period.

(d) Filing at the Panel. The Clerk of the Panel shall file the notice of multicircuit petitions for review and endorse thereon the date of filing.

(e) Filing with Each Circuit Clerk. The affected agency shall file copies of notices of multicircuit petitions for review with the clerk of each circuit court of appeals in which a petition for review is pending.

(Amended July 6, 2011)

Rule 25.3. Service of Notices

(a) Proof of Service. Notices of multicircuit petitions for review shall include proof of service on all other parties in the petitions for review included in the notice. Rule 25 of the Federal Rules of Appellate Procedure governs service and proof of service. The proof of service shall state the name, address and email address of each person served and shall indicate the party represented by each and the manner in which service was accomplished on each party. If a party is not represented by counsel, the proof of service shall indicate the name of the party and his or her last known address. The affected party shall submit proof of service for filing with the Clerk of the Panel and shall send copies thereof to each person included within the proof of service.

(b) Service on Clerk of Circuit. The proof of service pertaining to notices of multicircuit petitions for review shall certify the affected party has mailed or delivered copies of the notices to the clerk of each circuit court of appeals in which a petition for review is pending that is included in the notice. The Clerk shall file the notice with the circuit court.

Rule 25.4. Form of Notices; Place of Filing

(a) Unless otherwise provided here, Rule 3.2 governs the form of a notice of multicircuit petitions for review. Each notice shall bear the heading ["] Notice to the United States Judicial Panel on Multidistrict Litigation of Multicircuit Petitions for Review," followed by a brief caption identifying the involved agency, the relevant agency order, and the date of the order.

(b) Rule 3.2(b) and (c) govern the manner of filing a notice of multicircuit petitions for review.

Rule 25.5. Random Selection

(a) Selection Process. Upon filing a notice of multicircuit petitions for review, the Clerk of the Panel shall randomly select a circuit court of appeals from a drum containing an entry for each circuit wherein a constituent petition for review is pending. Multiple petitions for review pending in a single circuit shall be allotted only a single entry in the drum. A designated deputy other than the random selector shall witness the random selection. Thereafter, an order on behalf of the Panel shall be issued, signed by the random selector and the witness,

(i) consolidating the petitions for review in the court of appeals for the circuit that was randomly selected; and

(ii) designating that circuit as the one in which the record is to be filed pursuant to Rules 16 and 17 of the Federal Rules of Appellate Procedure.

(b) Effective Date. A consolidation of petitions for review shall be effective when the Clerk of the Panel enters the consolidation order.

Rule 25.6. Service of Panel Consolidation Order

(a) The Clerk of the Panel shall serve the Panel's consolidation order on the affected agency through the individual or individuals, as identified in Rule 25.2(a), who submitted the notice of multicircuit petitions for review on behalf of the agency.

(b) That individual or individuals, or anyone else designated by the agency, shall promptly serve the Panel's consolidation order on all other parties in all petitions for review included in the Panel's consolidation order, and shall promptly submit a proof of that service to the Clerk of the Panel. Rule 25.3 governs service.

(c) The Clerk of the Panel shall serve the Panel's consolidation order on the clerks of all circuit courts of appeals that were among the candidates for the Panel's random selection.

FEDERAL RULES OF CRIMINAL PROCEDURE

I. APPLICABILITY

Rule 1. Scope; Definitions

(a) Scope. (1) *In General.* These rules govern the procedure in all criminal proceedings in the United States district courts, the United States courts of appeals, and the Supreme Court of the United States.

(2) *State or Local Judicial Officer.* When a rule so states, it applies to a proceeding before a state or local judicial officer.

(3) *Territorial Courts.* These rules also govern the procedure in all criminal proceedings in the following courts:

(A) the district court of Guam;

(B) the district court for the Northern Mariana Islands, except as otherwise provided by law; and

(C) the district court of the Virgin Islands, except that the prosecution of offenses in that court must be by indictment or information as otherwise provided by law.

(4) *Removed Proceedings.* Although these rules govern all proceedings after removal from a state

court, state law governs a dismissal by the prosecution.

(5) *Excluded Proceedings.* Proceedings not governed by these rules include:

(A) the extradition and rendition of a fugitive;

(B) a civil property forfeiture for violating a federal statute;

(C) the collection of a fine or penalty;

(D) a proceeding under a statute governing juvenile delinquency to the extent the procedure is inconsistent with the statute, unless Rule 20(d) provides otherwise;

(E) a dispute between seamen under 22 U.S.C. §§ 256–258; and

(F) a proceeding against a witness in a foreign country under 28 U.S.C. § 1784.

(b) Definitions. The following definitions apply to these rules:

(1) "Attorney for the government" means:

(A) the Attorney General or an authorized assistant;

(B) a United States attorney or an authorized assistant;

(C) when applicable to cases arising under Guam law, the Guam Attorney General or other person whom Guam law authorizes to act in the matter; and

(D) any other attorney authorized by law to conduct proceedings under these rules as a prosecutor.

(2) "Court" means a federal judge performing functions authorized by law.

(3) "Federal judge" means:

(A) a justice or judge of the United States as these terms are defined in 28 U.S.C. § 451;

(B) a magistrate judge; and

(C) a judge confirmed by the United States Senate and empowered by statute in any commonwealth, territory, or possession to perform a function to which a particular rule relates.

(4) "Judge" means a federal judge or a state or local judicial officer.

(5) "Magistrate judge" means a United States magistrate judge as defined in 28 U.S.C. §§ 631–639.

(6) "Oath" includes an affirmation.

(7) "Organization" is defined in 18 U.S.C. § 18.

(8) "Petty offense" is defined in 18 U.S.C. § 19.

(9) "State" includes the District of Columbia, and any commonwealth, territory, or possession of the United States.

(10) "State or local judicial officer" means:

(A) a state or local officer authorized to act under 18 U.S.C. § 3041; and

(B) a judicial officer empowered by statute in the District of Columbia or in any commonwealth, territory, or possession to perform a function to which a particular rule relates.

(11) "Telephone" means any technology for transmitting live electronic voice communication.

(12) "Victim" means a "crime victim" as defined in 18 U.S.C. § 3771(e).

(c) Authority of a Justice or Judge of the United States. When these rules authorize a magistrate judge to act, any other federal judge may also act.

(Amended April 24, 1972, eff. Oct. 1, 1972; April 28, 1982, eff. Aug. 1, 1982; April 22, 1993, eff. Dec. 1, 1993; April 29, 2202, eff. Dec. 1, 2002; April 23, 2008, eff. Dec. 1, 2008; 26, 2011, eff. Dec. 1, 2011.)

Rule 2. Interpretation

These rules are to be interpreted to provide for the just determination of every criminal proceeding, to secure simplicity in procedure and fairness in administration, and to eliminate unjustifiable expense and delay.

(As amended April 29, 2002, eff. Dec. 1, 2002.)

II. PRELIMINARY PROCEEDINGS

Rule 3. The Complaint

The complaint is a written statement of the essential facts constituting the offense charged. Except as provided in Rule 4.1, it must be made under oath before a magistrate judge or, if none is reasonably available, before a state or local judicial officer.

(As amended April 24, 1972, eff. Oct. 1, 1972; April 22, 1993, eff. Dec. 1, 1993; April 29, 2002, eff. Dec. 1, 2002; April 26, 2011, eff. Dec. 1, 2011.)

Rule 4. Arrest Warrant or Summons on a Complaint

(a) Issuance. If the complaint or one or more affidavits filed with the complaint establish probable cause to believe that an offense has been committed and that the defendant committed it, the judge must issue an arrest warrant to an officer authorized to execute it. At the request of an attorney for the government, the judge must issue a summons, instead of a warrant, to a person authorized to serve it. A judge may issue more than one warrant or summons on the same complaint. If a defendant fails to appear in response to a summons, a judge may, and upon request of an attorney for the government must, issue a warrant.

(b) Form. (1) *Warrant.* A warrant must:

(A) contain the defendant's name or, if it is unknown, a name or description by which the defendant can be identified with reasonable certainty;

(B) describe the offense charged in the complaint;

(C) command that the defendant be arrested and brought without unnecessary delay before a magistrate judge or, if none is reasonably available, before a state or local judicial officer; and

(D) be signed by a judge.

(2) *Summons.* A summons must be in the same form as a warrant except that it must require the defendant to appear before a magistrate judge at a stated time and place.

(c) Execution or Service, and Return. (1) *By whom.* Only a marshal or other authorized officer may execute a warrant. Any person authorized to serve a summons in a federal civil action may serve a summons.

(2) *Location.* A warrant may be executed, or a summons served, within the jurisdiction of the United States or anywhere else a federal statute authorizes an arrest.

(3) *Manner.* (A) A warrant is executed by arresting the defendant. Upon arrest, an officer possessing the original or a duplicate original warrant must show it to the defendant. If the officer does not possess the warrant, the officer must inform the defendant of the warrant's existence and of the offense charged and, at the defendant's request, must show the original or a duplicate original warrant to the defendant as soon as possible.

(B) A summons is served on an individual defendant:

(i) by delivering a copy to the defendant personally; or

(ii) by leaving a copy at the defendant's residence or usual place of abode with a person of suitable age and discretion residing at that location and by mailing a copy to the defendant's last known address.

(C) A summons is served on an organization by delivering a copy to an officer, to a managing or general agent, or to another agent appointed or legally authorized to receive service of process. A copy must also be mailed to the organization's last known address within the district or to its principal place of business elsewhere in the United States.

(4) *Return.* (A) After executing a warrant, the officer must return it to the judge before whom the defendant is brought in accordance with Rule 5. The officer may do so by reliable electronic means. At the request of an attorney for the government, an unexecuted warrant must be brought back to and canceled by a magistrate judge or, if none is reasonably available, by a state or local judicial officer.

(B) The person to whom a summons was delivered for service must return it on or before the return day.

(C) At the request of an attorney for the government, a judge may deliver an unexecuted warrant, an unserved summons, or a copy of the warrant or summons to the marshal or other authorized person for execution or service.

(d) Warrant by Telephone or Other Reliable Electronic Means. In accordance with Rule 4.1, a magistrate judge may issue a warrant or summons based on information communicated by telephone or other reliable electronic means.

(Amended Feb. 28, 1966, eff. July 1, 1966; April 24, 1972, eff. Oct. 1, 1972; April 22, 1974, eff. Dec. 1, 1975; July 31, 1975, P. L. 94-64, §§ 3(1)–(3), 89 Stat. 370; March 9, 1987, eff. Aug. 1, 1987; April 22, 1993, eff. Dec. 1, 1993; April 29, 2002, eff. Dec. 1, 2002; April 26, 2011, eff. Dec. 1, 2011.)

Rule 4.1. Complaint, Warrant, or Summons by Telephone or Other Reliable Electronic Means

(a) In General. A magistrate judge may consider information communicated by telephone or other reliable electronic means when reviewing a complaint or deciding whether to issue a warrant or summons.

(b) Procedures. If a magistrate judge decides to proceed under this rule, the following procedures apply:

(1) *Taking Testimony Under Oath.* The judge must place under oath—and may examine—the applicant and any person on whose testimony the application is based.

(2) *Creating a Record of the Testimony and Exhibits.*

(A) Testimony Limited to Attestation. If the applicant does no more than attest to the contents of a written affidavit submitted by reliable electronic means, the judge must acknowledge the attestation in writing on the affidavit.

(B) Additional Testimony or Exhibits. If the judge considers additional testimony or exhibits, the judge must:

(i) have the testimony recorded verbatim by an electronic recording device, by a court reporter, or in writing;

(ii) have any recording or reporter's notes transcribed, have the transcription certified as accurate, and file it;

(iii) sign any other written record, certify its accuracy, and file it; and

(iv) make sure that the exhibits are filed.

(3) *Preparing a Proposed Duplicate Original of a Complaint, Warrant, or Summons.* The applicant must prepare a proposed duplicate original of a complaint, warrant, or summons, and must read or otherwise transmit its contents verbatim to the judge.

(4) *Preparing an Original Complaint, Warrant, or Summons.* If the applicant reads the contents of the proposed duplicate original, the judge must enter those contents into an original complaint, warrant, or summons. If the applicant transmits the contents by reliable electronic means, the transmission received by the judge may serve as the original.

(5) *Modification.* The judge may modify the complaint, warrant, or summons. The judge must then:

(A) transmit the modified version to the applicant by reliable electronic means; or

(B) file the modified original and direct the applicant to modify the proposed duplicate original accordingly.

(6) *Issuance.* To issue the warrant or summons, the judge must:

(A) sign the original documents;

(B) enter the date and time of issuance on the warrant or summons; and

(C) transmit the warrant or summons by reliable electronic means to the applicant or direct the applicant to sign the judge's name and enter the date and time on the duplicate original.

(c) Suppression Limited. Absent a finding of

bad faith, evidence obtained from a warrant issued under this rule is not subject to suppression on the ground that issuing the warrant in this manner was unreasonable under the circumstances.

(Added April 26, 2011, eff. Dec. 1, 2011.)

Rule 5. Initial Appearance

(a) In general. (1) *Appearance Upon an Arrest.* (A) A person making an arrest within the United States must take the defendant without unnecessary delay before a magistrate judge, or before a state or local judicial officer as Rule 5(c) provides, unless a statute provides otherwise.

(B) A person making an arrest outside the United States must take the defendant without unnecessary delay before a magistrate judge, unless a statute provides otherwise.

(2) *Exceptions.* (A) An officer making an arrest under a warrant issued upon a complaint charging solely a violation of 18 U.S.C. § 1073 need not comply with this rule if:

(i) the person arrested is transferred without unnecessary delay to the custody of appropriate state or local authorities in the district of arrest; and

(ii) an attorney for the government moves promptly, in the district where the warrant was issued, to dismiss the complaint.

(B) If a defendant is arrested for violating probation or supervised release, Rule 32.1 applies.

(C) If a defendant is arrested for failing to appear in another district, Rule 40 applies.

(3) *Appearance Upon a Summons.* When a defendant appears in response to a summons under Rule 4, a magistrate judge must proceed under Rule 5(d) or (e), as applicable.

(b) Arrest Without a Warrant. If a defendant is arrested without a warrant, a complaint meeting Rule 4(a)'s requirement of probable cause must be promptly filed in the district where the offense was allegedly committed.

(c) Place of Initial Appearance; Transfer to Another District. (1) *Arrest in the District Where the Offense Was Allegedly Committed.* If the defendant is arrested in the district where the offense was allegedly committed:

(A) the initial appearance must be in that district; and

(B) if a magistrate judge is not reasonably available, the initial appearance may be before a state or local judicial officer.

(2) *Arrest in a District Other Than Where the Offense Was Allegedly Committed.* If the defendant was arrested in a district other than where the offense was allegedly committed, the initial appearance must be:

(A) in the district of arrest; or

(B) in an adjacent district if:

(i) the appearance can occur more promptly there; or

(ii) the offense was allegedly committed there and the initial appearance will occur on the day of arrest.

(3) *Procedures in a District Other Than Where the Offense Was Allegedly Committed.* If the initial appearance occurs in a district other than where the offense was allegedly committed, the following procedures apply:

(A) the magistrate judge must inform the defendant about the provisions of Rule 20;

(B) if the defendant was arrested without a warrant, the district court where the offense was allegedly committed must first issue a warrant before the magistrate judge transfers the defendant to that district;

(C) the magistrate judge must conduct a preliminary hearing if required by Rule 5.1;

(D) the magistrate judge must transfer the defendant to the district where the offense was allegedly committed if:

(i) the government produces the warrant, a certified copy of the warrant, or a reliable electronic form of either; and

(ii) the judge finds that the defendant is the same person named in the indictment, information, or warrant; and

(E) when a defendant is transferred and discharged, the clerk must promptly transmit the papers and any bail to the clerk in the district where the offense was allegedly committed.

(4) *Procedure for Persons Extradited to the United States.* If the defendant is surrendered to the United States in accordance with a request for the defendant's extradition, the initial appearance must be in the district (or one of the districts) where the offense is charged.

(d) Procedure in a Felony Case. (1) *Advice.* If the defendant is charged with a felony, the judge must inform the defendant of the following:

(A) the complaint against the defendant, and any affidavit filed with it;

(B) the defendant's right to retain counsel or to request that counsel be appointed if the defendant cannot obtain counsel;

(C) the circumstances, if any, under which the defendant may secure pretrial release;

(D) any right to a preliminary hearing;

(E) the defendant's right not to make a statement, and that any statement made may be used against the defendant; and

(F) that a defendant who is not a United States citizen may request that an attorney for the government or a federal law enforcement official notify a consular officer from the defendant's country of nationality that the defendant has been arrested—but that even without the defendant's request, a treaty or other international agreement may require consular notification.

(2) *Consulting with Counsel.* The judge must allow the defendant reasonable opportunity to consult with counsel.

(3) *Detention or Release.* The judge must detain or release the defendant as provided by statute or these rules.

(4) *Plea.* A defendant may be asked to plead only under Rule 10.

(e) Procedure in a Misdemeanor Case. If the defendant is charged with a misdemeanor only, the judge must inform the defendant in accordance with Rule 58(b)(2).

(f) Video Teleconferencing. Video teleconferencing may be used to conduct an appearance under this rule if the defendant consents.

(Amended Feb. 28, 1966, eff. July 1, 1966; April 24, 1972, eff. Oct. 1, 1972; April 28, 1982, eff. Aug. 1, 1982; Oct. 12, 1984, P. L. 98-473, Title II, Ch I, § 209(a), 98 Stat. 1986; March 9, 1987, eff. Aug. 1, 1987; May 1, 1990, eff. Dec. 1, 1990; April 22, 1993, eff. Dec. 1, 1993; April 27, 1995, eff. Dec. 1, 1995; April 29, 2002, eff. Dec. 1, 2002; April 12, 2006, eff. Dec. 1, 2006; April 23, 2012, eff. Dec. 1, 2012; April 25, 2014, eff. Dec. 1, 2014.)

Rule 5.1. Preliminary Hearing

(a) In general. If a defendant is charged with an offense other than a petty offense, a magistrate judge must conduct a preliminary hearing unless:

(1) the defendant waives the hearing;

(2) the defendant is indicted;

(3) the government files an information under Rule 7(b) charging the defendant with a felony;

(4) the government files an information charging the defendant with a misdemeanor; or

(5) the defendant is charged with a misdemeanor and consents to trial before a magistrate judge.

(b) Selecting a District. A defendant arrested in a district other than where the offense was allegedly committed may elect to have the preliminary hearing conducted in the district where the prosecution is pending.

(c) Scheduling. The magistrate judge must hold the preliminary hearing within a reasonable time, but no later than 14 days after the initial appearance if the defendant is in custody and no later than 21 days if not in custody.

(d) Extending the Time. With the defendant's consent and upon a showing of good cause—taking into account the public interest in the prompt disposition of criminal cases—a magistrate judge may extend the time limits in Rule 5.1(c) one or more times. If the defendant does not consent, the magistrate judge may extend the time limits only on a showing that extraordinary circumstances exist and justice requires the delay.

(e) Hearing and Finding. At the preliminary hearing, the defendant may cross-examine adverse witnesses and may introduce evidence but may not object to evidence on the ground that it was unlawfully acquired. If the magistrate judge finds probable cause to believe an offense has been committed and the defendant committed it, the magistrate judge must promptly require the defendant to appear for further proceedings.

(f) Discharging the Defendant. If the magistrate judge finds no probable cause to believe an offense has been committed or the defendant committed it, the magistrate judge must dismiss the complaint and discharge the defendant. A discharge does not preclude the government from later prosecuting the defendant for the same offense.

(g) Recording the Proceedings. The preliminary hearing must be recorded by a court reporter or by a suitable recording device. A recording of the proceeding may be made available to any party upon request. A copy of the recording and a transcript may be provided to any party upon request and upon any payment required by applicable Judicial Conference regulations.

(h) Producing a Statement. (1) *In General.* Rule 26.2(a)–(d) and (f) applies at any hearing under this rule, unless the magistrate judge for good cause rules otherwise in a particular case.

(2) *Sanctions for Not Producing a Statement.* If a party disobeys a Rule 26.2 order to deliver a statement to the moving party, the magistrate judge must not consider the testimony of a witness whose statement is withheld.

(Added April 24, 1972, eff. Oct. 1, 1972; amended March 9, 1987, eff. Aug. 1, 1987; April 22, 1993, eff. Dec. 1, 1993; April 24, 1998, eff. Dec. 1, 1998; April 29, 2002, eff. Dec. 1, 2002; March 26, 2009, eff. Dec. 1, 2009.)

III. THE GRAND JURY, THE INDICTMENT, AND THE INFORMATION

Rule 6. The Grand Jury

(a) Summoning a Grand Jury. (1) *In General.* When the public interest so requires, the court must order that one or more grand juries be summoned. A grand jury must have 16 to 23 members, and the court must order that enough legally qualified persons be summoned to meet this requirement.

(2) *Alternate Jurors.* When a grand jury is selected, the court may also select alternate jurors. Alternate jurors must have the same qualifications and be selected in the same manner as any other juror. Alternate jurors replace jurors in the same sequence in which the alternates were selected. An alternate juror who replaces a juror is subject to the same challenges, takes the same oath, and has the same authority as the other jurors.

(b) Objection to the Grand Jury or to a Grand Juror. (1) *Challenges.* Either the government or a defendant may challenge the grand jury on the ground that it was not lawfully drawn, summoned, or selected, and may challenge an individual juror on the ground that the juror is not legally qualified.

(2) *Motion to Dismiss an Indictment.* A party may move to dismiss the indictment based on an objection to the grand jury or on an individual juror's lack of legal qualification, unless the court has previously ruled on the same objection under Rule 6(b)(1). The motion to dismiss is governed by 28 U.S.C. § 1867(e). The court must not dismiss the indict-

ment on the ground that a grand juror was not legally qualified if the record shows that at least 12 qualified jurors concurred in the indictment.

(c) Foreperson and Deputy Foreperson. The court will appoint one juror as the foreperson and another as the deputy foreperson. In the foreperson's absence, the deputy foreperson will act as the foreperson. The foreperson may administer oaths and affirmations and will sign all indictments. The foreperson—or another juror designated by the foreperson—will record the number of jurors concurring in every indictment and will file the record with the clerk, but the record may not be made public unless the court so orders.

(d) Who May Be Present. (1) *While the Grand Jury Is in Session.* The following persons may be present while the grand jury is in session: attorneys for the government, the witness being questioned, interpreters when needed, and a court reporter or an operator of a recording device.

(2) *During Deliberations and Voting.* No person other than the jurors, and any interpreter needed to assist a hearing-impaired or speech-impaired juror, may be present while the grand jury is deliberating or voting.

(e) Recording and Disclosing the Proceedings. (1) *Recording the Proceedings.* Except while the grand jury is deliberating or voting, all proceedings must be recorded by a court reporter or by a suitable recording device. But the validity of a prosecution is not affected by the unintentional failure to make a recording. Unless the court orders otherwise, an attorney for the government will retain control of the recording, the reporter's notes, and any transcript prepared from those notes.

(2) *Secrecy.* (A) No obligation of secrecy may be imposed on any person except in accordance with Rule 6(e)(2)(B).

(B) Unless these rules provide otherwise, the following persons must not disclose a matter occurring before the grand jury:

(i) a grand juror;

(ii) an interpreter;

(iii) a court reporter;

(iv) an operator of a recording device;

(v) a person who transcribes recorded testimony;

(vi) an attorney for the government; or

(vii) a person to whom disclosure is made under Rule 6(e)(3)(A)(ii) or (iii);

(3) *Exceptions.* (A) Disclosure of a grand-jury matter—other than the grand jury's deliberations or any grand juror's vote—may be made to:

(i) an attorney for the government for use in performing that attorney's duty;

(ii) any government personnel—including those of a state, state subdivision, Indian tribe, or foreign government—that an attorney for the government considers necessary to assist in performing that attorney's duty to enforce federal criminal law; or

(iii) a person authorized by 18 U.S.C. § 3322.

(B) A person to whom information is disclosed under Rule 6(e)(3)(A)(ii) may use that information only to assist an attorney for the government in performing that attorney's duty to enforce federal criminal law. An attorney for the government must promptly provide the court that impaneled the grand jury with the names of all persons to whom a disclosure has been made, and must certify that the attorney has advised those persons of their obligation of secrecy under this rule.

(C) An attorney for the government may disclose any grand-jury matter to another federal grand jury.

(D) An attorney for the government may disclose any grand-jury matter involving foreign intelligence, counterintelligence (as defined in 50 U.S.C. § 3003), or foreign intelligence information (as defined in Rule 6(e)(3)(D)(iii)) to any federal law enforcement, intelligence, protective, immigration, national defense, or national security official to assist the official receiving the information in the performance of that official's duties. An attorney for the government may also disclose any grand-jury matter involving, within the United States or elsewhere, a threat of attack or other grave hostile acts of a foreign power or its agent, a threat of domestic or international sabotage or terrorism, or clandestine intelligence gathering activities by an intelligence service or network of a foreign power or by its agent, to any appropriate federal, state, state subdivision, Indian tribal, or foreign government official, for the purpose of preventing or responding to such threat or activities.

(i) Any official who receives information under Rule 6(e)(3)(D) may use the information only as necessary in the conduct of that person's official duties subject to any limitations on the unauthorized disclosure of such information. Any state, state subdivision, Indian tribal, or foreign government official who receives information under Rule 6(e)(3)(D) may use the information only in a manner consistent with any guidelines issued by the Attorney General and the Director of National Intelligence.

(ii) Within a reasonable time after disclosure is made under Rule 6(e)(3)(D), an attorney for the government must file, under seal, a notice with the court in the district where the grand jury convened stating that such information was disclosed and the departments, agencies, or entities to which the disclosure was made.

(iii) As used in Rule 6(e)(3)(D), the term "foreign intelligence information" means:

(a) information, whether or not it concerns a United States person, that relates to the ability of the United States to protect against—

- actual or potential attack or other grave hostile acts of a foreign power or its agent;
- sabotage or international terrorism by a foreign power or its agent; or
- clandestine intelligence activities by an intelligence service or network of a foreign power or by its agent; or

(b) information, whether or not it concerns a United States person, with respect to a foreign power or foreign territory that relates to—

- the national defense or the security of the United States; or
- the conduct of the foreign affairs of the United States.

(E) The court may authorize disclosure—at a time, in a manner, and subject to any other conditions that it directs—of a grand-jury matter:

(i) preliminarily to or in connection with a judicial proceeding;

(ii) at the request of a defendant who shows that a ground may exist to dismiss the indictment because of a matter that occurred before the grand jury;

(iii) at the request of the government, when sought by a foreign court or prosecutor for use in an official criminal investigation;

(iv) at the request of the government if it shows that the matter may disclose a violation of State, Indian tribal, or foreign criminal law, as long as the disclosure is to an appropriate state, state subdivision, Indian tribal, or foreign government official for the purpose of enforcing that law; or

(v) at the request of the government if it shows that the matter may disclose a violation of military criminal law under the Uniform Code of Military Justice, as long as the disclosure is to an appropriate military official for the purpose of enforcing that law.

(F) A petition to disclose a grand-jury matter under Rule 6(e)(3)(E)(i) must be filed in the district where the grand jury convened. Unless the hearing is ex parte—as it may be when the government is the petitioner—the petitioner must serve the petition on, and the court must afford a reasonable opportunity to appear and be heard to:

(i) an attorney for the government;

(ii) the parties to the judicial proceeding; and

(iii) any other person whom the court may designate.

(G) If the petition to disclose arises out of a judicial proceeding in another district, the petitioned court must transfer the petition to the other court unless the petitioned court can reasonably determine whether disclosure is proper. If the petitioned court decides to transfer, it must send to the transferee court the material sought to be disclosed, if feasible, and a written evaluation of the need for continued grand jury secrecy. The transferee court must afford those persons identified in Rule 6(e)(3)(F) a reasonable opportunity to appear and be heard.

(4) *Sealed Indictment*. The magistrate judge to whom an indictment is returned may direct that the indictment be kept secret until the defendant is in custody or has been released pending trial. The clerk must then seal the indictment, and no person may disclose the indictment's existence except as necessary to issue or execute a warrant or summons.

(5) *Closed Hearing*. Subject to any right to an open hearing in a contempt proceeding, the court must close any hearing to the extent necessary to prevent disclosure of a matter occurring before a grand jury.

(6) *Sealed Records*. Records, orders, and subpoenas relating to grand-jury proceedings must be kept under seal to the extent and as long as necessary to prevent the unauthorized disclosure of a matter occurring before a grand jury.

(7) *Contempt*. A knowing violation of Rule 6, or of any guidelines jointly issued by the Attorney General and the Director of National Intelligence under Rule 6, may be punished as a contempt of court.

(f) Indictment and Return. A grand jury may indict only if at least 12 jurors concur. The grand jury—or its foreperson or deputy foreperson—must return the indictment to a magistrate judge in open court. To avoid unnecessary cost or delay, the magistrate judge may take the return by video teleconference from the court where the grand jury sits. If a complaint or information is pending against the defendant and 12 jurors do not concur in the indictment, the foreperson must promptly and in writing report the lack of concurrence to the magistrate judge.

(g) Discharging the Grand Jury. A grand jury must serve until the court discharges it, but it may serve more than 18 months only if the court, having determined that an extension is in the public interest, extends the grand jury's service. An extension may be granted for no more than 6 months, except as otherwise provided by statute.

(h) Excusing a Juror. At any time, for good cause, the court may excuse a juror either temporarily or permanently, and if permanently, the court may impanel an alternate juror in place of the excused juror.

(i) "Indian Tribe" Defined. "Indian tribe" means an Indian tribe recognized by the Secretary of the Interior on a list published in the Federal Register under 25 U.S.C. § 479a-1.

(Amended Feb. 28, 1966, eff. July 1, 1966; April 24, 1972, eff. Oct. 1, 1972; April 26 and July 8, 1976, eff. Aug. 1, 1976; July 30, 1977, P. L. 95-78, § 2(a), 91 Stat. 319; April 30, 1979, eff. Aug. 1, 1979; April 28, 1983, eff. Aug. 1, 1983; Oct. 12, 1984, P. L. 98-473, Title II, § 215(f), 98 Stat. 2016; April 29, 1985, eff. Aug. 1, 1985; March 9, 1987, eff. Aug. 1, 1987; April 22, 1993, eff. Dec. 1, 1993; April 26, 1999, eff. Dec. 1, 1999; Oct. 26, 2001, P. L. 107-56, Title II, § 203(a), 115 Stat. 278; April 29, 2002, eff. Dec. 1, 2002; Nov. 25, 2002, P. L. 107-296, Title VIII, Subtitle I, § 895, 116 Stat. 2256; Dec. 17, 2004, P. L. 108-458, Title VI, Subtitle F, § 6501(a), 118 Stat. 3760; April 12, 2006, eff. Dec. 1, 2006; April 26, 2011, eff. Dec. 1, 2011; April 25, 2014, eff. Dec. 1, 2014.)

Rule 7. The Indictment and the Information

(a) When Used. (1) *Felony.* An offense (other than criminal contempt) must be prosecuted by an indictment if it is punishable:

(A) by death; or

(B) by imprisonment for more than one year.

(2) *Misdemeanor.* An offense punishable by imprisonment for one year or less may be prosecuted in accordance with Rule 58(b)(1).

(b) Waiving Indictment. An offense punishable by imprisonment for more than one year may be prosecuted by information if the defendant—in open court and after being advised of the nature of the charge and of the defendant's rights—waives prosecution by indictment.

(c) Nature and Contents. (1) *In General.* The indictment or information must be a plain, concise, and definite written statement of the essential facts constituting the offense charged and must be signed by an attorney for the government. It need not contain a formal introduction or conclusion. A count may incorporate by reference an allegation made in another count. A count may allege that the means by which the defendant committed the offense are unknown or that the defendant committed it by one or more specified means. For each count, the indictment or information must give the official or customary citation of the statute, rule, regulation, or other provision of law that the defendant is alleged to have violated. For purposes of an indictment referred to in section 3282 of title 18, United States Code, for which the identity of the defendant is unknown, it shall be sufficient for the indictment to describe the defendant as an individual whose name is unknown, but who has a particular DNA profile, as that term is defined in that section 3282.

(2) *Citation Error.* Unless the defendant was misled and thereby prejudiced, neither an error in a citation nor a citation's omission is a ground to dismiss the indictment or information or to reverse a conviction.

(d) Surplusage. Upon the defendant's motion, the court may strike surplusage from the indictment or information.

(e) Amending an Information. Unless an additional or different offense is charged or a substantial right of the defendant is prejudiced, the court may permit an information to be amended at any time before the verdict or finding.

(f) Bill of Particulars. The court may direct the government to file a bill of particulars. The defendant may move for a bill of particulars before or within 14 days after arraignment or at a later time if the court permits. The government may amend a bill of particulars subject to such conditions as justice requires.

(Amended Feb. 28, 1966, eff. July 1, 1966; April 24, 1972, eff. Oct. 1, 1972; April 30, 1979, eff. Aug. 1, 1979; March 9, 1987, eff. Aug. 1, 1987; April 17, 2000, eff. Dec. 1, 2000; April 29, 2002, eff. Dec. 1, 2002; April 30, 2003, P. L. 108-21, Title VI, § 610(b), 117 Stat. 692; March 26, 2009, eff. Dec. 1, 2009.)

Rule 8. Joinder of Offenses or Defendants

(a) Joinder of Offenses. The indictment or information may charge a defendant in separate counts with 2 or more offenses if the offenses charged—whether felonies or misdemeanors or both—are of the same or similar character, or are based on the same act or transaction, or are connected with or constitute parts of a common scheme or plan.

(b) Joinder of Defendants. The indictment or information may charge 2 or more defendants if they are alleged to have participated in the same act or transaction, or in the same series of acts or transactions, constituting an offense or offenses. The defendants may be charged in one or more counts together or separately. All defendants need not be charged in each count.

(As amended April 29, 2002, eff. Dec. 1, 2002.)

Rule 9. Arrest Warrant or Summons on an Indictment or Information

(a) Issuance. The court must issue a warrant—or at the government's request, a summons—for each defendant named in an indictment or named in an information if one or more affidavits accompanying the information establish probable cause to believe that an offense has been committed and that the defendant committed it. The court may issue more than one warrant or summons for the same defendant. If a defendant fails to appear in response to a summons, the court may, and upon request of an attorney for the government must, issue a warrant. The court must issue the arrest warrant to an officer authorized to execute it or the summons to a person authorized to serve it.

(b) Form. (1) *Warrant.* The warrant must conform to Rule 4(b)(1) except that it must be signed by the clerk and must describe the offense charged in the indictment or information.

(2) *Summons.* The summons must be in the same form as a warrant except that it must require the defendant to appear before the court at a stated time and place.

(c) Execution or Service; Return; Initial Appearance. (1) *Execution or Service.* (A) The warrant must be executed or the summons served as provided in Rule 4(c)(1), (2), and (3).

(B) The officer executing the warrant must proceed in accordance with Rule 5(a)(1).

(2) *Return.* A warrant or summons must be returned in accordance with Rule 4(c)(4).

(3) *Initial Appearance.* When an arrested or summoned defendant first appears before the court, the judge must proceed under Rule 5.

(d) Warrant by Telephone or Other Means. In accordance with Rule 4.1, a magistrate judge may issue an arrest warrant or summons based on information communicated by telephone or other reliable electronic means.

(Amended April 24, 1972, eff. Oct. 1, 1972; April 22, 1974, eff. Dec. 1, 1975; July 31, 1975, P. L. 94-64, § 3(4), 89 Stat. 370; Dec. 12, 1975, P. L. 94-149, § 5, 89 Stat. 806; April 30, 1979, eff. Aug. 1, 1979; April 28, 1982, eff. Aug. 1, 1982; April 22, 1993, eff. Dec. 1, 1993; April 29, 2002, eff. Dec. 1, 2002; April 26, 2011, eff. Dec. 1, 2011.)

IV. ARRAIGNMENT AND PREPARATION FOR TRIAL

Rule 10. Arraignment

(a) In General. An arraignment must be conducted in open court and must consist of:

(1) ensuring that the defendant has a copy of the indictment or information;

(2) reading the indictment or information to the defendant or stating to the defendant the substance of the charge; and then

(3) asking the defendant to plead to the indictment or information.

(b) Waiving Appearance. A defendant need not be present for the arraignment if:

(1) the defendant has been charged by indictment or misdemeanor information;

(2) the defendant, in a written waiver signed by both the defendant and defense counsel, has waived appearance and has affirmed that the defendant received a copy of the indictment or information and that the plea is not guilty; and

(3) the court accepts the waiver.

(c) Video Teleconferencing. Video teleconferencing may be used to arraign a defendant if the defendant consents.

(Amended March 9, 1987, eff. Aug. 1, 1987; April 29, 2002, eff. Dec. 1, 2002.)

Rule 11. Pleas

(a) Entering a Plea. (1) *In general.* A defendant may plead not guilty, guilty, or (with the court's consent) nolo contendere.

(2) *Conditional Plea.* With the consent of the court and the government, a defendant may enter a conditional plea of guilty or nolo contendere, reserving in writing the right to have an appellate court review an adverse determination of a specified pretrial motion. A defendant who prevails on appeal may then withdraw the plea.

(3) *Nolo Contendere Plea.* Before accepting a plea of nolo contendere, the court must consider the parties' views and the public interest in the effective administration of justice.

(4) *Failure to Enter a Plea.* If a defendant refuses to enter a plea or if a defendant organization fails to appear, the court must enter a plea of not guilty.

(b) Considering and Accepting a Guilty or Nolo Contendere Plea. (1) *Advising and Questioning the Defendant.* Before the court accepts a plea of guilty or nolo contendere, the defendant may be placed under oath, and the court must address the defendant personally in open court. During this address, the court must inform the defendant of, and determine that the defendant understands, the following:

(A) the government's right, in a prosecution for perjury or false statement, to use against the defendant any statement that the defendant gives under oath;

(B) the right to plead not guilty, or having already so pleaded, to persist in that plea;

(C) the right to a jury trial;

(D) the right to be represented by counsel—and if necessary have the court appoint counsel—at trial and at every other stage of the proceeding;

(E) the right at trial to confront and cross-examine adverse witnesses, to be protected from compelled self-incrimination, to testify and present evidence, and to compel the attendance of witnesses;

(F) the defendant's waiver of these trial rights if the court accepts a plea of guilty or nolo contendere;

(G) the nature of each charge to which the defendant is pleading;

(H) any maximum possible penalty, including imprisonment, fine, and term of supervised release;

(I) any mandatory minimum penalty;

(J) any applicable forfeiture;

(K) the court's authority to order restitution;

(L) the court's obligation to impose a special assessment;

(M) in determining a sentence, the court's obligation to calculate the applicable sentencing-guideline range and to consider that range, possible departures under the Sentencing Guidelines, and other sentencing factors under 18 U.S.C. § 3553(a); and

(N) the terms of any plea-agreement provision waiving the right to appeal or to collaterally attack the sentence; and

(O) that, if convicted, a defendant who is not a United States citizen may be removed from the United States, denied citizenship, and denied admission to the United States in the future.

(2) *Ensuring That a Plea Is Voluntary.* Before accepting a plea of guilty or nolo contendere, the court must address the defendant personally in open court and determine that the plea is voluntary and did not result from force, threats, or promises (other than promises in a plea agreement).

(3) *Determining the Factual Basis for a Plea.* Before entering judgment on a guilty plea, the court must determine that there is a factual basis for the plea.

(c) Plea Agreement Procedure. (1) *In General.* An attorney for the government and the defendant's attorney, or the defendant when proceeding pro se, may discuss and reach a plea agreement. The court must not participate in these discussions. If the defendant pleads guilty or nolo contendere to either a charged offense or a lesser or related offense, the plea agreement may specify that an attorney for the government will:

(A) not bring, or will move to dismiss, other charges;

(B) recommend, or agree not to oppose the defendant's request, that a particular sentence or sentencing range is appropriate or that a particular provision of the Sentencing Guidelines, or policy statement, or sentencing factor does or does not apply (such a recommendation or request does not bind the court); or

(C) agree that a specific sentence or sentencing range is the appropriate disposition of the case, or that a particular provision of the Sentencing Guidelines, or policy statement, or sentencing factor does or does not apply (such a recommendation or request binds the court once the court accepts the plea agreement).

(2) *Disclosing a Plea Agreement.* The parties must disclose the plea agreement in open court when the plea is offered, unless the court for good cause allows the parties to disclose the plea agreement in camera.

(3) *Judicial Consideration of a Plea Agreement.* (A) To the extent the plea agreement is of the type specified in Rule 11(c)(1)(A) or (C), the court may accept the agreement, reject it, or defer a decision until the court has reviewed the presentence report.

(B) To the extent the plea agreement is of the type specified in Rule 11(c)(1)(B), the court must advise the defendant that the defendant has no right to withdraw the plea if the court does not follow the recommendation or request.

(4) *Accepting a Plea Agreement.* If the court accepts the plea agreement, it must inform the defendant that to the extent the plea agreement is of the type specified in Rule 11(c)(1)(A) or (C), the agreed disposition will be included in the judgment.

(5) *Rejecting a Plea Agreement.* If the court rejects a plea agreement containing provisions of the type specified in Rule 11(c)(1)(A) or (C), the court must do the following on the record and in open court (or, for good cause, in camera):

(A) inform the parties that the court rejects the plea agreement;

(B) advise the defendant personally that the court is not required to follow the plea agreement and give the defendant an opportunity to withdraw the plea; and

(C) advise the defendant personally that if the plea is not withdrawn, the court may dispose of the case less favorably toward the defendant than the plea agreement contemplated.

(d) Withdrawing a Guilty or Nolo Contendere Plea. A defendant may withdraw a plea of guilty or nolo contendere:

(1) before the court accepts the plea, for any reason or no reason; or

(2) after the court accepts the plea, but before it imposes sentence if:

(A) the court rejects a plea agreement under Rule 11(c)(5); or

(B) the defendant can show a fair and just reason for requesting the withdrawal.

(e) Finality of a Guilty or Nolo Contendere Plea. After the court imposes sentence, the defendant may not withdraw a plea of guilty or nolo contendere, and the plea may be set aside only on direct appeal or collateral attack.

(f) Admissibility or Inadmissibility of a Plea, Plea Discussions, and Related Statements. The admissibility or inadmissibility of a plea, a plea discussion, and any related statement is governed by Federal Rule of Evidence 410.

(g) Recording the Proceedings. The proceedings during which the defendant enters a plea must be recorded by a court reporter or by a suitable recording device. If there is a guilty plea or a nolo contendere plea, the record must include the inquiries and advice to the defendant required under Rule 11(b) and (c).

(h) Harmless Error. A variance from the requirements of this rule is harmless error if it does not affect substantial rights.

(Amended Feb. 28, 1966, eff. July 1, 1966; April 22, 1974, eff. Dec. 1, 1975; P. L. 94-64, §§ 2, 3(5)–(10), 89 Stat. 371, 372; April 30, 1979, eff. Aug. 1, 1979, and Dec. 1, 1980; April 28, 1982, eff. Aug. 1, 1982; April 28, 1983, eff. Aug. 1, 1983; April 29, 1985, eff. Aug. 1, 1985; March 9, 1987, eff. Aug. 1, 1987; Nov. 18, 1988, P. L. 100-690, Title VII, Subtitle B, § 7076, 102 Stat. 4406; April 25, 1989, eff. Dec. 1, 1989; April 26, 1999, eff. Dec. 1, 1999; April 29, 2002, eff. Dec. 1, 2002; April 30, 2007, eff. Dec. 1, 2007; April 16, 2013, eff. Dec. 1, 2013.)

Rule 12. Pleadings and Pretrial Motions

(a) Pleadings. The pleadings in a criminal proceeding are the indictment, the information, and the pleas of not guilty, guilty, and nolo contendere.

(b) Pretrial motions.

(1) *In general.* A party may raise by pretrial motion any defense, objection, or request that the court can determine without a trial on the merits. Rule 47 applies to a pretrial motion.

(2) *Motions that may be made at any time.* A motion that the court lacks jurisdiction may be made at any time while the case is pending.

(3) *Motions that must be made before trial.* The following defenses, objections, and requests must be raised by pretrial motion if the basis for the motion is then reasonably available and the motion can be determined without a trial on the merits:

(A) a defect in instituting the prosecution, including:

(i) improper venue;

(ii) preindictment delay;

(iii) a violation of the constitutional right to a speedy trial;

(iv) selective or vindictive prosecution; and

(v) an error in the grand-jury proceeding or preliminary hearing;

(B) a defect in the indictment or information, including:

(i) joining two or more offenses in the same count (duplicity);

(ii) charging the same offense in more than one count (multiplicity);

(iii) lack of specificity;

(iv) improper joinder; and

(v) failure to state an offense;

(C) suppression of evidence;

(D) severance of charges or defendants under Rule

14; and

(E) discovery under Rule 16. (4) Notice of the government's intent to use evidence.

(A) At the government's discretion. At the arraignment or as soon afterward as practicable, the government may notify the defendant of its intent to use specified evidence at trial in order to afford the defendant an opportunity to object before trial under Rule 12(b)(3)(C).

(B) At the defendant's request. At the arraignment or as soon afterward as practicable, the defendant may, in order to have an opportunity to move to suppress evidence under Rule 12(b)(3)(C), request notice of the government's intent to use (in its evidence-in-chief at trial) any evidence that the defendant may be entitled to discover under Rule 16.

(c) Deadline for a pretrial motion; consequences of not making a timely motion.

(1) *Setting the deadline.* The court may, at the arraignment or as soon afterward as practicable, set a deadline for the parties to make pretrial motions and may also schedule a motion hearing. If the court does not set one, the deadline is the start of trial.

(2) *Extending or resetting the deadline.* At any time before trial, the court may extend or reset the deadline for pretrial motions.

(3) *Consequences of not making a timely motion under Rule 12(b)(3).* If a party does not meet the deadline for making a Rule 12(b)(3) motion, the motion is untimely. But a court may consider the defense, objection, or request if the party shows good cause.

(d) Ruling on a motion. The court must decide every pretrial motion before trial unless it finds good cause to defer a ruling. The court must not defer ruling on a pretrial motion if the deferral will adversely affect a party's right to appeal. When factual issues are involved in deciding a motion, the court must state its essential findings on the record.

(e) [Reserved]

(f) Recording the Proceedings. All proceedings at a motion hearing, including any findings of fact and conclusions of law made orally by the court, must be recorded by a court reporter or a suitable recording device.

(g) Defendant's Continued Custody or Release Status. If the court grants a motion to dismiss based on a defect in instituting the prosecution, in the indictment, or in the information, it may order the defendant to be released or detained under 18 U.S.C. § 3142 for a specified time until a new indictment or information is filed. This rule does not affect any federal statutory period of limitations.

(h) Producing Statements at a Suppression Hearing. Rule 26.2 applies at a suppression hearing under Rule 12(b)(3)(C). At a suppression hearing, a law enforcement officer is considered a government witness.

(Amended April 22, 1974, eff. Dec. 1, 1975; July 31, 1975, P. L. 94-64, § 3(11), (12), 89 Stat. 372; April 28, 1983, eff. Aug. 1, 1983; March 9, 1987, eff. Aug. 1, 1987; April 22, 1993, eff. Dec. 1, 1993; April 29, 2002, eff. Dec. 1, 2002; April 25, 2014, eff. Dec. 1, 2014.)

Rule 12.1. Notice of an Alibi Defense

(a) Government's Request for Notice and Defendant's Response. (1) *Government's Request.* An attorney for the government may request in writing that the defendant notify an attorney for the government of any intended alibi defense. The request must state the time, date, and place of the alleged offense.

(2) *Defendant's Response.* Within 14 days after the request, or at some other time the court sets, the defendant must serve written notice on an attorney for the government of any intended alibi defense. The defendant's notice must state:

(A) each specific place where the defendant claims to have been at the time of the alleged offense; and

(B) the name, address, and telephone number of each alibi witness on whom the defendant intends to rely.

(b) Disclosing Government Witnesses. (1) *Disclosure.* (A) *In General.* If the defendant serves a Rule 12.1(a)(2) notice, an attorney for the government must disclose in writing to the defendant or the defendant's attorney:

(i) the name of each witness — and the address and telephone number of each witness other than a victim — that the government intends to rely on to establish that the defendant was present at the scene of the alleged offense; and

(ii) each government rebuttal witness to the defendant's alibi defense.

(B) *Victim's Address and Telephone Number.* If the government intends to rely on a victim's testimony to establish that the defendant was present at the scene of the alleged offense and the defendant establishes a need for the victim's address and telephone number, the court may:

(i) order the government to provide the information in writing to the defendant or the defendant's attorney; or

(ii) fashion a reasonable procedure that allows preparation of the defense and also protects the victim's interests.

(2) *Time to Disclose.* Unless the court directs otherwise, an attorney for the government must give its Rule 12.1(b)(1) disclosure within 14 days after the defendant serves notice of an intended alibi defense under Rule 12.1(a)(2), but no later than 14 days before trial.

(c) Continuing Duty to Disclose. (1) *In General.* Both an attorney for the government and the defendant must promptly disclose in writing to the other party the name of each additional witness — and the address and telephone number of each additional witness other than a victim — if:

(A) the disclosing party learns of the witness before or during trial; and

(B) the witness should have been disclosed under Rule 12.1(a) or (b) if the disclosing party had known of the witness earlier.

(2) *Address and Telephone Number of an Additional Victim Witness.* The address and telephone number of an additional victim witness must not be disclosed except as provided in Rule 12.1 (b)(1)(B).

(d) Exceptions. For good cause, the court may grant an exception to any requirement of Rule 12.1(a)–(c).

(e) Failure to Comply. If a party fails to comply with this rule, the court may exclude the testimony of any undisclosed witness regarding the defendant's alibi. This rule does not limit the defendant's right to testify.

(f) Inadmissibility of Withdrawn Intention. Evidence of an intention to rely on an alibi defense, later withdrawn, or of a statement made in connection with that intention, is not, in any civil or criminal proceeding, admissible against the person who gave notice of the intention.

(Added April 22, 1974, eff. Dec. 1, 1975; amended July 31, 1975, P. L. 94-64, § 3(13), 89 Stat. 372; April 29, 1985, eff. Aug. 1, 1985; March 9, 1987, eff. Aug. 1, 1987; April 29, 2002, eff. Dec. 1, 2002; April 23, 2008, eff. Dec. 1, 2008; March 26, 2009, eff. Dec. 1, 2009.)

Rule 12.2. Notice of an Insanity Defense; Mental Examination

(a) Notice of an Insanity Defense. A defendant who intends to assert a defense of insanity at the time of the alleged offense must so notify an attorney for the government in writing within the time provided for filing a pretrial motion, or at any later time the court sets, and file a copy of the notice with the clerk. A defendant who fails to do so cannot rely on an insanity defense. The court may, for good cause, allow the defendant to file the notice late, grant additional trial-preparation time, or make other appropriate orders.

(b) Notice of Expert Evidence of a Mental Condition. If a defendant intends to introduce expert evidence relating to a mental disease or defect or any other mental condition of the defendant bearing on either (1) the issue of guilt or (2) the issue of punishment in a capital case, the defendant must—within the time provided for filing a pretrial motion or at any later time the court sets—notify an attorney for the government in writing of this intention and file a copy of the notice with the clerk. The court may, for good cause, allow the defendant to file the notice late, grant the parties additional trial-preparation time, or make other appropriate orders.

(c) Mental Examination. (1) *Authority to Order an Examination; Procedures.* (A) The court may order the defendant to submit to a competency examination under 18 U.S.C. § 4241.

(B) If the defendant provides notice under Rule 12.2(a), the court must, upon the government's motion, order the defendant to be examined under 18 U.S.C. § 4242. If the defendant provides notice under Rule 12.2(b) the court may, upon the government's motion, order the defendant to be examined under procedures ordered by the court.

(2) *Disclosing Results and Reports of Capital Sentencing Examination.* The results and reports of any examination conducted solely under Rule 12.2(c)(1) after notice under Rule 12.2(b)(2) must be sealed and must not be disclosed to any attorney for the government or the defendant unless the defendant is found guilty of one or more capital crimes and the defendant confirms an intent to offer during sentencing proceedings expert evidence on mental condition.

(3) *Disclosing Results and Reports of the Defendant's Expert Examination.* After disclosure under Rule 12.2(c)(2) of the results and reports of the government's examination, the defendant must disclose to the government the results and reports of any examination on mental condition conducted by the defendant's expert about which the defendant intends to introduce expert evidence.

(4) *Inadmissibility of a Defendant's Statements.* No statement made by a defendant in the course of any examination conducted under this rule (whether conducted with or without the defendant's consent), no testimony by the expert based on the statement, and no other fruits of the statement may be admitted into evidence against the defendant in any criminal proceeding except on an issue regarding mental condition on which the defendant:

(A) has introduced evidence of incompetency or evidence requiring notice under Rule 12.2(a) or (b)(1), or

(B) has introduced expert evidence in a capital sentencing proceeding requiring notice under Rule 12.2(b)(2).

(d) Failure to Comply. (1) *Failure to Give Notice or to Submit to Examination.* The court may exclude any expert evidence from the defendant on the issue of the defendant's mental disease, mental defect, or any other mental condition bearing on the defendant's guilt or the issue of punishment in a capital case if the defendant fails to:

(A) give notice under Rule 12.2(b); or

(B) submit to an examination when ordered under Rule 12.2(c).

(2) *Failure to Disclose.* The court may exclude any expert evidence for which the defendant has failed to comply with the disclosure requirement of Rule 12.2(c)(3).

(e) Inadmissibility of Withdrawn Intention. Evidence of an intention as to which notice was given under Rule 12.2(a) or (b), later withdrawn, is not, in any civil or criminal proceeding, admissible against the person who gave notice of the intention.

(Added April 22, 1974, eff. Dec. 1, 1975; amended July 31, 1975, P. L. 94-64, § 3(14), 89 Stat. 370, 373; April 28, 1983, eff. Aug. 1, 1983; Oct. 12, 1984, P. L. 98-473, Title II, Ch IV, § 404, 98 Stat. 2067; Oct. 30, 1984, P. L. 98-596, § 11(a), (b), 98 Stat. 3138; Aug. 1, 1985; Nov. 10, 1986, P. L. 99-646, § 24, 100 Stat. 3597; March 9, 1987, eff. Aug. 1, 1987; April 29, 2002, eff. Dec. 1, 2002; April 25, 2005, eff. Dec. 1,

2005.)

Rule 12.3. Notice of a Public-Authority Defense

(a) Notice of the Defense and Disclosure of Witnesses. (1) *Notice in General.* If a defendant intends to assert a defense of actual or believed exercise of public authority on behalf of a law enforcement agency or federal intelligence agency at the time of the alleged offense, the defendant must so notify an attorney for the government in writing and must file a copy of the notice with the clerk within the time provided for filing a pretrial motion, or at any later time the court sets. The notice filed with the clerk must be under seal if the notice identifies a federal intelligence agency as the source of public authority.

(2) *Contents of Notice.* The notice must contain the following information:

(A) the law enforcement agency or federal intelligence agency involved;

(B) the agency member on whose behalf the defendant claims to have acted; and

(C) the time during which the defendant claims to have acted with public authority.

(3) *Response to the Notice.* An attorney for the government must serve a written response on the defendant or the defendant's attorney within 14 days after receiving the defendant's notice, but no later than 21 days before trial. The response must admit or deny that the defendant exercised the public authority identified in the defendant's notice.

(4) *Disclosing Witnesses.* (A) *Government's Request.* An attorney for the government may request in writing that the defendant disclose the name, address, and telephone number of each witness the defendant intends to rely on to establish a public-authority defense. An attorney for the government may serve the request when the government serves its response to the defendant's notice under Rule 12.3(a)(3), or later, but must serve the request no later than 21 days before trial.

(B) *Defendant's Response.* Within 14 days after receiving the government's request, the defendant must serve on an attorney for the government a written statement of the name, address, and telephone number of each witness.

(C) *Government's Reply.* Within 14 days after receiving the defendant's statement, an attorney for the government must serve on the defendant or the defendant's attorney a written statement of the name of each witness — and the address and telephone number of each witness other than a victim — that the government intends to rely on to oppose the defendant's public-authority defense.

(D) *Victim's Address and Telephone Number.* If the government intends to rely on a victim's testimony to oppose the defendant's public-authority defense and the defendant establishes a need for the victim's address and telephone number, the court may:

(i) order the government to provide the information in writing to the defendant or the defendant's attorney; or

(ii) fashion a reasonable procedure that allows for preparing the defense and also protects the victim's interests.

(5) *Additional Time.* The court may, for good cause, allow a party additional time to comply with this rule.

(b) Continuing Duty to Disclose. (1) *In General.* Both an attorney for the government and the defendant must promptly disclose in writing to the other party the name of any additional witness — and the address, and telephone number of any additional witness other than a victim — if:

(A) the disclosing party learns of the witness before or during trial; and

(B) the witness should have been disclosed under Rule 12.3(a)(4) if the disclosing party had known of the witness earlier.

(2) *Address and Telephone Number of an Additional Victim-Witness.* The address and telephone number of an additional victim-witness must not be disclosed except as provided in Rule 12.3(a)(4)(D).

(c) Failure to Comply. If a party fails to comply with this rule, the court may exclude the testimony of any undisclosed witness regarding the public-authority defense. This rule does not limit the defendant's right to testify.

(d) Protective Procedures Unaffected. This rule does not limit the court's authority to issue appropriate protective orders or to order that any filings be under seal.

(e) Inadmissibility of Withdrawn Intention. Evidence of an intention as to which notice was given under Rule 12.3(a), later withdrawn, is not, in any civil or criminal proceeding, admissible against the person who gave notice of the intention.

(Added Nov. 18, 1988, P. L. 100-690, Title VI, Subtitle N, § 6483, 102 Stat. 4382; amended April 29, 2002, eff. Dec. 1, 2002; March 26, 2009, eff. Dec. 1, 2009; April 28, 2010, eff. Dec. 1, 2010.)

Rule 12.4. Disclosure Statement

(a) Who Must File. (1) *Nongovernmental Corporate Party.* Any nongovernmental corporate party to a proceeding in a district court must file a statement that identifies any parent corporation and any publicly held corporation that owns 10% or more of its stock or states that there is no such corporation.

(2) *Organizational Victim.* If an organization is a victim of the alleged criminal activity, the government must file a statement identifying the victim. If the organizational victim is a corporation, the statement must also disclose the information required by Rule 12.4(a)(1) to the extent it can be obtained through due diligence.

(b) Time for Filing; Supplemental Filing. A party must:

(1) file the Rule 12.4(a) statement upon the defendant's initial appearance; and

(2) promptly file a supplemental statement upon

any change in the information that the statement requires.

(Added April 29, 2002, eff. Dec. 1, 2002.)

Rule 13. Joint Trial of Separate Cases

The court may order that separate cases be tried together as though brought in a single indictment or information if all offenses and all defendants could have been joined in a single indictment or information.

(As amended April 29, 2002, eff. Dec. 1, 2002.)

Rule 14. Relief from Prejudicial Joinder

(a) Relief. If the joinder of offenses or defendants in an indictment, an information, or a consolidation for trial appears to prejudice a defendant or the government, the court may order separate trials of counts, sever the defendants' trials, or provide any other relief that justice requires.

(b) Defendant's Statements. Before ruling on a defendant's motion to sever, the court may order an attorney for the government to deliver to the court for in camera inspection any defendant's statement that the government intends to use as evidence.

(Amended Feb. 28, 1966, eff. July 1, 1966; April 29, 2002, eff. Dec. 1, 2002.)

Rule 15. Depositions

(a) When taken. (1) *In General.* A party may move that a prospective witness be deposed in order to preserve testimony for trial. The court may grant the motion because of exceptional circumstances and in the interest of justice. If the court orders the deposition to be taken, it may also require the deponent to produce at the deposition any designated material that is not privileged, including any book, paper, document, record, recording, or data.

(2) *Detained Material Witness.* A witness who is detained under 18 U.S.C. § 3144 may request to be deposed by filing a written motion and giving notice to the parties. The court may then order that the deposition be taken and may discharge the witness after the witness has signed under oath the deposition transcript.

(b) Notice. (1) *In General.* A party seeking to take a deposition must give every other party reasonable written notice of the deposition's date and location. The notice must state the name and address of each deponent. If requested by a party receiving the notice, the court may, for good cause, change the deposition's date or location.

(2) *To the Custodial Officer.* A party seeking to take the deposition must also notify the officer who has custody of the defendant of the scheduled date and location.

(c) Defendant's presence. (1) *Defendant in custody.* Except as authorized by Rule 15(c)(3), the officer who has custody of the defendant must produce the defendant at the deposition and keep the defendant in the witness's presence during the examination, unless the defendant:

(A) waives in writing the right to be present; or

(B) persists in disruptive conduct justifying exclusion after being warned by the court that disruptive conduct will result in the defendant's exclusion.

(2) *Defendant Not in Custody.* Except as authorized by Rule 15(c)(3), a defendant who is not in custody has the right upon request to be present at the deposition, subject to any conditions imposed by the court. If the government tenders the defendant's expenses as provided in Rule 15(d) but the defendant still fails to appear, the defendant—absent good cause—waives both the right to appear and any objection to the taking and use of the deposition based on that right.

(3) *Taking Depositions Outside the United States Without the Defendant's Presence.* The deposition of a witness who is outside the United States may be taken without the defendant's presence if the court makes case-specific findings of all the following:

(A) the witness's testimony could provide substantial proof of a material fact in a felony prosecution;

(B) there is a substantial likelihood that the witness's attendance at trial cannot be obtained;

(C) the witness's presence for a deposition in the United States cannot be obtained;

(D) the defendant cannot be present because:

(i) the country where the witness is located will not permit the defendant to attend the deposition;

(ii) for an in-custody defendant, secure transportation and continuing custody cannot be assured at the witness's location; or

(iii) for an out-of-custody defendant, no reasonable conditions will assure an appearance at the deposition or at trial or sentencing; and

(E) the defendant can meaningfully participate in the deposition through reasonable means.

(d) Expenses. If the deposition was requested by the government, the court may—or if the defendant is unable to bear the deposition expenses, the court must—order the government to pay:

(1) any reasonable travel and subsistence expenses of the defendant and the defendant's attorney to attend the deposition; and

(2) the costs of the deposition transcript.

(e) Manner of Taking. Unless these rules or a court order provides otherwise, a deposition must be taken and filed in the same manner as a deposition in a civil action, except that:

(1) A defendant may not be deposed without that defendant's consent.

(2) The scope and manner of the deposition examination and cross-examination must be the same as would be allowed during trial.

(3) The government must provide to the defendant or the defendant's attorney, for use at the deposition, any statement of the deponent in the government's possession to which the defendant would be entitled at trial.

(f) Admissibility and Use as Evidence. An order authorizing a deposition to be taken under this rule does not determine its admissibility. A party may use all or part of a deposition as provided by the Federal Rules of Evidence.

(g) Objections. A party objecting to deposition testimony or evidence must state the grounds for the objection during the deposition.

(h) Depositions by Agreement Permitted. The parties may by agreement take and use a deposition with the court's consent.

(Amended April 22, 1974, eff. Dec. 1, 1975; July 31, 1975, P. L. 94-64, §§ 2, 3(15)–(19), 89 Stat. 370, 373; Oct. 12, 1984, P. L. 98-473, Title II, Ch I, § 209(b), 98 Stat. 1986; Mar. 9, 1987, eff. Aug. 1, 1987; April 29, 2002, eff. Dec. 1, 2002; April 23, 2012, eff. Dec. 1, 2012.)

Rule 16. Discovery and Inspection

(a) Government's Disclosure. (1) *Information Subject to Disclosure.* (A) *Defendant's Oral Statement.* Upon a defendant's request, the government must disclose to the defendant the substance of any relevant oral statement made by the defendant, before or after arrest, in response to interrogation by a person the defendant knew was a government agent if the government intends to use the statement at trial.

(B) *Defendant's Written or Recorded Statement.* Upon a defendant's request, the government must disclose to the defendant, and make available for inspection, copying, or photographing, all of the following:

(i) any relevant written or recorded statement by the defendant if:

• the statement is within the government's possession, custody, or control; and

• the attorney for the government knows—or through due diligence could know—that the statement exists;

(ii) the portion of any written record containing the substance of any relevant oral statement made before or after arrest if the defendant made the statement in response to interrogation by a person the defendant knew was a government agent; and

(iii) the defendant's recorded testimony before a grand jury relating to the charged offense.

(C) *Organizational Defendant.* Upon a defendant's request, if the defendant is an organization, the government must disclose to the defendant any statement described in Rule 16(a)(1)(A) and (B) if the government contends that the person making the statement:

(i) was legally able to bind the defendant regarding the subject of the statement because of that person's position as the defendant's director, officer, employee, or agent; or

(ii) was personally involved in the alleged conduct constituting the offense and was legally able to bind the defendant regarding that conduct because of that person's position as the defendant's director, officer, employee, or agent.

(D) *Defendant's Prior Record.* Upon a defendant's request, the government must furnish the defendant with a copy of the defendant's prior criminal record that is within the government's possession, custody, or control if the attorney for the government knows—or through due diligence could know—that the record exists.

(E) *Documents and Objects.* Upon a defendant's request, the government must permit the defendant to inspect and to copy or photograph books, papers, documents, data, photographs, tangible objects, buildings or places, or copies or portions of any of these items, if the item is within the government's possession, custody, or control and:

(i) the item is material to preparing the defense;

(ii) the government intends to use the item in its case-in-chief at trial; or

(iii) the item was obtained from or belongs to the defendant.

(F) *Reports of Examinations and Tests.* Upon a defendant's request, the government must permit a defendant to inspect and to copy or photograph the results or reports of any physical or mental examination and of any scientific test or experiment if:

(i) the item is within the government's possession, custody, or control;

(ii) the attorney for the government knows—or through due diligence could know—that the item exists; and

(iii) the item is material to preparing the defense or the government intends to use the item in its case-in-chief at trial.

(G) *Expert witnesses.* At the defendant's request, the government must give to the defendant a written summary of any testimony that the government intends to use under Rules 702, 703, or 705 of the Federal Rules of Evidence during its case-in-chief at trial. If the government requests discovery under subdivision (b)(1)(C)(ii) and the defendant complies, the government must, at the defendant's request, give to the defendant a written summary of testimony that the government intends to use under Rules 702, 703, or 705 of the Federal Rules of Evidence as evidence at trial on the issue of the defendant's mental condition. The summary provided under this subparagraph must describe the witness's opinions, the bases and reasons for those opinions, and the witness's qualifications.

(2) *Information Not Subject to Disclosure.* Except as permitted by Rule 16(a)(1)(A)–(D), (F), and (G), this rule does not authorize the discovery or inspection of reports, memoranda, or other internal government documents made by an attorney for the government or other government agent in connection with investigating or prosecuting the case. Nor does this rule authorize the discovery or inspection of statements made by prospective government witnesses except as provided in 18 U.S.C. § 3500.

(3) *Grand Jury Transcripts.* This rule does not apply to the discovery or inspection of a grand jury's recorded proceedings, except as provided in Rules 6, 12(h), 16(a)(1), and 26.2.

(b) Defendant's Disclosure. (1) *Information*

Subject to Disclosure. (A) *Documents and Objects.* If a defendant requests disclosure under Rule 16(a)(1)(E) and the government complies, then the defendant must permit the government, upon request, to inspect and to copy or photograph books, papers, documents, data, photographs, tangible objects, buildings or places, or copies or portions of any of these items if:

(i) the item is within the defendant's possession, custody, or control; and

(ii) the defendant intends to use the item in the defendant's case-in-chief at trial.

(B) *Reports of Examinations and Tests.* If a defendant requests disclosure under Rule 16(a)(1)(F) and the government complies, the defendant must permit the government, upon request, to inspect and to copy or photograph the results or reports of any physical or mental examination and of any scientific test or experiment if:

(i) the item is within the defendant's possession, custody, or control; and

(ii) the defendant intends to use the item in the defendant's case-in-chief at trial, or intends to call the witness who prepared the report and the report relates to the witness's testimony.

(C) *Expert witnesses.* The defendant must, at the government's request, give to the government a written summary of any testimony that the defendant intends to use under Rules 702, 703, or 705 of the Federal Rules of Evidence as evidence at trial, if—

(i) the defendant requests disclosure under subdivision (a)(1)(G) and the government complies; or

(ii) the defendant has given notice under Rule 12.2(b) of an intent to present expert testimony on the defendant's mental condition.

This summary must describe the witness's opinions, the bases and reasons for those opinions, and the witness's qualifications

(2) *Information Not Subject to Disclosure.* Except for scientific or medical reports, Rule 16(b)(1) does not authorize discovery or inspection of:

(A) reports, memoranda, or other documents made by the defendant, or the defendant's attorney or agent, during the case's investigation or defense; or

(B) a statement made to the defendant, or the defendant's attorney or agent, by:

(i) the defendant;

(ii) a government or defense witness; or

(iii) a prospective government or defense witness.

(c) Continuing Duty to Disclose. A party who discovers additional evidence or material before or during trial must promptly disclose its existence to the other party or the court if:

(1) the evidence or material is subject to discovery or inspection under this rule; and

(2) the other party previously requested, or the court ordered, its production.

(d) Regulating Discovery. (1) *Protective and Modifying Orders.* At any time the court may, for good cause, deny, restrict, or defer discovery or inspection, or grant other appropriate relief. The court may permit a party to show good cause by a written statement that the court will inspect ex parte. If relief is granted, the court must preserve the entire text of the party's statement under seal.

(2) *Failure to Comply.* If a party fails to comply with this rule, the court may:

(A) order that party to permit the discovery or inspection; specify its time, place, and manner; and prescribe other just terms and conditions;

(B) grant a continuance;

(C) prohibit that party from introducing the undisclosed evidence; or

(D) enter any other order that is just under the circumstances.

(Amended Feb. 28, 1966, eff. July 1, 1966; April 22, 1974, eff. Dec. 1, 1975; July 31, 1975, P. L. 94-64, §§ 2, 3(20)–(28), 89 Stat. 370, 374; Dec. 12, 1975, P. L. 94-149, § 5, 89 Stat. 806; April 28, 1983, eff. Aug. 1, 1983; Mar. 9, 1987, eff. Aug. 1, 1987; April 30, 1991, eff. Dec. 1, 1991; April 22, 1993, eff. Dec. 1, 1993; April 29, 1994, eff. Dec. 1, 1994; April 11, 1997, eff. Dec. 1, 1997; April 29, 2002, eff. Dec. 1, 2002; Nov. 2, 2002, P. L. 107-273, Div C, Title I, Subtitle A, § 11019(b), 116 Stat. 1825; Dec. 1, 2013.)

Rule 17. Subpoena

(a) Content. A subpoena must state the court's name and the title of the proceeding, include the seal of the court, and command the witness to attend and testify at the time and place the subpoena specifies. The clerk must issue a blank subpoena—signed and sealed—to the party requesting it, and that party must fill in the blanks before the subpoena is served.

(b) Defendant Unable to Pay. Upon a defendant's ex parte application, the court must order that a subpoena be issued for a named witness if the defendant shows an inability to pay the witness's fees and the necessity of the witness's presence for an adequate defense. If the court orders a subpoena to be issued, the process costs and witness fees will be paid in the same manner as those paid for witnesses the government subpoenas.

(c) Producing Documents and Objects. (1) *In General.* A subpoena may order the witness to produce any books, papers, documents, data, or other objects the subpoena designates. The court may direct the witness to produce the designated items in court before trial or before they are to be offered in evidence. When the items arrive, the court may permit the parties and their attorneys to inspect all or part of them.

(2) *Quashing or Modifying the Subpoena.* On motion made promptly, the court may quash or modify the subpoena if compliance would be unreasonable or oppressive.

(3) *Subpoena for Personal or Confidential Information About a Victim.* After a complaint, indictment, or information is filed, a subpoena requiring the production of personal or confidential information about a victim may be served on a third party

only by court order. Before entering the order and unless there are exceptional circumstances, the court must require giving notice to the victim so that the victim can move to quash or modify the subpoena or otherwise object.

(d) Service. A marshal, a deputy marshal, or any nonparty who is at least 18 years old may serve a subpoena. The server must deliver a copy of the subpoena to the witness and must tender to the witness one day's witness-attendance fee and the legal mileage allowance. The server need not tender the attendance fee or mileage allowance when the United States, a federal officer, or a federal agency has requested the subpoena.

(e) Place of Service. (1) *In the United States.* A subpoena requiring a witness to attend a hearing or trial may be served at any place within the United States.

(2) *In a Foreign Country.* If the witness is in a foreign country, 28 U.S.C. § 1783 governs the subpoena's service.

(f) Issuing a Deposition Subpoena. (1) *Issuance.* A court order to take a deposition authorizes the clerk in the district where the deposition is to be taken to issue a subpoena for any witness named or described in the order.

(2) *Place.* After considering the convenience of the witness and the parties, the court may order—and the subpoena may require—the witness to appear anywhere the court designates.

(g) Contempt. The court (other than a magistrate judge) may hold in contempt a witness who, without adequate excuse, disobeys a subpoena issued by a federal court in that district. A magistrate judge may hold in contempt a witness who, without adequate excuse, disobeys a subpoena issued by that magistrate judge as provided in 28 U.S.C. § 636(e).

(h) Information Not Subject to a Subpoena. No party may subpoena a statement of a witness or of a prospective witness under this rule. Rule 26.2 governs the production of the statement.

(Amended Dec. 27, 1948, eff. Oct. 20, 1949; Feb. 28, 1966, eff. July 1, 1966; April 24, 1972, eff. Oct. 1, 1972; April 22, 1974, eff. July 31, 1975, P. L. 94-64, §§ 2, 3(29), 89 Stat. 375; Dec. 1, 1975; April 30, 1979, eff. Dec. 1, 1980; Mar. 9, 1987, eff. Aug. 1, 1987; April 22, 1993, eff. Dec. 1, 1993; April 29, 2002, eff. Dec. 1, 2002; April 23, 2008, eff. Dec. 1, 2008.)

Rule 17.1. Pretrial Conference

On its own, or on a party's motion, the court may hold one or more pretrial conferences to promote a fair and expeditious trial. When a conference ends, the court must prepare and file a memorandum of any matters agreed to during the conference. The government may not use any statement made during the conference by the defendant or the defendant's attorney unless it is in writing and is signed by the defendant and the defendant's attorney.

(Added Feb. 28, 1966, eff. July 1, 1966; amended Mar. 9, 1987, eff. Aug. 1, 1987; April 29, 2002, eff. Dec. 1, 2002.)

V. VENUE

Rule 18. Place of Prosecution and Trial

Unless a statute or these rules permit otherwise, the government must prosecute an offense in a district where the offense was committed. The court must set the place of trial within the district with due regard for the convenience of the defendant, any victim, and the witnesses, and the prompt administration of justice.

(Amended Feb. 28, 1966, eff. July 1, 1966; April 30, 1979, eff. Aug. 1, 1979; April 29, 2002, eff. Dec. 1, 2002; April 23, 2008, eff. Dec. 1, 2008.)

Rule 19. [Reserved]

(As amended Dec. 1, 2002.)

Rule 20. Transfer for Plea and Sentence

(a) Consent to Transfer. A prosecution may be transferred from the district where the indictment or information is pending, or from which a warrant on a complaint has been issued, to the district where the defendant is arrested, held, or present if:

(1) the defendant states in writing a wish to plead guilty or nolo contendere and to waive trial in the district where the indictment, information, or complaint is pending, consents in writing to the court's disposing of the case in the transferee district, and files the statement in the transferee district; and

(2) the United States attorneys in both districts approve the transfer in writing.

(b) Clerk's Duties. After receiving the defendant's statement and the required approvals, the clerk where the indictment, information, or complaint is pending must send the file, or a certified copy, to the clerk in the transferee district.

(c) Effect of a Not Guilty Plea. If the defendant pleads not guilty after the case has been transferred under Rule 20(a), the clerk must return the papers to the court where the prosecution began, and that court must restore the proceeding to its docket. The defendant's statement that the defendant wished to plead guilty or nolo contendere is not, in any civil or criminal proceeding, admissible against the defendant.

(d) Juveniles. (1) *Consent to Transfer.* A juvenile, as defined in 18 U.S.C. § 5031, may be proceeded against as a juvenile delinquent in the district where the juvenile is arrested, held, or present if:

(A) the alleged offense that occurred in the other district is not punishable by death or life imprisonment;

(B) an attorney has advised the juvenile;

(C) the court has informed the juvenile of the juvenile's rights—including the right to be returned to the district where the offense allegedly occurred—and the consequences of waiving those rights;

(D) the juvenile, after receiving the court's information about rights, consents in writing to be proceeded against in the transferee district, and files the consent in the transferee district;

(E) the United States attorneys for both districts approve the transfer in writing; and

(F) the transferee court approves the transfer.

(2) *Clerk's Duties.* After receiving the juvenile's written consent and the required approvals, the clerk where the indictment, information, or complaint is pending or where the alleged offense occurred must send the file, or a certified copy, to the clerk in the transferee district.

(Amended Feb. 28, 1966, eff. July 1, 1966; April 22, 1974, eff. Dec. 1, 1975; July 31, 1975, P. L. 94-64, §§ 2, 3(30), 89 Stat. 370, 375; April 28, 1982, eff. Aug. 1, 1982; Mar. 9, 1987, eff. Aug. 1, 1987; April 29, 2002, eff. Dec. 1, 2002.)

Rule 21. Transfer for Trial

(a) For Prejudice. Upon the defendant's motion, the court must transfer the proceeding against that defendant to another district if the court is satisfied that so great a prejudice against the defendant exists in the transferring district that the defendant cannot obtain a fair and impartial trial there.

(b) For Convenience. Upon the defendant's motion, the court may transfer the proceeding, or one or more counts, against that defendant to another district for the convenience of the parties, any victim, and the witnesses, and in the interest of justice.

(c) Proceedings on Transfer. When the court orders a transfer, the clerk must send to the transferee district the file, or a certified copy, and any bail taken. The prosecution will then continue in the transferee district.

(d) Time to File a Motion to Transfer. A motion to transfer may be made at or before arraignment or at any other time the court or these rules prescribe.

(Amended Feb. 28, 1966, eff. July 1, 1966; Mar. 9, 1987, eff. Aug. 1, 1987; April 29, 2002, eff. Dec. 1, 2002; April 28, 2010, eff. Dec. 1, 2010.)

Rule 22. [Transferred]

(As amended Dec. 1, 2002.)

VI. TRIAL

Rule 23. Jury or Nonjury Trial

(a) Jury Trial. If the defendant is entitled to a jury trial, the trial must be by jury unless:

(1) the defendant waives a jury trial in writing;

(2) the government consents; and

(3) the court approves.

(b) Jury Size. (1) *In General.* A jury consists of 12 persons unless this rule provides otherwise.

(2) *Stipulation for a Smaller Jury.* At any time before the verdict, the parties may, with the court's approval, stipulate in writing that:

(A) the jury may consist of fewer than 12 persons; or

(B) a jury of fewer than 12 persons may return a verdict if the court finds it necessary to excuse a juror for good cause after the trial begins.

(3) *Court Order for a Jury of 11.* After the jury has retired to deliberate, the court may permit a jury of 11 persons to return a verdict, even without a stipulation by the parties, if the court finds good cause to excuse a juror.

(c) Nonjury Trial. In a case tried without a jury, the court must find the defendant guilty or not guilty. If a party requests before the finding of guilty or not guilty, the court must state its specific findings of fact in open court or in a written decision or opinion.

(Amended Feb. 28, 1966, eff. July 1, 1966; July 30, 1977, P. L. 95-78, § 2(b), 91 Stat. 320; April 28, 1983, eff. Aug. 1, 1983; April 29, 2002, eff. Dec. 1, 2002.)

Rule 24. Trial Jurors

(a) Examination. (1) *In General.* The court may examine prospective jurors or may permit the attorneys for the parties to do so.

(2) *Court Examination.* If the court examines the jurors, it must permit the attorneys for the parties to:

(A) ask further questions that the court considers proper; or

(B) submit further questions that the court may ask if it considers them proper.

(b) Peremptory Challenges. Each side is entitled to the number of peremptory challenges to prospective jurors specified below. The court may allow additional peremptory challenges to multiple defendants, and may allow the defendants to exercise those challenges separately or jointly.

(1) *Capital Case.* Each side has 20 peremptory challenges when the government seeks the death penalty.

(2) *Other Felony Case.* The government has 6 peremptory challenges and the defendant or defendants jointly have 10 peremptory challenges when the defendant is charged with a crime punishable by imprisonment of more than one year.

(3) *Misdemeanor Case.* Each side has peremptory challenges when the defendant is charged with a crime punishable by fine, imprisonment of one year or less, or both.

(c) Alternate Jurors. (1) *In General.* The court may impanel up to 6 alternate jurors to replace any jurors who are unable to perform or who are disqualified from performing their duties.

(2) *Procedure.* (A) Alternate jurors must have the same qualifications and be selected and sworn in the same manner as any other juror.

(B) Alternate jurors replace jurors in the same sequence in which the alternates were selected. An alternate juror who replaces a juror has the same authority as the other jurors.

(3) *Retaining Alternate Jurors.* The court may retain alternate jurors after the jury retires to deliberate. The court must ensure that a retained

alternate does not discuss the case with anyone until that alternate replaces a juror or is discharged. If an alternate replaces a juror after deliberations have begun, the court must instruct the jury to begin its deliberations anew.

(4) *Peremptory Challenges.* Each side is entitled to the number of additional peremptory challenges to prospective alternate jurors specified below. These additional challenges may be used only to remove alternate jurors.

(A) *One or Two Alternates.* One additional peremptory challenge is permitted when one or two alternates are impaneled.

(B) *Three or Four Alternates.* Two additional peremptory challenges are permitted when three or four alternates are impaneled.

(C) *Five or Six Alternates.* Three additional peremptory challenges are permitted when five or six alternates are impaneled.

(Amended Feb. 28, 1966, eff. July 1, 1966; Mar. 9, 1987, eff. Aug. 1, 1987; April 26, 1999, eff. Dec. 1, 1999; April 29, 2002, eff. Dec. 1, 2002.)

Rule 25. Judge's Disability

(a) During trial. Any judge regularly sitting in or assigned to the court may complete a jury trial if:

(1) the judge before whom the trial began cannot proceed because of death, sickness, or other disability; and

(2) the judge completing the trial certifies familiarity with the trial record.

(b) After a Verdict or Finding of Guilty. (1) *In General.* After a verdict or finding of guilty, any judge regularly sitting in or assigned to a court may complete the court's duties if the judge who presided at trial cannot perform those duties because of absence, death, sickness, or other disability.

(2) *Granting a New Trial.* The successor judge may grant a new trial if satisfied that:

(A) a judge other than the one who presided at the trial cannot perform the post-trial duties; or

(B) a new trial is necessary for some other reason.

(Amended Feb. 28, 1966, eff. July 1, 1966; Mar. 9, 1987, eff. Aug. 1, 1987; Apr. 29, 2002, eff. Dec. 1, 2002.)

Rule 26. Taking Testimony

In every trial the testimony of witnesses must be taken in open court, unless otherwise provided by a statute or by rules adopted under 28 U.S.C. §§ 2072–2077.

(Amended Nov. 20, 1972, eff. July 1, 1975; Jan. 2, 1975, P. L. 93-595, § 3, 88 Stat. 1959; Apr. 29, 2002, eff. Dec. 1, 2002.)

Rule 26.1. Foreign Law Determination

A party intending to raise an issue of foreign law must provide the court and all parties with reasonable written notice. Issues of foreign law are questions of law, but in deciding such issues a court may consider any relevant material or source—including testimony—without regard to the Federal Rules of Evidence.

(As added Feb. 28, 1966, eff. July 1, 1966; amended Nov. 20, 1972, eff. July 1, 1975; Jan. 2, 1975, P. L. 93-595, § 3, 88 Stat. 1949; July 1, 1975; April 29, 2002, eff. Dec. 1, 2002.)

Rule 26.2. Producing a Witness's Statement

(a) Motion to Produce. After a witness other than the defendant has testified on direct examination, the court, on motion of a party who did not call the witness, must order an attorney for the government or the defendant and the defendant's attorney to produce, for the examination and use of the moving party, any statement of the witness that is in their possession and that relates to the subject matter of the witness's testimony.

(b) Producing the Entire Statement. If the entire statement relates to the subject matter of the witness's testimony, the court must order that the statement be delivered to the moving party.

(c) Producing a Redacted Statement. If the party who called the witness claims that the statement contains information that is privileged or does not relate to the subject matter of the witness's testimony, the court must inspect the statement in camera. After excising any privileged or unrelated portions, the court must order delivery of the redacted statement to the moving party. If the defendant objects to an excision, the court must preserve the entire statement with the excised portion indicated, under seal, as part of the record.

(d) Recess to Examine a Statement. The court may recess the proceedings to allow time for a party to examine the statement and prepare for its use.

(e) Sanction for Failure to Produce or Deliver a Statement. If the party who called the witness disobeys an order to produce or deliver a statement, the court must strike the witness's testimony from the record. If an attorney for the government disobeys the order, the court must declare a mistrial if justice so requires.

(f) "Statement" Defined. As used in this rule, a witness's "statement" means:

(1) a written statement that the witness makes and signs, or otherwise adopts or approves;

(2) a substantially verbatim, contemporaneously recorded recital of the witness's oral statement that is contained in any recording or any transcription of a recording; or

(3) the witness's statement to a grand jury, however taken or recorded, or a transcription of such a statement.

(g) Scope. This rule applies at trial, at a suppression hearing under Rule 12, and to the extent specified in the following rules:

(1) Rule 5.1(h) (preliminary hearing);

(2) Rule 32(i)(2) (sentencing);

(3) Rule 32.1(e) (hearing to revoke or modify probation or supervised release);

(4) Rule 46(j) (detention hearing); and

(5) Rule 8 of the Rules Governing Proceedings under 28 U.S.C. § 2255.

(Amended April 30, 1979, eff. Dec. 1, 1980; July 31, 1979, P. L. 96-42, § 1(1), 93 Stat. 326; Mar. 9, 1987, eff. Aug. 1, 1987; April 22, 1993, eff. Dec. 1, 1993; April 24, 1998, eff. Dec. 1, 1998; April 29, 2002, eff. Dec. 1, 2002.)

Rule 26.3. Mistrial

Before ordering a mistrial, the court must give each defendant and the government an opportunity to comment on the propriety of the order, to state whether that party consents or objects, and to suggest alternatives.

(Added April 22, 1993, eff. Dec. 1, 1993; amended April 29, 2002, eff. Dec. 1, 2002.)

Rule 27. Proving an Official Record

A party may prove an official record, an entry in such a record, or the lack of a record or entry in the same manner as in a civil action.

(As amended April 29, 2002, eff. Dec. 1, 2002.)

Rule 28. Interpreters

The court may select, appoint, and set the reasonable compensation for an interpreter. The compensation must be paid from funds provided by law or by the government, as the court may direct.

(Amended Feb. 28, 1966, eff. July 1, 1966; Nov. 20, 1972, eff. July 1, 1975; Jan. 2, 1975, P. L. 93-595, § 3, 88 Stat. 1949; April 29, 2002, eff. Dec. 1, 2002.)

Rule 29. Motion for a Judgment of Acquittal

(a) Before Submission to the Jury. After the government closes its evidence or after the close of all the evidence, the court on the defendant's motion must enter a judgment of acquittal of any offense for which the evidence is insufficient to sustain a conviction. The court may on its own consider whether the evidence is insufficient to sustain a conviction. If the court denies a motion for a judgment of acquittal at the close of the government's evidence, the defendant may offer evidence without having reserved the right to do so.

(b) Reserving Decision. The court may reserve decision on the motion, proceed with the trial (where the motion is made before the close of all the evidence), submit the case to the jury, and decide the motion either before the jury returns a verdict or after it returns a verdict of guilty or is discharged without having returned a verdict. If the court reserves decision, it must decide the motion on the basis of the evidence at the time the ruling was reserved.

(c) After Jury Verdict or Discharge. (1) *Time for a Motion.* A defendant may move for a judgment of acquittal, or renew such a motion, within 14 days after a guilty verdict or after the court discharges the jury, whichever is later.

(2) *Ruling on the Motion.* If the jury has returned a guilty verdict, the court may set aside the verdict and enter an acquittal. If the jury has failed to return a verdict, the court may enter a judgment of acquittal.

(3) *No Prior Motion Required.* A defendant is not required to move for a judgment of acquittal before the court submits the case to the jury as a prerequisite for making such a motion after jury discharge.

(d) Conditional Ruling on a Motion for a New Trial. (1) *Motion for a New Trial.* If the court enters a judgment of acquittal after a guilty verdict, the court must also conditionally determine whether any motion for a new trial should be granted if the judgment of acquittal is later vacated or reversed. The court must specify the reasons for that determination.

(2) *Finality.* The court's order conditionally granting a motion for a new trial does not affect the finality of the judgment of acquittal.

(3) *Appeal.* (A) *Grant of a Motion for a New Trial.* If the court conditionally grants a motion for a new trial and an appellate court later reverses the judgment of acquittal, the trial court must proceed with the new trial unless the appellate court orders otherwise.

(B) *Denial of a Motion for a New Trial.* If the court conditionally denies a motion for a new trial, an appellee may assert that the denial was erroneous. If the appellate court later reverses the judgment of acquittal, the trial court must proceed as the appellate court directs.

(Amended Feb. 28, 1966, eff. July 1, 1966; Nov. 10, 1986, P. L. 99-646, § 54(a), 100 Stat. 3607; April. 29, 1994, eff. Dec. 1, 1994; April 29, 2002, eff. Dec. 1, 2002; April 25, 2005, eff. Dec. 1, 2005; Mar. 26, 2009, eff. Dec. 1, 2009.)

Rule 29.1. Closing Argument

Closing arguments proceed in the following order:

(1) the government argues;

(2) the defense argues; and

(3) the government rebuts.

(Added April 22, 1974, eff. Dec. 1, 1975; July 31, 1975, P. L. 94-64, § 2, 89 Stat. 370; April 29, 2002, eff. Dec. 1, 2002.)

Rule 30. Jury Instructions

(a) In General. Any party may request in writing that the court instruct the jury on the law as specified in the request. The request must be made at the close of the evidence or at any earlier time that the court reasonably sets. When the request is made, the requesting party must furnish a copy to every other party.

(b) Ruling on a Request. The court must inform the parties before closing arguments how it intends to rule on the requested instructions.

(c) Time for Giving Instructions. The court may instruct the jury before or after the arguments are completed, or at both times.

(d) Objections to Instructions. A party who

objects to any portion of the instructions or to a failure to give a requested instruction must inform the court of the specific objection and the grounds for the objection before the jury retires to deliberate. An opportunity must be given to object out of the jury's hearing and, on request, out of the jury's presence. Failure to object in accordance with this rule precludes appellate review, except as permitted under Rule 52(b).

(Amended Feb. 28, 1966, eff. July 1, 1966; Mar. 9, 1987, eff. Aug. 1, 1987; April 25, 1988, eff. Aug. 1, 1988; April 29, 2002, eff. Dec. 1, 2002.)

Rule 31. Jury Verdict

(a) Return. The jury must return its verdict to a judge in open court. The verdict must be unanimous.

(b) Partial Verdicts, Mistrial, and Retrial. (1) *Multiple Defendants.* If there are multiple defendants, the jury may return a verdict at any time during its deliberations as to any defendant about whom it has agreed.

(2) *Multiple Counts.* If the jury cannot agree on all counts as to any defendant, the jury may return a verdict on those counts on which it has agreed.

(3) *Mistrial and Retrial.* If the jury cannot agree on a verdict on one or more counts, the court may declare a mistrial on those counts. The government may retry any defendant on any count on which the jury could not agree.

(c) Lesser Offense or Attempt. A defendant may be found guilty of any of the following:

(1) an offense necessarily included in the offense charged;

(2) an attempt to commit the offense charged; or

(3) an attempt to commit an offense necessarily included in the offense charged, if the attempt is an offense in its own right.

(d) Jury Poll. After a verdict is returned but before the jury is discharged, the court must on a party's request, or may on its own, poll the jurors individually. If the poll reveals a lack of unanimity, the court may direct the jury to deliberate further or may declare a mistrial and discharge the jury.

(Amended Oct. 1, 1972; Dec. 1, 1998; Dec. 1, 2000; Dec. 1, 2002.)

VII. POST-CONVICTION PROCEDURES

Rule 32. Sentencing and Judgment

(a) [Reserved]

(b) Time of Sentencing. (1) *In General.* The court must impose sentence without unnecessary delay.

(2) *Changing Time Limits.* The court may, for good cause, change any time limits prescribed in this rule.

(c) Presentence Investigation. (1) *Required Investigation.* (A) In General. The probation officer must conduct a presentence investigation and submit a report to the court before it imposes sentence unless:

(i) 18 U.S.C. § 3593(c) or another statute requires otherwise; or

(ii) the court finds that the information in the record enables it to meaningfully exercise its sentencing authority under 18 U.S.C. § 3553, and the court explains its finding on the record.

(B) Restitution. If the law permits restitution, the probation officer must conduct an investigation and submit a report that contains sufficient information for the court to order restitution.

(2) *Interviewing the Defendant.* The probation officer who interviews a defendant as part of a presentence investigation must, on request, give the defendant's attorney notice and a reasonable opportunity to attend the interview.

(d) Presentence Report. (1) *Applying the Advisory Sentencing Guidelines.* The presentence report must:

(A) identify all applicable guidelines and policy statements of the Sentencing Commission;

(B) calculate the defendant's offense level and criminal history category;

(C) state the resulting sentencing range and kinds of sentences available;

(D) identify any factor relevant to:

(i) the appropriate kind of sentence, or

(ii) the appropriate sentence within the applicable sentencing range; and

(E) identify any basis for departing from the applicable sentencing range.

(2) *Additional Information.* The presentence report must also contain the following:

(A) the defendant's history and characteristics, including:

(i) any prior criminal record;

(ii) the defendant's financial condition; and

(iii) any circumstances affecting the defendant's behavior that may be helpful in imposing sentence or in correctional treatment;

(B) information that assesses any financial, social, psychological, and medical impact on any victim;

(C) when appropriate, the nature and extent of nonprison programs and resources available to the defendant;

(D) when the law provides for restitution, information sufficient for a restitution order;

(E) if the court orders a study under 18 U.S.C. § 3552(b), any resulting report and recommendation;

(F) a statement of whether the government seeks forfeiture under Rule 32.2 and any other law; and

(G) any other information that the court requires, including information relevant to the factors under 18 U.S.C. § 3553(a).

(3) *Exclusions.* The presentence report must exclude the following:

(A) any diagnoses that, if disclosed, might seriously disrupt a rehabilitation program;

(B) any sources of information obtained upon a promise of confidentiality; and

(C) any other information that, if disclosed, might

result in physical or other harm to the defendant or others.

(e) Disclosing the Report and Recommendation. (1) *Time to Disclose.* Unless the defendant has consented in writing, the probation officer must not submit a presentence report to the court or disclose its contents to anyone until the defendant has pleaded guilty or nolo contendere, or has been found guilty.

(2) *Minimum Required Notice.* The probation officer must give the presentence report to the defendant, the defendant's attorney, and an attorney for the government at least 35 days before sentencing unless the defendant waives this minimum period.

(3) *Sentence Recommendation.* By local rule or by order in a case, the court may direct the probation officer not to disclose to anyone other than the court the officer's recommendation on the sentence.

(f) Objecting to the Report. (1) *Time to Object.* Within 14 days after receiving the presentence report, the parties must state in writing any objections, including objections to material information, sentencing guideline ranges, and policy statements contained in or omitted from the report.

(2) *Serving Objections.* An objecting party must provide a copy of its objections to the opposing party and to the probation officer.

(3) *Action on Objections.* After receiving objections, the probation officer may meet with the parties to discuss the objections. The probation officer may then investigate further and revise the presentence report as appropriate.

(g) Submitting the Report. At least 7 days before sentencing, the probation officer must submit to the court and to the parties the presentence report and an addendum containing any unresolved objections, the grounds for those objections, and the probation officer's comments on them.

(h) Notice of Possible Departure From Sentencing Guidelines. Before the court may depart from the applicable sentencing range on a ground not identified for departure either in the presentence report or in a party's prehearing submission, the court must give the parties reasonable notice that it is contemplating such a departure. The notice must specify any ground on which the court is contemplating a departure.

(i) Sentencing. (1) *In General.* At sentencing, the court:

(A) must verify that the defendant and the defendant's attorney have read and discussed the presentence report and any addendum to the report;

(B) must give to the defendant and an attorney for the government a written summary of—or summarize in camera—any information excluded from the presentence report under Rule 32(d)(3) on which the court will rely in sentencing, and give them a reasonable opportunity to comment on that information;

(C) must allow the parties' attorneys to comment on the probation officer's determinations and other matters relating to an appropriate sentence; and

(D) may, for good cause, allow a party to make a new objection at any time before sentence is imposed.

(2) *Introducing Evidence; Producing a Statement.* The court may permit the parties to introduce evidence on the objections. If a witness testifies at sentencing, Rule 26.2(a)–(d) and (f) applies. If a party fails to comply with a Rule 26.2 order to produce a witness's statement, the court must not consider that witness's testimony.

(3) *Court Determinations.* At sentencing, the court:

(A) may accept any undisputed portion of the presentence report as a finding of fact;

(B) must—for any disputed portion of the presentence report or other controverted matter—rule on the dispute or determine that a ruling is unnecessary either because the matter will not affect sentencing, or because the court will not consider the matter in sentencing; and

(C) must append a copy of the court's determinations under this rule to any copy of the presentence report made available to the Bureau of Prisons.

(4) *Opportunity to Speak.* (A) By a Party. Before imposing sentence, the court must:

(i) provide the defendant's attorney an opportunity to speak on the defendant's behalf;

(ii) address the defendant personally in order to permit the defendant to speak or present any information to mitigate the sentence; and

(iii) provide an attorney for the government an opportunity to speak equivalent to that of the defendant's attorney.

(B) By a Victim. Before imposing sentence, the court must address any victim of the crime who is present at sentencing and must permit the victim to be reasonably heard.

(C) In Camera Proceedings. Upon a party's motion and for good cause, the court may hear in camera any statement made under Rule 32(i)(4).

(j) Defendant's Right to Appeal. (1) *Advice of a Right to Appeal.* (A) Appealing a Conviction. If the defendant pleaded not guilty and was convicted, after sentencing the court must advise the defendant of the right to appeal the conviction.

(B) Appealing a Sentence. After sentencing—regardless of the defendant's plea—the court must advise the defendant of any right to appeal the sentence.

(C) Appeal Costs. The court must advise a defendant who is unable to pay appeal costs of the right to ask for permission to appeal in forma pauperis.

(2) *Clerk's Filing of Notice.* If the defendant so requests, the clerk must immediately prepare and file a notice of appeal on the defendant's behalf.

(k) Judgment. (1) *In General.* In the judgment of conviction, the court must set forth the plea, the jury verdict or the court's findings, the adjudication, and the sentence. If the defendant is found not guilty or is otherwise entitled to be discharged, the court must so order. The judge must sign the judgment, and the clerk must enter it.

(2) *Criminal Forfeiture.* Forfeiture procedures are governed by Rule 32.2.

(Dec. 26, 1944, eff. March 21, 1946, as amended Feb. 28, 1966, eff. July 1, 1966; April 24, 1972, eff. Oct. 1, 1972; April 22, 1974, eff. Dec. 1, 1975; Act July 31, 1975, P. L. 94-64, §§ 2, 3(31)–(34), 89 Stat. 370, 376, eff. Dec. 1, 1975; April 30, 1979, eff. Dec. 1, 1980, as provided by Act July 31, 1979, P. L. 96-42, § 1(1), 93 Stat. 326; Oct. 12, 1982, P. L. 97-291, § 3, 96 Stat. 1249, eff. Oct. 12, 1982; April 28, 1983, eff. Aug. 1, 1983; Oct. 12, 1984, P. L. 98-473, Title II, Ch II, § 215(a), 98 Stat. 2014, eff. Nov. 1, 1987; Nov. 10, 1986, P. L. 99-646, § 25(a), 100 Stat. 3597; March 9, 1987, eff. Aug. 1, 1987; April 25, 1989, eff. Dec. 1, 1989; April 30, 1991, eff. Dec. 1, 1991; April 22, 1993, eff. Dec. 1, 1993; April 29, 1994, eff. Dec. 1, 1994; Sept. 13, 1994, P. L. 103-322, Title XXIII, Subtitle A, § 230101(a), (b), 108 Stat. 2077; April 23, 1996, eff. Dec. 1, 1996; April 24, 1996, P. L. 104-132, Title II, Subtitle A, § 207(a), 110 Stat. 1236; April 17, 2000, eff. Dec. 1, 2000; April 29, 2002, eff. Dec. 1, 2002; April 30, 2007, eff. Dec. 1, 2007; April 23, 2008, eff. Dec. 1, 2008; March 26, 2009, eff. Dec. 1, 2009; April 26, 2011, eff. Dec. 1, 2011.)

Rule 32.1. Revoking or Modifying Probation or Supervised Release

(a) Initial Appearance. (1) *Person In Custody.* A person held in custody for violating probation or supervised release must be taken without unnecessary delay before a magistrate judge.

(A) If the person is held in custody in the district where an alleged violation occurred, the initial appearance must be in that district.

(B) If the person is held in custody in a district other than where an alleged violation occurred, the initial appearance must be in that district, or in an adjacent district if the appearance can occur more promptly there.

(2) *Upon a Summons.* When a person appears in response to a summons for violating probation or supervised release, a magistrate judge must proceed under this rule.

(3) *Advice.* The judge must inform the person of the following:

(A) the alleged violation of probation or supervised release;

(B) the person's right to retain counsel or to request that counsel be appointed if the person cannot obtain counsel; and

(C) the person's right, if held in custody, to a preliminary hearing under Rule 32.1(b)(1).

(4) *Appearance in the District With Jurisdiction.* If the person is arrested or appears in the district that has jurisdiction to conduct a revocation hearing—either originally or by transfer of jurisdiction—the court must proceed under Rule 32.1(b)–(e).

(5) *Appearance in a District Lacking Jurisdiction.* If the person is arrested or appears in a district that does not have jurisdiction to conduct a revocation hearing, the magistrate judge must:

(A) if the alleged violation occurred in the district of arrest, conduct a preliminary hearing under Rule 32.1(b) and either:

(i) transfer the person to the district that has jurisdiction, if the judge finds probable cause to believe that a violation occurred; or

(ii) dismiss the proceedings and so notify the court that has jurisdiction, if the judge finds no probable cause to believe that a violation occurred; or

(B) if the alleged violation did not occur in the district of arrest, transfer the person to the district that has jurisdiction if:

(i) the government produces certified copies of the judgment, warrant, and warrant application, or produces copies of those certified documents by reliable electronic means; and

(ii) the judge finds that the person is the same person named in the warrant

(6) *Release or Detention.* The magistrate judge may release or detain the person under 18 U.S.C. § 3143(a)(1) pending further proceedings. The burden of establishing by clear and convincing evidence that the person will not flee or pose a danger to any other person or to the community rests with the person.

(b) Revocation. (1) *Preliminary Hearing.* (A) *In General.* If a person is in custody for violating a condition of probation or supervised release, a magistrate judge must promptly conduct a hearing to determine whether there is probable cause to believe that a violation occurred. The person may waive the hearing.

(B) *Requirements.* The hearing must be recorded by a court reporter or by a suitable recording device. The judge must give the person:

(i) notice of the hearing and its purpose, the alleged violation, and the person's right to retain counsel or to request that counsel be appointed if the person cannot obtain counsel;

(ii) an opportunity to appear at the hearing and present evidence; and

(iii) upon request, an opportunity to question any adverse witness, unless the judge determines that the interest of justice does not require the witness to appear.

(C) *Referral.* If the judge finds probable cause, the judge must conduct a revocation hearing. If the judge does not find probable cause, the judge must dismiss the proceeding.

(2) *Revocation Hearing.* Unless waived by the person, the court must hold the revocation hearing within a reasonable time in the district having jurisdiction. The person is entitled to:

(A) written notice of the alleged violation;

(B) disclosure of the evidence against the person;

(C) an opportunity to appear, present evidence, and question any adverse witness unless the court determines that the interest of justice does not require the witness to appear;

(D) notice of the person's right to retain counsel or to request that counsel be appointed if the person cannot obtain counsel; and

(E) an opportunity to make a statement and present any information in mitigation.

(c) Modification. (1) *In General.* Before modifying the conditions of probation or supervised release, the court must hold a hearing, at which the person has the right to counsel and an opportunity to make a statement and present any information in mitigation.

(2) *Exceptions.* A hearing is not required if:

(A) the person waives the hearing; or

(B) the relief sought is favorable to the person and does not extend the term of probation or of supervised release; and

(C) an attorney for the government has received notice of the relief sought, has had a reasonable opportunity to object, and has not done so.

(d) Disposition of the Case. The court's disposition of the case is governed by 18 U.S.C. § 3563 and § 3565 (probation) and § 3583 (supervised release).

(e) Producing a Statement. Rule 26.2(a)–(d) and (f) applies at a hearing under this rule. If a party fails to comply with a Rule 26.2 order to produce a witness's statement, the court must not consider that witness's testimony.

(Added April 30, 1979; effective Dec. 1, 1980, as provided by Act July 31, 1979, P. L. 96-42, § 1(1), 93 Stat. 326; Nov. 10, 1986, P. L. 99-646, § 12(b), 100 Stat. 3594; Marc. 9, 1987, eff.Aug. 1, 1987; April 25, 1989, eff. Dec. 1, 1989; April 30, 1991, eff. Dec. 1, 1991; April 22, 1993, eff. Dec. 1, 1993; April 29, 2002, eff. Dec. 1, 2002; April 25, 2005, eff. Dec. 1, 2005; April 12, 2006, eff. Dec. 1, 2006; April 28, 2010, eff. Dec. 1, 2010.)

Rule 32.2. Criminal Forfeiture

(a) Notice to the defendant. A court must not enter a judgment of forfeiture in a criminal proceeding unless the indictment or information contains notice to the defendant that the government will seek the forfeiture of property as part of any sentence in accordance with the applicable statute. The notice should not be designated as a count of the indictment or information. The indictment or information need not identify the property subject to forfeiture or specify the amount of any forfeiture money judgment that the government seeks.

(b) Entering a Preliminary Order of Forfeiture. (1) *Forfeiture phase of the trial.* (A) Forfeiture determinations. As soon as practical after a verdict or finding of guilty, or after a plea of guilty or nolo contendere is accepted, on any count in an indictment or information regarding which criminal forfeiture is sought, the court must determine what property is subject to forfeiture under the applicable statute. If the government seeks forfeiture of specific property, the court must determine whether the government has established the requisite nexus between the property and the offense. If the government seeks a personal money judgment, the court must determine the amount of money that the defendant will be ordered to pay.

(B) Evidence and hearing. The court's determination may be based on evidence already in the record, including any written plea agreement, and on any additional evidence or information submitted by the parties and accepted by the court as relevant and reliable. If the forfeiture is contested, on either party's request the court must conduct a hearing after the verdict or finding of guilty.

(2) *Preliminary order.* (A) Contents of a specific order. If the court finds that property is subject to forfeiture, it must promptly enter a preliminary order of forfeiture setting forth the amount of any money judgment, directing the forfeiture of specific property, and directing the forfeiture of any substitute property if the government has met the statutory criteria. The court must enter the order without regard to any third party's interest in the property. Determining whether a third party has such an interest must be deferred until any third party files a claim in an ancillary proceeding under Rule 32.2(c).

(B) Timing. Unless doing so is impractical, the court must enter the preliminary order sufficiently in advance of sentencing to allow the parties to suggest revisions or modifications before the order becomes final as to the defendant under Rule 32.2(b)(4).

(C) General order. If, before sentencing, the court cannot identify all the specific property subject to forfeiture or calculate the total amount of the money judgment, the court may enter a forfeiture order that:

(i) lists any identified property;

(ii) describes other property in general terms; and

(iii) states that the order will be amended under Rule 32.2(e)(1) when additional specific property is identified or the amount of the money judgment has been calculated.

(3) *Seizing property.* The entry of a preliminary order of forfeiture authorizes the Attorney General (or a designee) to seize the specific property subject to forfeiture; to conduct any discovery the court considers proper in identifying, locating, or disposing of the property; and to commence proceedings that comply with any statutes governing third-party rights. The court may include in the order of forfeiture conditions reasonably necessary to preserve the property's value pending any appeal.

(4) *Sentence and judgment.* (A) When final. At sentencing—or at any time before sentencing if the defendant consents—the preliminary forfeiture order becomes final as to the defendant. If the order directs the defendant to forfeit specific property, it remains preliminary as to third parties until the ancillary proceeding is concluded under Rule 32.2(c).

(B) Notice and inclusion in the judgment. The court must include the forfeiture when orally announcing the sentence or must otherwise ensure that the defendant knows of the forfeiture at sentencing. The court must also include the forfeiture order, directly or by reference, in the judgment, but the court's failure to do so may be corrected at any time under Rule 36.

(C) Time to appeal. The time for the defendant or the government to file an appeal from the forfeiture order, or from the court's failure to enter an order, begins to run when judgment is entered. If the court later amends or declines to amend a forfeiture order to include additional property under Rule 32.2(e), the defendant or the government may file an appeal regarding that property under Federal Rule of Appellate Procedure 4(b). The time for that appeal runs from the date when the order granting or denying the amendment becomes final.

(5) *Jury determination.* (A) Retaining the jury. In any case tried before a jury, if the indictment or information states that the government is seeking forfeiture, the court must determine before the jury begins deliberating whether either party requests that the jury be retained to determine the forfeitability of specific property if it returns a guilty verdict.

(B) Special verdict form. If a party timely requests to have the jury determine forfeiture, the government must submit a proposed Special Verdict Form listing each property subject to forfeiture and asking the jury to determine whether the government has established the requisite nexus between the property and the offense committed by the defendant.

(6) *Notice of the forfeiture order.* (A) Publishing and sending notice. If the court orders the forfeiture of specific property, the government must publish notice of the order and send notice to any person who reasonably appears to be a potential claimant with standing to contest the forfeiture in the ancillary proceeding.

(B) Content of the notice. The notice must describe the forfeited property, state the times under the applicable statute when a petition contesting the forfeiture must be filed, and state the name and contact information for the government attorney to be served with the petition.

(C) Means of publication; Exceptions to Publication Requirement. Publication must take place as described in Supplemental Rule G(4)(a)(iii) of the Federal Rules of Civil Procedure, and may be by any means described in Supplemental Rule G(4)(a)(iv). Publication is unnecessary if any exception in Supplemental Rule G(4)(a)(i) applies.

(D) Means of sending the notice. The notice may be sent in accordance with Supplemental Rules G(4)(b)(iii)–(v) of the Federal Rules of Civil Procedure.

(7) *Interlocutory sale.* At any time before entry of a final forfeiture order, the court, in accordance with Supplemental Rule G(7) of the Federal Rules of Civil Procedure, may order the interlocutory sale of property alleged to be forfeitable.

(c) Ancillary Proceeding; Entering a Final Order of Forfeiture. (1) *In General.* If, as prescribed by statute, a third party files a petition asserting an interest in the property to be forfeited, the court must conduct an ancillary proceeding, but no ancillary proceeding is required to the extent that the forfeiture consists of a money judgment.

(A) In the ancillary proceeding, the court may, on motion, dismiss the petition for lack of standing, for failure to state a claim, or for any other lawful reason. For purposes of the motion, the facts set forth in the petition are assumed to be true.

(B) After disposing of any motion filed under Rule 32.2(c)(1)(A) and before conducting a hearing on the petition, the court may permit the parties to conduct discovery in accordance with the Federal Rules of Civil Procedure if the court determines that discovery is necessary or desirable to resolve factual issues. When discovery ends, a party may move for summary judgment under Federal Rule of Civil Procedure 56.

(2) *Entering a Final Order.* When the ancillary proceeding ends, the court must enter a final order of forfeiture by amending the preliminary order as necessary to account for any third-party rights. If no third party files a timely petition, the preliminary order becomes the final order of forfeiture if the court finds that the defendant (or any combination of defendants convicted in the case) had an interest in the property that is forfeitable under the applicable statute. The defendant may not object to the entry of the final order on the ground that the property belongs, in whole or in part, to a codefendant or third party; nor may a third party object to the final order on the ground that the third party had an interest in the property.

(3) *Multiple Petitions.* If multiple third-party petitions are filed in the same case, an order dismissing or granting one petition is not appealable until rulings are made on all the petitions, unless the court determines that there is no just reason for delay.

(4) *Ancillary Proceeding Not Part of Sentencing.* An ancillary proceeding is not part of sentencing.

(d) Stay Pending Appeal. If a defendant appeals from a conviction or an order of forfeiture, the court may stay the order of forfeiture on terms appropriate to ensure that the property remains available pending appellate review. A stay does not delay the ancillary proceeding or the determination of a third party's rights or interests. If the court rules in favor of any third party while an appeal is pending, the court may amend the order of forfeiture but must not transfer any property interest to a third party until the decision on appeal becomes final, unless the defendant consents in writing or on the record.

(e) Subsequently Located Property; Substitute Property. (1) *In General.* On the government's motion, the court may at any time enter an order of forfeiture or amend an existing order of forfeiture to include property that:

(A) is subject to forfeiture under an existing order of forfeiture but was located and identified after that order was entered; or

(B) is substitute property that qualifies for forfeiture under an applicable statute.

(2) *Procedure.* If the government shows that the property is subject to forfeiture under Rule 32.2(e)(1), the court must:

(A) enter an order forfeiting that property, or amend an existing preliminary or final order to include it; and

(B) if a third party files a petition claiming an interest in the property, conduct an ancillary proceeding under Rule 32.2(c).

(3) *Jury Trial Limited.* There is no right to a jury trial under Rule 32.2(e).

(Added April 17, 2000, eff. Dec. 1, 2000; April 29, 2002, eff. Dec. 1, 2002; March 26, 2009, eff. Dec. 1, 2009.)

Rule 33. New trial

(a) Defendant's Motion. Upon the defendant's motion, the court may vacate any judgment and grant a new trial if the interest of justice so requires. If the case was tried without a jury, the court may take additional testimony and enter a new judgment.

(b) Time to File. (1) *Newly Discovered Evidence.* Any motion for a new trial grounded on newly discovered evidence must be filed within 3 years after the verdict or finding of guilty. If an appeal is pending, the court may not grant a motion for a new trial until the appellate court remands the case.

(2) *Other Grounds.* Any motion for a new trial grounded on any reason other than newly discovered evidence must be filed within 14 days after the verdict or finding of guilty.

(Dec. 26, 1944, eff. March 21, 1946, as amended Feb. 28, 1966, eff. July 1, 1966; March 9, 1987, eff. Aug. 1, 1987; April 24, 1998, eff. Dec. 1, 1998; April 29, 2002, eff. Dec. 1, 2002; April 25, 2005, eff. Dec. 1, 2005; March 26, 2009, eff. Dec. 1, 2009.)

Rule 34. Arresting Judgment

(a) In General. Upon the defendant's motion or on its own, the court must arrest judgment if the court does not have jurisdiction of the charged offense.

(b) Time to File. The defendant must move to arrest judgment within 14 days after the court accepts a verdict or finding of guilty, or after a plea of guilty or nolo contendere.

(Dec. 26, 1944, eff. March 21, 1946, as amended Feb. 28, 1966, eff. July 1, 1966; April 29, 2002, eff. Dec. 1, 2002; April 25, 2005, eff. Dec. 1, 2005; March 26, 2009, eff. Dec. 1, 2009; April 25, 2014, eff. Dec. 1, 2014.)

Rule 35. Correcting or Reducing a Sentence

(a) Correcting Clear Error. Within 14 days after sentencing, the court may correct a sentence that resulted from arithmetical, technical, or other clear error.

(b) Reducing a Sentence for Substantial Assistance. (1) *In General.* Upon the government's motion made within one year of sentencing, the court may reduce a sentence if the defendant, after sentencing, provided substantial assistance in investigating or prosecuting another person.

(2) *Later Motion.* Upon the government's motion made more than one year after sentencing, the court may reduce a sentence if the defendant's substantial assistance involved:

(A) information not known to the defendant until one year or more after sentencing;

(B) information provided by the defendant to the government within one year of sentencing, but which did not become useful to the government until more than one year after sentencing; or

(C) information the usefulness of which could not reasonably have been anticipated by the defendant until more than one year after sentencing and which was promptly provided to the government after its usefulness was reasonably apparent to the defendant.

(3) *Evaluating Substantial Assistance.* In evaluating whether the defendant has provided substantial assistance, the court may consider the defendant's presentence assistance.

(4) *Below Statutory Minimum.* When acting under Rule 35(b), the court may reduce the sentence to a level below the minimum sentence established by statute.

(c) "Sentencing" Defined. As used in this rule, "sentencing" means the oral announcement of the sentence.

(Dec. 26, 1944, eff. March 21, 1946, as amended Feb. 28, 1966, eff. July 1, 1966; April 30, 1979, eff. Aug. 1, 1979; April 28, 1983, eff. Aug. 1, 1983; Oct. 12, 1984, P. L. 98-473, Title II, Ch II, § 215(b), 98 Stat. 2015; April 29, 1985, eff. Aug 1, 1985 until Nov. 1, 1986, extended to Nov. 1, 1987; Oct. 27, 1986, P. L. 99-570, Title I, Subtitle A, § 1009(a), 100 Stat. 3207-8; April 26, 1998, eff. Dec. 1, 1991; April 24, 1998, eff. Dec. 1, 1998; April 29, 2002, eff. Dec. 1, 2002; April 26, 2004, eff. Dec. 1, 2004; April 30, 2007, eff. Dec. 1, 2007; March 26, 2009, eff. Dec. 1, 2009.)

Rule 36. Clerical Error

After giving any notice it considers appropriate, the court may at any time correct a clerical error in a judgment, order, or other part of the record, or correct an error in the record arising from oversight or omission.

(Dec. 26, 1944, eff. March 21, 1946; April 29, 2002, eff. Dec. 1, 2002.)

Rule 37. Indicative Ruling on a Motion for Relief That Is Barred by a Pending Appeal

(a) Relief pending appeal. If a timely motion is made for relief that the court lacks authority to grant because of an appeal that has been docketed and is pending, the court may:

(1) defer considering the motion;

(2) deny the motion; or

(3) state either that it would grant the motion if the court of appeals remands for that purpose or that the motion raises a substantial issue.

(b) Notice to the Court of Appeals. The movant must promptly notify the circuit clerk under Federal Rule of Appellate Procedure 12.1 if the district court states that it would grant the motion or that the motion raises a substantial issue.

(c) Remand. The district court may decide the motion if the court of appeals remands for that purpose.

(Added Dec. 1, 2012.)

Rule 38. Staying a Sentence or a Disability

(a) Death Sentence. The court must stay a death sentence if the defendant appeals the conviction or sentence.

(b) Imprisonment. (1) *Stay Granted.* If the defendant is released pending appeal, the court must stay a sentence of imprisonment.

(2) *Stay Denied; Place of Confinement.* If the defendant is not released pending appeal, the court may recommend to the Attorney General that the defendant be confined near the place of the trial or appeal for a period reasonably necessary to permit the defendant to assist in preparing the appeal.

(c) Fine. If the defendant appeals, the district court, or the court of appeals under Federal Rule of Appellate Procedure 8, may stay a sentence to pay a fine or a fine and costs. The court may stay the sentence on any terms considered appropriate and may require the defendant to:

(1) deposit all or part of the fine and costs into the district court's registry pending appeal;

(2) post a bond to pay the fine and costs; or

(3) submit to an examination concerning the defendant's assets and, if appropriate, order the defendant to refrain from dissipating assets.

(d) Probation. If the defendant appeals, the court may stay a sentence of probation. The court must set the terms of any stay.

(e) Restitution and Notice to Victims. (1) *In General.* If the defendant appeals, the district court, or the court of appeals under Federal Rule of Appellate Procedure 8, may stay—on any terms considered appropriate—any sentence providing for restitution under 18 U.S.C. § 3556 or notice under 18 U.S.C. § 3555.

(2) *Ensuring Compliance.* The court may issue any order reasonably necessary to ensure compliance with a restitution order or a notice order after disposition of an appeal, including:

(A) a restraining order;

(B) an injunction;

(C) an order requiring the defendant to deposit all or part of any monetary restitution into the district court's registry; or

(D) an order requiring the defendant to post a bond.

(f) Forfeiture. A stay of a forfeiture order is governed by Rule 32.2(d).

(g) Disability. If the defendant's conviction or sentence creates a civil or employment disability under federal law, the district court, or the court of appeals under Federal Rule of Appellate Procedure 8, may stay the disability pending appeal on any terms considered appropriate. The court may issue any order reasonably necessary to protect the interest represented by the disability pending appeal, including a restraining order or an injunction.

(As amended Dec. 27, 1948, eff. Jan. 1, 1949; Feb. 28, 1966, eff. July 1, 1966; Dec. 4, 1967, eff. July 1, 1968; April 24, 1972, eff. Oct. 1, 1972; Oct. 12, 1984, P. L. 98-473, Title II, Ch II, § 215(c), 98 Stat. 2016; March 9, 1987, eff. Aug. 1, 1987; April 17, 2000, eff. Dec. 1, 2000; April 29, 2002, eff. Dec. 1, 2002.)

Rule 39. [Reserved]

(As amended Dec. 1, 2002.)

VIII. SUPPLEMENTARY AND SPECIAL PROCEEDINGS

Rule 40. Arrest for Failing to Appear in Another District or for Violating Conditions of Release Set in Another District

(a) In General. A person must be taken without unnecessary delay before a magistrate judge in the district of arrest if the person has been arrested under a warrant issued in another district for:

(i) failing to appear as required by the terms of that person's release under 18 U.S.C. §§ 3141–3156 or by a subpoena; or

(ii) violating conditions of release set in another district.

(b) Proceedings. The judge must proceed under Rule 5(c)(3) as applicable.

(c) Release or Detention Order. The judge may modify any previous release or detention order issued in another district, but must state in writing the reasons for doing so.

(d) Video Teleconferencing. Video teleconferencing may be used to conduct an appearance under this rule if the defendant consents.

(Dec. 26, 1944, eff. March 21, 1946, as amended Feb. 28, 1966, eff. July 1, 1966; April 24, 1972, eff. Oct. 1, 1972; April 30, 1979, eff. Aug. 1, 1979; July 31, 1979, P. L. 96-42, § 1(2), 93 Stat. 326; April 28, 1982, eff. August 1, 1982; Oct. 12, 1984, P. L. 98-473, Title II, Ch I, § 209(c), Ch II, § 215(d), 98 Stat. 1986, 2016; March 9, 1987, eff. Aug. 1, 1987; April 25, 1989, eff. Dec. 1, 1989; April 22, 1993, eff. Dec. 1, 1993; April 29, 1994, eff. Dec. 1, 1994; April 27, 1995, eff. Dec. 1, 1995; April 29, 2002, eff. Dec. 1, 2002; April 12, 2006, eff. Dec. 1, 2006; April 26, 2011, eff. Dec. 1, 2011.)

Rule 41. Search and Seizure

(a) Scope and Definitions. (1) *Scope.* This rule

does not modify any statute regulating search or seizure, or the issuance and execution of a search warrant in special circumstances.

(2) *Definitions.* The following definitions apply under this rule:

(A) "Property" includes documents, books, papers, any other tangible objects, and information.

(B) "Daytime" means the hours between 6:00 a.m. and 10:00 p.m. according to local time.

(C) "Federal law enforcement officer" means a government agent (other than an attorney for the government) who is engaged in enforcing the criminal laws and is within any category of officers authorized by the Attorney General to request a search warrant.

(D) "Domestic terrorism" and "international terrorism" have the meanings set out in 18 U.S.C. § 2331.

(E) "Tracking device" has the meaning set out in 18 U.S.C. § 3117(b).

(b) Authority to Issue a Warrant. At the request of a federal law enforcement officer or an attorney for the government:

(1) a magistrate judge with authority in the district—or if none is reasonably available, a judge of a state court of record in the district—has authority to issue a warrant to search for and seize a person or property located within the district;

(2) a magistrate judge with authority in the district has authority to issue a warrant for a person or property outside the district if the person or property is located within the district when the warrant is issued but might move or be moved outside the district before the warrant is executed;

(3) a magistrate judge — in an investigation of domestic terrorism or international terrorism — with authority in any district in which activities related to the terrorism may have occurred has authority to issue a warrant for a person or property within or outside that district;

(4) a magistrate judge with authority in the district has authority to issue a warrant to install within the district a tracking device; the warrant may authorize use of the device to track the movement of a person or property located within the district, outside the district, or both; and

(5) a magistrate judge having authority in any district where activities related to the crime may have occurred, or in the District of Columbia, may issue a warrant for property that is located outside the jurisdiction of any state or district, but within any of the following:

(A) a United States territory, possession, or commonwealth;

(B) the premises — no matter who owns them — of a United States diplomatic or consular mission in a foreign state, including any appurtenant building, part of a building, or land used for the mission's purposes; or

(C) a residence and any appurtenant land owned or leased by the United States and used by United States personnel assigned to a United States diplomatic or consular mission in a foreign state.

(c) Persons or Property Subject to Search or Seizure. A warrant may be issued for any of the following:

(1) evidence of a crime;

(2) contraband, fruits of crime, or other items illegally possessed;

(3) property designed for use, intended for use, or used in committing a crime; or

(4) a person to be arrested or a person who is unlawfully restrained.

(d) Obtaining a Warrant. (1) *In General.* After receiving an affidavit or other information, a magistrate judge—or if authorized by Rule 41(b), a judge of a state court of record—must issue the warrant if there is probable cause to search for and seize a person or property or to install and use a tracking device.

(2) *Requesting a Warrant in the Presence of a Judge.* (A) Warrant on an Affidavit. When a federal law enforcement officer or an attorney for the government presents an affidavit in support of a warrant, the judge may require the affiant to appear personally and may examine under oath the affiant and any witness the affiant produces.

(B) Warrant on Sworn Testimony. The judge may wholly or partially dispense with a written affidavit and base a warrant on sworn testimony if doing so is reasonable under the circumstances.

(C) Recording Testimony. Testimony taken in support of a warrant must be recorded by a court reporter or by a suitable recording device, and the judge must file the transcript or recording with the clerk, along with any affidavit.

(3) *Requesting a Warrant by Telephonic or Other Means.* In accordance with Rule 4.1, a magistrate judge may issue a warrant based on information communicated by telephone or other reliable electronic means.

(e) Issuing the Warrant. (1) *In General.* The magistrate judge or a judge of a state court of record must issue the warrant to an officer authorized to execute it.

(2) *Contents of the Warrant.*

(A) Warrant to Search for and Seize a Person or Property. Except for a tracking-device warrant, the warrant must identify the person or property to be searched, identify any person or property to be seized, and designate the magistrate judge to whom it must be returned. The warrant must command the officer to:

(i) execute the warrant within a specified time no longer than 14 days;

(ii) execute the warrant during the daytime, unless the judge for good cause expressly authorizes execution at another time; and

(iii) return the warrant to the magistrate judge designated in the warrant.

(B) Warrant Seeking Electronically Stored Information. A warrant under Rule 41(e)(2)(A) may authorize the seizure of electronic storage media or the seizure or copying of electronically stored information. Unless otherwise specified, the warrant authorizes a later review of the media or information consistent with the warrant. The time for executing the warrant in Rule 41(e)(2)(A) and (f)(1)(A) refers to the seizure or on-site copying of the media or information, and not to any later off-site copying or review.

(C) Warrant for a Tracking Device. A tracking-device warrant must identify the person or property to be tracked, designate the magistrate judge to whom it must be returned, and specify a reasonable length of time that the device may be used. The time must not exceed 45 days from the date the warrant was issued. The court may, for good cause, grant one or more extensions for a reasonable period not to exceed 45 days each. The warrant must command the officer to:

(i) complete any installation authorized by the warrant within a specified time no longer than 10 days;

(ii) perform any installation authorized by the warrant during the daytime, unless the judge for good cause expressly authorizes installation at another time; and

(iii) return the warrant to the judge designated in the warrant.

(3) *Warrant by Telephonic or Other Means.* If a magistrate judge decides to proceed under Rule 41(d)(3)(A), the following additional procedures apply:

(A) Preparing a Proposed Duplicate Original Warrant. The applicant must prepare a "proposed duplicate original warrant" and must read or otherwise transmit the contents of that document verbatim to the magistrate judge.

(B) Preparing an Original Warrant. If the applicant reads the contents of the proposed duplicate original warrant, the magistrate judge must enter those contents into an original warrant. If the applicant transmits the contents by reliable electronic means, that transmission may serve as the original warrant.

(C) Modification. The magistrate judge may modify the original warrant. The judge must transmit any modified warrant to the applicant by reliable electronic means under Rule 41(e)(3)(D) or direct the applicant to modify the proposed duplicate original warrant accordingly.

(D) Signing the Warrant. Upon determining to issue the warrant, the magistrate judge must immediately sign the original warrant, enter on its face the exact date and time it is issued, and transmit it by reliable electronic means to the applicant or direct the applicant to sign the judge's name on the duplicate original warrant.

(f) Executing and Returning the Warrant. (1) *Warrant to Search for and Seize a Person or Property.* (A) Noting the Time. The officer executing the warrant must enter on it the exact date and time it was executed.

(B) Inventory. An officer present during the execution of the warrant must prepare and verify an inventory of any property seized. The officer must do so in the presence of another officer and the person from whom, or from whose premises, the property was taken. If either one is not present, the officer must prepare and verify the inventory in the presence of at least one other credible person. In a case involving the seizure of electronic storage media or the seizure or copying of electronically stored information, the inventory may be limited to describing the physical storage media that were seized or copied. The officer may retain a copy of the electronically stored information that was seized or copied.

(C) Receipt. The officer executing the warrant must give a copy of the warrant and a receipt for the property taken to the person from whom, or from whose premises, the property was taken or leave a copy of the warrant and receipt at the place where the officer took the property.

(D) Return. The officer executing the warrant must promptly return it—together with a copy of the inventory—to the magistrate judge designated on the warrant. The officer may do so by reliable electronic means. The judge must, on request, give a copy of the inventory to the person from whom, or from whose premises, the property was taken and to the applicant for the warrant.

(2) *Warrant for a Tracking Device.*

(A) Noting the Time. The officer executing a tracking-device warrant must enter on it the exact date and time the device was installed and the period during which it was used.

(B) Return. Within 10 days after the use of the tracking device has ended, the officer executing the warrant must return it to the judge designated in the warrant. The officer may do so by reliable electronic means.

(C) Service. Within 10 days after the use of the tracking device has ended, the officer executing a tracking-device warrant must serve a copy of the warrant on the person who was tracked or whose property was tracked. Service may be accomplished by delivering a copy to the person who, or whose property, was tracked; or by leaving a copy at the person's residence or usual place of abode with an individual of suitable age and discretion who resides at that location and by mailing a copy to the person's last known address. Upon request of the government, the judge may delay notice as provided in Rule 41(f)(3).

(3) *Delayed Notice.* Upon the government's request, a magistrate judge—or if authorized by Rule 41(b), a judge of a state court of record—may delay any notice required by this rule if the delay is authorized by statute.

(4) *Return.* The officer executing the warrant must promptly return it—together with a copy of the inventory—to the magistrate judge designated on

the warrant. The judge must, on request, give a copy of the inventory to the person from whom, or from whose premises, the property was taken and to the applicant for the warrant.

(g) Motion to Return Property. A person aggrieved by an unlawful search and seizure of property or by the deprivation of property may move for the property's return. The motion must be filed in the district where the property was seized. The court must receive evidence on any factual issue necessary to decide the motion. If it grants the motion, the court must return the property to the movant, but may impose reasonable conditions to protect access to the property and its use in later proceedings.

(h) Motion to Suppress. A defendant may move to suppress evidence in the court where the trial will occur, as Rule 12 provides.

(i) Forwarding Papers to the Clerk. The magistrate judge to whom the warrant is returned must attach to the warrant a copy of the return, of the inventory, and of all other related papers and must deliver them to the clerk in the district where the property was seized.

(Dec. 26, 1944, eff. March 21, 1946, as amended Dec. 27, 1948, eff. Oct. 20, 1949; April 9, 1956, eff. 90 days after April 9, 1956; April 24, 1972, eff. Oct. 1, 1972; March 18, 1974, eff. July 1, 1974; April 26, 1976, eff. Aug. 1, 1976 and Oct. 1, 1977; Act July 8, 1976, P.L. 94-349, § 1, 90 Stat. 822; Act July 30, 1977, P.L. 95-78, §§ 2(e), 4, 91 Stat. 320, 322, eff. Oct. 1, 1977; April 30, 1979, eff. Aug. 1, 1979; March 9, 1987, eff. Aug. 1, 1987; April 25, 1989, eff. Dec. 1, 1989; May 1, 1990, eff. Dec. 1, 1990; April 22, 1993, eff. Dec. 1, 1993; Oct. 26, 2001, P. L. 107-56, Title II, § 219, 115 Stat. 291; April 29, 2002, eff. Dec. 1, 2002; April 12, 2006, eff. Dec. 1, 2006; April 23, 2008, eff. Dec. 1, 2008; March 26, 2009, eff. Dec. 1, 2009; April 26, 2011, eff. Dec. 1, 2011.)

Rule 42. Criminal Contempt

(a) Disposition After Notice. Any person who commits criminal contempt may be punished for that contempt after prosecution on notice.

(1) *Notice.* The court must give the person notice in open court, in an order to show cause, or in an arrest order. The notice must:

(A) state the time and place of the trial;

(B) allow the defendant a reasonable time to prepare a defense; and

(C) state the essential facts constituting the charged criminal contempt and describe it as such.

(2) *Appointing a Prosecutor.* The court must request that the contempt be prosecuted by an attorney for the government, unless the interest of justice requires the appointment of another attorney. If the government declines the request, the court must appoint another attorney to prosecute the contempt.

(3) *Trial and Disposition.* A person being prosecuted for criminal contempt is entitled to a jury trial in any case in which federal law so provides and must be released or detained as Rule 46 provides. If the criminal contempt involves disrespect toward or criticism of a judge, that judge is disqualified from presiding at the contempt trial or hearing unless the defendant consents. Upon a finding or verdict of guilty, the court must impose the punishment.

(b) Summary Disposition. Notwithstanding any other provision of these rules, the court (other than a magistrate judge) may summarily punish a person who commits criminal contempt in its presence if the judge saw or heard the contemptuous conduct and so certifies; a magistrate judge may summarily punish a person as provided in 28 U.S.C. § 636(e). The contempt order must recite the facts, be signed by the judge, and be filed with the clerk.

(Dec. 26, 1944, eff. March 21, 1946; March 9, 1987, eff. Aug. 1, 1987; April 29, 2002, eff. Dec. 1, 2002.)

IX. GENERAL PROVISIONS

Rule 43. Defendant's Presence

(a) When Required. Unless this rule, Rule 5, or Rule 10 provides otherwise, the defendant must be present at:

(1) the initial appearance, the initial arraignment, and the plea;

(2) every trial stage, including jury impanelment and the return of the verdict; and

(3) sentencing.

(b) When Not Required. A defendant need not be present under any of the following circumstances:

(1) *Organizational Defendant.* The defendant is an organization represented by counsel who is present.

(2) *Misdemeanor Offense.* The offense is punishable by fine or by imprisonment for not more than one year, or both, and with the defendant's written consent, the court permits arraignment, plea, trial, and sentencing to occur by video teleconferencing or in the defendant's absence.

(3) *Conference or Hearing on a Legal Question.* The proceeding involves only a conference or hearing on a question of law.

(4) *Sentence Correction.* The proceeding involves the correction or reduction of sentence under Rule 35 or 18 U.S.C. § 3582(c).

(c) Waiving Continued Presence. (1) *In General.* A defendant who was initially present at trial, or who had pleaded guilty or nolo contendere, waives the right to be present under the following circumstances:

(A) when the defendant is voluntarily absent after the trial has begun, regardless of whether the court informed the defendant of an obligation to remain during trial;

(B) in a noncapital case, when the defendant is voluntarily absent during sentencing; or

(C) when the court warns the defendant that it will remove the defendant from the courtroom for disruptive behavior, but the defendant persists in conduct that justifies removal from the courtroom.

(2) *Waiver's Effect.* If the defendant waives the

right to be present, the trial may proceed to completion, including the verdict's return and sentencing, during the defendant's absence.

(Dec. 26, 1944, eff. March 21, 1946, as amended April 22, 1974, eff. Dec. 1, 1975; Act July 31, 1975, P. L. 94-64, §§ 2, 3(35), 89 Stat. 370, 376, eff. Dec. 1, 1975; March 9, 1987, eff. Aug. 1, 1987; April 27, 1995, eff. Dec. 1, 1995; April 24, 1998, eff. Dec. 1, 1998; April 29, 2002, eff. Dec. 1, 2002; April 26, 2011, eff. Dec. 1, 2011.)

Rule 44. Right to and Appointment of Counsel

(a) Right to Appointed Counsel. A defendant who is unable to obtain counsel is entitled to have counsel appointed to represent the defendant at every stage of the proceeding from initial appearance through appeal, unless the defendant waives this right.

(b) Appointment Procedure. Federal law and local court rules govern the procedure for implementing the right to counsel.

(c) Inquiry Into Joint Representation. (1) *Joint Representation.* Joint representation occurs when:

(A) two or more defendants have been charged jointly under Rule 8(b) or have been joined for trial under Rule 13; and

(B) the defendants are represented by the same counsel, or counsel who are associated in law practice.

(2) *Court's Responsibilities in Cases of Joint Representation.* The court must promptly inquire about the propriety of joint representation and must personally advise each defendant of the right to the effective assistance of counsel, including separate representation. Unless there is good cause to believe that no conflict of interest is likely to arise, the court must take appropriate measures to protect each defendant's right to counsel.

(Dec. 26, 1944, eff. March 21, 1946, as amended Feb. 28, 1966, eff. July 1, 1966; April 24, 1972, eff. Oct. 1, 1972; April 30, 1979, eff. Dec. 1, 1980, as provided by Act July 31, 1979, P. L. 96-42, § 1(1), 93 Stat. 362; March 9, 1987, eff. Aug. 1, 1987; April 22, 1993, eff. Dec. 1, 1993; April 29, 2002, eff. Dec. 1, 2002.)

Rule 45. Computing and Extending Time

(a) Computing Time. The following rules apply in computing any time period specified in these rules, in any local rule or court order, or in any statute that does not specify a method of computing time.

(1) *Period stated in days or a longer unit.* When the period is stated in days or a longer unit of time:

(A) exclude the day of the event that triggers the period;

(B) count every day, including intermediate Saturdays, Sundays, and legal holidays; and

(C) include the last day of the period, but if the last day is a Saturday, Sunday, or legal holiday, the period continues to run until the end of the next day that is not a Saturday, Sunday, or legal holiday.

(2) *Period stated in hours.* When the period is stated in hours:

(A) begin counting immediately on the occurrence of the event that triggers the period;

(B) count every hour, including hours during intermediate Saturdays, Sundays, and legal holidays; and

(C) if the period would end on a Saturday, Sunday, or legal holiday, the period continues to run until the same time on the next day that is not a Saturday, Sunday, or legal holiday.

(3) *Inaccessibility of the clerk's office.* Unless the court orders otherwise, if the clerk's office is inaccessible:

(A) on the last day for filing under Rule 45(a)(1), then the time for filing is extended to the first accessible day that is not a Saturday, Sunday, or legal holiday; or

(B) during the last hour for filing under Rule 45(a)(2), then the time for filing is extended to the same time on the first accessible day that is not a Saturday, Sunday, or legal holiday.

(4) *"Last day" defined.* Unless a different time is set by a statute, local rule, or court order, the last day ends:

(A) for electronic filing, at midnight in the court's time zone; and

(B) for filing by other means, when the clerk's office is scheduled to close.

(5) *"Next day" defined.* The "next day" is determined by continuing to count forward when the period is measured after an event and backward when measured before an event.

(6) *"Legal holiday" defined.* "Legal holiday" means:

(A) the day set aside by statute for observing New Year's Day, Martin Luther King Jr.'s Birthday, Washington's Birthday, Memorial Day, Independence Day, Labor Day, Columbus Day, Veterans' Day, Thanksgiving Day, or Christmas Day;

(B) any day declared a holiday by the President or Congress; and

(C) for periods that are measured after an event, any other day declared a holiday by the state where the district court is located.

(b) Extending Time. (1) *In General.* When an act must or may be done within a specified period, the court on its own may extend the time, or for good cause may do so on a party's motion made:

(A) before the originally prescribed or previously extended time expires; or

(B) after the time expires if the party failed to act because of excusable neglect.

(2) *Exception.* The court may not extend the time to take any action under Rule 35, except as stated in that rule.

(c) Additional Time After Certain Kinds of Service. Whenever a party must or may act within a specified period after service and service is made in the manner provided under Federal Rule of Civil Procedure 5(b)(2)(C), (D), (E), or (F), 3 days are added after the period would otherwise expire under subdivision (a).

(Dec. 26, 1944, eff. March 21, 1946, as amended Feb. 28, 1966, eff. July 1, 1966; Dec. 4, 1967, eff. July 1, 1968; March 1, 1971, eff. July 1, 1971; April 28, 1982, eff. Aug. 1, 1982; April 29, 1985, eff. Aug. 1, 1985; March 9, 1987, eff. Aug. 1, 1987; April 29, 2002, eff. Dec. 1, 2002; April 25, 2005, eff. Dec. 1, 2005; April 30, 2007, eff. Dec. 1, 2007; April 23, 2008, eff. Dec. 1, 2008; March 26, 2009, eff. Dec. 1, 2009.)

Rule 46. Release from Custody; Supervising Detention

(a) Before Trial. The provisions of 18 U.S.C. §§ 3142 and 3144 govern pretrial release.

(b) During Trial. A person released before trial continues on release during trial under the same terms and conditions. But the court may order different terms and conditions or terminate the release if necessary to ensure that the person will be present during trial or that the person's conduct will not obstruct the orderly and expeditious progress of the trial.

(c) Pending Sentencing or Appeal. The provisions of 18 U.S.C. § 3143 govern release pending sentencing or appeal. The burden of establishing that the defendant will not flee or pose a danger to any other person or to the community rests with the defendant.

(d) Pending Hearing on a Violation of Probation or Supervised Release. Rule 32.1(a)(6) governs release pending a hearing on a violation of probation or supervised release.

(e) Surety. The court must not approve a bond unless any surety appears to be qualified. Every surety, except a legally approved corporate surety, must demonstrate by affidavit that its assets are adequate. The court may require the affidavit to describe the following:

(1) the property that the surety proposes to use as security;

(2) any encumbrance on that property;

(3) the number and amount of any other undischarged bonds and bail undertakings the surety has issued; and

(4) any other liability of the surety.

(f) Bail Forfeiture. (1) *Declaration.* The court must declare the bail forfeited if a condition of the bond is breached.

(2) *Setting Aside.* The court may set aside in whole or in part a bail forfeiture upon any condition the court may impose if:

(A) the surety later surrenders into custody the person released on the surety's appearance bond; or

(B) it appears that justice does not require bail forfeiture.

(3) *Enforcement.* (A) *Default Judgment and Execution.* If it does not set aside a bail forfeiture, the court must, upon the government's motion, enter a default judgment.

(B) *Jurisdiction and Service.* By entering into a bond, each surety submits to the district court's jurisdiction and irrevocably appoints the district clerk as its agent to receive service of any filings affecting its liability.

(C) *Motion to Enforce.* The court may, upon the government's motion, enforce the surety's liability without an independent action. The government must serve any motion, and notice as the court prescribes, on the district clerk. If so served, the clerk must promptly mail a copy to the surety at its last known address.

(4) *Remission.* After entering a judgment under Rule 46(f)(3), the court may remit in whole or in part the judgment under the same conditions specified in Rule 46(f)(2).

(g) Exoneration. The court must exonerate the surety and release any bail when a bond condition has been satisfied or when the court has set aside or remitted the forfeiture. The court must exonerate a surety who deposits cash in the amount of the bond or timely surrenders the defendant into custody.

(h) Supervising Detention Pending Trial. (1) *In General.* To eliminate unnecessary detention, the court must supervise the detention within the district of any defendants awaiting trial and of any persons held as material witnesses.

(2) *Reports.* An attorney for the government must report biweekly to the court, listing each material witness held in custody for more than 10 days pending indictment, arraignment, or trial. For each material witness listed in the report, an attorney for the government must state why the witness should not be released with or without a deposition being taken under Rule 15(a).

(i) Forfeiture of Property. The court may dispose of a charged offense by ordering the forfeiture of 18 U.S.C. § 3142(c)(1)(B)(xi) property under 18 U.S.C. § 3146(d), if a fine in the amount of the property's value would be an appropriate sentence for the charged offense.

(j) Producing a Statement. (1) *In General.* Rule 26.2(a)–(d) and (f) applies at a detention hearing under 18 U.S.C. § 3142, unless the court for good cause rules otherwise.

(2) *Sanctions for Not Producing a Statement.* If a party disobeys a Rule 26.2 order to produce a witness's statement, the court must not consider that witness's testimony at the detention hearing.

(Dec. 26, 1944, eff. March 1, 1946, as amended April 9, 1956, eff. 90 days after April 9, 1956; Feb. 28, 1966, eff. July 1, 1966; April 24, 1972, eff. Oct. 1, 1972; Oct. 12, 1984, P. L. 98-473, Title II, Ch I, § 209(d), 98 Stat. 1987; March 9, 1987, eff. Aug. 1, 1987; April 30, 1991, eff. Dec. 1, 1991; April 22, 1993, eff. Dec. 1, 1993; Sept. 13, 1994; P. L. 103-322, Title XXXIII, § 330003(h), 108 Stat. 2141; April 29, 2002, eff. Dec. 1, 2002.)

Rule 47. Motions and Supporting Affidavits

(a) In General. A party applying to the court for an order must do so by motion.

(b) Form and Content of a Motion. A motion—except when made during a trial or hearing—must be in writing, unless the court permits the party to make the motion by other means. A motion must state the grounds on which it is based and the relief or order sought. A motion may be supported by affidavit.

(c) Timing of a Motion. A party must serve a written motion—other than one that the court may hear ex parte—and any hearing notice at least 7 days before the hearing date, unless a rule or court order sets a different period. For good cause, the court may set a different period upon ex parte application.

(d) Affidavit Supporting a Motion. The moving party must serve any supporting affidavit with the motion. A responding party must serve any opposing affidavit at least one day before the hearing, unless the court permits later service.

(Dec. 26, 1944, eff. March 21, 1946; April 29, 2002, eff. Dec. 1, 2002; March 26, 2009, eff. Dec. 1, 2009.)

Rule 48. Dismissal

(a) By the Government. The government may, with leave of court, dismiss an indictment, information, or complaint. The government may not dismiss the prosecution during trial without the defendant's consent.

(b) By the Court. The court may dismiss an indictment, information, or complaint if unnecessary delay occurs in:

(1) presenting a charge to a grand jury;

(2) filing an information against a defendant; or

(3) bringing a defendant to trial.

(Dec. 26, 1944, eff. March 21, 1946; April 29, 2002, eff. Dec. 1, 2002.)

Rule 49. Serving and Filing Papers

(a) When Required. A party must serve on every other party any written motion (other than one to be heard ex parte), written notice, designation of the record on appeal, or similar paper.

(b) How Made. Service must be made in the manner provided for a civil action. When these rules or a court order requires or permits service on a party represented by an attorney, service must be made on the attorney instead of the party, unless the court orders otherwise.

(c) Notice of a Court Order. When the court issues an order on any post-arraignment motion, the clerk must provide notice in a manner provided for in a civil action. Except as Federal Rule of Appellate Procedure 4(b) provides otherwise, the clerk's failure to give notice does not affect the time to appeal, or relieve—or authorize the court to relieve—a party's failure to appeal within the allowed time.

(d) Filing. A party must file with the court a copy of any paper the party is required to serve. A paper must be filed in a manner provided for in a civil action.

(e) Electronic Service and Filing. A court may, by local rule, allow papers to be filed, signed, or verified by electronic means that are consistent with any technical standards established by the Judicial Conference of the United States. A local rule may require electronic filing only if reasonable exceptions are allowed. A paper filed electronically in compliance with a local rule is written or in writing under these rules.

(Dec. 26, 1944, eff. March 21, 1946, as amended Feb. 28, 1966, eff. July 1, 1966; Dec. 4, 1967, eff. July 1, 1968; April 29, 1985, eff. Aug. 1, 1985; March 9, 1987, eff. Aug. 1, 1987; April 22, 1993, eff. Dec. 1, 1993; April 27, 1995, eff. Dec. 1, 1995; April 29, 2002, eff. Dec. 1, 2002; April 26, 2011, eff. Dec. 1, 2011.)

Rule 49.1. Privacy Protection For Filings Made with the Court

(a) Redacted Filings. Unless the court orders otherwise, in an electronic or paper filing with the court that contains an individual's social-security number, taxpayer-identification number, or birth date, the name of an individual known to be a minor, a financial-account number, or the home address of an individual, a party or nonparty making the filing may include only:

(1) the last four digits of the social-security number and taxpayer-identification number;

(2) the year of the individual's birth;

(3) the minor's initials;

(4) the last four digits of the financial-account number; and

(5) the city and state of the home address.

(b) Exemptions from the Redaction Requirement. The redaction requirement does not apply to the following:

(1) a financial-account number or real property address that identifies the property allegedly subject to forfeiture in a forfeiture proceeding;

(2) the record of an administrative or agency proceeding;

(3) the official record of a state-court proceeding;

(4) the record of a court or tribunal, if that record was not subject to the redaction requirement when originally filed;

(5) a filing covered by Rule 49.1(d);

(6) a pro se filing in an action brought under 28 U.S.C. §§ 2241, 2254, or 2255;

(7) a court filing that is related to a criminal matter or investigation and that is prepared before the filing of a criminal charge or is not filed as part of any docketed criminal case;

(8) an arrest or search warrant; and

(9) a charging document and an affidavit filed in support of any charging document.

(c) Immigration Cases. A filing in an action brought under 28 U.S.C. § 2241 that relates to the petitioner's immigration rights is governed by Federal Rule of Civil Procedure 5.2.

(d) Filings Made Under Seal. The court may order that a filing be made under seal without redaction. The court may later unseal the filing or order the person who made the filing to file a redacted version for the public record.

(e) Protective Orders. For good cause, the court may by order in a case:

(1) require redaction of additional information; or

(2) limit or prohibit a nonparty's remote electronic access to a document filed with the court.

(f) Option for Additional Unredacted Filing Under Seal. A person making a redacted filing may also file an unredacted copy under seal. The court must retain the unredacted copy as part of the record.

(g) Option for Filing a Reference List. A filing that contains redacted information may be filed together with a reference list that identifies each item of redacted information and specifies an appropriate identifier that uniquely corresponds to each item listed. The list must be filed under seal and may be amended as of right. Any reference in the case to a listed identifier will be construed to refer to the corresponding item of information.

(h) Waiver of Protection of Identifiers. A person waives the protection of Rule 49.1(a) as to the person's own information by filing it without redaction and not under seal.

(As added April 30, 2007, eff. Dec. 1, 2007.)

Rule 50. Prompt Disposition

Scheduling preference must be given to criminal proceedings as far as practicable.

(Dec. 26, 1944, eff. March 21, 1946, as amended April 24, 1972, eff. Oct. 1, 1972; March 18, 1974, eff. July 1, 1974; April 26, 1976, eff. Aug. 1, 1976; July 8, 1976, P.L. 94-349, § 1, 90 Stat. 822; April 22, 1993, eff. Dec. 1, 1993; April 29, 2002, eff. Dec. 1, 2002.)

Rule 51. Preserving Claimed Error

(a) Exceptions Unnecessary. Exceptions to rulings or orders of the court are unnecessary.

(b) Preserving a Claim of Error. A party may preserve a claim of error by informing the court—when the court ruling or order is made or sought—of the action the party wishes the court to take, or the party's objection to the court's action and the grounds for that objection. If a party does not have an opportunity to object to a ruling or order, the absence of an objection does not later prejudice that party. A ruling or order that admits or excludes evidence is governed by Federal Rule of Evidence 103.

(Dec. 26, 1944, eff. March 21, 1946; March 9, 1987, eff. eff. Aug. 1, 1987; April 29, 2002, eff. Dec. 1, 2002.)

Rule 52. Harmless and Plain Error.

(a) Harmless error. Any error, defect, irregularity, or variance that does not affect substantial rights must be disregarded.

(b) Plain error. A plain error that affects substantial rights may be considered even though it was not brought to the court's attention.

(Dec. 26, 1944, eff. March 21, 1946l; April 29, 2002, eff. Dec. 1, 2002.)

Rule 53. Courtroom Photographing and Broadcasting Prohibited

Except as otherwise provided by a statute or these rules, the court must not permit the taking of photographs in the courtroom during judicial proceedings or the broadcasting of judicial proceedings from the courtroom.

(Dec. 26, 1944, eff. March 21, 1946l April 29, 2002, eff. Dec. 1, 2002.)

Rule 54. [Transferred]

(Dec. 26, 1944, eff. March 21, 1946, as amended Dec. 27, 1948, eff. Oct. 20, 1949; April 9, 1956, eff. 90 days after April 9, 1956; Feb. 28, 1966, eff. July 1, 1966; April 24, 1972, eff. Oct. 1, 1972; April 29, 1982, eff. Aug. 1, 1982; Oct. 12, 1984, P. L. 98-473, Title II, Ch I, § 209(e), Ch II, § 215(e) 98 Stat. 1987, 2016; Nov. 18, 1988, P. L. 100-690, Title VII, Subtitle B, § 7089(c), 102 Stat. 4409; May 1, 1990, eff. Dec. 1, 1990; April 30, 1991, eff. Dec. 1, 1991; April 22, 1993, eff. Dec. 1, 1993; April 26, 1999, eff. Dec. 1, 1999; April 29, 2002, eff. Dec. 1, 2002.)

Rule 55. Records

The clerk of the district court must keep records of criminal proceedings in the form prescribed by the Director of the Administrative Office of the United States Courts. The clerk must enter in the records every court order or judgment and the date of entry.

(Dec. 26, 1944, eff. March 21, 1946, as amended Dec. 27, 1948, eff. Oct. 20, 1949; Feb. 28, 1966, eff. July 1, 1966; April 24, 1972, eff. Oct. 1, 1972; April 22, 1993, eff. Dec. 1, 1993; April 29, 2002, eff. Dec. 1, 2002.)

Rule 56. When Court Is Open

(a) In General. A district court is considered always open for any filing, and for issuing and returning process, making a motion, or entering an order.

(b) Office Hours. The clerk's office—with the clerk or a deputy in attendance—must be open during business hours on all days except Saturdays, Sundays, and legal holidays.

(c) Special Hours. A court may provide by local rule or order that its clerk's office will be open for specified hours on Saturdays or legal holidays other than those set aside by statute for observing New Year's Day, Martin Luther King, Jr.'s Birthday, Washington's Birthday, Memorial Day, Independence Day, Labor Day, Columbus Day, Veterans' Day, Thanksgiving Day, and Christmas Day.

(Dec. 26, 1944, eff. March 21, 1946, as amended Dec. 27, 1948, eff. Oct. 20, 1949; Feb. 28, 1966, eff.

July 1, 1966; Dec. 4, 1967, eff. July 1, 1968; March 1, 1971, eff. July 1, 1971; April 25, 1988, eff. Aug. 1, 1988; April 29, 2002, eff. Dec. 1, 2002.)

Rule 57. District Court Rules

(a) In General. (1) *Adopting Local Rules.* Each district court acting by a majority of its district judges may, after giving appropriate public notice and an opportunity to comment, make and amend rules governing its practice. A local rule must be consistent with—but not duplicative of—federal statutes and rules adopted under 28 U.S.C. § 2072 and must conform to any uniform numbering system prescribed by the Judicial Conference of the United States.

(2) *Limiting Enforcement.* A local rule imposing a requirement of form must not be enforced in a manner that causes a party to lose rights because of an unintentional failure to comply with the requirement.

(b) Procedure When There Is No Controlling Law. A judge may regulate practice in any manner consistent with federal law, these rules, and the local rules of the district. No sanction or other disadvantage may be imposed for noncompliance with any requirement not in federal law, federal rules, or the local district rules unless the alleged violator was furnished with actual notice of the requirement before the noncompliance.

(c) Effective Date and Notice. A local rule adopted under this rule takes effect on the date specified by the district court and remains in effect unless amended by the district court or abrogated by the judicial council of the circuit in which the district is located. Copies of local rules and their amendments, when promulgated, must be furnished to the judicial council and the Administrative Office of the United States Courts and must be made available to the public.

(Dec. 26, 1944, eff. March 21, 1946, as amended Dec. 27, 1948, eff. Oct. 20, 1949; Dec. 4, 1967, eff. July 1, 1968; April 29, 1985, eff. August 1, 1985; April 22, 1993, eff. Dec. 1, 1993; April 27, 1995, eff. Dec. 1, 1995; April 29, 2002, eff. Dec. 1, 2002.)

Rule 58. Petty Offenses and Other Misdemeanors

(a) Scope. (1) *In General.* These rules apply in petty offense and other misdemeanor cases and on appeal to a district judge in a case tried by a magistrate judge, unless this rule provides otherwise.

(2) *Petty Offense Case Without Imprisonment.* In a case involving a petty offense for which no sentence of imprisonment will be imposed, the court may follow any provision of these rules that is not inconsistent with this rule and that the court considers appropriate.

(3) *Definition.* As used in this rule, the term "petty offense for which no sentence of imprisonment will be imposed" means a petty offense for which the court determines that, in the event of conviction, no sentence of imprisonment will be imposed.

(b) Pretrial Procedure. (1) *Charging Document.* The trial of a misdemeanor may proceed on an indictment, information, or complaint. The trial of a petty offense may also proceed on a citation or violation notice.

(2) *Initial Appearance.* At the defendant's initial appearance on a petty offense or other misdemeanor charge, the magistrate judge must inform the defendant of the following:

(A) the charge, and the minimum and maximum penalties, including imprisonment, fines, any special assessment under 18 U.S.C. § 3013, and restitution under 18 U.S.C. § 3556;

(B) the right to retain counsel;

(C) the right to request the appointment of counsel if the defendant is unable to retain counsel—unless the charge is a petty offense for which the appointment of counsel is not required;

(D) the defendant's right not to make a statement, and that any statement made may be used against the defendant;

(E) the right to trial, judgment, and sentencing before a district judge—unless:

(i) the charge is a petty offense; or

(ii) the defendant consents to trial, judgment, and sentencing before a magistrate judge.

(F) the right to a jury trial before either a magistrate judge or a district judge—unless the charge is a petty offense;

(G) any right to a preliminary hearing under Rule 5.1, and the general circumstances, if any, under which the defendant may secure pretrial release; and

(H) that a defendant who is not a United States citizen may request that an attorney for the government or a federal law enforcement official notify a consular officer from the defendant's country of nationality that the defendant has been arrested—but that even without the defendant's request, a treaty or other international agreement may require consular notification.

(3) *Arraignment.* (A) Plea Before a Magistrate Judge. A magistrate judge may take the defendant's plea in a petty offense case. In every other misdemeanor case, a magistrate judge may take the plea only if the defendant consents either in writing or on the record to be tried before a magistrate judge and specifically waives trial before a district judge. The defendant may plead not guilty, guilty, or (with the consent of the magistrate judge) nolo contendere.

(B) Failure to Consent. Except in a petty offense case, the magistrate judge must order a defendant who does not consent to trial before a magistrate judge to appear before a district judge for further proceedings.

(c) Additional Procedures in Certain Petty Offense Cases. The following procedures also apply in a case involving a petty offense for which no sentence of imprisonment will be imposed:

(1) *Guilty or Nolo Contendere Plea.* The court must not accept a guilty or nolo contendere plea unless satisfied that the defendant understands the nature of the charge and the maximum possible penalty.

(2) *Waiving Venue.* (A) Conditions of Waiving Venue. If a defendant is arrested, held, or present in a district different from the one where the indictment, information, complaint, citation, or violation notice is pending, the defendant may state in writing a desire to plead guilty or nolo contendere; to waive venue and trial in the district where the proceeding is pending; and to consent to the court's disposing of the case in the district where the defendant was arrested, is held, or is present.

(B) Effect of Waiving Venue. Unless the defendant later pleads not guilty, the prosecution will proceed in the district where the defendant was arrested, is held, or is present. The district clerk must notify the clerk in the original district of the defendant's waiver of venue. The defendant's statement of a desire to plead guilty or nolo contendere is not admissible against the defendant.

(3) *Sentencing.* The court must give the defendant an opportunity to be heard in mitigation and then proceed immediately to sentencing. The court may, however, postpone sentencing to allow the probation service to investigate or to permit either party to submit additional information.

(4) *Notice of a Right to Appeal.* After imposing sentence in a case tried on a not-guilty plea, the court must advise the defendant of a right to appeal the conviction and of any right to appeal the sentence. If the defendant was convicted on a plea of guilty or nolo contendere, the court must advise the defendant of any right to appeal the sentence.

(d) Paying a Fixed Sum in Lieu of Appearance. (1) *In General.* If the court has a local rule governing forfeiture of collateral, the court may accept a fixed-sum payment in lieu of the defendant's appearance and end the case, but the fixed sum may not exceed the maximum fine allowed by law.

(2) *Notice to Appear.* If the defendant fails to pay a fixed sum, request a hearing, or appear in response to a citation or violation notice, the district clerk or a magistrate judge may issue a notice for the defendant to appear before the court on a date certain. The notice may give the defendant an additional opportunity to pay a fixed sum in lieu of appearance. The district clerk must serve the notice on the defendant by mailing a copy to the defendant's last known address.

(3) *Summons or Warrant.* Upon an indictment, or upon a showing by one of the other charging documents specified in Rule 58(b)(1) of probable cause to believe that an offense has been committed and that the defendant has committed it, the court may issue an arrest warrant or, if no warrant is requested by an attorney for the government, a summons. The showing of probable cause must be made under oath or under penalty of perjury, but the affiant need not appear before the court. If the defendant fails to appear before the court in response to a summons, the court may summarily issue a warrant for the defendant's arrest.

(e) Recording the Proceedings. The court must record any proceedings under this rule by using a court reporter or a suitable recording device.

(f) New Trial. Rule 33 applies to a motion for a new trial.

(g) Appeal. (1) *From a District Judge's Order or Judgment.* The Federal Rules of Appellate Procedure govern an appeal from a district judge's order or a judgment of conviction or sentence.

(2) *From a Magistrate Judge's Order or Judgment.* (A) Interlocutory Appeal. Either party may appeal an order of a magistrate judge to a district judge within 14 days of its entry if a district judge's order could similarly be appealed. The party appealing must file a notice with the clerk specifying the order being appealed and must serve a copy on the adverse party.

(B) Appeal from a Conviction or Sentence. A defendant may appeal a magistrate judge's judgment of conviction or sentence to a district judge within 14 days of its entry. To appeal, the defendant must file a notice with the clerk specifying the judgment being appealed and must serve a copy on an attorney for the government.

(C) Record. The record consists of the original papers and exhibits in the case; any transcript, tape, or other recording of the proceedings; and a certified copy of the docket entries. For purposes of the appeal, a copy of the record of the proceedings must be made available to a defendant who establishes by affidavit an inability to pay or give security for the record. The Director of the Administrative Office of the United States Courts must pay for those copies.

(D) Scope of Appeal. The defendant is not entitled to a trial de novo by a district judge. The scope of the appeal is the same as in an appeal to the court of appeals from a judgment entered by a district judge.

(3) *Stay of Execution and Release Pending Appeal.* Rule 38 applies to a stay of a judgment of conviction or sentence. The court may release the defendant pending appeal under the law relating to release pending appeal from a district court to a court of appeals.

(Added May 1, 1990, eff. Dec. 1, 1990; amended April 30, 1991, eff. Dec. 1, 1991; April 22, 1993, eff. Dec. 1, 1993; April 11, 1997, eff. Dec. 1, 1997; April 29, 2002, eff. Dec. 1, 2002; April 12, 2006, eff. Dec. 1, 2006; March 26, 2009, eff. Dec. 1, 2009; April 25, 2014, eff. Dec. 1, 2014.)

Rule 59. Matters Before a Magistrate Judge

(a) Nondispositive Matters. A district judge may refer to a magistrate judge for determination any matter that does not dispose of a charge or defense. The magistrate judge must promptly conduct the required proceedings and, when appropriate, enter on the record an oral or written order stating the determination. A party may serve and file objections to the order within 14 days after being served with a copy of a written order or after the oral order is stated on the record, or at some other time the court sets. The district judge must consider timely objections and modify or set aside any part of the order that is contrary to law or clearly erroneous. Failure to object in accordance with this rule waives a party's right to review.

(b) Dispositive Matters. (1) *Referral to Magistrate Judge.* A district judge may refer to a magistrate judge for recommendation a defendant's motion to dismiss or quash an indictment or information, a motion to suppress evidence, or any matter that may dispose of a charge or defense. The magistrate judge must promptly conduct the required proceedings. A record must be made of any evidentiary proceeding and of any other proceeding if the magistrate judge considers it necessary. The magistrate judge must enter on the record a recommendation for disposing of the matter, including any proposed findings of fact. The clerk must immediately serve copies on all parties.

(2) *Objections to Findings and Recommendations.* Within 14 days after being served with a copy of the recommended disposition, or at some other time the court sets, a party may serve and file specific written objections to the proposed findings and recommendations. Unless the district judge directs otherwise, the objecting party must promptly arrange for transcribing the record, or whatever portions of it the parties agree to or the magistrate judge considers sufficient. Failure to object in accordance with this rule waives a party's right to review.

(3) *De Novo Review of Recommendations.* The district judge must consider de novo any objection to the magistrate judge's recommendation. The district judge may accept, reject, or modify the recommendation, receive further evidence, or resubmit the matter to the magistrate judge with instructions.

(Added April 25, 2005, eff. Dec. 1, 2005; March 26, 2009, eff. Dec. 1, 2009.)

Rule 60. Victim's Rights

(a) In General. (1) *Notice of a Proceeding.* The government must use its best efforts to give the victim reasonable, accurate, and timely notice of any public court proceeding involving the crime.

(2) *Attending the Proceeding.* The court must not exclude a victim from a public court proceeding involving the crime, unless the court determines by clear and convincing evidence that the victim's testimony would be materially altered if the victim heard other testimony at that proceeding. In determining whether to exclude a victim, the court must make every effort to permit the fullest attendance possible by the victim and must consider reasonable alternatives to exclusion. The reasons for any exclusion must be clearly stated on the record.

(3) *Right to Be Heard on Release, a Plea, or Sentencing.* The court must permit a victim to be reasonably heard at any public proceeding in the district court concerning release, plea, or sentencing involving the crime.

(b) Enforcement and Limitations. (1) *Time for Deciding a Motion.* The court must promptly decide any motion asserting a victim's rights described in these rules.

(2) *Who May Assert the Rights.* A victim's rights described in these rules may be asserted by the victim, the victim's lawful representative, the attorney for the government, or any other person as authorized by 18 U.S.C. § 3771(d) and (e).

(3) *Multiple Victims.* If the court finds that the number of victims makes it impracticable to accord all of them their rights described in these rules, the court must fashion a reasonable procedure that gives effect to these rights without unduly complicating or prolonging the proceedings.

(4) *Where Rights May Be Asserted.* A victim's rights described in these rules must be asserted in the district where a defendant is being prosecuted for the crime.

(5) *Limitations on Relief.* A victim may move to reopen a plea or sentence only if:

(A) the victim asked to be heard before or during the proceeding at issue, and the request was denied;

(B) the victim petitions the court of appeals for a writ of mandamus within 10 days after the denial, and the writ is granted; and

(C) in the case of a plea, the accused has not pleaded to the highest offense charged.

(6) *No New Trial.* A failure to afford a victim any right described in these rules is not grounds for a new trial.

(Added April 23, 2008, eff. Dec. 1, 2008.)

Rule 61. Title

These rules may be known and cited as the Federal Rules of Criminal Procedure.

(Dec. 26, 1944, eff. March 21, 1946; as amended, April 29, 2002, eff. Dec. 1, 2002; April 23, 2008, eff. Dec. 1, 2008.)

APPENDIX OF FORMS [ABROGATED]

[illegible]

FEDERAL RULES OF EVIDENCE

ARTICLE I. GENERAL PROVISIONS

ARTICLE II. JUDICIAL NOTICE

ARTICLE III. PRESUMPTIONS IN CIVIL CASES

ARTICLE IV. RELEVANCE AND ITS LIMITS

ARTICLE V. PRIVILEGES

ARTICLE VI. WITNESSES

ARTICLE VII. OPINIONS AND EXPERT TESTIMONY

ARTICLE VIII. HEARSAY

ARTICLE IX. AUTHENTICATION AND IDENTIFICATION

ARTICLE X. CONTENTS OF WRITINGS, RECORDINGS, AND PHOTOGRAPHS

ARTICLE XI. MISCELLANEOUS RULES

ARTICLE I. GENERAL PROVISIONS

Rule 101. Scope; Definitions

(a) Scope. These rules apply to proceedings in United States courts. The specific courts and proceedings to which the rules apply, along with exceptions, are set out in Rule 1101.

(b) Definitions. In these rules:

(1) "civil case" means a civil action or proceeding;

(2) "criminal case" includes a criminal proceeding;

(3) "public office" includes a public agency;

(4) "record" includes a memorandum, report, or data compilation;

(5) a "rule prescribed by the Supreme Court" means a rule adopted by the Supreme Court under statutory authority; and

(6) a reference to any kind of written material or any other medium includes electronically stored

information.

(Jan. 2, 1975, P. L. 93-595, § 1, 88 Stat. 1929; March 2, 1987, eff. Oct. 1, 1987; April 25, 1988, eff. Nov. 1, 1988; April 22, 1993, eff. Dec. 1, 1993; April 26, 2011, eff. Dec. 1, 2011.)

Rule 102. Purpose

These rules should be construed so as to administer every proceeding fairly, eliminate unjustifiable expense and delay, and promote the development of evidence law, to the end of ascertaining the truth and securing a just determination.

(Jan. 2, 1975, P. L. 93-595, § 1, 88 Stat. 1929; April 26, 2011, eff. Dec. 1, 2011.)

Rule 103. Rulings on Evidence

(a) Preserving a Claim of Error. A party may claim error in a ruling to admit or exclude evidence only if the error affects a substantial right of the party and:

(1) if the ruling admits evidence, a party, on the record:

(A) timely objects or moves to strike; and

(B) states the specific ground, unless it was apparent from the context; or

(2) if the ruling excludes evidence, a party informs the court of its substance by an offer of proof, unless the substance was apparent from the context.

(b) Not Needing to Renew an Objection or Offer of Proof. Once the court rules definitively on the record—either before or at trial—a party need not renew an objection or offer of proof to preserve a claim of error for appeal.

(c) Court's Statement About the Ruling; Directing an Offer of Proof. The court may make any statement about the character or form of the evidence, the objection made, and the ruling. The court may direct that an offer of proof be made in question-and-answer form.

(d) Preventing the Jury from Hearing Inadmissible Evidence. To the extent practicable, the court must conduct a jury trial so that inadmissible evidence is not suggested to the jury by any means.

(e) Taking Notice of Plain Error. A court may take notice of a plain error affecting a substantial right, even if the claim of error was not properly preserved.

(Jan. 2, 1975, P. L. 93-595, § 1, 88 Stat. 1929; April 17, 2000, eff. Dec. 1, 2000; April 26, 2011, eff. Dec. 1, 2011.)

Rule 104. Preliminary Questions

(a) In General. The court must decide any preliminary question about whether a witness is qualified, a privilege exists, or evidence is admissible. In so deciding, the court is not bound by evidence rules, except those on privilege.

(b) Relevance That Depends on a Fact. When the relevance of evidence depends on whether a fact exists, proof must be introduced sufficient to support a finding that the fact does exist. The court may admit the proposed evidence on the condition that the proof be introduced later.

(c) Conducting a Hearing So That the Jury Cannot Hear It. The court must conduct any hearing on a preliminary question so that the jury cannot hear it if:

(1) the hearing involves the admissibility of a confession;

(2) a defendant in a criminal case is a witness and so requests; or

(3) justice so requires.

(d) Cross-Examining a Defendant in a Criminal Case. By testifying on a preliminary question, a defendant in a criminal case does not become subject to cross-examination on other issues in the case.

(e) Evidence Relevant to Weight and Credibility. This rule does not limit a party's right to introduce before the jury evidence that is relevant to the weight or credibility of other evidence.

(Jan. 2, 1975, P. L. 93-595, § 1, 88 Stat. 1929; March 2, 1987, eff. Oct. 1, 1987; April 26, 2011, eff. Dec. 1, 2011.)

Rule 105. Limiting Evidence That Is Not Admissible Against Other Parties or for Other Purposes

If the court admits evidence that is admissible against a party or for a purpose—but not against another party or for another purpose—the court, on timely request, must restrict the evidence to its proper scope and instruct the jury accordingly.

(Jan. 2, 1975, P. L. 93-595, § 1, 88 Stat. 1930; April 26, 2011, eff. Dec. 1, 2011.)

Rule 106. Remainder of or Related Writings or Recorded Statements

If a party introduces all or part of a writing or recorded statement, an adverse party may require the introduction, at that time, of any other part—or any other writing or recorded statement—that in fairness ought to be considered at the same time.

(Jan. 2, 1975, P. L. 93-595, § 1, 88 Stat. 1929; March 2, 1987, eff. Oct. 1, 1987; April 26, 2011, eff. Dec. 1, 2011.)

ARTICLE II. JUDICIAL NOTICE

Rule 201. Judicial Notice of Adjudicative Facts

(a) Scope. This rule governs judicial notice of an adjudicative fact only, not a legislative fact.

(b) Kinds of Facts That May Be Judicially Noticed. The court may judicially notice a fact that is not subject to reasonable dispute because it:

(1) is generally known within the trial court's territorial jurisdiction; or

(2) can be accurately and readily determined from sources whose accuracy cannot reasonably be questioned.

(c) Taking Notice. The court:

(1) may take judicial notice on its own; or

(2) must take judicial notice if a party requests it

and the court is supplied with the necessary information.

(d) Timing. The court may take judicial notice at any stage of the proceeding.

(e) Opportunity to Be Heard. On timely request, a party is entitled to be heard on the propriety of taking judicial notice and the nature of the fact to be noticed. If the court takes judicial notice before notifying a party, the party, on request, is still entitled to be heard.

(f) Instructing the Jury. In a civil case, the court must instruct the jury to accept the noticed fact as conclusive. In a criminal case, the court must instruct the jury that it may or may not accept the noticed fact as conclusive.

(Jan. 2, 1975, P. L. 93-595, § 1, 88 Stat. 1930; April 26, 2011, eff. Dec. 1, 2011 .)

ARTICLE III. PRESUMPTIONS IN CIVIL CASES

Rule 301. Presumptions in Civil Cases Generally

In a civil case, unless a federal statute or these rules provide otherwise, the party against whom a presumption is directed has the burden of producing evidence to rebut the presumption. But this rule does not shift the burden of persuasion, which remains on the party who had it originally.

(Jan. 2, 1975, P. L. 93-595, § 1, 88 Stat. 1931; April 26, 2011, eff. Dec. 1, 2011.)

Rule 302. Applying State Law to Presumptions in Civil Cases

In a civil case, state law governs the effect of a presumption regarding a claim or defense for which state law supplies the rule of decision.

(Jan. 2, 1975, P. L. 93-595, § 1, 88 Stat. 1931; April 26, 2011, eff. Dec. 1, 2011.)

ARTICLE IV. RELEVANCE AND ITS LIMITS

Rule 401. Test for Relevant Evidence

Evidence is relevant if:

(a) it has any tendency to make a fact more or less probable than it would be without the evidence; and

(b) the fact is of consequence in determining the action.

(Jan. 2, 1975, P. L. 93-595, § 1, 88 Stat. 1931; April 26, 2011, eff. Dec. 1, 2011.)

Rule 402. General Admissibility of Relevant Evidence

Relevant evidence is admissible unless any of the following provides otherwise:

- the United States Constitution;
- a federal statute;
- these rules; or
- other rules prescribed by the Supreme Court.

Irrelevant evidence is not admissible.

(Jan. 2, 1975, P. L. 93-595, § 1, 88 Stat. 1931; April 26, 2011, eff. Dec. 1, 2011.)

Rule 403. Excluding Relevant Evidence for Prejudice, Confusion, Waste of Time, or Other Reasons

The court may exclude relevant evidence if its probative value is substantially outweighed by a danger of one or more of the following: unfair prejudice, confusing the issues, misleading the jury, undue delay, wasting time, or needlessly presenting cumulative evidence.

(Jan. 2, 1975, P. L. 93-595, § 1, 88 Stat. 1932; April. 26, 2011, eff. Dec. 1, 2011.)

Rule 404. Character Evidence; Crimes or Other Acts

(a) Character Evidence.

(1) *Prohibited Uses.* Evidence of a person's character or character trait is not admissible to prove that on a particular occasion the person acted in accordance with the character or trait.

(2) *Exceptions for a Defendant or Victim in a Criminal Case.* The following exceptions apply in a criminal case:

(A) a defendant may offer evidence of the defendant's pertinent trait, and if the evidence is admitted, the prosecutor may offer evidence to rebut it;

(B) subject to the limitations in Rule 412, a defendant may offer evidence of an alleged victim's pertinent trait, and if the evidence is admitted, the prosecutor may:

(i) offer evidence to rebut it; and

(ii) offer evidence of the defendant's same trait; and

(C) in a homicide case, the prosecutor may offer evidence of the alleged victim's trait of peacefulness to rebut evidence that the victim was the first aggressor. (3) Exceptions for a Witness. Evidence of a witness's character may be admitted under Rules 607, 608, and 609.

(b) Crimes, Wrongs, or Other Acts.

(1) *Prohibited Uses.* Evidence of a crime, wrong, or other act is not admissible to prove a person's character in order to show that on a particular occasion the person acted in accordance with the character.

(2) *Permitted Uses; Notice in a Criminal Case.* This evidence may be admissible for another purpose, such as proving motive, opportunity, intent, preparation, plan, knowledge, identity, absence of mistake, or lack of accident. On request by a defendant in a criminal case, the prosecutor must:

(A) provide reasonable notice of the general nature of any such evidence that the prosecutor intends to offer at trial; and

(B) do so before trial—or during trial if the court, for good cause, excuses lack of pretrial notice.

(Jan. 2, 1975, P. L. 93-595, § 1, 88 Stat. 1932; March 2, 1987, eff. Oct. 1, 1987; April 30, 1991, eff. Dec.1, 1991; April 17, 2000, eff. Dec. 1, 2000; April

12, 2006, eff. Dec. 1, 2006; April 26, 2011, eff. Dec. 1, 2011.)

Rule 405. Methods of Proving Character

(a) By Reputation or Opinion. When evidence of a person's character or character trait is admissible, it may be proved by testimony about the person's reputation or by testimony in the form of an opinion. On cross-examination of the character witness, the court may allow an inquiry into relevant specific instances of the person's conduct.

(b) By Specific Instances of Conduct. When a person's character or character trait is an essential element of a charge, claim, or defense, the character or trait may also be proved by relevant specific instances of the person's conduct.

(Jan. 2, 1975, P. L. 93-595, § 1, 88 Stat. 1932; March 2, 1987, eff. Oct. 1, 1987; April 26, 2011, eff. Dec. 1, 2011.)

Rule 406. Habit; Routine Practice

Evidence of a person's habit or an organization's routine practice may be admitted to prove that on a particular occasion the person or organization acted in accordance with the habit or routine practice. The court may admit this evidence regardless of whether it is corroborated or whether there was an eyewitness.

(Jan. 2, 1975, P. L. 93-595, § 1, 88 Stat. 1932; April 26, 2011, eff. Dec. 1, 2011.)

Rule 407. Subsequent Remedial Measures

When measures are taken that would have made an earlier injury or harm less likely to occur, evidence of the subsequent measures is not admissible to prove:

- negligence;
- culpable conduct;
- a defect in a product or its design; or
- a need for a warning or instruction.

But the court may admit this evidence for another purpose, such as impeachment or—if disputed—proving ownership, control, or the feasibility of precautionary measures.

(Jan. 2, 1975, P. L. 93-595, § 1, 88 Stat. 1932; April 11, 1997, eff. Dec. 1, 1997; April 26, 2011, eff. Dec. 1, 2011.)

Rule 408. Compromise Offers and Negotiations

(a) Prohibited Uses. Evidence of the following is not admissible—on behalf of any party—either to prove or disprove the validity or amount of a disputed claim or to impeach by a prior inconsistent statement or a contradiction:

(1) furnishing, promising, or offering—or accepting, promising to accept, or offering to accept—a valuable consideration in compromising or attempting to compromise the claim; and

(2) conduct or a statement made during compromise negotiations about the claim—except when offered in a criminal case and when the negotiations related to a claim by a public office in the exercise of its regulatory, investigative, or enforcement authority.

(b) Exceptions. The court may admit this evidence for another purpose, such as proving a witness's bias or prejudice, negating a contention of undue delay, or proving an effort to obstruct a criminal investigation or prosecution.

(Jan. 2, 1975, P. L. 93-595, § 1, 88 Stat. 1933; April 12, 2006, eff. Dec. 1, 2006; April 26, 2011, eff. Dec. 1, 2011.)

Rule 409. Offers to Pay Medical and Similar Expenses

Evidence of furnishing, promising to pay, or offering to pay medical, hospital, or similar expenses resulting from an injury is not admissible to prove liability for the injury.

(Jan. 2, 1975, P. L. 93-595, § 1, 88 Stat. 1933; April 26, 2011, eff. Dec. 1, 2011.)

Rule 410. Pleas, Plea Discussions, and Related Statements

(a) Prohibited Uses. In a civil or criminal case, evidence of the following is not admissible against the defendant who made the plea or participated in the plea discussions:

(1) a guilty plea that was later withdrawn;

(2) a nolo contendere plea;

(3) a statement made during a proceeding on either of those pleas under Federal Rule of Criminal Procedure 11 or a comparable state procedure; or

(4) a statement made during plea discussions with an attorney for the prosecuting authority if the discussions did not result in a guilty plea or they resulted in a later-withdrawn guilty plea.

(b) Exceptions. The court may admit a statement described in Rule 410(a)(3) or (4):

(1) in any proceeding in which another statement made during the same plea or plea discussions has been introduced, if in fairness the statements ought to be considered together; or

(2) in a criminal proceeding for perjury or false statement, if the defendant made the statement under oath, on the record, and with counsel present.

(Jan. 2, 1975, P. L. 93-595, § 1, 88 Stat. 1933; Dec. 12, 1975, P. L. 94-149, § 1(9), 89 Stat. 805; April 30, 1979, eff. Dec. 1, 1980; April 26, 2011, eff. Dec. 1, 2011.)

Rule 411. Liability Insurance

Evidence that a person was or was not insured against liability is not admissible to prove whether the person acted negligently or otherwise wrongfully. But the court may admit this evidence for another purpose, such as proving a witness's bias or prejudice or proving agency, ownership, or control.

(Jan. 2, 1975, P. L. 93-595, § 1, 88 Stat. 1933; March 2, 1987, eff. Oct. 1, 1987; April 26, 2011, eff.

Dec. 1, 2011.)

Rule 412. Sex-Offense Cases: The Victim's Sexual Behavior or Predisposition

(a) Prohibited Uses. The following evidence is not admissible in a civil or criminal proceeding involving alleged sexual misconduct:

(1) evidence offered to prove that a victim engaged in other sexual behavior; or

(2) evidence offered to prove a victim's sexual predisposition.

(b) Exceptions.

(1) *Criminal Cases.* The court may admit the following evidence in a criminal case:

(A) evidence of specific instances of a victim's sexual behavior, if offered to prove that someone other than the defendant was the source of semen, injury, or other physical evidence;

(B) evidence of specific instances of a victim's sexual behavior with respect to the person accused of the sexual misconduct, if offered by the defendant to prove consent or if offered by the prosecutor; and

(C) evidence whose exclusion would violate the defendant's constitutional rights.

(2) *Civil Cases.* In a civil case, the court may admit evidence offered to prove a victim's sexual behavior or sexual predisposition if its probative value substantially outweighs the danger of harm to any victim and of unfair prejudice to any party. The court may admit evidence of a victim's reputation only if the victim has placed it in controversy.

(c) Procedure to Determine Admissibility.

(1) *Motion.* If a party intends to offer evidence under Rule 412(b), the party must:

(A) file a motion that specifically describes the evidence and states the purpose for which it is to be offered;

(B) do so at least 14 days before trial unless the court, for good cause, sets a different time;

(C) serve the motion on all parties; and

(D) notify the victim or, when appropriate, the victim's guardian or representative.

(2) *Hearing.* Before admitting evidence under this rule, the court must conduct an in camera hearing and give the victim and parties a right to attend and be heard. Unless the court orders otherwise, the motion, related materials, and the record of the hearing must be and remain sealed.

(d) Definition of "Victim." In this rule, "victim" includes an alleged victim.

(Oct. 28, 1978, P. L. 95-540, § 2(a), 92 Stat. 2046; Nov. 18, 1988, P. L. 100-690, Title VII, Subtitle B, § 7046(a), 102 Stat. 4400; April 29, 1994, eff. Dec. 1, 1994; Sept. 13, 1994, P. L. 103-322, Title IV, Subtitle A, Ch 4, § 40141(b), 109 Stat. 1919; April 26, 2011, eff. Dec. 1, 2011.)

Rule 413. Similar Crimes in Sexual-Assault Cases

(a) Permitted Uses. In a criminal case in which a defendant is accused of a sexual assault, the court may admit evidence that the defendant committed any other sexual assault. The evidence may be considered on any matter to which it is relevant.

(b) Disclosure to the Defendant. If the prosecutor intends to offer this evidence, the prosecutor must disclose it to the defendant, including witnesses' statements or a summary of the expected testimony. The prosecutor must do so at least 15 days before trial or at a later time that the court allows for good cause.

(c) Effect on Other Rules. This rule does not limit the admission or consideration of evidence under any other rule.

(d) Definition of "Sexual Assault." In this rule and Rule 415, "sexual assault" means a crime under federal law or under state law (as "state" is defined in 18 U.S.C. § 513) involving:

(1) any conduct prohibited by 18 U.S.C. chapter 109A;

(2) contact, without consent, between any part of the defendant's body—or an object—and another person's genitals or anus;

(3) contact, without consent, between the defendant's genitals or anus and any part of another person's body;

(4) deriving sexual pleasure or gratification from inflicting death, bodily injury, or physical pain on another person; or

(5) an attempt or conspiracy to engage in conduct described in subparagraphs (1)–(4).

(Sept. 13, 1994, P. L. 103-322, Title XXXII, Subtitle I, § 320935(a), 108 Stat. 2136; April 26, 2011, eff. Dec. 1, 2011.)

Rule 414. Similar Crimes in Child-Molestation Cases

(a) Permitted Uses. In a criminal case in which a defendant is accused of child molestation, the court may admit evidence that the defendant committed any other child molestation. The evidence may be considered on any matter to which it is relevant.

(b) Disclosure to the Defendant. If the prosecutor intends to offer this evidence, the prosecutor must disclose it to the defendant, including witnesses' statements or a summary of the expected testimony. The prosecutor must do so at least 15 days before trial or at a later time that the court allows for good cause.

(c) Effect on Other Rules. This rule does not limit the admission or consideration of evidence under any other rule.

(d) Definition of "Child" and "Child Molestation." In this rule and Rule 415:

(1) "child" means a person below the age of 14; and

(2) "child molestation" means a crime under federal law or under state law (as "state" is defined in 18 U.S.C. § 513) involving:

(A) any conduct prohibited by 18 U.S.C. chapter 109A and committed with a child;

(B) any conduct prohibited by 18 U.S.C. chapter 110;

(C) contact between any part of the defendant's body—or an object—and a child's genitals or anus;

(D) contact between the defendant's genitals or anus and any part of a child's body;

(E) deriving sexual pleasure or gratification from inflicting death, bodily injury, or physical pain on a child; or

(F) an attempt or conspiracy to engage in conduct described in subparagraphs (A)–(E).

(Sept. 13, 1994, P. L. 103-322, Title XXXII, Subtitle I, § 320935(a), 108 Stat. 2136; April 26, 2011, eff. Dec. 1, 2011.)

Rule 415. Similar Acts in Civil Cases Involving Sexual Assault or Child Molestation

(a) Permitted Uses. In a civil case involving a claim for relief based on a party's alleged sexual assault or child molestation, the court may admit evidence that the party committed any other sexual assault or child molestation. The evidence may be considered as provided in Rules 413 and 414.

(b) Disclosure to the Opponent. If a party intends to offer this evidence, the party must disclose it to the party against whom it will be offered, including witnesses' statements or a summary of the expected testimony. The party must do so at least 15 days before trial or at a later time that the court allows for good cause.

(c) Effect on Other Rules. This rule does not limit the admission or consideration of evidence under any other rule.

(Sept. 13, 1994, P. L. 103-322, Title XXXII, Subtitle I, § 320935(a), 108 Stat. 2137; April 26, 2011, eff. Dec. 1, 2011.)

ARTICLE V. PRIVILEGES

Rule 501. Privilege in General

The common law—as interpreted by United States courts in the light of reason and experience—governs a claim of privilege unless any of the following provides otherwise:

- the United States Constitution;
- a federal statute; or
- rules prescribed by the Supreme Court.

But in a civil case, state law governs privilege regarding a claim or defense for which state law supplies the rule of decision.

(Jan. 2, 1975, P. L. 93-595, § 1, 88 Stat. 1933; April 26, 2011, eff. Dec. 1, 2011.)

Rule 502. Attorney-Client Privilege and Work Product; Limitations on Waiver

The following provisions apply, in the circumstances set out, to disclosure of a communication or information covered by the attorney-client privilege or work-product protection.

(a) Disclosure Made in a Federal Proceeding or to a Federal Office or Agency; Scope of a Waiver. When the disclosure is made in a federal proceeding or to a federal office or agency and waives the attorney-client privilege or work-product protection, the waiver extends to an undisclosed communication or information in a federal or state proceeding only if:

(1) the waiver is intentional;

(2) the disclosed and undisclosed communications or information concern the same subject matter; and

(3) they ought in fairness to be considered together.

(b) Inadvertent Disclosure. When made in a federal proceeding or to a federal office or agency, the disclosure does not operate as a waiver in a federal or state proceeding if:

(1) the disclosure is inadvertent;

(2) the holder of the privilege or protection took reasonable steps to prevent disclosure; and

(3) the holder promptly took reasonable steps to rectify the error, including (if applicable) following Federal Rule of Civil Procedure 26(b)(5)(B).

(c) Disclosure Made in a State Proceeding. When the disclosure is made in a state proceeding and is not the subject of a state-court order concerning waiver, the disclosure does not operate as a waiver in a federal proceeding if the disclosure:

(1) would not be a waiver under this rule if it had been made in a federal proceeding; or

(2) is not a waiver under the law of the state where the disclosure occurred.

(d) Controlling Effect of a Court Order. A federal court may order that the privilege or protection is not waived by disclosure connected with the litigation pending before the court—in which event the disclosure is also not a waiver in any other federal or state proceeding.

(e) Controlling Effect of a Party Agreement. An agreement on the effect of disclosure in a federal proceeding is binding only on the parties to the agreement, unless it is incorporated into a court order.

(f) Controlling Effect of this Rule. Notwithstanding Rules 101 and 1101, this rule applies to state proceedings and to federal court-annexed and federal court-mandated arbitration proceedings, in the circumstances set out in the rule. And notwithstanding Rule 501, this rule applies even if state law provides the rule of decision.

(g) Definitions. In this rule:

(1) "attorney-client privilege" means the protection that applicable law provides for confidential attorney-client communications; and

(2) "work-product protection" means the protection that applicable law provides for tangible material (or its intangible equivalent) prepared in anticipation of litigation or for trial.

(Sept. 19, 2008, P. L. 110-322, § 1(a), 122 Stat. 3537; April 26, 2011, eff. Dec. 1, 2011.)

ARTICLE VI. WITNESSES

Rule 601. Competency to Testify in General

Every person is competent to be a witness unless these rules provide otherwise. But in a civil case, state law governs the witness's competency regarding a claim or defense for which state law supplies the rule of decision.

(Jan. 2, 1975, P. L. 93-595, § 1, 88 Stat. 1934; April 26, 2011, eff. Dec. 1, 2011.)

Rule 602. Need for Personal Knowledge

A witness may testify to a matter only if evidence is introduced sufficient to support a finding that the witness has personal knowledge of the matter. Evidence to prove personal knowledge may consist of the witness's own testimony. This rule does not apply to a witness's expert testimony under Rule 703.

(Jan. 2, 1975, P. L. 93-595, § 1, 88 Stat. 1934; March 2, 1987, eff. Oct. 1, 1987; April 25, 1988, eff. Nov. 1, 1988; April 26, 2011, eff. Dec. 1, 2011.)

Rule 603. Oath or Affirmation to Testify Truthfully

Before testifying, a witness must give an oath or affirmation to testify truthfully. It must be in a form designed to impress that duty on the witness's conscience.

(Jan. 2, 1975, P. L. 93-595, § 1, 88 Stat. 1934; March 2, 1987, eff. Oct. 1, 1987; April 26, 2011, eff. Dec. 1, 2011.)

Rule 604. Interpreter

An interpreter must be qualified and must give an oath or affirmation to make a true translation.

(Jan. 2, 1975, P. L. 93-595, § 1, 88 Stat. 1934; March 2, 1987, eff. Oct. 1, 1987; April 26, 2011, eff. Dec. 1, 2011.)

Rule 605. Judge's Competency as a Witness

The presiding judge may not testify as a witness at the trial. A party need not object to preserve the issue.

(Jan. 2, 1975, P. L. 93-595, § 1, 88 Stat. 1934; April 26, 2011, eff. Dec. 1, 2011.)

Rule 606. Juror's Competency as a Witness

(a) At the Trial. A juror may not testify as a witness before the other jurors at the trial. If a juror is called to testify, the court must give a party an opportunity to object outside the jury's presence.

(b) During an Inquiry into the Validity of a Verdict or Indictment.

(1) *Prohibited Testimony or Other Evidence.* During an inquiry into the validity of a verdict or indictment, a juror may not testify about any statement made or incident that occurred during the jury's deliberations; the effect of anything on that juror's or another juror's vote; or any juror's mental processes concerning the verdict or indictment. The court may not receive a juror's affidavit or evidence of a juror's statement on these matters.

(2) *Exceptions.* A juror may testify about whether:

(A) extraneous prejudicial information was improperly brought to the jury's attention;

(B) an outside influence was improperly brought to bear on any juror; or

(C) a mistake was made in entering the verdict on the verdict form.

(Jan. 2, 1975, P. L. 93-595, § 1, 88 Stat. 1934; Dec. 12, 1975, P.L. 94-149, § 1(10), 89 Stat. 805; March 2, 1987, eff. Oct. 1, 1987; April 12, 2006, eff. Dec. 1, 2006; April 26, 2011, eff. Dec. 1, 2011.)

Rule 607. Who May Impeach a Witness

Any party, including the party that called the witness, may attack the witness's credibility.

(Jan. 2, 1975, P. L. 93-595, § 1, 88 Stat. 1934; March 2, 1987, eff. Oct. 1, 1987; April 26, 2011, eff. Dec. 1, 2011.)

Rule 608. A Witness's Character for Truthfulness or Untruthfulness

(a) Reputation or Opinion Evidence. A witness's credibility may be attacked or supported by testimony about the witness's reputation for having a character for truthfulness or untruthfulness, or by testimony in the form of an opinion about that character. But evidence of truthful character is admissible only after the witness's character for truthfulness has been attacked.

(b) Specific Instances of Conduct. Except for a criminal conviction under Rule 609, extrinsic evidence is not admissible to prove specific instances of a witness's conduct in order to attack or support the witness's character for truthfulness. But the court may, on cross-examination, allow them to be inquired into if they are probative of the character for truthfulness or untruthfulness of:

(1) the witness; or

(2) another witness whose character the witness being cross-examined has testified about.

By testifying on another matter, a witness does not waive any privilege against self-incrimination for testimony that relates only to the witness's character for truthfulness.

(Jan. 2, 1975, P. L. 93-595, § 1, 88 Stat. 1935; March 2, 1987, eff. Oct. 1, 1987; April 25, 1988, eff. Nov. 1, 1988; March 27, 2003, eff. Dec. 1, 2003; April 26, 2011, eff. Dec. 1, 2011.)

Rule 609. Impeachment by Evidence of a Criminal Conviction

(a) In General. The following rules apply to attacking a witness's character for truthfulness by evidence of a criminal conviction:

(1) for a crime that, in the convicting jurisdiction, was punishable by death or by imprisonment for more than one year, the evidence:

(A) must be admitted, subject to Rule 403, in a civil case or in a criminal case in which the witness is not a defendant; and

(B) must be admitted in a criminal case in which the witness is a defendant, if the probative value of the evidence outweighs its prejudicial effect to that defendant; and

(2) for any crime regardless of the punishment, the evidence must be admitted if the court can readily determine that establishing the elements of the crime required proving—or the witness's admitting—a dishonest act or false statement.

(b) Limit on Using the Evidence After 10 Years. This subdivision (b) applies if more than 10 years have passed since the witness's conviction or release from confinement for it, whichever is later. Evidence of the conviction is admissible only if:

(1) its probative value, supported by specific facts and circumstances, substantially outweighs its prejudicial effect; and

(2) the proponent gives an adverse party reasonable written notice of the intent to use it so that the party has a fair opportunity to contest its use.

(c) Effect of a Pardon, Annulment, or Certificate of Rehabilitation. Evidence of a conviction is not admissible if:

(1) the conviction has been the subject of a pardon, annulment, certificate of rehabilitation, or other equivalent procedure based on a finding that the person has been rehabilitated, and the person has not been convicted of a later crime punishable by death or by imprisonment for more than one year; or

(2) the conviction has been the subject of a pardon, annulment, or other equivalent procedure based on a finding of innocence.

(d) Juvenile Adjudications. Evidence of a juvenile adjudication is admissible under this rule only if:

(1) it is offered in a criminal case;

(2) the adjudication was of a witness other than the defendant;

(3) an adult's conviction for that offense would be admissible to attack the adult's credibility; and

(4) admitting the evidence is necessary to fairly determine guilt or innocence.

(e) Pendency of an Appeal. A conviction that satisfies this rule is admissible even if an appeal is pending. Evidence of the pendency is also admissible.

(Jan. 2, 1975, P. L. 93-595, § 1, 88 Stat. 1935; March 2, 1987, eff. Oct. 1, 1987; Jan. 26, 1990, eff. Dec. 1, 1990; April 12, 2006, eff. Dec. 1, 2006; April 26, 2011, eff. Dec. 1, 2011.)

Rule 610. Religious Beliefs or Opinions

Evidence of a witness's religious beliefs or opinions is not admissible to attack or support the witness's credibility.

(Jan. 2, 1975, P. L. 93-595, § 1, 88 Stat. 1936; March 2, 1987, eff. Oct. 1, 1987; April 26, 2011, eff. Dec. 1, 2011.)

Rule 611. Mode and Order of Examining Witnesses and Presenting Evidence

(a) Control by the Court; Purposes. The court should exercise reasonable control over the mode and order of examining witnesses and presenting evidence so as to:

(1) make those procedures effective for determining the truth;

(2) avoid wasting time; and

(3) protect witnesses from harassment or undue embarrassment.

(b) Scope of Cross-Examination. Cross-examination should not go beyond the subject matter of the direct examination and matters affecting the witness's credibility. The court may allow inquiry into additional matters as if on direct examination.

(c) Leading Questions. Leading questions should not be used on direct examination except as necessary to develop the witness's testimony. Ordinarily, the court should allow leading questions:

(1) on cross-examination; and

(2) when a party calls a hostile witness, an adverse party, or a witness identified with an adverse party.

(Jan. 2, 1975, P. L. 93-595, § 1, 88 Stat. 1936; March 2, 1987, eff. Oct. 1, 1987; April 26, 2011, eff. Dec. 1, 2011.)

Rule 612. Writing Used to Refresh a Witness's Memory

(a) Scope. This rule gives an adverse party certain options when a witness uses a writing to refresh memory:

(1) while testifying; or

(2) before testifying, if the court decides that justice requires the party to have those options.

(b) Adverse Party's Options; Deleting Unrelated Matter. Unless 18 U.S.C. § 3500 provides otherwise in a criminal case, an adverse party is entitled to have the writing produced at the hearing, to inspect it, to cross-examine the witness about it, and to introduce in evidence any portion that relates to the witness's testimony. If the producing party claims that the writing includes unrelated matter, the court must examine the writing in camera, delete any unrelated portion, and order that the rest be delivered to the adverse party. Any portion deleted over objection must be preserved for the record.

(c) Failure to Produce or Deliver the Writing. If a writing is not produced or is not delivered as ordered, the court may issue any appropriate order. But if the prosecution does not comply in a criminal case, the court must strike the witness's testimony or—if justice so requires—declare a mistrial.

(Jan. 2, 1975, P. L. 93-595, § 1, 88 Stat. 1936; March 2, 1987, eff. Oct. 1, 1987; April 26, 2011, eff. Dec. 1, 2011.)

Rule 613. Witness's Prior Statement

(a) Showing or Disclosing the Statement During Examination. When examining a witness about the witness's prior statement, a party need not show it or disclose its contents to the witness. But the party must, on request, show it or disclose its contents to an adverse party's attorney.

(b) Extrinsic Evidence of a Prior Inconsistent Statement. Extrinsic evidence of a witness's prior inconsistent statement is admissible only if the witness is given an opportunity to explain or deny the statement and an adverse party is given an opportunity to examine the witness about it, or if justice so requires. This subdivision (b) does not apply to an opposing party's statement under Rule 801(d)(2).

(Jan. 2, 1975, P. L. 93-595, § 1, 88 Stat. 1936; March 2, 1987, eff. Oct. 1, 1987; April 25, 1988, eff. Nov. 1, 1988; April 26, 2011, eff. Dec. 1, 2011.)

Rule 614. Court's Calling or Examining a Witness

(a) Calling. The court may call a witness on its own or at a party's request. Each party is entitled to crossexamine the witness.

(b) Examining. The court may examine a witness regardless of who calls the witness.

(c) Objections. A party may object to the court's calling or examining a witness either at that time or at the next opportunity when the jury is not present.

(Jan. 2, 1975, P. L. 93-595, § 1, 88 Stat. 1937; April 26, 2011,eff. Dec. 1, 2011.)

Rule 615. Excluding Witnesses

At a party's request, the court must order witnesses excluded so that they cannot hear other witnesses' testimony. Or the court may do so on its own. But this rule does not authorize excluding:

(a) a party who is a natural person;

(b) an officer or employee of a party that is not a natural person, after being designated as the party's representative by its attorney;

(c) a person whose presence a party shows to be essential to presenting the party's claim or defense; or

(d) a person authorized by statute to be present.

(Jan. 2, 1975, P. L. 93-595, § 1, 88 Stat. 1937; March 2, 1987, eff. Oct. 1, 1987; April 25, 1988, eff. Nov. 1, 1988; Nov. 18, 1988, P. L. 100-690, Title VII, Subtitle B, § 7075(a), 102 Stat. 4405; Apr. 24, 1998, eff. Dec. 1, 1998; Apr. 26, 2011, eff. Dec. 1, 2011.)

ARTICLE VII. OPINIONS AND EXPERT TESTIMONY

Rule 701. Opinion Testimony by Lay Witnesses

If a witness is not testifying as an expert, testimony in the form of an opinion is limited to one that is:

(a) rationally based on the witness's perception;

(b) helpful to clearly understanding the witness's testimony or to determining a fact in issue; and

(c) not based on scientific, technical, or other specialized knowledge within the scope of Rule 702.

(Jan. 2, 1975, P. L. 93-595, § 1, 88 Stat. 1937; March 2, 1987, eff. Oct. 1, 1987; April 17, 2000, eff. Dec. 1, 2000; April 26, 2011, eff. Dec. 1, 2011.)

Rule 702. Testimony by Expert Witnesses

A witness who is qualified as an expert by knowledge, skill, experience, training, or education may testify in the form of an opinion or otherwise if:

(a) the expert's scientific, technical, or other specialized knowledge will help the trier of fact to understand the evidence or to determine a fact in issue;

(b) the testimony is based on sufficient facts or data;

(c) the testimony is the product of reliable principles and methods; and

(d) the expert has reliably applied the principles and methods to the facts of the case.

(Jan. 2, 1975, P. L. 93-595, § 1, 88 Stat. 1937; April 17, 2000, eff. Dec. 1, 2000; April 26, 2011, eff. Dec. 1, 2011.)

Rule 703. Bases of an Expert's Opinion Testimony

An expert may base an opinion on facts or data in the case that the expert has been made aware of or personally observed. If experts in the particular field would reasonably rely on those kinds of facts or data in forming an opinion on the subject, they need not be admissible for the opinion to be admitted. But if the facts or data would otherwise be inadmissible, the proponent of the opinion may disclose them to the jury only if their probative value in helping the jury evaluate the opinion substantially outweighs their prejudicial effect.

(Jan. 2, 1975, P. L. 93-595, § 1, 88 Stat. 1937; March 2, 1987, eff. Oct. 1, 1987; April 17, 2000, eff. Dec. 1, 2000; April 26, 2011, eff. Dec. 1, 2011.)

Rule 704. Opinion on an Ultimate Issue

(a) In General—Not Automatically Objectionable. An opinion is not objectionable just because it embraces an ultimate issue.

(b) Exception. In a criminal case, an expert witness must not state an opinion about whether the defendant did or did not have a mental state or condition that constitutes an element of the crime charged or of a defense. Those matters are for the trier of fact alone.

(Jan. 2, 1975, P. L. 93-595, § 1, 88 Stat. 1937; Oct. 12, 1984, P. L. 98-473, Title IV, Ch IV, § 406, 98 Stat. 2067; April 26, 2011, eff. Dec. 1, 2011.)

Rule 705. Disclosing the Facts or Data Underlying an Expert's Opinion

Unless the court orders otherwise, an expert may state an opinion—and give the reasons for it—without first testifying to the underlying facts or data. But the expert may be required to disclose those facts or data on cross-examination.

(Jan. 2, 1975, P. L. 93-595, § 1, 88 Stat. 1938; March 2, 1987, eff. Oct. 1, 1987; April 22, 1993, eff. Dec. 1, 1993; April 26, 2011, eff. Dec. 1, 2011.)

Rule 706. Court-Appointed Expert Witnesses

(a) Appointment Process. On a party's motion or on its own, the court may order the parties to show cause why expert witnesses should not be appointed and may ask the parties to submit nominations. The court may appoint any expert that the parties agree on and any of its own choosing. But the court may only appoint someone who consents to act.

(b) Expert's Role. The court must inform the expert of the expert's duties. The court may do so in writing and have a copy filed with the clerk or may do so orally at a conference in which the parties have an opportunity to participate. The expert:

(1) must advise the parties of any findings the expert makes;

(2) may be deposed by any party;

(3) may be called to testify by the court or any party; and

(4) may be cross-examined by any party, including the party that called the expert.

(c) Compensation. The expert is entitled to a reasonable compensation, as set by the court. The compensation is payable as follows:

(1) in a criminal case or in a civil case involving just compensation under the Fifth Amendment, from any funds that are provided by law; and

(2) in any other civil case, by the parties in the proportion and at the time that the court directs—and the compensation is then charged like other costs.

(d) Disclosing the Appointment to the Jury. The court may authorize disclosure to the jury that the court appointed the expert.

(e) Parties' Choice of Their Own Experts. This rule does not limit a party in calling its own experts.

(Jan. 2, 1975, P. L. 93-595, § 1, 88 Stat. 1938; March 2, 1987, eff. Oct. 1, 1987; April 26, 2011, eff. Dec. 1, 2011.)

ARTICLE VIII. HEARSAY

Rule 801. Definitions That Apply to This Article; Exclusions from Hearsay

(a) Statement. "Statement" means a person's oral assertion, written assertion, or nonverbal conduct, if the person intended it as an assertion.

(b) Declarant. "Declarant" means the person who made the statement.

(c) Hearsay. "Hearsay" means a statement that:

(1) the declarant does not make while testifying at the current trial or hearing; and

(2) a party offers in evidence to prove the truth of the matter asserted in the statement.

(d) Statements That Are Not Hearsay. A statement that meets the following conditions is not hearsay:

(1) *A Declarant-Witness's Prior Statement.* The declarant testifies and is subject to cross-examination about a prior statement, and the statement:

(A) is inconsistent with the declarant's testimony and was given under penalty of perjury at a trial, hearing, or other proceeding or in a deposition;

(B) is consistent with the declarant's testimony and is offered:

(i) to rebut an express or implied charge that the declarant recently fabricated it or acted from a recent improper influence or motive in so testifying; or

(ii) to rehabilitate the declarant's credibility as a witness when attacked on another ground; or

(C) identifies a person as someone the declarant perceived earlier.

(2) *An Opposing Party's Statement.* The statement is offered against an opposing party and:

(A) was made by the party in an individual or representative capacity;

(B) is one the party manifested that it adopted or believed to be true;

(C) was made by a person whom the party authorized to make a statement on the subject;

(D) was made by the party's agent or employee on a matter within the scope of that relationship and while it existed; or

(E) was made by the party's coconspirator during and in furtherance of the conspiracy.

The statement must be considered but does not by itself establish the declarant's authority under (C); the existence or scope of the relationship under (D); or the existence of the conspiracy or participation in it under (E).

(Jan. 2, 1975, P. L. 93-595, § 1, 88 Stat. 1938; Oct. 16, 1975, P. L. 94-113, § 1, 89 Stat. 576; March 2, 1987, eff. Oct. 1, 1987; April 22, 1997, eff. Dec. 1, 1997; April 26, 2011, eff. Dec. 1, 2011; April 25, 2014, eff. Dec. 1, 2014.)

Rule 802. The Rule Against Hearsay

Hearsay is not admissible unless any of the following provides otherwise:

- a federal statute;
- these rules; or
- other rules prescribed by the Supreme Court.

(Jan. 2, 1975, P. L. 93-595, § 1, 88 Stat. 1939; April 26, 2011, eff. Dec. 1, 2011.)

Rule 803. Exceptions to the Rule Against Hearsay—Regardless of Whether the Declarant Is Available as a Witness

The following are not excluded by the rule against hearsay, regardless of whether the declarant is available as a witness:

(1) *Present Sense Impression.* A statement describing or explaining an event or condition, made while or immediately after the declarant perceived it.

(2) *Excited Utterance.* A statement relating to a

startling event or condition, made while the declarant was under the stress of excitement that it caused.

(3) *Then-Existing Mental, Emotional, or Physical Condition.* A statement of the declarant's then-existing state of mind (such as motive, intent, or plan) or emotional, sensory, or physical condition (such as mental feeling, pain, or bodily health), but not including a statement of memory or belief to prove the fact remembered or believed unless it relates to the validity or terms of the declarant's will.

(4) *Statement Made for Medical Diagnosis or Treatment.* A statement that:

(A) is made for—and is reasonably pertinent to—medical diagnosis or treatment; and

(B) describes medical history; past or present symptoms or sensations; their inception; or their general cause.

(5) *Recorded Recollection.* A record that:

(A) is on a matter the witness once knew about but now cannot recall well enough to testify fully and accurately;

(B) was made or adopted by the witness when the matter was fresh in the witness's memory; and

(C) accurately reflects the witness's knowledge.

If admitted, the record may be read into evidence but may be received as an exhibit only if offered by an adverse party.

(6) *Records of a regularly conducted activity.* A record of an act, event, condition, opinion, or diagnosis if:

(A) the record was made at or near the time by—or from information transmitted by—someone with knowledge;

(B) the record was kept in the course of a regularly conducted activity of a business, organization, occupation, or calling, whether or not for profit;

(C) making the record was a regular practice of that activity;

(D) all these conditions are shown by the testimony of the custodian or another qualified witness, or by a certification that complies with Rule 902(11) or (12) or with a statute permitting certification; and

(E) the opponent does not show that the source of information or the method or circumstances of preparation indicate a lack of trustworthiness.

(7) *Absence of a record of a regularly conducted activity.* Evidence that a matter is not included in a record described in paragraph (6) if:

(A) the evidence is admitted to prove that the matter did not occur or exist;

(B) a record was regularly kept for a matter of that kind; and

(C) the opponent does not show that the possible source of the information or other circumstances indicate a lack of trustworthiness.

(8) *Public records.* A record or statement of a public office if:

(A) it sets out:

(i) the offices activities;

(ii) a matter observed while under a legal duty to report, but not including, in a criminal case, a matter observed by law-enforcement personnel; or

(iii) in a civil case or against the government in a criminal case, factual findings from a legally authorized investigation; and

(B) the opponent does not show that the source of information or other circumstances indicate a lack of trustworthiness.

(6) *Records of a Regularly Conducted Activity.* A record of an act, event, condition, opinion, or diagnosis if:

(A) the record was made at or near the time by—or from information transmitted by—someone with knowledge;

(B) the record was kept in the course of a regularly conducted activity of a business, organization, occupation, or calling, whether or not for profit;

(C) making the record was a regular practice of that activity;

(D) all these conditions are shown by the testimony of the custodian or another qualified witness, or by a certification that complies with Rule 902(11) or (12) or with a statute permitting certification; and

(E) neither the source of information nor the method or circumstances of preparation indicate a lack of trustworthiness.

(7) *Absence of a Record of a Regularly Conducted Activity.* Evidence that a matter is not included in a record described in paragraph (6) if:

(A) the evidence is admitted to prove that the matter did not occur or exist;

(B) a record was regularly kept for a matter of that kind; and

(C) neither the possible source of the information nor other circumstances indicate a lack of trustworthiness.

(8) *Public Records.* A record or statement of a public office if:

(A) it sets out:

(i) the office's activities;

(ii) a matter observed while under a legal duty to report, but not including, in a criminal case, a matter observed by law-enforcement personnel; or

(iii) in a civil case or against the government in a criminal case, factual findings from a legally authorized investigation; and

(B) neither the source of information nor other circumstances indicate a lack of trustworthiness.

(9) *Public Records of Vital Statistics.* A record of a birth, death, or marriage, if reported to a public office in accordance with a legal duty.

(10) *Absence of a Public Record.* Testimony—or a certification under Rule 902—that a diligent search failed to disclose a public record or statement if:

(A) the testimony or certification is admitted to prove that

(i) the record or statement does not exist; or

(ii) a matter did not occur or exist, if a public office regularly kept a record or statement for a matter of that kind; and

(B) in a criminal case, a prosecutor who intends to offer a certification provides written notice of that intent at least 14 days before trial, and the defendant does not object in writing within 7 days of receiving the notice—unless the court sets a different time for the notice or the objection.

(11) *Records of Religious Organizations Concerning Personal or Family History.* A statement of birth, legitimacy, ancestry, marriage, divorce, death, relationship by blood or marriage, or similar facts of personal or family history, contained in a regularly kept record of a religious organization.

(12) *Certificates of Marriage, Baptism, and Similar Ceremonies.* A statement of fact contained in a certificate:

(A) made by a person who is authorized by a religious organization or by law to perform the act certified;

(B) attesting that the person performed a marriage or similar ceremony or administered a sacrament; and

(C) purporting to have been issued at the time of the act or within a reasonable time after it.

(13) *Family Records.* A statement of fact about personal or family history contained in a family record, such as a Bible, genealogy, chart, engraving on a ring, inscription on a portrait, or engraving on an urn or burial marker.

(14) *Records of Documents That Affect an Interest in Property.* The record of a document that purports to establish or affect an interest in property if:

(A) the record is admitted to prove the content of the original recorded document, along with its signing and its delivery by each person who purports to have signed it;

(B) the record is kept in a public office; and

(C) a statute authorizes recording documents of that kind in that office.

(15) *Statements in Documents That Affect an Interest in Property.* A statement contained in a document that purports to establish or affect an interest in property if the matter stated was relevant to the document's purpose—unless later dealings with the property are inconsistent with the truth of the statement or the purport of the document.

(16) *Statements in Ancient Documents.* A statement in a document that is at least 20 years old and whose authenticity is established.

(17) *Market Reports and Similar Commercial Publications.* Market quotations, lists, directories, or other compilations that are generally relied on by the public or by persons in particular occupations.

(18) *Statements in Learned Treatises, Periodicals, or Pamphlets.* A statement contained in a treatise, periodical, or pamphlet if:

(A) the statement is called to the attention of an expert witness on cross-examination or relied on by the expert on direct examination; and

(B) the publication is established as a reliable authority by the expert's admission or testimony, by another expert's testimony, or by judicial notice.

If admitted, the statement may be read into evidence but not received as an exhibit.

(19) *Reputation Concerning Personal or Family History.* A reputation among a person's family by blood, adoption, or marriage—or among a person's associates or in the community—concerning the person's birth, adoption, legitimacy, ancestry, marriage, divorce, death, relationship by blood, adoption, or marriage, or similar facts of personal or family history.

(20) *Reputation Concerning Boundaries or General History.* A reputation in a community—arising before the controversy—concerning boundaries of land in the community or customs that affect the land, or concerning general historical events important to that community, state, or nation.

(21) *Reputation Concerning Character.* A reputation among a person's associates or in the community concerning the person's character.

(22) *Judgment of a Previous Conviction.* Evidence of a final judgment of conviction if:

(A) the judgment was entered after a trial or guilty plea, but not a nolo contendere plea;

(B) the conviction was for a crime punishable by death or by imprisonment for more than a year;

(C) the evidence is admitted to prove any fact essential to the judgment; and

(D) when offered by the prosecutor in a criminal case for a purpose other than impeachment, the judgment was against the defendant.

The pendency of an appeal may be shown but does not affect admissibility.

(23) *Judgments Involving Personal, Family, or General History, or a Boundary.* A judgment that is admitted to prove a matter of personal, family, or general history, or boundaries, if the matter:

(A) was essential to the judgment; and

(B) could be proved by evidence of reputation.

(24) [*Other Exceptions.*] [Transferred to Rule 807.]

(Jan. 2, 1975, P. L. 93-595, § 1, 88 Stat. 1939; Dec. 12, 1975, P. L. 94-149, § 1(11), 89 Stat. 905; March 2, 1987, eff. Oct. 1, 1987; April 11, 1997, eff. Dec. 1, 1997; April 17, 2000, eff. Dec. 1, 2000; April 26, 2011, eff. Dec. 1, 2011; April 16, 2013, eff. Dec. 1, 2013; April 25, 2014, eff. Dec. 1, 2014.)

Rule 804. Exceptions to the Rule Against Hearsay—When the Declarant Is Unavailable as a Witness

(a) Criteria for Being Unavailable. A declarant is considered to be unavailable as a witness if the declarant:

(1) is exempted from testifying about the subject matter of the declarant's statement because the court rules that a privilege applies;

(2) refuses to testify about the subject matter despite a court order to do so;

(3) testifies to not remembering the subject matter;

(4) cannot be present or testify at the trial or hearing because of death or a then-existing infir-

mity, physical illness, or mental illness; or

(5) is absent from the trial or hearing and the statement's proponent has not been able, by process or other reasonable means, to procure:

(A) the declarant's attendance, in the case of a hearsay exception under Rule 804(b)(1) or (6); or

(B) the declarant's attendance or testimony, in the case of a hearsay exception under Rule 804(b)(2), (3), or (4).

But this subdivision (a) does not apply if the statement's proponent procured or wrongfully caused the declarant's unavailability as a witness in order to prevent the declarant from attending or testifying.

(b) The Exceptions. The following are not excluded by the rule against hearsay if the declarant is unavailable as a witness:

(1) *Former Testimony.* Testimony that:

(A) was given as a witness at a trial, hearing, or lawful deposition, whether given during the current proceeding or a different one; and

(B) is now offered against a party who had—or, in a civil case, whose predecessor in interest had—an opportunity and similar motive to develop it by direct, cross-, or redirect examination.

(2) *Statement Under the Belief of Imminent Death.* In a prosecution for homicide or in a civil case, a statement that the declarant, while believing the declarant's death to be imminent, made about its cause or circumstances.

(3) *Statement Against Interest.* A statement that:

(A) a reasonable person in the declarant's position would have made only if the person believed it to be true because, when made, it was so contrary to the declarant's proprietary or pecuniary interest or had so great a tendency to invalidate the declarant's claim against someone else or to expose the declarant to civil or criminal liability; and

(B) is supported by corroborating circumstances that clearly indicate its trustworthiness, if it is offered in a criminal case as one that tends to expose the declarant to criminal liability.

(4) *Statement of Personal or Family History.* A statement about:

(A) the declarant's own birth, adoption, legitimacy, ancestry, marriage, divorce, relationship by blood, adoption, or marriage, or similar facts of personal or family history, even though the declarant had no way of acquiring personal knowledge about that fact; or

(B) another person concerning any of these facts, as well as death, if the declarant was related to the person by blood, adoption, or marriage or was so intimately associated with the person's family that the declarant's information is likely to be accurate.

(5) [*Other Exceptions.*] [Transferred to Rule 807.]

(6) *Statement Offered Against a Party That Wrongfully Caused the Declarant's Unavailability.* A statement offered against a party that wrongfully caused—or acquiesced in wrongfully causing—the declarant's unavailability as a witness, and did so intending that result.

(Jan. 2, 1975, P. L. 93-595, § 1, 88 Stat. 1942; Dec. 12, 1975, P. L. 94-149, § 1(12), (13), 89 Stat. 806; March 2, 1987, eff. Oct. 1, 1987; Nov. 18, 1988, P. L. 100-690, Title VII, Subtitle B, § 7075(b), 102 Stat. 4405; April 26, 1997, eff. Dec. 1, 1997; April 28, 2010, eff. Dec. 1, 2010; April 26, 2011, eff. Dec. 1, 2011.)

Rule 805. Hearsay Within Hearsay

Hearsay within hearsay is not excluded by the rule against hearsay if each part of the combined statements conforms with an exception to the rule.

(Jan. 2, 1975, P. L. 93-595, § 1, 88 Stat. 1943; April 26, 2011, eff. Dec. 1, 2011.)

Rule 806. Attacking and Supporting the Declarant's Credibility

When a hearsay statement—or a statement described in Rule 801(d)(2)(C), (D), or (E)—has been admitted in evidence, the declarant's credibility may be attacked, and then supported, by any evidence that would be admissible for those purposes if the declarant had testified as a witness. The court may admit evidence of the declarant's inconsistent statement or conduct, regardless of when it occurred or whether the declarant had an opportunity to explain or deny it. If the party against whom the statement was admitted calls the declarant as a witness, the party may examine the declarant on the statement as if on cross-examination.

(Jan. 2, 1975, P. L. 93-595, § 1, 88 Stat. 1943; March 2, 1987, eff. Oct. 1, 1987; April 11, 1997, eff. Dec. 1, 1997; April 26, 2011, eff. Dec. 1, 2011.)

Rule 807. Residual Exception

(a) In General. Under the following circumstances, a hearsay statement is not excluded by the rule against hearsay even if the statement is not specifically covered by a hearsay exception in Rule 803 or 804:

(1) the statement has equivalent circumstantial guarantees of trustworthiness;

(2) it is offered as evidence of a material fact;

(3) it is more probative on the point for which it is offered than any other evidence that the proponent can obtain through reasonable efforts; and

(4) admitting it will best serve the purposes of these rules and the interests of justice.

(b) Notice. The statement is admissible only if, before the trial or hearing, the proponent gives an adverse party reasonable notice of the intent to offer the statement and its particulars, including the declarant's name and address, so that the party has a fair opportunity to meet it.

(Added April 11, 1997, eff. Dec. 1, 1997; April 26, 2011, eff. Dec. 1, 2011.)

ARTICLE IX. AUTHENTICATION AND IDENTIFICATION

Rule 901. Authenticating or Identifying Evidence

(a) In General. To satisfy the requirement of authenticating or identifying an item of evidence, the proponent must produce evidence sufficient to support a finding that the item is what the proponent claims it is.

(b) Examples. The following are examples only—not a complete list—of evidence that satisfies the requirement:

(1) *Testimony of a Witness with Knowledge.* Testimony that an item is what it is claimed to be.

(2) *Nonexpert Opinion About Handwriting.* A nonexpert's opinion that handwriting is genuine, based on a familiarity with it that was not acquired for the current litigation.

(3) *Comparison by an Expert Witness or the Trier of Fact.* A comparison with an authenticated specimen by an expert witness or the trier of fact.

(4) *Distinctive Characteristics and the Like.* The appearance, contents, substance, internal patterns, or other distinctive characteristics of the item, taken together with all the circumstances.

(5) *Opinion About a Voice.* An opinion identifying a person's voice—whether heard firsthand or through mechanical or electronic transmission or recording—based on hearing the voice at any time under circumstances that connect it with the alleged speaker.

(6) *Evidence About a Telephone Conversation.* For a telephone conversation, evidence that a call was made to the number assigned at the time to:

(A) a particular person, if circumstances, including self-identification, show that the person answering was the one called; or

(B) a particular business, if the call was made to a business and the call related to business reasonably transacted over the telephone.

(7) *Evidence About Public Records.* Evidence that:

(A) a document was recorded or filed in a public office as authorized by law; or

(B) a purported public record or statement is from the office where items of this kind are kept.

(8) *Evidence About Ancient Documents or Data Compilations.* For a document or data compilation, evidence that it:

(A) is in a condition that creates no suspicion about its authenticity;

(B) was in a place where, if authentic, it would likely be; and

(C) is at least 20 years old when offered.

(9) *Evidence About a Process or System.* Evidence describing a process or system and showing that it produces an accurate result.

(10) *Methods Provided by a Statute or Rule.* Any method of authentication or identification allowed by a federal statute or a rule prescribed by the Supreme Court.

(Jan. 2, 1975, P. L. 93-595, § 1, 88 Stat. 1943; April 26, 2011, eff. Dec. 1, 2011.)

Rule 902. Evidence That Is Self-Authenticating

The following items of evidence are self-authenticating; they require no extrinsic evidence of authenticity in order to be admitted:

(1) *Domestic Public Documents That Are Sealed and Signed.* A document that bears:

(A) a seal purporting to be that of the United States; any state, district, commonwealth, territory, or insular possession of the United States; the former Panama Canal Zone; the Trust Territory of the Pacific Islands; a political subdivision of any of these entities; or a department, agency, or officer of any entity named above; and

(B) a signature purporting to be an execution or attestation.

(2) *Domestic Public Documents That Are Not Sealed but Are Signed and Certified.* A document that bears no seal if:

(A) it bears the signature of an officer or employee of an entity named in Rule 902(1)(A); and

(B) another public officer who has a seal and official duties within that same entity certifies under seal—or its equivalent—that the signer has the official capacity and that the signature is genuine.

(3) *Foreign Public Documents.* A document that purports to be signed or attested by a person who is authorized by a foreign country's law to do so. The document must be accompanied by a final certification that certifies the genuineness of the signature and official position of the signer or attester—or of any foreign official whose certificate of genuineness relates to the signature or attestation or is in a chain of certificates of genuineness relating to the signature or attestation. The certification may be made by a secretary of a United States embassy or legation; by a consul general, vice consul, or consular agent of the United States; or by a diplomatic or consular official of the foreign country assigned or accredited to the United States. If all parties have been given a reasonable opportunity to investigate the document's authenticity and accuracy, the court may, for good cause, either:

(A) order that it be treated as presumptively authentic without final certification; or

(B) allow it to be evidenced by an attested summary with or without final certification.

(4) *Certified Copies of Public Records.* A copy of an official record—or a copy of a document that was recorded or filed in a public office as authorized by law—if the copy is certified as correct by:

(A) the custodian or another person authorized to make the certification; or

(B) a certificate that complies with Rule 902(1), (2), or (3), a federal statute, or a rule prescribed by the Supreme Court.

(5) *Official Publications.* A book, pamphlet, or other publication purporting to be issued by a public

authority.

(6) *Newspapers and Periodicals.* Printed material purporting to be a newspaper or periodical.

(7) *Trade Inscriptions and the Like.* An inscription, sign, tag, or label purporting to have been affixed in the course of business and indicating origin, ownership, or control.

(8) *Acknowledged Documents.* A document accompanied by a certificate of acknowledgment that is lawfully executed by a notary public or another officer who is authorized to take acknowledgments.

(9) *Commercial Paper and Related Documents.* Commercial paper, a signature on it, and related documents, to the extent allowed by general commercial law.

(10) *Presumptions Under a Federal Statute.* A signature, document, or anything else that a federal statute declares to be presumptively or prima facie genuine or authentic.

(11) *Certified Domestic Records of a Regularly Conducted Activity.* The original or a copy of a domestic record that meets the requirements of Rule 803(6)(A)–(C), as shown by a certification of the custodian or another qualified person that complies with a federal statute or a rule prescribed by the Supreme Court. Before the trial or hearing, the proponent must give an adverse party reasonable written notice of the intent to offer the record—and must make the record and certification available for inspection—so that the party has a fair opportunity to challenge them.

(12) *Certified Foreign Records of a Regularly Conducted Activity.* In a civil case, the original or a copy of a foreign record that meets the requirements of Rule 902(11), modified as follows: the certification, rather than complying with a federal statute or Supreme Court rule, must be signed in a manner that, if falsely made, would subject the maker to a criminal penalty in the country where the certification is signed. The proponent must also meet the notice requirements of Rule 902(11).

(Jan. 2, 1975, P. L. 93-595, § 1, 88 Stat. 1944; March 2, 1987, eff. Oct. 1, 1987; April 25, 1988, eff. Nov. 1, 1988; April 17, 2000, eff. Dec. 1, 2000; April 26, 2011, eff. Dec. 1, 2011.)

Rule 903. Subscribing Witness's Testimony

A subscribing witness's testimony is necessary to authenticate a writing only if required by the law of the jurisdiction that governs its validity.

(Jan. 2, 1975, P. L. 93-595, § 1, 88 Stat. 1945; April 26, 2011, eff. Dec. 1, 2011.)

ARTICLE X. CONTENTS OF WRITINGS, RECORDINGS, AND PHOTOGRAPHS

Rule 1001. Definitions That Apply to This Article

In this article:

(a) A "writing" consists of letters, words, numbers, or their equivalent set down in any form.

(b) A "recording" consists of letters, words, numbers, or their equivalent recorded in any manner.

(c) A "photograph" means a photographic image or its equivalent stored in any form.

(d) An "original" of a writing or recording means the writing or recording itself or any counterpart intended to have the same effect by the person who executed or issued it. For electronically stored information, "original" means any printout—or other output readable by sight—if it accurately reflects the information. An "original" of a photograph includes the negative or a print from it.

(e) A "duplicate" means a counterpart produced by a mechanical, photographic, chemical, electronic, or other equivalent process or technique that accurately reproduces the original.

(Jan. 2, 1975, P. L. 93-595, § 1, 88 Stat. 1945; April 26, 2011, eff. Dec. 1, 2011.)

Rule 1002. Requirement of the Original

An original writing, recording, or photograph is required in order to prove its content unless these rules or a federal statute provides otherwise.

(Jan. 2, 1975, P. L. 93-595, § 1, 88 Stat. 1946; April 26, 2011, eff. Dec. 1, 2011.)

Rule 1003. Admissibility of Duplicates

A duplicate is admissible to the same extent as the original unless a genuine question is raised about the original's authenticity or the circumstances make it unfair to admit the duplicate.

(Jan. 2, 1975, P. L. 93-595, § 1, 88 Stat. 1946; April 26, 2011, eff. Dec. 1, 2011.)

Rule 1004. Admissibility of Other Evidence of Content

An original is not required and other evidence of the content of a writing, recording, or photograph is admissible if:

(a) all the originals are lost or destroyed, and not by the proponent acting in bad faith;

(b) an original cannot be obtained by any available judicial process;

(c) the party against whom the original would be offered had control of the original; was at that time put on notice, by pleadings or otherwise, that the original would be a subject of proof at the trial or hearing; and fails to produce it at the trial or hearing; or

(d) the writing, recording, or photograph is not closely related to a controlling issue.

(Jan. 2, 1975, P. L. 93-595, § 1, 88 Stat. 1946; March 2, 1987, eff. Oct. 1, 1987; April 26, 2011, eff. Dec. 1, 2011.)

Rule 1005. Copies of Public Records to Prove Content

The proponent may use a copy to prove the content of an official record—or of a document that was recorded or filed in a public office as authorized by law—if these conditions are met: the record or document is otherwise admissible; and the copy is certified as correct in accordance with Rule 902(4) or is testified to be correct by a witness who has compared it with the original. If no such copy can be obtained by reasonable diligence, then the proponent may use other evidence to prove the content.

(Jan. 2, 1975, P. L. 93-595, § 1, 88 Stat. 1946; April 26, 2011, eff. Dec. 1, 2011.)

Rule 1006. Summaries to Prove Content

The proponent may use a summary, chart, or calculation to prove the content of voluminous writings, recordings, or photographs that cannot be conveniently examined in court. The proponent must make the originals or duplicates available for examination or copying, or both, by other parties at a reasonable time and place. And the court may order the proponent to produce them in court.

(Jan. 2, 1975, P. L. 93-595, § 1, 88 Stat. 1946; April 26, 2011, eff. Dec. 1, 2011.)

Rule 1007. Testimony or Statement of a Party to Prove Content

The proponent may prove the content of a writing, recording, or photograph by the testimony, deposition, or written statement of the party against whom the evidence is offered. The proponent need not account for the original.

(Jan. 2, 1975, P. L. 93-595, § 1, 88 Stat. 1947; March 2, 1987, eff. Oct. 1, 1987; April 26, 2011, eff. Dec. 1, 2011.)

Rule 1008. Functions of the Court and Jury

Ordinarily, the court determines whether the proponent has fulfilled the factual conditions for admitting other evidence of the content of a writing, recording, or photograph under Rule 1004 or 1005. But in a jury trial, the jury determines—in accordance with Rule 104(b)—any issue about whether:

(a) an asserted writing, recording, or photograph ever existed;

(b) another one produced at the trial or hearing is the original; or

(c) other evidence of content accurately reflects the content.

(Jan. 2, 1975, P. L. 93-595, § 1, 88 Stat. 1947; April 26, 2011, eff. Dec. 1, 2011.)

ARTICLE XI. MISCELLANEOUS RULES

Rule 1101. Applicability of the Rules

(a) To Courts and Judges. These rules apply to proceedings before:

- United States district courts;
- United States bankruptcy and magistrate judges;
- United States courts of appeals;
- the United States Court of Federal Claims; and
- the district courts of Guam, the Virgin Islands, and the Northern Mariana Islands.

(b) To Cases and Proceedings. These rules apply in:

- civil cases and proceedings, including bankruptcy, admiralty, and maritime cases;
- criminal cases and proceedings; and
- contempt proceedings, except those in which the court may act summarily.

(c) Rules on Privilege. The rules on privilege apply to all stages of a case or proceeding.

(d) Exceptions. These rules—except for those on privilege—do not apply to the following:

(1) the court's determination, under Rule 104(a), on a preliminary question of fact governing admissibility;

(2) grand-jury proceedings; and

(3) miscellaneous proceedings such as:

- extradition or rendition;
- issuing an arrest warrant, criminal summons, or search warrant;
- a preliminary examination in a criminal case;
- sentencing;
- granting or revoking probation or supervised release; and
- considering whether to release on bail or otherwise.

(e) Other Statutes and Rules. A federal statute or a rule prescribed by the Supreme Court may provide for admitting or excluding evidence independently from these rules.

(Jan. 2, 1975, P. L. 93-595, § 1, 88 Stat. 1947; Dec. 12, 1975, P. L. 94-149, § 1(14), 89 Stat. 806; Nov. 6, 1978, P. L. 95-598, Title II, §§ 251, 252, 92 Stat. 2673; Apr. 2, 1982, P. L. 97-164, Title I, Part A, § 142, 96 Stat. 45; March 2, 1987, eff. Oct. 1, 1987; April 25, 1988, eff. Nov. 1, 1988; Nov. 18, 1988, P. L. 100-690, Title VII, Subtitle B, § 7075(c), 102 Stat. 4405; April 22, 1993, eff. Dec. 1, 1993; April 26, 2011, eff. Dec. 1, 2011.)

Rule 1102. Amendments

These rules may be amended as provided in 28 U.S.C. § 2072.

(Jan. 2, 1975, P. L. 93-595, § 1, 88 Stat. 1948; Dec. 1, 1991; Apr. 26, 2011, eff. Dec. 1, 2011.)

Rule 1103. Title

These rules may be cited as the Federal Rules of Evidence.

(Jan. 2, 1975, P. L. 93-595, § 1, 88 Stat. 1948; April 26, 2011, eff. Dec. 1, 2011.)

RULES GOVERNING SECTION 2254 CASES

Rule 1. Scope

(a) Cases involving a petition under 28 U.S.C. § 2254. These rules govern a petition for a writ of habeas corpus filed in a United States district court under 28 U.S.C. § 2254 by:

(1) a person in custody under a state-court judgment who seeks a determination that the custody violates the Constitution, laws, or treaties of the United States; and

(2) a person in custody under a state-court or federal-court judgment who seeks a determination that future custody under a state-court judgment would violate the Constitution, laws, or treaties of the United States.

(b) Other cases. The district court may apply any or all of these rules to a habeas corpus petition not covered by Rule 1(a).

(As amended April 26, 2004, eff. Dec. 1, 2004.)

Rule 2. The Petition

(a) Current custody; naming the respondent. If the petitioner is currently in custody under a state-court judgment, the petition must name as respondent the state officer who has custody.

(b) Future custody; naming the respondents and specifying the judgment. If the petitioner is not yet in custody—-but may be subject to future custody—-under the state-court judgment being contested, the petition must name as respondents both the officer who has current custody and the attorney general of the state where the judgment was entered. The petition must ask for relief from the state-court judgment being contested.

(c) Form. The petition must:

(1) specify all the grounds for relief available to the petitioner;

(2) state the facts supporting each ground;

(3) state the relief requested;

(4) be printed, typewritten, or legibly handwritten; and

(5) be signed under penalty of perjury by the petitioner or by a person authorized to sign it for the petitioner under 28 U.S.C. § 2242.

(d) Standard form. The petition must substantially follow either the form appended to these rules or a form prescribed by a local district-court rule. The clerk must make forms available to petitioners without charge.

(e) Separate petitions for judgments of separate courts. A petitioner who seeks relief from judgments of more than one state court must file a separate petition covering the judgment or judgments of each court.

(As amended Sept. 28, 1976, P.L. 94-426, § 2(1), (2), 90 Stat. 1334; April 28, 1982, eff. Aug. 1, 1982; April 26, 2004, eff. Dec. 1, 2004.)

Rule 3. Filing the Petition; Inmate Filing

(a) Where to file; copies; filing fee. An original and two copies of the petition must be filed with the clerk and must be accompanied by:

(1) the applicable filing fee, or

(2) a motion for leave to proceed in forma pauperis, the affidavit required by 28 U.S.C. § 1915, and a certificate from the warden or other appropriate officer of the place of confinement showing the amount of money or securities that the petitioner has in any account in the institution.

(b) Filing. The clerk must file the petition and enter it on the docket.

(c) Time to file. The time for filing a petition is governed by 28 U.S.C. § 2244(d).

(d) Inmate filing. A paper filed by an inmate confined in an institution is timely if deposited in the institution's internal mailing system on or before the last day for filing. If an institution has a system designed for legal mail, the inmate must use that system to receive the benefit of this rule. Timely filing may be shown by a declaration in compliance with 28 U.S.C. § 1746 or by a notarized statement, either of which must set forth the date of deposit and state that first-class postage has been prepaid.

(As amended April 26, 2004, eff. Dec. 1, 2004.)

Rule 4. Preliminary Review; Serving the Petition and Order

The clerk must promptly forward the petition to a judge under the court's assignment procedure, and the judge must promptly examine it. If it plainly appears from the petition and any attached exhibits that the petitioner is not entitled to relief in the district court, the judge must dismiss the petition and direct the clerk to notify the petitioner. If the petition is not dismissed, the judge must order the respondent to file an answer, motion, or other response within a fixed time, or to take other action the judge may order. In every case, the clerk must serve a copy of the petition and any order on the respondent and on the attorney general or other appropriate officer of the state involved.

(As amended April 26, 2004, eff. Dec. 1, 2004.)

Rule 5. The Answer and the Reply

(a) When required. The respondent is not required to answer the petition unless a judge so orders.

(b) Contents: addressing the allegations; stating a bar. The answer must address the allegations in the petition. In addition, it must state whether any claim in the petition is barred by a failure to exhaust state remedies, a procedural bar, non-retroactivity, or a statute of limitations.

(c) Contents: transcripts. The answer must also indicate what transcripts (of pretrial, trial, sentencing, or post-conviction proceedings) are available, when they can be furnished, and what proceedings have been recorded but not transcribed. The respondent must attach to the answer parts of the transcript that the respondent considers relevant. The judge may order that the respondent furnish other parts of existing transcripts or that parts of untranscribed recordings be transcribed and furnished. If a transcript cannot be obtained,the respondent may submit a narrative summary of the evidence.

(d) Contents: briefs on appeal and opinions. The respondent must also file with the answer a copy of:

(1) any brief that the petitioner submitted in an appellate court contesting the conviction or sentence, or contesting an adverse judgment or order in a post-conviction proceeding;

(2) any brief that the prosecution submitted in an appellate court relating to the conviction or sentence; and

(3) the opinions and dispositive orders of the appellate court relating to the conviction or the sentence.

(e) Reply. The petitioner may submit a reply to the respondent's answer or other pleading within a time fixed by the judge.

(As amended April 26, 2004, eff. Dec. 1, 2004.)

Rule 6. Discovery

(a) Leave of court required. A judge may, for good cause, authorize a party to conduct discovery under the Federal Rules of Civil Procedure and may limit the extent of discovery. If necessary for effective discovery, the judge must appoint an attorney for a petitioner who qualifies to have counsel appointed under 18 U.S.C. § 3006A.

(b) Requesting discovery. A party requesting discovery must provide reasons for the request. The request must also include any proposed interrogatories and requests for admission, and must specify any requested documents.

(c) Deposition expenses. If the respondent is granted leave to take a deposition, the judge may require the respondent to pay the travel expenses, subsistence expenses, and fees of the petitioner's attorney to attend the deposition.

(As amended April 26, 2004, eff. Dec. 1, 2004.)

Rule 7. Expanding the record

(a) In general. If the petition is not dismissed, the judge may direct the parties to expand the record by submitting additional materials relating to the petition. The judge may require that these materials be authenticated.

(b) Types of materials. The materials that may be required include letters predating the filing of the petition, documents,exhibits, and answers under oath to written interrogatories propounded by the judge. Affidavits may also be submitted and considered as part of the record.

(c) Review by the opposing party. The judge must give the party against whom the additional materials are offered an opportunity to admit or deny their correctness.

(As amended April 26, 2004, eff. Dec. 1, 2004.)

Rule 8. Evidentiary Hearing

(a) Determining whether to hold a hearing. If the petition is not dismissed, the judge must review the answer, any transcripts and records of state-court proceedings, and any materials submitted under Rule 7 to determine whether an evidentiary hearing is warranted.

(b) Reference to a magistrate judge. A judge may, under 28 U.S.C. § 636(b), refer the petition to a magistrate judge to conduct hearings and to file proposed findings of fact and recommendations for disposition. When they are filed, the clerk must promptly serve copies of the proposed findings and recommendations on all parties. Within 14 days after being served, a party may file objections as provided by local court rule. The judge must determine de novo any proposed finding or recommendation to which objection is made. The judge may accept, reject, or modify any proposed finding or recommendation.

(c) Appointing counsel; time of hearing. If an evidentiary hearing is warranted, the judge must appoint an attorney to represent a petitioner who qualifies to have counsel appointed under 18 U.S.C. § 3006A. The judge must conduct the hearing as soon as practicable after giving the attorneys adequate time to investigate and prepare. These rules do not limit the appointment of counsel under § 3006A at any stage of the proceeding.

(As amended Sept. 28, 1976, P.L. 94-426, § 2(5), 90 Stat. 1334; Oct. 21, 1976, P.L. 94-577, § 2(a)(1), (b)(1), 90 Stat. 2730, 2731; April 26, 2004, eff. Dec. 1, 2004; March 26, 2009, eff. Dec. 1, 2009.)

Rule 9. Second or Successive Petitions

Before presenting a second or successive petition, the petitioner must obtain an order from the appropriate court of appeals authorizing the district court to consider the petition as required by 28 U.S.C. § 2244(b)(3)and (4).

(As amended Sept. 28, 1976, P.L. 94-426, § 2(7), (8), 90 Stat. 1335.; April 26, 2004, eff. Dec. 1, 2004.)

Rule 10. Powers of a Magistrate Judge

A magistrate judge may perform the duties of a district judge under these rules, as authorized under 28 U.S.C. § 636.

(As amended Sept. 28, 1976, P.L. 94-426, § 2(11) 90 Stat. 1335; April 30, 1979, eff. Aug. 1, 1979; April 26, 2004, eff. Dec. 1, 2004.)

Rule 11. Certificate of Appealability; Time to Appeal

(a) Certificate of appealability. The district court must issue or deny a certificate of appealability when it enters a final order adverse to the applicant. Before entering the final order, the court may direct the parties to submit arguments on whether a certificate should issue. If the court issues a certificate, the court must state the specific issue or issues that satisfy the showing required by 28 U.S.C. § 2253(c)(2). If the court denies a certificate, the parties may not appeal the denial but may seek a certificate from the court of appeals under Federal Rule of Appellate Procedure 22. A motion to reconsider a denial does not extend the time to appeal.

(b) Time to appeal. Federal Rule of Appellate Procedure 4(a) governs the time to appeal an order entered under these rules. A timely notice of appeal must be filed even if the district court issues a certificate of appealability.

(Added March 26, 2009, eff. Dec. 1, 2009.)

Rule 12. Applicability of the Federal Rules of Civil Procedure

The Federal Rules of Civil Procedure, to the extent that they are not inconsistent with any statutory provisions or these rules, may be applied to a proceeding under these rules.

(As amended April 26, 2004, eff. Dec. 1, 2004; March 26, 2009, eff. Dec. 1, 2009.)

APPENDIX

APPENDIX OF FORMS

Form No. 1. PETITION FOR RELIEF FROM A CONVICTION OR SENTENCE BY A PERSON IN STATE CUSTODY

Petition for Relief From a Conviction or Sentence By a Person in State Custody

(Petition Under 28 U.S.C. § 2254 for a Writ of Habeas Corpus)

Instructions

1. To use this form, you must be a person who is currently serving a sentence under a judgment against you in a state court. You are asking for relief from the conviction or the sentence. This form is your petition for relief.
2. You may also use this form to challenge a state judgment that imposed a sentence to be served in the future, but you must fill in the name of the state where the judgment was entered. If you want to challenge a federal judgment that imposed a sentence to be served in the future, you should file a motion under 28 U.S.C. § 2255 in the federal court that entered the judgment.
3. Make sure the form is typed or neatly written.
4. You must tell the truth and sign the form. If you make a false statement of a material fact, you may be prosecuted for perjury.
5. Answer all the questions. You do not need to cite law. You may submit additional pages if necessary. If you do not fill out the form properly, you will be asked to submit additional or correct information. If you want to submit a brief or arguments, you must submit them in a separate memorandum.
6. You must pay a fee of $5. If the fee is paid, your petition will be filed. If you cannot pay the fee, you may ask to proceed *in forma pauperis* (as a poor person). To do that, you must fill out the last page of this form. Also, you must submit a certificate signed by an officer at the institution where you are confined showing the amount of money that the institution is holding for you. If your account exceeds $, you must pay the filing fee.
7. In this petition, you may challenge the judgment entered by only one court. If you want to challenge a judgment entered by a different court (either in the same state or in different states), you must file a separate petition.
8. When you have completed the form, send the original and two copies to the Clerk of the United States District Court at this address:

   Clerk, United States District Court for
   Address
   City, State Zip Code
9. **CAUTION : You must include in this petition all the grounds for relief from the conviction or sentence that you challenge. And you must state the facts that support each ground. If you fail to set forth all the grounds in this petition, you may be barred from presenting additional grounds at a later date.**
10. **CAPITAL CASES : If you are under a sentence of death, you are entitled to the assistance of counsel and should request the appointment of counsel.**

PETITION UNDER 28 U.S.C. § 2254 FOR WRIT OF HABEAS CORPUS BY A PERSON IN STATE CUSTODY

United States District Court	District
Name (under which you were convicted):	Docket or Case No.:
Place of Confinement:	Prisoner No.:
Petitioner (include the name under which were convicted) v.	Respondent (authorized person having custody of petitioner)
The Attorney General of the State of	

PETITION

1. (a) Name and location of court which entered the judgment of conviction you are challenging:
   (b) Criminal docket or case number (if you know): ______
2. (a) Date of judgment of conviction (if you know): ______
   (b) Date of sentencing: ______
3. Length of sentence: ______
4. In this case, were you convicted on more than one count or of more than one crime? Yes ☐ No ☐
5. Identify all crimes of which you were convicted and sentenced in this case: ______
6. (a) What was your plea? (Check one)
   (1) Not guilty ☐ (3) Nolo contendere (no contest) ☐
   (2) Guilty ☐ (4) Insanity plea ☐
   (b) If you entered a guilty plea to one count or charge and a not guilty plea to another count or charge, what did you plead not guilty to?
   (c) If you went to trial, what kind of trial did you have? (Check one)
   Jury ☐ Judge only ☐
7. Did you testify at a pretrial hearing, trial, or a post-trial hearing?
   Yes ☐ No ☐
8. Did you appeal from the judgment of conviction?
   Yes ☐ No ☐
9. If you did appeal, answer the following: ______
(a) Name of court: ______
(b) Docket or case number (if you know): ______
(c) Result: ______
(d) Date of result (if you know): ______
(e) Citation to the case (if you know): ______
(f) Grounds raised: ______

(g) Did you seek further review by a higher state court? Yes ☐ No ☐
   If yes, answer the following:
   (1) Name of court: ______
   (2) Docket or case number (if you know): ______
   (3) Result: ______
   (4) Date of result (if you know): ______
   (5) Citation to the case (if you know): ______
   (6) Grounds raised: ______

(h) Did you file a petition for certiorari in the United States Supreme Court? Yes ☐ No ☐
   If yes, answer the following: ______
   (1) Docket or case number (if you know): ______
   (2) Result: ______
   (3) Date of result (if you know): ______
   (4) Citation to the case (if you know): ______

10. Other than the direct appeals listed above, have you previously filed any other petitions, applications, or motions concerning this judgment of conviction in any state court? Yes ☐ No ☐
11. If your answer to Question 10 was "Yes," give the following information: ______
   (a) (1) Name of court: ______
   (2) Docket or case number (if you know): ______
   (3) Date of filing (if you know): ______
   (4) Nature of proceeding: ______
   (5) Grounds raised: ______

(6) Did you receive a hearing where evidence was given on your petition, application, or motion? Yes ☐ No ☐

(7) Result: ____

(8) Date of result (if you know): ____

(b) If you filed any second petition, application or motion give the same information:

(1) Name of court: ____

(2) Docket or case number (if you know): ____

(3) Date of filing (if you know): ____

(4) Nature of proceeding: ____

(5) Grounds raised: ____

(6) Did you receive a hearing where evidence was given on your petition, application, or motion? Yes ☐ No ☐

(7) Result: ____

(8) Date of result (if you know): ____

(c) If you filed any third petition, application, or motion, give the same information:

(1) Name of court: ____

(2) Docket or case number (if you know): ____

(3) Date of filing (if you know): ____

(4) Nature of proceeding: ____

(5) Grounds raised: ____

(6) Did you receive a hearing where evidence was given on your petition, application, or motion? Yes ☐ No ☐

(7) Result: ____

(8) Date of result (if you know): ____

(d) Did you appeal to the highest state court having jurisdiction over the action taken on your petition, application, or motion?

(1) First petition: Yes ☐ No ☐

(2) Second petition: Yes ☐ No ☐

(3) Third petition: Yes ☐ No ☐

(e) If you did not appeal to the highest state court having jurisdiction, explain why you did not:

12. For this petition, state every ground on which you claim that you are being held in violation of the Constitution, laws, or treaties of the United States. Attach additional pages if you have more than four grounds. State the facts supporting each ground.

CAUTION: To proceed in the federal court, you must ordinarily first exhaust (use up) your available state-court remedies on each ground on which you request action by the federal court. Also, if you fail to set forth all the grounds in this petition, you may be barred from presenting additional grounds at a later date.

GROUND ONE: ____

(a) Supporting facts (Do not argue or cite law. Just state the specific facts that support your claim.):

(b) If you did not exhaust your state remedies on Ground One, explain why: ____

(c) **Direct Appeal of Ground One:**

(1) If you appealed from the judgment of conviction, did you raise this issue?

Yes ☐ No ☐

(2) If you did not raise this issue in your direct appeal, explain why: ____

(d) **Post-Conviction Proceedings:**

(1) Did you raise this issue through a post-conviction motion or petition for habeas corpus in a state trial court? Yes ☐ No ☐

(2) If your answer to Question (d)(1) is "Yes," state:

Type of motion or petition: ____

Name and location of the court where the motion or petition was filed: ____

Docket or case number (if you know): ____

Date of the court's decision: ____

Result (attach a copy of the court's opinion or order, if available): ____

(3) Did you receive a hearing on your motion or petition?

Yes ☐ No ☐

(4) Did you appeal from the denial of your motion or petition?

Yes ☐ No ☐

(5) If your answer to Question (d)(4) is "Yes," did you raise this issue in the appeal?

Yes ☐ No ☐

(6) If your answer to Question (d)(4) is "Yes," state: ____

Name and location of the court where the appeal was filed: ____

Docket or case number (if you know): ____

Date of the court's decision: ____

Result (attach a copy of the court's opinion or order, if available):

(7) If your answer to Question (d)(4) or Question (d)(5) is "No," explain why you did not raise this issue: ____

(e) **Other Remedies:** Describe any other procedures (such as habeas corpus, administrative remedies, etc.) that you have used to exhaust your state remedies on Ground One: ____

GROUND TWO: ____

(a) Supporting facts (Do not argue or cite law. Just state the specific facts that support your claim.):

(b) If you did not exhaust your state remedies on Ground Two, explain why: ______

(c) **Direct Appeal of Ground Two:**

(1) If you appealed from the judgment of conviction, did you raise this issue?

Yes ☐ No ☐

(2) If you did not raise this issue in your direct appeal, explain why: ______

(d) **Post-Conviction Proceedings:**

(1) Did you raise this issue through a post-conviction motion or petition for habeas corpus in a state trial court? Yes ☐ No ☐

(2) If your answer to Question (d)(1) is "Yes," state:

Type of motion or petition: ______

Name and location of the court where the motion or petition was filed: ______

Docket or case number (if you know): ______

Date of the court's decision: ______

Result (attach a copy of the court's opinion or order, if available): ______

(3) Did you receive a hearing on your motion or petition?

Yes ☐ No ☐

(4) Did you appeal from the denial of your motion or petition?

Yes ☐ No ☐

(5) If your answer to Question (d)(4) is "Yes," did you raise this issue in the appeal?

Yes ☐ No ☐

(6) If your answer to Question (d)(4) is "Yes," state:

Name and location of the court where the appeal was filed: ______

Docket or case number (if you know): ______

Date of the court's decision: ______

Result (attach a copy of the court's opinion or order, if available): ______

(7) If your answer to Question (d)(4) or Question (d)(5) is "No," explain why you did not raise this issue: ______

(e) **Other Remedies:** Describe any other procedures (such as habeas corpus, administrative remedies, etc.) that you have used to exhaust your state remedies on Ground Two: ______

GROUND THREE:

(a) Supporting facts (Do not argue or cite law. Just state the specific facts that support your claim.):

(b) If you did not exhaust your state remedies on Ground Three, explain why:

(c) **Direct Appeal of Ground Three:**

(1) If you appealed from the judgment of conviction, did you raise this issue?

Yes ☐ No ☐

(2) If you did not raise this issue in your direct appeal, explain why: ______

(d) **Post-Conviction Proceedings:**

(1) Did you raise this issue through a post-conviction motion or petition for habeas corpus in a state trial court? Yes ☐ No ☐

(2) If your answer to Question (d)(1) is "Yes," state:

Type of motion or petition: ______

Name and location of the court where the motion or petition was filed: ______

Docket or case number (if you know): ______

Date of the court's decision: ______

Result (attach a copy of the court's opinion or order, if available): ______

(3) Did you receive a hearing on your motion or petition?

Yes ☐ No ☐

(4) Did you appeal from the denial of your motion or petition?

Yes ☐ No ☐

(5) If your answer to Question (d)(4) is "Yes," did you raise this issue in the appeal?

Yes ☐ No ☐

(6) If your answer to Question (d)(4) is "Yes," state:

Name and location of the court where the appeal was filed: ______

Docket or case number (if you know): ______

Date of the court's decision: ______

Result (attach a copy of the court's opinion or order, if available): ______

(7) If your answer to Question (d)(4) or Question (d)(5) is "No," explain why you did not raise this issue: ______

(e) **Other Remedies:** Describe any other procedures (such as habeas corpus, administrative remedies, etc.) that you have used to exhaust your state remedies on Ground Three: ______

GROUND FOUR: ______

(a) Supporting facts (Do not argue or cite law. Just state the specific facts that support your claim.):

(b) If you did not exhaust your state remedies on Ground Four, explain why: ______

(c) **Direct Appeal of Ground Four:**

(1) If you appealed from the judgment of conviction, did you raise this issue?

Yes ☐ No ☐

(2) If you did not raise this issue in your direct appeal, explain why: ____________

(d) **Post-Conviction Proceedings:**

(1) Did you raise this issue through a post-conviction motion or petition for habeas corpus in a state trial court? Yes ☐ No ☐

(2) If your answer to Question (d)(1) is "Yes," state:

Type of motion or petition: ____________

Name and location of the court where the motion or petition was filed: ____________

Docket or case number (if you know): ____________

Date of the court's decision: ____________

Result (attach a copy of the court's opinion or order, if available: ____________

____

____

(3) Did you receive a hearing on your motion or petition?

Yes ☐ No ☐

(4) Did you appeal from the denial of your motion or petition?

Yes ☐ No ☐

(5) If your answer to Question (d)(4) is "Yes," did you raise this issue in the appeal?

Yes ☐ No ☐

(6) If your answer to Question (d)(4) is "Yes," state:

Name and location of the court where the motion or petition was filed: ____________

Docket or case number (if you know): ____________

Date of the court's decision: ____________

Result (attach a copy of the court's opinion or order, if available: ____________

(7) If your answer to Question (d)(4) or Question (d)(5) is "No," explain why you did not raise this issue:

(e) **Other Remedies:** Describe any other procedures (such as habeas corpus, administrative remedies, etc.) that you have used to exhaust your state remedies on Ground Four:

13. Please answer these additional questions about the petition you are filing:

(a) Have all grounds for relief that you have raised in this petition been presented to the highest state court having jurisdiction? Yes ☐ No ☐

If your answer is "No," state which grounds have not been so presented and give your reason(s) for not presenting them:

(b) Is there any ground in this petition that has not been presented in some state or federal court? If so, which ground or grounds have not been presented, and state your reasons for not presenting them: ____________

14. Have you previously filed any type of petition, application, or motion in a federal court regarding the conviction that you challenge in this petition? Yes ☐ No ☐

If "Yes," state the name and location of the court, the docket or case number, the type of proceeding, the issues raised, the date of the court's decision, and the result for each petition, application, or motion filed. Attach a copy of any court opinion or order, if available.

15. Do you have any petition or appeal now pending (filed and not decided yet) in any court, either state or federal, for the judgment you are challenging? Yes ☐ No ☐

If "Yes," state the name and location of the court, the docket or case number, the type of proceeding, and the issues raised.

16. Give the name and address, if you know, of each attorney who represented you in the following stages of the judgment you are challenging:

(a) At preliminary hearing: ____________

(b) At arraignment and plea: ____________

(c) At trial: ____________

(d) At sentencing: ____________

(e) On appeal: ____________

(f) In any post-conviction proceeding: ____________

(g) On appeal from any ruling against you in a post-conviction proceeding: ____________

17. Do you have any future sentence to serve after you complete the sentence for the judgment that you are challenging? Yes ☐ No ☐

(a) If so, give name and location of court that imposed the other sentence you will serve in the future: ____________

(b) Give the date the other sentence was imposed: ____________

(c) Give the length of the other sentence: ____________

(c) Have you filed, or do you plan to file, any petition that challenges the judgment or sentence to be served in the future? Yes ☐ No ☐

18. TIMELINESS OF PETITION: If your judgment of conviction became final over one year ago, you must explain why the one-year statute of limitations as contained in 28 U.S.C. § 2244(d) does not bar your petition.*

Therefore, petitioner asks that the Court grant the following relief: ____________

or any other relief to which petitioner may be entitled.

____

Signature of Attorney (if any)

I declare (or certify, verify, or state) under penalty of perjury that the foregoing is true and correct and that this Petition for Writ of Habeas Corpus was placed in the prison mailing system on (month, date, year).

Executed (signed) on ________________ (date).
Signature of Petitioner

If the person signing is not petitioner, state relationship to petitioner and explain why petitioner is not signing this petition.

____

* The Antiterrorism and Effective Death Penalty Act of 1996 ("AEDPA") as contained in 28 U.S.C. § 2244(d) provides in part that:

(1) A one-year period of limitation shall apply to an application for a writ of habeas corpus by a person in custody pursuant to the judgment of a State court. The limitation period shall run from the latest of—
(A) the date on which the judgment became final by the conclusion of direct review or the expiration of the time for seeking such review;
(B) the date on which the impediment to filing an application created by State action in violation of the Constitution or laws of the United States is removed,if the applicant was prevented from filing by such state action;
(C) the date on which the constitutional right asserted was initially recognized by the Supreme Court, if the right has been newly recognized by the Supreme Court and made retroactively applicable to cases on collateral review; or
(D) the date on which the factual predicate of the claim or claims presented could have been discovered through the exercise of due diligence.

(2) The time during which a properly filed application for State post-conviction or other collateral review with respect to the pertinent judgment or claim is pending shall not be counted toward any period of limitation under this subsection.

____
Signature of Petitioner

Section 2254 Cases Form No. 1

IN FORMA PAUPERIS DECLARATION

____
[Insert appropriate court]

______________________ DECLARATION IN SUPPORT
(Petitioner) OF REQUEST
v. TO PROCEED
______________________ IN FORMA PAUPERIS
(Respondent(s))

I, __________, declare that I am the petitioner in the above entitled case; that in support of my motion to proceed without being required to prepay fees, costs or give security therefor, I state that because of my poverty I am unable to pay the costs of said proceeding or to give security therefor; that I believe I am entitled to relief.

1. Are you presently employed? Yes ☐ No ☐

a. If the answer is "yes," state the amount of your salary or wages per month, and give the name and address of your employer.

____

____

b. If the answer is "no," state the date of last employment and the amount of the salary and wages per month which you received.

____

____

2. Have you received within the past twelve months any money from any of the following sources?

a. Business, profession or form of self-employment? Yes ☐ No ☐

b. Rent payments, interest or dividends?
Yes ☐ No ☐

c. Pensions, annuities or life insurance payments?
Yes ☐ No ☐

d. Gifts or inheritances? Yes ☐ No ☐

e. Any other sources? Yes ☐ No ☐

If the answer to any of the above is "yes," describe each source of money and state the amount received from each during the past twelve months. ________

____

3. Do you own cash, or do you have money in checking or savings account?
Yes ☐ No ☐
(Include any funds in prison accounts.)
If the answer is "yes," state the total value of the items owned. ______________________

____

4. Do you own any real estate, stocks, bonds, notes, automobiles, or other valuable property (excluding ordinary household furnishings and clothing)?
Yes ☐ No ☐
If the answer is "yes," describe the property and state its approximate value. ______________

____

5. List the persons who are dependent upon you for support, state your relationship to those persons, and indicate how much you contribute toward their support. ______________________

____

I declare (or certify, verify, or state) under penalty of perjury that the foregoing is true and correct. Executed on ______ (date).

____
Signature of Petitioner

Certificate

I hereby certify that the petitioner herein has the sum of $______ on account to his credit at the __________ institution where he is confined. I further certify that petitioner likewise has the following securities to his credit according to the records of said ____________ institution:

____

____
Authorized Officer of

(Amended, effective August 1, 1982; effective December 1, 2004.)

Form 2. Model Form for Use in 28 U.S.C. § 2254 Cases Involving a Rule 9 Issue under Section 2254 of Title 28, United States Code [Abrogated.]

(Amended Aug. 1, 1982; Apr. 30, 2007, eff. Dec. 1, 2007.)

RULES GOVERNING SECTION 2255 PROCEEDINGS

Rule 1. Scope

These rules govern a motion filed in a United States district court under 28 U.S.C. § 2255 by:

(a) a person in custody under a judgment of that court who seeks a determination that:

(1) the judgment violates the Constitution or laws of the United States;

(2) the court lacked jurisdiction to enter the judgment;

(3) the sentence exceeded the maximum allowed by law; or

(4) the judgment or sentence is otherwise subject to collateral review; and

(b) a person in custody under a judgment of a state court or another federal court, and subject to future custody under a judgment of the district court, who seeks a determination that:

(1) future custody under a judgment of the district court would violate the Constitution or laws of the United States;

(2) the district court lacked jurisdiction to enter the judgment;

(3) the district court's sentence exceeded the maximum allowed by law; or

(4) the district court's judgment or sentence is otherwise subject to collateral review.

(As amended April 26, 2004, eff. Dec. 1, 2004.)

Rule 2. The Motion

(a) Applying for relief. The application must be in the form of a motion to vacate, set aside, or correct the sentence.

(b) Form. The motion must:

(1) specify all the grounds for relief available to the moving party;

(2) state the facts supporting each ground;

(3) state the relief requested;

(4) be printed, typewritten, or legibly handwritten; and

(5) be signed under penalty of perjury by the movant or by a person authorized to sign it for the movant.

(c) Standard form. The motion must substantially follow either the form appended to these rules or a form prescribed by a local district-court rule. The clerk must make forms available to moving parties without charge.

(d) Separate motions for separate judgments. A moving party who seeks relief from more than one judgment must file a separate motion covering each judgment.

(As amended Sept. 28, 1976, P.L. 94-426, § 2(3), (4), 90 Stat. 1334; April 28, 1982, eff. Aug. 1, 1982; April 26, 2004, eff. Dec. 1, 2004.)

Rule 3. Filing the Motion; Inmate Filing

(a) Where to file; copies. An original and two copies of the motion must be filed with the clerk.

(b) Filing and service. The clerk must file the motion and enter it on the criminal docket of the case in which the challenged judgment was entered. The clerk must then deliver or serve a copy of the motion on the United States attorney in that district, together with a notice of its filing.

(c) Time to file. The time for filing a motion is governed by 28 U.S.C. § 2255 para. 6.

(d) Inmate filing. A paper filed by an inmate confined in an institution is timely if deposited in the institution's internal mailing system on or before the last day for filing. If an institution has a system designed for legal mail, the inmate must use that system to receive the benefit of this rule. Timely filing may be shown by a declaration in compliance with 28 U.S.C. § 1746 or by a notarized statement, either of which must set forth the date of deposit and state that first-class postage has been prepaid.

(As amended April 26, 2004, eff. Dec. 1, 2004.)

Rule 4. Preliminary Review

(a) Referral to a judge. The clerk must promptly forward the motion to the judge who conducted the trial and imposed sentence or, if the judge who imposed sentence was not the trial judge, to the judge who conducted the proceedings being challenged. If the appropriate judge is not available, the clerk must forward the motion to a judge under the court's assignment procedure.

(b) Initial consideration by the judge. The judge who receives the motion must promptly examine it. If it plainly appears from the motion, any attached exhibits, and the record of prior proceedings that the moving party is not entitled to relief, the judge must dismiss the motion and direct the clerk to notify the moving party. If the motion is not dismissed, the judge must order the United States attorney to file an answer, motion, or other response within a fixed time, or to take other action the judge may order.

(As amended April 26, 2004, eff. Dec. 1, 2004.)

Rule 5. The Answer and the Reply

(a) When required. The respondent is not required to answer the motion unless a judge so orders.

(b) Contents. The answer must address the allegations in the motion. In addition, it must state whether the moving party has used any other federal remedies, including any prior post-conviction motions under these rules or any previous rules, and whether the moving party received an evidentiary hearing.

(c) Records of prior proceedings. If the answer refers to briefs or transcripts of the prior proceedings that are not available in the court's records,the judge must order the government to furnish them within a reasonable time that will not unduly delay the proceedings.

(d) Reply. The moving party may submit a reply to the respondent's answer or other pleading within a time fixed by the judge.

(As amended April 26, 2004, eff. Dec. 1, 2004.)

Rule 6. Discovery

(a) Leave of court required. A judge may, for good cause, authorize a party to conduct discovery under the Federal Rules of Criminal Procedure or Civil Procedure, or in accordance with the practices and principles of law. If necessary for effective discovery, the judge must appoint an attorney for a moving party who qualifies to have counsel appointed under 18 U.S.C. § 3006A.

(b) Requesting discovery. A party requesting discovery must provide reasons for the request. The request must also include any proposed interrogatories and requests for admission, and must specify any requested documents.

(c) Deposition expenses. If the government is granted leave to take a deposition, the judge may require the government to pay the travel expenses, subsistence expenses, and fees of the moving party's attorney to attend the deposition.

(As amended April 26, 2004, eff. Dec. 1, 2004.)

Rule 7. Expanding the Record

(a) In general. If the motion is not dismissed, the judge may direct the parties to expand the record by submitting additional materials relating to the motion. The judge may require that these materials be authenticated.

(b) Types of materials. The materials that may be required include letters predating the filing of the motion, documents, exhibits, and answers under oath to written interrogatories propounded by the judge. Affidavits also may be submitted and considered as part of the record.

(c) Review by the opposing party. The judge must give the party against whom the additional materials are offered an opportunity to admit or deny their correctness.

(As amended April 26, 2004, eff. Dec. 1, 2004.)

Rule 8. Evidentiary Hearing

(a) Determining whether to hold a hearing. If the motion is not dismissed, the judge must review the answer, any transcripts and records of prior proceedings, and any materials submitted under Rule 7 to determine whether an evidentiary hearing is warranted.

(b) Reference to a magistrate judge. A judge may, under 28 U.S.C. § 636(b), refer the motion to a magistrate judge to conduct hearings and to file proposed findings of fact and recommendations for disposition. When they are filed, the clerk must promptly serve copies of the proposed findings and recommendations on all parties. Within 14 days after being served, a party may file objections as provided by local court rule. The judge must determine de novo any proposed finding or recommendation to which objection is made. The judge may accept, reject, or modify any proposed finding or recommendation.

(c) Appointing counsel; time of hearing. If an evidentiary hearing is warranted, the judge must appoint an attorney to represent a moving party who qualifies to have counsel appointed under 18 U.S.C. § 3006A. The judge must conduct the hearing as soon as practicable after giving the attorneys adequate time to investigate and prepare. These rules do not limit the appointment of counsel under § 3006A at any stage of the proceeding.

(d) Producing a statement. Federal Rule of Criminal Procedure 26.2(a)–(d) and (f) applies at a hearing under this rule. If a party does not comply with a Rule 26.2(a)order to produce a witness's statement, the court must not consider that witness's testimony.

(As amended Sept. 28, 1976, P.L. 94-426, § 2(6), 90 Stat. 1335; Oct. 21, 1976, P.L. 94-577, § 2(a)(2), (b)(2), 90 Stat. 2730, 2731; April 22, 1993, eff. Dec. 1, 1993; April 26, 2004, eff. Dec. 1, 2004; March 26, 2009, eff. Dec. 1, 2009.)

Rule 9. Second or Successive Motions

Before presenting a second or successive motion, the moving party must obtain an order from the appropriate court of appeals authorizing the district court to consider the motion, as required by 28 U.S.C. § 2255, para. 8.

(As amended Sept. 28, 1976, P.L. 94-426, § 2(9), (10), 90 Stat. 1335; April 26, 2004, eff. Dec. 1, 2004.)

Rule 10. Powers of a Magistrate Judge

A magistrate judge may perform the duties of a district judge under these rules, as authorized by 28 U.S.C. § 636.

(As amended Sept. 28, 1976, P. L. 94-426, § 2(12),

90 Stat. 1335; April 30, 1979, eff. Aug. 1, 1979; April 26, 2004, eff. Dec. 1, 2004.)

Rule 11. Certificate of Appealability; Time to Appeal

(a) Certificate of appealability. The district court must issue or deny a certificate of appealability when it enters a final order adverse to the applicant. Before entering the final order, the court may direct the parties to submit arguments on whether a certificate should issue. If the court issues a certificate, the court must state the specific issue or issues that satisfy the showing required by 28 U.S.C. § 2253(c)(2). If the court denies a certificate, a party may not appeal the denial but may seek a certificate from the court of appeals under Federal Rule of Appellate Procedure 22. A motion to reconsider a denial does not extend the time to appeal.

(b) Time to appeal. Federal Rule of Appellate Procedure 4(a) governs the time to appeal an order entered under these rules. A timely notice of appeal must be filed even if the district court issues a certificate of appealability. These rules do not extend the time to appeal the original judgment of conviction.

(Amended April 30, 1979, effective Aug. 1, 1979; April 26, 2004, eff. Dec. 1, 2004; March 26, 2009, eff. Dec. 1, 2009.)

Rule 12. Applicability of the Federal Rules of Civil Procedure and the Federal Rules of Criminal Procedure

The Federal Rules of Civil Procedure and the Federal Rules of Criminal Procedure, to the extent that they are not inconsistent with any statutory provisions or these rules, may be applied to a proceeding under these rules.

(As amended April 26, 2004, eff. Dec. 1, 2004.)

APPENDIX

APPENDIX OF FORMS

Form No. 1. MOTION TO VACATE, SET ASIDE, OR CORRECT A SENTENCE BY A PERSON IN FEDERAL CUSTODY

Motion to Vacate, Set Aside, or Correct a Sentence By a Person in Federal Custody

(Motion Under 28 U.S.C. § 2255)

Instructions

1. To use this form, you must be a person who is serving a sentence under a judgment against you in a federal court. You are asking for relief from the conviction or the sentence. This form is your motion for relief.
2. You must file the form in the United States district court that entered the judgment that you are challenging. If you want to challenge a federal judgment that imposed a sentence to be served in the future, you should file a motion in the federal court that entered that judgment.
3. Make sure the form is typed or neatly written.
4. You must tell the truth and sign the form. If you make a false statement of a material fact, you may be prosecuted for perjury.
5. Answer all the questions. You do not need to cite law. You may submit additional pages if necessary. If you do not fill out the form properly, you will be asked to submit additional or correct information. If you want to submit a brief or arguments, you must submit them in a separate memorandum.
6. If you cannot pay for the costs of this motion (such as costs for an attorney or transcripts), you may ask to proceed *in forma pauperis* (as a poor person). To do that, you must fill out the last page of this form. Also, you must submit a certificate signed by an officer at the institution where you are confined showing the amount of money that the institution is holding for you.
7. In this motion, you may challenge the judgment entered by only one court. If you want to challenge a judgment entered by a different judge or division (either in the same district or in a different district), you must file a separate motion.
8. When you have completed the form, send the original and two copies to the Clerk of the United States District Court at this address:

   Clerk, United States District Court
   for ________________
   Address
   City, State Zip Code
9. **CAUTION : You must include in this motion all the grounds for relief from the conviction or sentence that you challenge. And you must state the facts that support each ground. If you fail to set forth all the grounds in this motion, you may be barred from presenting additional grounds at a later date.**
10. **CAPITAL CASES : If you are under a sentence of death, you are entitled to the assistance of counsel and should request the appointment of counsel.**

MOTION UNDER 28 U.S.C. § 2255 TO VACATE, SET ASIDE, OR CORRECT SENTENCE BY A PERSON IN FEDERAL CUSTODY

United States District Court	District
Name (under which you were convicted):	Docket or Case No.:
Place of Confinement:	Prisoner No.:
UNITED STATES OF AMERICA	Movant (include name under which you were convicted)
v.	

MOTION

1. Name and location of court which entered the judgment of conviction under attack ______
2. Date of judgment of conviction ______
3. Length of sentence ______
4. Nature of crime (all counts) ______

5.(a) What was your plea? (Check one)
(1) Not guilty ☐
(2) Guilty ☐
(3) Nolo contendere ☐
(b) If you entered a guilty plea to one count or indictment, and a not guilty plea to another count or indictment, what did you plead guilty to and what did you plead not guilty to?
6. If you went to trial, what kind of trial did you have? (Check one)
Jury ☐ Judge only ☐
7. Did you testify at a pretrial hearing, trial, or a post-trial hearing?
Yes ☐ No ☐
8. Did you appeal from the judgment of conviction?
Yes ☐ No ☐
9. If you did appeal, answer the following:
(a) Name of court: ______
(b) Docket or case number: ______
(c) Result: ______
(d) Date of result (if you know): ______
(e) Citation to the case (if you know): ______
(f) Grounds raised: ______
(g) Did you file a petition for certiorari in the United States Supreme Court?
Yes ☐ No ☐
If yes, answer the following:
(1) Docket or case number (if you know): ______
(2) Result: ______
(3) Date of result (if you know): ______
(4) Citation to the case (if you know): ______
(5) Grounds raised: ______

10. Other than the direct appeals listed above, have you previously filed any other motions, petitions, or applications concerning this judgment of conviction in any court?
Yes ☐ No ☐
11. If your answer to Question 10 was "Yes," give the following information:
(a) (1) Name of court: ______
(2) Docket or case number (if you know): ______
(3) Date of filing (if you know): ______
(4) Nature of proceeding: ______
(5) Grounds raised: ______

(6) Did you receive a hearing where evidence was given on your motion, petition, or application? Yes ☐ No ☐
(7) Result: ______
(8) Date of result (if you know): ______
(b) If you filed any second motion, petition, or application, give the same information:
(1) Name of court: ______
(2) Docket or case number (if you know): ______
(3) Date of filing (if you know): ______
(4) Nature of proceeding: ______
(5) Grounds raised: ______

(6) Did you receive a hearing where evidence was given on your motion, petition, or application? Yes ☐ No ☐
(7) Result: ______
(8) Date of result (if you know): ______
(c) Did you appeal to a federal appellate court

having jurisdiction over the action taken on your motion, petition, or application?

(1) First petition: Yes ☐ No ☐

(2) Second petition: Yes ☐ No ☐

(d) If you did not appeal from the action on any motion, petition, or application, explain briefly why you did not: ______

12. For this motion, state every ground on which you claim that you are being held in violation of the Constitution, laws, or treaties of the United States. Attach additional pages if you have more than four grounds. State the facts supporting each ground.

GROUND ONE: ______

(a) Supporting facts (Do not argue or cite law. Just state the specific facts that support your claim.): ______

(b) **Direct Appeal of Ground One:**

(1) If you appealed from the judgment of conviction, did you raise this issue?

Yes ☐ No ☐

(2) If you did not raise this issue in your direct appeal, explain why:

(c) **Post-Conviction Proceedings:**

(1) Did you raise this issue in any post-conviction motion, petition, or application? Yes ☐ No ☐

(2) If your answer to Question (c)(1) is "Yes," state:

Type of motion or petition ______

Name and location of the court where the motion or petition was filed: ______

Docket or case number (if you know): ______

Date of the court's decision: ______

Result (attach a copy of the court's opinion or order, if available: ______

(3) Did you receive a hearing on your motion, petition, or application?

Yes ☐ No ☐

(4) Did you appeal from the denial of your motion, petition, or application?

Yes ☐ No ☐

(5) If your answer to Question (c)(4) is "Yes," did you raise this issue in the appeal?

Yes ☐ No ☐

(6) If your answer to Question (c)(4) is "Yes," state:

Name and location of the court where the appeal was filed: ______

Docket or case number (if you know): ______

Date of the court's decision: ______

Result (attach a copy of the court's opinion or order, if available: ______

(7) If your answer to Question (c)(4) or (c)(5) is "No," explain why you did not appeal or raise this issue: ______

GROUND TWO: ______

(a) Supporting facts (Do not argue or cite law. Just state the specific facts that support your claim.): ______

(b) **Direct Appeal of Ground Two:**

(1) If you appealed from the judgment of conviction, did you raise this issue?

Yes ☐ No ☐

(2) If you did not raise this issue in your direct appeal, explain why: ______

(c) **Post-Conviction Proceedings:**

(1) Did you raise this issue in any post-conviction motion, petition, or application? Yes ☐ No ☐

(2) If your answer to Question (c)(1) is "Yes," state:

Type of motion or petition

Name and location of the court where the motion or petition was filed: ______

Docket or case number (if you know): ______

Date of the court's decision: ______

Result (attach a copy of the court's opinion or order, if available: ______

(3) Did you receive a hearing on your motion, petition, or application?

Yes ☐ No ☐

(4) Did you appeal from the denial of your motion, petition, or application?

Yes ☐ No ☐

(5) If your answer to Question (c)(4) is "Yes," did you raise this issue in the appeal?

Yes ☐ No ☐

(6) If your answer to Question (c)(4) is "Yes," state:

Name and location of the court where the appeal was filed: ______

Docket or case number (if you know): ______

Date of the court's decision: ______

Result (attach a copy of the court's opinion

or order, if available: ____________________

(7) If your answer to Question (c)(4) or (c)(5) is "No," explain why you did not appeal or raise this issue: ____________________

GROUND THREE: ____________________

(a) Supporting facts (Do not argue or cite law. Just state the specific facts that support your claim.):

____

(b) **Direct Appeal of Ground Three:**

(1) If you appealed from the judgment of conviction, did you raise this issue?

Yes ☐ No ☐

(2) If you did not raise this issue in your direct appeal, explain why: ____________________

(c) **Post-Conviction Proceedings:**

(1) Did you raise this issue in any post-conviction motion, petition or application? Yes ☐ No ☐

(2) If your answer to Question (c)(1) is "Yes," state:

Type of motion or petition ____________________

Name and location of the court where the motion or petition was filed: ____________________

Docket or case number (if you know):

Date of the court's decision: ____________________

Result (attach a copy of the court's opinion or order, if available: ____________________

(3) Did you receive a hearing on your motion, petition, or application?

Yes ☐ No ☐

(4) Did you appeal from the denial of your motion, petition, or application?

Yes ☐ No ☐

(5) If your answer to Question (c)(4) is "Yes," did you raise this issue in the appeal?

Yes ☐ No ☐

(6) If your answer to Question (c)(4) is "Yes," state:

Name and location of the court where the appeal was filed: ____________________

Docket or case number (if you know):

Date of the court's decision: ____________________

Result (attach a copy of the court's opinion or order, if available: ____________________

(7) If your answer to Question (c)(4) or (c)(5) is "No," explain why you did not appeal or raise this issue: ____________________

GROUND FOUR: ____________________

(a) Supporting facts (Do not argue or cite law. Just state the specific facts that support your claim.):

____

(b) **Direct Appeal of Ground Four:**

(1) If you appealed from the judgment of conviction, did you raise this issue?

Yes ☐ No ☐

(2) If you did not raise this issue in your direct appeal, explain why: ____________________

(c) **Post-Conviction Proceedings:**

(1) Did you raise this issue in any post-conviction motion, petition or application? Yes ☐ No ☐

(2) If your answer to Question (c)(1) is "Yes," state:

Type of motion or petition ____________________

Name and location of the court where the motion or petition was filed:

____

Docket or case number (if you know):

Date of the court's decision: ____________________

Result (attach a copy of the court's opinion or order, if available: ____________________

(3) Did you receive a hearing on your motion, petition, or application?

Yes ☐ No ☐

(4) Did you appeal from the denial of your motion, petition, or application?

Yes ☐ No ☐

(5) If your answer to Question (c)(4) is "Yes," did you raise this issue in the appeal?

Yes ☐ No ☐

(6) If your answer to Question (c)(4) is "Yes," state:

Name and location of the court where the appeal was filed: ____________________

Docket or case number (if you know): ______

Date of the court's decision: ____________________

Result (attach a copy of the court's opinion

or order, if available: ______

(7) If your answer to Question (c)(4) or (c)(5) is "No," explain why you did not appeal or raise this issue: ______

13. Is there any ground in this motion that you have not previously presented in some federal court?

    If so, which groung or grounds have not been presented, and state your reasons for not presenting them:

    ______

14. Do you have any motion, petition, or appeal now pending (filed and not decided yet) in any court for the judgment you are challenging? Yes ☐ No ☐

    If "Yes," state the name and location of the court, the docket or case number, the type of proceeding, and the issues raised.

    ______

15. Give the name and address, if known, of each attorney who represented you in the following stages of the judgment you are challenging:

    (a) At preliminary hearing: ______

    (b) At arraignment and plea: ______

    (c) At trial: ______

    (d) At sentencing: ______
    t

    (e) On appeal: ______

    (f) In any post-conviction proceeding: ______

    (g) On appeal from any ruling against you in a post-conviction proceeding: ______

16. Were you sentenced on more than one count of an indictment, or on more than one indictment, in the same court and at the same time? Yes ☐ No ☐

17. Do you have any future sentence to serve after you complete the sentence for the judgment that you are challenging? Yes ☐ No ☐

    (a) If so, give name and location of court that imposed the other sentence you will serve in the future: ______

    (b) Give the date the other sentence was imposed: ______

    (c) Give the length of the other sentence:

    (d) Have you filed, or do you plan to file, any motion, petition, or application that challenges the judgment or sentence to be served in the future? Yes ☐ No ☐

18. TIMELINESS OF MOTION: If your judgment of conviction became final over one year ago, you must explain why the one-year statute of limitations as contained in 28 U.S.C. § 2255 does not bar your petition.*

    ______

Therefore, movant asks that the Court grant the following relief: ______

or any other relief to which movant may be entitled.

______
Signature of Attorney (if any)

I declare (or certify, verify, or state) under penalty of perjury that the foregoing is true and correct and that this Motion under 28 U.S.C. § 2255 was placed in the prison mailing system on ______(month, date, year).

Executed (signed) on ______(date).

______
Signature of Movant

If the person signing is not movant, state relationship to movant and explain why movant is not signing this motion.

______

* The Antiterrorism and Effective Death Penalty Act of 1996 ("AEDPA") as contained in 28 U.S.C. § 2255 provides in part that:

(1) A one-year period of limitation shall apply to a a motion under this section. The limitation period shall run from the latest of—
(1) the date on which the judgment of conviction became final;
(2) the date on which the impediment to making a motion created by governmental action in violation of the Constitution or laws of the United States is removed, if the movant was prevented from making such a motion by such governmental action;
(3) the date on which the right asserted was initially recognized by the Supreme Court, if the right has been newly recognized by the Supreme Court and made retroactively applicable to cases on collateral review; or
(4) the date on which the facts supporting the claim or claims presented could have been discovered through the exercise of due diligence.

IN FORMA PAUPERIS DECLARATION

____

(Insert appropriate court)

United States
v.
____
(Movant)

DECLARATION IN SUPPORT OF REQUEST TO PROCEED IN FORMA PAUPERIS

I, __________, declare that I am the movant in the above entitled case; that in support of my motion to proceed without being required to prepay fees, costs or give security therefor, I state that because of my poverty, I am unable to pay the costs of said proceeding or to give security therefor; that I believe I am entitled to relief.

1. Are you presently employed?
Yes ☐ No ☐

a. If the answer is "yes," state the amount of your salary or wages per month, and give the name and address of your employer.______________________

____

b. If the answer is "no," state the date of last employment and the amount of the salary and wages per month which you received.______________________

____

2. Have you received within the past twelve months any money from any of the following sources?

a. Business, profession or form of self-employment?
Yes ☐ No ☐

b. Rent payments, interest or dividends?
Yes ☐ No ☐

c. Pensions, annuities or life insurance payments?
Yes ☐ No ☐

d. Gifts or inheritances?
Yes ☐ No ☐

e. Any other sources?

Yes ☐ No ☐

If the answer to any of the above is "yes," describe each source of money and state the amount received from each during the past twelve months. ________

____

____

3. Do you own any cash, or do you have money in a checking or savings account?
Yes ☐ No ☐ (Include any funds in prison accounts)

If the answer is "yes," state the total value of the items owned. ______________________

____

4. Do you own real estate, stocks, bonds, notes, automobiles, or other valuable property (excluding ordinary household furnishings and clothing)?
Yes ☐ No ☐

If the answer is "yes," describe the property and state its approximate value. ______________________

____

5. List the persons who are dependent upon you for support, state your relationship to those persons, and indicate how much you contribute toward their support. ______________________

____

I declare (or certify, verify, or state) under penalty of perjury that the foregoing is true and correct. Executed on ______ (date).

____
Signature of Movant

CERTIFICATE

I hereby certify that the movant herein has the sum of $________ on account to his credit at the ____________ institution where he is confined.

I further certify that movant likewise has the following securities to his credit according to the records of said____ institution: ______________

____

____

____
Authorized Officer of Institution

(Amended, effective August 1, 1982; effective December 1, 2004.)

FEDERAL RULES OF BANKRUPTCY PROCEDURE AND OFFICIAL BANKRUPTCY FORMS

FEDERAL RULES OF BANKRUPTCY PROCEDURE

FEDERAL RULES OF BANKRUPTCY PROCEDURE

Rule 1001. Scope of Rules and Forms; Short Title

The Bankruptcy Rules and Forms govern procedure in cases under title 11 of the United States

Code. The rules shall be cited as the Federal Rules of Bankruptcy Procedure and the forms as the Official Bankruptcy Forms. These rules shall be construed to secure the just, speedy, and inexpensive determination of every case and proceeding.

(Amended Aug. 1, 1987; Aug. 1, 1991.)

PART I. COMMENCEMENT OF CASE; PROCEEDINGS RELATING TO PETITION AND ORDER FOR RELIEF

Rule 1002. Commencement of Case

(a) Petition. A petition commencing a case under the Code shall be filed with the clerk.

(b) Transmission to United States trustee. The clerk shall forthwith transmit to the United States trustee a copy of the petition filed pursuant to subdivision (a) of this rule.

(Amended Aug. 1, 1987; Aug. 1, 1991.)

Rule 1003. Involuntary Petition

(a) Transferor or transferee of claim. A transferor or transferee of a claim shall annex to the original and each copy of the petition a copy of all documents evidencing the transfer, whether transferred unconditionally, for security, or otherwise, and a signed statement that the claim was not transferred for the purpose of commencing the case and setting forth the consideration for and terms of the transfer. An entity that has transferred or acquired a claim for the purpose of commencing a case for liquidation under chapter 7 or for reorganization under chapter 11 shall not be a qualified petitioner.

(b) Joinder of petitioners after filing. If the answer to an involuntary petition filed by fewer than three creditors avers the existence of 12 or more creditors, the debtor shall file with the answer a list of all creditors with their addresses, a brief statement of the nature of their claims, and the amounts thereof. If it appears that there are 12 or more creditors as provided in § 303(b) of the Code [11 USCS § 303(b)], the court shall afford a reasonable opportunity for other creditors to join in the petition before a hearing is held thereon.

(Amended Aug. 1, 1987.)

Rule 1004. Involuntary Petition Against a Partnership

After filing of an involuntary petition under § 303(b)(3) of the Code [11 USCS § 303(b)(3)], (1) the petitioning partners or other petitioners shall promptly send to or serve on each general partner who is not a petitioner a copy of the petition; and (2) the clerk shall promptly issue a summons for service on each general partner who is not a petitioner. Rule 1010 applies to the form and service of the summons.

(Amended Dec. 1, 2002.)

Rule 1004.1. Petition for an Infant or Incompetent Person

If an infant or incompetent person has a representative, including a general guardian, committee, conservator, or similar fiduciary, the representative may file a voluntary petition on behalf of the infant or incompetent person. An infant or incompetent person who does not have a duly appointed representative may file a voluntary petition by next friend or guardian ad litem. The court shall appoint a guardian ad litem for an infant or incompetent person who is a debtor and is not otherwise represented or shall make any other order to protect the infant or incompetent debtor.

(Added Dec. 1, 2002.)

Rule 1004.2. Petition in Chapter 15 Cases

(a) Designating center of main interests. A petition for recognition of a foreign proceeding under chapter 15 of the Code [11 USCS §§ 1501 et seq.] shall state the country where the debtor has its center of main interests. The petition shall also identify each country in which a foreign proceeding by, regarding, or against the debtor is pending.

(b) Challenging designation. The United States trustee or a party in interest may file a motion for a determination that the debtor's center of main interests is other than as stated in the petition for recognition commencing the chapter 15 case. Unless the court orders otherwise, the motion shall be filed no later than seven days before the date set for the hearing on the petition. The motion shall be transmitted to the United States trustee and served on the debtor, all persons or bodies authorized to administer foreign proceedings of the debtor, all entities against whom provisional relief is being sought under § 1519 of the Code [11 USCS § 1519], all parties to litigation pending in the United States in which the debtor was a party as of the time the petition was filed, and such other entities as the court may direct.

(Added Dec. 1, 2011.)

Rule 1005. Caption of Petition

The caption of a petition commencing a case under the Code shall contain the name of the court, the title of the case, and the docket number. The title of the case shall include the following information about the debtor: name, employer identification number, last four digits of the social-security number or individual debtor's taxpayer-identification number, any other federal taxpayer-identification number, and all other names used within eight years before filing the petition. If the petition is not filed by the debtor, it shall include all names used by the debtor which are known to the petitioners.

(Amended Aug. 1, 1987; Dec. 1, 2003; Dec. 1, 2008.)

Rule 1006. Filing Fee

(a) General requirement. Every petition Shall

be accompanied by the filing fee except as provided in subdivisions (b) and (c) of this rule. For the purpose of this rule, "filing fee" means the filing fee prescribed by 28 U.S.C. § 1930(a)(1)–(a)(5) and any other fee prescribed by the Judicial Conference of the United States under 28 U.S.C. § 1930(b) that is payable to the clerk upon the commencement of a case under the Code.

(b) Payment of filing fee in installments. (1) *Application to pay filing fee in installments.* A voluntary petition by an individual shall be accepted for filing if accompanied by the debtor's signed application, prepared as prescribed by the appropriate Official Form, stating that the debtor is unable to pay the filing fee except in installments.

(2) *Action on application.* Prior to the meeting of creditors, the court may order the filing fee paid to the clerk or grant leave to pay in installments and fix the number, amount and dates of payment. The number of installments shall not exceed four, and the final installment shall be payable not later than 120 days after filing the petition. For cause shown, the court may extend the time of any installment, provided the last installment is paid not later than 180 days after filing the petition.

(3) *Postponement of attorney's fees.* All installments of the filing fee must be paid in full before the debtor or chapter 13 trustee may make further payments to an attorney or any other person who renders services to the debtor in connection with the case.

(c) Waiver of filing fee. A voluntary chapter 7 petition filed by an individual shall be accepted for filing if accompanied by the debtor's application requesting a waiver under 28 U.S.C. § 1930(f), prepared as prescribed by the appropriate Official Form.

(Amended Aug. 1, 1987; Dec. 1, 1996; Dec. 1, 2008.)

Rule 1007. Lists, Schedules, Statements, and Other Documents; Time Limits

(a) Corporate ownership statement, list of creditors and equity security holders, and other lists. (1) *Voluntary case.* In a voluntary case, the debtor shall file with the petition a list containing the name and address of each entity included or to be included on Schedules D, E, F, G, and H as prescribed by the Official Forms. If the debtor is a corporation, other than a governmental unit, the debtor shall file with the petition a corporate ownership statement containing the information described in Rule 7007.1. The debtor shall file a supplemental statement promptly upon any change in circumstances that renders the corporate ownership statement inaccurate.

(2) *Involuntary case.* In an involuntary case, the debtor shall file, within seven days after entry of the order for relief, a list containing the name and address of each entity included or to be included on Schedules D, E, F, G, and H as prescribed by the Official Forms.

(3) *Equity security holders.* In a chapter 11 reorganization case, unless the court orders otherwise, the debtor shall file within 14 days after entry of the order for relief a list of the debtor's equity security holders of each class showing the number and kind of interests registered in the name of each holder, and the last known address or place of business of each holder.

(4) *Chapter 15 case.* In addition to the documents required under § 1515 of the Code [11 USCS § 1515], a foreign representative filing a petition for recognition under chapter 15 shall file with the petition: (A) a corporate ownership statement containing the information described in Rule 7007.1; and (B) unless the court orders otherwise, a list containing the names and addresses of all persons or bodies authorized to administer foreign proceedings of the debtor, all parties to litigation pending in the United States in which the debtor is a party at the time of the filing of the petition, and all entities against whom provisional relief is being sought under § 1519 of the Code [11 USCS § 1519].

(5) *Extension of time.* Any extension of time for the filing of the lists required by this subdivision may be granted only on motion for cause shown and on notice to the United States trustee and to any trustee, committee elected under § 705 [11 USCS § 705] or appointed under § 1102 of the Code [11 USCS § 1102], or other party as the court may direct.

(b) Schedules, statements, and other documents required. (1) Except in a chapter 9 municipality case, the debtor, unless the court orders otherwise, shall file the following schedules, statements, and other documents, prepared as prescribed by the appropriate Official Forms, if any:

(A) schedules of assets and liabilities;

(B) a schedule of current income and expenditures;

(C) a schedule of executory contracts and unexpired leases;

(D) a statement of financial affairs;

(E) copies of all payment advices or other evidence of payment, if any, received by the debtor from an employer within 60 days before the filing of the petition, with redaction of all but the last four digits of the debtor's social-security number or individual taxpayer-identification number; and

(F) a record of any interest that the debtor has in an account or program of the type specified in § 521(c) of the Code [11 USCS § 521(c)].

(2) An individual debtor in a chapter 7 case shall file a statement of intention as required by § 521(a) of the Code [11 USCS § 521(a)], prepared as prescribed by the appropriate Official Form. A copy of the statement of intention shall be served on the trustee and the creditors named in the statement on or before the filing of the statement.

(3) Unless the United States trustee has determined that the credit counseling requirement of

§ 109(h) [11 USCS § 109(h)] does not apply in the district, an individual debtor must file a statement of compliance with the credit counseling requirement, prepared as prescribed by the appropriate Official Form which must include one of the following:

(A) an attached certificate and debt repayment plan, if any, required by § 521(b) [11 USCS § 521(b)];

(B) a statement that the debtor has received the credit counseling briefing required by § 109(h)(1) [11 USCS § 109(h)(1)] but does not have the certificate required by § 521(b) [11 USCS § 521(b)];

(C) a certification under § 109(h)(3) [11 USCS § 109(h)(3)]; or

(D) a request for a determination by the court under § 109(h)(4) [11 USCS § 109(h)(4)].

(4) Unless § 707(b)(2)(D) [11 USCS § 707(b)(2)(D)] applies, an individual debtor in a chapter 7 case shall file a statement of current monthly income prepared as prescribed by the appropriate Official Form, and, if the current monthly income exceeds the median family income for the applicable state and household size, the information, including calculations, required by § 707(b) [11 USCS § 707(b)], prepared as prescribed by the appropriate Official Form.

(5) An individual debtor in a chapter 11 case shall file a statement of current monthly income, prepared as prescribed by the appropriate Official Form.

(6) A debtor in a chapter 13 case shall file a statement of current monthly income, prepared as prescribed by the appropriate Official Form, and, if the current monthly income exceeds the median family income for the applicable state and household size, a calculation of disposable income made in accordance with § 1325(b)(3) [11 USCS § 1325(b)(3)], prepared as prescribed by the appropriate Official Form.

(7) Unless an approved provider of an instructional course concerning personal financial management has notified the court that a debtor has completed the course after filing the petition:

(A) An individual debtor in a chapter 7 or chapter 13 case shall file a statement of completion of the course, prepared as prescribed by the appropriate Official Form; and

(B) An individual debtor in a chapter 11 case shall file the statement if § 1141(d)(3) applies.

(8) If an individual debtor in a chapter 11, 12, or 13 case has claimed an exemption under § 522(b)(3)(A) [11 USCS § 522(b)(3)(A)] in property of the kind described in § 522(p)(1) [11 USCS § 522(p)(1)] with a value in excess of the amount set out in § 522(q)(1) [11 USCS § 522(q)(1)], the debtor shall file a statement as to whether there is any proceeding pending in which the debtor may be found guilty of a felony of a kind described in § 522(q)(1)(A) [11 USCS § 522(q)(1)(A)] or found liable for a debt of the kind described in § 522(q)(1)(B) [11 USCS § 522(q)(1)(B)].

(c) Time limits. In a voluntary case, the schedules, statements, and other documents required by subdivision (b)(1), (4), (5), and (6) shall be filed with the petition or within 14 days thereafter, except as otherwise provided in subdivisions (d), (e), (f), and (h) of this rule. In an involuntary case, the schedules, statements, and other documents required by subdivision (b)(1) shall be filed by the debtor within 14 days after the entry of the order for relief. In a voluntary case, the documents required by paragraphs (A), (C), and (D) of subdivision (b)(3) shall be filed with the petition. Unless the court orders otherwise, a debtor who has filed a statement under subdivision (b)(3)(B), shall file the documents required by subdivision (b)(3)(A) within 14 days of the order for relief. In a chapter 7 case, the debtor shall file the statement required by subdivision (b)(7) within 60 days after the first date set for the meeting of creditors under § 341 of the Code [11 USCS § 341], and in a chapter 11 or 13 case no later than the date when the last payment was made by the debtor as required by the plan or the filing of a motion for a discharge under § 1141(d)(5)(B) or § 1328(b) of the Code [11 USCS § 1141(d)(5)(B) or 1328(b)]. The court may, at any time and in its discretion, enlarge the time to file the statement required by subdivision (b)(7). The debtor shall file the statement required by subdivision (b)(8) no earlier than the date of the last payment made under the plan or the date of the filing of a motion for a discharge under §§ 1141(d)(5)(B), 1228(b), or 1328(b) of the Code [11 USCS § 1141(d)(5)(B), 1228(b), or 1328(b)]. Lists, schedules, statements, and other documents filed prior to the conversion of a case to another chapter shall be deemed filed in the converted case unless the court directs otherwise. Except as provided in § 1116(3) [11 USCS § 1116(3)], any extension of time to file schedules, statements, and other documents required under this rule may be granted only on motion for cause shown and on notice to the United States trustee, any committee elected under § 705 [11 USCS § 705] or appointed under § 1102 of the Code [11 USCS § 1102], trustee, examiner, or other party as the court may direct. Notice of an extension shall be given to the United States trustee and to any committee, trustee, or other party as the court may direct.

(d) List of 20 largest creditors in chapter 9 municipality case or chapter 11 reorganization case. In addition to the list required by subdivision (a) of this rule, a debtor in a chapter 9 municipality case or a debtor in a voluntary chapter 11 reorganization case shall file with the petition a list containing the name, address and claim of the creditors that hold the 20 largest unsecured claims, excluding insiders, as prescribed by the appropriate Official Form. In an involuntary chapter 11 reorganization case, such list shall be filed by the debtor within 2 days after entry of the order for relief under

§ 303(h) of the Code [11 USCS § 303(h)].

(e) List in chapter 9 municipality cases. The list required by subdivision (a) of this rule shall be filed by the debtor in a chapter 9 municipality case within such time as the court shall fix. If a proposed plan requires a revision of assessments so that the proportion of special assessments or special taxes to be assessed against some real property will be different from the proportion in effect at the date the petition is filed, the debtor shall also file a list showing the name and address of each known holder of title, legal or equitable, to real property adversely affected. On motion for cause shown, the court may modify the requirements of this subdivision and subdivision (a) of this rule.

(f) Statement of social security number. An individual debtor shall submit a verified statement that sets out the debtor's social security number, or states that the debtor does not have a social security number. In a voluntary case, the debtor shall submit the statement with the petition. In an involuntary case, the debtor shall submit the statement within 14 days after the entry of the order for relief.

(g) Partnership and partners. The general partners of a debtor partnership shall prepare and file the list required under subdivision (a), the schedules of the assets and liabilities, schedule of current income and expenditures, schedule of executory contracts and unexpired leases, and statement of financial affairs of the partnership. The court may order any general partner to file a statement of personal assets and liabilities within such time as the court may fix.

(h) Interests acquired or arising after petition. If, as provided by § 541(a)(5) of the Code [11 USCS § 541(a)(5)], the debtor acquires or becomes entitled to acquire any interest in property, the debtor shall within 14 days after the information comes to the debtor's knowledge or within such further time the court may allow, file a supplemental schedule in the chapter 7 liquidation case, chapter 11 reorganization case, chapter 12 family farmer's debt adjustment case, or chapter 13 individual debt adjustment case. If any of the property required to be reported under this subdivision is claimed by the debtor as exempt, the debtor shall claim the exemptions in the supplemental schedule. The duty to file a supplemental schedule in accordance with this subdivision continues notwithstanding the closing of the case, except that the schedule need not be filed in a chapter 11, chapter 12, or chapter 13 case with respect to property acquired after entry of the order confirming a chapter 11 plan or discharging the debtor in a chapter 12 or chapter 13 case.

(i) Disclosure of list of security holders. After notice and hearing and for cause shown, the court may direct an entity other than the debtor or trustee to disclose any list of security holders of the debtor in its possession or under its control, indicating the name, address and security held by any of them. The entity possessing this list may be required either to produce the list or a true copy thereof, or permit inspection or copying, or otherwise disclose the information contained on the list.

(j) Impounding of lists. On motion of a party in interest and for cause shown the court may direct the impounding of the lists filed under this rule, and may refuse to permit inspection by any entity. The court may permit inspection or use of the lists, however, by any party in interest on terms prescribed by the court.

(k) Preparation of list, schedules, or statements on default of debtor. If a list, schedule, or statement, other than a statement of intention, is not prepared and filed as required by this rule, the court may order the trustee, a petitioning creditor, committee, or other party to prepare and file any of these papers within a time fixed by the court. The court may approve reimbursement of the cost incurred in complying with such an order as an administrative expense.

(l) Transmission to United States trustee. The clerk shall forthwith transmit to the United States trustee a copy of every list, schedule, and statement filed pursuant to subdivision (a)(1), (a)(2), (b), (d), or (h) of this rule.

(m) Infants and incompetent persons. If the debtor knows that a person on the list of creditors or schedules is an infant or incompetent person, the debtor also shall include the name, address, and legal relationship of any person upon whom process would be served in an adversary proceeding against the infant or incompetent person in accordance with Rule 7004(b)(2).

(Amended Aug. 1, 1987; Aug. 1, 1991; Dec. 1, 1996; Dec. 1, 2001; Dec. 1, 2003; Dec. 1, 2005; Dec. 1, 2008; Dec. 1, 2009; Dec. 1, 2010; Dec. 1, 2012; Dec. 1, 2013.)

Rule 1008. Verification of Petitions and Accompanying Papers

All petitions, lists, schedules, statements and amendments thereto shall be verified or contain an unsworn declaration as provided in 28 U.S.C. § 1746.

(Amended Aug. 1, 1991.)

Rule 1009. Amendments of Voluntary Petitions, Lists, Schedules and Statements

(a) General right to amend. A voluntary petition, list, schedule, or statement may be amended by the debtor as a matter of course at any time before the case is closed. The debtor shall give notice of the amendment to the trustee and to any entity affected thereby. On motion of a party in interest, after notice and a hearing, the court may order any voluntary petition, list, schedule, or statement to be amended and the clerk shall give notice of the amendment to entities designated by the court.

(b) Statement of intention. The statement of intention may be amended by the debtor at any time before the expiration of the period provided in

§ 521(a) of the Code [11 USCS § 521(a)]. The debtor shall give notice of the amendment to the trustee and to any entity affected thereby.

(c) Statement of social security number. If a debtor becomes aware that the statement of social security number submitted under Rule 1007(f) is incorrect, the debtor shall promptly submit an amended verified statement setting forth the correct social security number. The debtor shall give notice of the amendment to all of the entities required to be included on the list filed under Rule 1007(a)(1) or (a)(2).

(d) Transmission to United States trustee. The clerk shall promptly transmit to the United States trustee a copy of every amendment filed or submitted under subdivision (a), (b), or (c) of this rule.

(Amended Aug. 1, 1987; Aug. 1, 1991; April 12, 2006, eff. Dec. 1, 2006; Dec. 1, 2008.)

Rule 1010. Service of Involuntary Petition and Summons; Petition For Recognition of a Foreign Nonmain Proceeding

(a) Service of involuntary petition and summons; service of petition for recognition of foreign nonmain proceeding. On the filing of an involuntary petition or a petition for recognition of a foreign nonmain proceeding, the clerk shall forthwith issue a summons for service. When an involuntary petition is filed, service shall be made on the debtor. When a petition for recognition of a foreign nonmain proceeding is filed, service shall be made on the debtor, any entity against whom provisional relief is sought under § 1519 of the Code [11 USCS § 1519], and on any other party as the court may direct. The summons shall be served with a copy of the petition in the manner provided for service of a summons and complaint by Rule 7004(a) or (b). If service cannot be so made, the court may order that the summons and petition be served by mailing copies to the party's last known address, and by at least one publication in a manner and form directed by the court. The summons and petition may be served on the party anywhere. Rule 7004(e) and Rule 4(l) F.R.Civ.P. apply when service is made or attempted under this rule.

(b) Corporate ownership statement. Each petitioner that is a corporation shall file with the involuntary petition a corporate ownership statement containing the information described in Rule 7007.1.

(Amended Aug. 1, 1987; Aug. 1, 1991; Aug. 1, 1993; Dec. 1, 1997; Dec. 1, 2008.)

Rule 1011. Responsive Pleading or Motion in Involuntary and Cross-Border Cases

(a) Who may contest petition. The debtor named in an involuntary petition, or a party in interest to a petition for recognition of a foreign proceeding, may contest the petition. In the case of a petition against a partnership under Rule 1004, a nonpetitioning general partner, or a person who is alleged to be a general partner but denies the allegation, may contest the petition.

(b) Defenses and objections; when presented. Defenses and objections to the petition shall be presented in the manner prescribed by Rule 12 F. R. Civ. P. and shall be filed and served within 21 days after service of the summons, except that if service is made by publication on a party or partner not residing or found within the state in which the court sits, the court shall prescribe the time for filing and serving the response.

(c) Effect of motion. Service of a motion under Rule 12(b) F.R. Civ. P. shall extend the time for filing and serving a responsive pleading as permitted by Rule 12(a) F. R. Civ. P.

(d) Claims against petitioners. A claim against a petitioning creditor may not be asserted in the answer except for the purpose of defeating the petition.

(e) Other pleadings. No other pleadings shall be permitted, except that the court may order a reply to an answer and prescribe the time for filing and service.

(f) Corporate ownership statement. If the entity responding to the involuntary petition or the petition for recognition of a foreign proceeding is a corporation, the entity shall file with its first appearance, pleading, motion, response, or other request addressed to the court a corporate ownership statement containing the information described in Rule 7007.1.

(Amended Aug. 1, 1987; Dec. 1, 2004; Dec. 1, 2008; Dec. 1, 2009.)

Rule 1012. Examination of Debtor, Including Discovery, on Issue of Nonpayment of Debts in Involuntary Cases [Abrogated Aug. 1, 1987]

Rule 1013. Hearing and Disposition of a Petition in an Involuntary Case

(a) Contested petition. The court shall determine the issues of a contested petition at the earliest practicable time and forthwith enter an order for relief, dismiss the petition, or enter any other appropriate order.

(b) Default. If no pleading or other defense to a petition is filed within the time provided by Rule 1011, the court, on the next day, or as soon thereafter as practicable, shall enter an order for the relief requested in the petition.

(c) [Abrogated]

(Amended Aug. 1, 1991; Aug. 1, 1993.)

Rule 1014. Dismissal and Change of Venue

(a) Dismissal and transfer of cases. (1) *Cases filed in proper district.* If a petition is filed in the proper district, the court, on the timely motion of a party in interest or on its own motion, and after hearing on notice to the petitioners, the United States trustee, and other entities as directed by the court, may transfer the case to any other district if the court determines that the transfer is in the interest of justice or for the convenience of the parties.

(2) *Cases filed in improper district.* If a petition is filed in an improper district, the court, on the timely motion of a party in interest or on its own motion, and after hearing on notice to the petitioners, the United States trustee, and other entities as directed by the court, may dismiss the case or transfer it to any other district if the court determines that transfer is in the interest of justice or for the convenience of the parties.

(b) Procedure when petitions involving the same debtor or related debtors are filed in different courts. If petitions commencing cases under the Code or seeking recognition under chapter 15 are filed in different districts by, regarding, or against (1) the same debtor, (2) a partnership and one or more of its general partners, (3) two or more general partners, or (4) a debtor and an affiliate, the court in the district in which the first-filed petition is pending may determine, in the interest of justice or for the convenience of the parties, the district or districts in which any of the cases should proceed. The court may so determine on motion and after a hearing, with notice to the following entities in the affected cases: the United States trustee, entities entitled to notice under Rule 2002(a), and other entities as the court directs. The court may order the parties to the later-filed cases not to proceed further until it makes the determination.

(Amended Aug. 1, 1987; Aug. 1, 1991; Dec. 1, 2007; Dec. 1, 2010; Dec. 1, 2014.)

Rule 1015. Consolidation or Joint Administration of Cases Pending in Same Court

(a) Cases involving same debtor. If two or more petitions by, regarding, or against the same debtor are pending in the same court, the court may order consolidation of the cases.

(b) Cases involving two or more related debtors. If a joint petition or two or more petitions are pending in the same court by or against (1) a husband and wife, or (2) a partnership and one or more of its general partners, or (3) two or more general partners, or (4) a debtor and an affiliate, the court may order a joint administration of the estates. Prior to entering an order the court shall give consideration to protecting creditors of different estates against potential conflicts of interest. An order directing joint administration of individual cases of a husband and wife shall, if one spouse has elected the exemptions under § 522(b)(2) of the Code [11 USCS § 522(b)(2)] and the other has elected the exemptions under § 522(b)(3) [11 USCS § 522(b)(3)], fix a reasonable time within which either may amend the election so that both shall have elected the same exemptions. The order shall notify the debtors that unless they elect the same exemptions within the time fixed by the court, they will be deemed to have elected the exemptions provided by § 522(b)(2) [11 USCS § 522(b)(2)].

(c) Expediting and protective orders. When an order for consolidation or joint administration of a joint case or two or more cases is entered pursuant to this rule, while protecting the rights of the parties under the Code, the court may enter orders as may tend to avoid unnecessary costs and delay.

(Amended Aug. 1, 1987; Dec. 1, 2008; Dec. 1, 2010.)

Rule 1016. Death or Incompetency of Debtor

Death or incompetency of the debtor shall not abate a liquidation case under chapter 7 of the Code [11 USCS §§ 701 et seq.]. In such event the estate shall be administered and the case concluded in the same manner, so far as possible, as though the death or incompetency had not occurred. If a reorganization, family farmer's debt adjustment, or individual's debt adjustment case is pending under chapter 11, chapter 12, or chapter 13, the case may be dismissed; or if further administration is possible and in the best interest of the parties, the case may proceed and be concluded in the same manner, so far as possible, as though the death or incompetency had not occurred.

(Amended Aug. 1, 1991.)

Rule 1017. Dismissal or Conversion of Case; Suspension

(a) Voluntary dismissal; dismissal for want of prosecution or other cause. Except as provided in §§ 707(a)(3), 707(b), 1208(b), and 1307(b) of the Code [11 USCS §§ 707(a)(3), (b), 1208(b), and 1307(b)], and in Rule 1017(b), (c), and (e), a case shall not be dismissed on motion of the petitioner, for want of prosecution or other cause, or by consent of the parties, before a hearing on notice as provided in Rule 2002. For the purpose of the notice, the debtor shall file a list of creditors with their addresses within the time fixed by the court unless the list was previously filed. If the debtor fails to file the list, the court may order the debtor or another entity to prepare and file it.

(b) Dismissal for failure to pay filing fee. (1) If any installment of the filing fee has not been paid, the court may, after a hearing on notice to the debtor and the trustee, dismiss the case.

(2) If the case is dismissed or closed without full payment of the filing fee, the installments collected shall be distributed in the same manner and proportions as if the filing fee had been paid in full.

(c) Dismissal of voluntary chapter 7 or chapter 13 case for failure to timely file list of creditors, schedules, and statement of financial affairs. The court may dismiss a voluntary chapter 7 or chapter 13 case under § 707(a)(3) or § 1307(c)(9) [11 USCS § 707(a)(3) or 1307(c)(9)] after a hearing on notice served by the United States trustee on the debtor, the trustee, and any other entities as the court directs.

(d) Suspension. The court shall not dismiss a case or suspend proceedings under § 305 [11 USCS § 305] before a hearing on notice as provided in Rule 2002(a).

(e) Dismissal of an individual debtor's chapter 7 case, or conversion to a case under chapter 11 or 13, for abuse. The court may dismiss or, with the debtor's consent, convert an individual debtor's case for abuse under § 707(b) [11 USCS § 707(b)] only on motion and after a hearing on notice to the debtor, the trustee, the United States trustee, and any other entity as the court directs.

(1) Except as otherwise provided in § 704(b)(2) [11 USCS § 704(b)(2)], a motion to dismiss a case for abuse under § 707(b) or (c) [11 USCS § 707(b) or (c)] may be filed only within 60 days after the first date set for the meeting of creditors under § 341(a) [11 USCS § 341(a)], unless, on request filed before the time has expired, the court for cause extends the time for filing the motion to dismiss. The party filing the motion shall set forth in the motion all matters to be considered at the hearing. In addition, a motion to dismiss under § 707(b)(1) and (3) [11 USCS § 707(b)(1) and (3)] shall state with particularity the circumstances alleged to constitute abuse.

(2) If the hearing is set on the court's own motion, notice of the hearing shall be served on the debtor no later than 60 days after the first date set for the meeting of creditors under § 341(a) [11 USCS § 341(a)]. The notice shall set forth all matters to be considered by the court at the hearing.

(f) Procedure for dismissal, conversion, or suspension. (1) Rule 9014 governs a proceeding to dismiss or suspend a case, or to convert a case to another chapter, except under §§ 706(a), 1112(a), 1208(a) or (b), or 1307(a) or (b) [11 USCS § 706(a), 1112(a), 1208(a) or (b), or 1307(a) or (b)].

(2) Conversion or dismissal under §§ 706(a), 1112(a), 1208(b), or 1307(b) [11 USCS § 706(a), 1112(a), 1208(b), or 1307(b)] shall be on motion filed and served as required by Rule 9013.

(3) A chapter 12 or chapter 13 case shall be converted without court order when the debtor files a notice of conversion under §§ 1208(a) or 1307(a) [11 USCS § 1208(a) or 1307(a)]. The filing date of the notice becomes the date of the conversion order for the purposes of applying § 348(c) [11 USCS § 348(c)] and Rule 1019. The clerk shall promptly transmit a copy of the notice to the United States trustee.

(Amended Aug. 1, 1987; Aug. 1, 1991; Aug. 1, 1993; Dec. 1, 1999; Dec. 1, 2000; Dec. 1, 2008.)

Rule 1018. Contested Involuntary Petitions; Contested Petitions Commencing Chapter 15 Cases; Proceedings to Vacate Order for Relief; Applicability of Rules in Part VII Governing Adversary Proceedings

Unless the court otherwise directs and except as otherwise prescribed in Part I of these rules, the following rules in Part VII apply to all proceedings contesting an involuntary petition or a chapter 15 petition for recognition, and to all proceedings to vacate an order for relief: Rules 7005, 7008–7010, 7015, 7016, 7024–7026, 7028–7037, 7052, 7054, 7056, and 7062. The court may direct that other rules in Part VII shall also apply. For the purposes of this rule a reference in the Part VII rules to adversary proceedings shall be read as a reference to proceedings contesting an involuntary petition or a chapter 15 petition for recognition, or proceedings to vacate an order for relief. Reference in the Federal Rules of Civil Procedure to the complaint shall be read as a reference to the petition.

(Amended Aug. 1, 1987; Dec. 1, 2010.)

Rule 1019. Conversion of Chapter 11 Reorganization Case, Chapter 12 Family Farmer's Debt Adjustment Case, or Chapter 13 Individual's Debt Adjustment Case to a Chapter 7 Liquidation Case

When a chapter 11, chapter 12, or chapter 13 case has been converted or reconverted to a chapter 7 case:

(1) *Filing of lists, inventories, schedules, statements.* (A) Lists, inventories, schedules, and statements of financial affairs theretofore filed shall be deemed to be filed in the chapter 7 case, unless the court directs otherwise. If they have not been previously filed, the debtor shall comply with Rule 1007 as if an order for relief had been entered on an involuntary petition on the date of the entry of the order directing that the case continue under chapter 7.

(B) If a statement of intention is required, it shall be filed within 30 days after entry of the order of conversion or before the first date set for the meeting of creditors, whichever is earlier. The court may grant an extension of time for cause only on written motion filed, or oral request made during a hearing, before the time has expired. Notice of an extension shall be given to the United States trustee and to any committee, trustee, or other party as the court may direct.

(2) *New filing periods.* (A) A new time period for filing a motion under § 707(b) or (c) [11 USCS § 707(b) or (c)], a claim, a complaint objecting to discharge, or a complaint to obtain a determination of dischargeability of any debt shall commence under Rules 1017, 3002, 4004, or 4007, but a new time period shall not commence if a chapter 7 case had been converted to a chapter 11, 12, or 13 case and thereafter reconverted to a chapter 7 case and the time for filing a motion under § 707(b) or (c) [11 USCS § 707(b) or (c)], a claim, a complaint objecting to discharge, or a complaint to obtain a determination of the dischargeability of any debt, or any extension thereof, expired in the original chapter 7 case.

(B) A new time period for filing an objection to a claim of exemptions shall commence under Rule 4003(b) after conversion of a case to chapter 7 unless:

(i) the case was converted to chapter 7 more than one year after the entry of the first order confirming a plan under chapter 11, 12, or 13; or

(ii) the case was previously pending in chapter 7 and the time to object to a claimed exemption had expired in the original chapter 7 case.

(3) *Claims filed before conversion.* All claims actually filed by a creditor before conversion of the case are deemed filed in the chapter 7 case.

(4) *Turnover of records and property.* After qualification of, or assumption of duties by the chapter 7 trustee, any debtor in possession or trustee previously acting in the chapter 11, 12, or 13 case shall, forthwith, unless otherwise ordered, turn over to the chapter 7 trustee all records and property of the estate in the possession or control of the debtor in possession or trustee.

(5) *Filing final report and schedule of postpetition debts.* (A) Conversion of chapter 11 or chapter 12 case. Unless the court directs otherwise, if a chapter 11 or chapter 12 case is converted to chapter 7, the debtor in possession or, if the debtor is not a debtor in possession, the trustee serving at the time of conversion, shall:

(i) not later than 14 days after conversion of the case, file a schedule of unpaid debts incurred after the filing of the petition and before conversion of the case, including the name and address of each holder of a claim; and

(ii) not later than 30 days after conversion of the case, file and transmit to the United States trustee a final report and account; (B) Conversion of chapter 13 case. Unless the court directs otherwise, if a chapter 13 case is converted to chapter 7,

(i) the debtor, not later than 14 days after conversion of the case, shall file a schedule of unpaid debts incurred after the filing of the petition and before conversion of the case, including the name and address of each holder of a claim; and

(ii) the trustee, not later than 30 days after conversion of the case, shall file and transmit to the United States trustee a final report and account; (C) Conversion after confirmation of a plan. Unless the court orders otherwise, if a chapter 11, chapter 12, or chapter 13 case is converted to chapter 7 after confirmation of a plan, the debtor shall file:

(i) a schedule of property not listed in the final report and account acquired after the filing of the petition but before conversion, except if the case is converted from chapter 13 to chapter 7 and § 348(f)(2) [11 USCS § 348(f)(2)] does not apply;

(ii) a schedule of unpaid debts not listed in the final report and account incurred after confirmation but before the conversion; and

(iii) a schedule of executory contracts and unexpired leases entered into or assumed after the filing of the petition but before conversion. (D) Transmission to United States trustee. The clerk shall forthwith transmit to the United States trustee a copy of every schedule filed pursuant to Rule 1019(5).

(6) *Postpetition claims; preconversion administrative expenses; notice.* A request for payment of an administrative expense incurred before conversion of the case is timely filed under § 503(a) of the Code [11 USCS § 503(a)] if it is filed before conversion or a time fixed by the court. If the request is filed by a governmental unit, it is timely if it is filed before conversion or within the later of a time fixed by the court or 180 days after the date of the conversion. A claim of a kind specified in § 348(d) [11 USCS § 348(d)] may be filed in accordance with Rules 3001(a)–(d) and 3002. Upon the filing of the schedule of unpaid debts incurred after commencement of the case and before conversion, the clerk, or some other person as the court may direct, shall give notice to those entities listed on the schedule of the time for filing a request for payment of an administrative expense and, unless a notice of insufficient assets to pay a dividend is mailed in accordance with Rule 2002(e), the time for filing a claim of a kind specified in § 348(d) [11 USCS § 348(d)].

(Amended Aug. 1, 1987; Aug. 1, 1991; Dec. 1, 1996; Dec. 1, 1997; Dec. 1, 1999; Dec. 1, 2008; Dec. 1, 2009; Dec. 1, 2010.)

Rule 1020. Small Business Chapter 11 Reorganization Case

(a) Small business debtor designation. In a voluntary chapter 11 case, the debtor shall state in the petition whether the debtor is a small business debtor. In an involuntary chapter 11 case, the debtor shall file within 14 days after entry of the order for relief a statement as to whether the debtor is a small business debtor. Except as provided in subdivision (c), the status of the case as a small business case shall be in accordance with the debtor's statement under this subdivision, unless and until the court enters an order finding that the debtor's statement is incorrect.

(b) Objecting to designation. Except as provided in subdivision (c), the United States trustee or a party in interest may file an objection to the debtor's statement under subdivision (a) no later than 30 days after the conclusion of the meeting of creditors held under § 341(a) of the Code [11 USCS § 341(a)], or within 30 days after any amendment to the statement, whichever is later.

(c) Appointment of committee of unsecured creditors. If a committee of unsecured creditors has been appointed under § 1102(a)(1) [11 USCS § 1102(a)(1)], the case shall proceed as a small business case only if, and from the time when, the court enters an order determining that the committee has not been sufficiently active and representative to provide effective oversight of the debtor and that the debtor satisfies all the other requirements for being a small business. A request for a determination under this subdivision may be filed by the United States trustee or a party in interest only within a reasonable time after the failure of the committee to be sufficiently active and representative. The debtor may file a request for a determination at any time as to whether the committee has been sufficiently active and representative.

(d) Procedure for objection or determination. Any objection or request for a determination under this rule shall be governed by Rule 9014 and served on: the debtor; the debtor's attorney; the United States trustee; the trustee; any committee appointed under § 1102 [11 USCS § 1102] or its authorized agent, or, if no committee of unsecured creditors has been appointed under § 1102 [11 USCS § 1102], the creditors included on the list filed under Rule 1007(d); and any other entity as the court directs.

(Added December 1, 1997; Dec. 1, 2008; Dec. 1, 2009.)

Rule 1021. Health Care Business Case

(a) Health care business designation. Unless the court orders otherwise, if a petition in a case under chapter 7, chapter 9, or chapter 11 states that the debtor is a health care business, the case shall proceed as a case in which the debtor is a health care business.

(b) Motion. The United States trustee or a party in interest may file a motion to determine whether the debtor is a health care business. The motion shall be transmitted to the United States trustee and served on: the debtor; the trustee; any committee elected under § 705 [11 USCS § 705] or appointed under § 1102 of the Code [11 USCS § 1102] or its authorized agent, or, if the case is a chapter 9 municipality case or a chapter 11 reorganization case and no committee of unsecured creditors has been appointed under § 1102 [11 USCS § 1102], the creditors included on the list filed under Rule 1007(d); and any other entity as the court directs. The motion shall be governed by Rule 9014.

(As added Dec. 1, 2008.)

PART II. OFFICERS AND ADMINISTRATION; NOTICES; MEETINGS; EXAMINATIONS; ELECTIONS; ATTORNEYS AND ACCOUNTANTS

Rule 2001. Appointment of Interim Trustee Before Order for Relief in a Chapter 7 Liquidation Case

(a) Appointment. At any time following the commencement of an involuntary liquidation case and before an order for relief, the court on written motion of a party in interest may order the appointment of an interim trustee under § 303(g) of the Code [11 USCS § 303(g)]. The motion shall set forth the necessity for the appointment and may be granted only after hearing on notice to the debtor, the petitioning creditors, the United States trustee, and other parties in interest as the court may designate.

(b) Bond of movant. An interim trustee may not be appointed under this rule unless the movant furnishes a bond in an amount approved by the court, conditioned to indemnify the debtor for costs, attorney's fee, expenses, and damages allowable under § 303(i) of the Code [11 USCS § 303(i)].

(c) Order of appointment. The order directing the appointment of an interim trustee shall state the reason the appointment is necessary and shall specify the trustee's duties.

(d) Turnover and report. Following qualification of the trustee selected under § 702 of the Code [11 USCS § 702], the interim trustee, unless otherwise ordered, shall (1) forthwith deliver to the trustee all the records and property of the estate in possession or subject to control of the interim trustee and, (2) within 30 days thereafter file a final report and account.

(Amended Aug. 1, 1987; Aug. 1, 1991.)

Rule 2002. Notices to Creditors, Equity Security Holders, Administrators in Foreign Proceedings, Persons Against Whom Provisional Relief is Sought in Ancillary and Other Cross-Border Cases, United States, and United States Trustee

(a) Twenty-one-day notices to parties in interest. Except as provided in subdivisions (h), (i), (*l*), (p), and (q) of this rule, the clerk, or some other person as the court may direct, shall give the debtor, the trustee, all creditors and indenture trustees at least 21 days' notice by mail of:

(1) the meeting of creditors under § 341 or § 1104(b) of the Code [11 USCS § 341 or 1104(b)], which notice, unless the court orders otherwise, shall include the debtor's employer identification number, social security number, and any other federal taxpayer identification number;

(2) a proposed use, sale, or lease of property of the estate other than in the ordinary course of business, unless the court for cause shown shortens the time or directs another method of giving notice;

(3) the hearing on approval of a compromise or settlement of a controversy other than approval of an agreement pursuant to Rule 4001(d), unless the court for cause shown directs that notice not be sent;

(4) in a chapter 7 liquidation, a chapter 11 reorganization case, or a chapter 12 family farmer debt adjustment case, the hearing on the dismissal of the case or the conversion of the case to another chapter, unless the hearing is under § 707(a)(3) or § 707(b) [11 USCS § 707(a)(3) or (b)] or is on dismissal of the case for failure to pay the filing fee;

(5) the time fixed to accept or reject a proposed modification of a plan;

(6) a hearing on any entity's request for compensation or reimbursement of expenses if the request exceeds $1,000;

(7) the time fixed for filing proofs of claims pursuant to Rule 3003(c); and

(8) the time fixed for filing objections and the hearing to consider confirmation of a chapter 12 plan.

(b) Twenty-eight-day notices to parties in interest. Except as provided in subdivision (*l*) of this rule, the clerk, or some other person as the court may direct, shall give the debtor, the trustee, all creditors and indenture trustees not less than 28 days' notice by mail of the time fixed (1) for filing objections and the hearing to consider approval of a disclosure statement or, under § 1125(f) [11 USCS § 1125(f)], to make a final determination whether the plan provides adequate information so that a separate disclosure statement is not necessary; and (2) for filing objections and the hearing to consider confirmation of a chapter 9, chapter 11, or chapter 13 plan.

(c) Content of notice. (1) *Proposed use, sale, or lease of property.* Subject to Rule 6004, the notice of a proposed use, sale, or lease of property required by subdivision (a)(2) of this rule shall include the time and place of any public sale, the terms and conditions of any private sale and the time fixed for filing objections. The notice of a proposed use, sale, or lease of property, including real estate, is sufficient if it generally describes the property. The notice of a proposed sale or lease of personally identifiable information under § 363(b)(1) of the Code [11 USCS § 363(b)(1)] shall state whether the sale is consistent with any policy prohibiting the transfer of the information.

(2) *Notice of hearing on compensation.* The notice of a hearing on an application for compensation or reimbursement of expenses required by subdivision (a)(6) of this rule shall identify the applicant and the amounts requested.

(3) *Notice of hearing on confirmation when plan provides for an injunction.* If a plan provides for an injunction against conduct not otherwise enjoined under the Code, the notice required under Rule 2002(b)(2) shall:

(A) include in conspicuous language (bold, italic, or underlined text) a statement that the plan proposes an injunction;

(B) describe briefly the nature of the injunction; and

(C) identify the entities that would be subject to the injunction.

(d) Notice to equity security holders. In a chapter 11 reorganization case, unless otherwise ordered by the court, the clerk, or some other person as the court may direct, shall in the manner and form directed by the court give notice to all equity security holders of (1) the order for relief; (2) any meeting of equity security holders held pursuant to § 341 of the Code [11 USCS § 341]; (3) the hearing on the proposed sale of all or substantially all of the debtor's assets; (4) the hearing on the dismissal or conversion of a case to another chapter; (5) the time fixed for filing objections to and the hearing to consider approval of a disclosure statement; (6) the time fixed for filing objections to and the hearing to consider confirmation of a plan; and (7) the time fixed to accept or reject a proposed modification of a plan.

(e) Notice of no dividend. In a chapter 7 liquidation case, if it appears from the schedules that there are no assets from which a dividend can be paid, the notice of the meeting of creditors may include a statement to that effect; that it is unnecessary to file claims; and that if sufficient assets become available for the payment of a dividend, further notice will be given for the filing of claims.

(f) Other notices. Except as provided in subdivision (*l*) of this rule, the clerk, or some other person as the court may direct, shall give the debtor, all creditors, and indenture trustees notice by mail of:

(1) the order for relief;

(2) the dismissal or the conversion of the case to another chapter, or the suspension of proceedings under § 305 [11 USCS § 305];

(3) the time allowed for filing claims pursuant to Rule 3002;

(4) the time fixed for filing a complaint objecting to the debtor's discharge pursuant to § 727 of the Code [11 USCS § 727] as provided in Rule 4004;

(5) the time fixed for filing a complaint to determine the dischargeability of a debt pursuant to § 523 of the Code [11 USCS § 523] as provided in Rule 4007;

(6) the waiver, denial, or revocation of a discharge as provided in Rule 4006;

(7) entry of an order confirming a chapter 9, 11, or 12 plan;

(8) a summary of the trustee's final report in a chapter 7 case if the net proceeds realized exceed $1,500;

(9) a notice under Rule 5008 regarding the presumption of abuse;

(10) a statement under § 704(b)(1) [11 USCS § 704(b)(1)] as to whether the debtor's case would be presumed to be an abuse under § 707(b) [11 USCS § 707(b)]; and

(11) the time to request a delay in the entry of the discharge under §§ 1141(d)(5)(C), 1228(f), and 1328(h). Notice of the time fixed for accepting or rejecting a plan pursuant to Rule 3017(c) shall be given in accordance with Rule 3017(d).

(g) Addressing notices. (1) Notices required to be mailed under Rule 2002 to a creditor, indenture trustee, or equity security holder shall be addressed as such entity or an authorized agent has directed in its last request filed in the particular case. For the purposes of this subdivision—

(A) a proof of claim filed by a creditor or indenture trustee that designates a mailing address constitutes a filed request to mail notices to that address, unless a notice of no dividend has been given under Rule 2002(e)and a later notice of possible dividend under Rule 3002(c)(5) has not been given; and

(B) a proof of interest filed by an equity security holder that designates a mailing address constitutes a filed request to mail notices to that address.

(2) Except as provided in § 342(f) of the Code [11 USCS § 342(f)], if a creditor or indenture trustee has not filed a request designating a mailing address under Rule 2002(g)(1) or Rule 5003(e), the notices shall be mailed to the address shown on the list of creditors or schedule of liabilities, whichever is filed later. If an equity security holder has not filed a request designating a mailing address under Rule 2002(g)(1) or Rule 5003(e), the notices shall be mailed to the address shown on the list of equity security holders.

(3) If a list or schedule filed under Rule 1007 includes the name and address of a legal representative of an infant or incompetent person, and a person other than that representative files a request or proof of claim designating a name and mailing address that differs from the name and address of the representative included in the list or schedule,unless the court orders otherwise, notices under Rule 2002 shall be mailed to the representative included in the list or schedules and to the name and address designated in the request or proof of claim.

(4) Notwithstanding Rule 2002(g)(1)–(3), an entity and a notice provider may agree that when the notice provider is directed by the court to give a notice, the notice provider shall give the notice to the entity in the manner agreed to and at the address or addresses the entity supplies to the notice provider. That address is conclusively presumed to be a proper address for the notice. The notice provider's failure to use the supplied address does not invalidate any notice that is otherwise effective under applicable law.

(5) A creditor may treat a notice as not having been brought to the creditor's attention under § 342(g)(1) [11 USCS § 342(g)(1)] only if, prior to issuance of the notice, the creditor has filed a statement that designates the name and address of the person or organizational subdivision of the creditor responsible for receiving notices under the Code, and that describes the procedures established by the creditor to cause such notices to be delivered to the designated person or subdivision.

(h) Notices to creditors whose claims are filed. In a chapter 7 case, after 90 days following the first date set for the meeting of creditors under § 341 of the Code [11 USCS § 341], the court may direct that all notices required by subdivision (a) of this rule be mailed only to the debtor, the trustee, all indenture trustees, creditors that hold claims for which proofs of claim have been filed, and creditors, if any, that are still permitted to file claims by reason of an extension granted pursuant to Rule 3002(c)(1) or (c)(2). In a case where notice of insufficient assets to pay a dividend has been given to creditors pursuant to subdivision (e) of this rule, after 90 days following the mailing of a notice of the time for filing claims pursuant to Rule 3002(c)(5), the court may direct that notices be mailed only to the entities specified in the preceding sentence.

(i) Notices to committees. Copies of all notices required to be mailed pursuant to this rule shall be mailed to the committees elected under § 705 [11 USCS § 705] or appointed under § 1102 of the Code [11 USCS § 1102] or to their authorized agents. Notwithstanding the foregoing subdivisions, the court may order that notices required by subdivision (a)(2), (3) and (6) of this rule be transmitted to the United States trustee and be mailed only to the committees elected under § 705 [11 USCS § 705] or appointed under § 1102 of the Code [11 USCS § 1102] or to their authorized agents and to the creditors and equity security holders who serve on the trustee or debtor in possession and file a request that all notices be mailed to them. A committee appointed under § 1114 [11 USCS § 1114] shall receive copies of all notices required by subdivisions (a)(1), (a)(5), (b), (f)(2), and (f)(7), and such other notices as the court may direct.

(j) Notices to the United States. Copies of notices required to be mailed to all creditors under this rule shall be mailed (1) in a chapter 11 reorganization case, to the Securities and Exchange Commission at any place the Commission designates, if the Commission has filed either a notice of appearance in the case or a written request to receive notices; (2) in a commodity broker case, to the Commodity Futures Trading Commission at Washington, D.C.; (3) in a chapter 11 case, to the Internal Revenue Service at its address set out in the register maintained under Rule 5003(e) for the district in which the case is pending; (4) if the papers in the case disclose a debt to the United States other than for taxes, to the United States attorney for the district in which the case is pending and to the department, agency, or instrumentality of the United States through which the debtor became indebted; or (5) if the filed papers disclose a stock interest of the United States, to the Secretary of the Treasury at Washington, D.C.

(k) Notices to United States trustee. Unless the case is a chapter 9 municipality case or unless the United States trustee requests otherwise, the clerk, or some other person as the court may direct, shall transmit to the United States trustee notice of the matters described in subdivisions (a)(2), (a)(3), (a)(4), (a)(8), (b), (f)(1), (f)(2), (f)(4), (f)(6), (f)(7), (f)(8), and (q) of this rule and notice of hearings on all applications for compensation or reimbursement of expenses. Notices to the United States trustee shall be transmitted within the time prescribed in subdivision (a) or (b) of this rule. The United States trustee shall also receive notice of any other matter if such notice is requested by the United States trustee or ordered by the court. Nothing in these rules requires the clerk or any other person to transmit to the United States trustee any notice, schedule, report, application or other document in a case under the Securities Investor Protection Act, 15 U.S.C. § 78aaa *et. seq.*

(l) Notice by publication. The court may order notice by publication if it finds that notice by mail is impracticable or that it is desirable to supplement the notice.

(m) Orders designating matter of notices. The court may from time to time enter orders designating the matters in respect to which, the entity to whom, and the form and manner in which notices shall be sent except as otherwise provided by these rules.

(n) Caption. The caption of every notice given under this rule shall comply with Rule 1005. The caption of every notice required to be given by the debtor to a creditor shall include the information required to be in the notice by § 342(c) of the Code [11 USCS § 342(c)].

(o) Notice of order for relief in consumer case. In a voluntary case commenced by an individual debtor whose debts are primarily consumer debts, the clerk or some other person as the court may direct shall give the trustee and all creditors notice by mail of the order for relief within 21 days from the date thereof.

(p) Notice to a creditor with a foreign address. (1) If, at the request of the United States trustee or a party in interest, or on its own initiative, the court finds that a notice mailed within the time prescribed by these rules would not be sufficient to give a creditor with a foreign address to which notices under these rules are mailed reasonable notice under the circumstances, the court may order that the notice be supplemented with notice by other means or that the time prescribed for the notice by mail be enlarged.

(2) Unless the court for cause orders otherwise, a creditor with a foreign address to which notices under this rule are mailed shall be given at least 30 days' notice of the time fixed for filing a proof of claim under Rule 3002(c) or Rule 3003(c).

(3) Unless the court for cause orders otherwise, the mailing address of a creditor with a foreign address shall be determined under Rule 2002(g).

(q) Notice of petition for recognition of foreign proceeding and of court's intention to communicate with foreign courts and foreign representatives. (1) *Notice of petition for recognition.* The clerk, or some other person as the court may direct, shall forthwith give the debtor, all persons or bodies authorized to administer foreign proceedings of the debtor, all entities against whom provisional relief is being sought under § 1519 of the Code [11 USCS § 1519], all parties to litigation pending in the United States in which the debtor is a party at the time of the filing of the petition, and such other entities as the court may direct, at least 21 days' notice by mail of the hearing on the petition for recognition of a foreign proceeding. The notice shall state whether the petition seeks recognition as a foreign main proceeding or foreign nonmain proceeding.

(2) *Notice of court's intention to communicate with foreign courts and foreign representatives.* The clerk, or some other person as the court may direct, shall give the debtor, all persons or bodies authorized to administer foreign proceedings of the debtor, all entities against whom provisional relief is being sought under § 1519 of the Code [11 USCS § 1519], all parties to litigation pending in the United States in which the debtor is a party at the time of the filing of the petition, and such other entities as the court may direct, notice by mail of the court's intention to communicate with a foreign court or foreign representative.

(Amended Aug. 30, 1983, P. L. 98-91, § 2(a), 97 Stat. 607; July 10, 1984, P. L. 98-353, Title III, Subtitle A, § 321, 98 Stat 357; Aug. 1, 1987; Aug. 1, 1993; Dec. 1, 1996; Dec. 1, 1997; Dec. 1, 1999; Dec. 1, 2000; Dec. 1, 2001; Dec. 1, 2003; Dec. 1, 2004; Dec. 1, 2005; Dec. 1, 2008; Dec. 1, 2009.)

Rule 2003. Meeting of Creditors or Equity Security Holders

(a) Date and place. Except as otherwise provided in § 341(e) of the Code [11 USCS § 341(e)], in a chapter 7 liquidation or a chapter 11 reorganization case, the United States trustee shall call a meeting of creditors to be held no fewer than 21 and no more than 40 days after the order for relief. In a chapter 12 family farmer debt adjustment case, the United States trustee shall call a meeting of creditors to be held no fewer than 21 and no more than 35 days after the order for relief. In a chapter 13 individual's debt adjustment case, the United States trustee shall call a meeting of creditors to be held no fewer than 21 and no more than 50 days after the order for relief. If there is an appeal from or a motion to vacate the order for relief, or if there is a motion to dismiss the case, the United States trustee may set a later date for the meeting. The meeting may be held at a regular place for holding court or at any other place designated by the United States trustee within the district convenient for the parties in interest. If the United States trustee designates a place for the meeting which is not regularly staffed by the United States trustee or an assistant who may preside at the meeting, the meeting may be held not more than 60 days after the order for relief.

(b) Order of meeting. (1) *Meeting of creditors.* The United States trustee shall preside at the meeting of creditors. The business of the meeting shall include the examination of the debtor under oath and, in a chapter 7 liquidation case, may include the election of a creditors' committee and, if the case is not under subchapter V of chapter 7 [11 USCS §§ 781 et seq.], the election of a trustee. The presiding officer shall have the authority to administer oaths.

(2) *Meeting of equity security holders.* If the United States trustee convenes a meeting of equity security holders pursuant to § 341(b) of the Code [11 USCS § 341(b)], the United States trustee shall fix a date for the meeting and shall preside.

(3) *Right to vote.* In a chapter 7 liquidation case, a creditor is entitled to vote at a meeting if, at or before the meeting, the creditor has filed a proof of claim or a writing setting forth facts evidencing a right to vote pursuant to § 702(a) of the Code [11 USCS § 702(a)] unless objection is made to the claim or the proof of claim is insufficient on its face. A creditor of a partnership may file a proof of claim or writing evidencing a right to vote for the trustee for the estate of a general partner notwithstanding that a trustee for the estate of the partnership has previously qualified. In the event of an objection to the amount or allowability of a claim for the purpose of voting, unless the court orders otherwise, the United States trustee shall tabulate the votes for each alternative presented by the dispute and, if resolution of such dispute is necessary to determine the result of the election, the tabulations for each alternative shall be reported to the court.

(c) Record of meeting. Any examination under oath at the meeting of creditors held pursuant to § 341(a) of the Code [11 USCS § 341(a)] shall be recorded verbatim by the United States trustee using electronic sound recording equipment or other means of recording, and such record shall be preserved by the United States trustee and available for public access until two years after the conclusion of the meeting of creditors. Upon request of any entity, the United States trustee shall certify and provide a copy or transcript of such recording at the entity's expense.

(d) Report of election and resolution of disputes in a chapter 7 case. (1) *Report of undisputed election.* In a chapter 7 case, if the election of a trustee or a member of a creditors' committee is not disputed, the United States trustee shall promptly file a report of the election, including the name and address of the person or entity elected and a statement that the election is undisputed.

(2) *Disputed election.* If the election is disputed, the United States trustee shall promptly file a report stating that the election is disputed, informing the court of the nature of the dispute, and listing the name and address of any candidate elected under any alternative presented by the dispute. No later than the date on which the report is filed, the United States trustee shall mail a copy of the report to any party in interest that has made a request to receive a copy of the report. Pending disposition by the court of a disputed election for trustee, the interim trustee shall continue in office. Unless a motion for the resolution of the dispute is filed no later than 14 days after the United States trustee files a report of a disputed election for trustee, the interim trustee shall serve as trustee in the case.

(e) Adjournment. The meeting may be adjourned from time to time by announcement at the meeting of the adjourned date and time. The presiding official shall promptly file a statement specifying the date and time to which the meeting is adjourned.

(f) Special meetings. The United States trustee may call a special meeting of creditors on request of a party in interest or on the United States trustee's own initiative.

(g) Final meeting. If the United States trustee calls a final meeting of creditors in a case in which the net proceeds realized exceed $1,500, the clerk shall mail a summary of the trustee's final account to the creditors with a notice of the meeting, together with a statement of the amount of the claims allowed. The trustee shall attend the final meeting and shall, if requested, report on the administration of the estate.

(Amended Aug. 1, 1987; Aug. 1, 1991; Aug. 1, 1993; Dec. 1, 1999; Dec. 1, 2003; Dec. 1, 2008; Dec. 1, 2009; Dec. 1, 2011.)

Rule 2004. Examination

(a) Examination on motion. On motion of any party in interest, the court may order the examination of any entity.

(b) Scope of examination. The examination of an entity under this rule or of the debtor under § 343 of the Code [11 USCS § 343] may relate only to the acts, conduct, or property or to the liabilities and financial condition of the debtor, or to any matter which may affect the administration of the debtor's estate, or to the debtor's right to a discharge. In a family farmer's debt adjustment case under chapter 12 [11 USCS §§ 1201 et seq.], an individual's debt adjustment case under chapter 13 [11 USCS §§ 1301 et seq.], or a reorganization case under chapter 11 of the Code [11 USCS §§ 1101 et seq.], other than for the reorganization of a railroad, the examination may also relate to the operation of any business and the desirability of its continuance, the source of any money or property acquired or to be acquired by the debtor for purposes of consummating a plan and the consideration given or offered therefor, and any other matter relevant to the case or to the formulation of a plan.

(c) Compelling attendance and production of documents. The attendance of an entity for examination and for the production of documents, whether the examination is to be conducted within or without the district in which the case is pending, may be compelled as provided in Rule 9016 for the attendance of a witness at a hearing or trial. As an officer of the court, an attorney may issue and sign a subpoena on behalf of the court for the district in which the examination is to be held if the attorney is admitted to practice in that court or in the court in which the case is pending.

(d) Time and place of examination of debtor. The court may for cause shown and on terms as it may impose order the debtor to be examined under this rule at any time or place it designates, whether within or without the district wherein the case is pending.

(e) Mileage. An entity other than a debtor shall not be required to attend as a witness unless lawful mileage and witness fee for one day's attendance shall be first tendered. If the debtor resides more than 100 miles from the place of examination when required to appear for an examination under this rule, the mileage allowed by law to a witness shall be tendered for any distance more than 100 miles from the debtor's residence at the date of the filing of the first petition commencing a case under the Code or the residence at the time the debtor is required to appear for the examination, whichever is the lesser.

(Amended Aug. 1, 1987; Aug. 1, 1991; Dec. 1, 2002.)

Rule 2005. Apprehension and Removal of Debtor to Compel Attendance for Examination

(a) Order to compel attendance for examination. On motion of any party in interest supported by an affidavit alleging (1) that the examination of the debtor is necessary for the proper administration of the estate and that there is reasonable cause to believe that the debtor is about to leave or has left the debtor's residence or principal place of business to avoid examination, or (2) that the debtor has evaded service of a subpoena or of an order to attend for examination, or (3) that the debtor has willfully disobeyed a subpoena or order to attend for examination, duly served, the court may issue to the marshal, or some other officer authorized by law, an order directing the officer to bring the debtor before the court without unnecessary delay. If, after hearing, the court finds the allegations to be true, the court shall thereupon cause the debtor to be examined forthwith. If necessary, the court shall fix conditions for further examination and for the debtor's obedience to all orders made in reference thereto.

(b) Removal. Whenever any order to bring the debtor before the court is issued under this rule and the debtor is found in a district other than that of the court issuing the order, the debtor may be taken into custody under the order and removed in accordance with the following rules:

(1) If the debtor is taken into custody under the order at a place less than 100 miles from the place of issue of the order, the debtor shall be brought forthwith before the court that issued the order.

(2) If the debtor is taken into custody under the order at a place 100 miles or more from the place of issue of the order, the debtor shall be brought without unnecessary delay before the nearest available United States magistrate judge, bankruptcy judge, or district judge. If, after hearing, the magistrate judge, bankruptcy judge, or district judge finds that an order has issued under this rule and that the person in custody is the debtor, or if the person in custody waives a hearing, the magistrate judge, bankruptcy judge, or district judge shall order removal, and the person in custody shall be released on conditions ensuring prompt appearance before the court that issued the order to compel the attendance.

(c) Conditions of release. In determining what conditions will reasonably assure attendance or obedience under subdivision (a) of this rule or appearance under subdivision (b) of this rule, the court shall be governed by the provisions and policies of title 18, U.S.C., § 3146(a) and (b).

(Amended Aug. 1, 1987; Aug. 1, 1993.)

Rule 2006. Solicitation and Voting of Proxies in Chapter 7 Liquidation Cases

(a) Applicability. This rule applies only in a liquidation case pending under chapter 7 of the Code [11 USCS §§ 701 et seq.].

(b) Definitions. (1) *Proxy.* A proxy is a written power of attorney authorizing any entity to vote the claim or otherwise act as the owner's attorney in fact in connection with the administration of the estate.

(2) *Solicitation of proxy.* The solicitation of a proxy is any communication, other than one from an attorney to a regular client who owns a claim or from an attorney to the owner of a claim who has requested the attorney to represent the owner, by which a creditor is asked, directly or indirectly, to give a proxy after or in contemplation of the filing of a petition by or against the debtor.

(c) Authorized solicitation. (1) A proxy may be solicited only by (A) a creditor owning an allowable unsecured claim against the estate on the date of the filing of the petition; (B) a committee elected pursuant to § 705 of the Code [11 USCS § 705]; (C) a committee of creditors selected by a majority in number and amount of claims of creditors (i) whose claims are not contingent or unliquidated, (ii) who are not disqualified from voting under § 702(a) of the Code [11 USCS § 702(a)] and (iii) who were present or represented at a meeting of which all creditors having claims of over $500 or the 100 creditors having the largest claims had at least seven days' notice in writing and of which meeting written minutes were kept and are available reporting the names of the creditors present or represented and voting and the amounts of their claims; or (D) a bona fide trade or credit association, but such association may solicit only creditors who were its members or subscribers in good standing and had allowable unsecured claims on the date of the filing of the petition.

(2) A proxy may be solicited only in writing.

(d) Solicitation not authorized. This rule does not permit solicitation (1) in any interest other than that of general creditors; (2) by or on behalf of any custodian; (3) by the interim trustee or by or on behalf of any entity not qualified to vote under § 702(a) of the Code [11 USCS § 702(a)]; (4) by or on behalf of an attorney at law; or (5) by or on behalf of a transferee of a claim for collection only.

(e) Data required from holders of multiple proxies. At any time before the voting commences at any meeting of creditors pursuant to § 341(a) of the Code [11 USCS § 341(a)], or at any other time as the court may direct, a holder of two or more proxies shall file and transmit to the United States trustee a verified list of the proxies to be voted and a verified statement of the pertinent facts and circumstances in connection with the execution and delivery of each proxy, including:

(1) a copy of the solicitation;

(2) identification of the solicitor, the forwarder, if the forwarder is neither the solicitor nor the owner of the claim, and the proxyholder, including their connections with the debtor and with each other. If the solicitor, forwarder, or proxyholder is an association, there shall also be included a statement that the creditors whose claims have been solicited and the creditors whose claims are to be voted were members or subscribers in good standing and had allowable unsecured claims on the date of the filing of the petition. If the solicitor, forwarder, or proxyholder is a committee of creditors, the statement shall also set forth the date and place the committee was organized, that the committee was organized in accordance with clause (B) or (C) of paragraph (c)(1) of this rule, the members of the committee, the amounts of their claims, when the claims were acquired, the amounts paid therefor, and the extent to which the claims of the committee members are secured or entitled to priority;

(3) a statement that no consideration has been paid or promised by the proxyholder for the proxy;

(4) a statement as to whether there is any agreement and, if so, the particulars thereof, between the proxyholder and any other entity for the payment of any consideration in connection with voting the proxy, or for the sharing of compensation with any entity, other than a member or regular associate of the proxyholder's law firm, which may be allowed the trustee or any entity for services rendered in the case, or for the employment of any person as attorney, accountant, appraiser, auctioneer, or other employee for the estate;

(5) if the proxy was solicited by an entity other than the proxyholder, or forwarded to the holder by an entity who is neither a solicitor of the proxy nor the owner of the claim, a statement signed and verified by the solicitor or forwarder that no consideration has been paid or promised for the proxy, and whether there is any agreement, and, if so, the particulars thereof, between the solicitor or forwarder and any other entity for the payment of any consideration in connection with voting the proxy, or for sharing compensation with any entity, other than a member or regular associate of the solicitor's or forwarder's law firm which may be allowed the trustee or any entity for services rendered in the case, or for the employment of any person as attorney, accountant, appraiser, auctioneer, or other employee for the estate;

(6) if the solicitor, forwarder, or proxyholder is a committee, a statement signed and verified by each member as to the amount and source of any consideration paid or to be paid to such member in connection with the case other than by way of dividend on the member's claim.

(f) Enforcement of restrictions on solicitation. On motion of any party in interest or on its own initiative, the court may determine whether there has been a failure to comply with the provisions of this rule or any other impropriety in connection with the solicitation or voting of a proxy. After notice and a hearing the court may reject any proxy for cause, vacate any order entered in consequence of the voting of any proxy which should have been rejected, or take any other appropriate action.

(Amended Aug. 1, 1987; Aug. 1, 1991; Dec. 1, 2009.)

Rule 2007. Review of Appointment of Creditors' Committee Organized Before Commencement of the Case

(a) Motion to review appointment. If a committee appointed by the United States trustee pursuant to § 1102(a) of the Code [11 USCS § 1102(a)] consists of the members of a committee organized by creditors before the commencement of a chapter 9 or chapter 11 case, on motion of a party in interest and after a hearing on notice to the United States trustee and other entities as the court may direct, the court may determine whether the appointment of the committee satisfies the requirements of § 1102(b)(1) of the Code [11 USCS § 1102(b)(1)].

(b) Selection of members of committee. The court may find that a committee organized by unsecured creditors before the commencement of a chapter 9 or chapter 11 case was fairly chosen if:

(1) it was selected by a majority in number and amount of claims of unsecured creditors who may vote under § 702(a) of the Code [11 USCS § 702(a)] and were present in person or represented at a meeting of which all creditors having unsecured claims of over $1,000 or the 100 unsecured creditors having the largest claims had at least seven days' notice in writing, and of which meeting written minutes reporting the names of the creditors present or represented and voting and the amounts of their claims were kept and are available for inspection;

(2) all proxies voted at the meeting for the elected committee were solicited pursuant to Rule 2006 and the lists and statements required by subdivision (e) thereof have been transmitted to the United States trustee; and

(3) the organization of the committee was in all other respects fair and proper.

(c) Failure to comply with requirements for appointment. After a hearing on notice pursuant to subdivision (a) of this rule, the court shall direct the United States trustee to vacate the appointment of the committee and may order other appropriate action if the court finds that such appointment failed to satisfy the requirements of § 1102(b)(1) of the Code [11 USCS § 1102(b)(1)].

(Amended Aug. 1, 1987; Aug. 1, 1991; Dec. 1, 2009.)

Rule 2007.1. Appointment of Trustee or Examiner in a Chapter 11 Reorganization Case

(a) Order to appoint trustee or examiner. In a chapter 11 reorganization case, a motion for an order to appoint a trustee or an examiner under § 1104(a) or § 1104(c) of the Code [11 USCS § 1104(a) or (c)] shall be made in accordance with Rule 9014.

(b) Election of trustee. (1) *Request for an election.* A request to convene a meeting of creditors for the purpose of electing a trustee in a chapter 11 reorganization case shall be filed and transmitted to the United States trustee in accordance with Rule 5005 within the time prescribed by § 1104(b) of the Code [11 USCS § 1104(b)]. Pending court approval of the person elected, any person appointed by the United States trustee under § 1104(d) [11 USCS § 1104(d)] and approved in accordance with subdivision (c) of this rule shall serve as trustee.

(2) *Manner of election and notice.* An election of a trustee under § 1104(b) of the Code [11 USCS § 1104(b)] shall be conducted in the manner provided in Rules 2003(b)(3) and 2006. Notice of the meeting of creditors convened under § 1104(b) [11 USCS § 1104(b)] shall be given as provided in Rule 2002. The United States trustee shall preside at the meeting. A proxy for the purpose of voting in the election may be solicited only by a committee of creditors appointed under § 1102 of the Code or by any other party entitled to solicit a proxy pursuant to Rule 2006.

(3) *Report of election and resolution of disputes.* (A) Report of undisputed election. If no dispute arises out of the election, the United States trustee shall promptly file a report certifying the election, including the name and address of the person elected and a statement that the election is undisputed. The report shall be accompanied by a verified statement of the person elected setting forth that person's connections with the debtor, creditors, any other party in interest, their respective attorneys and accountants, the United States trustee, or any person employed in the office of the United States trustee.

(B) Dispute arising out of an election. f a dispute arises out of an election, the United States trustee shall promptly file a report stating that the election is disputed, informing the court of the nature of the dispute, and listing the name and address of any candidate elected under any alternative presented by the dispute. The report shall be accompanied by a verified statement by each candidate elected under each alternative presented by the dispute, setting forth the person's connections with the debtor, creditors, any other party in interest, their respective attorneys and accountants, the United States trustee, or any person employed in the office of the United States trustee. Not later than the date on which the report of the disputed election is filed, the United States trustee shall mail a copy of the report and each verified statement to any party in interest that has made a request to convene a meeting under § 1104(b) [11 USCS § 1104(b)] or to receive a copy of the report, and to any committee appointed under § 1102 of the Code [11 USCS § 1102].

(c) Approval of appointment. An order approving the appointment of a trustee or an examiner under § 1104(d) of the Code [11 USCS § 1104(d)] shall be made on application of the United States trustee. The application shall state the name of the person appointed and, to the best of the applicant's knowledge, all the person's connections with the debtor, creditors, any other parties in interest, their respective attorneys and accountants, the United States trustee, or persons employed in the office of the United States trustee. The application shall state the names of the parties in interest with whom the United States trustee consulted regarding the appointment. The application shall be accompanied by a verified statement of the person appointed setting forth the person's connections with the debtor, creditors, any other party in interest, their respective attorneys and accountants, the United States trustee, or any person employed in the office of the United States trustee.

(Added Aug. 1, 1991; Dec. 1, 1997; Dec. 1, 2008.)

Rule 2007.2. Appointment of Patient Care Ombudsman in a Health Care Business Case

(a) Order to appoint patient care ombudsman. In a chapter 7, chapter 9, or chapter 11 case in which the debtor is a health care business, the court shall order the appointment of a patient care ombudsman under § 333 of the Code [11 USCS § 333], unless the court, on motion of the United States trustee or a party in interest filed no later than 21 days after the commencement of the case or within another time fixed by the court, finds that the appointment of a patient care ombudsman is not necessary under the specific circumstances of the case for the protection of patients.

(b) Motion for order to appoint ombudsman. If the court has found that the appointment of an ombudsman is not necessary, or has terminated the appointment, the court, on motion of the United States trustee or a party in interest, may order the appointment at a later time if it finds that the appointment has become necessary to protect patients.

(c) Notice of appointment. If a patient care ombudsman is appointed under § 333 [11 USCS § 333], the United States trustee shall promptly file a notice of the appointment, including the name and address of the person appointed. Unless the person appointed is a State Long-Term Care Ombudsman, the notice shall be accompanied by a verified statement of the person appointed setting forth the person's connections with the debtor, creditors, patients, any other party in interest, their respective attorneys and accountants, the United States trustee, and any person employed in the office of the United States trustee.

(d) Termination of appointment. On motion of

the United States trustee or a party in interest, the court may terminate the appointment of a patient care ombudsman if the court finds that the appointment is not necessary to protect patients.

(e) Motion. A motion under this rule shall be governed by Rule 9014. The motion shall be transmitted to the United States trustee and served on: the debtor; the trustee; any committee elected under § 705 [11 USCS § 705] or appointed under § 1102 of the Code [11 USCS § 1102] or its authorized agent, or, if the case is a chapter 9 municipality case or a chapter 11 reorganization case and no committee of unsecured creditors has been appointed under § 1102 [11 USCS § 1102], on the creditors included on the list filed under Rule 1007(d); and such other entities as the court may direct.

(As added Dec. 1, 2008; Dec. 1, 2009.)

Rule 2008. Notice to Trustee of Selection

The United States trustee shall immediately notify the person selected as trustee how to qualify and, if applicable, the amount of the trustee's bond. A trustee that has filed a blanket bond pursuant to Rule 2010 and has been selected as trustee in a chapter 7, chapter 12, or chapter 13 case that does not notify the court and the United States trustee in writing of rejection of the office within seven days after receipt of notice of selection shall be deemed to have accepted the office. Any other person selected as trustee shall notify the court and the United States trustee in writing of acceptance of the office within seven days after receipt of notice of selection or shall be deemed to have rejected the office.

(Amended Aug. 1, 1987; Aug. 1, 1991; Dec. 1, 2009.)

Rule 2009. Trustees for Estates When Joint Administration Ordered

(a) Election of single trustee for estates being jointly administered. If the court orders a joint administration of two or more estates under Rule 1015(b), creditors may elect a single trustee for the estates being jointly administered, unless the case is under subchapter V of chapter 7 of the Code [11 USCS §§ 781 et seq.].

(b) Right of creditors to elect separate trustee. Notwithstanding entry of an order for joint administration under Rule 1015(b), the creditors of any debtor may elect a separate trustee for the estate of the debtor as provided in § 702 of the Code [11 USCS § 702], unless the case is under subchapter V of chapter 7 [11 USCS §§ 781 et seq.].

(c) Appointment of trustees for estates being jointly administered. (1) *Chapter 7 liquidation cases.* Except in a case governed by subchapter V of chapter 7 [11 USCS §§ 781 et seq.], the United States trustee may appoint one or more interim trustees for estates being jointly administered in chapter 7 cases.

(2) *Chapter 11 reorganization cases.* If the appointment of a trustee is ordered, the United States trustee may appoint one or more trustees for estates being jointly administered in chapter 11 cases.

(3) *Chapter 12 family farmer's debt adjustment cases.* The United States trustee may appoint one or more trustees for estates being jointly administered in chapter 12 cases.

(4) *Chapter 13 individual's debt adjustment cases.* The United States trustee may appoint one or more trustees for estates being jointly administered in chapter 13 cases.

(d) Potential conflicts of interest. On a showing that creditors or equity security holders of the different estates will be prejudiced by conflicts of interest of a common trustee who has been elected or appointed, the court shall order the selection of separate trustees for estates being jointly administered.

(e) Separate accounts. The trustee or trustees of estates being jointly administered shall keep separate accounts of the property and distribution of each estate.

(Amended Aug. 1, 1987; Aug. 1, 1991; Dec. 1, 2003.)

Rule 2010. Qualification by Trustee; Proceeding on Bond

(a) Blanket bond. The United States trustee may authorize a blanket bond in favor of the United States conditioned on the faithful performance of official duties by the trustee or trustees to cover (1) a person who qualifies as trustee in a number of cases, and (2) a number of trustees each of whom qualifies in a different case.

(b) Proceeding on bond. A proceeding on the trustee's bond may be brought by any party in interest in the name of the United States for the use of the entity injured by the breach of the condition.

(Amended Aug. 1, 1987; Aug. 1, 1991.)

Rule 2011. Evidence of Debtor in Possession or Qualification of Trustee

(a) Whenever evidence is required that a debtor is a debtor in possession or that a trustee has qualified, the clerk may so certify and the certificate shall constitute conclusive evidence of that fact.

(b) If a person elected or appointed as trustee does not qualify within the time prescribed by § 322(a) of the Code [11 USCS § 322(a)], the clerk shall so notify the court and the United States trustee.

(Amended Aug. 1, 1991.)

Rule 2012. Substitution of Trustee or Successor Trustee; Accounting

(a) Trustee. If a trustee is appointed in a chapter 11 case or the debtor is removed as debtor in possession in a chapter 12 case, the trustee is substituted automatically for the debtor in possession as a party in any pending action, proceeding, or matter.

(b) Successor trustee. When a trustee dies, resigns, is removed, or otherwise ceases to hold office during the pendency of a case under the Code (1) the successor is automatically substituted as a party in any pending action, proceeding, or matter; and (2) the successor trustee shall prepare, file, and transmit to the United States trustee an accounting of the prior administration of the estate.

(Amended Aug. 1, 1987; Aug. 1, 1991.)

Rule 2013. Public Record of Compensation Awarded to Trustees, Examiners, and Professionals

(a) Record to be kept. The clerk shall maintain a public record listing fees awarded by the court (1) to trustees and attorneys, accountants, appraisers, auctioneers and other professionals employed by trustees, and (2) to examiners. The record shall include the name and docket number of the case, the name of the individual or firm receiving the fee and the amount of the fee awarded. The record shall be maintained chronologically and shall be kept current and open to examination by the public without charge. "Trustees," as used in this rule, does not include debtors in possession.

(b) Summary of record. At the close of each annual period, the clerk shall prepare a summary of the public record by individual or firm name, to reflect total fees awarded during the preceding year. The summary shall be open to examination by the public without charge. The clerk shall transmit a copy of the summary to the United States trustee.

(Amended Aug. 1, 1987; Aug. 1, 1991.)

Rule 2014. Employment of Professional Persons

(a) Application for an order of employment. An order approving the employment of attorneys, accountants, appraisers, auctioneers, agents, or other professionals pursuant to § 327, § 1103, or § 1114 of the Code [11 USCS § 327, 1103, or 1114] shall be made only on application of the trustee or committee. The application shall be filed and, unless the case is a chapter 9 municipality case, a copy of the application shall be transmitted by the applicant to the United States trustee. The application shall state the specific facts showing the necessity for the employment, the name of the person to be employed, the reasons for the selection, the professional services to be rendered, any proposed arrangement for compensation, and, to the best of the applicant's knowledge, all of the person's connections with the debtor, creditors, any other party in interest, their respective attorneys and accountants, the United States trustee, or any person employed in the office of the United States trustee. The application shall be accompanied by a verified statement of the person to be employed setting forth the person's connections with the debtor, creditors, any other party in interest, their respective attorneys and accountants, the United States trustee, or any person employed in the office of the United States trustee.

(b) Services rendered by member or associate of firm of attorneys or accountants. If, under the Code and this rule, a law partnership or corporation is employed as an attorney, or an accounting partnership or corporation is employed as an accountant, or if a named attorney or accountant is employed, any partner, member, or regular associate of the partnership, corporation or individual may act as attorney or accountant so employed, without further order of the court.

(Amended Aug. 1, 1987; Aug. 1, 1991.)

Rule 2015. Duty to Keep Records, Make Reports, and Give Notice of Case or Change of Status

(a) Trustee or debtor in possession. A trustee or debtor in possession shall:

(1) in a chapter 7 liquidation case and, if the court directs, in a chapter 11 reorganization case file and transmit to the United States trustee a complete inventory of the property of the debtor within 30 days after qualifying as a trustee or debtor in possession, unless such an inventory has already been filed;

(2) keep a record of receipts and the disposition of money and property received;

(3) file the reports and summaries required by § 704(a)(8) of the Code [11 USCS § 704(a)(8)], which shall include a statement, if payments are made to employees, of the amounts of deductions for all taxes required to be withheld or paid for and in behalf of employees and the place where these amounts are deposited;

(4) as soon as possible after the commencement of the case, give notice of the case to every entity known to be holding money or property subject to withdrawal or order of the debtor, including every bank, savings or building and loan association, public utility company, and landlord with whom the debtor has a deposit, and to every insurance company which has issued a policy having a cash surrender value payable to the debtor, except that notice need not be given to any entity who has knowledge or has previously been notified of the case;

(5) in a chapter 11 reorganization case, on or before the last day of the month after each calendar quarter during which there is a duty to pay fees under 28 U.S.C. § 1930(a)(6), file and transmit to the United States trustee a statement of any disbursements made during that quarter and of any fees payable under 28 U.S.C. § 1930(a)(6) for that quarter; and

(6) in a chapter 11 small business case, unless the court, for cause, sets another reporting interval, file and transmit to the United States trustee for each calendar month after the order for relief, on the appropriate Official Form, the report required by § 308 [11 USCS § 308]. If the order for relief is within the first 15 days of a calendar month, a report shall be filed for the portion of the month that follows the order for relief. If the order for relief is

after the 15th day of a calendar month, the period for the remainder of the month shall be included in the report for the next calendar month. Each report shall be filed no later than 21 days after the last day of the calendar month following the month covered by the report. The obligation to file reports under this subparagraph terminates on the effective date of the plan, or conversion or dismissal of the case.

(b) Chapter 12 trustee and debtor in possession. In a chapter 12 family farmer's debt adjustment case, the debtor in possession shall perform the duties prescribed in clauses (2)–(4) of subdivision (a) of this rule and, if the court directs, shall file and transmit to the United States trustee a complete inventory of the property of the debtor within the time fixed by the court. If the debtor is removed as debtor in possession, the trustee shall perform the duties of the debtor in possession prescribed in this paragraph.

(c) Chapter 13 trustee and debtor. (1) *Business cases.* In a chapter 13 individual's debt adjustment case, when the debtor is engaged in business, the debtor shall perform the duties prescribed by clauses (2)–(4) of subdivision (a) of this rule and, if the court directs, shall file and transmit to the United States trustee a complete inventory of the property of the debtor within the time fixed by the court.

(2) *Nonbusiness cases.* In a chapter 13 individual's debt adjustment case, when the debtor is not engaged in business, the trustee shall perform the duties prescribed by clause (2) of subdivision (a) of this rule.

(d) Foreign representative. In a case in which the court has granted recognition of a foreign proceeding under chapter 15, the foreign representative shall file any notice required under § 1518 of the Code [11 USCS § 1518] within 14 days after the date when the representative becomes aware of the subsequent information.

(e) Transmission of reports. In a chapter 11 case the court may direct that copies or summaries of annual reports and copies or summaries of other reports shall be mailed to the creditors, equity security holders, and indenture trustees. The court may also direct the publication of summaries of any such reports. A copy of every report or summary mailed or published pursuant to this subdivision shall be transmitted to the United States trustee.

(Amended Aug. 1, 1987; Aug. 1, 1991; Dec. 1, 1996; Dec. 1, 2002; Dec. 1, 2008; Dec. 1, 2009; Dec. 1, 2012.)

Rule 2015.1. Patient Care Ombudsman

(a) Reports. A patient care ombudsman, at least 14 days before making a report under § 333(b)(2) of the Code [11 USCS § 333(b)(2)], shall give notice that the report will be made to the court, unless the court orders otherwise. The notice shall be transmitted to the United States trustee, posted conspicuously at the health care facility that is the subject of the report, and served on: the debtor; the trustee; all patients; and any committee elected under § 705 [11 USCS § 705] or appointed under § 1102 of the Code [11 USCS § 1102] or its authorized agent, or, if the case is a chapter 9 municipality case or a chapter 11 reorganization case and no committee of unsecured creditors has been appointed under § 1102 [11 USCS § 1102], on the creditors included on the list filed under Rule 1007(d); and such other entities as the court may direct. The notice shall state the date and time when the report will be made, the manner in which the report will be made, and, if the report is in writing, the name, address, telephone number, email address, and website, if any, of the person from whom a copy of the report may be obtained at the debtor's expense.

(b) Authorization to review confidential patient records. A motion by a patient care ombudsman under § 333(c) [11 USCS § 333(c)] to review confidential patient records shall be governed by Rule 9014, served on the patient and any family member or other contact person whose name and address have been given to the trustee or the debtor for the purpose of providing information regarding the patient's health care, and transmitted to the United States trustee subject to applicable nonbankruptcy law relating to patient privacy. Unless the court orders otherwise, a hearing on the motion may not be commenced earlier than 14 days after service of the motion.

(As added Dec. 1, 2008; Dec. 1, 2009.)

Rule 2015.2. Transfer of Patient in Health Care Business Case

Unless the court orders otherwise, if the debtor is a health care business, the trustee may not transfer a patient to another health care business under § 704(a)(12) of the Code [11 USCS § 704(a)(12)] unless the trustee gives at least 14 days' notice of the transfer to the patient care ombudsman, if any, the patient, and any family member or other contact person whose name and address has been given to the trustee or the debtor for the purpose of providing information regarding the patient's health care. The notice is subject to applicable nonbankruptcy law relating to patient privacy.

(As added Dec. 1, 2008; Dec. 1, 2009.)

Rule 2015.3. Reports of Financial Information on Entities in Which a Chapter 11 Estate Holds a Controlling or Substantial Interest

(a) Reporting requirement. In a chapter 11 case, the trustee or debtor in possession shall file periodic financial reports of the value, operations, and profitability of each entity that is not a publicly traded corporation or a debtor in a case under title 11, and in which the estate holds a substantial or controlling interest. The reports shall be prepared as prescribed by the appropriate Official Form, and shall be based upon the most recent information reasonably available to the trustee or debtor in possession.

(b) Time for filing; service. The first report required by this rule shall be filed no later than seven days before the first date set for the meeting of creditors under § 341 of the Code [11 USCS § 341]. Subsequent reports shall be filed no less frequently than every six months thereafter, until the effective date of a plan or the case is dismissed or converted. Copies of the report shall be served on the United States trustee, any committee appointed under § 1102 of the Code [11 USCS § 1102], and any other party in interest that has filed a request therefor.

(c) Presumption of substantial or controlling interest; judicial determination. For purposes of this rule, an entity of which the estate controls or owns at least a 20 percent interest, shall be presumed to be an entity in which the estate has a substantial or controlling interest. An entity in which the estate controls or owns less than a 20 percent interest shall be presumed not to be an entity in which the estate has a substantial or controlling interest. Upon motion, the entity, any holder of an interest therein, the United States trustee, or any other party in interest may seek to rebut either presumption, and the court shall, after notice and a hearing, determine whether the estate's interest in the entity is substantial or controlling.

(d) Modification of reporting requirement. The court may, after notice and a hearing, vary the reporting requirement established by subdivision (a) of this rule for cause, including that the trustee or debtor in possession is not able, after a good faith effort, to comply with those reporting requirements, or that the information required by subdivision (a) is publicly available.

(e) Notice and protective orders. No later than 14 days before filing the first report required by this rule, the trustee or debtor in possession shall send notice to the entity in which the estate has a substantial or controlling interest, and to all holders — known to the trustee or debtor in possession — of an interest in that entity, that the trustee or debtor in possession expects to file and serve financial information relating to the entity in accordance with this rule. The entity in which the estate has a substantial or controlling interest, or a person holding an interest in that entity, may request protection of the information under § 107 of the Code [11 USCS § 107].

(f) Effect of request. Unless the court orders otherwise, the pendency of a request under subdivisions (c), (d), or (e) of this rule shall not alter or stay the requirements of subdivision (a).

(As added Dec. 1, 2008; Dec. 1, 2009.)

Rule 2016. Compensation for Services Rendered and Reimbursement of Expenses

(a) Application for compensation or reimbursement. An entity seeking interim or final compensation for services, or reimbursement of necessary expenses, from the estate shall file an application setting forth a detailed statement of (1) the services rendered, time expended and expenses incurred, and (2) the amounts requested. An application for compensation shall include a statement as to what payments have theretofore been made or promised to the applicant for services rendered or to be rendered in any capacity whatsoever in connection with the case, the source of the compensation so paid or promised, whether any compensation previously received has been shared and whether an agreement or understanding exists between the applicant and any other entity for the sharing of compensation received or to be received for services rendered in or in connection with the case, and the particulars of any sharing of compensation or agreement or understanding therefor, except that details of any agreement by the applicant for the sharing of compensation as a member or regular associate of a firm of lawyers or accountants shall not be required. The requirements of this subdivision shall apply to an application for compensation for services rendered by an attorney or accountant even though the application is filed by a creditor or other entity. Unless the case is a chapter 9 municipality case, the applicant shall transmit to the United States trustee a copy of the application.

(b) Disclosure of compensation paid or promised to attorney for debtor. Every attorney for a debtor, whether or not the attorney applies for compensation, shall file and transmit to the United States trustee within 14 days after the order for relief, or at another time as the court may direct, the statement required by § 329 of the Code [11 USCS § 329] including whether the attorney has shared or agreed to share the compensation with any other entity. The statement shall include the particulars of any such sharing or agreement to share by the attorney, but the details of any agreement for the sharing of the compensation with a member or regular associate of the attorney's law firm shall not be required. A supplemental statement shall be filed and transmitted to the United States trustee within 14 days after any payment or agreement not previously disclosed.

(c) Disclosure of compensation paid or promised to bankruptcy petition preparer. Before a petition is filed, every bankruptcy petition preparer for a debtor shall deliver to the debtor, the declaration under penalty of perjury required by § 110(h)(2) [11 USCS § 110(h)(2)]. The declaration shall disclose any fee, and the source of any fee, received from or on behalf of the debtor within 12 months of the filing of the case and all unpaid fees charged to the debtor. The declaration shall also describe the services performed and documents prepared or caused to be prepared by the bankruptcy petition preparer. The declaration shall be filed with the petition. The petition preparer shall file a supplemental statement within 14 days after any payment or agreement not previously disclosed.

(Amended Aug. 1, 1987; Aug. 1, 1991; Dec. 1, 2003;

Dec. 1, 2009.)

Rule 2017. Examination of Debtor's Transactions with Debtor's Attorney

(a) Payment or transfer to attorney before order for relief. On motion by any party in interest or on the court's own initiative, the court after notice and a hearing may determine whether any payment of money or any transfer of property by the debtor, made directly or indirectly and in contemplation of the filing of a petition under the Code by or against the debtor or before entry of the order for relief in an involuntary case, to an attorney for services rendered or to be rendered is excessive.

(b) Payment or transfer to attorney after order for relief. On motion by the debtor, the United States trustee, or on the court's own initiative, the court after notice and a hearing may determine whether any payment of money or any transfer of property, or any agreement therefor, by the debtor to an attorney after entry of an order for relief in a case under the Code is excessive, whether the payment or transfer is made or is to be made directly or indirectly, if the payment, transfer, or agreement therefor is for services in any way related to the case.

(Amended Aug. 1, 1991.)

Rule 2018. Intervention; Right to Be Heard

(a) Permissive intervention. In a case under the Code, after hearing on such notice as the court directs and for cause shown, the court may permit any interested entity to intervene generally or with respect to any specified matter.

(b) Intervention by attorney general of a state. In a chapter 7, 11, 12, or 13 case, the Attorney General of a State may appear and be heard on behalf of consumer creditors if the court determines the appearance is in the public interest, but the Attorney General may not appeal from any judgment, order, or decree in the case.

(c) Chapter 9 municipality case. The Secretary of the Treasury of the United States may, or if requested by the court shall, intervene in a chapter 9 case. Representatives of the state in which the debtor is located may intervene in a chapter 9 case with respect to matters specified by the court.

(d) Labor unions. In a chapter 9, 11, or 12 case, a labor union or employees' association, representative of employees of the debtor, shall have the right to be heard on the economic soundness of a plan affecting the interests of the employees. A labor union or employees' association which exercises its right to be heard under this subdivision shall not be entitled to appeal any judgment, order, or decree relating to the plan, unless otherwise permitted by law.

(e) Service on entities covered by this rule. The court may enter orders governing the service of notice and papers on entities permitted to intervene or be heard pursuant to this rule.

(Amended Aug. 1, 1987; Aug. 1, 1991.)

Rule 2019. Disclosure Regarding Creditors and Equity Security Holders in Chapter 9 and Chapter 11 Cases

(a) Definitions. In this rule the following terms have the meanings indicated:

(1) "Disclosable economic interest" means any claim, interest, pledge, lien, option, participation, derivative instrument, or any other right or derivative right granting the holder an economic interest that is affected by the value, acquisition, or disposition of a claim or interest.

(2) "Represent" or "represents" means to take a position before the court or to solicit votes regarding the confirmation of a plan on behalf of another.

(b) Disclosure by groups, committees, and entities.

(1) In a chapter 9 or 11 case, a verified statement setting forth the information specified in subdivision (c) of this rule shall be filed by every group or committee that consists of or represents, and every entity that represents, multiple creditors or equity security holders that are (A) acting in concert to advance their common interests, and (B) not composed entirely of affiliates or insiders of one another.

(2) Unless the court orders otherwise, an entity is not required to file the verified statement described in paragraph (1) of this subdivision solely because of its status as:

(A) an indenture trustee;

(B) an agent for one or more other entities under an agreement for the extension of credit;

(C) a class action representative; or

(D) a governmental unit that is not a person.

(c) Information required. The verified statement shall include:

(1) the pertinent facts and circumstances concerning:

(A) with respect to a group or committee, other than a committee appointed under § 1102 or § 1114 of the Code [11 USCS § 1102 or 1114], the formation of the group or committee, including the name of each entity at whose instance the group or committee was formed or for whom the group or committee has agreed to act; or

(B) with respect to an entity, the employment of the entity, including the name of each creditor or equity security holder at whose instance the employment was arranged;

(2) if not disclosed under subdivision (c)(1), with respect to an entity, and with respect to each member of a group or committee:

(A) name and address;

(B) the nature and amount of each disclosable economic interest held in relation to the debtor as of the date the entity was employed or the group or committee was formed; and

(C) with respect to each member of a group or committee that claims to represent any entity in addition to the members of the group or committee, other than a committee appointed under § 1102 or § 1114 of the Code [11 USCS § 1102 or 1114], the date of acquisition by quarter and year of each disclosable economic interest, unless acquired more than one year before the petition was filed;

(3) if not disclosed under subdivision (c)(1) or (c)(2), with respect to each creditor or equity security holder represented by an entity, group, or committee, other than a committee appointed under § 1102 or § 1114 of the Code [11 USCS § 1102 or 1114]:

(A) name and address; and

(B) the nature and amount of each disclosable economic interest held in relation to the debtor as of the date of the statement; and

(4) a copy of the instrument, if any, authorizing the entity, group, or committee to act on behalf of creditors or equity security holders.

(d) Supplemental statements. If any fact disclosed in its most recently filed statement has changed materially, an entity, group, or committee shall file a verified supplemental statement whenever it takes a position before the court or solicits votes on the confirmation of a plan. The supplemental statement shall set forth the material changes in the facts required by subdivision (c) to be disclosed.

(e) Determination of failure to comply; sanctions.

(1) On motion of any party in interest, or on its own motion, the court may determine whether there has been a failure to comply with any provision of this rule.

(2) If the court finds such a failure to comply, it may:

(A) refuse to permit the entity, group, or committee to be heard or to intervene in the case;

(B) hold invalid any authority, acceptance, rejection, or objection given, procured, or received by the entity, group, or committee; or

(C) grant other appropriate relief.

(Amended Aug. 1, 1987; Aug. 1, 1991; Dec. 1, 2011.)

Rule 2020. Review of Acts by United States Trustee

A proceeding to contest any act or failure to act by the United States trustee is governed by Rule 9014.

(Added Aug. 1, 1991.)

PART III. CLAIMS AND DISTRIBUTION TO CREDITORS AND EQUITY INTEREST HOLDERS; PLANS

Rule 3001. Proof of Claim

(a) Form and content. A proof of claim is a written statement setting forth a creditor's claim. A proof of claim shall conform substantially to the appropriate Official Form.

(b) Who may execute. A proof of claim shall be executed by the creditor or the creditor's authorized agent except as provided in Rules 3004 and 3005.

(c) Supporting information.

(1) *Claim based on a writing.* Except for a claim governed by paragraph (3) of this subdivision, when a claim, or an interest in property of the debtor securing the claim, is based on a writing, a copy of the writing shall be filed with the proof of claim. If the writing has been lost or destroyed, a statement of the circumstances of the loss or destruction shall be filed with the claim.

(2) *Additional requirements in an individual debtor case; sanctions for failure to comply.* In a case in which the debtor is an individual:

(A) If, in addition to its principal amount, a claim includes interest, fees, expenses, or other charges incurred before the petition was filed, an itemized statement of the interest, fees, expenses, or charges shall be filed with the proof of claim.

(B) If a security interest is claimed in the debtor's property, a statement of the amount necessary to cure any default as of the date of the petition shall be filed with the proof of claim.

(C) If a security interest is claimed in property that is the debtor's principal residence, the attachment prescribed by the appropriate Official Form shall be filed with the proof of claim. If an escrow account has been established in connection with the claim, an escrow account statement prepared as of the date the petition was filed and in a form consistent with applicable nonbankruptcy law shall be filed with the attachment to the proof of claim.

(D) If the holder of a claim fails to provide any information required by this subdivision (c), the court may, after notice and hearing, take either or both of the following actions:

(i) preclude the holder from presenting the omitted information, in any form, as evidence in any contested matter or adversary proceeding in the case, unless the court determines that the failure was substantially justified or is harmless; or

(ii) award other appropriate relief, including reasonable expenses and attorney's fees caused by the failure.

(3) *Claim Based on an Open-End or Revolving Consumer Credit Agreement.* (A) When a claim is based on an open-end or revolving consumer credit agreement—except one for which a security interest is claimed in the debtor's real property—a statement shall be filed with the proof of claim, including all of the following information that applies to the account:

(i) the name of the entity from whom the creditor purchased the account;

(ii) the name of the entity to whom the debt was owed at the time of an account holder's last transaction on the account;

(iii) the date of an account holder's last transaction;

(iv) the date of the last payment on the account; and

(v) the date on which the account was charged to profit and loss.

(B) On written request by a party in interest, the holder of a claim based on an open-end or revolving consumer credit agreement shall, within 30 days after the request is sent, provide the requesting party a copy of the writing specified in paragraph (1) of this subdivision.

(d) Evidence of perfection of security interest. If a security interest in property of the debtor is claimed, the proof of claim shall be accompanied by evidence that the security interest has been perfected.

(e) Transferred claim. (1) *Transfer of claim other than for security before proof filed.* If a claim has been transferred other than for security before proof of the claim has been filed, the proof of claim may be filed only by the transferee or an indenture trustee.

(2) *Transfer of claim other than for security after proof filed.* If a claim other than one based on a publicly traded note, bond, or debenture has been transferred other than for security after the proof of claim has been filed, evidence of the transfer shall be filed by the transferee. The clerk shall immediately notify the alleged transferor by mail of the filing of the evidence of transfer and that objection thereto, if any, must be filed within 21 days of the mailing of the notice or within any additional time allowed by the court. If the alleged transferor files a timely objection and the court finds, after notice and a hearing, that the claim has been transferred other than for security, it shall enter an order substituting the transferee for the transferor. If a timely objection is not filed by the alleged transferor, the transferee shall be substituted for the transferor.

(3) *Transfer of claim for security before proof filed.* If a claim other than one based on a publicly traded note, bond, or debenture has been transferred for security before proof of the claim has been filed, the transferor or transferee or both may file a proof of claim for the full amount. The proof shall be supported by a statement setting forth the terms of the transfer. If either the transferor or the transferee files a proof of claim, the clerk shall immediately notify the other by mail of the right to join in the filed claim. If both transferor and transferee file proofs of the same claim, the proofs shall be consolidated. If the transferor or transferee does not file an agreement regarding its relative rights respecting voting of the claim, payment of dividends thereon, or participation in the administration of the estate, on motion by a party in interest and after notice and a hearing, the court shall enter such orders respecting these matters as may be appropriate.

(4) *Transfer of claim for security after proof filed.* If a claim other than one based on a publicly traded note, bond, or debenture has been transferred for security after the proof of claim has been filed, evidence of the terms of the transfer shall be filed by the transferee. The clerk shall immediately notify the alleged transferor by mail of the filing of the evidence of transfer and that objection thereto, if any, must be filed within 21 days of the mailing of the notice or within any additional time allowed by the court. If a timely objection is filed by the alleged transferor, the court, after notice and a hearing, shall determine whether the claim has been transferred for security. If the transferor or transferee does not file an agreement regarding its relative rights respecting voting of the claim, payment of dividends thereon, or participation in the administration of the estate, on motion by a party in interest and after notice and a hearing, the court shall enter such orders respecting these matters as may be appropriate.

(5) *Service of objection or motion; notice of hearing.* A copy of an objection filed pursuant to paragraph (2) or (4) or a motion filed pursuant to paragraph (3) or (4) of this subdivision together with a notice of a hearing shall be mailed or otherwise delivered to the transferor or transferee, whichever is appropriate, at least 30 days prior to the hearing.

(f) Evidentiary effect. A proof of claim executed and filed in accordance with these rules shall constitute prima facie evidence of the validity and amount of the claim.

(g) [Evidence of title.] To the extent not inconsistent with the United States Warehouse Act or applicable State law, a warehouse receipt, scale ticket, or similar document of the type routinely issued as evidence of title by a grain storage facility, as defined in section 557 of title 11, shall constitute prima facie evidence of the validity and amount of a claim of ownership of a quantity of grain.

(Amended July 10, 1984, P. L. 98-353, Title III, Subtitle B, § 354, 98 Stat. 361; Aug. 1, 1991; Dec. 1, 2009; Dec. 1, 2011; Dec. 1, 2012.)

Rule 3002. Filing Proof of Claim or Interest

(a) Necessity for filing. An unsecured creditor or an equity security holder must file a proof of claim or interest for the claim or interest to be allowed, except as provided in Rules 1019(3), 3003, 3004, and 3005.

(b) Place of filing. A proof of claim or interest shall be filed in accordance with Rule 5005.

(c) Time for filing. In a chapter 7 liquidation, chapter 12 family farmer's debt adjustment, or chapter 13 individual's debt adjustment case, a proof of claim is timely filed if it is filed not later than 90 days after the first date set for the meeting of creditors called under § 341(a) of the Code [11 USCS § 341(a)], except as follows:

(1) A proof of claim filed by a governmental unit, other than for a claim resulting from a tax return filed under § 1308 [11 USCS § 1308], is timely filed if it is filed not later than 180 days after the date of the order for relief. A proof of claim filed by a governmental unit for a claim resulting from a tax return filed under § 1308 [11 USCS § 1308] is timely filed if it is filed no later than 180 days after

the date of the order for relief or 60 days after the date of the filing of the tax return. The court may, for cause, enlarge the time for a governmental unit to file a proof of claim only upon motion of the governmental unit made before expiration of the period for filing a timely proof of claim.

(2) In the interest of justice and if it will not unduly delay the administration of the case, the court may extend the time for filing a proof of claim by an infant or incompetent person or the representative of either.

(3) An unsecured claim which arises in favor of an entity or becomes allowable as a result of a judgment may be filed within 30 days after the judgment becomes final if the judgment is for the recovery of money or property from that entity or denies or avoids the entity's interest in property. If the judgment imposes a liability which is not satisfied, or a duty which is not performed within such period or such further time as the court may permit, the claim shall not be allowed.

(4) A claim arising from the rejection of an executory contract or unexpired lease of the debtor may be filed within such time as the court may direct.

(5) If notice of insufficient assets to pay a dividend was given to creditors under Rule 2002(e), and subsequently the trustee notifies the court that payment of a dividend appears possible, the clerk shall give at least 90 days' notice by mail to creditors of that fact and of the date by which proofs of claim must be filed.

(6) If notice of the time to file a proof of claim has been mailed to a creditor at a foreign address, on motion filed by the creditor before or after the expiration of the time, the court may extend the time by not more than 60 days if the court finds that the notice was insufficient under the circumstances to give the creditor a reasonable time to file a proof of claim.

(Amended Aug. 1, 1987; Aug. 1, 1991; Dec. 1, 1996; Dec. 1, 2008.)

Rule 3002.1. Notice Relating to Claims Secured by Security Interest in the Debtor's Principal Residence

(a) In general. This rule applies in a chapter 13 case to claims that are (1) secured by a security interest in the debtor's principal residence, and (2) provided for under § 1322(b)(5) of the Code [11 USCS § 1322(b)(5)] in the debtor's plan.

(b) Notice of payment changes. The holder of the claim shall file and serve on the debtor, debtor's counsel, and the trustee a notice of any change in the payment amount, including any change that results from an interest rate or escrow account adjustment, no later than 21 days before a payment in the new amount is due.

(c) Notice of fees, expenses, and charges. The holder of the claim shall file and serve on the debtor, debtor's counsel, and the trustee a notice itemizing all fees, expenses, or charges (1) that were incurred in connection with the claim after the bankruptcy case was filed, and (2) that the holder asserts are recoverable against the debtor or against the debtor's principal residence. The notice shall be served within 180 days after the date on which the fees, expenses, or charges are incurred.

(d) Form and content. A notice filed and served under subdivision (b) or (c) of this rule shall be prepared as prescribed by the appropriate Official Form, and filed as a supplement to the holder's proof of claim. The notice is not subject to Rule 3001(f).

(e) Determination of fees, expenses, or charges. On motion of the debtor or trustee filed within one year after service of a notice under subdivision (c) of this rule, the court shall, after notice and hearing, determine whether payment of any claimed fee, expense, or charge is required by the underlying agreement and applicable nonbankruptcy law to cure a default or maintain payments in accordance with § 1322(b)(5) of the Code [11 USCS § 1322(b)(5)].

(f) Notice of final cure payment. Within 30 days after the debtor completes all payments under the plan, the trustee shall file and serve on the holder of the claim, the debtor, and debtor's counsel a notice stating that the debtor has paid in full the amount required to cure any default on the claim. The notice shall also inform the holder of its obligation to file and serve a response under subdivision (g). If the debtor contends that final cure payment has been made and all plan payments have been completed, and the trustee does not timely file and serve the notice required by this subdivision, the debtor may file and serve the notice.

(g) Response to notice of final cure payment. Within 21 days after service of the notice under subdivision (f) of this rule, the holder shall file and serve on the debtor, debtor's counsel, and the trustee a statement indicating (1) whether it agrees that the debtor has paid in full the amount required to cure the default on the claim, and (2) whether the debtor is otherwise current on all payments consistent with § 1322(b)(5) of the Code [11 USCS § 1322(b)(5)]. The statement shall itemize the required cure or postpetition amounts, if any, that the holder contends remain unpaid as of the date of the statement. The statement shall be filed as a supplement to the holder's proof of claim and is not subject to Rule 3001(f).

(h) Determination of final cure and payment. On motion of the debtor or trustee filed within 21 days after service of the statement under subdivision (g) of this rule, the court shall, after notice and hearing, determine whether the debtor has cured the default and paid all required postpetition amounts.

(i) Failure to notify. If the holder of a claim fails to provide any information as required by subdivision (b), (c), or (g) of this rule, the court may, after notice and hearing, take either or both of the following actions:

(1) preclude the holder from presenting the omitted information, in any form, as evidence in any contested matter or adversary proceeding in the case, unless the court determines that the failure was substantially justified or is harmless; or

(2) award other appropriate relief, including reasonable expenses and attorney's fees caused by the failure.

(Added Dec. 1, 2011.)

Rule 3003. Filing Proof of Claim or Equity Security Interest in Chapter 9 Municipality or Chapter 11 Reorganization Cases

(a) Applicability of rule. This rule applies in chapter 9 and 11 cases.

(b) Schedule of liabilities and list of equity security holders. (1) *Schedule of liabilities.* The schedule of liabilities filed pursuant to § 521(1) of the Code [11 USCS § 521(1)] shall constitute prima facie evidence of the validity and amount of the claims of creditors, unless they are scheduled as disputed, contingent, or unliquidated. It shall not be necessary for a creditor or equity security holder to file a proof of claim or interest except as provided in subdivision (c) (2) of this rule.

(2) *List of equity security holders.* The list of equity security holders filed pursuant to Rule 1007(a)(3) shall constitute prima facie evidence of the validity and amount of the equity security interests and it shall not be necessary for the holders of such interests to file a proof of interest.

(c) Filing proof of claim. (1) *Who may file.* Any creditor or indenture trustee may file a proof of claim within the time prescribed by subdivision (c)(3) of this rule.

(2) *Who must file.*Any creditor or equity security holder whose claim or interest is not scheduled or scheduled as disputed, contingent, or unliquidated shall file a proof of claim or interest within the time prescribed by subdivision (c)(3) of this rule; any creditor who fails to do so shall not be treated as a creditor with respect to such claim for the purposes of voting and distribution.

(3) *Time for filing.* The court shall fix and for cause shown may extend the time within which proofs of claim or interest may be filed. Notwithstanding the expiration of such time, a proof of claim may be filed to the extent and under the conditions stated in Rule 3002(c)(2), (c)(3), (c)(4), and (c)(6).

(4) *Effect of filing claim or interest.* A proof of claim or interest executed and filed in accordance with this subdivision shall supersede any scheduling of that claim or interest pursuant to § 521(a)(1) of the Code [11 USCS § 521(a)(1)].

(5) *Filing by indenture trustee.* An indenture trustee may file a claim on behalf of all known or unknown holders of securities issued pursuant to the trust instrument under which it is trustee.

(d) Proof of right to record status. For the purposes of Rules 3017, 3018 and 3021 and for receiving notices, an entity who is not the record holder of a security may file a statement setting forth facts which entitle that entity to be treated as the record holder. An objection to the statement may be filed by any party in interest.

(Amended Aug. 1, 1987; Aug. 1, 1991; Dec. 1, 2008.)

Rule 3004. Filing of Claims by Debtor or Trustee

If a creditor does not timely file a proof of claim under Rule 3002(c)or 3003(c), the debtor or trustee may file a proof of the claim within 30 days after the expiration of the time for filing claims prescribed by Rule 3002(c) or 3003(c), whichever is applicable. The clerk shall forthwith give notice of the filing to the creditor, the debtor and the trustee.

(Amended Aug. 1, 1987; Dec. 1, 2005.)

Rule 3005. Filing of Claim, Acceptance, or Rejection by Guarantor, Surety, Indorser, or Other Codebtor

(a) Filing of claim. If a creditor does not timely file a proof of claim under Rule 3002(c) or 3003(c), any entity that is or may be liable with the debtor to that creditor, or who has secured that creditor, may file a proof of the claim within 30 days after the expiration of the time for filing claims prescribed by Rule 3002(c) or Rule 3003(c) whichever is applicable. No distribution shall be made on the claim except on satisfactory proof that the original debt will be diminished by the amount of distribution.

(b) Filing of acceptance or rejection; substitution of creditor. An entity which has filed a claim pursuant to the first sentence of subdivision (a) of this rule may file an acceptance or rejection of a plan in the name of the creditor, if known, or if unknown, in the entity's own name but if the creditor files a proof of claim within the time permitted by Rule 3003(c) or files a notice prior to confirmation of a plan of the creditor's intention to act in the creditor's own behalf, the creditor shall be substituted for the obligor with respect to that claim.

(Amended Aug. 1, 1987; Aug. 1, 1991; Dec. 1, 2005.)

Rule 3006. Withdrawal of Claim; Effect on Acceptance or Rejection of Plan

A creditor may withdraw a claim as of right by filing a notice of withdrawal, except as provided in this rule. If after a creditor has filed a proof of claim an objection is filed thereto or a complaint is filed against that creditor in an adversary proceeding, or the creditor has accepted or rejected the plan or otherwise has participated significantly in the case, the creditor may not withdraw the claim except on order of the court after a hearing on notice to the trustee or debtor in possession, and any creditors' committee elected pursuant to § 705(a) [11 USCS § 705(a)] or appointed pursuant to § 1102 of the Code [11 USCS § 1102]. The order of the court shall contain such terms and conditions as the court deems proper. Unless the court orders otherwise, an authorized withdrawal of a claim shall constitute withdrawal of any related acceptance or rejection of a plan.

(Amended Aug. 1, 1991.)

Rule 3007. Objections to Claims

(a) Objections to claims. An objection to the allowance of a claim shall be in writing and filed. A copy of the objection with notice of the hearing thereon shall be mailed or otherwise delivered to the claimant, the debtor or debtor in possession, and the trustee at least 30 days prior to the hearing.

(b) Demand for relief requiring an adversary proceeding. A party in interest shall not include a demand for relief of a kind specified in Rule 7001 in an objection to the allowance of a claim, but may include the objection in an adversary proceeding.

(c) Limitation on joinder of claims objections. Unless otherwise ordered by the court or permitted by subdivision (d), objections to more than one claim shall not be joined in a single objection.

(d) Omnibus objection. Subject to subdivision (e), objections to more than one claim may be joined in an omnibus objection if all the claims were filed by the same entity, or the objections are based solely on the grounds that the claims should be disallowed, in whole or in part, because:

(1) they duplicate other claims;

(2) they have been filed in the wrong case;

(3) they have been amended by subsequently filed proofs of claim;

(4) they were not timely filed;

(5) they have been satisfied or released during the case in accordance with the Code, applicable rules, or a court order;

(6) they were presented in a form that does not comply with applicable rules, and the objection states that the objector is unable to determine the validity of the claim because of the noncompliance;

(7) they are interests, rather than claims; or

(8) they assert priority in an amount that exceeds the maximum amount under § 507 of the Code [11 USCS § 507].

(e) Requirements for omnibus objection. An omnibus objection shall:

(1) state in a conspicuous place that claimants receiving the objection should locate their names and claims in the objection;

(2) list claimants alphabetically, provide a cross-reference to claim numbers, and, if appropriate, list claimants by category of claims;

(3) state the grounds of the objection to each claim and provide a cross-reference to the pages in the omnibus objection pertinent to the stated grounds;

(4) state in the title the identity of the objector and the grounds for the objections;

(5) be numbered consecutively with other omnibus objections filed by the same objector; and

(6) contain objections to no more than 100 claims.

(f) Finality of objection. The finality of any order regarding a claim objection included in an omnibus objection shall be determined as though the claim had been subject to an individual objection.

(Amended Aug. 1, 1991; Dec. 1, 2007.)

Rule 3008. Reconsideration of Claims

A party in interest may move for reconsideration of an order allowing or disallowing a claim against the estate. The court after a hearing on notice shall enter an appropriate order.

Rule 3009. Declaration and Payment of Dividends in Chapter 7 Liquidation Cases

In a chapter 7 case, dividends to creditors shall be paid as promptly as practicable. Dividend checks shall be made payable to and mailed to each creditor whose claim has been allowed, unless a power of attorney authorizing another entity to receive dividends has been executed and filed in accordance with Rule 9010. In that event, dividend checks shall be made payable to the creditor and to the other entity and shall be mailed to the other entity.

(Amended Aug. 1, 1987; Aug. 1, 1993.)

Rule 3010. Small Dividends and Payments in Chapter 7 Liquidation, Chapter 12 Family Farmer's Debt Adjustment, and Chapter 13 Individual's Debt Adjustment Cases

(a) Chapter 7 cases. In a chapter 7 case no dividend in an amount less than $5 shall be distributed by the trustee to any creditor unless authorized by local rule or order of the court. Any dividend not distributed to a creditor shall be treated in the same manner as unclaimed funds as provided in § 347 of the Code [11 USCS § 347].

(b) Chapter 12 and chapter 13 cases. In a chapter 12 or chapter 13 case no payment in an amount less than $15 shall be distributed by the trustee to any creditor unless authorized by local rule or order of the court. Funds not distributed because of this subdivision shall accumulate and shall be paid whenever the accumulation aggregates $15. Any funds remaining shall be distributed with the final payment.

(Amended Aug. 1, 1987; Aug. 1, 1991.)

Rule 3011. Unclaimed Funds in Chapter 7 Liquidation, Chapter 12 Family Farmer's Debt Adjustment, and Chapter 13 Individual's Debt Adjustment Cases

The trustee shall file a list of all known names and addresses of the entities and the amounts which they are entitled to be paid from remaining property of the estate that is paid into court pursuant to § 347(a) of the Code [11 USCS § 347(a)].

(Amended Aug. 1, 1987; Aug. 1, 1991.)

Rule 3012. Valuation of Security

The court may determine the value of a claim secured by a lien on property in which the estate has an interest on motion of any party in interest and after a hearing on notice to the holder of the secured claim and any other entity as the court may direct.

(Amended Aug. 1, 1987.)

Rule 3013. Classification of Claims and Interests

For the purposes of the plan and its acceptance, the court may, on motion after hearing on notice as the court may direct, determine classes of creditors and equity security holders pursuant to §§ 1122, 1222(b)(1), and 1322(b)(1) of the Code [11 USCS §§ 1122, 1222(b)(1), and 1322(b)(1)].

(Amended Aug. 1, 1991.)

Rule 3014. Election Under § 1111(b) by Secured Creditor in Chapter 9 Municipality or Chapter 11 Reorganization Case

An election of application of § 1111(b)(2) of the Code [11 USCS § 1111(b)(2)] by a class of secured creditors in a chapter 9 or 11 case may be made at any time prior to the conclusion of the hearing on the disclosure statement or within such later time as the court may fix. If the disclosure statement is conditionally approved pursuant to Rule 3017.1, and a final hearing on the disclosure statement is not held, the election of application of § 1111(b)(2) [11 USCS § 1111(b)(2)] may be made not later than the date fixed pursuant to Rule 3017.1(a)(2) or another date the court may fix. The election shall be in writing and signed unless made at the hearing on the disclosure statement. The election, if made by the majorities required by § 1111(b)(1)(A)(i) [11 USCS § 1111(b)(1)(A)(i)], shall be binding on all members of the class with respect to the plan.

(Amended Dec. 1, 1997.)

Rule 3015. Filing, Objection to Confirmation, and Modification of a Plan in a Chapter 12 Family Farmer's Debt Adjustment or a Chapter 13 Individual's Debt Adjustment Case

(a) Chapter 12 plan. The debtor may file a chapter 12 plan with the petition. If a plan is not filed with the petition, it shall be filed within the time prescribed by § 1221 of the Code [11 USCS § 1221].

(b) Chapter 13 plan. The debtor may file a chapter 13 plan with the petition. If a plan is not filed with the petition, it shall be filed within 14 days thereafter, and such time may not be further extended except for cause shown and on notice as the court may direct. If a case is converted to chapter 13, a plan shall be filed within 14 days thereafter, and such time may not be further extended except for cause shown and on notice as the court may direct.

(c) Dating. Every proposed plan and any modification thereof shall be dated.

(d) Notice and copies. The plan or a summary of the plan shall be included with each notice of the hearing on confirmation mailed pursuant to Rule 2002. If required by the court, the debtor shall furnish a sufficient number of copies to enable the clerk to include a copy of the plan with the notice of the hearing.

(e) Transmission to United States trustee. The clerk shall forthwith transmit to the United States trustee a copy of the plan and any modification thereof filed pursuant to subdivision (a) or (b) of this rule.

(f) Objection to confirmation; determination of good faith in the absence of an objection. An objection to confirmation of a plan shall be filed and served on the debtor, the trustee, and any other entity designated by the court, and shall be transmitted to the United States trustee, before confirmation of the plan. An objection to confirmation is governed by Rule 9014. If no objection is timely filed, the court may determine that the plan has been proposed in good faith and not by any means forbidden by law without receiving evidence on such issues.

(g) Modification of plan after confirmation. A request to modify a plan pursuant to § 1229 or § 1329 of the Code [11 USCS § 1229 or 1329] shall identify the proponent and shall be filed together with the proposed modification. The clerk, or some other person as the court may direct, shall give the debtor, the trustee, and all creditors not less than 21 days' notice by mail of the time fixed for filing objections and, if an objection is filed, the hearing to consider the proposed modification, unless the court orders otherwise with respect to creditors who are not affected by the proposed modification. A copy of the notice shall be transmitted to the United States trustee. A copy of the proposed modification, or a summary thereof, shall be included with the notice. If required by the court, the proponent shall furnish a sufficient number of copies of the proposed modification, or a summary thereof, to enable the clerk to include a copy with each notice. Any objection to the proposed modification shall be filed and served on the debtor, the trustee, and any other entity designated by the court, and shall be transmitted to the United States trustee. An objection to a proposed modification is governed by Rule 9014.

(Amended Aug. 1, 1991; Aug. 1, 1993; Dec. 1, 2009.)

Rule 3016. Filing of Plan and Disclosure Statement in a Chapter 9 Municipality or Chapter 11 Reorganization Case

(a) Identification of plan. Every proposed plan and any modification thereof shall be dated and, in a chapter 11 case, identified with the name of the entity or entities submitting or filing it.

(b) Disclosure statement. In a chapter 9 or 11 case, a disclosure statement under § 1125 of the Code [11 USCS § 1125] or evidence showing compliance with § 1126(b) [11 USCS § 1126(b)] shall be filed with the plan or within a time fixed by the court, unless the plan is intended to provide adequate information under § 1125(f)(1) [11 USCS § 1125(f)]. If the plan is intended to provide adequate information under § 1125(f)(1) [11 USCS § 1125(f)(1)], it shall be so designated and Rule 3017.1 shall apply as if the plan is a disclosure statement.

(c) Injunction under a plan. If a plan provides for an injunction against conduct not otherwise enjoined under the Code, the plan and disclosure statement shall describe in specific and conspicuous language (bold, italic, or underlined text) all acts to be enjoined and identify the entities that would be subject to the injunction.

(d) Standard form small business disclosure statement and plan. In a small business case, the court may approve a disclosure statement and may confirm a plan that conform substantially to the appropriate Official Forms or other standard forms approved by the court.

(Amended Aug. 1, 1987; Aug. 1, 1991; Dec. 1, 1996; Dec. 1, 2001; Dec. 1, 2008.)

Rule 3017. Court Consideration of Disclosure Statement in a Chapter 9 Municipality or Chapter 11 Reorganization Case

(a) Hearing on disclosure statement and objections. Except as provided in Rule 3017.1, after a disclosure statement is filed in accordance with Rule 3016(b), the court shall hold a hearing on at least 28 days' notice to the debtor, creditors, equity security holders and other parties in interest as provided in Rule 2002 to consider the disclosure statement and any objections or modifications thereto. The plan and the disclosure statement shall be mailed with the notice of the hearing only to the debtor, any trustee or committee appointed under the Code, the Securities and Exchange Commission and any party in interest who requests in writing a copy of the statement or plan. Objections to the disclosure statement shall be filed and served on the debtor, the trustee, any committee appointed under the Code, and any other entity designated by the court, at any time before the disclosure statement is approved or by an earlier date as the court may fix. In a chapter 11 reorganization case, every notice, plan, disclosure statement, and objection required to be served or mailed pursuant to this subdivision shall be transmitted to the United States trustee within the time provided in this subdivision.

(b) Determination on disclosure statement. Following the hearing the court shall determine whether the disclosure statement should be approved.

(c) Dates fixed for voting on plan and confirmation. On or before approval of the disclosure statement, the court shall fix a time within which the holders of claims and interests may accept or reject the plan and may fix a date for the hearing on confirmation.

(d) Transmission and notice to United States trustee, creditors, and equity security holders. Upon approval of a disclosure statement,—except to the extent that the court orders otherwise with respect to one or more unimpaired classes of creditors or equity security holders—the debtor in possession, trustee, proponent of the plan, or clerk as the court orders shall mail to all creditors and equity security holders, and in a chapter 11 reorganization case shall transmit to the United States trustee,

(1) the plan or a court-approved summary of the plan;

(2) the disclosure statement approved by the court;

(3) notice of the time within which acceptances and rejections of the plan may be filed; and

(4) any other information as the court may direct, including any court opinion approving the disclosure statement or a court-approved summary of the opinion.

In addition, notice of the time fixed for filing objections and the hearing on confirmation shall be mailed to all creditors and equity security holders in accordance with Rule 2002(b), and a form of ballot conforming to the appropriate Official Form shall be mailed to creditors and equity security holders entitled to vote on the plan. If the court opinion is not transmitted or only a summary of the plan is transmitted, the court opinion or the plan shall be provided on request of a party in interest at the plan proponent's expense. If the court orders that the disclosure statement and the plan or a summary of the plan shall not be mailed to any unimpaired class, notice that the class is designated in the plan as unimpaired and notice of the name and address of the person from whom the plan or summary of the plan and disclosure statement may be obtained upon request and at the plan proponent's expense, shall be mailed to members of the unimpaired class together with the notice of the time fixed for filing objections to and the hearing on confirmation. For the purposes of this subdivision, creditors and equity security holders shall include holders of stock, bonds, debentures, notes, and other securities of record on the date the order approving the disclosure statement is entered or another date fixed by the court, for cause, after notice and a hearing.

(e) Transmission to beneficial holders of securities. At the hearing held pursuant to subdivision (a) of this rule, the court shall consider the procedures for transmitting the documents and information required by subdivision (d) of this rule to beneficial holders of stock, bonds, debentures, notes, and other securities, determine the adequacy of the procedures, and enter any orders the court deems appropriate.

(f) Notice and transmission of documents to entities subject to an injunction under a plan. If a plan provides for an injunction against conduct not otherwise enjoined under the Code and an entity that would be subject to the injunction is not a creditor or equity security holder, at the hearing held under Rule 3017(a), the court shall consider procedures for providing the entity with:

(1) at least 28 days' notice of the time fixed for

filing objections and the hearing on confirmation of the plan containing the information described in Rule 2002(c)(3); and

(2) to the extent feasible, a copy of the plan and disclosure statement.

(Amended Aug. 1, 1987; Aug. 1, 1991; Dec. 1, 1997; Dec. 1, 2001; Dec. 1, 2009.)

Rule 3017.1. Court Consideration of Disclosure Statement in a Small Business Case

(a) Conditional approval of disclosure statement. In a small business case, the court may, on application of the plan proponent or on its own initiative, conditionally approve a disclosure statement filed in accordance with Rule 3016. On or before conditional approval of the disclosure statement, the court shall:

(1) fix a time within which the holders of claims and interests may accept or reject the plan;

(2) fix a time for filing objections to the disclosure statement;

(3) fix a date for the hearing on final approval of the disclosure statement to be held if a timely objection is filed; and

(4) fix a date for the hearing on confirmation.

(b) Application of Rule 3017. Rule 3017(a), (b), (c), and (e) do not apply to a conditionally approved disclosure statement. Rule 3017(d) applies to a conditionally approved disclosure statement, except that conditional approval is considered approval of the disclosure statement for the purpose of applying Rule 3017(d).

(c) Final approval. (1) *Notice.* Notice of the time fixed for filing objections and the hearing to consider final approval of the disclosure statement shall be given in accordance with Rule 2002 and may be combined with notice of the hearing on confirmation of the plan.

(2) *Objections.* Objections to the disclosure statement shall be filed, transmitted to the United States trustee, and served on the debtor, the trustee, any committee appointed under the Code and any other entity designated by the court at any time before final approval of the disclosure statement or by an earlier date as the court may fix.

(3) *Hearing.* If a timely objection to the disclosure statement is filed, the court shall hold a hearing to consider final approval before or combined with the hearing on confirmation of the plan.

(Added December 1, 1997; Dec. 1, 2008.)

Rule 3018. Acceptance or Rejection of Plan in a Chapter 9 Municipality or a Chapter 11 Reorganization Case

(a) Entities entitled to accept or reject plan; time for acceptance or rejection. A plan may be accepted or rejected in accordance with § 1126 of the Code [11 USCS § 1126] within the time fixed by the court pursuant to Rule 3017. Subject to subdivision (b) of this rule, an equity security holder or creditor whose claim is based on a security of record shall not be entitled to accept or reject a plan unless the equity security holder or creditor is the holder of record of the security on the date the order approving the disclosure statement is entered or on another date fixed by the court, for cause, after notice and a hearing. For cause shown, the court after notice and hearing may permit a creditor or equity security holder to change or withdraw an acceptance or rejection. Notwithstanding objection to a claim or interest, the court after notice and hearing may temporarily allow the claim or interest in an amount which the court deems proper for the purpose of accepting or rejecting a plan.

(b) Acceptances or rejections obtained before petition. An equity security holder or creditor whose claim is based on a security of record who accepted or rejected the plan before the commencement of the case shall not be deemed to have accepted or rejected the plan pursuant to § 1126(b) of the Code [11 USCS § 1126(b)] unless the equity security holder or creditor was the holder of record of the security on the date specified in the solicitation of such acceptance or rejection for the purposes of such solicitation. A holder of a claim or interest who has accepted or rejected a plan before the commencement of the case under the Code shall not be deemed to have accepted or rejected the plan if the court finds after notice and hearing that the plan was not transmitted to substantially all creditors and equity security holders of the same class, that an unreasonably short time was prescribed for such creditors and equity security holders to accept or reject the plan, or that the solicitation was not in compliance with § 1126(b) of the Code [11 USCS § 1126(b)].

(c) Form of acceptance or rejection. An acceptance or rejection shall be in writing, identify the plan or plans accepted or rejected, be signed by the creditor or equity security holder or an authorized agent, and conform to the appropriate Official Form. If more than one plan is transmitted pursuant to Rule 3017, an acceptance or rejection may be filed by each creditor or equity security holder for any number of plans transmitted and if acceptances are filed for more than one plan, the creditor or equity security holder may indicate a preference or preferences among the plans so accepted.

(d) Acceptance or rejection by partially secured creditor. A creditor whose claim has been allowed in part as a secured claim and in part as an unsecured claim shall be entitled to accept or reject a plan in both capacities.

(Amended Aug. 1, 1987; Aug. 1, 1991; Aug. 1, 1993; Dec. 1, 1997.)

Rule 3019. Modification of Accepted Plan in a Chapter 9 Municipality or a Chapter 11 Reorganization Case

(a) Modification of plan before confirmation. In a chapter 9 or chapter 11 case, after a plan has been accepted and before its confirmation, the proponent may file a modification of the plan. If the court finds after hearing on notice to the trustee, any committee appointed under the Code, and any other entity designated by the court that the proposed modification does not adversely change the treatment of the claim of any creditor or the interest of any equity security holder who has not accepted in writing the modification, it shall be deemed accepted by all creditors and equity security holders who have previously accepted the plan.

(b) Modification of plan after confirmation in individual debtor case. If the debtor is an individual, a request to modify the plan under § 1127(e) of the Code [11 USCS § 1127(e)] is governed by Rule 9014. The request shall identify the proponent and shall be filed together with the proposed modification. The clerk, or some other person as the court may direct, shall give the debtor, the trustee, and all creditors not less than 21 days' notice by mail of the time fixed to file objections and, if an objection is filed, the hearing to consider the proposed modification, unless the court orders otherwise with respect to creditors who are not affected by the proposed modification. A copy of the notice shall be transmitted to the United States trustee, together with a copy of the proposed modification. Any objection to the proposed modification shall be filed and served on the debtor, the proponent of the modification, the trustee, and any other entity designated by the court, and shall be transmitted to the United States trustee.

(Amended Aug. 1, 1987; Aug. 1, 1993; Dec. 1, 2008; Dec. 1, 2009.)

Rule 3020. Deposit; Confirmation of Plan in a Chapter 9 Municipality or Chapter 11 Reorganization Case

(a) Deposit. In a chapter 11 case, prior to entry of the order confirming the plan, the court may order the deposit with the trustee or debtor in possession of the consideration required by the plan to be distributed on confirmation. Any money deposited shall be kept in a special account established for the exclusive purpose of making the distribution.

(b) Objection to and hearing on confirmation in a chapter 9 or chapter 11 case. (1) *Objection.* An objection to confirmation of the plan shall be filed and served on the debtor, the trustee, the proponent of the plan, any committee appointed under the Code, and any other entity designated by the court, within a time fixed by the court. Unless the case is a chapter 9 municipality case, a copy of every objection to confirmation shall be transmitted by the objecting party to the United States trustee within the time fixed for filing objections. An objection to confirmation is governed by Rule 9014. (2) *Hearing.* The court shall rule on confirmation of the plan after notice and hearing as provided in Rule 2002. If no objection is timely filed, the court may determine that the plan has been proposed in good faith and not by any means forbidden by law without receiving evidence on such issues.

(c) Order of confirmation. (1) The order of confirmation shall conform to the appropriate Official Form. If the plan provides for an injunction against conduct not otherwise enjoined under the Code, the order of confirmation shall (1) describe in reasonable detail all acts enjoined; (2) be specific in its terms regarding the injunction; and (3) identify the entities subject to the injunction.

(2) Notice of entry of the order of confirmation shall be mailed promptly to the debtor, the trustee, creditors, equity security holders, other parties in interest, and, if known, to any identified entity subject to an injunction provided for in the plan against conduct not otherwise enjoined under the Code.

(3) Except in a chapter 9 municipality case, notice of entry of the order of confirmation shall be transmitted to the United States trustee as provided in Rule 2002(k).

(d) Retained power. Notwithstanding the entry of the order of confirmation, the court may issue any other order necessary to administer the estate.

(e) Stay of confirmation order. An order confirming a plan is stayed until the expiration of 14 days after the entry of the order, unless the court orders otherwise.

(Amended Aug. 1, 1987; Aug. 1, 1991; Aug. 1, 1993; Dec. 1, 1999; Dec. 1, 2001; Dec. 1, 2009.)

Rule 3021. Distribution Under Plan

Except as provided in Rule 3020(e), after a plan is confirmed, distribution shall be made to creditors whose claims have been allowed, to interest holders whose interests have not been disallowed, and to indenture trustees who have filed claims under Rule 3003(c)(5) that have been allowed. For purposes of this rule, creditors include holders of bonds, debentures, notes, and other debt securities, and interest holders include the holders of stock and other equity securities, of record at the time of commencement of distribution, unless a different time is fixed by the plan or the order confirming the plan.

(Amended Dec. 1, 1997; Dec. 1, 1999.)

Rule 3022. Final Decree in Chapter 11 Reorganization Case

After an estate is fully administered in a chapter 11 reorganization case, the court, on its own motion or on motion of a party in interest, shall enter a final decree closing the case.

(Amended Aug. 1, 1987; Aug. 1, 1991.)

PART IV. THE DEBTOR: DUTIES AND BENEFITS

Rule 4001. Relief from Automatic Stay; Prohibiting or Conditioning the Use, Sale, or Lease of Property; Use of Cash Collateral; Obtaining Credit; Agreements

(a) Relief from stay; prohibiting or conditioning the use, sale, or lease of property. (1) *Motion.* A motion for relief from an automatic stay provided by the Code or a motion to prohibit or condition the use, sale, or lease of property pursuant to § 363(e) [11 USCS § 363(e)] shall be made in accordance with Rule 9014 and shall be served on any committee elected pursuant to § 705 [11 USCS § 705] or appointed pursuant to § 1102 of the Code [11 USCS § 1102] or its authorized agent, or, if the case is a chapter 9 municipality case or a chapter 11 reorganization case and no committee of unsecured creditors has been appointed pursuant to § 1102 [11 USCS § 1102], on the creditors included on the list filed pursuant to Rule 1007(d), and on such other entities as the court may direct.

(2) *Ex parte relief.* Relief from a stay under § 362(a) [11 USCS § 362(a)] or a request to prohibit or condition the use, sale, or lease of property pursuant to § 363(e) [11 USCS § 363(e)] may be granted without prior notice only if (A) it clearly appears from specific facts shown by affidavit or by a verified motion that immediate and irreparable injury, loss, or damage will result to the movant before the adverse party or the attorney for the adverse party can be heard in opposition, and (B) the movant's attorney certifies to the court in writing the efforts, if any, which have been made to give notice and the reasons why notice should not be required. The party obtaining relief under this subdivision and § 362(f) or § 363(e) [11 USCS § 362(f) or 363(e)] shall immediately give oral notice thereof to the trustee or debtor in possession and to the debtor and forthwith mail or otherwise transmit to such adverse party or parties a copy of the order granting relief. On two days notice to the party who obtained relief from the stay without notice or on shorter notice to that party as the court may prescribe, the adverse party may appear and move reinstatement of the stay or reconsideration of the order prohibiting or conditioning the use, sale, or lease of property. In that event, the court shall proceed expeditiously to hear and determine the motion.

(3) *Stay of order.* An order granting a motion for relief from an automatic stay made in accordance with Rule 4001(a)(1) is stayed until the expiration of 14 days after the entry of the order, unless the court orders otherwise.

(b) Use of cash collateral. (1) *Motion; service.* (A) Motion. A motion for authority to use cash collateral shall be made in accordance with Rule 9014 and shall be accompanied by a proposed form of order.

(B) Contents. The motion shall consist of or (if the motion is more than five pages in length) begin with a concise statement of the relief requested, not to exceed five pages, that lists or summarizes, and sets out the location within the relevant documents of, all material provisions, including:

(i) the name of each entity with an interest in the cash collateral;

(ii) the purposes for the use of the cash collateral;

(iii) the material terms, including duration, of the use of the cash collateral; and

(iv) any liens, cash payments, or other adequate protection that will be provided to each entity with an interest in the cash collateral or, if no additional adequate protection is proposed, an explanation of why each entity's interest is adequately protected.

(C) Service. The motion shall be served on: (1) any entity with an interest in the cash collateral; (2) any committee elected under § 705 [11 USCS § 705] or appointed under § 1102 of the Code [11 USCS § 1102], or its authorized agent, or, if the case is a chapter 9 municipality case or a chapter 11 reorganization case and no committee of unsecured creditors has been appointed under § 1102 [11 USCS § 1102], the creditors included on the list filed under Rule 1007(d); and (3) any other entity that the court directs.

(2) *Hearing.* The court may commence a final hearing on a motion for authorization to use cash collateral no earlier than 14 days after service of the motion. If the motion so requests, the court may conduct a preliminary hearing before such 14-day period expires, but the court may authorize the use of only that amount of cash collateral as is necessary to avoid immediate and irreparable harm to the estate pending a final hearing.

(3) *Notice.* Notice of hearing pursuant to this subdivision shall be given to the parties on whom service of the motion is required by paragraph (1) of this subdivision and to such other entities as the court may direct.

(c) Obtaining credit. (1) *Motion; service.* (A) Motion. A motion for authority to obtain credit shall be made in accordance with Rule 9014 and shall be accompanied by a copy of the credit agreement and a proposed form of order.

(B) Contents. The motion shall consist of or (if the motion is more than five pages in length) begin with a concise statement of the relief requested, not to exceed five pages, that lists or summarizes, and sets out the location within the relevant documents of, all material provisions of the proposed credit agreement and form of order, including interest rate, maturity, events of default, liens, borrowing limits, and borrowing conditions. If the proposed credit agreement or form of order includes any of the provisions listed below, the concise statement shall also: briefly list or summarize each one; identify its specific location in the proposed agreement and form of order; and identify any such provision that is proposed to remain in effect if interim approval is granted, but final relief is denied, as provided under Rule 4001(c)(2). In addition, the motion shall describe the nature and extent of each provision listed below:

(i) a grant of priority or a lien on property of the estate under § 364(c) or (d) [11 USCS § 364(c) or (d)];

(ii) the providing of adequate protection or priority

for a claim that arose before the commencement of the case, including the granting of a lien on property of the estate to secure the claim, or the use of property of the estate or credit obtained under § 364 [11 USCS § 364] to make cash payments on account of the claim;

(iii) a determination of the validity, enforceability, priority, or amount of a claim that arose before the commencement of the case, or of any lien securing the claim;

(iv) a waiver or modification of Code provisions or applicable rules relating to the automatic stay;

(v) a waiver or modification of any entity's authority or right to file a plan, seek an extension of time in which the debtor has the exclusive right to file a plan, request the use of cash collateral under § 363(c) [11 USCS § 363(c)], or request authority to obtain credit under § 364 [11 USCS § 364];

(vi) the establishment of deadlines for filing a plan of reorganization, for approval of a disclosure statement, for a hearing on confirmation, or for entry of a confirmation order;

(vii) a waiver or modification of the applicability of nonbankruptcy law relating to the perfection of a lien on property of the estate, or on the foreclosure or other enforcement of the lien;

(viii) a release, waiver, or limitation on any claim or other cause of action belonging to the estate or the trustee, including any modification of the statute of limitations or other deadline to commence an action;

(ix) the indemnification of any entity;

(x) a release, waiver, or limitation of any right under § 506(c) [11 USCS § 506(c)]; or

(xi) the granting of a lien on any claim or cause of action arising under §§ 544, 545, 547, 548, 549, 553(b), 723(a), or 724(a) [11 USCS § 544, 545, 547, 548, 549, 553(b), 723(a), or 724(a)].

(C) Service. The motion shall be served on: (1) any committee elected under § 705 [11 USCS § 705] or appointed under § 1102 of the Code [11 USCS § 1102], or its authorized agent, or, if the case is a chapter 9 municipality case or a chapter 11 reorganization case and no committee of unsecured creditors has been appointed under § 1102 [11 USCS § 1102], on the creditors included on the list filed under Rule 1007(d); and (2) on any other entity that the court directs.

(2) *Hearing.* The court may commence a final hearing on a motion for authority to obtain credit no earlier than 14 days after service of the motion. If the motion so requests, the court may conduct a hearing before such 14-day period expires, but the court may authorize the obtaining of credit only to the extent necessary to avoid immediate and irreparable harm to the estate pending a final hearing.

(3) *Notice.* Notice of hearing pursuant to this subdivision shall be given to the parties on whom service of the motion is required by paragraph (1) of this subdivision and to such other entities as the court may direct.

(d) Agreement relating to relief from the automatic stay, prohibiting or conditioning the use, sale, or lease of property, providing adequate protection, use of cash collateral, and obtaining credit. (1) *Motion; service.* (A) Motion. A motion for approval of any of the following shall be accompanied by a copy of the agreement and a proposed form of order:

(i) an agreement to provide adequate protection;

(ii) an agreement to prohibit or condition the use, sale, or lease of property;

(iii) an agreement to modify or terminate the stay provided for in § 362 [11 USCS § 362];

(iv) an agreement to use cash collateral; or

(v) an agreement between the debtor and an entity that has a lien or interest in property of the estate pursuant to which the entity consents to the creation of a lien senior or equal to the entity's lien or interest in such property.

(B) Contents. The motion shall consist of or (if the motion is more than five pages in length) begin with a concise statement of the relief requested, not to exceed five pages, that lists or summarizes, and sets out the location within the relevant documents of, all material provisions of the agreement. In addition, the concise statement shall briefly list or summarize, and identify the specific location of, each provision in the proposed form of order, agreement, or other document of the type listed in subdivision (c)(1)(B). The motion shall also describe the nature and extent of each such provision.

(C) Service. The motion shall be served on: (1) any committee elected under § 705 [11 USCS § 705] or appointed under § 1102 of the Code [11 USCS § 1102], or its authorized agent, or, if the case is a chapter 9 municipality case or a chapter 11 reorganization case and no committee of unsecured creditors has been appointed under § 1102 [11 USCS § 1102], on the creditors included on the list filed under Rule 1007(d); and (2) on any other entity the court directs.

(2) *Objection.* Notice of the motion and the time within which objections may be filed and served on the debtor in possession or trustee shall be mailed to the parties on whom service is required by paragraph (1) of this subdivision and to such other entities as the court may direct. Unless the court fixes a different time, objections may be filed within 14 days of the mailing of the notice.

(3) *Disposition; hearing.* If no objection is filed, the court may enter an order approving or disapproving the agreement without conducting a hearing. If an objection is filed or if the court determines a hearing is appropriate, the court shall hold a hearing on no less than seven days' notice to the objector, the movant, the parties on whom service is required by paragraph (1) of this subdivision and such other entities as the court may direct.

(4) *Agreement in settlement of motion.* The court may direct that the procedures prescribed in paragraphs (1), (2), and (3) of this subdivision shall not apply and the agreement may be approved without

further notice if the court determines that a motion made pursuant to subdivisions (a), (b), or (c) of this rule was sufficient to afford reasonable notice of the material provisions of the agreement and opportunity for a hearing.

(Amended Aug. 1, 1987; Aug. 1, 1991; Dec. 1, 1999; Dec. 1, 2007; Dec. 1, 2009; Dec. 1, 2010.)

Rule 4002. Duties of Debtor

(a) In general. In addition to performing other duties prescribed by the Code and rules, the debtor shall:

(1) attend and submit to an examination at the times ordered by the court;

(2) attend the hearing on a complaint objecting to discharge and testify, if called as a witness;

(3) inform the trustee immediately in writing as to the location of real property in which the debtor has an interest and the name and address of every person holding money or property subject to the debtor's withdrawal or order if a schedule of property has not yet been filed pursuant to Rule 1007;

(4) cooperate with the trustee in the preparation of an inventory, the examination of proofs of claim, and the administration of the estate; and

(5) file a statement of any change of the debtor's address.

(b) Individual debtor's duty to provide documentation. (1) *Personal identification.* Every individual debtor shall bring to the meeting of creditors under § 341 [11 USCS § 341]:

(A) a picture identification issued by a governmental unit, or other personal identifying information that establishes the debtor's identity; and

(B) evidence of social-security number(s), or a written statement that such documentation does not exist.

(2) *Financial information.* Every individual debtor shall bring to the meeting of creditors under § 341 [11 USCS § 341], and make available to the trustee, the following documents or copies of them, or provide a written statement that the documentation does not exist or is not in the debtor's possession:

(A) evidence of current income such as the most recent payment advice;

(B) unless the trustee or the United States trustee instructs otherwise, statements for each of the debtor's depository and investment accounts, including checking, savings, and money market accounts, mutual funds and brokerage accounts for the time period that includes the date of the filing of the petition; and

(C) documentation of monthly expenses claimed by the debtor if required by § 707(b)(2)(A) or (B) [11 USCS § 707(b)(2)(A) or (B)].

(3) *Tax return.* At least 7 days before the first date set for the meeting of creditors under § 341 [11 USCS § 341], the debtor shall provide to the trustee a copy of the debtor's federal income tax return for the most recent tax year ending immediately before the commencement of the case and for which a return was filed, including any attachments, or a transcript of the tax return, or provide a written statement that the documentation does not exist.

(4) *Tax returns provided to creditors.* If a creditor, at least 14 days before the first date set for the meeting of creditors under § 341 [11 USCS § 341], requests a copy of the debtor's tax return that is to be provided to the trustee under subdivision (b)(3), the debtor, at least 7 days before the first date set for the meeting of creditors under § 341 [11 USCS § 341], shall provide to the requesting creditor a copy of the return, including any attachments, or a transcript of the tax return, or provide a written statement that the documentation does not exist.

(5) *Confidentiality of tax information.* The debtor's obligation to provide tax returns under Rule 4002(b)(3) and (b)(4) is subject to procedures for safeguarding the confidentiality of tax information established by the Director of the Administrative Office of the United States Courts.

(Amended Aug. 1, 1987; Dec. 1, 2008; Dec. 1, 2009.)

Rule 4003. Exemptions

(a) Claim of exemptions. A debtor shall list the property claimed as exempt under § 522 of the Code [11 USCS § 522] on the schedule of assets required to be filed by Rule 1007. If the debtor fails to claim exemptions or file the schedule within the time specified in Rule 1007, a dependent of the debtor may file the list within 30 days thereafter.

(b) Objecting to a claim of exemptions. (1) Except as provided in paragraphs (2) and (3), a party in interest may file an objection to the list of property claimed as exempt within 30 days after the meeting of creditors held under § 341(a) [11 USCS § 341(a)] is concluded or within 30 days after any amendment to the list or supplemental schedules is filed, whichever is later. The court may, for cause, extend the time for filing objections if, before the time to object expires, a party in interest files a request for an extension.

(2) The trustee may file an objection to a claim of exemption at any time prior to one year after the closing of the case if the debtor fraudulently asserted the claim of exemption. The trustee shall deliver or mail the objection to the debtor and the debtor's attorney, and to any person filing the list of exempt property and that person's attorney.

(3) An objection to a claim of exemption based on § 522(q) [11 USCS § 522(q)] shall be filed before the closing of the case. If an exemption is first claimed after a case is reopened, an objection shall be filed before the reopened case is closed.

(4) A copy of any objection shall be delivered or mailed to the trustee, the debtor and the debtor's attorney, and the person filing the list and that person's attorney.

(c) Burden of proof. In any hearing under this rule, the objecting party has the burden of proving that the exemptions are not properly claimed. After hearing on notice, the court shall determine the issues presented by the objections.

(d) Avoidance by debtor of transfers of exempt property. A proceeding by the debtor to avoid a lien or other transfer of property exempt under § 522(f) of the Code [11 USCS § 522(f)] shall be by motion in accordance with Rule 9014. Notwithstanding the provisions of subdivision (b), a creditor may object to a motion filed under § 522(f) [11 USCS § 522(f)] by challenging the validity of the exemption asserted to be impaired by the lien.

(Amended Aug. 1, 1987; Aug. 1, 1991; Dec. 1, 2000; Dec. 1, 2008.)

Rule 4004. Grant or Denial of Discharge

(a) Time for objecting to discharge; notice of time fixed. In a chapter 7 case, a complaint, or a motion under § 727(a)(8) or (a)(9) of the Code [11 USCS § 727 (a)(8) or (a)(9)], objecting to the debtor's discharge shall be filed no later than 60 days after the first date set for the meeting of creditors under § 341(a) [11 USCS § 341(a)]. In a chapter 11 case, the complaint shall be filed no later than the first date set for the hearing on confirmation. In a chapter 13 case, a motion objecting to the debtor's discharge under § 1328(f) [11 USCS § 1328(f)] shall be filed no later than 60 days after the first date set for the meeting of creditors under § 341(a) [11 USCS § 341(a)]. At least 28 days' notice of the time so fixed shall be given to the United States trustee and all creditors as provided in Rule 2002(f) and (k) and to the trustee and the trustee's attorney.

(b) Extension of time.

(1) On motion of any party in interest, after notice and hearing, the court may for cause extend the time to object to discharge. Except as provided in subdivision (b)(2), the motion shall be filed before the time has expired.

(2) A motion to extend the time to object to discharge may be filed after the time for objection has expired and before discharge is granted if (A) the objection is based on facts that, if learned after the discharge, would provide a basis for revocation under § 727(d) of the Code [11 USCS § 727(d)], and (B) the movant did not have knowledge of those facts in time to permit an objection. The motion shall be filed promptly after the movant discovers the facts on which the objection is based.

(c) Grant of discharge. (1) In a chapter 7 case, on expiration of the times fixed for objecting to discharge and for filing a motion to dismiss the case under Rule 1017(e), the court shall forthwith grant the discharge, except that the court shall not grant the discharge if:

(A) the debtor is not an individual;

(B) a complaint, or a motion under § 727(a)(8) or (a)(9) [11 USCS § 727(a)(8) or (a)(9)], objecting to the discharge has been filed and not decided in the debtor's favor;

(C) the debtor has filed a waiver under § 727(a)(10) [11 USCS § 727(a)(10)];

(D) a motion to dismiss the case under § 707 [11 USCS § 707] is pending;

(E) a motion to extend the time for filing a complaint objecting to discharge is pending;

(F) a motion to extend the time for filing a motion to dismiss the case under Rule 1017(e)(1) is pending;

(G) the debtor has not paid in full the filing fee prescribed by 28 U.S.C. § 1930(a) and any other fee prescribed by the Judicial Conference of the United States under 28 U.S.C. § 1930(b) that is payable to the clerk upon the commencement of a case under the Code, unless the court has waived the fees under 28 U.S.C. § 1930(f);

(H) the debtor has not filed with the court a statement of completion of a course concerning personal financial management if required by Rule 1007(b)(7);

(I) a motion to delay or postpone discharge under § 727(a)(12) [11 USCS § 727(a)(12)] is pending;

(J) a motion to enlarge the time to file a reaffirmation agreement under Rule 4008(a) is pending;

(K) a presumption is in effect under § 524(m) [11 USCS § 524(m)] that a reaffirmation agreement is an undue hardship and the court has not concluded a hearing on the presumption; or

(L) a motion is pending to delay discharge, because the debtor has not filed with the court all tax documents required to be filed under § 521(f) [11 USCS § 521(f)].

(2) Notwithstanding Rule 4004(c)(1), on motion of the debtor, the court may defer the entry of an order granting a discharge for 30 days and, on motion within that period, the court may defer entry of the order to a date certain.

(3) If the debtor is required to file a statement under Rule 1007(b)(8), the court shall not grant a discharge earlier than 30 days after the statement is filed.

(4) In a chapter 11 case in which the debtor is an individual, or a chapter 13 case, the court shall not grant a discharge if the debtor has not filed any statement required by Rule 1007(b)(7).

(d) Applicability of rules in Part VII and Rule 9014. An objection to discharge is governed by Part VII of these rules, except that an objection to discharge under §§ 727(a)(8), (a)(9), or 1328(f) [11 USCS § 727(a)(8), (a)(9), or 1328(f)] is commenced by motion and governed by Rule 9014.

(e) Order of discharge. An order of discharge shall conform to the appropriate Official Form.

(f) Registration in other districts. An order of discharge that has become final may be registered in any other district by filing a certified copy of the order in the office of the clerk of that district. When so registered the order of discharge shall have the same effect as an order of the court of the district where registered.

(g) Notice of discharge. The clerk shall promptly mail a copy of the final order of discharge to those specified in subdivision (a) of this rule.

(Amended Aug. 1, 1987; Aug. 1, 1991; Dec. 1, 1996; Dec. 1, 1999; Dec. 1, 2000; Dec. 1, 2002; Dec. 1, 2008; Dec. 1, 2009; Dec. 1, 2010; Dec. 1, 2011; Dec. 1, 2013.)

Rule 4005. Burden of Proof in Objecting to Discharge

At the trial on a complaint objecting to a discharge, the plaintiff has the burden of proving the objection.

(Amended Aug. 1, 1987.)

Rule 4006. Notice of No Discharge

If an order is entered: denying a discharge; revoking a discharge; approving a waiver of discharge; or, in the case of an individual debtor, closing the case without the entry of a discharge, the clerk shall promptly notify all parties in interest in the manner provided by Rule 2002.

(Amended Aug. 1, 1987; Dec. 1, 2008.)

Rule 4007. Determination of Dischargeability of a Debt

(a) Persons entitled to file complaint. A debtor or any creditor may file a complaint to obtain a determination of the dischargeability of any debt.

(b) Time for commencing proceeding other than under § 523(c) of the code. A complaint other than under § 523(c) [11 USCS § 523(c)] may be filed at any time. A case may be reopened without payment of an additional filing fee for the purpose of filing a complaint to obtain a determination under this rule.

(c) Time for filing complaint under § 523(c) in a chapter 7 liquidation, chapter 11 reorganization, chapter 12 family farmer's debt adjustment case, or chapter 13 individual's debt adjustment case; notice of time fixed. Except as otherwise provided in subdivision (d), a complaint to determine the dischargeability of a debt under § 523(c) [11 USCS § 523(c)] shall be filed no later than 60 days after the first date set for the meeting of creditors under § 341(a) [11 USCS § 341(a)]. The court shall give all creditors no less than 30 days' notice of the time so fixed in the manner provided in Rule 2002. On motion of a party in interest, after hearing on notice, the court may for cause extend the time fixed under this subdivision. The motion shall be filed before the time has expired.

(d) Time for filing complaint under § 523(a)(6) in a chapter 13 individual's debt adjustment case; notice of time fixed. On motion by a debtor for a discharge under § 1328(b) [11 USCS § 1328(b)], the court shall enter an order fixing the time to file a complaint to determine the dischargeability of any debt under § 523(a)(6) [11 USCS § 523(a)(6)] and shall give no less than 30 days' notice of the time fixed to all creditors in the manner provided in Rule 2002. On motion of any party in interest, after hearing on notice, the court may for cause extend the time fixed under this subdivision. The motion shall be filed before the time has expired.

(e) Applicability of rules in part VII. A proceeding commenced by a complaint filed under this rule is governed by Part VII of these rules.

(Amended Aug. 1, 1987; Aug. 1, 1991; Dec. 1, 1999; Dec. 1, 2008.)

Rule 4008. Filing of Reaffirmation Agreement; Statement in Support of Reaffirmation Agreement

(a) Filing of reaffirmation agreement. A reaffirmation agreement shall be filed no later than 60 days after the first date set for the meeting of creditors under § 341(a) of the Code [11 USCS § 341(a)]. The reaffirmation agreement shall be accompanied by a cover sheet, prepared as prescribed by the appropriate Official Form. The court may, at any time and in its discretion, enlarge the time to file a reaffirmation agreement.

(b) Statement in support of reaffirmation agreement. The debtor's statement required under § 524(k)(6)(A) of the Code [11 USCS § 524(k)(6)(A)] shall be accompanied by a statement of the total income and expenses stated on schedules I and J. If there is a difference between the total income and expenses stated on those schedules and the statement required under § 524(k)(6)(A) [11 USCS § 524(k)(6)(A)], the statement required by this subdivision shall include an explanation of the difference.

(Amended Aug. 1, 1991; Dec. 1, 2008; Dec. 1, 2009.)

PART V. COURTS AND CLERKS

Rule 5001. Courts and Clerks' Offices

(a) Courts always open. The courts shall be deemed always open for the purpose of filing any pleading or other proper paper, issuing and returning process, and filing, making, or entering motions, orders and rules.

(b) Trials and hearings; orders in chambers. All trials and hearings shall be conducted in open court and so far as convenient in a regular court room. Except as otherwise provided in 28 U.S.C. § 152(c), all other acts or proceedings may be done or conducted by a judge in chambers and at any place either within or without the district; but no hearing, other than one ex parte, shall be conducted outside the district without the consent of all parties affected thereby.

(c) Clerk's office. The clerk's office with the clerk or a deputy in attendance shall be open during business hours on all days except Saturdays, Sundays and the legal holidays listed in Rule 9006(a).

(Amended Aug. 1, 1987; Aug. 1, 1991; Dec. 1, 2008.)

Rule 5002. Restrictions on Approval of Appointments

(a) Approval of appointment of relatives pro-

hibited. The appointment of an individual as a trustee or examiner pursuant to § 1104 of the Code [11 USCS § 1104] shall not be approved by the court if the individual is a relative of the bankruptcy judge approving the appointment or the United States trustee in the region in which the case is pending. The employment of an individual as an attorney, accountant, appraiser, auctioneer, or other professional person pursuant to §§ 327, 1103, or 1114 [11 USCS § 327, 1103, or 1114] shall not be approved by the court if the individual is a relative of the bankruptcy judge approving the employment. The employment of an individual as attorney, accountant, appraiser, auctioneer, or other professional person pursuant to §§ 327, 1103, or 1114 [11 USCS § 327, 1103, or 1114] may be approved by the court if the individual is a relative of the United States trustee in the region in which the case is pending, unless the court finds that the relationship with the United States trustee renders the employment improper under the circumstances of the case. Whenever under this subdivision an individual may not be approved for appointment or employment, the individual's firm, partnership, corporation, or any other form of business association or relationship, and all members, associates and professional employees thereof also may not be approved for appointment or employment.

(b) Judicial determination that approval of appointment or employment is improper. A bankruptcy judge may not approve the appointment of a person as a trustee or examiner pursuant to § 1104 of the Code [11 USCS § 1104] or approve the employment of a person as an attorney, accountant, appraiser, auctioneer, or other professional person pursuant to §§ 327, 1103, or 1114 of the Code [11 USCS § 327, 1103, or 1114] if that person is or has been so connected with such judge or the United States trustee as to render the appointment or employment improper.

(Amended Aug. 1, 1985; Aug. 1, 1991.)

Rule 5003. Records Kept By the Clerk

(a) Bankruptcy dockets. The clerk shall keep a docket in each case under the Code and shall enter thereon each judgment, order, and activity in that case as prescribed by the Director of the Administrative Office of the United States Courts. The entry of a judgment or order in a docket shall show the date the entry is made.

(b) Claims register. The clerk shall keep in a claims register a list of claims filed in a case when it appears that there will be a distribution to unsecured creditors.

(c) Judgments. The clerk shall keep, in the form and manner as the Director of the Administrative Office of the United States Courts may prescribe, a correct copy of every final judgment or order affecting title to or lien on real property or for the recovery of money or property, and any other order which the court may direct to be kept. On request of the prevailing party, a correct copy of every judgment or order affecting title to or lien upon real or personal property or for the recovery of money or property shall be kept and indexed with the civil judgments of the district court.

(d) Index of cases; certificate of search. The clerk shall keep indices of all cases and adversary proceedings as prescribed by the Director of the Administrative Office of the United States Courts. On request, the clerk shall make a search of any index and papers in the clerk's custody and certify whether a case or proceeding has been filed in or transferred to the court or if a discharge has been entered in its records.

(e) Register of mailing addresses of federal and state governmental units and certain taxing authorities. The United States or the state or territory in which the court is located may file a statement designating its mailing address. The United States, state, territory, or local governmental unit responsible for collecting taxes within the district in which the case is pending may also file a statement designating an address for service of requests under § 505(b) of the Code [11 USCS § 505(b)], and the designation shall describe where further information concerning additional requirements for filing such requests may be found. The clerk shall keep, in the form and manner as the Director of the Administrative Office of the United States Courts may prescribe, a register that includes the mailing addresses designated under the first sentence of this subdivision, and a separate register of the addresses designated for the service of requests under § 505(b) of the Code [11 USCS § 505(b)]. The clerk is not required to include in any single register more than one mailing address for each department, agency, or instrumentality of the United States or the state or territory. If more than one address for a department, agency, or instrumentality is included in the register, the clerk shall also include information that would enable a user of the register to determine the circumstances when each address is applicable, and mailing notice to only one applicable address is sufficient to provide effective notice. The clerk shall update the register annually, effective January 2 of each year. The mailing address in the register is conclusively presumed to be a proper address for the governmental unit, but the failure to use that mailing address does not invalidate any notice that is otherwise effective under applicable law.

(f) Other books and records of the clerk. The clerk shall keep any other books and records required by the Director of the Administrative Office of the United States Courts.

(Amended Aug. 1, 1987; Dec. 1, 2000; Dec. 1, 2008.)

Rule 5004. Disqualification

(a) Disqualification of judge. A bankruptcy judge shall be governed by 28 U.S.C. § 455, and disqualified from presiding over the proceeding or contested matter in which the disqualifying circumstance arises or, if appropriate, shall be disqualified from presiding over the case.

(b) Disqualification of judge from allowing compensation. A bankruptcy judge shall be disqualified from allowing compensation to a person who is a relative of the bankruptcy judge or with whom the judge is so connected as to render it improper for the judge to authorize such compensation.

(Amended Aug. 1, 1985; Aug. 1, 1987.)

Rule 5005. Filing and Transmittal of Papers

(a) Filing. (1) *Place of filing.* The lists, schedules, statements, proofs of claim or interest, complaints, motions, applications, objections and other papers required to be filed by these rules, except as provided in 28 U.S.C. § 1409, shall be filed with the clerk in the district where the case under the Code is pending. The judge of that court may permit the papers to be filed with the judge, in which event the filing date shall be noted thereon, and they shall be forthwith transmitted to the clerk. The clerk shall not refuse to accept for filing any petition or other paper presented for the purpose of filing solely because it is not presented in proper form as required by these rules or any local rules or practices.

(2) *Filing by electronic means.* A court may by local rule permit or require documents to be filed, signed, or verified by electronic means that are consistent with technical standards, if any, that the Judicial Conference of the United States establishes. A local rule may require filing by electronic means only if reasonable exceptions are allowed. A document filed by electronic means in compliance with a local rule constitutes a written paper for the purpose of applying these rules, the Federal Rules of Civil Procedure made applicable by these rules, and § 107 of the Code [11 USCS § 107].

(b) Transmittal to the United States trustee. (1) The complaints, motions, applications, objections and other papers required to be transmitted to the United States trustee by these rules shall be mailed or delivered to an office of the United States trustee, or to another place designated by the United States trustee, in the district where the case under the Code is pending.

(2) The entity, other than the clerk, transmitting a paper to the United States trustee shall promptly file as proof of such transmittal a verified statement identifying the paper and stating the date on which it was transmitted to the United States trustee.

(3) Nothing in these rules shall require the clerk to transmit any paper to the United States trustee if the United States trustee requests in writing that the paper not be transmitted.

(c) Error in filing or transmittal. A paper intended to be filed with the clerk but erroneously delivered to the United States trustee, the trustee, the attorney for the trustee, a bankruptcy judge, a district judge, the clerk of the bankruptcy appellate panel, or the clerk of the district court shall, after the date of its receipt has been noted thereon, be transmitted forthwith to the clerk of the bankruptcy court. A paper intended to be transmitted to the United States trustee but erroneously delivered to the clerk, the trustee, the attorney for the trustee, a bankruptcy judge, a district judge, the clerk of the bankruptcy appellate panel, or the clerk of the district court shall, after the date of its receipt has been noted thereon, be transmitted forthwith to the United States trustee. In the interest of justice, the court may order that a paper erroneously delivered shall be deemed filed with the clerk or transmitted to the United States trustee as of the date of its original delivery.

(Amended Aug. 1, 1987; Aug. 1, 1991; Aug. 1, 1993; Dec. 1, 1996; Dec. 1, 2006.)

Rule 5006. Certification of Copies of Papers

The clerk shall issue a certified copy of the record of any proceeding in a case under the Code or of any paper filed with the clerk on payment of any prescribed fee.

(Amended Aug. 1, 1991.)

Rule 5007. Record of Proceedings and Transcripts

(a) Filing of record or transcript. The reporter or operator of a recording device shall certify the original notes of testimony, tape recording, or other original record of the proceeding and promptly file them with the clerk. The person preparing any transcript shall promptly file a certified copy.

(b) Transcript fees. The fees for copies of transcripts shall be charged at rates prescribed by the Judicial Conference of the United States. No fee may be charged for the certified copy filed with the clerk.

(c) Admissibility of record in evidence. A certified sound recording or a transcript of a proceeding shall be admissible as prima facie evidence to establish the record.

(Amended Aug. 1, 1987; Aug. 1, 1991.)

Rule 5008. Notice Regarding Presumption of Abuse in Chapter 7 Cases of Individual Debtors

If a presumption of abuse has arisen under § 707(b) [11 USCS § 707(b)] in a chapter 7 case of an individual with primarily consumer debts, the clerk shall within 10 days after the date of the filing of the petition notify creditors of the presumption of abuse in accordance with Rule 2002. If the debtor has not filed a statement indicating whether a presumption of abuse has arisen, the clerk shall within 10 days after the date of the filing of the petition notify creditors that the debtor has not filed the statement and that further notice will be given if a later filed statement indicates that a presumption of abuse has arisen. If a debtor later files a statement indicating that a presumption of abuse has arisen, the clerk shall notify creditors of the presumption of abuse as promptly as practicable.

(As added Dec. 1, 2008.)

Rule 5009. Closing Chapter 7 Liquidation, Chapter 12 Family Farmer's Debt Adjustment, Chapter 13 Individual's Debt Adjustment, and Chapter 15 Ancillary and Cross-Border Cases

(a) Cases under chapters 7, 12, and 13. If in a chapter 7, chapter 12, or chapter 13 case the trustee has filed a final report and final account and has certified that the estate has been fully administered, and if within 30 days no objection has been filed by the United States trustee or a party in interest, there shall be a presumption that the estate has been fully administered.

(b) Notice of failure to file Rule 1007(b)(7) statement. If an individual debtor in a chapter 7 or 13 case is required to file a statement under Rule 1007(b)(7) and fails to do so within 45 days after the first date set for the meeting of creditors under § 341(a) of the Code, the clerk shall promptly notify the debtor that the case will be closed without entry of a discharge unless the required statement is filed within the applicable time limit under Rule 1007(c).

(c) Cases under chapter 15. A foreign representative in a proceeding recognized under § 1517 of the Code [11 USCS § 1517] shall file a final report when the purpose of the representative's appearance in the court is completed. The report shall describe the nature and results of the representative's activities in the court. The foreign representative shall transmit the report to the United States trustee, and give notice of its filing to the debtor, all persons or bodies authorized to administer foreign proceedings of the debtor, all parties to litigation pending in the United States in which the debtor was a party at the time of the filing of the petition, and such other entities as the court may direct. The foreign representative shall file a certificate with the court that notice has been given. If no objection has been filed by the United States trustee or a party in interest within 30 days after the certificate is filed, there shall be a presumption that the case has been fully administered.

(Amended Aug. 1, 1991; Dec. 1, 2010; Dec. 1, 2013.)

Rule 5010. Reopening Cases

A case may be reopened on motion of the debtor or other party in interest pursuant to § 350(b) of the Code [11 USCS § 350(b)]. In a chapter 7, 12, or 13 case a trustee shall not be appointed by the United States trustee unless the court determines that a trustee is necessary to protect the interests of creditors and the debtor or to insure efficient administration of the case.

(Amended Aug. 1, 1987; Aug. 1, 1991.)

Rule 5011. Withdrawal and Abstention from Hearing a Proceeding

(a) Withdrawal. A motion for withdrawal of a case or proceeding shall be heard by a district judge.

(b) Abstention from hearing a proceeding. A motion for abstention pursuant to 28 U.S.C. § 1334(c) shall be governed by Rule 9014 and shall be served on the parties to the proceeding.

(c) Effect of filing of motion for withdrawal or abstention. The filing of a motion for withdrawal of a case or proceeding or for abstention pursuant to 28 U.S.C. § 1334(c) shall not stay the administration of the case or any proceeding therein before the bankruptcy judge except that the bankruptcy judge may stay, on such terms and conditions as are proper, proceedings pending disposition of the motion. A motion for a stay ordinarily shall be presented first to the bankruptcy judge. A motion for a stay or relief from a stay filed in the district court shall state why it has not been presented to or obtained from the bankruptcy judge. Relief granted by the district judge shall be on such terms and conditions as the judge deems proper.

(Added Aug. 1, 1987; Aug. 1, 1991.)

Rule 5012. Agreements Concerning Coordination of Proceedings in Chapter 15 Cases

Approval of an agreement under § 1527(4) of the Code [11 USCS § 1527(4)] shall be sought by motion. The movant shall attach to the motion a copy of the proposed agreement or protocol and, unless the court directs otherwise, give at least 30 days' notice of any hearing on the motion by transmitting the motion to the United States trustee, and serving it on the debtor, all persons or bodies authorized to administer foreign proceedings of the debtor, all entities against whom provisional relief is being sought under § 1519 [11 USCS § 1519], all parties to litigation pending in the United States in which the debtor was a party at the time of the filing of the petition, and such other entities as the court may direct.

(As added Dec. 1, 2010.)

PART VI. COLLECTION AND LIQUIDATION OF THE ESTATE

Rule 6001. Burden of Proof As to Validity of Postpetition Transfer

Any entity asserting the validity of a transfer under § 549 of the Code [11 USCS § 549] shall have the burden of proof.

Rule 6002. Accounting by Prior Custodian of Property of the Estate

(a) Accounting required. Any custodian required by the Code to deliver property in the custodian's possession or control to the trustee shall promptly file and transmit to the United States trustee a report and account with respect to the property of the estate and the administration thereof.

(b) Examination of administration. On the filing and transmittal of the report and account required by subdivision (a) of this rule and after an examination has been made into the superseded administration, after notice and a hearing, the court shall determine the propriety of the administration, including the reasonableness of all disbursements.

(Amended Aug. 1, 1987; Aug. 1, 1991; Aug. 1, 1993.)

Rule 6003. Interim and Final Relief Immediately Following the Commencement of the Case—Applications for Employment; Motions for Use, Sale, or Lease of Property; and Motions for Assumption or Assignment of Executory Contracts

Except to the extent that relief is necessary to avoid immediate and irreparable harm, the court shall not, within 21 days after the filing of the petition, issue an order granting the following:

(a) an application under Rule 2014;

(b) a motion to use, sell, lease, or otherwise incur an obligation regarding property of the estate, including a motion to pay all or part of a claim that arose before the filing of the petition, but not a motion under Rule 4001; or

(c) a motion to assume or assign an executory contract or unexpired lease in accordance with § 365 [11 USCS § 365].

(As added Dec. 1, 2007; Dec. 1, 2009; Dec. 1, 2011.)

Rule 6004. Use, Sale, or Lease of Property

(a) Notice of proposed use, sale, or lease of property. Notice of a proposed use, sale, or lease of property, other than cash collateral, not in the ordinary course of business shall be given pursuant to Rule 2002(a)(2), (c)(1), (i), and (k) and, if applicable, in accordance with § 363(b)(2) of the Code [11 USCS § 363(b)(2)].

(b) Objection to proposal. Except as provided in subdivisions (c) and (d) of this rule, an objection to a proposed use, sale, or lease of property shall be filed and served not less than seven days before the date set for the proposed action or within the time fixed by the court. An objection to the proposed use, sale, or lease of property is governed by Rule 9014.

(c) Sale free and clear of liens and other interests. A motion for authority to sell property free and clear of liens or other interests shall be made in accordance with Rule 9014 and shall be served on the parties who have liens or other interests in the property to be sold. The notice required by subdivision (a) of this rule shall include the date of the hearing on the motion and the time within which objections may be filed and served on the debtor in possession or trustee.

(d) Sale of property under $2,500. Notwithstanding subdivision (a) of this rule, when all of the nonexempt property of the estate has an aggregate gross value less than $2,500, it shall be sufficient to give a general notice of intent to sell such property other than in the ordinary course of business to all creditors, indenture trustees, committees appointed or elected pursuant to the Code, the United States trustee and other persons as the court may direct. An objection to any such sale may be filed and served by a party in interest within 14 days of the mailing of the notice, or within the time fixed by the court. An objection is governed by Rule 9014.

(e) Hearing. If a timely objection is made pursuant to subdivision (b) or (d) of this rule, the date of the hearing thereon may be set in the notice given pursuant to subdivision (a) of this rule.

(f) Conduct of sale not in the ordinary course of business. (1) *Public or private sale.* All sales not in the ordinary course of business may be by private sale or by public auction. Unless it is impracticable, an itemized statement of the property sold, the name of each purchaser, and the price received for each item or lot or for the property as a whole if sold in bulk shall be filed on completion of a sale. If the property is sold by an auctioneer, the auctioneer shall file the statement, transmit a copy thereof to the United States trustee, and furnish a copy to the trustee, debtor in possession, or chapter 13 debtor. If the property is not sold by an auctioneer, the trustee, debtor in possession, or chapter 13 debtor shall file the statement and transmit a copy thereof to the United States trustee.

(2) *Execution of instruments.* After a sale in accordance with this rule the debtor, the trustee, or debtor in possession, as the case may be, shall execute any instrument necessary or ordered by the court to effectuate the transfer to the purchaser.

(g) Sale of personally identifiable information. (1) *Motion.* A motion for authority to sell or lease personally identifiable information under § 363(b)(1)(B) [11 USCS § 363(b)(1)(B)] shall include a request for an order directing the United States trustee to appoint a consumer privacy ombudsman under § 332 [11 USCS § 332]. Rule 9014 governs the motion which shall be served on: any committee elected under § 705 [11 USCS § 705] or appointed under § 1102 of the Code [11 USCS § 1102], or if the case is a chapter 11 reorganization case and no committee of unsecured creditors has been appointed under § 1102 [11 USCS § 1102], on the creditors included on the list of creditors filed under Rule 1007(d); and on such other entities as the court may direct. The motion shall be transmitted to the United States trustee.

(2) *Appointment.* If a consumer privacy ombudsman is appointed under § 332 [11 USCS § 332], no later than seven days before the hearing on the motion under § 363(b)(1)(B) [11 USCS § 363(b)(1)(B)], the United States trustee shall file a notice of the appointment, including the name and address of the person appointed. The United States trustee's notice shall be accompanied by a verified statement of the person appointed setting forth the person's connections with the debtor, creditors, any

other party in interest, their respective attorneys and accountants, the United States trustee, or any person employed in the office of the United States trustee.

(h) Stay of order authorizing use, sale, or lease of property. An order authorizing the use, sale, or lease of property other than cash collateral is stayed until the expiration of 14 days after entry of the order, unless the court orders otherwise.

(Amended Aug. 1, 1987; Aug. 1, 1991; Dec. 1, 1999; Dec. 1, 2008; Dec. 1, 2009.)

Rule 6005. Appraisers and Auctioneers

The order of the court approving the employment of an appraiser or auctioneer shall fix the amount or rate of compensation. No officer or employee of the Judicial Branch of the United States or the United States Department of Justice shall be eligible to act as appraiser or auctioneer. No residence or licensing requirement shall disqualify an appraiser or auctioneer from employment.

(Amended Aug. 1, 1991.)

Rule 6006. Assumption, Rejection or Assignment of an Executory Contract or Unexpired Lease

(a) Proceeding to assume, reject, or assign. A proceeding to assume, reject, or assign an executory contract or unexpired lease, other than as part of a plan, is governed by Rule 9014.

(b) Proceeding to require trustee to act. A proceeding by a party to an executory contract or unexpired lease in a chapter 9 municipality case, chapter 11 reorganization case, chapter 12 family farmer's debt adjustment case, or chapter 13 individual's debt adjustment case, to require the trustee, debtor in possession, or debtor to determine whether to assume or reject the contract or lease is governed by Rule 9014.

(c) Notice. Notice of a motion made pursuant to subdivision (a) or (b) of this rule shall be given to the other party to the contract or lease, to other parties in interest as the court may direct, and, except in a chapter 9 municipality case, to the United States trustee.

(d) Stay of order authorizing assignment. An order authorizing the trustee to assign an executory contract or unexpired lease under § 365(f) [11 USCS § 365(f)] is stayed until the expiration of 14 days after the entry of the order, unless the court orders otherwise.

(e) Limitations. The trustee shall not seek authority to assume or assign multiple executory contracts or unexpired leases in one motion unless: (1) all executory contracts or unexpired leases to be assumed or assigned are between the same parties or are to be assigned to the same assignee; (2) the trustee seeks to assume, but not assign to more than one assignee, unexpired leases of real property; or (3) the court otherwise authorizes the motion to be filed. Subject to subdivision (f), the trustee may join requests for authority to reject multiple executory contracts or unexpired leases in one motion.

(f) Omnibus motions. A motion to reject or, if permitted under subdivision (e), a motion to assume or assign multiple executory contracts or unexpired leases that are not between the same parties shall:

(1) state in a conspicuous place that parties receiving the omnibus motion should locate their names and their contracts or leases listed in the motion;

(2) list parties alphabetically and identify the corresponding contract or lease;

(3) specify the terms, including the curing of defaults, for each requested assumption or assignment;

(4) specify the terms, including the identity of each assignee and the adequate assurance of future performance by each assignee, for each requested assignment;

(5) be numbered consecutively with other omnibus motions to assume, assign, or reject executory contracts or unexpired leases; and

(6) be limited to no more than 100 executory contracts or unexpired leases.

(g) Finality of determination. The finality of any order respecting an executory contract or unexpired lease included in an omnibus motion shall be determined as though such contract or lease had been the subject of a separate motion.

(Amended Aug. 1, 1987; Aug. 1, 1991; Aug. 1, 1993; Dec. 1, 1999; Dec. 1, 2007; Dec. 1, 2009.)

Rule 6007. Abandonment or Disposition of Property

(a) Notice of proposed abandonment or disposition; objections; hearing. Unless otherwise directed by the court, the trustee or debtor in possession shall give notice of a proposed abandonment or disposition of property to the United States trustee, all creditors, indenture trustees, and committees elected pursuant to § 705 [11 USCS § 705] or appointed pursuant to § 1102 of the Code [11 USCS § 1102]. A party in interest may file and serve an objection within 14 days of the mailing of the notice, or within the time fixed by the court. If a timely objection is made, the court shall set a hearing on notice to the United States trustee and to other entities as the court may direct.

(b) Motion by party in interest. A party in interest may file and serve a motion requiring the trustee or debtor in possession to abandon property of the estate.

(c) [Abrogated]

(Amended Aug. 1, 1987; Aug. 1, 1991; Aug. 1, 1993; Dec. 1, 2009.)

Rule 6008. Redemption of Property from Lien or Sale

On motion by the debtor, trustee, or debtor in possession and after hearing on notice as the court may direct, the court may authorize the redemption of property from a lien or from a sale to enforce a lien in accordance with applicable law.

Rule 6009. Prosecution and Defense of Proceedings by Trustee or Debtor in Possession

With or without court approval, the trustee or debtor in possession may prosecute or may enter an appearance and defend any pending action or proceeding by or against the debtor, or commence and prosecute any action or proceeding in behalf of the estate before any tribunal.

Rule 6010. Proceeding to Avoid Indemnifying Lien or Transfer to Surety

If a lien voidable under § 547 of the Code [11 USCS § 547] has been dissolved by the furnishing of a bond or other obligation and the surety thereon has been indemnified by the transfer of, or the creation of a lien upon, nonexempt property of the debtor, the surety shall be joined as a defendant in any proceeding to avoid the indemnifying transfer or lien. Such proceeding is governed by the rules in Part VII.

(Amended Aug. 1, 1991.)

Rule 6011. Disposal of Patient Records in Health Care Business Case

(a) Notice by publication under § 351(1)(A). A notice regarding the claiming or disposing of patient records under § 351(1)(A) [11 USCS § 351(1)(A)]shall not identify any patient by name or other identifying information, but shall:

(1) identify with particularity the health care facility whose patient records the trustee proposes to destroy;

(2) state the name, address, telephone number, email address, and website, if any, of a person from whom information about the patient records may be obtained;

(3) state how to claim the patient records; and

(4) state the date by which patient records must be claimed, and that if they are not so claimed the records will be destroyed.

(b) Notice by mail under § 351(1)(B). Subject to applicable nonbankruptcy law relating to patient privacy, a notice regarding the claiming or disposing of patient records under § 351(1)(B) [11 USCS § 351(1)(B)] shall, in addition to including the information in subdivision (a), direct that a patient's family member or other representative who receives the notice inform the patient of the notice. Any notice under this subdivision shall be mailed to the patient and any family member or other contact person whose name and address have been given to the trustee or the debtor for the purpose of providing information regarding the patient's health care, to the Attorney General of the State where the health care facility is located, and to any insurance company known to have provided health care insurance to the patient.

(c) Proof of compliance with notice requirement. Unless the court orders the trustee to file proof of compliance with § 351(1)(B) [11 USCS § 351(1)(B)] under seal, the trustee shall not file, but shall maintain, the proof of compliance for a reasonable time.

(d) Report of destruction of records. The trustee shall file, no later than 30 days after the destruction of patient records under § 351(3) [11 USCS § 351(3)], a report certifying that the unclaimed records have been destroyed and explaining the method used to effect the destruction. The report shall not identify any patient by name or other identifying information.

(As added Dec. 1, 2008.)

PART VII. ADVERSARY PROCEEDINGS

Rule 7001. Scope of Rules of Part VII

An adversary proceeding is governed by the rules of this Part VII. The following are adversary proceedings:

(1) a proceeding to recover money or property, other than a proceeding to compel the debtor to deliver property to the trustee, or a proceeding under § 554(b) or § 725 of the Code [11 USCS § 554(b) or 725], Rule 2017, or Rule 6002;

(2) a proceeding to determine the validity, priority, or extent of a lien or other interest in property, other than a proceeding under Rule 4003(d);

(3) a proceeding to obtain approval under § 363(h) [11 USCS § 363(h)] for the sale of both the interest of the estate and of a co-owner in property;

(4) a proceeding to object to or revoke a discharge, other than an objection to discharge under §§ 727(a)(8), (a)(9), or 1328(f) [11 USCS § 727(a)(8), (a)(9), or 1328(f)];

(5) a proceeding to revoke an order of confirmation of a chapter 11, chapter 12, or chapter 13 plan;

(6) a proceeding to determine the dischargeability of a debt;

(7) a proceeding to obtain an injunction or other equitable relief, except when a chapter 9, chapter 11, chapter 12, or chapter 13 plan provides for the relief;

(8) a proceeding to subordinate any allowed claim or interest, except when a chapter 9, chapter 11, chapter 12, or chapter 13 plan provides for subordination;

(9) a proceeding to obtain a declaratory judgment relating to any of the foregoing; or

(10) a proceeding to determine a claim or cause of action removed under 28 U.S.C. § 1452.

(Amended Aug. 1, 1987; Aug. 1, 1991; Dec. 1, 1999; Dec. 1, 2010.)

Rule 7002. References to Federal Rules of Civil Procedure

Whenever a Federal Rule of Civil Procedure applicable to adversary proceedings makes reference to another Federal Rule of Civil Procedure, the reference shall be read as a reference to the Federal Rule of Civil Procedure as modified in this Part VII.

Rule 7003. Commencement of Adversary Proceeding

Rule 3 F.R.Civ.P. applies in adversary proceedings.

Rule 7004. Process; Service of Summons, Complaint

(a) Summons; service; proof of service. (1) Except as provided in Rule 7004(a)(2), Rule 4(a), (b), (c)(1), (d)(1), (e)–(j), (*l*), and (m) F. R. Civ. P. applies in adversary proceedings. Personal service under Rule 4(e)–(j) F. R. Civ. P. may be made by any person at least 18 years of age who is not a party, and the summons may be delivered by the clerk to any such person.

(2) The clerk may sign, seal, and issue a summons electronically by putting an "s/" before the clerk's name and including the court's seal on the summons.

(b) Service by first class mail. Except as provided in subdivision (h), in addition to the methods of service authorized by Rule 4(e)–(j) F.R.Civ.P., service may be made within the United States by first class mail postage prepaid as follows:

(1) Upon an individual other than an infant or incompetent, by mailing a copy of the summons and complaint to the individual's dwelling house or usual place of abode or to the place where the individual regularly conducts a business or profession.

(2) Upon an infant or an incompetent person, by mailing a copy of the summons and complaint to the person upon whom process is prescribed to be served by the law of the state in which service is made when an action is brought against such a defendant in the courts of general jurisdiction of that state. The summons and complaint in that case shall be addressed to the person required to be served at that person's dwelling house or usual place of abode or at the place where the person regularly conducts a business or profession.

(3) Upon a domestic or foreign corporation or upon a partnership or other unincorporated association, by mailing a copy of the summons and complaint to the attention of an officer, a managing or general agent, or to any other agent authorized by appointment or by law to receive service of process and, if the agent is one authorized by statute to receive service and the statute so requires, by also mailing a copy to the defendant.

(4) Upon the United States, by mailing a copy of the summons and complaint addressed to the civil process clerk at the office of the United States attorney for the district in which the action is brought and by mailing a copy of the summons and complaint to the Attorney General of the United States at Washington, District of Columbia, and in any action attacking the validity of an order of an officer or an agency of the United States not made a party, by also mailing a copy of the summons and complaint to that officer or agency. The court shall allow a reasonable time for service pursuant to this subdivision for the purpose of curing the failure to mail a copy of the summons and complaint to multiple officers, agencies, or corporations of the United States if the plaintiff has mailed a copy of the summons and complaint either to the civil process clerk at the office of the United States attorney or to the Attorney General of the United States.

(5) Upon any officer or agency of the United States, by mailing a copy of the summons and complaint to the United States as prescribed in paragraph (4) of this subdivision and also to the officer or agency. If the agency is a corporation, the mailing shall be as prescribed in paragraph (3) of this subdivision of this rule. The court shall allow a reasonable time for service pursuant to this subdivision for the purpose of curing the failure to mail a copy of the summons and complaint to multiple officers, agencies, or corporations of the United States if the plaintiff has mailed a copy of the summons and complaint either to the civil process clerk at the office of the United States attorney or to the Attorney General of the United States. If the United States trustee is the trustee in the case and service is made upon the United States trustee solely as trustee, service may be made as prescribed in paragraph (10) of this subdivision of this rule.

(6) Upon a state or municipal corporation or other governmental organization thereof subject to suit, by mailing a copy of the summons and complaint to the person or office upon whom process is prescribed to be served by the law of the state in which service is made when an action is brought against such a defendant in the courts of general jurisdiction of that state, or in the absence of the designation of any such person or office by state law, then to the chief executive officer thereof.

(7) Upon a defendant of any class referred to in paragraph (1) or (3) of this subdivision of this rule, it is also sufficient if a copy of the summons and complaint is mailed to the entity upon whom service is prescribed to be served by any statute of the United States or by the law of the state in which service is made when an action is brought against such a defendant in the court of general jurisdiction of that state.

(8) Upon any defendant, it is also sufficient if a copy of the summons and complaint is mailed to an agent of such defendant authorized by appointment or by law to receive service of process, at the agent's dwelling house or usual place of abode or at the place where the agent regularly carries on a business or profession and, if the authorization so requires, by mailing also a copy of the summons and complaint to the defendant as provided in this subdivision.

(9) Upon the debtor, after a petition has been filed by or served upon the debtor and until the case is

dismissed or closed, by mailing a copy of the summons and complaint to the debtor at the address shown in the petition or to such other address as the debtor may designate in a filed writing.

(10) Upon the United States trustee, when the United States trustee is the trustee in the case and service is made upon the United States trustee solely as trustee, by mailing a copy of the summons and complaint to an office of the United States trustee or another place designated by the United States trustee in the district where the case under the Code is pending.

(c) Service by publication. If a party to an adversary proceeding to determine or protect rights in property in the custody of the court cannot be served as provided in Rule 4(e)–(j) F.R.Civ.P. or subdivision (b) of this rule, the court may order the summons and complaint to be served by mailing copies thereof by first class mail, postage prepaid, to the party's last known address, and by at least one publication in such manner and form as the court may direct.

(d) Nationwide service of process. The summons and complaint and all other process except a subpoena may be served anywhere in the United States.

(e) Summons: time limit for service within the United States. Service made under Rule 4(e), (g), (h)(1), (i), or (j)(2) F.R.Civ.P. shall be by delivery of the summons and complaint within 7 days after the summons is issued. If service is by any authorized form of mail, the summons and complaint shall be deposited in the mail within 7 days after the summons is issued. If a summons is not timely delivered or mailed, another summons will be issued for service. This subdivision does not apply to service in a foreign country.

(f) Personal jurisdiction. If the exercise of jurisdiction is consistent with the Constitution and laws of the United States, serving a summons or filing a waiver of service in accordance with this rule or the subdivisions of Rule 4 F.R.Civ.P. made applicable by these rules is effective to establish personal jurisdiction over the person of any defendant with respect to a case under the Code or a civil proceeding arising under the Code, or arising in or related to a case under the Code.

(g) Service on debtor's attorney. If the debtor is represented by an attorney, whenever service is made upon the debtor under this Rule, service shall also be made upon the debtor's attorney by any means authorized under Rule 5(b) F. R. Civ. P.

(h) Service of process on an insured depository institution. Service on an insured depository institution (as defined in section 3 of the Federal Deposit Insurance Act) in a contested matter or adversary proceeding shall be made by certified mail addressed to an officer of the institution unless—

(1) the institution has appeared by its attorney, in which case the attorney shall be served by first class mail;

(2) the court orders otherwise after service upon the institution by certified mail of notice of an application to permit service on the institution by first class mail sent to an officer of the institution designated by the institution; or

(3) the institution has waived in writing its entitlement to service by certified mail by designating an officer to receive service.

(Amended Aug. 1, 1987; Aug. 1, 1991; Oct. 22, 1994, P. L. 103-394, Title I, § 114, 108 Stat. 4118; Dec. 1, 1996; Dec. 1, 1999; April 25, 2005, eff. Dec. 1, 2005; April 12, 2006, eff. Dec. 1, 2006; Dec. 1, 2009; April 25, 2014, eff. Dec. 1, 2014.)

Rule 7005. Service and Filing of Pleadings and Other Papers

Rule 5 F.R.Civ.P. applies in adversary proceedings.

Rule 7007. Pleadings Allowed

Rule 7 F.R.Civ.P. applies in adversary proceedings.

Rule 7007.1. Corporate Ownership Statement

(a) Required disclosure. Any corporation that is a party to an adversary proceeding, other than the debtor or a governmental unit, shall file two copies of a statement that identifies any corporation, other than a governmental unit, that directly or indirectly owns 10% or more of any class of the corporation's equity interests, or states that there are no entities to report under this subdivision.

(b) Time for filing. A party shall file the statement required under Rule 7007.1(a) with its first appearance, pleading, motion, response, or other request addressed to the court. A party shall file a supplemental statement promptly upon any change in circumstances that this rule requires the party to identify or disclose.

(As added Dec. 1, 2003; Dec. 1, 2007.)

Rule 7008. General Rules of Pleading

Rule 8 F.R.Civ.P. applies in adversary proceedings. The allegation of jurisdiction required by Rule 8(a) shall also contain a reference to the name, number, and chapter of the case under the Code to which the adversary proceeding relates and to the district and division where the case under the Code is pending. In an adversary proceeding before a bankruptcy judge, the complaint, counterclaim, cross-claim, or third-party complaint shall contain a statement that the proceeding is core or non-core and, if non-core, that the pleader does or does not consent to entry of final orders or judgment by the bankruptcy judge.

(Amended Aug. 1, 1987; April 25, 2014, eff. Dec. 1, 2014.)

Rule 7009. Pleading Special Matters

Rule 9 F.R.Civ.P. applies in adversary

proceedings.

Rule 7010. Form of Pleadings

Rule 10 F.R.Civ.P. applies in adversary proceedings, except that the caption of each pleading in such a proceeding shall conform substantially to the appropriate Official Form.

(Amended Aug. 1, 1991.)

Rule 7012. Defenses and Objections—When and How Presented—By Pleading or Motion—Motion for Judgment on the Pleadings

(a) When presented. If a complaint is duly served, the defendant shall serve an answer within 30 days after the issuance of the summons, except when a different time is prescribed by the court. The court shall prescribe the time for service of the answer when service of a complaint is made by publication or upon a party in a foreign country. A party served with a pleading stating a cross-claim shall serve an answer thereto within 21 days after service. The plaintiff shall serve a reply to a counterclaim in the answer within 21 days after service of the answer or, if a reply is ordered by the court, within 21 days after service of the order, unless the order otherwise directs. The United States or an officer or agency thereof shall serve an answer to a complaint within 35 days after the issuance of the summons, and shall serve an answer to a cross-claim, or a reply to a counterclaim, within 35 days after service upon the United States attorney of the pleading in which the claim is asserted. The service of a motion permitted under this rule alters these periods of time as follows, unless a different time is fixed by order of the court: (1) if the court denies the motion or postpones its disposition until the trial on the merits, the responsive pleading shall be served within 14 days after notice of the court's action; (2) if the court grants a motion for a more definite statement, the responsive pleading shall be served within 14 days after the service of a more definite statement.

(b) Applicability of Rule 12(b)–(i) F.R.Civ.P. Rule 12(b)–(i) F.R.Civ.P. applies in adversary proceedings. A responsive pleading shall admit or deny an allegation that the proceeding is core or non-core. If the response is that the proceeding is non-core, it shall include a statement that the party does or does not consent to entry of final orders or judgment by the bankruptcy judge. In non-core proceedings final orders and judgments shall not be entered on the bankruptcy judge's order except with the express consent of the parties.

(Amended Aug. 1, 1987; Dec. 1, 2008; Dec. 1, 2009.)

Rule 7013. Counterclaim and Cross-Claim

Rule 13 F.R.Civ.P. applies in adversary proceedings, except that a party sued by a trustee or debtor in possession need not state as a counterclaim any claim that the party has against the debtor, the debtor's property, or the estate, unless the claim arose after the entry of an order for relief. A trustee or debtor in possession who fails to plead a counterclaim through oversight, inadvertence, or excusable neglect, or when justice so requires, may by leave of court amend the pleading, or commence a new adversary proceeding or separate action.

(Amended Aug. 1, 1987.)

Rule 7014. Third-Party Practice

Rule 14 F.R.Civ.P. applies in adversary proceedings.

Rule 7015. Amended and Supplemental Pleadings

Rule 15 F.R.Civ.P. applies in adversary proceedings.

Rule 7016. Pre-Trial Procedure; Formulating Issues

Rule 16 F.R.Civ.P. applies in adversary proceedings.

Rule 7017. Parties Plaintiff and Defendant; Capacity

Rule 17 F.R.Civ.P. applies in adversary proceedings, except as provided in Rule 2010(b).

(Amended Aug. 1, 1991.)

Rule 7018. Joinder of Claims and Remedies

Rule 18 F.R.Civ.P. applies in adversary proceedings.

Rule 7019. Joinder of Persons Needed for Just Determination

Rule 19 F.R.Civ.P. applies in adversary proceedings, except that (1) if an entity joined as a party raises the defense that the court lacks jurisdiction over the subject matter and the defense is sustained, the court shall dismiss such entity from the adversary proceedings and (2) if an entity joined as a party properly and timely raises the defense of improper venue, the court shall determine, as provided in 28 U.S.C. § 1412, whether that part of the proceeding involving the joined party shall be transferred to another district, or whether the entire adversary proceeding shall be transferred to another district.

(Amended Aug. 1, 1987.)

Rule 7020. Permissive Joinder of Parties

Rule 20 F.R.Civ.P. applies in adversary proceedings.

Rule 7021. Misjoinder and Non-Joinder of Parties

Rule 21 F.R.Civ.P. applies in adversary proceedings.

Rule 7022. Interpleader

Rule 22(a) F.R.Civ.P. applies in adversary proceedings. This rule supplements — and does not limit — the joinder of parties allowed by Rule 7020.

(As amended Dec. 1, 2008.)

Rule 7023. Class Proceedings

Rule 23 F.R.Civ.P. applies in adversary proceedings.

Rule 7023.1. Derivative Actions

Rule 23.1 F.R.Civ.P. applies in adversary proceedings.

(As amended Dec. 1, 2008.)

Rule 7023.2. Adversary Proceedings Relating to Unincorporated Associations

Rule 23.2 F.R.Civ.P. applies in adversary proceedings.

Rule 7024. Intervention

Rule 24 F.R.Civ.P. applies in adversary proceedings.

Rule 7025. Substitution of Parties

Subject to the provisions of Rule 2012, Rule 25 F.R.Civ.P. applies in adversary proceedings.

Rule 7026. General Provisions Governing Discovery

Rule 26 F.R.Civ.P. applies in adversary proceedings.

Rule 7027. Depositions Before Adversary Proceedings or Pending Appeal

Rule 27 F.R.Civ.P. applies to adversary proceedings.

Rule 7028. Persons Before Whom Depositions May Be Taken

Rule 28 F.R.Civ.P. applies in adversary proceedings.

Rule 7029. Stipulations Regarding Discovery Procedure

Rule 29 F.R.Civ.P. applies in adversary proceedings.

Rule 7030. Depositions Upon Oral Examination

Rule 30 F.R.Civ.P. applies in adversary proceedings.

Rule 7031. Deposition Upon Written Questions

Rule 31 F.R.Civ.P. applies in adversary proceedings.

Rule 7032. Use of Depositions in Adversary Proceedings

Rule 32 F.R.Civ.P. applies in adversary proceedings.

Rule 7033. Interrogatories to Parties

Rule 33 F.R.Civ.P. applies in adversary proceedings.

Rule 7034. Production of Documents and Things and Entry Upon Land for Inspection and Other Purposes

Rule 34 F.R.Civ.P. applies in adversary proceedings.

Rule 7035. Physical and Mental Examination of Persons

Rule 35 F.R.Civ.P. applies in adversary proceedings.

Rule 7036. Requests for Admission

Rule 36 F.R.Civ.P. applies in adversary proceedings.

Rule 7037. Failure to Make Discovery: Sanctions

Rule 37 F.R.Civ.P. applies in adversary proceedings.

Rule 7040. Assignment of Cases for Trial

Rule 40 F.R.Civ.P. applies in adversary proceedings.

Rule 7041. Dismissal of Adversary Proceedings

Rule 41 F.R.Civ.P. applies in adversary proceedings, except that a complaint objecting to the debtor's discharge shall not be dismissed at the plaintiff's instance without notice to the trustee, the United States trustee, and such other persons as the court may direct, and only on order of the court containing terms and conditions which the court deems proper.

(Amended Aug. 1, 1991.)

Rule 7042. Consolidation of Adversary Proceedings; Separate Trials

Rule 42 F.R.Civ.P. applies in adversary proceedings.

Rule 7052. Findings by the Court

Rule 52 F. R. Civ. P. applies in adversary proceedings, except that any motion under subdivision (b) of that rule for amended or additional findings shall be filed no later than 14 days after entry of judgment. In these proceedings, the reference in Rule 52 F. R. Civ. P. to the entry of judgment under Rule 58 F. R. Civ. P. shall be read as a reference to the entry of a judgment or order under Rule 5003(a).

(As amended Dec. 1, 2009.)

Rule 7054. Judgments; Costs

(a) Judgments. Rule 54(a)–(c) F.R.Civ.P. applies in adversary proceedings.

(b) Costs; attorney's fees. (1) *Costs other than attorney's fees.* The court may allow costs to the prevailing party except when a statute of the United States or these rules otherwise provides. Costs against the United States, its officers and agencies shall be imposed only to the extent permitted by law. Costs may be taxed by the clerk on 14 days' notice; on motion served within seven days thereafter, the action of the clerk may be reviewed by the court. (2) *Attorney's fees.*

(A) Rule 54(d)(2)(A)–(C) and (E) F.R.Civ.P. applies in adversary proceedings except for the reference in Rule 54(d)(2)(C) to Rule 78.

(B) By local rule, the court may establish special procedures to resolve fee-related issues without extensive evidentiary hearings.

(Amended Dec. 1, 2012; Dec. 1, 2014.)

Rule 7055. Default

Rule 55 F.R.Civ.P. applies in adversary proceedings.

Rule 7056. Summary Judgment

Rule 56 F.R.Civ.P. applies in adversary proceedings, except that any motion for summary judgment must be made at least 30 days before the initial date set for an evidentiary hearing on any issue for which summary judgment is sought, unless a different time is set by local rule or the court orders otherwise.

(Amended Dec. 1, 2012.)

Rule 7058. Entering Judgment in Adversary Proceeding

Rule 58 F. R. Civ. P. applies in adversary proceedings. In these proceedings, the reference in Rule 58 F. R. Civ. P. to the civil docket shall be read as a reference to the docket maintained by the clerk under Rule 5003(a).

(As added Dec. 1, 2009.)

Rule 7062. Stay of Proceedings to Enforce a Judgment

Rule 62 F.R.Civ.P. applies in adversary proceedings.

(Amended Aug. 1, 1991; Dec. 1, 1999.)

Rule 7064. Seizure of Person or Property

Rule 64 F.R.Civ.P. applies in adversary proceedings.

Rule 7065. Injunctions

Rule 65 F.R.Civ.P. applies in adversary proceedings, except that a temporary restraining order or preliminary injunction may be issued on application of a debtor, trustee, or debtor in possession without compliance with Rule 65(c).

Rule 7067. Deposit in Court

Rule 67 F.R.Civ.P. applies in adversary proceedings.

Rule 7068. Offer of Judgment

Rule 68 F.R.Civ.P. applies in adversary proceedings.

Rule 7069. Execution

Rule 69 F.R.Civ.P. applies in adversary proceedings.

Rule 7070. Judgment for Specific Acts; Vesting Title

Rule 70 F.R.Civ.P. applies in adversary proceedings and the court may enter a judgment divesting the title of any party and vesting title in others whenever the real or personal property involved is within the jurisdiction of the court.

(Amended Aug. 1, 1987.)

Rule 7071. Process in Behalf of and Against Persons Not Parties

Rule 71 F.R.Civ.P. applies in adversary proceedings.

Rule 7087. Transfer of Adversary Proceeding

On motion and after a hearing, the court may transfer an adversary proceeding or any part thereof to another district pursuant to 28 U.S.C. § 1412, except as provided in Rule 7019(2).

(Amended Aug. 1, 1987.)

PART VIII. APPEALS TO DISTRICT COURT OR BANKRUPTCY APPELLATE PANEL

Rule 8001. Scope of Part VIII Rules; Definition of "BAP"; Method of Transmission

(a) General scope. These Part VIII rules govern the procedure in a United States district court and a bankruptcy appellate panel on appeal from a judgment, order, or decree of a bankruptcy court. They also govern certain procedures on appeal to a United States court of appeals under 28 U.S.C. § 158(d).

(b) Definition of "BAP". "BAP" means a bankruptcy appellate panel established by a circuit's judicial council and authorized to hear appeals from a bankruptcy court under 28 U.S.C. § 158.

(c) Method of transmitting documents. A document must be sent electronically under these Part VIII rules, unless it is being sent by or to an individual who is not represented by counsel or the court's governing rules permit or require mailing or other means of delivery.

(Amended Aug. 1, 1987; Aug. 1, 1991; Dec. 1, 1997; Dec. 1, 2008; Dec. 1, 2009; Dec. 1, 2014.)

Rule 8002. Time for Filing Notice of Appeal

(a) In general. (1) *Fourteen-day period.* Except as provided in subdivisions (b) and (c), a notice of appeal must be filed with the bankruptcy clerk within 14 days after entry of the judgment, order, or decree being appealed.

(2) *Filing before the entry of judgment.* A notice of appeal filed after the bankruptcy court announces a decision or order—but before entry of the judgment, order, or decree—is treated as filed on the date of and after the entry.

(3) *Multiple appeals.* If one party files a timely notice of appeal, any other party may file a notice of appeal within 14 days after the date when the first notice was filed, or within the time otherwise allowed by this rule, whichever period ends later.

(4) *Mistaken filing in another court.* If a notice of appeal is mistakenly filed in a district court, BAP, or court of appeals, the clerk of that court must state on the notice the date on which it was received and transmit it to the bankruptcy clerk. The notice of appeal is then considered filed in the bankruptcy court on the date so stated.

(b) Effect of a motion on the time to appeal. (1) *In general.* If a party timely files in the bankruptcy court any of the following motions, the time to file an appeal runs for all parties from the entry of the order disposing of the last such remaining motion:

(A) to amend or make additional findings under Rule 7052, whether or not granting the motion would alter the judgment;

(B) to alter or amend the judgment under Rule 9023;

(C) for a new trial under Rule 9023; or

(D) for relief under Rule 9024 if the motion is filed within 14 days after the judgment is entered.

(2) *Filing an appeal before the motion is decided.* If a party files a notice of appeal after the court announces or enters a judgment, order, or decree—but before it disposes of any motion listed in subdivision (b)(1)—the notice becomes effective when the order disposing of the last such remaining motion is entered.

(3) *Appealing the ruling on the motion.* If a party intends to challenge an order disposing of any motion listed in subdivision (b)(1)—or the alteration or amendment of a judgment, order, or decree upon the motion—the party must file a notice of appeal or an amended notice of appeal. The notice or amended notice must comply with Rule 8003 or 8004 and be filed within the time prescribed by this rule, measured from the entry of the order disposing of the last such remaining motion.

(4) *No additional fee.* No additional fee is required to file an amended notice of appeal.

(c) Appeal by an inmate confined in an institution. (1) *In general.* If an inmate confined in an institution files a notice of appeal from a judgment, order, or decree of a bankruptcy court, the notice is timely if it is deposited in the institution's internal mail system on or before the last day for filing. If the institution has a system designed for legal mail, the inmate must use that system to receive the benefit of this rule. Timely filing may be shown by a declaration in compliance with 28 U.S.C. § 1746 or by a notarized statement, either of which must set forth the date of deposit and state that first-class postage has been prepaid.

(2) *Multiple appeals.* If an inmate files under this subdivision the first notice of appeal, the 14-day period provided in subdivision (a)(3) for another party to file a notice of appeal runs from the date when the bankruptcy clerk dockets the first notice.

(d) Extending the time to appeal. (1) *When the time may be extended.* Except as provided in subdivision (d)(2), the bankruptcy court may extend the time to file a notice of appeal upon a party's motion that is filed: (A) within the time prescribed by this rule; or (B) within 21 days after that time, if the party shows excusable neglect.

(2) *When the time may not be extended.* The bankruptcy court may not extend the time to file a notice of appeal if the judgment, order, or decree appealed from:

(A) grants relief from an automatic stay under § 362, 922, 1201, or 1301 of the Code [11 USCS § 362, 922, 1201, or 1301];

(B) authorizes the sale or lease of property or the use of cash collateral under § 363 of the Code [11 USCS § 363];

(C) authorizes the obtaining of credit under § 364 of the Code [11 USCS § 364];

(D) authorizes the assumption or assignment of an executory contract or unexpired lease under § 365 of the Code [11 USCS § 365];

(E) approves a disclosure statement under § 1125 of the Code [11 USCS § 1125]; or

(F) confirms a plan under § 943, 1129, 1225, or 1325 of the Code [11 USCS § 943, 1129, 1225, or 1325].

(3) *Time limits on an extension.* No extension of time may exceed 21 days after the time prescribed by this rule, or 14 days after the order granting the motion to extend time is entered, whichever is later.

(Amended Aug. 1, 1987; Aug. 1, 1991; Aug. 1, 1994; Dec. 1, 1997; Dec. 1, 2009; Dec. 1, 2014.)

Rule 8003. Appeal as of Right—How Taken; Docketing the Appeal

(a) Filing the notice of appeal. (1) *In general.* An appeal from a judgment, order, or decree of a bankruptcy court to a district court or BAP under 28 U.S.C. § 158(a)(1) or (a)(2) may be taken only by filing a notice of appeal with the bankruptcy clerk within the time allowed by Rule 8002.

(2) *Effect of not taking other steps.* An appellant's failure to take any step other than the timely filing of a notice of appeal does not affect the validity of the appeal, but is ground only for the district court or BAP to act as it considers appropriate, including dismissing the appeal.

(3) *Contents.* The notice of appeal must:

(A) conform substantially to the appropriate Official Form;

(B) be accompanied by the judgment, order, or decree, or the part of it, being appealed; and

(C) be accompanied by the prescribed fee.

(4) *Additional copies.* If requested to do so, the appellant must furnish the bankruptcy clerk with enough copies of the notice to enable the clerk to comply with subdivision (c).

(b) Joint or consolidated appeals. (1) *Joint notice of appeal.* When two or more parties are entitled to appeal from a judgment, order, or decree of a bankruptcy court and their interests make joinder practicable, they may file a joint notice of appeal. They may then proceed on appeal as a single appellant.

(2) *Consolidating appeals.* When parties have separately filed timely notices of appeal, the district court or BAP may join or consolidate the appeals.

(c) Serving the notice of appeal. (1) *Serving parties and transmitting to the United States trustee.* The bankruptcy clerk must serve the notice of appeal on counsel of record for each party to the appeal, excluding the appellant, and transmit it to the United States trustee. If a party is proceeding pro se, the clerk must send the notice of appeal to the party's last known address. The clerk must note, on each copy, the date when the notice of appeal was filed.

(2) *Effect of failing to serve or transmit notice.* The bankruptcy clerk's failure to serve notice on a party or transmit notice to the United States trustee does not affect the validity of the appeal.

(3) *Noting service on the docket.* The clerk must note on the docket the names of the parties served and the date and method of the service.

(d) Transmitting the notice of appeal to the district court or BAP; docketing the appeal. (1) *Transmitting the Notice.* The bankruptcy clerk must promptly transmit the notice of appeal to the BAP clerk if a BAP has been established for appeals from that district and the appellant has not elected to have the district court hear the appeal. Otherwise, the bankruptcy clerk must promptly transmit the notice to the district clerk.

(2) *Docketing in the District Court or BAP.* Upon receiving the notice of appeal, the district or BAP clerk must docket the appeal under the title of the bankruptcy case and the title of any adversary proceeding, and must identify the appellant, adding the appellant's name if necessary.

(Amended Aug. 1, 1987; Dec. 1, 2008; Dec. 1, 2009; Dec. 1, 2014.)

Rule 8004. Appeal by Leave—How Taken; Docketing the Appeal

(a) Notice of appeal and motion for leave to appeal. To appeal from an interlocutory order or decree of a bankruptcy court under 28 U.S.C. § 158(a)(3), a party must file with the bankruptcy clerk a notice of appeal as prescribed by Rule 8003(a). The notice must:

(1) be filed within the time allowed by Rule 8002;

(2) be accompanied by a motion for leave to appeal prepared in accordance with subdivision (b); and

(3) unless served electronically using the court's transmission equipment, include proof of service in accordance with Rule 8011(d).

(b) Contents of the motion; response. (1) *Contents.* A motion for leave to appeal under 28 U.S.C. § 158(a)(3) must include the following:

(A) the facts necessary to understand the question presented;

(B) the question itself;

(C) the relief sought;

(D) the reasons why leave to appeal should be granted; and

(A) a copy of the interlocutory order or decree and any related opinion or memorandum.

(2) *Response.* A party may file with the district or BAP clerk a response in opposition or a cross-motion within 14 days after the motion is served.

(c) Transmitting the notice of appeal and the motion; docketing the appeal; determining the motion. (1) *Transmitting to the District Court or BAP.* The bankruptcy clerk must promptly transmit the notice of appeal and the motion for leave to the BAP clerk if a BAP has been established for appeals from that district and the appellant has not elected to have the district court hear the appeal. Otherwise, the bankruptcy clerk must promptly transmit the notice and motion to the district clerk.

(2) *Docketing in the District Court or BAP.* Upon receiving the notice and motion, the district or BAP clerk must docket the appeal under the title of the bankruptcy case and the title of any adversary proceeding, and must identify the appellant, adding the appellant's name if necessary.

(3) *Oral argument not required.* The motion and any response or cross-motion are submitted without oral argument unless the district court or BAP orders otherwise.

(d) Failure to file a motion with a notice of appeal. If an appellant timely files a notice of appeal under this rule but does not include a motion for leave, the district court or BAP may order the appellant to file a motion for leave, or treat the notice of appeal as a motion for leave and either grant or deny it. If the court orders that a motion for leave be filed, the appellant must do so within 14 days after the order is entered, unless the order provides otherwise.

(e) Direct appeal to a court of appeals. If leave to appeal an interlocutory order or decree is required under 28 U.S.C. § 158(a)(3), an authorization of a direct appeal by the court of appeals under 28 U.S.C. § 158(d)(2) satisfies the requirement.

(Amended Aug. 1, 1987; Aug. 1, 1991; Dec. 1, 2014.)

Rule 8005. Election to Have an Appeal Heard

by the District Court Instead of the BAP

(a) Filing of a statement of election. To elect to have an appeal heard by the district court, a party must:

(1) file a statement of election that conforms substantially to the appropriate Official Form; and

(2) do so within the time prescribed by 28 U.S.C. § 158(c)(1).

(b) Transmitting the documents related to the appeal. Upon receiving an appellant's timely statement of election, the bankruptcy clerk must transmit to the district clerk all documents related to the appeal. Upon receiving a timely statement of election by a party other than the appellant, the BAP clerk must transmit to the district clerk all documents related to the appeal and notify the bankruptcy clerk of the transmission.

(c) Determining the validity of an election. A party seeking a determination of the validity of an election must file a motion in the court where the appeal is then pending. The motion must be filed within 14 days after the statement of election is filed.

(d) Motion for leave without a notice of appeal—effect on the timing of an election. If an appellant moves for leave to appeal under Rule 8004 but fails to file a separate notice of appeal with the motion, the motion must be treated as a notice of appeal for purposes of determining the timeliness of a statement of election.

(Amended Aug. 1, 1987; Dec. 1, 2014.)

Rule 8006. Certifying a Direct Appeal to the Court of Appeals

(a) Effective date of a certification. A certification of a judgment, order, or decree of a bankruptcy court for direct review in a court of appeals under 28 U.S.C. § 158(d)(2) is effective when:

(1) the certification has been filed;

(2) a timely appeal has been taken under Rule 8003 or 8004; and

(3) the notice of appeal has become effective under Rule 8002.

(b) Filing the certification. The certification must be filed with the clerk of the court where the matter is pending. For purposes of this rule, a matter remains pending in the bankruptcy court for 30 days after the effective date under Rule 8002 of the first notice of appeal from the judgment, order, or decree for which direct review is sought. A matter is pending in the district court or BAP thereafter.

(c) Joint certification by all appellants and appellees. A joint certification by all the appellants and appellees under 28 U.S.C. § 158(d)(2)(A) must be made by using the appropriate Official Form. The parties may supplement the certification with a short statement of the basis for the certification, which may include the information listed in subdivision (f)(2).

(d) The court that may make the certification. Only the court where the matter is pending, as provided in subdivision (b), may certify a direct review on request of parties or on its own motion.

(e) Certification on the court's own motion. (1) *How accomplished.* A certification on the court's own motion must be set forth in a separate document. The clerk of the certifying court must serve it on the parties to the appeal in the manner required for service of a notice of appeal under Rule 8003(c)(1). The certification must be accompanied by an opinion or memorandum that contains the information required by subdivision (f)(2)(A)–(D).

(2) *Supplemental statement by a party.* Within 14 days after the court's certification, a party may file with the clerk of the certifying court a short supplemental statement regarding the merits of certification.

(f) Certification by the court on request. (1) *How requested.* A request by a party for certification that a circumstance specified in 28 U.S.C. § 158(d)(2)(A)(i)–(iii) applies—or a request by a majority of the appellants and a majority of the appellees—must be filed with the clerk of the court where the matter is pending within 60 days after the entry of the judgment, order, or decree.

(2) *Service and contents.* The request must be served on all parties to the appeal in the manner required for service of a notice of appeal under Rule 8003(c)(1), and it must include the following:

(A) the facts necessary to understand the question presented;

(B) the question itself;

(C) the relief sought;

(D) the reasons why the direct appeal should be allowed, including which circumstance specified in 28 U.S.C. § 158(d)(2)(A)(i)–(iii) applies; and

(E) a copy of the judgment, order, or decree and any related opinion or memorandum.

(3) *Time to file a response or a cross-request.* A party may file a response to the request within 14 days after the request is served, or such other time as the court where the matter is pending allows. A party may file a cross-request for certification within 14 days after the request is served, or within 60 days after the entry of the judgment, order, or decree, whichever occurs first.

(4) *Oral argument not required.* The request, cross-request, and any response are submitted without oral argument unless the court where the matter is pending orders otherwise.

(5) *Form and service of the certification.* If the court certifies a direct appeal in response to the request, it must do so in a separate document. The certification must be served on the parties to the appeal in the manner required for service of a notice of appeal under Rule 8003(c)(1).

(g) Proceeding in the court of appeals following a certification. Within 30 days after the date the certification becomes effective under subdivision (a), a request for permission to take a direct appeal to the court of appeals must be filed with the circuit clerk in accordance with F.R.App.P. 6(c).

(Amended Aug. 1, 1987; Aug. 1, 1991; Aug. 1, 1994; Dec. 1, 2009; Dec. 1, 2014.)

Rule 8007. Stay Pending Appeal; Bonds; Suspension of Proceedings

(a) Initial motion in the bankruptcy court. (1) *In general.* Ordinarily, a party must move first in the bankruptcy court for the following relief:

(A) a stay of a judgment, order, or decree of the bankruptcy court pending appeal;

(B) the approval of a supersedeas bond;

(C) an order suspending, modifying, restoring, or granting an injunction while an appeal is pending; or

(D) the suspension or continuation of proceedings in a case or other relief permitted by subdivision (e).

(2) *Time to file.* The motion may be made either before or after the notice of appeal is filed.

(b) Motion in the district court, the BAP, or the court of appeals on direct appeal. (1) *Request for relief.* A motion for the relief specified in subdivision (a)(1)—or to vacate or modify a bankruptcy court's order granting such relief—may be made in the court where the appeal is pending.

(2) *Showing or statement required.* The motion must:

(A) show that moving first in the bankruptcy court would be impracticable; or

(B) if a motion was made in the bankruptcy court, either state that the court has not yet ruled on the motion, or state that the court has ruled and set out any reasons given for the ruling.

(3) *Additional content.* The motion must also include:

(A) the reasons for granting the relief requested and the facts relied upon;

(B) affidavits or other sworn statements supporting facts subject to dispute; and

(C) relevant parts of the record.

(4) Serving Notice. The movant must give reasonable notice of the motion to all parties.

(c) Filing a bond or other security. The district court, BAP, or court of appeals may condition relief on filing a bond or other appropriate security with the bankruptcy court.

(d) Bond for a trustee or the United States. The court may require a trustee to file a bond or other appropriate security when the trustee appeals. A bond or other security is not required when an appeal is taken by the United States, its officer, or its agency or by direction of any department of the federal government.

(e) Continuation of proceedings in the bankruptcy court. Despite Rule 7062 and subject to the authority of the district court, BAP, or court of appeals, the bankruptcy court may:

(1) suspend or order the continuation of other proceedings in the case; or

(2) issue any other appropriate orders during the pendency of an appeal to protect the rights of all parties in interest.

(Amended Aug. 1, 1987; Aug. 1, 1991; Dec. 1, 2014.)

Rule 8008. Indicative Rulings

(a) Relief pending appeal. If a party files a timely motion in the bankruptcy court for relief that the court lacks authority to grant because of an appeal that has been docketed and is pending, the bankruptcy court may:

(1) defer considering the motion;

(2) deny the motion; or

(3) state that the court would grant the motion if the court where the appeal is pending remands for that purpose, or state that the motion raises a substantial issue.

(b) Notice to the court where the appeal is pending. The movant must promptly notify the clerk of the court where the appeal is pending if the bankruptcy court states that it would grant the motion or that the motion raises a substantial issue.

(c) Remand after an indicative ruling. If the bankruptcy court states that it would grant the motion or that the motion raises a substantial issue, the district court or BAP may remand for further proceedings, but it retains jurisdiction unless it expressly dismisses the appeal. If the district court or BAP remands but retains jurisdiction, the parties must promptly notify the clerk of that court when the bankruptcy court has decided the motion on remand.

(Amended Aug. 1, 1987; Dec. 1, 1996; Dec. 1, 2014.)

Rule 8009. Record on Appeal; Sealed Documents

(a) Designating the record on appeal; statement of the issues. (1) *Appellant.* (A) The appellant must file with the bankruptcy clerk and serve on the appellee a designation of the items to be included in the record on appeal and a statement of the issues to be presented.

(B) The appellant must file and serve the designation and statement within 14 days after:

(i) the appellant's notice of appeal as of right becomes effective under Rule 8002; or

(ii) an order granting leave to appeal is entered.

A designation and statement served prematurely must be treated as served on the first day on which filing is timely.

(2) *Appellee and cross-appellant.* Within 14 days after being served, the appellee may file with the bankruptcy clerk and serve on the appellant a designation of additional items to be included in the record. An appellee who files a cross-appeal must file and serve a designation of additional items to be included in the record and a statement of the issues to be presented on the cross-appeal.

(3) *Cross-appellee.* Within 14 days after service of the cross-appellant's designation and statement, a cross-appellee may file with the bankruptcy clerk and serve on the cross-appellant a designation of

additional items to be included in the record.

(4) *Record on appeal.* The record on appeal must include the following:

- docket entries kept by the bankruptcy clerk;
- items designated by the parties;
- the notice of appeal;
- the judgment, order, or decree being appealed;
- any order granting leave to appeal;
- any certification required for a direct appeal to the court of appeals;
- any opinion, findings of fact, and conclusions of law relating to the issues on appeal, including transcripts of all oral rulings;
- any transcript ordered under subdivision (b);
- any statement required by subdivision (c); and
- any additional items from the record that the court where the appeal is pending orders.

(5) *Copies for the bankruptcy clerk.* If paper copies are needed, a party filing a designation of items must provide a copy of any of those items that the bankruptcy clerk requests. If the party fails to do so, the bankruptcy clerk must prepare the copy at the party's expense.

(b) Transcript of proceedings. (1) *Appellant's duty to order.* Within the time period prescribed by subdivision (a)(1), the appellant must:

(A) order in writing from the reporter, as defined in Rule 8010(a)(1), a transcript of such parts of the proceedings not already on file as the appellant considers necessary for the appeal, and file a copy of the order with the bankruptcy clerk; or

(B) file with the bankruptcy clerk a certificate stating that the appellant is not ordering a transcript.

(2) *Cross-appellant's duty to order.* Within 14 days after the appellant files a copy of the transcript order or a certificate of not ordering a transcript, the appellee as cross-appellant must:

(A) order in writing from the reporter, as defined in Rule 8010(a)(1), a transcript of such additional parts of the proceedings as the cross-appellant considers necessary for the appeal, and file a copy of the order with the bankruptcy clerk; or

(B) file with the bankruptcy clerk a certificate stating that the cross-appellant is not ordering a transcript.

(3) *Appellee's or cross-appellee's right to order.* Within 14 days after the appellant or cross-appellant files a copy of a transcript order or certificate of not ordering a transcript, the appellee or cross-appellee may order in writing from the reporter a transcript of such additional parts of the proceedings as the appellee or cross-appellee considers necessary for the appeal. A copy of the order must be filed with the bankruptcy clerk.

(4) *Payment.* At the time of ordering, a party must make satisfactory arrangements with the reporter for paying the cost of the transcript.

(5) *Unsupported finding or conclusion.* If the appellant intends to argue on appeal that a finding or conclusion is unsupported by the evidence or is contrary to the evidence, the appellant must include in the record a transcript of all relevant testimony and copies of all relevant exhibits.

(c) Statement of the evidence when a transcript is unavailable. If a transcript of a hearing or trial is unavailable, the appellant may prepare a statement of the evidence or proceedings from the best available means, including the appellant's recollection. The statement must be filed within the time prescribed by subdivision (a)(1) and served on the appellee, who may serve objections or proposed amendments within 14 days after being served. The statement and any objections or proposed amendments must then be submitted to the bankruptcy court for settlement and approval. As settled and approved, the statement must be included by the bankruptcy clerk in the record on appeal.

(d) Agreed statement as the record on appeal. Instead of the record on appeal as defined in subdivision (a), the parties may prepare, sign, and submit to the bankruptcy court a statement of the case showing how the issues presented by the appeal arose and were decided in the bankruptcy court. The statement must set forth only those facts alleged and proved or sought to be proved that are essential to the court's resolution of the issues. If the statement is accurate, it—together with any additions that the bankruptcy court may consider necessary to a full presentation of the issues on appeal—must be approved by the bankruptcy court and must then be certified to the court where the appeal is pending as the record on appeal. The bankruptcy clerk must then transmit it to the clerk of that court within the time provided by Rule 8010. A copy of the agreed statement may be filed in place of the appendix required by Rule 8018(b) or, in the case of a direct appeal to the court of appeals, by F.R.App.P. 30.

(e) Correcting or modifying the record. (1) *Submitting to the bankruptcy court.* If any difference arises about whether the record accurately discloses what occurred in the bankruptcy court, the difference must be submitted to and settled by the bankruptcy court and the record conformed accordingly. If an item has been improperly designated as part of the record on appeal, a party may move to strike that item.

(2) *Correcting in other ways.* If anything material to either party is omitted from or misstated in the record by error or accident, the omission or misstatement may be corrected, and a supplemental record may be certified and transmitted:

(A) on stipulation of the parties;

(B) by the bankruptcy court before or after the record has been forwarded; or

(C) by the court where the appeal is pending.

(3) *Remaining questions.* All other questions as to the form and content of the record must be presented to the court where the appeal is pending.

(f) Sealed documents. A document placed under seal by the bankruptcy court may be designated as part of the record on appeal. In doing so, a party must identify it without revealing confidential or secret information, but the bankruptcy clerk must not transmit it to the clerk of the court where the appeal is pending as part of the record. Instead, a party must file a motion with the court where the appeal is pending to accept the document under seal. If the motion is granted, the movant must notify the bankruptcy court of the ruling, and the bankruptcy clerk must promptly transmit the sealed document to the clerk of the court where the appeal is pending.

(g) Other necessary actions. All parties to an appeal must take any other action necessary to enable the bankruptcy clerk to assemble and transmit the record.

(Amended Aug. 1, 1987; Dec. 1, 2009; Dec. 1, 2014.)

Rule 8010. Completing and Transmitting the Record

(a) Reporter's duties. (1) *Proceedings recorded without a reporter present.* If proceedings were recorded without a reporter being present, the person or service selected under bankruptcy court procedures to transcribe the recording is the reporter for purposes of this rule.

(2) *Preparing and filing the transcript.* The reporter must prepare and file a transcript as follows:

(A) Upon receiving an order for a transcript in accordance with Rule 8009(b), the reporter must file in the bankruptcy court an acknowledgment of the request that shows when it was received, and when the reporter expects to have the transcript completed.

(B) After completing the transcript, the reporter must file it with the bankruptcy clerk, who will notify the district, BAP, or circuit clerk of its filing.

(C) If the transcript cannot be completed within 30 days after receiving the order, the reporter must request an extension of time from the bankruptcy clerk. The clerk must enter on the docket and notify the parties whether the extension is granted.

(D) If the reporter does not file the transcript on time, the bankruptcy clerk must notify the bankruptcy judge.

(b) Clerk's duties. (1) *Transmitting the record—in general.* Subject to Rule 8009(f) and subdivision (b)(5) of this rule, when the record is complete, the bankruptcy clerk must transmit to the clerk of the court where the appeal is pending either the record or a notice that the record is available electronically.

(2) *Multiple appeals.* If there are multiple appeals from a judgment, order, or decree, the bankruptcy clerk must transmit a single record.

(3) *Receiving the record.* Upon receiving the record or notice that it is available electronically, the district, BAP, or circuit clerk must enter that information on the docket and promptly notify all parties to the appeal.

(4) *If paper copies are ordered.* If the court where the appeal is pending directs that paper copies of the record be provided, the clerk of that court must so notify the appellant. If the appellant fails to provide them, the bankruptcy clerk must prepare them at the appellant's expense.

(5) *When leave to appeal is requested.* Subject to subdivision (c), if a motion for leave to appeal has been filed under Rule 8004, the bankruptcy clerk must prepare and transmit the record only after the district court, BAP, or court of appeals grants leave.

(c) Record for a preliminary motion in the district court, BAP, or court of appeals. This subdivision (c) applies if, before the record is transmitted, a party moves in the district court, BAP, or court of appeals for any of the following relief:

- leave to appeal;
- dismissal;
- a stay pending appeal;
- approval of a supersedeas bond, or additional security on a bond or undertaking on appeal; or
- any other intermediate order.

The bankruptcy clerk must then transmit to the clerk of the court where the relief is sought any parts of the record designated by a party to the appeal or a notice that those parts are available electronically.

(Amended Dec. 1, 2014)

Rule 8011. Filing and Service; Signature

(a) Filing. (1) *With the clerk.* A document required or permitted to be filed in a district court or BAP must be filed with the clerk of that court.

(2) *Method and timeliness.* (A) In general. Filing may be accomplished by transmission to the clerk of the district court or BAP. Except as provided in subdivision (a)(2)(B) and (C), filing is timely only if the clerk receives the document within the time fixed for filing.

(B) Brief or appendix. A brief or appendix is also timely filed if, on or before the last day for filing, it is:

(i) mailed to the clerk by first-class mail—or other class of mail that is at least as expeditious—postage prepaid, if the district court's or BAP's procedures permit or require a brief or appendix to be filed by mailing; or

(ii) dispatched to a third-party commercial carrier for delivery within 3 days to the clerk, if the court's procedures so permit or require.

(C) Inmate filing. A document filed by an inmate confined in an institution is timely if deposited in the institution's internal mailing system on or before the last day for filing. If the institution has a system designed for legal mail, the inmate must use that system to receive the benefit of this rule. Timely filing may be shown by a declaration in compliance with 28 U.S.C. § 1746 or by a notarized statement, either of which must set forth the date of deposit and state that first-class postage has been prepaid.

(D) Copies. If a document is filed electronically, no paper copy is required. If a document is filed by mail or delivery to the district court or BAP, no additional copies are required. But the district court or BAP may require by local rule or by order in a particular case the filing or furnishing of a specified number of paper copies.

(3) *Clerk's refusal of documents.* The court's clerk must not refuse to accept for filing any document transmitted for that purpose solely because it is not presented in proper form as required by these rules or by any local rule or practice.

(b) Service of all documents required. Unless a rule requires service by the clerk, a party must, at or before the time of the filing of a document, serve it on the other parties to the appeal. Service on a party represented by counsel must be made on the party's counsel.

(c) Manner of service. (1) *Methods.* Service must be made electronically, unless it is being made by or on an individual who is not represented by counsel or the court's governing rules permit or require service by mail or other means of delivery. Service may be made by or on an unrepresented party by any of the following methods:

(A) personal delivery;

(B) mail; or

(C) third-party commercial carrier for delivery within 3 days.

(2) *When service is complete.* Service by electronic means is complete on transmission, unless the party making service receives notice that the document was not transmitted successfully. Service by mail or by commercial carrier is complete on mailing or delivery to the carrier.

(d) Proof of service. (1) *What is required.* A document presented for filing must contain either:

(A) an acknowledgment of service by the person served; or

(B) proof of service consisting of a statement by the person who made service certifying:

(i) the date and manner of service;

(ii) the names of the persons served; and

(iii) the mail or electronic address, the fax number, or the address of the place of delivery, as appropriate for the manner of service, for each person served.

(2) *Delayed proof.* The district or BAP clerk may permit documents to be filed without acknowledgment or proof of service, but must require the acknowledgment or proof to be filed promptly thereafter.

(3) *Brief or appendix.* When a brief or appendix is filed, the proof of service must also state the date and manner by which it was filed.

(e) Signature. Every document filed electronically must include the electronic signature of the person filing it or, if the person is represented, the electronic signature of counsel. The electronic signature must be provided by electronic means that are consistent with any technical standards that the Judicial Conference of the United States establishes. Every document filed in paper form must be signed by the person filing the document or, if the person is represented, by counsel.

(Amended Dec. 1, 2014)

Rule 8012. Corporate Disclosure Statement

(a) Who must file. Any nongovernmental corporate party appearing in the district court or BAP must file a statement that identifies any parent corporation and any publicly held corporation that owns 10% or more of its stock or states that there is no such corporation.

(b) Time to file; supplemental filing. A party must file the statement with its principal brief or upon filing a motion, response, petition, or answer in the district court or BAP, whichever occurs first, unless a local rule requires earlier filing. Even if the statement has already been filed, the party's principal brief must include a statement before the table of contents. A party must supplement its statement whenever the required information changes.

(As amended Dec. 1, 2014.)

Rule 8013. Motions; Intervention

(a) Contents of a motion; response; reply. (1) *Request for relief.* A request for an order or other relief is made by filing a motion with the district or BAP clerk, with proof of service on the other parties to the appeal.

(2) *Contents of a motion.* (A) Grounds and the relief sought. A motion must state with particularity the grounds for the motion, the relief sought, and the legal argument necessary to support it.

(B) Motion to expedite an appeal. A motion to expedite an appeal must explain what justifies considering the appeal ahead of other matters. If the district court or BAP grants the motion, it may accelerate the time to transmit the record, the deadline for filing briefs and other documents, oral argument, and the resolution of the appeal. A motion to expedite an appeal may be filed as an emergency motion under subdivision (d).

(C) Accompanying documents. (i) Any affidavit or other document necessary to support a motion must be served and filed with the motion.

(ii) An affidavit must contain only factual information, not legal argument.

(iii) A motion seeking substantive relief must include a copy of the bankruptcy court's judgment, order, or decree, and any accompanying opinion as a separate exhibit.

(D) Documents barred or not required. (i) A separate brief supporting or responding to a motion must not be filed.

(ii) Unless the court orders otherwise, a notice of motion or a proposed order is not required.

(3) *Response and reply; time to file.* Unless the district court or BAP orders otherwise,

(A) any party to the appeal may file a response to the motion within 7 days after service of the motion; and

(B) the movant may file a reply to a response within 7 days after service of the response, but may only address matters raised in the response.

(b) Disposition of a motion for a procedural order. The district court or BAP may rule on a motion for a procedural order—including a motion under Rule 9006(b) or (c)—at any time without awaiting a response. A party adversely affected by the ruling may move to reconsider, vacate, or modify it within 7 days after the procedural order is served.

(c) Oral argument. A motion will be decided without oral argument unless the district court or BAP orders otherwise.

(d) Emergency motion. (1) *Noting the emergency.* When a movant requests expedited action on a motion because irreparable harm would occur during the time needed to consider a response, the movant must insert the word "Emergency" before the title of the motion.

(2) *Contents of the motion.* The emergency motion must

(A) be accompanied by an affidavit setting out the nature of the emergency;

(B) state whether all grounds for it were submitted to the bankruptcy court and, if not, why the motion should not be remanded for the bankruptcy court to consider;

(C) include the e-mail addresses, office addresses, and telephone numbers of moving counsel and, when known, of opposing counsel and any unrepresented parties to the appeal; and

(D) be served as prescribed by Rule 8011.

(3) *Notifying opposing parties.* Before filing an emergency motion, the movant must make every practicable effort to notify opposing counsel and any unrepresented parties in time for them to respond. The affidavit accompanying the emergency motion must state when and how notice was given or state why giving it was impracticable.

(e) Power of a single BAP judge to entertain a motion. (1) *Single judge's authority.* A BAP judge may act alone on any motion, but may not dismiss or otherwise determine an appeal, deny a motion for leave to appeal, or deny a motion for a stay pending appeal if denial would make the appeal moot.

(2) *Reviewing a single judge's action.* The BAP may review a single judge's action, either on its own motion or on a party's motion.

(f) Form of documents; page limits; number of copies. (1) *Format of a paper document.* Rule 27(d)(1) F.R.App.P. applies in the district court or BAP to a paper version of a motion, response, or reply.

(2) *Format of an electronically filed document.* A motion, response, or reply filed electronically must comply with the requirements for a paper version regarding covers, line spacing, margins, typeface, and type style. It must also comply with the page limits under paragraph (3).

(3) *Page limits.* Unless the district court or BAP orders otherwise:

(A) a motion or a response to a motion must not exceed 20 pages, exclusive of the corporate disclosure statement and accompanying documents authorized by subdivision (a)(2)(C); and

(B) a reply to a response must not exceed 10 pages.

(4) *Paper copies.* Paper copies must be provided only if required by local rule or by an order in a particular case.

(g) Intervening in an appeal. Unless a statute provides otherwise, an entity that seeks to intervene in an appeal pending in the district court or BAP must move for leave to intervene and serve a copy of the motion on the parties to the appeal. The motion or other notice of intervention authorized by statute must be filed within 30 days after the appeal is docketed. It must concisely state the movant's interest, the grounds for intervention, whether intervention was sought in the bankruptcy court, why intervention is being sought at this stage of the proceeding, and why participating as an amicus curiae would not be adequate.

(Amended Aug. 1, 1987; Dec. 1, 2014.)

Rule 8014. Briefs

(a) Appellant's brief. The appellant's brief must contain the following under appropriate headings and in the order indicated:

(1) a corporate disclosure statement, if required by Rule 8012;

(2) a table of contents, with page references;

(3) a table of authorities—cases (alphabetically arranged), statutes, and other authorities—with references to the pages of the brief where they are cited;

(4) a jurisdictional statement, including:

(A) the basis for the bankruptcy court's subject-matter jurisdiction, with citations to applicable statutory provisions and stating relevant facts establishing jurisdiction;

(B) the basis for the district court's or BAP's jurisdiction, with citations to applicable statutory provisions and stating relevant facts establishing jurisdiction;

(C) the filing dates establishing the timeliness of the appeal; and

(D) an assertion that the appeal is from a final judgment, order, or decree, or information establishing the district court's or BAP's jurisdiction on another basis;

(5) a statement of the issues presented and, for each one, a concise statement of the applicable standard of appellate review;

(6) a concise statement of the case setting out the facts relevant to the issues submitted for review, describing the relevant procedural history, and identifying the rulings presented for review, with appropriate references to the record;

(7) a summary of the argument, which must contain a succinct, clear, and accurate statement of the arguments made in the body of the brief, and which must not merely repeat the argument headings;

(8) the argument, which must contain the appellant's contentions and the reasons for them, with citations to the authorities and parts of the record on which the appellant relies;

(9) a short conclusion stating the precise relief

sought; and

(10) the certificate of compliance, if required by Rule 8015(a)(7) or (b).

(b) Appellee's brief. The appellee's brief must conform to the requirements of subdivision (a)(1)–(8) and (10), except that none of the following need appear unless the appellee is dissatisfied with the appellant's statement:

(1) the jurisdictional statement;

(2) the statement of the issues and the applicable standard of appellate review; and

(3) the statement of the case.

(c) Reply brief. The appellant may file a brief in reply to the appellee's brief. A reply brief must comply with the requirements of subdivision (a)(2)–(3).

(d) Statutes, rules, regulations, or similar authority. If the court's determination of the issues presented requires the study of the Code or other statutes, rules, regulations, or similar authority, the relevant parts must be set out in the brief or in an addendum.

(e) Briefs in a case involving multiple appellants or appellees. In a case involving more than one appellant or appellee, including consolidated cases, any number of appellants or appellees may join in a brief, and any party may adopt by reference a part of another's brief. Parties may also join in reply briefs.

(f) Citation of supplemental authorities. If pertinent and significant authorities come to a party's attention after the party's brief has been filed—or after oral argument but before a decision—a party may promptly advise the district or BAP clerk by a signed submission setting forth the citations. The submission, which must be served on the other parties to the appeal, must state the reasons for the supplemental citations, referring either to the pertinent page of a brief or to a point argued orally. The body of the submission must not exceed 350 words. Any response must be made within 7 days after the party is served, unless the court orders otherwise, and must be similarly limited.

(Amended Aug. 1, 1987; Dec. 1, 2014.)

Rule 8015. Form and Length of Briefs; Form of Appendices and Other Papers

(a) Paper copies of a brief. If a paper copy of a brief may or must be filed, the following provisions apply: (1) *Reproduction.* (A) A brief may be reproduced by any process that yields a clear black image on light paper. The paper must be opaque and unglazed. Only one side of the paper may be used.

(B) Text must be reproduced with a clarity that equals or exceeds the output of a laser printer.

(C) Photographs, illustrations, and tables may be reproduced by any method that results in a good copy of the original. A glossy finish is acceptable if the original is glossy.

(2) *Cover.* The front cover of a brief must contain:

(A) the number of the case centered at the top;

(B) the name of the court;

(C) the title of the case as prescribed by Rule 8003(d)(2) or 8004(c)(2);

(D) the nature of the proceeding and the name of the court below;

(E) the title of the brief, identifying the party or parties for whom the brief is filed; and

(F) the name, office address, telephone number, and e-mail address of counsel representing the party for whom the brief is filed.

(3) *Binding.* The brief must be bound in any manner that is secure, does not obscure the text, and permits the brief to lie reasonably flat when open.

(4) *Paper size, line spacing, and margins.* The brief must be on 8½-by-11 inch paper. The text must be double-spaced, but quotations more than two lines long may be indented and single-spaced. Headings and footnotes may be single-spaced. Margins must be at least one inch on all four sides. Page numbers may be placed in the margins, but no text may appear there.

(5) *Typeface.* Either a proportionally spaced or monospaced face may be used.

(A) A proportionally spaced face must include serifs, but sans-serif type may be used in headings and captions. A proportionally spaced face must be 14-point or larger.

(B) A monospaced face may not contain more than 10½ characters per inch.

(6) *Type styles.* A brief must be set in plain, roman style, although italics or boldface may be used for emphasis. Case names must be italicized or underlined.

(7) *Length.* (A) Page limitation. A principal brief must not exceed 30 pages, or a reply brief 15 pages, unless it complies with (B) and (C).

(B) Type-volume limitation. (i) A principal brief is acceptable if:

- it contains no more than 14,000 words; or
- it uses a monospaced face and contains no more than 1,300 lines of text.

(ii) A reply brief is acceptable if it contains no more than half of the type volume specified in item (i).

(iii) Headings, footnotes, and quotations count toward the word and line limitations. The corporate disclosure statement, table of contents, table of citations, statement with respect to oral argument, any addendum containing statutes, rules, or regulations, and any certificates of counsel do not count toward the limitation.

(C) Certificate of compliance. (i) A brief submitted under subdivision (a)(7)(B) must include a certificate signed by the attorney, or an unrepresented party, that the brief complies with the type-volume limitation. The person preparing the certificate may rely on the word or line count of the word-processing system used to prepare the brief. The certificate must state either:

- the number of words in the brief; or
- the number of lines of monospaced type in the brief.

(ii) The certification requirement is satisfied by a certificate of compliance that conforms substantially to the appropriate Official Form.

(b) Electronically filed briefs. A brief filed electronically must comply with subdivision (a), except for (a)(1), (a)(3), and the paper requirement of (a)(4).

(c) Paper copies of appendices. A paper copy of an appendix must comply with subdivision (a)(1), (2), (3), and (4), with the following exceptions:

(1) An appendix may include a legible photocopy of any document found in the record or of a printed decision.

(2) When necessary to facilitate inclusion of odd-sized documents such as technical drawings, an appendix may be a size other than 8½-by-11 inches, and need not lie reasonably flat when opened.

(d) Electronically filed appendices. An appendix filed electronically must comply with subdivision (a)(2) and (4), except for the paper requirement of (a)(4).

(e) Other documents. (1) *Motion.* Rule 8013(f) governs the form of a motion, response, or reply.

(2) *Paper copies of other documents.* A paper copy of any other document, other than a submission under Rule 8014(f), must comply with subdivision (a), with the following exceptions:

(A) A cover is not necessary if the caption and signature page together contain the information required by subdivision (a)(2).

(B) Subdivision (a)(7) does not apply.

(3) *Other documents filed electronically.* Any other document filed electronically, other than a submission under Rule 8014(f), must comply with the appearance requirements of paragraph (2).

(f) Local variation. A district court or BAP must accept documents that comply with the applicable requirements of this rule. By local rule, a district court or BAP may accept documents that do not meet all of the requirements of this rule.

(Amended Aug. 1, 1987; Dec. 1, 2009; Dec. 1, 2014.)

Rule 8016. Cross-Appeals

(a) Applicability. This rule applies to a case in which a cross-appeal is filed. Rules 8014(a)–(c), 8015(a)(7)(A)–(B), and 8018(a)(1)–(3) do not apply to such a case, except as otherwise provided in this rule.

(b) Designation of appellant. The party who files a notice of appeal first is the appellant for purposes of this rule and Rule 8018(a)(4) and (b) and Rule 8019. If notices are filed on the same day, the plaintiff, petitioner, applicant, or movant in the proceeding below is the appellant. These designations may be modified by the parties' agreement or by court order.

(c) Briefs. In a case involving a cross-appeal:

(1) *Appellant's principal brief.* The appellant must file a principal brief in the appeal. That brief must comply with Rule 8014(a).

(2) *Appellee's principal and response brief.* The appellee must file a principal brief in the cross-appeal and must, in the same brief, respond to the principal brief in the appeal. That brief must comply with Rule 8014(a), except that the brief need not include a statement of the case unless the appellee is dissatisfied with the appellant's statement.

(3) *Appellant's response and reply brief.* The appellant must file a brief that responds to the principal brief in the cross-appeal and may, in the same brief, reply to the response in the appeal. That brief must comply with Rule 8014(a)(2)–(8) and (10), except that none of the following need appear unless the appellant is dissatisfied with the appellee's statement in the cross-appeal:

(A) the jurisdictional statement;

(B) the statement of the issues and the applicable standard of appellate review; and

(C) the statement of the case.

(4) Appellee's reply brief. The appellee may file a brief in reply to the response in the cross-appeal. That brief must comply with Rule 8014(a)(2)–(3) and (10) and must be limited to the issues presented by the cross-appeal.

(d) Length. (1) *Page limitation.* Unless it complies with paragraphs (2) and (3), the appellant's principal brief must not exceed 30 pages; the appellee's principal and response brief, 35 pages; the appellant's response and reply brief, 30 pages; and the appellee's reply brief, 15 pages.

(2) *Type-volume limitation.* (A) The appellant's principal brief or the appellant's response and reply brief is acceptable if:

(i) it contains no more than 14,000 words; or

(ii) it uses a monospaced face and contains no more than 1,300 lines of text.

(B) The appellee's principal and response brief is acceptable if:

(i) it contains no more than 16,500 words; or

(ii) it uses a monospaced face and contains no more than 1,500 lines of text.

(C) The appellee's reply brief is acceptable if it contains no more than half of the type volume specified in subparagraph (A).

(D) Headings, footnotes, and quotations count toward the word and line limitations. The corporate disclosure statement, table of contents, table of citations, statement with respect to oral argument, any addendum containing statutes, rules, or regulations, and any certificates of counsel do not count toward the limitation.

(3) *Certificate of compliance.* A brief submitted either electronically or in paper form under paragraph (2) must comply with Rule 8015(a)(7)(C).

(e) Time to serve and file a brief. Briefs must be served and filed as follows, unless the district court or BAP by order in a particular case excuses the filing of briefs or specifies different time limits: (1) the appellant's principal brief, within 30 days after the docketing of notice that the record has been transmitted or is available electronically; (2) the appellee's principal and response brief, within 30 days after the appellant's principal brief is served; (3) the appellant's response and reply brief, within 30 days after the appellee's principal and response brief is served; and (4) the appellee's reply brief, within 14 days after the appellant's response and reply brief is served, but at least 7 days before scheduled argument unless the district court or BAP, for good cause, allows a later filing.

(Amended Aug. 1, 1987; Aug. 1, 1991; Dec. 1, 2014.)

Rule 8017. Brief of an Amicus Curiae

(a) When permitted. The United States or its officer or agency or a state may file an amicus-curiae brief without the consent of the parties or leave of court. Any other amicus curiae may file a brief only by leave of court or if the brief states that all parties have consented to its filing. On its own motion, and with notice to all parties to an appeal, the district court or BAP may request a brief by an amicus curiae.

(b) Motion for leave to file. The motion must be accompanied by the proposed brief and state:

(1) the movant's interest; and

(2) the reason why an amicus brief is desirable and why the matters asserted are relevant to the disposition of the appeal.

(c) Contents and form. An amicus brief must comply with Rule 8015. In addition to the requirements of Rule 8015, the cover must identify the party or parties supported and indicate whether the brief supports affirmance or reversal. If an amicus curiae is a corporation, the brief must include a disclosure statement like that required of parties by Rule 8012. An amicus brief need not comply with Rule 8014, but must include the following:

(1) a table of contents, with page references;

(2) a table of authorities—cases (alphabetically arranged), statutes, and other authorities—with references to the pages of the brief where they are cited;

(3) a concise statement of the identity of the amicus curiae, its interest in the case, and the source of its authority to file;

(4) unless the amicus curiae is one listed in the first sentence of subdivision (a), a statement that indicates whether:

(A) a party's counsel authored the brief in whole or in part;

(B) a party or a party's counsel contributed money that was intended to fund preparing or submitting the brief; and

(C) a person—other than the amicus curiae, its members, or its counsel—contributed money that was intended to fund preparing or submitting the brief and, if so, identifies each such person;

(5) an argument, which may be preceded by a summary and need not include a statement of the applicable standard of review; and

(6) a certificate of compliance, if required by Rule 8015(a)(7)(C) or 8015(b).

(d) Length. Except by the district court's or BAP's permission, an amicus brief must be no more than one-half the maximum length authorized by these rules for a party's principal brief. If the court grants a party permission to file a longer brief, that extension does not affect the length of an amicus brief.

(e) Time for filing. An amicus curiae must file its brief, accompanied by a motion for filing when necessary, no later than 7 days after the principal brief of the party being supported is filed. An amicus curiae that does not support either party must file its brief no later than 7 days after the appellant's principal brief is filed. The district court or BAP may grant leave for later filing, specifying the time within which an opposing party may answer.

(f) Reply brief. Except by the district court's or BAP's permission, an amicus curiae may not file a reply brief.

(g) Oral argument. An amicus curiae may participate in oral argument only with the district court's or BAP's permission.

(As amended Dec. 1, 2009; Dec. 1, 2014.)

Rule 8018. Serving and Filing Briefs; Appendices

(a) Time to serve and file a brief. The following rules apply unless the district court or BAP by order in a particular case excuses the filing of briefs or specifies different time limits:

(1) The appellant must serve and file a brief within 30 days after the docketing of notice that the record has been transmitted or is available electronically.

(2) The appellee must serve and file a brief within 30 days after service of the appellant's brief.

(3) The appellant may serve and file a reply brief within 14 days after service of the appellee's brief, but a reply brief must be filed at least 7 days before scheduled argument unless the district court or BAP, for good cause, allows a later filing.

(4) If an appellant fails to file a brief on time or within an extended time authorized by the district court or BAP, an appellee may move to dismiss the appeal—or the district court or BAP, after notice, may dismiss the appeal on its own motion. An appellee who fails to file a brief will not be heard at oral argument unless the district court or BAP grants permission.

(b) Duty to serve and file an appendix to the brief. (1) *Appellant.* Subject to subdivision (e) and Rule 8009(d), the appellant must serve and file with its principal brief excerpts of the record as an appendix. It must contain the following:

(A) the relevant entries in the bankruptcy docket;

(B) the complaint and answer, or other equivalent filings;

(C) the judgment, order, or decree from which the appeal is taken;

(D) any other orders, pleadings, jury instructions,

findings, conclusions, or opinions relevant to the appeal;

(E) the notice of appeal; and

(F) any relevant transcript or portion of it.

(2) *Appellee.* The appellee may also serve and file with its brief an appendix that contains material required to be included by the appellant or relevant to the appeal or cross-appeal, but omitted by the appellant.

(3) *Cross-appellee.* The appellant as cross-appellee may also serve and file with its response an appendix that contains material relevant to matters raised initially by the principal brief in the cross-appeal, but omitted by the cross-appellant.

(c) Format of the appendix. The appendix must begin with a table of contents identifying the page at which each part begins. The relevant docket entries must follow the table of contents. Other parts of the record must follow chronologically. When pages from the transcript of proceedings are placed in the appendix, the transcript page numbers must be shown in brackets immediately before the included pages. Omissions in the text of documents or of the transcript must be indicated by asterisks. Immaterial formal matters (captions, subscriptions, acknowledgments, and the like) should be omitted.

(d) Exhibits. Exhibits designated for inclusion in the appendix may be reproduced in a separate volume or volumes, suitably indexed.

(e) Appeal on the original record without an appendix. The district court or BAP may, either by rule for all cases or classes of cases or by order in a particular case, dispense with the appendix and permit an appeal to proceed on the original record, with the submission of any relevant parts of the record that the district court or BAP orders the parties to file.

(Amended Dec. 1, 1995; Dec. 1, 2014.)

Rule 8019. Oral Argument

(a) Party's statement. Any party may file, or a district court or BAP may require, a statement explaining why oral argument should, or need not, be permitted.

(b) Presumption of oral argument and exceptions. Oral argument must be allowed in every case unless the district judge—or all the BAP judges assigned to hear the appeal—examine the briefs and record and determine that oral argument is unnecessary because

(1) the appeal is frivolous;

(2) the dispositive issue or issues have been authoritatively decided; or

(3) the facts and legal arguments are adequately presented in the briefs and record, and the decisional process would not be significantly aided by oral argument.

(c) Notice of argument; postponement. The district court or BAP must advise all parties of the date, time, and place for oral argument, and the time allowed for each side. A motion to postpone the argument or to allow longer argument must be filed reasonably in advance of the hearing date.

(d) Order and contents of argument. The appellant opens and concludes the argument. Counsel must not read at length from briefs, the record, or authorities.

(e) Cross-appeals and separate appeals. If there is a cross-appeal, Rule 8016(b) determines which party is the appellant and which is the appellee for the purposes of oral argument. Unless the district court or BAP directs otherwise, a cross-appeal or separate appeal must be argued when the initial appeal is argued. Separate parties should avoid duplicative argument.

(f) Nonappearance of a party. If the appellee fails to appear for argument, the district court or BAP may hear the appellant's argument. If the appellant fails to appear for argument, the district court or BAP may hear the appellee's argument. If neither party appears, the case will be decided on the briefs unless the district court or BAP orders otherwise.

(g) Submission on briefs. The parties may agree to submit a case for decision on the briefs, but the district court or BAP may direct that the case be argued.

(h) Use of physical exhibits at argument; removal. Counsel intending to use physical exhibits other than documents at the argument must arrange to place them in the courtroom on the day of the argument before the court convenes. After the argument, counsel must remove the exhibits from the courtroom unless the district court or BAP directs otherwise. The clerk may destroy or dispose of the exhibits if counsel does not reclaim them within a reasonable time after the clerk gives notice to remove them.

(Amended Aug. 1, 1987; Dec. 1, 2014.)

Rule 8020. Frivolous Appeal and Other Misconduct

(a) Frivolous appeal—damages and costs. If the district court or BAP determines that an appeal is frivolous, it may, after a separately filed motion or notice from the court and reasonable opportunity to respond, award just damages and single or double costs to the appellee.

(b) Other misconduct. The district court or BAP may discipline or sanction an attorney or party appearing before it for other misconduct, including failure to comply with any court order. First, however, the court must afford the attorney or party reasonable notice, an opportunity to show cause to the contrary, and, if requested, a hearing.

(Added Dec. 1, 1997; Dec. 1, 2014.)

Rule 8021. Costs

(a) Against whom assessed. The following rules apply unless the law provides or the district court or BAP orders otherwise:

(1) if an appeal is dismissed, costs are taxed

against the appellant, unless the parties agree otherwise;

(2) if a judgment, order, or decree is affirmed, costs are taxed against the appellant;

(3) if a judgment, order, or decree is reversed, costs are taxed against the appellee;

(4) if a judgment, order, or decree is affirmed or reversed in part, modified, or vacated, costs are taxed only as the district court or BAP orders.

(b) Costs for and against the United States. Costs for or against the United States, its agency, or its officer may be assessed under subdivision (a) only if authorized by law.

(c) Costs on appeal taxable in the bankruptcy court. The following costs on appeal are taxable in the bankruptcy court for the benefit of the party entitled to costs under this rule:

(1) the production of any required copies of a brief, appendix, exhibit, or the record;

(2) the preparation and transmission of the record;

(3) the reporter's transcript, if needed to determine the appeal;

(4) premiums paid for a supersedeas bond or other bonds to preserve rights pending appeal; and

(5) the fee for filing the notice of appeal.

(d) Bill of costs; objections. A party who wants costs taxed must, within 14 days after entry of judgment on appeal, file with the bankruptcy clerk, with proof of service, an itemized and verified bill of costs. Objections must be filed within 14 days after service of the bill of costs, unless the bankruptcy court extends the time.

(Added Dec. 1, 2014.)

Rule 8022. Motion for Rehearing

(a) Time to file; contents; response; action by the district court or BAP if granted.

(1) *Time.* Unless the time is shortened or extended by order or local rule, any motion for rehearing by the district court or BAP must be filed within 14 days after entry of judgment on appeal.

(2) *Contents.* The motion must state with particularity each point of law or fact that the movant believes the district court or BAP has overlooked or misapprehended and must argue in support of the motion. Oral argument is not permitted.

(3) *Response.* Unless the district court or BAP requests, no response to a motion for rehearing is permitted. But ordinarily, rehearing will not be granted in the absence of such a request.

(4) *Action by the district court or BAP.* If a motion for rehearing is granted, the district court or BAP may do any of the following:

(A) make a final disposition of the appeal without reargument;

(B) restore the case to the calendar for reargument or resubmission; or

(C) issue any other appropriate order.

(b) Form of the motion; length. The motion must comply in form with Rule 8013(f)(1) and (2). Copies must be served and filed as provided by Rule 8011. Unless the district court or BAP orders otherwise, a motion for rehearing must not exceed 15 pages.

(Added Dec. 1, 2014.)

Rule 8023. Voluntary Dismissal

The clerk of the district court or BAP must dismiss an appeal if the parties file a signed dismissal agreement specifying how costs are to be paid and pay any fees that are due. An appeal may be dismissed on the appellant's motion on terms agreed to by the parties or fixed by the district court or BAP.

(Added Dec. 1, 2014.)

Rule 8024. Clerk's Duties on Disposition of the Appeal

(a) Judgment on appeal. The district or BAP clerk must prepare, sign, and enter the judgment after receiving the court's opinion or, if there is no opinion, as the court instructs. Noting the judgment on the docket constitutes entry of judgment.

(b) Notice of a judgment. Immediately upon the entry of a judgment, the district or BAP clerk must:

(1) transmit a notice of the entry to each party to the appeal, to the United States trustee, and to the bankruptcy clerk, together with a copy of any opinion; and

(2) note the date of the transmission on the docket.

(c) Returning physical items. If any physical items were transmitted as the record on appeal, they must be returned to the bankruptcy clerk on disposition of the appeal.

(Added Dec. 1, 2014.)

Rule 8025. Stay of a District Court or BAP Judgment

(a) Automatic stay of judgment on appeal. Unless the district court or BAP orders otherwise, its judgment is stayed for 14 days after entry.

(b) Stay pending appeal to the court of appeals. (1) *In general.* On a party's motion and notice to all other parties to the appeal, the district court or BAP may stay its judgment pending an appeal to the court of appeals.

(2) *Time limit.* The stay must not exceed 30 days after the judgment is entered, except for cause shown.

(3) *Stay continued.* If, before a stay expires, the party who obtained the stay appeals to the court of appeals, the stay continues until final disposition by the court of appeals.

(4) *Bond or other security.* A bond or other security may be required as a condition for granting or continuing a stay of the judgment. A bond or other security may be required if a trustee obtains a stay, but not if a stay is obtained by the United States or its officer or agency or at the direction of any department of the United States government.

(c) Automatic stay of an order, judgment, or

decree of a bankruptcy court. If the district court or BAP enters a judgment affirming an order, judgment, or decree of the bankruptcy court, a stay of the district court's or BAP's judgment automatically stays the bankruptcy court's order, judgment, or decree for the duration of the appellate stay.

(d) Power of a court of appeals not limited. This rule does not limit the power of a court of appeals or any of its judges to do the following:

(1) stay a judgment pending appeal;

(2) stay proceedings while an appeal is pending;

(3) suspend, modify, restore, vacate, or grant a stay or an injunction while an appeal is pending; or

(4) issue any order appropriate to preserve the status quo or the effectiveness of any judgment to be entered.

(Added Dec. 1, 2014.)

Rule 8026. Rules by Circuit Councils and District Courts; Procedure When There is No Controlling Law

(a) Local rules by circuit councils and district courts. (1) *Adopting local rules.* A circuit council that has authorized a BAP under 28 U.S.C. § 158(b) may make and amend rules governing the practice and procedure on appeal from a judgment, order, or decree of a bankruptcy court to the BAP. A district court may make and amend rules governing the practice and procedure on appeal from a judgment, order, or decree of a bankruptcy court to the district court. Local rules must be consistent with, but not duplicative of, Acts of Congress and these Part VIII rules. Rule 83 F.R.Civ.P. governs the procedure for making and amending rules to govern appeals.

(2) *Numbering.* Local rules must conform to any uniform numbering system prescribed by the Judicial Conference of the United States.

(3) *Limitation on imposing requirements of form.* A local rule imposing a requirement of form must not be enforced in a way that causes a party to lose any right because of a nonwillful failure to comply.

(b) Procedure when there is no controlling law. (1) *In general.* A district court or BAP may regulate practice in any manner consistent with federal law, applicable federal rules, the Official Forms, and local rules.

(2) *Limitation on sanctions.* No sanction or other disadvantage may be imposed for noncompliance with any requirement not in federal law, applicable federal rules, the Official Forms, or local rules unless the alleged violator has been furnished in the particular case with actual notice of the requirement.

(Added Dec. 1, 2014.)

Rule 8027. Notice of a Mediation Procedure

If the district court or BAP has a mediation procedure applicable to bankruptcy appeals, the clerk must notify the parties promptly after docketing the appeal of:

(a) the requirements of the mediation procedure; and

(b) any effect the mediation procedure has on the time to file briefs.

(Added Dec. 1, 2014.)

Rule 8028. Suspension of Rules in Part VIII

In the interest of expediting decision or for other cause in a particular case, the district court or BAP, or where appropriate the court of appeals, may suspend the requirements or provisions of the rules in Part VIII, except Rules 8001, 8002, 8003, 8004, 8005, 8006, 8007, 8012, 8020, 8024, 8025, 8026, and 8028.

(Added Dec. 1, 2014.)

PART IX. GENERAL PROVISIONS

Rule 9001. General Definitions

The definitions of words and phrases in §§ 101, 902, 1101, and 1502 of the Code [11 USCS §§ 101, 902, 1101, and 1502], and the rules of construction in § 102 [11 USCS § 102], govern their use in these rules. In addition, the following words and phrases used in these rules have the meanings indicated:

(1) "Bankruptcy clerk" means a clerk appointed pursuant to 28 U.S.C. § 156(b).

(2) "Bankruptcy Code" or "Code" means title 11 of the United States Code.

(3) "Clerk" means bankruptcy clerk, if one has been appointed, otherwise clerk of the district court.

(4) "Court" or "judge" means the judicial officer before whom a case or proceeding is pending.

(5) "Debtor." When any act is required by these rules to be performed by a debtor or when it is necessary to compel attendance of a debtor for examination and the debtor is not a natural person: (A) if the debtor is a corporation, "debtor" includes, if designated by the court, any or all of its officers, members of its board of directors or trustees or of a similar controlling body, a controlling stockholder or member, or any other person in control; (B) if the debtor is a partnership, "debtor" includes any or all of its general partners or, if designated by the court, any other person in control.

(6) "Firm" includes a partnership or professional corporation of attorneys or accountants.

(7) "Judgment" means any appealable order.

(8) "Mail" means first class, postage prepaid.

(9) "Notice provider" means any entity approved by the Administrative Office of the United States Courts to give notice to creditors under Rule 2002(g)(4).

(10) "Regular associate" means any attorney regularly employed by, associated with, or counsel to an individual or firm.

(11) "Trustee" includes a debtor in possession in a chapter 11 case.

(12) "United States trustee" includes an assistant

United States trustee and any designee of the United States trustee.

(Amended Aug. 1, 1987; Aug. 1, 1991; Dec. 1, 2005; Dec. 1, 2010.)

Rule 9002. Meanings of Words in the Federal Rules of Civil Procedure When Applicable to Cases Under The Code

The following words and phrases used in the Federal Rules of Civil Procedure made applicable to cases under the Code by these rules have the meanings indicated unless they are inconsistent with the context:

(1) "Action" or "civil action" means an adversary proceeding or, when appropriate, a contested petition, or proceedings to vacate an order for relief or to determine any other contested matter.

(2) "Appeal" means an appeal as provided by 28 U.S.C. § 158.

(3) "Clerk" or "clerk of the district court" means the court officer responsible for the bankruptcy records in the district.

(4) "District court," "trial court," "court," "district judge," or "judge" means bankruptcy judge if the case or proceeding is pending before a bankruptcy judge.

(5) "Judgment" includes any order appealable to an appellate court.

(Amended Aug. 1, 1987; Aug. 1, 1993.)

Rule 9003. Prohibition of Ex Parte Contacts

(a) General prohibition. Except as otherwise permitted by applicable law, any examiner, any party in interest, and any attorney, accountant, or employee of a party in interest shall refrain from ex parte meetings and communications with the court concerning matters affecting a particular case or proceeding.

(b) United States trustee. Except as otherwise permitted by applicable law, the United States trustee and assistants to and employees or agents of the United States trustee shall refrain from ex parte meetings and communications with the court concerning matters affecting a particular case or proceeding. This rule does not preclude communications with the court to discuss general problems of administration and improvement of bankruptcy administration, including the operation of the United States trustee system.

(Amended Aug. 1, 1987; Aug. 1, 1991.)

Rule 9004. General Requirements of Form

(a) Legibility; abbreviations. All petitions, pleadings, schedules and other papers shall be clearly legible. Abbreviations in common use in the English language may be used.

(b) Caption. Each paper filed shall contain a caption setting forth the name of the court, the title of the case, the bankruptcy docket number, and a brief designation of the character of the paper.

Rule 9005. Harmless Error

Rule 61 F.R.Civ.P. applies in cases under the Code. When appropriate, the court may order the correction of any error or defect or the cure of any omission which does not affect substantial rights.

Rule 9005.1. Constitutional Challenge to a Statute—Notice, Certification, and Intervention

Rule 5.1 F. R. Civ. P. applies in cases under the Code.

(As added Dec. 1, 2007.)

Rule 9006. Computing and Extending Time; Time for Motion Papers

(a) Computing Time. The following rules apply in computing any time period specified in these rules, in the Federal Rules of Civil Procedure, in any local rule or court order, or in any statute that does not specify a method of computing time.

(1) *Period stated in days or a longer unit.* When the period is stated in days or a longer unit of time:

(A) exclude the day of the event that triggers the period;

(B) count every day, including intermediate Saturdays, Sundays, and legal holidays; and

(C) include the last day of the period, but if the last day is a Saturday, Sunday, or legal holiday, the period continues to run until the end of the next day that is not a Saturday, Sunday, or legal holiday.

(2) *Period stated in hours.* When the period is stated in hours:

(A) begin counting immediately on the occurrence of the event that triggers the period;

(B) count every hour, including hours during intermediate Saturdays, Sundays, and legal holidays; and

(C) if the period would end on a Saturday, Sunday, or legal holiday, then continue the period until the same time on the next day that is not a Saturday, Sunday, or legal holiday.

(3) *Inaccessibility of clerk's office.* Unless the court orders otherwise, if the clerk's office is inaccessible:

(A) on the last day for filing under Rule 9006(a)(1), then the time for filing is extended to the first accessible day that is not a Saturday, Sunday, or legal holiday; or

(B) during the last hour for filing under Rule 9006(a)(2), then the time for filing is extended to the same time on the first accessible day that is not a Saturday, Sunday, or legal holiday.

(4) *"Last day" defined.* Unless a different time is set by a statute, local rule, or order in the case, the last day ends:

(A) for electronic filing, at midnight in the court's time zone; and

(B) for filing by other means, when the clerk's office is scheduled to close.

(5) *"Next day" defined.* The "next day" is determined by continuing to count forward when the period is measured after an event and backward

when measured before an event.

(6) *"Legal holiday" defined.* "Legal holiday" means:

(A) the day set aside by statute for observing New Year's Day, Martin Luther King Jr.'s Birthday, Washington's Birthday, Memorial Day, Independence Day, Labor Day, Columbus Day, Veterans' Day, Thanksgiving Day, or Christmas Day;

(B) any day declared a holiday by the President or Congress; and

(C) for periods that are measured after an event, any other day declared a holiday by the state where the district court is located. (In this rule, "state" includes the District of Columbia and any United States commonwealth or territory.)

(b) Enlargement. (1) *In general.* Except as provided in paragraphs (2) and (3) of this subdivision, when an act is required or allowed to be done at or within a specified period by these rules or by a notice given thereunder or by order of court, the court for cause shown may at any time in its discretion (1) with or without motion or notice order the period enlarged if the request therefor is made before the expiration of the period originally prescribed or as extended by a previous order or (2) on motion made after the expiration of the specified period permit the act to be done where the failure to act was the result of excusable neglect.

(2) *Enlargement not permitted.* The court may not enlarge the time for taking action under Rules 1007(d), 2003(a) and (d), 7052, 9023, and 9024.

(3) *Enlargement governed by other rules.* The court may enlarge the time for taking action under Rules 1006(b)(2), 1017(e), 3002(c), 4003(b), 4004(a), 4007(c), 4008(a), 8002, and 9033, only to the extent and under the conditions stated in those rules. In addition, the court may enlarge the time to file the statement required under Rule 1007(b)(7), and to file schedules and statements in a small business case under § 1116(3) of the Code [11 USCS § 1116(3)], only to the extent and under the conditions stated in Rule 1007(c).

(c) Reduction. (1) *In general.* Except as provided in paragraph (2) of this subdivision, when an act is required or allowed to be done at or within a specified time by these rules or by a notice given thereunder or by order of court, the court for cause shown may in its discretion with or without motion or notice order the period reduced.

(2) *Reduction not permitted.* The court may not reduce the time for taking action under Rules 2002(a)(7), 2003(a), 3002(c), 3014, 3015, 4001(b)(2), (c)(2), 4003(a), 4004(a), 4007(c), 4008(a), 8002, and 9033(b). In addition, the court may not reduce the time under Rule 1007(c) to file the statement required by Rule 1007(b)(7).

(d) Motion papers. A written motion, other than one which may be heard ex parte, and notice of any hearing shall be served not later than seven days before the time specified for such hearing, unless a different period is fixed by these rules or by order of the court. Such an order may for cause shown be made on ex parte application. When a motion is supported by affidavit, the affidavit shall be served with the motion. Except as otherwise provided in Rule 9023, any written response shall be served not later than one day before the hearing, unless the court permits otherwise.

(e) Time of service. Service of process and service of any paper other than process or of notice by mail is complete on mailing.

(f) Additional time after service by mail or under Rule 5(b)(2)(D), (E), or (F) F. R. Civ. P. When there is a right or requirement to act or undertake some proceedings within a prescribed period after service and that service is by mail or under Rule 5(b)(2)(D), (E), or (F) F.R.Civ.P., three days are added after the prescribed period would otherwise expire under Rule 9006(a).

(g) Grain storage facility cases. This rule shall not limit the court's authority under § 557 of the Code [11 USCS § 557]to enter orders governing procedures in cases in which the debtor is an owner or operator of a grain storage facility.

(Amended Aug. 1, 1987; Aug. 1, 1989; Aug. 1, 1991; Dec. 1, 1996; Dec. 1, 1999; Dec. 1, 2001; Dec. 1, 2005; Dec. 1, 2008; Dec. 1, 2009; Dec. 1, 2013.)

Rule 9007. General Authority to Regulate Notices

When notice is to be given under these rules, the court shall designate, if not otherwise specified herein, the time within which, the entities to whom, and the form and manner in which the notice shall be given. When feasible, the court may order any notices under these rules to be combined.

(Amended Aug. 1, 1987.)

Rule 9008. Service or Notice by Publication

Whenever these rules require or authorize service or notice by publication, the court shall, to the extent not otherwise specified in these rules, determine the form and manner thereof, including the newspaper or other medium to be used and the number of publications.

Rule 9009. Forms

Except as otherwise provided in Rule 3016(d), the Official Forms prescribed by the Judicial Conference of the United States shall be observed and used with alterations as may be appropriate. Forms may be combined and their contents rearranged to permit economies in their use. The Director of the Administrative Office of the United States Courts may issue additional forms for use under the Code. The forms shall be construed to be consistent with these rules and the Code.

(Amended Aug. 1, 1991; Dec. 1, 2008.)

Rule 9010. Representation and Appearances; Powers of Attorney

(a) Authority to act personally or by attor-

ney. A debtor, creditor, equity security holder, indenture trustee, committee or other party may (1) appear in a case under the Code and act either in the entity's own behalf or by an attorney authorized to practice in the court, and (2) perform any act not constituting the practice of law, by an authorized agent, attorney in fact, or proxy.

(b) Notice of appearance. An attorney appearing for a party in a case under the Code shall file a notice of appearance with the attorney's name, office address and telephone number, unless the attorney's appearance is otherwise noted in the record.

(c) Power of attorney. The authority of any agent, attorney in fact, or proxy to represent a creditor for any purpose other than the execution and filing of a proof of claim or the acceptance or rejection of a plan shall be evidenced by a power of attorney conforming substantially to the appropriate Official Form. The execution of any such power of attorney shall be acknowledged before one of the officers enumerated in 28 U.S.C. § 459, § 953, Rule 9012, or a person authorized to administer oaths under the laws of the state where the oath is administered.

(Amended Aug. 1, 1987; Aug. 1, 1991.)

Rule 9011. Signing of Papers; Representations to the Court; Sanctions; Verification and Copies of Papers

(a) Signature. Every petition, pleading, written motion, and other paper, except a list, schedule, or statement, or amendments thereto, shall be signed by at least one attorney of record in the attorney's individual name. A party who is not represented by an attorney shall sign all papers. Each paper shall state the signer's address and telephone number, if any. An unsigned paper shall be stricken unless omission of the signature is corrected promptly after being called to the attention of the attorney or party.

(b) Representations to the court. By presenting to the court (whether by signing, filing, submitting, or later advocating) a petition, pleading, written motion, or other paper, an attorney or unrepresented party is certifying that to the best of the person's knowledge, information, and belief, formed after an inquiry reasonable under the circumstances,—

(1) it is not being presented for any improper purpose, such as to harass or to cause unnecessary delay or needless increase in the cost of litigation;

(2) the claims, defenses, and other legal contentions therein are warranted by existing law or by a nonfrivolous argument for the extension, modification, or reversal of existing law or the establishment of new law;

(3) the allegations and other factual contentions have evidentiary support or, if specifically so identified, are likely to have evidentiary support after a reasonable opportunity for further investigation or discovery; and

(4) the denials of factual contentions are warranted on the evidence or, if specifically so identified, are reasonably based on a lack of information or belief.

(c) Sanctions. If, after notice and a reasonable opportunity to respond, the court determines that subdivision (b) has been violated, the court may, subject to the conditions stated below, impose an appropriate sanction upon the attorneys, law firms, or parties that have violated subdivision (b) or are responsible for the violation.

(1) *How initiated.* (A) By motion. A motion for sanctions under this rule shall be made separately from other motions or requests and shall describe the specific conduct alleged to violate subdivision (b). It shall be served as provided in Rule 7004. The motion for sanctions may not be filed with or presented to the court unless, within 21 days after service of the motion (or such other period as the court may prescribe), the challenged paper, claim, defense, contention, allegation, or denial is not withdrawn or appropriately corrected, except that this limitation shall not apply if the conduct alleged is the filing of a petition in violation of subdivision (b). If warranted, the court may award to the party prevailing on the motion the reasonable expenses and attorney's fees incurred in presenting or opposing the motion. Absent exceptional circumstances, a law firm shall be held jointly responsible for violations committed by its partners, associates, and employees.

(B) On court's initiative. On its own initiative, the court may enter an order describing the specific conduct that appears to violate subdivision (b) and directing an attorney, law firm, or party to show cause why it has not violated subdivision (b) with respect thereto.

(2) *Nature of sanction; limitations.* A sanction imposed for violation of this rule shall be limited to what is sufficient to deter repetition of such conduct or comparable conduct by others similarly situated. Subject to the limitations in subparagraphs (A) and (B), the sanction may consist of, or include, directives of a nonmonetary nature, an order to pay a penalty into court, or, if imposed on motion and warranted for effective deterrence, an order directing payment to the movant of some or all of the reasonable attorneys' fees and other expenses incurred as a direct result of the violation.

(A) Monetary sanctions may not be awarded against a represented party for a violation of subdivision (b)(2).

(B) Monetary sanctions may not be awarded on the court's initiative unless the court issues its order to show cause before a voluntary dismissal or settlement of the claims made by or against the party which is, or whose attorneys are, to be sanctioned.

(3) *Order.* When imposing sanctions, the court shall describe the conduct determined to constitute a violation of this rule and explain the basis for the sanction imposed.

(d) Inapplicability to discovery. Subdivisions

(a) through (c) of this rule do not apply to disclosures and discovery requests, responses, objections, and motions that are subject to the provisions of Rules 7026 through 7037.

(e) Verification. Except as otherwise specifically provided by these rules, papers filed in a case under the Code need not be verified. Whenever verification is required by these rules, an unsworn declaration as provided in 28 U.S.C. § 1746 satisfies the requirement of verification.

(f) Copies of signed or verified papers. When these rules require copies of a signed or verified paper, it shall suffice if the original is signed or verified and the copies are conformed to the original.

(Amended Aug. 1, 1987; Aug. 1, 1991; Dec. 1, 1997.)

Rule 9012. Oaths and Affirmations

(a) Persons authorized to administer oaths. The following persons may administer oaths and affirmations and take acknowledgments: a bankruptcy judge, clerk, deputy clerk, United States trustee, officer authorized to administer oaths in proceedings before the courts of the United States or under the laws of the state where the oath is to be taken, or a diplomatic or consular officer of the United States in any foreign country.

(b) Affirmation in lieu of oath. When in a case under the Code an oath is required to be taken, a solemn affirmation may be accepted in lieu thereof.

(Amended Aug. 1, 1987; Aug. 1, 1991.)

Rule 9013. Motions: Form and Service

A request for an order, except when an application is authorized by the rules, shall be by written motion, unless made during a hearing. The motion shall state with particularity the grounds therefor, and shall set forth the relief or order sought. Every written motion, other than one which may be considered ex parte, shall be served by the moving party within the time determined under Rule 9006(d). The moving party shall serve the motion on:

(a) the trustee or debtor in possession and on those entities specified by these rules; or

(b) the entities the court directs if these rules do not require service or specify the entities to be served.

(Amended Aug. 1, 1987; Dec. 1, 2013.)

Rule 9014. Contested Matters

(a) Motion. In a contested matter not otherwise governed by these rules, relief shall be requested by motion, and reasonable notice and opportunity for hearing shall be afforded the party against whom relief is sought. No response is required under this rule unless the court directs otherwise.

(b) Service. The motion shall be served in the manner provided for service of a summons and complaint by Rule 7004 and within the time determined under Rule 9006(d). Any written response to the motion shall be served within the time determined under Rule 9006(d). Any paper served after the motion shall be served in the manner provided by Rule 5(b) F.R. Civ. P.

(c) Application of Part VII rules. Except as otherwise provided in this rule,and unless the court directs otherwise, the following rules shall apply: 7009, 7017, 7021, 7025, 7026, 7028–7037, 7041, 7042, 7052, 7054–7056, 7064, 7069, and 7071. The following subdivisions of Fed.R.Civ.P. 26, as incorporated by Rule 7026, shall not apply in a contested matter unless the court directs otherwise: 26(a)(1) (mandatory disclosure), 26(a)(2) (disclosures regarding expert testimony)and 26(a)(3) (additional pretrial disclosure), and 26(f) (mandatory meeting before scheduling conference/discovery plan). An entity that desires to perpetuate testimony may proceed in the same manner as provided in Rule 7027 for the taking of a deposition before an adversary proceeding. The court may at any stage in a particular matter direct that one or more of the other rules in Part VII shall apply. The court shall give the parties notice of any order issued under this paragraph to afford them a reasonable opportunity to comply with the procedures prescribed by the order.

(d) Testimony of witnesses. Testimony of witnesses with respect to disputed material factual issues shall be taken in the same manner as testimony in an adversary proceeding.

(e) Attendance of witnesses. The court shall provide procedures that enable parties to ascertain at a reasonable time before any scheduled hearing whether the hearing will be an evidentiary hearing at which witnesses may testify.

(Amended Aug. 1, 1987; Dec. 1, 1999; Dec. 1, 2002; Dec. 1, 2004; Dec. 1, 2013.)

Rule 9015. Jury Trials

(a) **Applicability of certain Federal Rules of Civil Procedure.** Rules 38, 39, 47–49, and 51, F. R. Civ. P., and Rule 81(c) F. R. Civ. P. insofar as it applies to jury trials, apply in cases and proceedings, except that a demand made under Rule 38(b) F. R. Civ. P. shall be filed in accordance with Rule 5005.

(b) **Consent to have trial conducted by bankruptcy judge.** If the right to a jury trial applies, a timely demand has been filed pursuant to Rule 38(b) F.R.Civ.P., and the bankruptcy judge has been specially designated to conduct the jury trial, the parties may consent to have a jury trial conducted by a bankruptcy judge under 28 U.S.C. § 157(e) by jointly or separately filing a statement of consent within any applicable time limits specified by local rule.

(c) **Applicability of Rule 50 F. R. Civ. P.** Rule 50 F. R. Civ. P. applies in cases and proceedings, except that any renewed motion for judgment or request for a new trial shall be filed no later than 14 days after the entry of judgment.

(Added December 1, 1997; Dec. 1, 2009.)

Rule 9016. Subpoena

Rule 45 F.R.Civ.P. applies in cases under the Code.

(Amended Aug. 1, 1987.)

Rule 9017. Evidence

The Federal Rules of Evidence and Rules 43, 44 and 44.1 F.R.Civ.P. apply in cases under the Code.

Rule 9018. Secret, Confidential, Scandalous, or Defamatory Matter

On motion or on its own initiative, with or without notice, the court may make any order which justice requires (1) to protect the estate or any entity in respect of a trade secret or other confidential research, development, or commercial information, (2) to protect any entity against scandalous or defamatory matter contained in any paper filed in a case under the Code, or (3) to protect governmental matters that are made confidential by statute or regulation. If an order is entered under this rule without notice, any entity affected thereby may move to vacate or modify the order, and after a hearing on notice the court shall determine the motion.

(Amended Aug. 1, 1987.)

Rule 9019. Compromise and Arbitration

(a) Compromise. On motion by the trustee and after notice and a hearing, the court may approve a compromise or settlement. Notice shall be given to creditors, the United States trustee, the debtor, and indenture trustees as provided in Rule 2002 and to any other entity as the court may direct.

(b) Authority to compromise or settle controversies within classes. After a hearing on such notice as the court may direct, the court may fix a class or classes of controversies and authorize the trustee to compromise or settle controversies within such class or classes without further hearing or notice.

(c) Arbitration. On stipulation of the parties to any controversy affecting the estate the court may authorize the matter to be submitted to final and binding arbitration.

(Amended Aug. 1, 1987; Aug. 1, 1991; Aug. 1, 1993.)

Rule 9020. Contempt Proceedings

Rule 9014 governs a motion for an order of contempt made by the United States trustee or a party in interest.

(Amended Aug. 1, 1987; Aug. 1, 1991; Dec. 1, 2001.)

Rule 9021. Entry of Judgment

A judgment or order is effective when entered under Rule 5003.

(Amended Aug. 1, 1987; Dec. 1, 2009.)

Rule 9022. Notice of Judgment or Order

(a) Judgment or order of bankruptcy judge. Immediately on the entry of a judgment or order the clerk shall serve a notice of entry in the manner provided in Rule 5(b) Fed. R. Civ. P. on the contesting parties and on other entities as the court directs. Unless the case is a chapter 9 municipality case, the clerk shall forthwith transmit to the United States trustee a copy of the judgment or order. Service of the notice shall be noted in the docket. Lack of notice of the entry does not affect the time to appeal or relieve or authorize the court to relieve a party for failure to appeal within the time allowed, except as permitted in Rule 8002.

(b) Judgment or order of district judge. Notice of a judgment or order entered by a district judge is governed by Rule 77(d) F.R.Civ.P. Unless the case is a chapter 9 municipality case, the clerk shall forthwith transmit to the United States trustee a copy of a judgment or order entered by a district judge.

(Amended Aug. 1, 1987; Aug. 1, 1991; Dec. 1, 2001.)

Rule 9023. New Trials; Amendment of Judgments

Except as provided in this rule and Rule 3008, Rule 59 F.R.Civ.P. applies in cases under the Code. A motion for a new trial or to alter or amend a judgment shall be filed, and a court may on its own order a new trial, no later than 14 days after entry of judgment. In some circumstances, Rule 8008 governs post-judgment motion practice after an appeal has been docketed and is pending.

(As amended Dec. 1, 2009; Dec. 1, 2014.)

Rule 9024. Relief from Judgment or Order

Rule 60 F.R.Civ.P. applies in cases under the Code except that (1) a motion to reopen a case under the Code or for the reconsideration of an order allowing or disallowing a claim against the estate entered without a contest is not subject to the one year limitation prescribed in Rule 60(c), (2) a complaint to revoke a discharge in a chapter 7 liquidation case may be filed only within the time allowed by § 727(e) of the Code [11 USCS § 727(e)], and (3) a complaint to revoke an order confirming a plan may be filed only within the time allowed by § 1144, § 1230, or § 1330 [11 USCS § 1144, 1230, or 1330]. In some circumstances, Rule 8008 governs post-judgment motion practice after an appeal has been docketed and is pending.

(Amended Aug. 1, 1991; Dec. 1, 2008; Dec. 1, 2014.)

Rule 9025. Security: Proceedings Against Sureties

Whenever the Code or these rules require or permit the giving of security by a party, and security is given in the form of a bond or stipulation or other undertaking with one or more sureties, each surety submits to the jurisdiction of the court, and liability may be determined in an adversary proceeding governed by the rules in Part VII.

Rule 9026. Exceptions Unnecessary

Rule 46 F.R.Civ.P. applies in cases under the Code.

Rule 9027. Removal

(a) Notice of removal. (1) *Where filed; form and content.* A notice of removal shall be filed with the clerk for the district and division within which is located the state or federal court where the civil action is pending. The notice shall be signed pursuant to Rule 9011 and contain a short and plain statement of the facts which entitle the party filing the notice to remove, contain a statement that upon removal of the claim or cause of action the proceeding is core or non-core and, if non-core, that the party filing the notice does or does not consent to entry of final orders or judgment by the bankruptcy judge, and be accompanied by a copy of all process and pleadings.

(2) *Time for filing; civil action initiated before commencement of the case under the Code.* If the claim or cause of action in a civil action is pending when a case under the Code is commenced, a notice of removal may be filed only within the longest of (A) 90 days after the order for relief in the case under the Code, (B) 30 days after entry of an order terminating a stay, if the claim or cause of action in a civil action has been stayed under § 362 of the Code [11 USCS § 362], or (C) 30 days after a trustee qualifies in a chapter 11 reorganization case but not later than 180 days after the order for relief.

(3) *Time for filing; civil action initiated after commencement of the case under the Code.* If a claim or cause of action is asserted in another court after the commencement of a case under the Code, a notice of removal may be filed with the clerk only within the shorter of (A) 30 days after receipt, through service or otherwise, of a copy of the initial pleading setting forth the claim or cause of action sought to be removed, or (B) 30 days after receipt of the summons if the initial pleading has been filed with the court but not served with the summons.

(b) Notice. Promptly after filing the notice of removal, the party filing the notice shall serve a copy of it on all parties to the removed claim or cause of action.

(c) Filing in non-bankruptcy court. Promptly after filing the notice of removal, the party filing the notice shall file a copy of it with the clerk of the court from which the claim or cause of action is removed. Removal of the claim or cause of action is effected on such filing of a copy of the notice of removal. The parties shall proceed no further in that court unless and until the claim or cause of action is remanded.

(d) Remand. A motion for remand of the removed claim or cause of action shall be governed by Rule 9014 and served on the parties to the removed claim or cause of action.

(e) Procedure after removal. (1) After removal of a claim or cause of action to a district court the district court or, if the case under the Code has been referred to a bankruptcy judge of the district, the bankruptcy judge, may issue all necessary orders and process to bring before it all proper parties whether served by process issued by the court from which the claim or cause of action was removed or otherwise.

(2) The district court or, if the case under the Code has been referred to a bankruptcy judge of the district, the bankruptcy judge, may require the party filing the notice of removal to file with the clerk copies of all records and proceedings relating to the claim or cause of action in the court from which the claim or cause of action was removed.

(3) Any party who has filed a pleading in connection with the removed claim or cause of action, other than the party filing the notice of removal, shall file a statement admitting or denying any allegation in the notice of removal that upon removal of the claim or cause of action the proceeding is core or non-core. If the statement alleges that the proceeding is non-core, it shall state that the party does or does not consent to entry of final orders or judgment by the bankruptcy judge. A statement required by this paragraph shall be signed pursuant to Rule 9011 and shall be filed not later than 14 days after the filing of the notice of removal. Any party who files a statement pursuant to this paragraph shall mail a copy to every other party to the removed claim or cause of action.

(f) Process after removal. If one or more of the defendants has not been served with process, the service has not been perfected prior to removal, or the process served proves to be defective, such process or service may be completed or new process issued pursuant to Part VII of these rules. This subdivision shall not deprive any defendant on whom process is served after removal of the defendant's right to move to remand the case.

(g) Applicability of part VII. The rules of Part VII apply to a claim or cause of action removed to a district court from a federal or state court and govern procedure after removal. Repleading is not necessary unless the court so orders. In a removed action in which the defendant has not answered, the defendant shall answer or present the other defenses or objections available under the rules of Part VII within 21 days following the receipt through service or otherwise of a copy of the initial pleading setting forth the claim for relief on which the action or proceeding is based, or within 21 days following the service of summons on such initial pleading, or within seven days following the filing of the notice of removal, whichever period is longest.

(h) Record supplied. When a party is entitled to copies of the records and proceedings in any civil action or proceeding in a federal or a state court, to be used in the removed civil action or proceeding, and the clerk of the federal or state court, on demand accompanied by payment or tender of the lawful fees, fails to deliver certified copies, the court may, on affidavit reciting the facts, direct such record to be supplied by affidavit or otherwise. Thereupon the proceedings, trial and judgment may be had in the court, and all process awarded, as if certified copies had been filed.

(i) Attachment or sequestration; securities. When a claim or cause of action is removed to a district court, any attachment or sequestration of property in the court from which the claim or cause of action was removed shall hold the property to answer the final judgment or decree in the same manner as the property would have been held to answer final judgment or decree had it been rendered by the court from which the claim or cause of action was removed. All bonds, undertakings, or security given by either party to the claim or cause of action prior to its removal shall remain valid and effectual notwithstanding such removal. All injunctions issued, orders entered and other proceedings had prior to removal shall remain in full force and effect until dissolved or modified by the court.

(Amended Aug. 1, 1987; Aug. 1, 1991; Dec. 1, 2002; Dec. 1, 2009.)

Rule 9028. Disability of a Judge

Rule 63 F.R.Civ.P. applies in cases under the Code.

(Amended Aug. 1, 1987)

Rule 9029. Local Bankruptcy Rules; Procedure When There is No Controlling Law

(a) Local Bankruptcy Rules. (1) Each district court acting by a majority of its district judges may make and amend rules governing practice and procedure in all cases and proceedings within the district court's bankruptcy jurisdiction which are consistent with—but not duplicative of—Acts of Congress and these rules and which do not prohibit or limit the use of the Official Forms. Rule 83 F.R.Civ.P. governs the procedure for making local rules. A district court may authorize the bankruptcy judges of the district, subject to any limitation or condition it may prescribe and the requirements of 83 F.R.Civ.P., to make and amend rules of practice and procedure which are consistent with—but not duplicative of—Acts of Congress and these rules and which do not prohibit or limit the use of the Official Forms. Local rules shall conform to any uniform numbering system prescribed by the Judicial Conference of the United States.

(2) A local rule imposing a requirement of form shall not be enforced in a manner that causes a party to lose rights because of a nonwillful failure to comply with the requirement.

(b) Procedure When There is No Controlling Law. A judge may regulate practice in any manner consistent with federal law, these rules, Official Forms, and local rules of the district. No sanction or other disadvantage may be imposed for noncompliance with any requirement not in federal law, federal rules, Official Forms, or the local rules of the district unless the alleged violator has been furnished in the particular case with actual notice of the requirement.

(Amended Aug. 1, 1987; Aug. 1, 1991; Dec. 1, 1995.)

Rule 9030. Jurisdiction and Venue Unaffected

These rules shall not be construed to extend or limit the jurisdiction of the courts or the venue of any matters therein.

(Amended Aug. 1, 1987)

Rule 9031. Masters Not Authorized

Rule 53 F.R.Civ.P. does not apply in cases under the Code.

Rule 9032. Effect of Amendment of Federal Rules of Civil Procedure

The Federal Rules of Civil Procedure which are incorporated by reference and made applicable by these rules shall be the Federal Rules of Civil Procedure in effect on the effective date of these rules and as thereafter amended, unless otherwise provided by such amendment or by these rules.

(Amended Aug. 1, 1991.)

Rule 9033. Review of Proposed Findings of Fact and Conclusions of Law in Non-Core Proceedings

(a) Service. In non-core proceedings heard pursuant to 28 U.S.C. § 157(c)(1), the bankruptcy judge shall file proposed findings of fact and conclusions of law. The clerk shall serve forthwith copies on all parties by mail and note the date of mailing on the docket.

(b) Objections: time for filing. Within 14 days after being served with a copy of the proposed findings of fact and conclusions of law a party may serve and file with the clerk written objections which identify the specific proposed findings or conclusions objected to and state the grounds for such objection. A party may respond to another party's objections within 14 days after being served with a copy thereof. A party objecting to the bankruptcy judge's proposed findings or conclusions shall arrange promptly for the transcription of the record, or such portions of it as all parties may agree upon or the bankruptcy judge deems sufficient, unless the district judge otherwise directs.

(c) Extension of time. The bankruptcy judge may for cause extend the time for filing objections by any party for a period not to exceed 21 days from the expiration of the time otherwise prescribed by this rule. A request to extend the time for filing objections must be made before the time for filing objections has expired, except that a request made no more than 21 days after the expiration of the time for filing objections may be granted upon a showing of excusable neglect.

(d) Standard of review. The district judge shall make a de novo review upon the record or, after additional evidence, of any portion of the bankruptcy judge's findings of fact or conclusions of law to which specific written objection has been made in accordance with this rule. The district judge may accept, reject, or modify the proposed findings of fact or conclusions of law, receive further evidence, or recommit the matter to the bankruptcy judge with instructions.

(Added Aug. 1, 1987; Dec. 1, 2009.)

Rule 9034. Transmittal of Pleadings, Motion Papers, Objections, and Other Papers to the United States Trustee

Unless the United States trustee requests otherwise or the case is a chapter 9 municipality case, any entity that files a pleading, motion, objection, or similar paper relating to any of the following matters shall transmit a copy thereof to the United States trustee within the time required by these rules for service of the paper:

(a) a proposed use, sale, or lease of property of the estate other than in the ordinary course of business;

(b) the approval of a compromise or settlement of a controversy;

(c) the dismissal or conversion of a case to another chapter;

(d) the employment of professional persons;

(e) an application for compensation or reimbursement of expenses;

(f) a motion for, or approval of an agreement relating to, the use of cash collateral or authority to obtain credit;

(g) the appointment of a trustee or examiner in a chapter 11 reorganization case;

(h) the approval of a disclosure statement;

(i) the confirmation of a plan;

(j) an objection to, or waiver or revocation of, the debtor's discharge;

(k) any other matter in which the United States trustee requests copies of filed papers or the court orders copies transmitted to the United States trustee.

(Added Aug. 1, 1991.)

Rule 9035. Applicability of Rules in Judicial Districts in Alabama and North Carolina

In any case under the Code that is filed in or transferred to a district in the State of Alabama or the State of North Carolina and in which a United States trustee is not authorized to act, these rules apply to the extent that they are not inconsistent with any federal statute effective in the case.

(Added Aug. 1, 1991; Dec. 1, 1997.)

Rule 9036. Notice by Electronic Transmission

Whenever the clerk or some other person as directed by the court is required to send notice by mail and the entity entitled to receive the notice requests in writing that, instead of notice by mail, all or part of the information required to be contained in the notice be sent by a specified type of electronic transmission, the court may direct the clerk or other person to send the information by such electronic transmission. Notice by electronic means is complete on transmission.

(Added Aug. 1, 1993; Dec. 1, 2005.)

Rule 9037. Privacy Protection For Filings Made with the Court

(a) Redacted filings. Unless the court orders otherwise, in an electronic or paper filing made with the court that contains an individual's social-security number, taxpayer-identification number, or birth date, the name of an individual, other than the debtor, known to be and identified as a minor, or a financial-account number, a party or nonparty making the filing may include only:

(1) the last four digits of the social-security number and taxpayer-identification number;

(2) the year of the individual's birth;

(3) the minor's initials; and

(4) the last four digits of the financial-account number.

(b) Exemptions from the redaction requirement. The redaction requirement does not apply to the following:

(1) a financial-account number that identifies the property allegedly subject to forfeiture in a forfeiture proceeding;

(2) the record of an administrative or agency proceeding unless filed with a proof of claim;

(3) the official record of a state-court proceeding;

(4) the record of a court or tribunal, if that record was not subject to the redaction requirement when originally filed;

(5) a filing covered by subdivision (c) of this rule; and

(6) a filing that is subject to § 110 of the Code [11 USCS § 110].

(c) Filings made under seal. The court may order that a filing be made under seal without redaction. The court may later unseal the filing or order the entity that made the filing to file a redacted version for the public record.

(d) Protective orders. For cause, the court may by order in a case under the Code:

(1) require redaction of additional information; or

(2) limit or prohibit a nonparty's remote electronic access to a document filed with the court.

(e) Option for additional unredacted filing under seal. An entity making a redacted filing may also file an unredacted copy under seal. The court must retain the unredacted copy as part of the record.

(f) Option for filing a reference list. A filing that contains redacted information may be filed together with a reference list that identifies each item of redacted information and specifies an appropriate identifier that uniquely corresponds to each item listed. The list must be filed under seal and may be amended as of right. Any reference in the case to a listed identifier will be construed to refer to the corresponding item of information.

(g) Waiver of protection of identifiers. An entity waives the protection of subdivision (a) as to the entity's own information by filing it without redaction and not under seal.

(As added Dec. 1, 2007.)

PART X. UNITED STATES TRUSTEES [ABROGATED]

Rules X-1001—X-1010. [Abrogated Aug. 1, 1991]

OFFICIAL BANKRUPTCY FORMS

Form 1. Voluntary Petition

B1 (Official Form 1) (04/13)

UNITED STATES BANKRUPTCY COURT

VOLUNTARY PETITION

Name of Debtor (if individual, enter Last, First, Middle):	Name of Joint Debtor (Spouse) (Last, First, Middle):
All Other Names used by the Debtor in the last 8 years (include married, maiden, and trade names):	All Other Names used by the Joint Debtor in the last 8 years (include married, maiden, and trade names):
Last four digits of Soc. Sec. or Individual-Taxpayer I.D. (ITIN)/Complete EIN (if more than one, state all):	Last four digits of Soc. Sec. or Individual-Taxpayer I.D. (ITIN)/Complete EIN (if more than one, state all):
Street Address of Debtor (No. and Street, City, and State): ZIP CODE	Street Address of Joint Debtor (No. and Street, City, and State): ZIP CODE
County of Residence or of the Principal Place of Business:	County of Residence or of the Principal Place of Business:
Mailing Address of Debtor (if different from street address): ZIP CODE	Mailing Address of Joint Debtor (if different from street address): ZIP CODE

Location of Principal Assets of Business Debtor (if different from street address above): ZIP CODE

Type of Debtor
(Form of Organization)
(Check **one** box.)

☐ Individual (includes Joint Debtors)
See Exhibit D on page 2 of this form.
☐ Corporation (includes LLC and LLP)
☐ Partnership
☐ Other (If debtor is not one of the above entities, check this box and state type of entity below.)

Nature of Business
(Check **one** box.)

☐ Health Care Business
☐ Single Asset Real Estate as defined in 11 U.S.C. § 101(51B)
☐ Railroad
☐ Stockbroker
☐ Commodity Broker
☐ Clearing Bank
☐ Other

Chapter of Bankruptcy Code Under Which the Petition is Filed (Check **one** box.)

☐ Chapter 7
☐ Chapter 9
☐ Chapter 11
☐ Chapter 12
☐ Chapter 13
☐ Chapter 15 Petition for Recognition of a Foreign Main Proceeding
☐ Chapter 15 Petition for Recognition of a Foreign Nonmain Proceeding

Chapter 15 Debtors

Country of debtor's center of main interests:

Each country in which a foreign proceeding by, regarding, or against debtor is pending:

Tax-Exempt Entity
(Check box, if applicable.)

☐ Debtor is a tax-exempt organization under title 26 of the United States Code (the Internal Revenue Code).

Nature of Debts
(Check **one** box.)

☐ Debts are primarily consumer debts, defined in 11 U.S.C. § 101(8) as "incurred by an individual primarily for a personal, family, or household purpose."
☐ Debts are primarily business debts.

Filing Fee (Check one box.)

☐ Full Filing Fee attached.

☐ Filing Fee to be paid in installments (applicable to individuals only). Must attach signed application for the court's consideration certifying that the debtor is unable to pay fee except in installments. Rule 1006(b). See Official Form 3A.

☐ Filing Fee waiver requested (applicable to chapter 7 individuals only). Must attach signed application for the court's consideration. See Official Form 3B.

Chapter 11 Debtors

Check one box:
☐ Debtor is a small business debtor as defined in 11 U.S.C. § 101(51D).
☐ Debtor is not a small business debtor as defined in 11 U.S.C. § 101(51D).

Check if:
☐ Debtor's aggregate noncontingent liquidated debts (excluding debts owed to insiders or affiliates) are less than $2,490,925 (*amount subject to adjustment on 4/01/16 and every three years thereafter*).

Check all applicable boxes:
☐ A plan is being filed with this petition.
☐ Acceptances of the plan were solicited prepetition from one or more classes of creditors, in accordance with 11 U.S.C. § 1126(b).

Statistical/Administrative Information

THIS SPACE IS FOR COURT USE ONLY

☐ Debtor estimates that funds will be available for distribution to unsecured creditors.
☐ Debtor estimates that, after any exempt property is excluded and administrative expenses paid, there will be no funds available for distribution to unsecured creditors.

Estimated Number of Creditors

☐	☐	☐	☐	☐	☐	☐	☐	☐	☐
1-49	50-99	100-199	200-999	1,000-5,000	5,001-10,000	10,001-25,000	25,001-50,000	50,001-100,000	Over 100,000

Estimated Assets

☐	☐	☐	☐	☐	☐	☐	☐	☐	☐
$0 to $50,000	$50,001 to $100,000	$100,001 to $500,000	$500,001 to $1 million	$1,000,001 to $10 million	$10,000,001 to $50 million	$50,000,001 to $100 million	$100,000,001 to $500 million	$500,000,001 to $1 billion	More than $1 billion

Estimated Liabilities

☐	☐	☐	☐	☐	☐	☐	☐	☐	☐
$0 to $50,000	$50,001 to $100,000	$100,001 to $500,000	$500,001 to $1 million	$1,000,001 to $10 million	$10,000,001 to $50 million	$50,000,001 to $100 million	$100,000,001 to $500 million	$500,000,001 to $1 billion	More than $1 billion

B1 (Official Form 1) (04/13)

Voluntary Petition *(This page must be completed and filed in every case.)*	Name of Debtor(s):	
All Prior Bankruptcy Cases Filed Within Last 8 Years (If more than two, attach additional sheet.)		
Location Where Filed:	Case Number:	Date Filed:
Location Where Filed:	Case Number:	Date Filed:
Pending Bankruptcy Case Filed by any Spouse, Partner, or Affiliate of this Debtor (If more than one, attach additional sheet.)		
Name of Debtor:	Case Number:	Date Filed:
District:	Relationship:	Judge:

Exhibit A

(To be completed if debtor is required to file periodic reports (e.g., forms 10K and 10Q) with the Securities and Exchange Commission pursuant to Section 13 or 15(d) of the Securities Exchange Act of 1934 and is requesting relief under chapter 11.)

☐ Exhibit A is attached and made a part of this petition.

Exhibit B

(To be completed if debtor is an individual whose debts are primarily consumer debts.)

I, the attorney for the petitioner named in the foregoing petition, declare that I have informed the petitioner that [he or she] may proceed under chapter 7, 11, 12, or 13 of title 11, United States Code, and have explained the relief available under each such chapter. I further certify that I have delivered to the debtor the notice required by 11 U.S.C. § 342(b).

X ______________________________

Signature of Attorney for Debtor(s) (Date)

Exhibit C

Does the debtor own or have possession of any property that poses or is alleged to pose a threat of imminent and identifiable harm to public health or safety?

☐ Yes, and Exhibit C is attached and made a part of this petition.

☐ No.

Exhibit D

(To be completed by every individual debtor. If a joint petition is filed, each spouse must complete and attach a separate Exhibit D.)

☐ Exhibit D, completed and signed by the debtor, is attached and made a part of this petition.

If this is a joint petition:

☐ Exhibit D, also completed and signed by the joint debtor, is attached and made a part of this petition.

Information Regarding the Debtor - Venue

(Check any applicable box.)

☐ Debtor has been domiciled or has had a residence, principal place of business, or principal assets in this District for 180 days immediately preceding the date of this petition or for a longer part of such 180 days than in any other District.

☐ There is a bankruptcy case concerning debtor's affiliate, general partner, or partnership pending in this District.

☐ Debtor is a debtor in a foreign proceeding and has its principal place of business or principal assets in the United States in this District, or has no principal place of business or assets in the United States but is a defendant in an action or proceeding [in a federal or state court] in this District, or the interests of the parties will be served in regard to the relief sought in this District.

Certification by a Debtor Who Resides as a Tenant of Residential Property

(Check all applicable boxes.)

☐ Landlord has a judgment against the debtor for possession of debtor's residence. (If box checked, complete the following.)

____

(Name of landlord that obtained judgment)

____

(Address of landlord)

☐ Debtor claims that under applicable nonbankruptcy law, there are circumstances under which the debtor would be permitted to cure the entire monetary default that gave rise to the judgment for possession, after the judgment for possession was entered, and

☐ Debtor has included with this petition the deposit with the court of any rent that would become due during the 30-day period after the filing of the petition.

☐ Debtor certifies that he/she has served the Landlord with this certification. (11 U.S.C. § 362(l)).

B1 (Official Form 1) (04/13)

Voluntary Petition
(This page must be completed and filed in every case.)

Name of Debtor(s):

Signatures

Signature(s) of Debtor(s) (Individual/Joint)

I declare under penalty of perjury that the information provided in this petition is true and correct.
[If petitioner is an individual whose debts are primarily consumer debts and has chosen to file under chapter 7] I am aware that I may proceed under chapter 7, 11, 12 or 13 of title 11, United States Code, understand the relief available under each such chapter, and choose to proceed under chapter 7.
[If no attorney represents me and no bankruptcy petition preparer signs the petition] I have obtained and read the notice required by 11 U.S.C. § 342(b).

I request relief in accordance with the chapter of title 11, United States Code, specified in this petition.

X ______________________________
Signature of Debtor

X ______________________________
Signature of Joint Debtor

____
Telephone Number (if not represented by attorney)

____
Date

Signature of a Foreign Representative

I declare under penalty of perjury that the information provided in this petition is true and correct, that I am the foreign representative of a debtor in a foreign proceeding, and that I am authorized to file this petition.

(Check only **one** box.)

☐ I request relief in accordance with chapter 15 of title 11, United States Code. Certified copies of the documents required by 11 U.S.C. § 1515 are attached.

☐ Pursuant to 11 U.S.C. § 1511, I request relief in accordance with the chapter of title 11 specified in this petition. A certified copy of the order granting recognition of the foreign main proceeding is attached.

X ______________________________
(Signature of Foreign Representative)

____
(Printed Name of Foreign Representative)

____
Date

Signature of Attorney*

X ______________________________
Signature of Attorney for Debtor(s)

____
Printed Name of Attorney for Debtor(s)

____
Firm Name

____
Address

____
Telephone Number

____
Date

*In a case in which § 707(b)(4)(D) applies, this signature also constitutes a certification that the attorney has no knowledge after an inquiry that the information in the schedules is incorrect.

Signature of Debtor (Corporation/Partnership)

I declare under penalty of perjury that the information provided in this petition is true and correct, and that I have been authorized to file this petition on behalf of the debtor.

The debtor requests the relief in accordance with the chapter of title 11, United States Code, specified in this petition.

X ______________________________
Signature of Authorized Individual

____
Printed Name of Authorized Individual

____
Title of Authorized Individual

____
Date

Signature of Non-Attorney Bankruptcy Petition Preparer

I declare under penalty of perjury that: (1) I am a bankruptcy petition preparer as defined in 11 U.S.C. § 110; (2) I prepared this document for compensation and have provided the debtor with a copy of this document and the notices and information required under 11 U.S.C. §§ 110(b), 110(h), and 342(b); and, (3) if rules or guidelines have been promulgated pursuant to 11 U.S.C. § 110(h) setting a maximum fee for services chargeable by bankruptcy petition preparers, I have given the debtor notice of the maximum amount before preparing any document for filing for a debtor or accepting any fee from the debtor, as required in that section. Official Form 19 is attached.

____
Printed Name and title, if any, of Bankruptcy Petition Preparer

____
Social-Security number (If the bankruptcy petition preparer is not an individual, state the Social-Security number of the officer, principal, responsible person or partner of the bankruptcy petition preparer.) (Required by 11 U.S.C. § 110.)

____
Address

X ______________________________
Signature

____
Date

Signature of bankruptcy petition preparer or officer, principal, responsible person, or partner whose Social-Security number is provided above.

Names and Social-Security numbers of all other individuals who prepared or assisted in preparing this document unless the bankruptcy petition preparer is not an individual.

If more than one person prepared this document, attach additional sheets conforming to the appropriate official form for each person.

A bankruptcy petition preparer's failure to comply with the provisions of title 11 and the Federal Rules of Bankruptcy Procedure may result in fines or imprisonment or both. 11 U.S.C. § 110; 18 U.S.C. § 156.

Form B1, Exh. A (9/97)

Exhibit "A"

[If debtor is required to file periodic reports (e.g., forms 10K and 10Q) with the Securities and Exchange Commission pursuant to Section 13 or 15(d) of the Securities Exchange Act of 1934 and is requesting relief under chapter 11 of the Bankruptcy Code, this Exhibit "A" shall be completed and attached to the petition.]

[Caption as in Form 16B]

Exhibit "A" to Voluntary Petition

1. If any of the debtor's securities are registered under Section 12 of the Securities Exchange Act of 1934, the SEC file number is ______________.

2. The following financial data is the latest available information and refers to the debtor's condition on _____________.

a. Total assets $ ________________

b. Total debts (including debts listed in 2.c., below) $ ________________

		Approximate number of holders
c. Debt securities held by more than 500 holders.		
secured / / unsecured / / subordinated / /	$ ____________	_________
secured / / unsecured / / subordinated / /	$ ____________	_________
secured / / unsecured / / subordinated / /	$ ____________	_________
secured / / unsecured / / subordinated / /	$ ____________	_________
secured / / unsecured / / subordinated / /	$ ____________	_________
d. Number of shares of preferred stock	____________	_________
e. Number of shares common stock	____________	_________

Comments, if any: ____

____

____

3. Brief description of debtor's business: ___________________________

____

____

4. List the names of any person who directly or indirectly owns, controls, or holds, with power to vote, 5% or more of the voting securities of debtor:

____

____

____

Form B1, Exhibit C
(9/01)

Exhibit "C"

[If, to the best of the debtor's knowledge, the debtor owns or has possession of property that poses or is alleged to pose a threat of imminent and identifiable harm to the public health or safety, attach this Exhibit "C" to the petition.]

[Caption as in Form 16B]

Exhibit "C" to Voluntary Petition

1. Identify and briefly describe all real or personal property owned by or in possession of the debtor that, to the best of the debtor's knowledge, poses or is alleged to pose a threat of imminent and identifiable harm to the public health or safety (attach additional sheets if necessary):

____
____
____
____

2. With respect to each parcel of real property or item of personal property identified in question 1, describe the nature and location of the dangerous condition, whether environmental or otherwise, that poses or is alleged to pose a threat of imminent and identifiable harm to the public health or safety (attach additional sheets if necessary):

____
____
____
____

Official Form 1, Exhibit D (12/09)

UNITED STATES BANKRUPTCY COURT

_______________District of_______________

In re______________________ Case No.__________
Debtor(s) (if known)

EXHIBIT D INDIVIDUAL DEBTOR'S STATEMENT OF COMPLIANCE WITH CREDIT COUNSELING REQUIREMENT

Warning: You must be able to check truthfully one of the five statements regarding credit counseling listed below. If you cannot do so, you are not eligible to file a bankruptcy case, and the court can dismiss any case you do file. If that happens, you will lose whatever filing fee you paid, and your creditors will be able to resume collection activities against you. If your case is dismissed and you file another bankruptcy case later, you may be required to pay a second filing fee and you may have to take extra steps to stop creditors' collection activities.

Every individual debtor must file this Exhibit D. If a joint petition is filed, each spouse must complete and file a separate Exhibit D. Check one of the five statements below and attach any documents as directed.

☐ 1. Within the 180 days **before the filing of my bankruptcy case,** I received a briefing from a credit counseling agency approved by the United States trustee or bankruptcy administrator that outlined the opportunities for available credit counseling and assisted me in performing a related budget analysis, and I have a certificate from the agency describing the services provided to me. *Attach a copy of the certificate and a copy of any debt repayment plan developed through the agency.*

☐ 2. Within the 180 days **before the filing of my bankruptcy case,** I received a briefing from a credit counseling agency approved by the United States trustee or bankruptcy administrator that outlined the opportunities for available credit counseling and assisted me in performing a related budget analysis, but I do not have a certificate from the agency describing the services provided to me. *You must file a copy of a certificate from the agency describing the services provided to you and a copy of any debt repayment plan developed through the agency no later than 14 days after your bankruptcy case is filed.*

☐ 3. I certify that I requested credit counseling services from an approved agency but was unable to obtain the services during the seven days from the time I made my request, and the following exigent circumstances merit a temporary waiver of the credit counseling requirement so I can file my bankruptcy case now. *[Summarize exigent circumstances here.]*

If your certification is satisfactory to the court, you must still obtain the credit counseling briefing within the first 30 days after you file your bankruptcy petition and promptly file a certificate from the agency that provided the counseling, together with a copy of any debt management plan developed through the agency. Failure to fulfill these requirements may result in dismissal of your case. Any extension of the 30-day deadline can be granted only for cause and is limited to a maximum of 15 days. Your case may also be dismissed if the court is not satisfied with your reasons for filing your bankruptcy case without first receiving a credit counseling briefing.

☐ 4. I am not required to receive a credit counseling briefing because of: *[Check the applicable statement.] [Must be accompanied by a motion for determination by the court.]*

☐ Incapacity. (Defined in 11 U.S.C. § 109(h)(4) as impaired by reason of mental illness or mental deficiency so as to be incapable of realizing and making rational decisions with respect to financial responsibilities.);

☐ Disability. (Defined in 11 U.S.C. § 109(h)(4) as physically impaired to the extent of being unable, after reasonable effort, to participate in a credit counseling briefing in person, by telephone, or through the Internet.);

☐ Active military duty in a military combat zone.

☐ 5. The United States trustee or bankruptcy administrator has determined that the credit counseling requirement of 11 U.S.C. § 109(h) does not apply in this district.

I certify under penalty of perjury that the information provided above is true and correct.

Signature of Debtor: ________________________

Date: _______________

(Amended Oct. 17, 2005; Oct. 1, 2006; April 1, 2007; Jan. 1, 2008; Dec. 1, 2009; April 1, 2010; Dec. 1, 2012; April 1, 2013.)

Form 2. Declaration under Penalty of Perjury on Behalf of a Corporation or Partnership

I, [the president *or* other officer *or* an authorized agent of the corporation] [*or* a member *or* an authorized agent of the partnership] named as the debtor in this case, declare under penalty of perjury that I have read the foregoing [list *or* schedule *or* amendment *or* other document (describe)] and that it is true and correct to the best of my information and belief.

Date______________________________

Signature______________________________

____

(Print Name and Title)

Form 3A. Application and Order to Pay Filing Fee in Installments

Fill in this information to identify your case:

Debtor 1 ______________________________
First Name Middle Name Last Name

Debtor 2 ______________________________
(Spouse, if filing) First Name Middle Name Last Name

United States Bankruptcy Court for the: ____________ District of ______

Case number ______________
(If known)

☐ Check if this is an amended filing

Official Form B 3A

Application for Individuals to Pay the Filing Fee in Installments

12/14

Be as complete and accurate as possible. If two married people are filing together, both are equally responsible for supplying correct information.

Part 1: Specify Your Proposed Payment Timetable

1. **Which chapter of the Bankruptcy Code are you choosing to file under?**

   ☐ Chapter 7
   ☐ Chapter 11
   ☐ Chapter 12
   ☐ Chapter 13

2. **You may apply to pay the filing fee in up to four installments. Fill in the amounts you propose to pay and the dates you plan to pay them. Be sure all dates are business days. Then add the payments you propose to pay.**

   You must propose to pay the entire fee no later than 120 days after you file this bankruptcy case. If the court approves your application, the court will set your final payment timetable.

   You propose to pay...

   $________ ☐ With the filing of the petition
   ☐ On or before this date........ MM / DD / YYYY

   $________ On or before this date........... MM / DD / YYYY

   $________ On or before this date........... MM / DD / YYYY

   \+ $________ On or before this date........... MM / DD / YYYY

   Total $________ ◀ Your total must equal the entire fee for the chapter you checked in line 1.

Part 2: Sign Below

By signing here, you state that you are unable to pay the full filing fee at once, that you want to pay the fee in installments, and that you understand that:

- You must pay your entire filing fee before you make any more payments or transfer any more property to an attorney, bankruptcy petition preparer, or anyone else for services in connection with your bankruptcy case.
- You must pay the entire fee no later than 120 days after you first file for bankruptcy, unless the court later extends your deadline. Your debts will not be discharged until your entire fee is paid.
- If you do not make any payment when it is due, your bankruptcy case may be dismissed, and your rights in other bankruptcy proceedings may be affected.

✘ ________________ Signature of Debtor 1 Date ________ MM / DD / YYYY

✘ ________________ Signature of Debtor 2 Date ________ MM / DD / YYYY

✘ ________________ Your attorney's name and signature, if you used one Date ________ MM / DD / YYYY

Fill in this information to identify the case:

Debtor 1 ______________________________
First Name Middle Name Last Name

Debtor 2 ______________________________
(Spouse, if filing) First Name Middle Name Last Name

United States Bankruptcy Court for the: ____________________ District of ______

Case number ____________________
(If known)

Chapter filing under:

- ☐ Chapter 7
- ☐ Chapter 11
- ☐ Chapter 12
- ☐ Chapter 13

Order Approving Payment of Filing Fee in Installments

After considering the *Application for Individuals to Pay the Filing Fee in Installments* (Official Form B 3A), the court orders that:

[ ] The debtor(s) may pay the filing fee in installments on the terms proposed in the application.

[ ] The debtor(s) must pay the filing fee according to the following terms:

	You must pay...	On or before this date...
	$________	________ Month / day / year
	$________	________ Month / day / year
	$________	________ Month / day / year
	+ $________	________ Month / day / year
Total	$________	

Until the filing fee is paid in full, the debtor(s) must not make any additional payment or transfer any additional property to an attorney or to anyone else for services in connection with this case.

________ By the court: ______________________________
Month / day / year United States Bankruptcy Judge

(Amended Oct. 17, 2005; Dec. 1, 2007; Dec. 1, 2013; June 1, 2014; Dec. 14, 2014.)

Form 3B. Application For Waiver of the Chapter 7 Filing Fee For Individuals Who Cannot Pay the Filing Fee In Full or In Installments

Fill in this information to identify your case:

Debtor 1 ______________________________
First Name Middle Name Last Name

Debtor 2 ______________________________
(Spouse, if filing) First Name Middle Name Last Name

United States Bankruptcy Court for the: ____________ District of ______

Case number ____________
(If known)

☐ Check if this is an amended filing

Official Form B 3B

Application to Have the Chapter 7 Filing Fee Waived

12/14

Be as complete and accurate as possible. If two married people are filing together, both are equally responsible for supplying correct information. If more space is needed, attach a separate sheet to this form. On the top of any additional pages, write your name and case number (if known).

Part 1: Tell the Court About Your Family and Your Family's Income

1. What is the size of your family?
Your family includes you, your spouse, and any dependents listed on *Schedule J: Current Expenditures of Individual Debtor(s)* (Official Form 6J).

Check all that apply:
☐ You
☐ Your spouse
☐ Your dependents ____________ How many dependents? ____________ Total number of people

2. Fill in your family's average monthly income.

Include your spouse's income if your spouse is living with you, even if your spouse is not filing.

Do not include your spouse's income if you are separated and your spouse is not filing with you.

Add your income and your spouse's income. Include the value (if known) of any non-cash governmental assistance that you receive, such as food stamps (benefits under the Supplemental Nutrition Assistance Program) or housing subsidies.

If you have already filled out *Schedule I: Your Income*, see line 10 of that schedule.

	That person's average monthly net income (take-home pay)
You................	$__________
Your spouse.... +	$__________
Subtotal...........	$__________
Subtract any non-cash governmental assistance that you included above. −	$__________
Your family's average monthly net income Total..................	$__________

3. Do you receive non-cash governmental assistance?
☐ No
☐ Yes. Describe.......... Type of assistance ______________

4. Do you expect your family's average monthly net income to increase or decrease by more than 10% during the next 6 months?
☐ No
☐ Yes. Explain.......... ______________

5. Tell the court why you are unable to pay the filing fee in installments within 120 days. If you have some additional circumstances that cause you to not be able to pay your filing fee in installments, explain them. ______________

Debtor 1 ______________________________ Case number (if known) ______________
First Name Middle Name Last Name

Part 2: Tell the Court About Your Monthly Expenses

6. Estimate your average monthly expenses.
Include amounts paid by any government assistance that you reported on line 2. $__________

If you have already filled out *Schedule J, Your Expenses*, copy line 22 from that form.

7. Do these expenses cover anyone who is not included in your family as reported in line 1?
☐ No
☐ Yes. Identify who........

8. Does anyone other than you regularly pay any of these expenses?
If you have already filled out *Schedule I: Your Income*, copy the total from line 11.
☐ No
☐ Yes. How much do you regularly receive as contributions? $________ monthly

9. Do you expect your average monthly expenses to increase or decrease by more than 10% during the next 6 months?
☐ No
☐ Yes. Explain ....

Part 3: Tell the Court About Your Property

If you have already filled out *Schedule A: Real Property (Official Form B 6A)* and *Schedule B: Personal Property (Official Form B 6B)*, attach copies to this application and go to Part 4.

10. How much cash do you have?
Examples: Money you have in your wallet, in your home, and on hand when you file this application

Cash: $__________

11. Bank accounts and other deposits of money?
Examples: Checking, savings, money market, or other financial accounts; certificates of deposit; shares in banks, credit unions, brokerage houses, and other similar institutions. If you have more than one account with the same institution, list each. Do not include 401(k) and IRA accounts.

	Institution name:	Amount:
Checking account:		$
Savings account:		$
Other financial accounts:		$
Other financial accounts:		$

12. Your home? (if you own it outright or are purchasing it)
Examples: House, condominium, manufactured home, or mobile home

Number Street
City State ZIP Code
Current value: $__________
Amount you owe on mortgage and liens: $__________

13. Other real estate?

Number Street
City State ZIP Code
Current value: $__________
Amount you owe on mortgage and liens: $__________

14. The vehicles you own?
Examples: Cars, vans, trucks, sports utility vehicles, motorcycles, tractors, boats

Make: __________
Model: __________
Year: __________
Mileage __________
Current value: $__________
Amount you owe on liens: $__________

Make: __________
Model: __________
Year: __________
Mileage __________
Current value: $__________
Amount you owe on liens: $__________

Debtor 1 ______________________________ Case number (if known) ______________
First Name Middle Name Last Name

15. Other assets?

Do not include household items and clothing.

Describe the other assets: [ ]

Current value: $__________

Amount you owe on liens: $__________

16. Money or property due you?

Examples: Tax refunds, past due or lump sum alimony, spousal support, child support, maintenance, divorce or property settlements, Social Security benefits, Workers' compensation, personal injury recovery

Who owes you the money or property? ______________ ______________

How much is owed? $__________ $__________

Do you believe you will likely receive payment in the next 180 days?

- [ ] No
- [ ] Yes. Explain: [ ]

Part 4: Answer These Additional Questions

17. Have you paid anyone for services for this case, including filling out this application, the bankruptcy filing package, or the schedules?

- [ ] No
- [ ] Yes. **Whom did you pay?** *Check all that apply:*
  - [ ] An attorney
  - [ ] A bankruptcy petition preparer, paralegal, or typing service
  - [ ] Someone else ______________

How much did you pay? $__________

18. Have you promised to pay or do you expect to pay someone for services for your bankruptcy case?

- [ ] No
- [ ] Yes. **Whom do you expect to pay?** *Check all that apply:*
  - [ ] An attorney
  - [ ] A bankruptcy petition preparer, paralegal, or typing service
  - [ ] Someone else ______________

How much do you expect to pay? $__________

19. Has anyone paid someone on your behalf for services for this case?

- [ ] No
- [ ] Yes. **Who was paid on your behalf?** *Check all that apply:*
  - [ ] An attorney
  - [ ] A bankruptcy petition preparer, paralegal, or typing service
  - [ ] Someone else __________

Who paid? *Check all that apply:*

- [ ] Parent
- [ ] Brother or sister
- [ ] Friend
- [ ] Pastor or clergy
- [ ] Someone else __________

How much did someone else pay? $__________

20. Have you filed for bankruptcy within the last 8 years?

- [ ] No
- [ ] Yes. District __________ When __________ (MM/ DD/ YYYY) Case number __________

District __________ When __________ (MM/ DD/ YYYY) Case number __________

District __________ When __________ (MM/ DD/ YYYY) Case number __________

Part 5: Sign Below

By signing here under penalty of perjury, I declare that I cannot afford to pay the filing fee either in full or in installments. I also declare that the information I provided in this application is true and correct.

✗ ______________________ Signature of Debtor 1

✗ ______________________ Signature of Debtor 2

Date __________ MM / DD / YYYY

Date __________ MM / DD / YYYY

Fill in this information to identify the case:

Debtor 1 ______________________________
First Name Middle Name Last Name

Debtor 2 ______________________________
(Spouse, if filing) First Name Middle Name Last Name

United States Bankruptcy Court for the: ______________ District of ______

Case number ______________________
(If known)

Order on the Application to Have the Chapter 7 Filing Fee Waived

After considering the debtor's *Application to Have the Chapter 7 Filing Fee Waived* (Official Form B 3B), the court orders that the application is:

[ ] **Granted.** However, the court may order the debtor to pay the fee in the future if developments in administering the bankruptcy case show that the waiver was unwarranted.

[ ] **Denied.** The debtor must pay the filing fee according to the following terms:

You must pay...	On or before this date...
$________	________ Month / day / year
$________	________ Month / day / year
$________	________ Month / day / year
+ $________	________ Month / day / year
Total	

If the debtor would like to propose a different payment timetable, the debtor must file a motion promptly with a payment proposal. The debtor may use *Application for Individuals to Pay the Filing Fee in Installments* (Official Form B 3A) for this purpose. The court will consider it.

The debtor must pay the entire filing fee before making any more payments or transferring any more property to an attorney, bankruptcy petition preparer, or anyone else in connection with the bankruptcy case. The debtor must also pay the entire filing fee to receive a discharge. If the debtor does not make any payment when it is due, the bankruptcy case may be dismissed and the debtor's rights in future bankruptcy cases may be affected.

[ ] **Scheduled for hearing.**

A hearing to consider the debtor's application will be held

on __________ at ________ AM / PM at ______________________________.
Month / day / year Address of courthouse

If the debtor does not appear at this hearing, the court may deny the application.

__________ **By the court:** ______________________________
Month / day / year United States Bankruptcy Judge

(As added Oct. 17, 2005; April 9, 2006; Dec. 1, 2007; Nov. 1, 2011; Dec. 1, 2013; June 1, 2014; Dec. 14, 2014.)

Form 4. List of Creditors Holding 20 Largest Unsecured Claims

Official Form 4 (12/07)

United States Bankruptcy Court

____________ District Of ___________

In re ____________________, Case No. ____________

Debtor

Chapter __________

LIST OF CREDITORS HOLDING 20 LARGEST UNSECURED CLAIMS

Following is the list of the debtor's creditors holding the 20 largest unsecured claims. The list is prepared in accordance with Fed. R. Bankr. P. 1007(d) for filing in this chapter 11 [*or* chapter 9] case. The list does not include (1) persons who come within the definition of "insider" set forth in 11 U.S.C. § 101, or (2) secured creditors unless the value of the collateral is such that the unsecured deficiency places the creditor among the holders of the 20 largest unsecured claims. If a minor child is one of the creditors holding the 20 largest unsecured claims, indicate that by stating "a minor child" and do not disclose the child's name. See 11 U.S.C. § 112. If "a minor child" is stated, also include the name, address, and legal relationship to the minor child of a person described in Fed. R. Bankr. P. 1007(m).

(1)	(2)	(3)	(4)	(5)
Name of creditor and complete mailing address including zip code	*Name, telephone number and complete mailing address, including zip code, of employee, agent, or department of creditor familiar with claim who may be contacted*	*Nature of claim (trade debt, bank loan, government contract, etc.)*	*Indicate if claim is contingent, unliquidated, disputed or subject to setoff*	*Amount of claim [if secured also state value of security]*

Date: ________________

____
Debtor

[Declaration as in Form 2]

(As amended Oct. 17, 2005; Dec. 1, 2007.)

Form 5. Involuntary Petition

B 5 (Official Form 5) (12/07)

UNITED STATES BANKRUPTCY COURT	INVOLUNTARY PETITION
IN RE (Name of Debtor – If Individual: Last, First, Middle)	ALL OTHER NAMES used by debtor in the last 8 years (Include married, maiden, and trade names.)
Last four digits of Social-Security or other Individual's Tax-I.D. No./Complete EIN (If more than one, state all.):	
STREET ADDRESS OF DEBTOR (No. and street, city, state, and zip code) COUNTY OF RESIDENCE OR PRINCIPAL PLACE OF BUSINESS ZIP CODE	MAILING ADDRESS OF DEBTOR (If different from street address) ZIP CODE

LOCATION OF PRINCIPAL ASSETS OF BUSINESS DEBTOR (If different from previously listed addresses)

CHAPTER OF BANKRUPTCY CODE UNDER WHICH PETITION IS FILED

☐ Chapter 7 ☐ Chapter 11

INFORMATION REGARDING DEBTOR (Check applicable boxes)

Nature of Debts (Check **one** box.)	**Type of Debtor** (Form of Organization)	**Nature of Business** (Check **one** box.)
Petitioners believe: ☐ Debts are primarily consumer debts ☐ Debts are primarily business debts	☐ Individual (Includes Joint Debtor) ☐ Corporation (Includes LLC and LLP) ☐ Partnership ☐ Other (If debtor is not one of the above entities, check this box and state type of entity below.) ____________________	☐ Health Care Business ☐ Single Asset Real Estate as defined in 11 U.S.C. § 101(51)(B) ☐ Railroad ☐ Stockbroker ☐ Commodity Broker ☐ Clearing Bank ☐ Other

VENUE	**FILING FEE** (Check one box)
☐ Debtor has been domiciled or has had a residence, principal place of business, or principal assets in the District for 180 days immediately preceding the date of this petition or for a longer part of such 180 days than in any other District. ☐ A bankruptcy case concerning debtor's affiliate, general partner or partnership is pending in this District.	☐ Full Filing Fee attached ☐ Petitioner is a child support creditor or its representative, and the form specified in § 304(g) of the Bankruptcy Reform Act of 1994 is attached. *[If a child support creditor or its representative is a petitioner, and if the petitioner files the form specified in § 304(g) of the Bankruptcy Reform Act of 1994, no fee is required.]*

PENDING BANKRUPTCY CASE FILED BY OR AGAINST ANY PARTNER OR AFFILIATE OF THIS DEBTOR (Report information for any additional cases on attached sheets.)

Name of Debtor	Case Number	Date
Relationship	District	Judge

ALLEGATIONS (Check applicable boxes)	COURT USE ONLY
1. ☐ Petitioner (s) are eligible to file this petition pursuant to 11 U.S.C. § 303 (b). 2. ☐ The debtor is a person against whom an order for relief may be entered under title 11 of the United States Code. 3.a. ☐ The debtor is generally not paying such debtor's debts as they become due, unless such debts are the subject of a bona fide dispute as to liability or amount; or b. ☐ Within 120 days preceding the filing of this petition, a custodian, other than a trustee receiver, or agent appointed or authorized to take charge of less than substantially all of the property of the debtor for the purpose of enforcing a lien against such property, was appointed or took possession.	

B 5 (Official Form 5) (12/07) – Page 2

Name of Debtor__________________

Case No.__________________

TRANSFER OF CLAIM

☐ Check this box if there has been a transfer of any claim against the debtor by or to any petitioner. Attach all documents that evidence the transfer and any statements that are required under Bankruptcy Rule 1003(a).

REQUEST FOR RELIEF

Petitioner(s) request that an order for relief be entered against the debtor under the chapter of title 11, United States Code, specified in this petition. If any petitioner is a foreign representative appointed in a foreign proceeding, a certified copy of the order of the court granting recognition is attached.

Petitioner(s) declare under penalty of perjury that the foregoing is true and correct according to the best of their knowledge, information, and belief.

x______________________ Signature of Petitioner or Representative (State title) ______________________ Name of Petitioner Date Signed Name & Mailing Address of Individual Signing in Representative Capacity ______ ______	x______________________ Signature of Attorney Date ______________________ Name of Attorney Firm (If any) ______________________ Address ______________________ Telephone No.
x______________________ Signature of Petitioner or Representative (State title) ______________________ Name of Petitioner Date Signed Name & Mailing Address of Individual Signing in Representative Capacity ______ ______	x______________________ Signature of Attorney Date ______________________ Name of Attorney Firm (If any) ______________________ Address ______________________ Telephone No.
x______________________ Signature of Petitioner or Representative (State title) ______________________ Name of Petitioner Date Signed Name & Mailing Address of Individual Signing in Representative Capacity ______ ______	x______________________ Signature of Attorney Date ______________________ Name of Attorney Firm (If any) ______________________ Address ______________________ Telephone No.

PETITIONING CREDITORS

Name and Address of Petitioner	Nature of Claim	Amount of Claim
Name and Address of Petitioner	Nature of Claim	Amount of Claim
Name and Address of Petitioner	Nature of Claim	Amount of Claim
Note: If there are more than three petitioners, attach additional sheets with the statement under penalty of perjury, each petitioner's signature under the statement and the name of attorney and petitioning creditor information in the format above.		Total Amount of Petitioners' Claims

_____continuation sheets attached

(Amended Oct. 17, 2005; Oct. 1, 2006; Dec. 1, 2007.)

Bankruptcy Form 5

Form 6. Schedules

Summary of Schedules
Statistical Summary of Certain Liabilities and Related Data (28 U.S.C. § 159)

Schedule A - Real Property
Schedule B - Personal Property
Schedule C - Property Claimed as Exempt
Schedule D - Creditors Holding Secured Claims
Schedule E - Creditors Holding Unsecured Priority Claims
Schedule F - Creditors Holding Unsecured Nonpriority Claims
Schedule G - Executory Contracts and Unexpired Leases
Schedule H - Codebtors
Schedule I - Current Income of Individual Debtor(s)
Schedule J - Current Expenditures of Individual Debtor(s)

Unsworn Declaration Under Penalty of Perjury

GENERAL INSTRUCTIONS: The first page of the debtor's schedules and the first page of any amendments thereto must contain a caption as in Form 16B. Subsequent pages should be identified with the debtor's name and case number. If the schedules are filed with the petition, the case number should be left blank.

Schedules D, E, and F have been designed for the listing of each claim only once. Even when a claim is secured only in part or entitled to priority only in part, it still should be listed only once. A claim which is secured in whole or in part should be listed on Schedule D only, and a claim which is entitled to priority in whole or in part should be listed on Schedule E only. Do not list the same claim twice. If a creditor has more than one claim, such as claims arising from separate transactions, each claim should be scheduled separately.

Review the specific instructions for each schedule before completing the schedule.

B 6 Summary (Official Form 6 - Summary) (12/14)

UNITED STATES BANKRUPTCY COURT

In re ______________________________,
Debtor

Case No. ________________

Chapter __________

STATISTICAL SUMMARY OF CERTAIN LIABILITIES AND RELATED DATA (28 U.S.C. § 159)

If you are an individual debtor whose debts are primarily consumer debts, as defined in § 101(8) of the Bankruptcy Code (11 U.S.C. § 101(8)), filing a case under chapter 7, 11 or 13, you must report all information requested below.

☐Check this box if you are an individual debtor whose debts are NOT primarily consumer debts. You are not required to report any information here.

This information is for statistical purposes only under 28 U.S.C. § 159.

Summarize the following types of liabilities, as reported in the Schedules, and total them.

Type of Liability	**Amount**
Domestic Support Obligations (from Schedule E)	$
Taxes and Certain Other Debts Owed to Governmental Units (from Schedule E)	$
Claims for Death or Personal Injury While Debtor Was Intoxicated (from Schedule E) (whether disputed or undisputed)	$
Student Loan Obligations (from Schedule F)	$
Domestic Support, Separation Agreement, and Divorce Decree Obligations Not Reported on Schedule E	$
Obligations to Pension or Profit-Sharing, and Other Similar Obligations (from Schedule F)	$
TOTAL	$

State the following:

Average Income (from Schedule I, Line 12)	$
Average Expenses (from Schedule J, Line 22)	$
Current Monthly Income (from Form 22A-1 Line 11; **OR**, Form 22B Line 14; **OR**, Form 22C-1 Line 14)	$

State the following:

1. Total from Schedule D, "UNSECURED PORTION, IF ANY" column		$
2. Total from Schedule E, "AMOUNT ENTITLED TO PRIORITY" column.	$	
3. Total from Schedule E, "AMOUNT NOT ENTITLED TO PRIORITY, IF ANY" column		$
4. Total from Schedule F		$
5. Total of non-priority unsecured debt (sum of 1, 3, and 4)		$

Bankruptcy Form 6

B 6 Summary (Official Form 6 - Summary) (12/13)

UNITED STATES BANKRUPTCY COURT

In re ______________________________, Case No. ________________
Debtor

Chapter __________

STATISTICAL SUMMARY OF CERTAIN LIABILITIES AND RELATED DATA (28 U.S.C. § 159)

If you are an individual debtor whose debts are primarily consumer debts, as defined in § 101(8) of the Bankruptcy Code (11 U.S.C. § 101(8)), filing a case under chapter 7, 11 or 13, you must report all information requested below.

☐ Check this box if you are an individual debtor whose debts are NOT primarily consumer debts. You are not required to report any information here.

This information is for statistical purposes only under 28 U.S.C. § 159.

Summarize the following types of liabilities, as reported in the Schedules, and total them.

Type of Liability	**Amount**
Domestic Support Obligations (from Schedule E)	$
Taxes and Certain Other Debts Owed to Governmental Units (from Schedule E)	$
Claims for Death or Personal Injury While Debtor Was Intoxicated (from Schedule E) (whether disputed or undisputed)	$
Student Loan Obligations (from Schedule F)	$
Domestic Support, Separation Agreement, and Divorce Decree Obligations Not Reported on Schedule E	$
Obligations to Pension or Profit-Sharing, and Other Similar Obligations (from Schedule F)	$
TOTAL	$

State the following:

Average Income (from Schedule I, Line 12)	$
Average Expenses (from Schedule J, Line 22)	$
Current Monthly Income (from Form 22A Line 12; **OR**, Form 22B Line 11; **OR**, Form 22C Line 20)	$

State the following:

1. Total from Schedule D, "UNSECURED PORTION, IF ANY" column		$
2. Total from Schedule E, "AMOUNT ENTITLED TO PRIORITY" column.	$	
3. Total from Schedule E, "AMOUNT NOT ENTITLED TO PRIORITY, IF ANY" column		$
4. Total from Schedule F		$
5. Total of non-priority unsecured debt (sum of 1, 3, and 4)		$

B 6 Summary (Official Form 6 - Summary) (12/07)

United States Bankruptcy Court

In re ______________________________, Case No. ________________
Debtor

Chapter ________

STATISTICAL SUMMARY OF CERTAIN LIABILITIES AND RELATED DATA (28 U.S.C. § 159)

If you are an individual debtor whose debts are primarily consumer debts, as defined in § 101(8) of the Bankruptcy Code (11 U.S.C. § 101(8)), filing a case under chapter 7, 11 or 13, you must report all information requested below.

☐ Check this box if you are an individual debtor whose debts are NOT primarily consumer debts. You are not required to report any information here.

This information is for statistical purposes only under 28 U.S.C. § 159.

Summarize the following types of liabilities, as reported in the Schedules, and total them.

Type of Liability	Amount
Domestic Support Obligations (from Schedule E)	$
Taxes and Certain Other Debts Owed to Governmental Units (from Schedule E)	$
Claims for Death or Personal Injury While Debtor Was Intoxicated (from Schedule E) (whether disputed or undisputed)	$
Student Loan Obligations (from Schedule F)	$
Domestic Support, Separation Agreement, and Divorce Decree Obligations Not Reported on Schedule E	$
Obligations to Pension or Profit-Sharing, and Other Similar Obligations (from Schedule F)	$
TOTAL	$

State the following:

Average Income (from Schedule I, Line 16)	$
Average Expenses (from Schedule J, Line 18)	$
Current Monthly Income (from Form 22A Line 12; **OR**, Form 22B Line 11; **OR**, Form 22C Line 20)	$

State the following:

1. Total from Schedule D, "UNSECURED PORTION, IF ANY" column		$
2. Total from Schedule E, "AMOUNT ENTITLED TO PRIORITY" column.	$	
3. Total from Schedule E, "AMOUNT NOT ENTITLED TO PRIORITY, IF ANY" column		$
4. Total from Schedule F		$
5. Total of non-priority unsecured debt (sum of 1, 3, and 4)		$

B6A (Official Form 6A) (12/07)

In re ______________________________________, **Case No.** ________________________
Debtor **(If known)**

SCHEDULE A - REAL PROPERTY

Except as directed below, list all real property in which the debtor has any legal, equitable, or future interest, including all property owned as a co-tenant, community property, or in which the debtor has a life estate. Include any property in which the debtor holds rights and powers exercisable for the debtor's own benefit. If the debtor is married, state whether the husband, wife, both, or the marital community own the property by placing an "H," "W," "J," or "C" in the column labeled "Husband, Wife, Joint, or Community." If the debtor holds no interest in real property, write "None" under "Description and Location of Property."

Do not include interests in executory contracts and unexpired leases on this schedule. List them in Schedule G - Executory Contracts and Unexpired Leases.

If an entity claims to have a lien or hold a secured interest in any property, state the amount of the secured claim. See Schedule D. If no entity claims to hold a secured interest in the property, write "None" in the column labeled "Amount of Secured Claim."

If the debtor is an individual or if a joint petition is filed, state the amount of any exemption claimed in the property only in Schedule C - Property Claimed as Exempt.

DESCRIPTION AND LOCATION OF PROPERTY	NATURE OF DEBTOR'S INTEREST IN PROPERTY	HUSBAND, WIFE, JOINT, OR COMMUNITY	CURRENT VALUE OF DEBTOR'S INTEREST IN PROPERTY, WITHOUT DEDUCTING ANY SECURED CLAIM OR EXEMPTION	AMOUNT OF SECURED CLAIM
		Total➤		

(Report also on Summary of Schedules.)

Bankruptcy Form 6

B 6B (Official Form 6B) (12/07)

In re ______________________________, **Case No.** ____________________
Debtor **(If known)**

SCHEDULE B - PERSONAL PROPERTY

Except as directed below, list all personal property of the debtor of whatever kind. If the debtor has no property in one or more of the categories, place an "x" in the appropriate position in the column labeled "None." If additional space is needed in any category, attach a separate sheet properly identified with the case name, case number, and the number of the category. If the debtor is married, state whether the husband, wife, both, or the marital community own the property by placing an "H," "W," "J," or "C" in the column labeled "Husband, Wife, Joint, or Community." If the debtor is an individual or a joint petition is filed, state the amount of any exemptions claimed only in Schedule C - Property Claimed as Exempt.

Do not list interests in executory contracts and unexpired leases on this schedule. List them in Schedule G - Executory Contracts and Unexpired Leases.

If the property is being held for the debtor by someone else, state that person's name and address under "Description and Location of Property." If the property is being held for a minor child, simply state the child's initials and the name and address of the child's parent or guardian, such as "A.B., a minor child, by John Doe, guardian." Do not disclose the child's name. See, 11 U.S.C. §112 and Fed. R. Bankr. P. 1007(m).

TYPE OF PROPERTY	NONE	DESCRIPTION AND LOCATION OF PROPERTY	HUSBAND, WIFE, JOINT, OR COMMUNITY	CURRENT VALUE OF DEBTOR'S INTEREST IN PROPERTY, WITHOUT DEDUCTING ANY SECURED CLAIM OR EXEMPTION
1. Cash on hand.				
2. Checking, savings or other financial accounts, certificates of deposit or shares in banks, savings and loan, thrift, building and loan, and homestead associations, or credit unions, brokerage houses, or cooperatives.				
3. Security deposits with public utilities, telephone companies, landlords, and others.				
4. Household goods and furnishings, including audio, video, and computer equipment.				
5. Books; pictures and other art objects; antiques; stamp, coin, record, tape, compact disc, and other collections or collectibles.				
6. Wearing apparel.				
7. Furs and jewelry.				
8. Firearms and sports, photographic, and other hobby equipment.				
9. Interests in insurance policies. Name insurance company of each policy and itemize surrender or refund value of each.				
10. Annuities. Itemize and name each issuer.				
11. Interests in an education IRA as defined in 26 U.S.C. § 530(b)(1) or under a qualified State tuition plan as defined in 26 U.S.C. § 529(b)(1). Give particulars. (File separately the record(s) of any such interest(s). 11 U.S.C. § 521(c).)				

B 6B (Official Form 6B) (12/07) -- Cont.

In re ______________________________, Case No. ____________________
Debtor (If known)

SCHEDULE B - PERSONAL PROPERTY

(Continuation Sheet)

TYPE OF PROPERTY	NONE	DESCRIPTION AND LOCATION OF PROPERTY	HUSBAND, WIFE, JOINT, OR COMMUNITY	CURRENT VALUE OF DEBTOR'S INTEREST IN PROPERTY, WITH-OUT DEDUCTING ANY SECURED CLAIM OR EXEMPTION
12. Interests in IRA, ERISA, Keogh, or other pension or profit sharing plans. Give particulars.				
13. Stock and interests in incorporated and unincorporated businesses. Itemize.				
14. Interests in partnerships or joint ventures. Itemize.				
15. Government and corporate bonds and other negotiable and non-negotiable instruments.				
16. Accounts receivable.				
17. Alimony, maintenance, support, and property settlements to which the debtor is or may be entitled. Give particulars.				
18. Other liquidated debts owed to debtor including tax refunds. Give particulars.				
19. Equitable or future interests, life estates, and rights or powers exercisable for the benefit of the debtor other than those listed in Schedule A – Real Property.				
20. Contingent and noncontingent interests in estate of a decedent, death benefit plan, life insurance policy, or trust.				
21. Other contingent and unliquidated claims of every nature, including tax refunds, counterclaims of the debtor, and rights to setoff claims. Give estimated value of each.				

B 6B (Official Form 6B) (12/07) -- Cont.

In re ______________________________, Case No. ____________________
Debtor (If known)

SCHEDULE B - PERSONAL PROPERTY

(Continuation Sheet)

TYPE OF PROPERTY	NONE	DESCRIPTION AND LOCATION OF PROPERTY	HUSBAND, WIFE, JOINT, OR COMMUNITY	CURRENT VALUE OF DEBTOR'S INTEREST IN PROPERTY, WITH-OUT DEDUCTING ANY SECURED CLAIM OR EXEMPTION
22. Patents, copyrights, and other intellectual property. Give particulars.				
23. Licenses, franchises, and other general intangibles. Give particulars.				
24. Customer lists or other compilations containing personally identifiable information (as defined in 11 U.S.C. § 101(41A)) provided to the debtor by individuals in connection with obtaining a product or service from the debtor primarily for personal, family, or household purposes.				
25. Automobiles, trucks, trailers, and other vehicles and accessories.				
26. Boats, motors, and accessories.				
27. Aircraft and accessories.				
28. Office equipment, furnishings, and supplies.				
29. Machinery, fixtures, equipment, and supplies used in business.				
30. Inventory.				
31. Animals.				
32. Crops - growing or harvested. Give particulars.				
33. Farming equipment and implements.				
34. Farm supplies, chemicals, and feed.				
35. Other personal property of any kind not already listed. Itemize.				

________ continuation sheets attached Total➤ $

(Include amounts from any continuation sheets attached. Report total also on Summary of Schedules.)

Bankruptcy Form 6

B6C (Official Form 6C) (04/13)

In re ______________________________, **Case No.** ______________________
Debtor *(If known)*

SCHEDULE C - PROPERTY CLAIMED AS EXEMPT

Debtor claims the exemptions to which debtor is entitled under:
(Check one box)
☐ 11 U.S.C. § 522(b)(2)
☐ 11 U.S.C. § 522(b)(3)

☐ Check if debtor claims a homestead exemption that exceeds $155,675.*

DESCRIPTION OF PROPERTY	SPECIFY LAW PROVIDING EACH EXEMPTION	VALUE OF CLAIMED EXEMPTION	CURRENT VALUE OF PROPERTY WITHOUT DEDUCTING EXEMPTION

* *Amount subject to adjustment on 4/01/16, and every three years thereafter with respect to cases commenced on or after the date of adjustment.*

B 6D (Official Form 6D) (12/07)

In re ______________________________, **Case No.** ______________________________
Debtor **(If known)**

SCHEDULE D - CREDITORS HOLDING SECURED CLAIMS

State the name, mailing address, including zip code, and last four digits of any account number of all entities holding claims secured by property of the debtor as of the date of filing of the petition. The complete account number of any account the debtor has with the creditor is useful to the trustee and the creditor and may be provided if the debtor chooses to do so. List creditors holding all types of secured interests such as judgment liens, garnishments, statutory liens, mortgages, deeds of trust, and other security interests.

List creditors in alphabetical order to the extent practicable. If a minor child is the creditor, state the child's initials and the name and address of the child's parent or guardian, such as "A.B., a minor child, by John Doe, guardian." Do not disclose the child's name. See, 11 U.S.C. §112 and Fed. R. Bankr. P. 1007(m). If all secured creditors will not fit on this page, use the continuation sheet provided.

If any entity other than a spouse in a joint case may be jointly liable on a claim, place an "X" in the column labeled "Codebtor," include the entity on the appropriate schedule of creditors, and complete Schedule H – Codebtors. If a joint petition is filed, state whether the husband, wife, both of them, or the marital community may be liable on each claim by placing an "H," "W," "J," or "C" in the column labeled "Husband, Wife, Joint, or Community."

If the claim is contingent, place an "X" in the column labeled "Contingent." If the claim is unliquidated, place an "X" in the column labeled "Unliquidated." If the claim is disputed, place an "X" in the column labeled "Disputed." (You may need to place an "X" in more than one of these three columns.)

Total the columns labeled "Amount of Claim Without Deducting Value of Collateral" and "Unsecured Portion, if Any" in the boxes labeled "Total(s)" on the last sheet of the completed schedule. Report the total from the column labeled "Amount of Claim Without Deducting Value of Collateral" also on the Summary of Schedules and, if the debtor is an individual with primarily consumer debts, report the total from the column labeled "Unsecured Portion, if Any" on the Statistical Summary of Certain Liabilities and Related Data.

☐ Check this box if debtor has no creditors holding secured claims to report on this Schedule D.

CREDITOR'S NAME AND MAILING ADDRESS INCLUDING ZIP CODE AND AN ACCOUNT NUMBER (*See Instructions Above.*)	CODEBTOR	HUSBAND, WIFE, JOINT, OR COMMUNITY	DATE CLAIM WAS INCURRED, NATURE OF LIEN , AND DESCRIPTION AND VALUE OF PROPERTY SUBJECT TO LIEN	CONTINGENT	UNLIQUIDATED	DISPUTED	AMOUNT OF CLAIM WITHOUT DEDUCTING VALUE OF COLLATERAL	UNSECURED PORTION, IF ANY
ACCOUNT NO.			VALUE $					
ACCOUNT NO.			VALUE $					
ACCOUNT NO.			VALUE $					
____ continuation sheets attached			Subtotal ▶ (Total of this page)				$	$
			Total ▶ (Use only on last page)				$	$
							(Report also on Summary of Schedules.)	(If applicable, report also on Statistical Summary of Certain Liabilities and Related Data.)

B 6D (Official Form 6D) (12/07) – Cont. 2

In re ______________________, **Case No.** ______________________
Debtor **(if known)**

SCHEDULE D - CREDITORS HOLDING SECURED CLAIMS
(Continuation Sheet)

CREDITOR'S NAME AND MAILING ADDRESS INCLUDING ZIP CODE AND AN ACCOUNT NUMBER (*See Instructions Above.*)	CODEBTOR	HUSBAND, WIFE, JOINT, OR COMMUNITY	DATE CLAIM WAS INCURRED, NATURE OF LIEN , AND DESCRIPTION AND VALUE OF PROPERTY SUBJECT TO LIEN	CONTINGENT	UNLIQUIDATED	DISPUTED	AMOUNT OF CLAIM WITHOUT DEDUCTING VALUE OF COLLATERAL	UNSECURED PORTION, IF ANY
ACCOUNT NO.			VALUE $					
ACCOUNT NO.			VALUE $					
ACCOUNT NO.			VALUE $					
ACCOUNT NO.			VALUE $					
ACCOUNT NO.			VALUE $					
Sheet no.____of____continuation sheets attached to Schedule of Creditors Holding Secured Claims			Subtotal (s)▶ (Total(s) of this page)				$	$
			Total(s) ▶ (Use only on last page)				$	$
							(Report also on Summary of Schedules.)	(If applicable, report also on Statistical Summary of Certain Liabilities and Related Data.)

Bankruptcy Form 6

B6E (Official Form 6E) (04/13)

In re ______________________________, Case No.____________________
Debtor *(if known)*

SCHEDULE E - CREDITORS HOLDING UNSECURED PRIORITY CLAIMS

A complete list of claims entitled to priority, listed separately by type of priority, is to be set forth on the sheets provided. Only holders of unsecured claims entitled to priority should be listed in this schedule. In the boxes provided on the attached sheets, state the name, mailing address, including zip code, and last four digits of the account number, if any, of all entities holding priority claims against the debtor or the property of the debtor, as of the date of the filing of the petition. Use a separate continuation sheet for each type of priority and label each with the type of priority.

The complete account number of any account the debtor has with the creditor is useful to the trustee and the creditor and may be provided if the debtor chooses to do so. If a minor child is a creditor, state the child's initials and the name and address of the child's parent or guardian, such as "A.B., a minor child, by John Doe, guardian." Do not disclose the child's name. See, 11 U.S.C. §112 and Fed. R. Bankr. P. 1007(m).

If any entity other than a spouse in a joint case may be jointly liable on a claim, place an "X" in the column labeled "Codebtor," include the entity on the appropriate schedule of creditors, and complete Schedule H-Codebtors. If a joint petition is filed, state whether the husband, wife, both of them, or the marital community may be liable on each claim by placing an "H," "W," "J," or "C" in the column labeled "Husband, Wife, Joint, or Community." If the claim is contingent, place an "X" in the column labeled "Contingent." If the claim is unliquidated, place an "X" in the column labeled "Unliquidated." If the claim is disputed, place an "X" in the column labeled "Disputed." (You may need to place an "X" in more than one of these three columns.)

Report the total of claims listed on each sheet in the box labeled "Subtotals" on each sheet. Report the total of all claims listed on this Schedule E in the box labeled "Total" on the last sheet of the completed schedule. Report this total also on the Summary of Schedules.

Report the total of amounts entitled to priority listed on each sheet in the box labeled "Subtotals" on each sheet. Report the total of all amounts entitled to priority listed on this Schedule E in the box labeled "Totals" on the last sheet of the completed schedule. Individual debtors with primarily consumer debts report this total also on the Statistical Summary of Certain Liabilities and Related Data.

Report the total of amounts not entitled to priority listed on each sheet in the box labeled "Subtotals" on each sheet. Report the total of all amounts not entitled to priority listed on this Schedule E in the box labeled "Totals" on the last sheet of the completed schedule. Individual debtors with primarily consumer debts report this total also on the Statistical Summary of Certain Liabilities and Related Data.

☐ Check this box if debtor has no creditors holding unsecured priority claims to report on this Schedule E.

TYPES OF PRIORITY CLAIMS (Check the appropriate box(es) below if claims in that category are listed on the attached sheets.)

☐ **Domestic Support Obligations**

Claims for domestic support that are owed to or recoverable by a spouse, former spouse, or child of the debtor, or the parent, legal guardian, or responsible relative of such a child, or a governmental unit to whom such a domestic support claim has been assigned to the extent provided in 11 U.S.C. § 507(a)(1).

☐ **Extensions of credit in an involuntary case**

Claims arising in the ordinary course of the debtor's business or financial affairs after the commencement of the case but before the earlier of the appointment of a trustee or the order for relief. 11 U.S.C. § 507(a)(3).

☐ **Wages, salaries, and commissions**

Wages, salaries, and commissions, including vacation, severance, and sick leave pay owing to employees and commissions owing to qualifying independent sales representatives up to $12,475* per person earned within 180 days immediately preceding the filing of the original petition, or the cessation of business, whichever occurred first, to the extent provided in 11 U.S.C. § 507(a)(4).

☐ **Contributions to employee benefit plans**

Money owed to employee benefit plans for services rendered within 180 days immediately preceding the filing of the original petition, or the cessation of business, whichever occurred first, to the extent provided in 11 U.S.C. § 507(a)(5).

* *Amount subject to adjustment on 4/01/16, and every three years thereafter with respect to cases commenced on or after the date of adjustment.*

B6E (Official Form 6E) (04/13) – Cont.

In re ______________________________, **Case No.**____________________
Debtor *(if known)*

☐ **Certain farmers and fishermen**

Claims of certain farmers and fishermen, up to $6,150* per farmer or fisherman, against the debtor, as provided in 11 U.S.C. § 507(a)(6).

☐ **Deposits by individuals**

Claims of individuals up to $2,775* for deposits for the purchase, lease, or rental of property or services for personal, family, or household use, that were not delivered or provided. 11 U.S.C. § 507(a)(7).

☐ **Taxes and Certain Other Debts Owed to Governmental Units**

Taxes, customs duties, and penalties owing to federal, state, and local governmental units as set forth in 11 U.S.C. § 507(a)(8).

☐ **Commitments to Maintain the Capital of an Insured Depository Institution**

Claims based on commitments to the FDIC, RTC, Director of the Office of Thrift Supervision, Comptroller of the Currency, or Board of Governors of the Federal Reserve System, or their predecessors or successors, to maintain the capital of an insured depository institution. 11 U.S.C. § 507 (a)(9).

☐ **Claims for Death or Personal Injury While Debtor Was Intoxicated**

Claims for death or personal injury resulting from the operation of a motor vehicle or vessel while the debtor was intoxicated from using alcohol, a drug, or another substance. 11 U.S.C. § 507(a)(10).

* *Amounts are subject to adjustment on 4/01/16, and every three years thereafter with respect to cases commenced on or after the date of adjustment.*

____ continuation sheets attached

B6E (Official Form 6E) (04/13) – Cont.

In re ______________________________, Case No. ______________________
Debtor (if known)

SCHEDULE E - CREDITORS HOLDING UNSECURED PRIORITY CLAIMS

(Continuation Sheet)

Type of Priority for Claims Listed on This Sheet

CREDITOR'S NAME, MAILING ADDRESS INCLUDING ZIP CODE, AND ACCOUNT NUMBER (*See instructions above.*)	CODEBTOR	HUSBAND, WIFE, JOINT, OR COMMUNITY	DATE CLAIM WAS INCURRED AND CONSIDERATION FOR CLAIM	CONTINGENT	UNLIQUIDATED	DISPUTED	AMOUNT OF CLAIM	AMOUNT ENTITLED TO PRIORITY	AMOUNT NOT ENTITLED TO PRIORITY, IF ANY
Account No.									
Account No.									
Account No.									
Account No.									
Sheet no. ___ of ___ continuation sheets attached to Schedule of Creditors Holding Priority Claims						Subtotals➤ (Totals of this page)	$	$	
						Total➤ (Use only on last page of the completed Schedule E. Report also on the Summary of Schedules.)	$		
						Totals➤ (Use only on last page of the completed Schedule E. If applicable, report also on the Statistical Summary of Certain Liabilities and Related Data.)		$	$

Bankruptcy Form 6

B 6F (Official Form 6F) (12/07)

In re ______________________________, **Case No.** ______________________
Debtor **(if known)**

SCHEDULE F - CREDITORS HOLDING UNSECURED NONPRIORITY CLAIMS

State the name, mailing address, including zip code, and last four digits of any account number, of all entities holding unsecured claims without priority against the debtor or the property of the debtor, as of the date of filing of the petition. The complete account number of any account the debtor has with the creditor is useful to the trustee and the creditor and may be provided if the debtor chooses to do so. If a minor child is a creditor, state the child's initials and the name and address of the child's parent or guardian, such as "A.B., a minor child, by John Doe, guardian." Do not disclose the child's name. See, 11 U.S.C. §112 and Fed. R. Bankr. P. 1007(m). Do not include claims listed in Schedules D and E. If all creditors will not fit on this page, use the continuation sheet provided.

If any entity other than a spouse in a joint case may be jointly liable on a claim, place an "X" in the column labeled "Codebtor," include the entity on the appropriate schedule of creditors, and complete Schedule H - Codebtors. If a joint petition is filed, state whether the husband, wife, both of them, or the marital community may be liable on each claim by placing an "H," "W," "J," or "C" in the column labeled "Husband, Wife, Joint, or Community."

If the claim is contingent, place an "X" in the column labeled "Contingent." If the claim is unliquidated, place an "X" in the column labeled "Unliquidated." If the claim is disputed, place an "X" in the column labeled "Disputed." (You may need to place an "X" in more than one of these three columns.)

Report the total of all claims listed on this schedule in the box labeled "Total" on the last sheet of the completed schedule. Report this total also on the Summary of Schedules and, if the debtor is an individual with primarily consumer debts, report this total also on the Statistical Summary of Certain Liabilities and Related Data..

☐ Check this box if debtor has no creditors holding unsecured claims to report on this Schedule F.

CREDITOR'S NAME, MAILING ADDRESS INCLUDING ZIP CODE, AND ACCOUNT NUMBER *(See instructions above.)*	CODEBTOR	HUSBAND, WIFE, JOINT, OR COMMUNITY	DATE CLAIM WAS INCURRED AND CONSIDERATION FOR CLAIM. IF CLAIM IS SUBJECT TO SETOFF, SO STATE.	CONTINGENT	UNLIQUIDATED	DISPUTED	AMOUNT OF CLAIM
ACCOUNT NO.							
ACCOUNT NO.							
ACCOUNT NO.							
ACCOUNT NO.							
						Subtotal➤	$
____continuation sheets attached						Total➤ (Use only on last page of the completed Schedule F.) (Report also on Summary of Schedules and, if applicable, on the Statistical Summary of Certain Liabilities and Related Data.)	$

Bankruptcy Form 6

B 6F (Official Form 6F) (12/07) - Cont.

In re ______________________________, Case No. ______________________
Debtor (if known)

SCHEDULE F - CREDITORS HOLDING UNSECURED NONPRIORITY CLAIMS

(Continuation Sheet)

CREDITOR'S NAME, MAILING ADDRESS INCLUDING ZIP CODE, AND ACCOUNT NUMBER (See instructions above.)	CODEBTOR	HUSBAND, WIFE, JOINT, OR COMMUNITY	DATE CLAIM WAS INCURRED AND CONSIDERATION FOR CLAIM. IF CLAIM IS SUBJECT TO SETOFF, SO STATE.	CONTINGENT	UNLIQUIDATED	DISPUTED	AMOUNT OF CLAIM
ACCOUNT NO.							
ACCOUNT NO.							
ACCOUNT NO.							
ACCOUNT NO.							
ACCOUNT NO.							

Sheet no._____ of_____ continuation sheets attached to Schedule of Creditors Holding Unsecured Nonpriority Claims

Subtotal➤ $

Total➤ $
(Use only on last page of the completed Schedule F.)
(Report also on Summary of Schedules and, if applicable on the Statistical Summary of Certain Liabilities and Related Data.)

Bankruptcy Form 6

B 6G (Official Form 6G) (12/07)

In re ______________________________, **Case No.**____________________
Debtor **(if known)**

SCHEDULE G - EXECUTORY CONTRACTS AND UNEXPIRED LEASES

Describe all executory contracts of any nature and all unexpired leases of real or personal property. Include any timeshare interests. State nature of debtor's interest in contract, i.e., "Purchaser," "Agent," etc. State whether debtor is the lessor or lessee of a lease. Provide the names and complete mailing addresses of all other parties to each lease or contract described. If a minor child is a party to one of the leases or contracts, state the child's initials and the name and address of the child's parent or guardian, such as "A.B., a minor child, by John Doe, guardian." Do not disclose the child's name. See, 11 U.S.C. §112 and Fed. R. Bankr. P. 1007(m).

☐ Check this box if debtor has no executory contracts or unexpired leases.

NAME AND MAILING ADDRESS, INCLUDING ZIP CODE, OF OTHER PARTIES TO LEASE OR CONTRACT.	DESCRIPTION OF CONTRACT OR LEASE AND NATURE OF DEBTOR'S INTEREST. STATE WHETHER LEASE IS FOR NONRESIDENTIAL REAL PROPERTY. STATE CONTRACT NUMBER OF ANY GOVERNMENT CONTRACT.

B 6H (Official Form 6H) (12/07)

In re ______________________________, **Case No.** ______________________
Debtor **(if known)**

SCHEDULE H - CODEBTORS

Provide the information requested concerning any person or entity, other than a spouse in a joint case, that is also liable on any debts listed by the debtor in the schedules of creditors. Include all guarantors and co-signers. If the debtor resides or resided in a community property state, commonwealth, or territory (including Alaska, Arizona, California, Idaho, Louisiana, Nevada, New Mexico, Puerto Rico, Texas, Washington, or Wisconsin) within the eight-year period immediately preceding the commencement of the case, identify the name of the debtor's spouse and of any former spouse who resides or resided with the debtor in the community property state, commonwealth, or territory. Include all names used by the nondebtor spouse during the eight years immediately preceding the commencement of this case. If a minor child is a codebtor or a creditor, state the child's initials and the name and address of the child's parent or guardian, such as "A.B., a minor child, by John Doe, guardian." Do not disclose the child's name. See, 11 U.S.C. §112 and Fed. R. Bankr. P. 1007(m).

☐ Check this box if debtor has no codebtors.

NAME AND ADDRESS OF CODEBTOR	NAME AND ADDRESS OF CREDITOR

Fill in this information to identify your case:

Debtor 1 ______ First Name ______ Middle Name ______ Last Name

Debtor 2 (Spouse, if filing) ______ First Name ______ Middle Name ______ Last Name

United States Bankruptcy Court for the: ______ District of ______

Case number (If known) ______

Check if this is:

☐ An amended filing

☐ A supplement showing post-petition chapter 13 income as of the following date:

______ MM / DD / YYYY

Official Form B 6I

Schedule I: Your Income

12/13

Be as complete and accurate as possible. If two married people are filing together (Debtor 1 and Debtor 2), both are equally responsible for supplying correct information. If you are married and not filing jointly, and your spouse is living with you, include information about your spouse. If you are separated and your spouse is not filing with you, do not include information about your spouse. If more space is needed, attach a separate sheet to this form. On the top of any additional pages, write your name and case number (if known). Answer every question.

Part 1: Describe Employment

1. **Fill in your employment information.**

   If you have more than one job, attach a separate page with information about additional employers.

   Include part-time, seasonal, or self-employed work.

   Occupation may Include student or homemaker, if it applies.

	Debtor 1	Debtor 2 or non-filing spouse
Employment status	☐ Employed ☐ Not employed	☐ Employed ☐ Not employed
Occupation	______	______
Employer's name	______	______
Employer's address	______ Number Street ______ ______ ______ City State ZIP Code	______ Number Street ______ ______ ______ City State ZIP Code
How long employed there?	______	______

Part 2: Give Details About Monthly Income

Estimate monthly income as of the date you file this form. If you have nothing to report for any line, write $0 in the space. Include your non-filing spouse unless you are separated.

If you or your non-filing spouse have more than one employer, combine the information for all employers for that person on the lines below. If you need more space, attach a separate sheet to this form.

		For Debtor 1	For Debtor 2 or non-filing spouse
2. **List monthly gross wages, salary, and commissions** (before all payroll deductions). If not paid monthly, calculate what the monthly wage would be.	2.	$______	$______
3. **Estimate and list monthly overtime pay.**	3.	+$______	+ $______
4. **Calculate gross income.** Add line 2 + line 3.	4.	$______	$______

Debtor 1 ______ First Name Middle Name Last Name Case number (if known) ______

		For Debtor 1	For Debtor 2 or non-filing spouse	
Copy line 4 here ...	→ 4.	$	$	
5. **List all payroll deductions:**				
5a. **Tax, Medicare, and Social Security deductions**	5a.	$	$	
5b. **Mandatory contributions for retirement plans**	5b.	$	$	
5c. **Voluntary contributions for retirement plans**	5c.	$	$	
5d. **Required repayments of retirement fund loans**	5d.	$	$	
5e. **Insurance**	5e.	$	$	
5f. **Domestic support obligations**	5f.	$	$	
5g. **Union dues**	5g.	$	$	
5h. **Other deductions.** Specify: ______	5h.	+ $	+ $	
6. **Add the payroll deductions.** Add lines 5a + 5b + 5c + 5d + 5e +5f + 5g +5h.	6.	$	$	
7. **Calculate total monthly take-home pay.** Subtract line 6 from line 4.	7.	$	$	
8. **List all other income regularly received:**				
8a. **Net income from rental property and from operating a business, profession, or farm** Attach a statement for each property and business showing gross receipts, ordinary and necessary business expenses, and the total monthly net income.	8a.	$	$	
8b. **Interest and dividends**	8b.	$	$	
8c. **Family support payments that you, a non-filing spouse, or a dependent regularly receive** Include alimony, spousal support, child support, maintenance, divorce settlement, and property settlement.	8c.	$	$	
8d. **Unemployment compensation**	8d.	$	$	
8e. **Social Security**	8e.	$	$	
8f. **Other government assistance that you regularly receive** Include cash assistance and the value (if known) of any non-cash assistance that you receive, such as food stamps (benefits under the Supplemental Nutrition Assistance Program) or housing subsidies. Specify: ______	8f.	$	$	
8g. **Pension or retirement income**	8g.	$	$	
8h. **Other monthly income.** Specify: ______	8h.	+ $	+ $	
9. **Add all other income.** Add lines 8a + 8b + 8c + 8d + 8e + 8f +8g + 8h.	9.	$	$	
10. **Calculate monthly income.** Add line 7 + line 9. Add the entries in line 10 for Debtor 1 and Debtor 2 or non-filing spouse.	10.	$	+ $	= $

11. **State all other regular contributions to the expenses that you list in *Schedule J.***
Include contributions from an unmarried partner, members of your household, your dependents, your roommates, and other friends or relatives.
Do not include any amounts already included in lines 2-10 or amounts that are not available to pay expenses listed in *Schedule J.*
Specify: ______ 11. + $______

12. **Add the amount in the last column of line 10 to the amount in line 11.** The result is the combined monthly income.
Write that amount on the *Summary of Schedules* and *Statistical Summary of Certain Liabilities and Related Data*, if it applies 12. $______
Combined monthly income

13. **Do you expect an increase or decrease within the year after you file this form?**
☐ No.
☐ Yes. Explain: ______

Official Form B 6I **Schedule I: Your Income** page 2

Bankruptcy Form 6

Fill in this information to identify your case:

Debtor 1 ____________ First Name ____________ Middle Name ____________ Last Name

Debtor 2 (Spouse, if filing) ____________ First Name ____________ Middle Name ____________ Last Name

United States Bankruptcy Court for the: ____________ District of ________

Case number (If known) ____________

Check if this is:

☐ An amended filing

☐ A supplement showing post-petition chapter 13 expenses as of the following date:

MM / DD / YYYY

☐ A separate filing for Debtor 2 because Debtor 2 maintains a separate household

Official Form B 6J

Schedule J: Your Expenses

12/13

Be as complete and accurate as possible. If two married people are filing together, both are equally responsible for supplying correct information. If more space is needed, attach another sheet to this form. On the top of any additional pages, write your name and case number (if known). Answer every question.

Part 1: Describe Your Household

1. **Is this a joint case?**

☐ No. Go to line 2.

☐ Yes. **Does Debtor 2 live in a separate household?**

☐ No

☐ Yes. Debtor 2 must file a separate Schedule J.

2. **Do you have dependents?**

Do not list Debtor 1 and Debtor 2.

Do not state the dependents' names.

☐ No

☐ Yes. Fill out this information for each dependent........................

Dependent's relationship to Debtor 1 or Debtor 2	Dependent's age	Does dependent live with you?
____________	______	☐ No ☐ Yes
____________	______	☐ No ☐ Yes
____________	______	☐ No ☐ Yes
____________	______	☐ No ☐ Yes
____________	______	☐ No ☐ Yes

3. **Do your expenses include expenses of people other than yourself and your dependents?**

☐ No

☐ Yes

Part 2: Estimate Your Ongoing Monthly Expenses

Estimate your expenses as of your bankruptcy filing date unless you are using this form as a supplement in a Chapter 13 case to report expenses as of a date after the bankruptcy is filed. If this is a supplemental *Schedule J*, check the box at the top of the form and fill in the applicable date.

Include expenses paid for with non-cash government assistance if you know the value of such assistance and have included it on *Schedule I: Your Income* (Official Form B 6I.)

		Your expenses
4. **The rental or home ownership expenses for your residence.** Include first mortgage payments and any rent for the ground or lot.	4.	$________
If not included in line 4:		
4a. Real estate taxes	4a.	$________
4b. Property, homeowner's, or renter's insurance	4b.	$________
4c. Home maintenance, repair, and upkeep expenses	4c.	$________
4d. Homeowner's association or condominium dues	4d.	$________

Debtor 1 ______________________ First Name Middle Name Last Name Case number (if known) ______________

		Your expenses
5. **Additional mortgage payments for your residence**, such as home equity loans	5.	$________
6. **Utilities:**		
6a. Electricity, heat, natural gas	6a.	$________
6b. Water, sewer, garbage collection	6b.	$________
6c. Telephone, cell phone, Internet, satellite, and cable services	6c.	$________
6d. Other. Specify: ______________	6d.	$________
7. **Food and housekeeping supplies**	7.	$________
8. **Childcare and children's education costs**	8.	$________
9. **Clothing, laundry, and dry cleaning**	9.	$________
10. **Personal care products and services**	10.	$________
11. **Medical and dental expenses**	11.	$________
12. **Transportation.** Include gas, maintenance, bus or train fare. Do not include car payments.	12.	$________
13. **Entertainment, clubs, recreation, newspapers, magazines, and books**	13.	$________
14. **Charitable contributions and religious donations**	14.	$________
15. **Insurance.** Do not include insurance deducted from your pay or included in lines 4 or 20.		
15a. Life insurance	15a.	$________
15b. Health insurance	15b.	$________
15c. Vehicle insurance	15c.	$________
15d. Other insurance. Specify: ______________	15d.	$________
16. **Taxes.** Do not include taxes deducted from your pay or included in lines 4 or 20. Specify: ______________	16.	$________
17. **Installment or lease payments:**		
17a. Car payments for Vehicle 1	17a.	$________
17b. Car payments for Vehicle 2	17b.	$________
17c. Other. Specify: ______________	17c.	$________
17d. Other. Specify: ______________	17d.	$________
18. **Your payments of alimony, maintenance, and support that you did not report as deducted from your pay on line 5, *Schedule I, Your Income* (Official Form B 6I).**	18.	$________
19. **Other payments you make to support others who do not live with you.** Specify: ______________	19.	$________
20. **Other real property expenses not included in lines 4 or 5 of this form or on *Schedule I: Your Income.***		
20a. Mortgages on other property	20a.	$________
20b. Real estate taxes	20b.	$________
20c. Property, homeowner's, or renter's insurance	20c.	$________
20d. Maintenance, repair, and upkeep expenses	20d.	$________
20e. Homeowner's association or condominium dues	20e.	$________

Debtor 1 ______________________________
First Name Middle Name Last Name

Case number (if known) ______________________________

21. **Other**. Specify: ______________________________ 21. +$______________

22. **Your monthly expenses.** Add lines 4 through 21.
The result is your monthly expenses. 22. $______________

23. **Calculate your monthly net income.**

23a. Copy line 12 (*your combined monthly income*) from *Schedule I.* 23a. $______________

23b. Copy your monthly expenses from line 22 above. 23b. –$______________

23c. Subtract your monthly expenses from your monthly income.
The result is your *monthly net income.* 23c. $______________

24. **Do you expect an increase or decrease in your expenses within the year after you file this form?**

For example, do you expect to finish paying for your car loan within the year or do you expect your mortgage payment to increase or decrease because of a modification to the terms of your mortgage?

☐ No.
☐ Yes. Explain here:

B6 Declaration (Official Form 6 - Declaration) (12/07)

In re ______________________________, **Case No.** ______________________
Debtor **(if known)**

DECLARATION CONCERNING DEBTOR'S SCHEDULES

DECLARATION UNDER PENALTY OF PERJURY BY INDIVIDUAL DEBTOR

I declare under penalty of perjury that I have read the foregoing summary and schedules, consisting of _____ sheets, and that they are true and correct to the best of my knowledge, information, and belief.

Date ____________________________ Signature: ______________________________________
Debtor

Date ____________________________ Signature: ______________________________________
(Joint Debtor, if any)

[If joint case, both spouses must sign.]

DECLARATION AND SIGNATURE OF NON-ATTORNEY BANKRUPTCY PETITION PREPARER (See 11 U.S.C. § 110)

I declare under penalty of perjury that: (1) I am a bankruptcy petition preparer as defined in 11 U.S.C. § 110; (2) I prepared this document for compensation and have provided the debtor with a copy of this document and the notices and information required under 11 U.S.C. §§ 110(b), 110(h) and 342(b); and, (3) if rules or guidelines have been promulgated pursuant to 11 U.S.C. § 110(h) setting a maximum fee for services chargeable by bankruptcy petition preparers, I have given the debtor notice of the maximum amount before preparing any document for filing for a debtor or accepting any fee from the debtor, as required by that section.

______________________________________ ______________________
Printed or Typed Name and Title, if any, of Bankruptcy Petition Preparer Social Security No. *(Required by 11 U.S.C. § 110.)*

If the bankruptcy petition preparer is not an individual, state the name, title (if any), address, and social security number of the officer, principal, responsible person, or partner who signs this document.

____

____

____
Address

X ______________________________________ ________________
Signature of Bankruptcy Petition Preparer Date

Names and Social Security numbers of all other individuals who prepared or assisted in preparing this document, unless the bankruptcy petition preparer is not an individual:

If more than one person prepared this document, attach additional signed sheets conforming to the appropriate Official Form for each person.

A bankruptcy petition preparer's failure to comply with the provisions of title 11 and the Federal Rules of Bankruptcy Procedure may result in fines or imprisonment or both. 11 U.S.C. § 110; 18 U.S.C. § 156.

DECLARATION UNDER PENALTY OF PERJURY ON BEHALF OF A CORPORATION OR PARTNERSHIP

I, the ______________________ [the president or other officer or an authorized agent of the corporation or a member or an authorized agent of the partnership] of the ______________________ [corporation or partnership] named as debtor in this case, declare under penalty of perjury that I have read the foregoing summary and schedules, consisting of _____ sheets (*Total shown on summary page plus 1*), and that they are true and correct to the best of my knowledge, information, and belief.

Date ____________________________

Signature: ______________________________________

____
[Print or type name of individual signing on behalf of debtor.]

[An individual signing on behalf of a partnership or corporation must indicate position or relationship to debtor.]

Penalty for making a false statement or concealing property: Fine of up to $500,000 or imprisonment for up to 5 years or both. 18 U.S.C. §§ 152 and 3571.

(Amended Oct. 17, 2005; Oct. 1, 2006; April 1, 2007; Dec. 1, 2007; April 1, 2010; April 1, 2013; Dec. 1, 2013; Dec. 14, 2014.)

Form 7. Statement of Financial Affairs

UNITED STATES BANKRUPTCY COURT

In re: ______________________________, Case No. ______________________
Debtor (if known)

STATEMENT OF FINANCIAL AFFAIRS

This statement is to be completed by every debtor. Spouses filing a joint petition may file a single statement on which the information for both spouses is combined. If the case is filed under chapter 12 or chapter 13, a married debtor must furnish information for both spouses whether or not a joint petition is filed, unless the spouses are separated and a joint petition is not filed. An individual debtor engaged in business as a sole proprietor, partner, family farmer, or self-employed professional, should provide the information requested on this statement concerning all such activities as well as the individual's personal affairs. To indicate payments, transfers and the like to minor children, state the child's initials and the name and address of the child's parent or guardian, such as "A.B., a minor child, by John Doe, guardian." Do not disclose the child's name. See, 11 U.S.C. §112 and Fed. R. Bankr. P. 1007(m).

Questions 1 - 18 are to be completed by all debtors. Debtors that are or have been in business, as defined below, also must complete Questions 19 - 25. **If the answer to an applicable question is "None," mark the box labeled "None."** If additional space is needed for the answer to any question, use and attach a separate sheet properly identified with the case name, case number (if known), and the number of the question.

DEFINITIONS

"In business." A debtor is "in business" for the purpose of this form if the debtor is a corporation or partnership. An individual debtor is "in business" for the purpose of this form if the debtor is or has been, within six years immediately preceding the filing of this bankruptcy case, any of the following: an officer, director, managing executive, or owner of 5 percent or more of the voting or equity securities of a corporation; a partner, other than a limited partner, of a partnership; a sole proprietor or self-employed full-time or part-time. An individual debtor also may be "in business" for the purpose of this form if the debtor engages in a trade, business, or other activity, other than as an employee, to supplement income from the debtor's primary employment.

"Insider." The term "insider" includes but is not limited to: relatives of the debtor; general partners of the debtor and their relatives; corporations of which the debtor is an officer, director, or person in control; officers, directors, and any persons in control of a corporate debtor and their relatives; affiliates of the debtor and insiders of such affiliates; and any managing agent of the debtor. 11 U.S.C. § 101(2), (31).

---

1. Income from employment or operation of business

None ☐ State the gross amount of income the debtor has received from employment, trade, or profession, or from operation of the debtor's business, including part-time activities either as an employee or in independent trade or business, from the beginning of this calendar year to the date this case was commenced. State also the gross amounts received during the **two years** immediately preceding this calendar year. (A debtor that maintains, or has maintained, financial records on the basis of a fiscal rather than a calendar year may report fiscal year income. Identify the beginning and ending dates of the debtor's fiscal year.) If a joint petition is filed, state income for each spouse separately. (Married debtors filing under chapter 12 or chapter 13 must state income of both spouses whether or not a joint petition is filed, unless the spouses are separated and a joint petition is not filed.)

AMOUNT SOURCE

2. Income other than from employment or operation of business

None ☐

State the amount of income received by the debtor other than from employment, trade, profession, operation of the debtor's business during the **two years** immediately preceding the commencement of this case. Give particulars. If a joint petition is filed, state income for each spouse separately. (Married debtors filing under chapter 12 or chapter 13 must state income for each spouse whether or not a joint petition is filed, unless the spouses are separated and a joint petition is not filed.)

AMOUNT	SOURCE

---

3. Payments to creditors

Complete a. or b., as appropriate, and c.

None ☐

a. *Individual or joint debtor(s) with primarily consumer debts:* List all payments on loans, installment purchases of goods or services, and other debts to any creditor made within **90 days** immediately preceding the commencement of this case unless the aggregate value of all property that constitutes or is affected by such transfer is less than $600. Indicate with an asterisk (*) any payments that were made to a creditor on account of a domestic support obligation or as part of an alternative repayment schedule under a plan by an approved nonprofit budgeting and credit counseling agency. (Married debtors filing under chapter 12 or chapter 13 must include payments by either or both spouses whether or not a joint petition is filed, unless the spouses are separated and a joint petition is not filed.)

NAME AND ADDRESS OF CREDITOR	DATES OF PAYMENTS	AMOUNT PAID	AMOUNT STILL OWING

None ☐

b. Debtor whose debts are not primarily consumer debts: List each payment or other transfer to any creditor made within **90 days** immediately preceding the commencement of the case unless the aggregate value of all property that constitutes or is affected by such transfer is less than $5,850*. If the debtor is an individual, indicate with an asterisk (*) any payments that were made to a creditor on account of a domestic support obligation or as part of an alternative repayment schedule under a plan by an approved nonprofit budgeting and credit counseling agency. (Married debtors filing under chapter 12 or chapter 13 must include payments and other transfers by either or both spouses whether or not a joint petition is filed, unless the spouses are separated and a joint petition is not filed.)

NAME AND ADDRESS OF CREDITOR	DATES OF PAYMENTS/ TRANSFERS	AMOUNT PAID OR VALUE OF TRANSFERS	AMOUNT STILL OWING

Bankruptcy Form 7

---

* *Amount subject to adjustment on 4/01/13, and every three years thereafter with respect to cases commenced on or after the date of adjustment.*

None ☐

c. *All debtors:* List all payments made within **one year** immediately preceding the commencement of this case to or for the benefit of creditors who are or were insiders. (Married debtors filing under chapter 12 or chapter 13 must include payments by either or both spouses whether or not a joint petition is filed, unless the spouses are separated and a joint petition is not filed.)

NAME AND ADDRESS OF CREDITOR AND RELATIONSHIP TO DEBTOR	DATE OF PAYMENT	AMOUNT PAID	AMOUNT STILL OWING

---

4. Suits and administrative proceedings, executions, garnishments and attachments

None ☐

a. List all suits and administrative proceedings to which the debtor is or was a party within **one year** immediately preceding the filing of this bankruptcy case. (Married debtors filing under chapter 12 or chapter 13 must include information concerning either or both spouses whether or not a joint petition is filed, unless the spouses are separated and a joint petition is not filed.)

CAPTION OF SUIT AND CASE NUMBER	NATURE OF PROCEEDING	COURT OR AGENCY AND LOCATION	STATUS OR DISPOSITION

None ☐

b. Describe all property that has been attached, garnished or seized under any legal or equitable process within **one year** immediately preceding the commencement of this case. (Married debtors filing under chapter 12 or chapter 13 must include information concerning property of either or both spouses whether or not a joint petition is filed, unless the spouses are separated and a joint petition is not filed.)

NAME AND ADDRESS OF PERSON FOR WHOSE BENEFIT PROPERTY WAS SEIZED	DATE OF SEIZURE	DESCRIPTION AND VALUE OF PROPERTY

---

5. Repossessions, foreclosures and returns

None ☐

List all property that has been repossessed by a creditor, sold at a foreclosure sale, transferred through a deed in lieu of foreclosure or returned to the seller, within **one year** immediately preceding the commencement of this case. (Married debtors filing under chapter 12 or chapter 13 must include information concerning property of either or both spouses whether or not a joint petition is filed, unless the spouses are separated and a joint petition is not filed.)

NAME AND ADDRESS OF CREDITOR OR SELLER	DATE OF REPOSSESSION, FORECLOSURE SALE, TRANSFER OR RETURN	DESCRIPTION AND VALUE OF PROPERTY

---

6. Assignments and receiverships

None ☐ a. Describe any assignment of property for the benefit of creditors made within **120 days** immediately preceding the commencement of this case. (Married debtors filing under chapter 12 or chapter 13 must include any assignment by either or both spouses whether or not a joint petition is filed, unless the spouses are separated and a joint petition is not filed.)

NAME AND ADDRESS OF ASSIGNEE	DATE OF ASSIGNMENT	TERMS OF ASSIGNMENT OR SETTLEMENT

None ☐ b. List all property which has been in the hands of a custodian, receiver, or court-appointed official within **one year** immediately preceding the commencement of this case. (Married debtors filing under chapter 12 or chapter 13 must include information concerning property of either or both spouses whether or not a joint petition is filed, unless the spouses are separated and a joint petition is not filed.)

NAME AND ADDRESS OF CUSTODIAN	NAME AND LOCATION OF COURT CASE TITLE & NUMBER	DATE OF ORDER	DESCRIPTION AND VALUE Of PROPERTY

7. Gifts

None ☐ List all gifts or charitable contributions made within **one year** immediately preceding the commencement of this case except ordinary and usual gifts to family members aggregating less than $200 in value per individual family member and charitable contributions aggregating less than $100 per recipient. (Married debtors filing under chapter 12 or chapter 13 must include gifts or contributions by either or both spouses whether or not a joint petition is filed, unless the spouses are separated and a joint petition is not filed.)

NAME AND ADDRESS OF PERSON OR ORGANIZATION	RELATIONSHIP TO DEBTOR, IF ANY	DATE OF GIFT	DESCRIPTION AND VALUE OF GIFT

8. Losses

None ☐ List all losses from fire, theft, other casualty or gambling within **one year** immediately preceding the commencement of this case **or since the commencement of this case**. (Married debtors filing under chapter 12 or chapter 13 must include losses by either or both spouses whether or not a joint petition is filed, unless the spouses are separated and a joint petition is not filed.)

DESCRIPTION AND VALUE OF PROPERTY	DESCRIPTION OF CIRCUMSTANCES AND, IF LOSS WAS COVERED IN WHOLE OR IN PART BY INSURANCE, GIVE PARTICULARS	DATE OF LOSS

9. Payments related to debt counseling or bankruptcy

None ☐ List all payments made or property transferred by or on behalf of the debtor to any persons, including attorneys, for consultation concerning debt consolidation, relief under the bankruptcy law or preparation of a petition in bankruptcy within **one year** immediately preceding the commencement of this case.

NAME AND ADDRESS OF PAYEE	DATE OF PAYMENT, NAME OF PAYER IF OTHER THAN DEBTOR	AMOUNT OF MONEY OR DESCRIPTION AND VALUE OF PROPERTY

---

10. Other transfers

None ☐ a. List all other property, other than property transferred in the ordinary course of the business or financial affairs of the debtor, transferred either absolutely or as security within **two years** immediately preceding the commencement of this case. (Married debtors filing under chapter 12 or chapter 13 must include transfers by either or both spouses whether or not a joint petition is filed, unless the spouses are separated and a joint petition is not filed.)

NAME AND ADDRESS OF TRANSFEREE, RELATIONSHIP TO DEBTOR	DATE	DESCRIBE PROPERTY TRANSFERRED AND VALUE RECEIVED

None ☐ b. List all property transferred by the debtor within **ten years** immediately preceding the commencement of this case to a self-settled trust or similar device of which the debtor is a beneficiary.

NAME OF TRUST OR OTHER DEVICE	DATE(S) OF TRANSFER(S)	AMOUNT OF MONEY OR DESCRIPTION AND VALUE OF PROPERTY OR DEBTOR'S INTEREST IN PROPERTY

---

11. Closed financial accounts

None ☐ List all financial accounts and instruments held in the name of the debtor or for the benefit of the debtor which were closed, sold, or otherwise transferred within **one year** immediately preceding the commencement of this case. Include checking, savings, or other financial accounts, certificates of deposit, or other instruments; shares and share accounts held in banks, credit unions, pension funds, cooperatives, associations, brokerage houses and other financial institutions. (Married debtors filing under chapter 12 or chapter 13 must include information concerning accounts or instruments held by or for either or both spouses whether or not a joint petition is filed, unless the spouses are separated and a joint petition is not filed.)

NAME AND ADDRESS OF INSTITUTION	TYPE OF ACCOUNT, LAST FOUR DIGITS OF ACCOUNT NUMBER, AND AMOUNT OF FINAL BALANCE	AMOUNT AND DATE OF SALE OR CLOSING

---

12. Safe deposit boxes

None ☐ List each safe deposit or other box or depository in which the debtor has or had securities, cash, or other valuables within **one year** immediately preceding the commencement of this case. (Married debtors filing under chapter 12 or chapter 13 must include boxes or depositories of either or both spouses whether or not a joint petition is filed, unless the spouses are separated and a joint petition is not filed.)

NAME AND ADDRESS OF BANK OR OTHER DEPOSITORY	NAMES AND ADDRESSES OF THOSE WITH ACCESS TO BOX OR DEPOSITORY	DESCRIPTION OF CONTENTS	DATE OF TRANSFER OR SURRENDER, IF ANY

---

13. Setoffs

None ☐ List all setoffs made by any creditor, including a bank, against a debt or deposit of the debtor within **90 days** preceding the commencement of this case. (Married debtors filing under chapter 12 or chapter 13 must include information concerning either or both spouses whether or not a joint petition is filed, unless the spouses are separated and a joint petition is not filed.)

NAME AND ADDRESS OF CREDITOR	DATE OF SETOFF	AMOUNT OF SETOFF

---

14. Property held for another person

None ☐ List all property owned by another person that the debtor holds or controls.

NAME AND ADDRESS OF OWNER	DESCRIPTION AND VALUE OF PROPERTY	LOCATION OF PROPERTY

---

15. Prior address of debtor

None ☐ If debtor has moved within **three years** immediately preceding the commencement of this case, list all premises which the debtor occupied during that period and vacated prior to the commencement of this case. If a joint petition is filed, report also any separate address of either spouse.

ADDRESS	NAME USED	DATES OF OCCUPANCY

---

16. Spouses and Former Spouses

None ☐ If the debtor resides or resided in a community property state, commonwealth, or territory (including Alaska, Arizona, California, Idaho, Louisiana, Nevada, New Mexico, Puerto Rico, Texas, Washington, or Wisconsin) within **eight years** immediately preceding the commencement of the case, identify the name of the debtor's spouse and of any former spouse who resides or resided with the debtor in the community property state.

NAME

---

17. Environmental Information.

For the purpose of this question, the following definitions apply:

"Environmental Law" means any federal, state, or local statute or regulation regulating pollution, contamination, releases of hazardous or toxic substances, wastes or material into the air, land, soil, surface water, groundwater, or other medium, including, but not limited to, statutes or regulations regulating the cleanup of these substances, wastes, or material.

"Site" means any location, facility, or property as defined under any Environmental Law, whether or not presently or formerly owned or operated by the debtor, including, but not limited to, disposal sites.

"Hazardous Material" means anything defined as a hazardous waste, hazardous substance, toxic substance, hazardous material, pollutant, or contaminant or similar term under an Environmental Law.

None ☐ a. List the name and address of every site for which the debtor has received notice in writing by a governmental unit that it may be liable or potentially liable under or in violation of an Environmental Law. Indicate the governmental unit, the date of the notice, and, if known, the Environmental Law:

SITE NAME AND ADDRESS	NAME AND ADDRESS OF GOVERNMENTAL UNIT	DATE OF NOTICE	ENVIRONMENTAL LAW

None ☐ b. List the name and address of every site for which the debtor provided notice to a governmental unit of a release of Hazardous Material. Indicate the governmental unit to which the notice was sent and the date of the notice.

SITE NAME AND ADDRESS	NAME AND ADDRESS OF GOVERNMENTAL UNIT	DATE OF NOTICE	ENVIRONMENTAL LAW

None ☐ c. List all judicial or administrative proceedings, including settlements or orders, under any Environmental Law with respect to which the debtor is or was a party. Indicate the name and address of the governmental unit that is or was a party to the proceeding, and the docket number.

NAME AND ADDRESS OF GOVERNMENTAL UNIT	DOCKET NUMBER	STATUS OR DISPOSITION

---

18 . Nature, location and name of business

None ☐ a. *If the debtor is an individual*, list the names, addresses, taxpayer-identification numbers, nature of the businesses, and beginning and ending dates of all businesses in which the debtor was an officer, director, partner, or managing executive of a corporation, partner in a partnership, sole proprietor, or was self-employed in a trade, profession, or other activity either full- or part-time within **six years** immediately preceding the commencement of this case, or in which the debtor owned 5 percent or more of the voting or equity securities within **six years** immediately preceding the commencement of this case.

If the debtor is a partnership, list the names, addresses, taxpayer-identification numbers, nature of the businesses, and beginning and ending dates of all businesses in which the debtor was a partner or owned 5 percent or more of the voting or equity securities, within **six years** immediately preceding the commencement of this case.

If the debtor is a corporation, list the names, addresses, taxpayer-identification numbers, nature of the businesses, and beginning and ending dates of all businesses in which the debtor was a partner or owned 5 percent or more of the voting or equity securities within **six years** immediately preceding the commencement of this case.

NAME	LAST FOUR DIGITS OF SOCIAL-SECURITY OR OTHER INDIVIDUAL TAXPAYER-I.D. NO. (ITIN)/ COMPLETE EIN	ADDRESS	NATURE OF BUSINESS	BEGINNING AND ENDING DATES

None ☐ b. Identify any business listed in response to subdivision a., above, that is "single asset real estate" as defined in 11 U.S.C. § 101.

NAME	ADDRESS

The following questions are to be completed by every debtor that is a corporation or partnership and by any individual debtor who is or has been, within **six years** immediately preceding the commencement of this case, any of the following: an officer, director, managing executive, or owner of more than 5 percent of the voting or equity securities of a corporation; a partner, other than a limited partner, of a partnership, a sole proprietor, or self-employed in a trade, profession, or other activity, either full- or part-time.

*(An individual or joint debtor should complete this portion of the statement **only** if the debtor is or has been in business, as defined above, within six years immediately preceding the commencement of this case. A debtor who has not been in business within those six years should go directly to the signature page.)*

---

19. Books, records and financial statements

None ☐ a. List all bookkeepers and accountants who within **two years** immediately preceding the filing of this bankruptcy case kept or supervised the keeping of books of account and records of the debtor.

NAME AND ADDRESS	DATES SERVICES RENDERED

None ☐ b. List all firms or individuals who within **two years** immediately preceding the filing of this bankruptcy case have audited the books of account and records, or prepared a financial statement of the debtor.

NAME	ADDRESS	DATES SERVICES RENDERED

None ☐ c. List all firms or individuals who at the time of the commencement of this case were in possession of the books of account and records of the debtor. If any of the books of account and records are not available, explain.

NAME ADDRESS

None ☐ d. List all financial institutions, creditors and other parties, including mercantile and trade agencies, to whom a financial statement was issued by the debtor within **two years** immediately preceding the commencement of this case.

NAME AND ADDRESS DATE ISSUED

---

20. Inventories

None ☐ a. List the dates of the last two inventories taken of your property, the name of the person who supervised the taking of each inventory, and the dollar amount and basis of each inventory.

DATE OF INVENTORY	INVENTORY SUPERVISOR	DOLLAR AMOUNT OF INVENTORY (Specify cost, market or other basis)

None ☐ b. List the name and address of the person having possession of the records of each of the inventories reported in a., above.

DATE OF INVENTORY	NAME AND ADDRESSES OF CUSTODIAN OF INVENTORY RECORDS

---

21 . Current Partners, Officers, Directors and Shareholders

None ☐ a. If the debtor is a partnership, list the nature and percentage of partnership interest of each member of the partnership.

NAME AND ADDRESS	NATURE OF INTEREST	PERCENTAGE OF INTEREST

None ☐ b. If the debtor is a corporation, list all officers and directors of the corporation, and each stockholder who directly or indirectly owns, controls, or holds 5 percent or more of the voting or equity securities of the corporation.

NAME AND ADDRESS	TITLE	NATURE AND PERCENTAGE OF STOCK OWNERSHIP

---

22 . Former partners, officers, directors and shareholders

None ☐ a. If the debtor is a partnership, list each member who withdrew from the partnership within **one year** immediately preceding the commencement of this case.

NAME	ADDRESS	DATE OF WITHDRAWAL

None ☐ b. If the debtor is a corporation, list all officers or directors whose relationship with the corporation terminated within **one year** immediately preceding the commencement of this case.

NAME AND ADDRESS	TITLE	DATE OF TERMINATION

---

23 . Withdrawals from a partnership or distributions by a corporation

None ☐ If the debtor is a partnership or corporation, list all withdrawals or distributions credited or given to an insider, including compensation in any form, bonuses, loans, stock redemptions, options exercised and any other perquisite during **one year** immediately preceding the commencement of this case.

NAME & ADDRESS OF RECIPIENT, RELATIONSHIP TO DEBTOR	DATE AND PURPOSE OF WITHDRAWAL	AMOUNT OF MONEY OR DESCRIPTION AND VALUE OF PROPERTY

---

24. Tax Consolidation Group.

None ☐ If the debtor is a corporation, list the name and federal taxpayer-identification number of the parent corporation of any consolidated group for tax purposes of which the debtor has been a member at any time within **six years** immediately preceding the commencement of the case.

NAME OF PARENT CORPORATION	TAXPAYER-IDENTIFICATION NUMBER (EIN)

---

25. Pension Funds.

None ☐ If the debtor is not an individual, list the name and federal taxpayer-identification number of any pension fund to which the debtor, as an employer, has been responsible for contributing at any time within **six years** immediately preceding the commencement of the case.

NAME OF PENSION FUND	TAXPAYER-IDENTIFICATION NUMBER (EIN)

* * * * * *

[If completed by an individual or individual and spouse]

I declare under penalty of perjury that I have read the answers contained in the foregoing statement of financial affairs and any attachments thereto and that they are true and correct.

Date ______________________ Signature of Debtor ______________________

Date ______________________ Signature of Joint Debtor (if any) ______________________

[If completed on behalf of a partnership or corporation]

I declare under penalty of perjury that I have read the answers contained in the foregoing statement of financial affairs and any attachments thereto and that they are true and correct to the best of my knowledge, information and belief.

Date ______________________ Signature ______________________

Print Name and Title ______________________

[An individual signing on behalf of a partnership or corporation must indicate position or relationship to debtor.]

___continuation sheets attached

Penalty for making a false statement: Fine of up to $500,000 or imprisonment for up to 5 years, or both. 18 U.S.C. §§ 152 and 3571

DECLARATION AND SIGNATURE OF NON-ATTORNEY BANKRUPTCY PETITION PREPARER (See 11 U.S.C. § 110)

I declare under penalty of perjury that: (1) I am a bankruptcy petition preparer as defined in 11 U.S.C. § 110; (2) I prepared this document for compensation and have provided the debtor with a copy of this document and the notices and information required under 11 U.S.C. §§ 110(b), 110(h), and 342(b); and, (3) if rules or guidelines have been promulgated pursuant to 11 U.S.C. § 110(h) setting a maximum fee for services chargeable by bankruptcy petition preparers, I have given the debtor notice of the maximum amount before preparing any document for filing for a debtor or accepting any fee from the debtor, as required by that section.

______________________ ______________________

Printed or Typed Name and Title, if any, of Bankruptcy Petition Preparer Social-Security No. (Required by 11 U.S.C. § 110.)

If the bankruptcy petition preparer is not an individual, state the name, title (if any), address, and social-security number of the officer, principal, responsible person, or partner who signs this document.

____

Address

______________________ ______________________

Signature of Bankruptcy Petition Preparer Date

Names and Social-Security numbers of all other individuals who prepared or assisted in preparing this document unless the bankruptcy petition preparer is not an individual:

If more than one person prepared this document, attach additional signed sheets conforming to the appropriate Official Form for each person

A bankruptcy petition preparer's failure to comply with the provisions of title 11 and the Federal Rules of Bankruptcy Procedure may result in fines or imprisonment or both. 18 U.S.C. § 156.

(Amended Oct. 17, 2005; April 1, 2007; Dec. 1, 2007; April 1, 2010; Dec. 1, 2012; April 1, 2013.)

Form 8. Chapter 7 Individual Debtor's Statement of Intention

B 8 (Official Form 8) (12/08)

UNITED STATES BANKRUPTCY COURT

In re ______________________________, Case No. ____________________
Debtor Chapter 7

CHAPTER 7 INDIVIDUAL DEBTOR'S STATEMENT OF INTENTION

PART A – Debts secured by property of the estate. *(Part A must be fully completed for **EACH** debt which is secured by property of the estate. Attach additional pages if necessary.)*

Property No. 1

Creditor's Name:	**Describe Property Securing Debt:**

Property will be *(check one)*:
❒ Surrendered ❒ Retained

If retaining the property, I intend to *(check at least one)*:
❒ Redeem the property
❒ Reaffirm the debt
❒ Other. Explain ______________________________ (for example, avoid lien using 11 U.S.C. § 522(f)).

Property is *(check one)*:
❒ Claimed as exempt ❒ Not claimed as exempt

Property No. 2 *(if necessary)*

Creditor's Name:	**Describe Property Securing Debt:**

Property will be *(check one)*:
❒ Surrendered ❒ Retained

If retaining the property, I intend to *(check at least one)*:
❒ Redeem the property
❒ Reaffirm the debt
❒ Other. Explain ______________________________ (for example, avoid lien using 11 U.S.C. § 522(f)).

Property is *(check one)*:
❒ Claimed as exempt ❒ Not claimed as exempt

B 8 (Official Form 8) (12/08) Page 2

PART B – Personal property subject to unexpired leases. *(All three columns of Part B must be completed for each unexpired lease. Attach additional pages if necessary.)*

Property No. 1		
Lessor's Name:	**Describe Leased Property:**	Lease will be Assumed pursuant to 11 U.S.C. § 365(p)(2): ❒ YES ❒ NO

Property No. 2 *(if necessary)*		
Lessor's Name:	**Describe Leased Property:**	Lease will be Assumed pursuant to 11 U.S.C. § 365(p)(2): ❒ YES ❒ NO

Property No. 3 *(if necessary)*		
Lessor's Name:	**Describe Leased Property:**	Lease will be Assumed pursuant to 11 U.S.C. § 365(p)(2): ❒ YES ❒ NO

____ continuation sheets attached *(if any)*

I declare under penalty of perjury that the above indicates my intention as to any property of my estate securing a debt and/or personal property subject to an unexpired lease.

Date: ____________________ ______________________________
Signature of Debtor

____
Signature of Joint Debtor

B 8 (Official Form 8) (12/08) Page 3

CHAPTER 7 INDIVIDUAL DEBTOR'S STATEMENT OF INTENTION

(Continuation Sheet)

PART A - Continuation

Property No.	
Creditor's Name:	**Describe Property Securing Debt:**

Property will be *(check one)*:
❒ Surrendered ❒ Retained

If retaining the property, I intend to *(check at least one)*:
❒ Redeem the property
❒ Reaffirm the debt
❒ Other. Explain ______________________________ (for example, avoid lien using 11 U.S.C. § 522(f)).

Property is *(check one)*:
❒ Claimed as exempt ❒ Not claimed as exempt

PART B - Continuation

Property No.		
Lessor's Name:	**Describe Leased Property:**	Lease will be Assumed pursuant to 11 U.S.C. § 365(p)(2): ❒ YES ❒ NO

Property No.		
Lessor's Name:	**Describe Leased Property:**	Lease will be Assumed pursuant to 11 U.S.C. § 365(p)(2): ❒ YES ❒ NO

(Amended Oct. 17, 2005; Dec. 1, 2008.)

Form 9. Notice of Commencement of Case Under the Bankruptcy Code, Meeting of Creditors, and Deadlines

Form 9A. Chapter 7 Individual or Joint Debtor No Asset Case

B9A (Official Form 9A) (Chapter 7 Individual or Joint Debtor No Asset Case) (12/12)

UNITED STATES BANKRUPTCY COURT ____________ **District of** ____________

Notice of
Chapter 7 Bankruptcy Case, Meeting of Creditors, & Deadlines

[A chapter 7 bankruptcy case concerning the debtor(s) listed below was filed on ____________ (date).]
or [A bankruptcy case concerning the debtor(s) listed below was originally filed under chapter ____________ on ____________ (date) and was converted to a case under chapter 7 on ____________ (date).]

You may be a creditor of the debtor. **This notice lists important deadlines.** You may want to consult an attorney to protect your rights. All documents filed in the case may be inspected at the bankruptcy clerk's office at the address listed below. NOTE: The staff of the bankruptcy clerk's office cannot give legal advice.

Creditors -- Do not file this notice in connection with any proof of claim you submit to the court.
See Reverse Side for Important Explanations.

Debtor(s) (name(s) and address):	Case Number:
	Last four digits of Social-Security or Individual Taxpayer-ID (ITIN) No(s)./Complete EIN:
All other names used by the Debtor(s) in the last 8 years (include married, maiden, and trade names):	Bankruptcy Trustee (name and address):
Attorney for Debtor(s) (name and address):	
Telephone number:	Telephone number:

Meeting of Creditors

Date: / / Time: ( ) A. M. ( ) P. M. Location:

Presumption of Abuse under 11 U.S.C. § 707(b)
See "Presumption of Abuse" on the reverse side.

Depending on the documents filed with the petition, one of the following statements will appear.

The presumption of abuse does not arise.
Or
The presumption of abuse arises.
Or
Insufficient information has been filed to date to permit the clerk to make any determination concerning the presumption of abuse. If more complete information, when filed, shows that the presumption has arisen, creditors will be notified.

Deadlines:
Papers must be *received* by the bankruptcy clerk's office by the following deadlines:
Deadline to Object to Debtor's Discharge or to Challenge Dischargeability of Certain Debts:

Deadline to Object to Exemptions:
Thirty (30) days after the *conclusion* of the meeting of creditors.

Creditors May Not Take Certain Actions:
In most instances, the filing of the bankruptcy case automatically stays certain collection and other actions against the debtor and the debtor's property. Under certain circumstances, the stay may be limited to 30 days or not exist at all, although the debtor can request the court to extend or impose a stay. If you attempt to collect a debt or take other action in violation of the Bankruptcy Code, you may be penalized. Consult a lawyer to determine your rights in this case.

Please Do Not File a Proof of Claim Unless You Receive a Notice To Do So.

Creditor with a Foreign Address:
A creditor to whom this notice is sent at a foreign address should read the information under "Do Not File a Proof of Claim at This Time" on the reverse side.

Address of the Bankruptcy Clerk's Office:	For the Court:
Telephone number:	Clerk of the Bankruptcy Court:
Hours Open:	Date:

EXPLANATIONS **B9A (Official Form 9A) (12/12)**

Filing of Chapter 7 Bankruptcy Case	A bankruptcy case under Chapter 7 of the Bankruptcy Code (title 11, United States Code) has been filed in this court by or against the debtor(s) listed on the front side, and an order for relief has been entered.
Legal Advice	The staff of the bankruptcy clerk's office cannot give legal advice. Consult a lawyer to determine your rights in this case.
Creditors Generally May Not Take Certain Actions	Prohibited collection actions are listed in Bankruptcy Code § 362. Common examples of prohibited actions include contacting the debtor by telephone, mail, or otherwise to demand repayment; taking actions to collect money or obtain property from the debtor; repossessing the debtor's property; starting or continuing lawsuits or foreclosures; and garnishing or deducting from the debtor's wages. Under certain circumstances, the stay may be limited to 30 days or not exist at all, although the debtor can request the court to extend or impose a stay.
Presumption of Abuse	If the presumption of abuse arises, creditors may have the right to file a motion to dismiss the case under § 707(b) of the Bankruptcy Code. The debtor may rebut the presumption by showing special circumstances.
Meeting of Creditors	A meeting of creditors is scheduled for the date, time, and location listed on the front side. *The debtor (both spouses in a joint case) must be present at the meeting to be questioned under oath by the trustee and by creditors.* Creditors are welcome to attend, but are not required to do so. The meeting may be continued and concluded at a later date specified in a notice filed with the court.
Do Not File a Proof of Claim at This Time	There does not appear to be any property available to the trustee to pay creditors. *You therefore should not file a proof of claim at this time.* If it later appears that assets are available to pay creditors, you will be sent another notice telling you that you may file a proof of claim, and telling you the deadline for filing your proof of claim. If this notice is mailed to a creditor at a foreign address, the creditor may file a motion requesting the court to extend the deadline. *Do not include this notice with any filing you make with the court.*
Discharge of Debts	The debtor is seeking a discharge of most debts, which may include your debt. A discharge means that you may never try to collect the debt from the debtor. If you believe that the debtor is not entitled to receive a discharge under Bankruptcy Code § 727(a) *or* that a debt owed to you is not dischargeable under Bankruptcy Code § 523(a)(2), (4), or (6), you must file a complaint -- or a motion if you assert the discharge should be denied under § 727(a)(8) or (a)(9) -- in the bankruptcy clerk's office by the "Deadline to Object to Debtor's Discharge or to Challenge the Dischargeability of Certain Debts" listed on the front of this form. The bankruptcy clerk's office must receive the complaint or motion and any required filing fee by that deadline.
Exempt Property	The debtor is permitted by law to keep certain property as exempt. Exempt property will not be sold and distributed to creditors. The debtor must file a list of all property claimed as exempt. You may inspect that list at the bankruptcy clerk's office. If you believe that an exemption claimed by the debtor is not authorized by law, you may file an objection to that exemption. The bankruptcy clerk's office must receive the objections by the "Deadline to Object to Exemptions" listed on the front side.
Bankruptcy Clerk's Office	Any paper that you file in this bankruptcy case should be filed at the bankruptcy clerk's office at the address listed on the front side. You may inspect all papers filed, including the list of the debtor's property and debts and the list of the property claimed as exempt, at the bankruptcy clerk's office.
Creditor with a Foreign Address	Consult a lawyer familiar with United States bankruptcy law if you have any questions regarding your rights in this case.

Refer To Other Side For Important Deadlines and Notices

(Amended Oct. 17, 2005; Dec. 1, 2007; Dec. 1, 2010; Dec. 1, 2011; Dec. 1, 2012.)

Form 9B. Chapter 7 Corporation/Partnership No Asset Case

B9B (Official Form 9B) (Chapter 7 Corporation/Partnership No Asset Case) (12/12)

UNITED STATES BANKRUPTCY COURT________________ **District of**________________

Notice of
Chapter 7 Bankruptcy Case, Meeting of Creditors, & Deadlines

[A chapter 7 bankruptcy case concerning the debtor(s) listed below was filed on ________________(date).]
or [A bankruptcy case concerning the debtor(s) listed below was originally filed under chapter ________ on ________________(date) and was converted to a case under chapter 7 on ________________(date).]

You may be a creditor of the debtor. **This notice lists important deadlines.** You may want to consult an attorney to protect your rights. All documents filed in the case may be inspected at the bankruptcy clerk's office at the address listed below. NOTE: The staff of the bankruptcy clerk's office cannot give legal advice.

Creditors -- Do not file this notice in connection with any proof of claim you submit to the court.
See Reverse Side for Important Explanations.

Debtor(s) (name(s) and address):	Case Number:
	Last four digits of Social-Security or Individual Taxpayer-ID (ITIN) No(s)./Complete EIN:
All other names used by the debtor(s) in the last 8 years (include trade names):	Bankruptcy Trustee (name and address):
Attorney for Debtor(s) (name and address):	
Telephone number:	Telephone number:

Meeting of Creditors

Date: / / Time: ( ) A. M. ( ) P. M. Location:

Creditors May Not Take Certain Actions:

In most instances, the filing of the bankruptcy case automatically stays certain collection and other actions against the debtor and the debtor's property. Under certain circumstances, the stay may be limited to 30 days or not exist at all, although the debtor can request the court to extend or impose a stay. If you attempt to collect a debt or take other action in violation of the Bankruptcy Code, you may be penalized. Consult a lawyer to determine your rights in this case.

Please Do Not File a Proof of Claim Unless You Receive a Notice To Do So.

Creditor with a Foreign Address:

A creditor to whom this notice is sent at a foreign address should read the information under "Do Not File a Proof of Claim at This Time" on the reverse side.

Address of the Bankruptcy Clerk's Office:	**For the Court:**
	Clerk of the Bankruptcy Court:
Telephone number:	
Hours Open:	Date:

EXPLANATIONS **B9B (Official Form 9B) (12/12)**

Filing of Chapter 7 Bankruptcy Case	A bankruptcy case under Chapter 7 of the Bankruptcy Code (title 11, United States Code) has been filed in this court by or against the debtor(s) listed on the front side, and an order for relief has been entered.
Legal Advice	The staff of the bankruptcy clerk's office cannot give legal advice. Consult a lawyer to determine your rights in this case.
Creditors Generally May Not Take Certain Actions	Prohibited collection actions are listed in Bankruptcy Code § 362. Common examples of prohibited actions include contacting the debtor by telephone, mail, or otherwise to demand repayment; taking actions to collect money or obtain property from the debtor; repossessing the debtor's property; and starting or continuing lawsuits or foreclosures. Under certain circumstances, the stay may be limited to 30 days or not exist at all, although the debtor can request the court to extend or impose a stay.
Meeting of Creditors	A meeting of creditors is scheduled for the date, time, and location listed on the front side. *The debtor's representative must be present at the meeting to be questioned under oath by the trustee and by creditors.* Creditors are welcome to attend, but are not required to do so. The meeting may be continued and concluded at a later date specified in a notice filed with the court.
Do Not File a Proof of Claim at This Time	There does not appear to be any property available to the trustee to pay creditors. *You therefore should not file a proof of claim at this time.* If it later appears that assets are available to pay creditors, you will be sent another notice telling you that you may file a proof of claim, and telling you the deadline for filing your proof of claim. If this notice is mailed to a creditor at a foreign address, the creditor may file a motion requesting the court to extend the deadline. *Do not include this notice with any filing you make with the court.*
Bankruptcy Clerk's Office	Any paper that you file in this bankruptcy case should be filed at the bankruptcy clerk's office at the address listed on the front side. You may inspect all papers filed, including the list of the debtor's property and debts and the list of the property claimed as exempt, at the bankruptcy clerk's office.
Creditor with a Foreign Address	Consult a lawyer familiar with United States bankruptcy law if you have any questions regarding your rights in this case.
Refer To Other Side For Important Deadlines and Notices	

(Amended Oct. 17, 2005; Dec. 1, 2007; Dec. 1, 2011; Dec. 1, 2012.)

Form 9C. Chapter 7 Individual or Joint Debtor Asset Case

B9C (Official Form 9C) (Chapter 7 Individual or Joint Debtor Asset Case) (12/12)

UNITED STATES BANKRUPTCY COURT ____________ **District of** ____________

Notice of
Chapter 7 Bankruptcy Case, Meeting of Creditors, & Deadlines

[A chapter 7 bankruptcy case concerning the debtor(s) listed below was filed on ____________(date).]
or [A bankruptcy case concerning the debtor(s) listed below was originally filed under chapter ________ on ____________(date) and was converted to a case under chapter 7 on ____________(date).]

You may be a creditor of the debtor. **This notice lists important deadlines.** You may want to consult an attorney to protect your rights. All documents filed in the case may be inspected at the bankruptcy clerk's office at the address listed below. NOTE: The staff of the bankruptcy clerk's office cannot give legal advice.

Creditors -- Do not file this notice in connection with any proof of claim you submit to the court.
See Reverse Side for Important Explanations.

Debtor(s) (name(s) and address):	Case Number:
	Last four digits of Social-Security or Individual Taxpayer-ID (ITIN) No(s)./Complete EIN:
All other names used by the Debtor(s) in the last 8 years (include married, maiden, and trade names):	Bankruptcy Trustee (name and address):
Attorney for Debtor(s) (name and address): Telephone number:	Telephone number:

Meeting of Creditors

Date: / / Time: ( ) A. M. ( ) P. M. Location:

Presumption of Abuse under 11 U.S.C. § 707(b)
See "Presumption of Abuse" on the reverse side.

Depending on the documents filed with the petition, one of the following statements will appear.

The presumption of abuse does not arise.
Or
The presumption of abuse arises.
Or
Insufficient information has been filed to date to permit the clerk to make any determination concerning the presumption of abuse. If more complete information, when filed, shows that the presumption has arisen, creditors will be notified.

Deadlines:
Papers must be *received* by the bankruptcy clerk's office by the following deadlines:

Deadline to File a Proof of Claim:
For all creditors (except a governmental unit): For a governmental unit:

Creditor with a Foreign Address:
A creditor to whom this notice is sent at a foreign address should read the information under "Claims" on the reverse side.

Deadline to Object to Debtor's Discharge or to Challenge Dischargeability of Certain Debts:

Deadline to Object to Exemptions:
Thirty (30) days after the *conclusion* of the meeting of creditors.

Creditors May Not Take Certain Actions:
In most instances, the filing of the bankruptcy case automatically stays certain collection and other actions against the debtor and the debtor's property. Under certain circumstances, the stay may be limited to 30 days or not exist at all, although the debtor can request the court to extend or impose a stay. If you attempt to collect a debt or take other action in violation of the Bankruptcy Code, you may be penalized. Consult a lawyer to determine your rights in this case.

Address of the Bankruptcy Clerk's Office:	**For the Court:**
Telephone number:	Clerk of the Bankruptcy Court:
Hours Open:	Date:

EXPLANATIONS B9C (Official Form 9C) (12/12)

Filing of Chapter 7 Bankruptcy Case	A bankruptcy case under Chapter 7 of the Bankruptcy Code (title 11, United States Code) has been filed in this court by or against the debtor(s) listed on the front side, and an order for relief has been entered.
Legal Advice	The staff of the bankruptcy clerk's office cannot give legal advice. Consult a lawyer to determine your rights in this case.
Creditors Generally May Not Take Certain Actions	Prohibited collection actions are listed in Bankruptcy Code § 362. Common examples of prohibited actions include contacting the debtor by telephone, mail, or otherwise to demand repayment; taking actions to collect money or obtain property from the debtor; repossessing the debtor's property; starting or continuing lawsuits or foreclosures; and garnishing or deducting from the debtor's wages. Under certain circumstances, the stay may be limited to 30 days or not exist at all, although the debtor can request the court to extend or impose a stay.
Meeting of Creditors	A meeting of creditors is scheduled for the date, time, and location listed on the front side. *The debtor (both spouses in a joint case) must be present at the meeting to be questioned under oath by the trustee and by creditors.* Creditors are welcome to attend, but are not required to do so. The meeting may be continued and concluded at a later date specified in a notice filed with the court.
Claims	A Proof of Claim is a signed statement describing a creditor's claim. If a Proof of Claim form is not included with this notice, you can obtain one at any bankruptcy clerk's office. A secured creditor retains rights in its collateral regardless of whether that creditor files a Proof of Claim. If you do not file a Proof of Claim by the "Deadline to File a Proof of Claim" listed on the front side, you might not be paid any money on your claim from other assets in the bankruptcy case. To be paid, you must file a Proof of Claim even if your claim is listed in the schedules filed by the debtor. Filing a Proof of Claim submits the creditor to the jurisdiction of the bankruptcy court, with consequences a lawyer can explain. For example, a secured creditor who files a Proof of Claim may surrender important nonmonetary rights, including the right to a jury trial. **Filing Deadline for a Creditor with a Foreign Address:** The deadlines for filing claims set forth on the front of this notice apply to all creditors. If this notice has been mailed to a creditor at a foreign address, the creditor may file a motion requesting the court to extend the deadline. *Do not include this notice with any filing you make with the court.*
Discharge of Debts	The debtor is seeking a discharge of most debts, which may include your debt. A discharge means that you may never try to collect the debt from the debtor. If you believe that the debtor is not entitled to receive a discharge under Bankruptcy Code § 727(a) *or* that a debt owed to you is not dischargeable under Bankruptcy Code § 523(a)(2), (4), or (6), you must file a complaint -- or a motion if you assert the discharge should be denied under § 727(a)(8) or (a)(9) -- in the bankruptcy clerk's office by the "Deadline to Object to Debtor's Discharge or to Challenge the Dischargeability of Certain Debts" listed on the front of this form. The bankruptcy clerk's office must receive the complaint or motion and any required filing fee by that deadline.
Exempt Property	The debtor is permitted by law to keep certain property as exempt. Exempt property will not be sold and distributed to creditors. The debtor must file a list of all property claimed as exempt. You may inspect that list at the bankruptcy clerk's office. If you believe that an exemption claimed by the debtor is not authorized by law, you may file an objection to that exemption. The bankruptcy clerk's office must receive the objections by the "Deadline to Object to Exemptions" listed on the front side.
Presumption of Abuse	If the presumption of abuse arises, creditors may have the right to file a motion to dismiss the case under § 707(b) of the Bankruptcy Code. The debtor may rebut the presumption by showing special circumstances.
Bankruptcy Clerk's Office	Any paper that you file in this bankruptcy case should be filed at the bankruptcy clerk's office at the address listed on the front side. You may inspect all papers filed, including the list of the debtor's property and debts and the list of the property claimed as exempt, at the bankruptcy clerk's office.
Liquidation of the Debtor's Property and Payment of Creditors' Claims	The bankruptcy trustee listed on the front of this notice will collect and sell the debtor's property that is not exempt. If the trustee can collect enough money, creditors may be paid some or all of the debts owed to them, in the order specified by the Bankruptcy Code. To make sure you receive any share of that money, you must file a Proof of Claim, as described above.
Creditor with a Foreign Address	Consult a lawyer familiar with United States bankruptcy law if you have any questions regarding your rights in this case.
Refer To Other Side For Important Deadlines and Notices	

(Amended Oct. 17, 2005; Dec. 1, 2007; Dec. 1, 2010; Dec. 1, 2011; Dec. 1, 2012.)

Form 9D. Chapter 7 Corporation/Partnership Asset Case

B9D (Official Form 9D) (Chapter 7 Corporation/Partnership Asset Case) (12/12)

UNITED STATES BANKRUPTCY COURT ____________ **District of** ______________

Notice of
Chapter 7 Bankruptcy Case, Meeting of Creditors, & Deadlines

[A chapter 7 bankruptcy case concerning the debtor(s) listed below was filed on ____________(date).]
or [A bankruptcy case concerning the debtor(s) listed below was originally filed under chapter __________ on ____________(date) and was converted to a case under chapter 7 on __________(date).]

You may be a creditor of the debtor. **This notice lists important deadlines.** You may want to consult an attorney to protect your rights. All documents filed in the case may be inspected at the bankruptcy clerk's office at the address listed below. NOTE: The staff of the bankruptcy clerk's office cannot give legal advice.

Creditors -- Do not file this notice in connection with any proof of claim you submit to the court.
See Reverse Side for Important Explanations.

Debtor(s) (name(s) and address):	Case Number:
	Last four digits of Social-Security or Individual Taxpayer-ID (ITIN) No(s)./Complete EIN:
All other names used by the Debtor(s) in the last 8 years (include trade names):	Bankruptcy Trustee (name and address):
Attorney for Debtor(s) (name and address): Telephone number:	Telephone number:

Meeting of Creditors

Date: / / Time: ( ) A. M. ( ) P. M. Location:

Deadline to File a Proof of Claim

Papers must be *received* by the bankruptcy clerk's office by the following deadlines:

For all creditors (except a governmental unit): For a governmental unit:

Creditor with a Foreign Address:
A creditor to whom this notice is sent at a foreign address should read the information under "Claims" on the reverse side.

Creditors May Not Take Certain Actions:

In most instances, the filing of the bankruptcy case automatically stays certain collection and other actions against the debtor and the debtor's property. Under certain circumstances, the stay may be limited to 30 days or not exist at all, although the debtor can request the court to extend or impose a stay. If you attempt to collect a debt or take other action in violation of the Bankruptcy Code, you may be penalized. Consult a lawyer to determine your rights in this case.

Address of the Bankruptcy Clerk's Office:	For the Court:
Telephone number:	Clerk of the Bankruptcy Court:
Hours Open:	Date:

EXPLANATIONS **B9D (Official Form 9D) (12/12)**

Filing of Chapter 7 Bankruptcy Case	A bankruptcy case under Chapter 7 of the Bankruptcy Code (title 11, United States Code) has been filed in this court by or against the debtor(s) listed on the front side, and an order for relief has been entered.
Legal Advice	The staff of the bankruptcy clerk's office cannot give legal advice. Consult a lawyer to determine your rights in this case.
Creditors Generally May Not Take Certain Actions	Prohibited collection actions are listed in Bankruptcy Code § 362. Common examples of prohibited actions include contacting the debtor by telephone, mail, or otherwise to demand repayment; taking actions to collect money or obtain property from the debtor; repossessing the debtor's property; and starting or continuing lawsuits or foreclosures. Under certain circumstances, the stay may be limited to 30 days or not exist at all, although the debtor can request the court to extend or impose a stay.
Meeting of Creditors	A meeting of creditors is scheduled for the date, time, and location listed on the front side. *The debtor's representative must be present at the meeting to be questioned under oath by the trustee and by creditors.* Creditors are welcome to attend, but are not required to do so. The meeting may be continued and concluded at a later date specified in a notice filed with the court.
Claims	A Proof of Claim is a signed statement describing a creditor's claim. If a Proof of Claim form is not included with this notice, you can obtain one at any bankruptcy clerk's office. A secured creditor retains rights in its collateral regardless of whether that creditor files a Proof of Claim. If you do not file a Proof of Claim by the "Deadline to File a Proof of Claim" listed on the front side, you might not be paid any money on your claim from other assets in the bankruptcy case. To be paid, you must file a Proof of Claim even if your claim is listed in the schedules filed by the debtor. Filing a Proof of Claim submits the creditor to the jurisdiction of the bankruptcy court, with consequences a lawyer can explain. For example, a secured creditor who files a Proof of Claim may surrender important nonmonetary rights, including the right to a jury trial. **Filing Deadline for a Creditor with a Foreign Address:** The deadlines for filing claims set forth on the front of this notice apply to all creditors. If this notice has been mailed to a creditor at a foreign address, the creditor may file a motion requesting the court to extend the deadline. *Do not include this notice with any filing you make with the court.*
Liquidation of the Debtor's Property and Payment of Creditors' Claims	The bankruptcy trustee listed on the front of this notice will collect and sell the debtor's property that is not exempt. If the trustee can collect enough money, creditors may be paid some or all of the debts owed to them, in the order specified by the Bankruptcy Code. To make sure you receive any share of that money, you must file a Proof of Claim, as described above.
Bankruptcy Clerk's Office	Any paper that you file in this bankruptcy case should be filed at the bankruptcy clerk's office at the address listed on the front side. You may inspect all papers filed, including the list of the debtor's property and debts and the list of the property claimed as exempt, at the bankruptcy clerk's office.
Creditor with a Foreign Address	Consult a lawyer familiar with United States bankruptcy law if you have any questions regarding your rights in this case.
Refer To Other Side For Important Deadlines and Notices	

(Amended Oct. 17, 2005; Dec. 1, 2007; Dec. 1, 2011; Dec. 1, 2012.)

Form 9E. Chapter 11 Individual or Joint Debtor Case

B9E (Official Form 9E) (Chapter 11 Individual or Joint Debtor Case) (12/12)

UNITED STATES BANKRUPTCY COURT__________ **District of**__________

Notice of
Chapter 11 Bankruptcy Case, Meeting of Creditors, & Deadlines

[A chapter 11 bankruptcy case concerning the debtor(s) listed below was filed on __________ (date).]
or [A bankruptcy case concerning the debtor(s) listed below was originally filed under chapter ______ on __________ (date) and was converted to a case under chapter 11 on __________ (date).]

You may be a creditor of the debtor. **This notice lists important deadlines.** You may want to consult an attorney to protect your rights. All documents filed in the case may be inspected at the bankruptcy clerk's office at the address listed below.
NOTE: The staff of the bankruptcy clerk's office cannot give legal advice

Creditors -- Do not file this notice in connection with any proof of claim you submit to the court.
See Reverse Side for Important Explanations.

Debtor(s) (name(s) and address):	Case Number:
	Last four digits of Social-Security or Individual Taxpayer-ID (ITIN) No(s)./Complete EIN:
All other names used by the Debtor(s) in the last 8 years (include married, maiden, and trade names):	Attorney for Debtor(s) (name and address): Telephone number:

Meeting of Creditors

Date: / / Time: ( ) A. M. ( ) P. M. Location:

Deadlines:
Papers must be *received* by the bankruptcy clerk's office by the following deadlines:

Deadline to File a Proof of Claim:
Notice of deadline will be sent at a later time.

Creditor with a Foreign Address:
A creditor to whom this notice is sent at a foreign address should read the information under "Claims" on the reverse side.

Deadline to File a Complaint to Determine Dischargeability of Certain Debts:

Deadline to File a Complaint Objecting to Discharge of the Debtor:

First date set for hearing on confirmation of plan
Notice of that date will be sent at a later time.

Deadline to Object to Exemptions:

Thirty (30) days after the *conclusion* of the meeting of creditors.

Creditors May Not Take Certain Actions:
In most instances, the filing of the bankruptcy case automatically stays certain collection and other actions against the debtor and the debtor's property. Under certain circumstances, the stay may be limited to 30 days or not exist at all, although the debtor can request the court to extend or impose a stay. If you attempt to collect a debt or take other action in violation of the Bankruptcy Code, you may be penalized. Consult a lawyer to determine your rights in this case.

Address of the Bankruptcy Clerk's Office:	For the Court:
  Telephone number:	Clerk of the Bankruptcy Court:
Hours Open:	Date:

EXPLANATIONS **B9E (Official Form 9E) (12/12)**

Filing of Chapter 11 Bankruptcy Case	A bankruptcy case under Chapter 11 of the Bankruptcy Code (title 11, United States Code) has been filed in this court by or against the debtor(s) listed on the front side, and an order for relief has been entered. Chapter 11 allows a debtor to reorganize or liquidate pursuant to a plan. A plan is not effective unless confirmed by the court. You may be sent a copy of the plan and a disclosure statement telling you about the plan, and you might have the opportunity to vote on the plan. You will be sent notice of the date of the confirmation hearing, and you may object to confirmation of the plan and attend the confirmation hearing. Unless a trustee is serving, the debtor will remain in possession of the debtor's property and may continue to operate any business.
Legal Advice	The staff of the bankruptcy clerk's office cannot give legal advice. Consult a lawyer to determine your rights in this case.
Creditors Generally May Not Take Certain Actions	Prohibited collection actions are listed in Bankruptcy Code § 362. Common examples of prohibited actions include contacting the debtor by telephone, mail, or otherwise to demand repayment; taking actions to collect money or obtain property from the debtor; repossessing the debtor's property; starting or continuing lawsuits or foreclosures; and garnishing or deducting from the debtor's wages. Under certain circumstances, the stay may be limited to 30 days or not exist at all, although the debtor can request the court to extend or impose a stay.
Meeting of Creditors	A meeting of creditors is scheduled for the date, time, and location listed on the front side. *The debtor (both spouses in a joint case) must be present at the meeting to be questioned under oath by the trustee and by creditors.* Creditors are welcome to attend, but are not required to do so. The meeting may be continued and concluded at a later date specified in a notice filed with the court. The court, after notice and a hearing, may order that the United States trustee not convene the meeting if the debtor has filed a plan for which the debtor solicited acceptances before filing the case.
Claims	A Proof of Claim is a signed statement describing a creditor's claim. If a Proof of Claim form is not included with this notice, you can obtain one at any bankruptcy clerk's office. You may look at the schedules that have been or will be filed at the bankruptcy clerk's office. If your claim is scheduled and is *not* listed as disputed, contingent, or unliquidated, it will be allowed in the amount scheduled unless you filed a Proof of Claim or you are sent further notice about the claim. Whether or not your claim is scheduled, you are permitted to file a Proof of Claim. If your claim is not listed at all *or* if your claim is listed as disputed, contingent, or unliquidated, then you must file a Proof of Claim or you might not be paid any money on your claim and may be unable to vote on a plan. The court has not yet set a deadline to file a Proof of Claim. If a deadline is set, you will be sent another notice. A secured creditor retains rights in its collateral regardless of whether that creditor files a Proof of Claim. Filing a Proof of Claim submits the creditor to the jurisdiction of the bankruptcy court, with consequences a lawyer can explain. For example, a secured creditor who files a Proof of Claim may surrender important nonmonetary rights, including the right to a jury trial. **Filing Deadline for a Creditor with a Foreign Address:** The deadline for filing claims will be set in a later court order and will apply to all creditors unless the order provides otherwise. If notice of the order setting the deadline is sent to a creditor at a foreign address, the creditor may file a motion requesting the court to extend the deadline. *Do not include this notice with any filing you make with the court.*
Discharge of Debts	Confirmation of a chapter 11 plan may result in a discharge of debts, which may include all or part of your debt. *See* Bankruptcy Code § 1141 (d). Unless the court orders otherwise, however, the discharge will not be effective until completion of all payments under the plan. A discharge means that you may never try to collect the debt from the debtor except as provided in the plan. If you believe that a debt owed to you is not dischargeable under Bankruptcy Code § 523 (a) (2), (4), or (6), you must start a lawsuit by filing a complaint in the bankruptcy clerk's office by the "Deadline to File a Complaint to Determine Dischargeability of Certain Debts" listed on the front side. The bankruptcy clerk's office must receive the complaint and any required filing fee by that Deadline. If you believe that the debtor is not entitled to receive a discharge under Bankruptcy Code § 1141 (d) (3), you must file a complaint with the required filing fee in the bankruptcy clerk's office not later than the first date set for the hearing on confirmation of the plan. You will be sent another notice informing you of that date.
Exempt Property	The debtor is permitted by law to keep certain property as exempt. Exempt property will not be sold and distributed to creditors, even if the debtor's case is converted to chapter 7. The debtor must file a list of property claimed as exempt. You may inspect that list at the bankruptcy clerk's office. If you believe that an exemption claimed by the debtor is not authorized by law, you may file an objection to that exemption. The bankruptcy clerk's office must receive the objection by the "Deadline to Object to Exemptions" listed on the front side.
Bankruptcy Clerk's Office	Any paper that you file in this bankruptcy case should be filed at the bankruptcy clerk's office at the address listed on the front side. You may inspect all papers filed, including the list of the debtor's property and debts and the list of the property claimed as exempt, at the bankruptcy clerk's office.
Creditor with a Foreign Address	Consult a lawyer familiar with United States bankruptcy law if you have any questions regarding your rights in this case.
Refer To Other Side For Important Deadlines and Notices	

(Amended Oct. 17, 2005; Dec. 1, 2007; Dec. 1, 2011; Dec. 1, 2012.)

Form 9E (Alt). Chapter 11 Individual or Joint Debtor Case

B9E ALT (Official Form 9E ALT) (Chapter 11 Individual or Joint Debtor Case) (12/12)

UNITED STATES BANKRUPTCY COURT____________ **District of**____________________

Notice of
Chapter 11 Bankruptcy Case, Meeting of Creditors, & Deadlines

[A chapter 11 bankruptcy case concerning the debtor(s) listed below was filed on _______________(date).]
or [A bankruptcy case concerning the debtor(s) listed below was originally filed under chapter__________ on
_________________(date) and was converted to a case under chapter 11 on _______________(date).]

You may be a creditor of the debtor. **This notice lists important deadlines.** You may want to consult an attorney to protect your rights. All documents filed in the case may be inspected at the bankruptcy clerk's office at the address listed below.
NOTE: The staff of the bankruptcy clerk's office cannot give legal advice.

Creditors -- Do not file this notice in connection with any proof of claim you submit to the court.
See Reverse Side for Important Explanations.

Debtor(s) (name(s) and address):	Case Number:
	Last four digits of Social-Security or Individual Taxpayer-ID (ITIN) No(s)./Complete EIN:
All other names used by the Debtor(s) in the last 8 years (include married, maiden, and trade names):	Attorney for Debtor(s) (name and address): Telephone number:

Meeting of Creditors

Date: / / Time: ( ) A. M. ( ) P. M. Location:

Deadlines:

Papers must be *received* by the bankruptcy clerk's office by the following deadlines:

Deadline to File a Proof of Claim:

For all creditors (except a governmental unit): For a governmental unit:

Creditor with a Foreign Address:
A creditor to whom this notice is sent at a foreign address should read the information under "Claims" on the reverse side.

Deadline to File a Complaint to Determine Dischargeability of Certain Debts:

Deadline to File a Complaint Objecting to Discharge of the Debtor:

First date set for hearing on confirmation of plan
Notice of that date will be sent at a later time.

Deadline to Object to Exemptions:

Thirty (30) days after the *conclusion* of the meeting of creditors.

Creditors May Not Take Certain Actions:
In most instances, the filing of the bankruptcy case automatically stays certain collection and other actions against the debtor and the debtor's property. Under certain circumstances, the stay may be limited to 30 days or not exist at all, although the debtor can request the court to extend or impose a stay. If you attempt to collect a debt or take other action in violation of the Bankruptcy Code, you may be penalized. Consult a lawyer to determine your rights in this case.

Address of the Bankruptcy Clerk's Office: **Telephone number:**	**For the Court:** Clerk of the Bankruptcy Court:
Hours Open:	Date:

EXPLANATIONS **B9E ALT (Official Form 9E ALT) (12/12)**

Filing of Chapter 11 Bankruptcy Case	A bankruptcy case under Chapter 11 of the Bankruptcy Code (title 11, United States Code) has been filed in this court by or against the debtor(s) listed on the front side, and an order for relief has been entered. Chapter 11 allows a debtor to reorganize or liquidate pursuant to a plan. A plan is not effective unless confirmed by the court. You may be sent a copy of the plan and a disclosure statement telling you about the plan, and you might have the opportunity to vote on the plan. You will be sent notice of the date of the confirmation hearing, and you may object to confirmation of the plan and attend the confirmation hearing. Unless a trustee is serving, the debtor will remain in possession of the debtor's property and may continue to operate any business.
Legal Advice	The staff of the bankruptcy clerk's office cannot give legal advice. Consult a lawyer to determine your rights in this case.
Creditors Generally May Not Take Certain Actions	Prohibited collection actions are listed in Bankruptcy Code § 362. Common examples of prohibited actions include contacting the debtor by telephone, mail, or otherwise to demand repayment; taking actions to collect money or obtain property from the debtor; repossessing the debtor's property; starting or continuing lawsuits or foreclosures; and garnishing or deducting from the debtor's wages. Under certain circumstances, the stay may be limited to 30 days or not exist at all, although the debtor can request the court to extend or impose a stay.
Meeting of Creditors	A meeting of creditors is scheduled for the date, time, and location listed on the front side. *The debtor (both spouses in a joint case) must be present at the meeting to be questioned under oath by the trustee and by creditors.* Creditors are welcome to attend, but are not required to do so. The meeting may be continued and concluded at a later date specified in a notice filed with the court. The court, after notice and a hearing, may order that the United States trustee not convene the meeting if the debtor has filed a plan for which the debtor solicited acceptances before filing the case.
Claims	A Proof of Claim is a signed statement describing a creditor's claim. If a Proof of Claim form is not included with this notice, you can obtain one at any bankruptcy clerk's office. You may look at the schedules that have been or will be filed at the bankruptcy clerk's office. If your claim is scheduled and is *not* listed as disputed, contingent, or unliquidated, it will be allowed in the amount scheduled unless you filed a Proof of Claim or you are sent further notice about the claim. Whether or not your claim is scheduled, you are permitted to file a Proof of Claim. If your claim is not listed at all *or* if your claim is listed as disputed, contingent, or unliquidated, then you must file a Proof of Claim by the "Deadline to File a Proof of Claim" listed on the front side or you might not be paid any money on your claim and may be unable to vote on a plan. A secured creditor retains rights in its collateral regardless of whether that creditor files a Proof of Claim. Filing a Proof of Claim submits the creditor to the jurisdiction of the bankruptcy court, with consequences a lawyer can explain. For example, a secured creditor who files a Proof of Claim may surrender important nonmonetary rights, including the right to a jury trial. **Filing Deadline for a Creditor with a Foreign Address:** The deadlines for filing claims set forth on the front of this notice apply to all creditors. If this notice has been mailed to a creditor at a foreign address, the creditor may file a motion requesting the court to extend the deadline. *Do not include this notice with any filing you make with the court.*
Discharge of Debts	Confirmation of a chapter 11 plan may result in a discharge of debts, which may include all or part of your debt. *See* Bankruptcy Code § 1141 (d). Unless the court orders otherwise, however, the discharge will not be effective until completion of all payments under the plan. A discharge means that you may never try to collect the debt from the debtor except as provided in the plan. If you believe that a debt owed to you is not dischargeable under Bankruptcy Code § 523 (a) (2), (4), or (6), you must start a lawsuit by filing a complaint in the bankruptcy clerk's office by the "Deadline to File a Complaint to Determine Dischargeability of Certain Debts" listed on the front side. The bankruptcy clerk's office must receive the complaint and any required filing fee by that Deadline. If you believe that the debtor is not entitled to receive a discharge under Bankruptcy Code § 1141 (d) (3), you must file a complaint with the required filing fee in the bankruptcy clerk's office not later than the first date set for the hearing on confirmation of the plan. You will be sent another notice informing you of that date.
Exempt Property	The debtor is permitted by law to keep certain property as exempt. Exempt property will not be sold and distributed to creditors, even if the debtor's case is converted to chapter 7. The debtor must file a list of property claimed as exempt. You may inspect that list at the bankruptcy clerk's office. If you believe that an exemption claimed by the debtor is not authorized by law, you may file an objection to that exemption. The bankruptcy clerk's office must receive the objection by the "Deadline to Object to Exemptions" listed on the front side.
Bankruptcy Clerk's Office	Any paper that you file in this bankruptcy case should be filed at the bankruptcy clerk's office at the address listed on the front side. You may inspect all papers filed, including the list of the debtor's property and debts and the list of the property claimed as exempt, at the bankruptcy clerk's office.
Creditor with a Foreign Address	Consult a lawyer familiar with United States bankruptcy law if you have any questions regarding your rights in this case.
Refer To Other Side For Important Deadlines and Notices	

(Amended Oct. 17, 2005; Dec. 1, 2007; Dec. 1, 2011; Dec. 1, 2012.)

Form 9F. Chapter 11 Corporation/Partnership Case

B9F (Official Form 9F) (Chapter 11 Corporation/Partnership Case) (12/12)

UNITED STATES BANKRUPTCY COURT____________ **District of**____________

Notice of
Chapter 11 Bankruptcy Case, Meeting of Creditors, & Deadlines

[A chapter 11 bankruptcy case concerning the debtor(s) listed below was filed on ____________(date).]
or [A bankruptcy case concerning the debtor(s) listed below was originally filed under chapter____________on ____________(date) and was converted to a case under chapter 11 on____________(date).]

You may be a creditor of the debtor. **This notice lists important deadlines.** You may want to consult an attorney to protect your rights. All documents filed in the case may be inspected at the bankruptcy clerk's office at the address listed below.
NOTE: The staff of the bankruptcy clerk's office cannot give legal advice.

Creditors -- Do not file this notice in connection with any proof of claim you submit to the court.
See Reverse Side for Important Explanations.

Debtor(s) (name(s) and address):	Case Number:
	Last four digits of Social-Security or Individual Taxpayer-ID (ITIN) No(s)./Complete EIN:
All other names used by the Debtor(s) in the last 8 years (include trade names):	Attorney for Debtor(s) (name and address): Telephone number:

Meeting of Creditors

Date: / / Time: ( ) A. M. Location:
( ) P. M.

Deadline to File a Proof of Claim

Proof of Claim must be *received* by the bankruptcy clerk's office by the following deadline:

Notice of deadline will be sent at a later time.

Creditor with a Foreign Address:
A creditor to whom this notice is sent at a foreign address should read the information under "Claims" on the reverse side.

Deadline to File a Complaint to Determine Dischargeability of Certain Debts:

Creditors May Not Take Certain Actions:
In most instances, the filing of the bankruptcy case automatically stays certain collection and other actions against the debtor and the debtor's property. Under certain circumstances, the stay may be limited to 30 days or not exist at all, although the debtor can request the court to extend or impose a stay. If you attempt to collect a debt or take other action in violation of the Bankruptcy Code, you may be penalized. Consult a lawyer to determine your rights in this case.

Address of the Bankruptcy Clerk's Office:	**For the Court:**
Telephone number:	Clerk of the Bankruptcy Court:
Hours Open:	Date:

EXPLANATIONS B9F (Official Form 9F) (12/12)

Filing of Chapter 11 Bankruptcy Case	A bankruptcy case under Chapter 11 of the Bankruptcy Code (title 11, United States Code) has been filed in this court by or against the debtor(s) listed on the front side, and an order for relief has been entered. Chapter 11 allows a debtor to reorganize or liquidate pursuant to a plan. A plan is not effective unless confirmed by the court. You may be sent a copy of the plan and a disclosure statement telling you about the plan, and you might have the opportunity to vote on the plan. You will be sent notice of the date of the confirmation hearing, and you may object to confirmation of the plan and attend the confirmation hearing. Unless a trustee is serving, the debtor will remain in possession of the debtor's property and may continue to operate any business.
Legal Advice	The staff of the bankruptcy clerk's office cannot give legal advice. Consult a lawyer to determine your rights in this case.
Creditors Generally May Not Take Certain Actions	Prohibited collection actions are listed in Bankruptcy Code § 362. Common examples of prohibited actions include contacting the debtor by telephone, mail, or otherwise to demand repayment; taking actions to collect money or obtain property from the debtor; repossessing the debtor's property; and starting or continuing lawsuits or foreclosures. Under certain circumstances, the stay may be limited to 30 days or not exist at all, although the debtor can request the court to extend or impose a stay.
Meeting of Creditors	A meeting of creditors is scheduled for the date, time, and location listed on the front side. *The debtor's representative must be present at the meeting to be questioned under oath by the trustee and by creditors.* Creditors are welcome to attend, but are not required to do so. The meeting may be continued and concluded at a later date specified in a notice filed with the court. The court, after notice and a hearing, may order that the United States trustee not convene the meeting if the debtor has filed a plan for which the debtor solicited acceptances before filing the case.
Claims	A Proof of Claim is a signed statement describing a creditor's claim. If a Proof of Claim form is not included with this notice, you can obtain one at any bankruptcy clerk's office. You may look at the schedules that have been or will be filed at the bankruptcy clerk's office. If your claim is scheduled and is *not* listed as disputed, contingent, or unliquidated, it will be allowed in the amount scheduled unless you filed a Proof of Claim or you are sent further notice about the claim. Whether or not your claim is scheduled, you are permitted to file a Proof of Claim. If your claim is not listed at all *or* if your claim is listed as disputed, contingent, or unliquidated, then you must file a Proof of Claim or you might not be paid any money on your claim and may be unable to vote on a plan. The court has not yet set a deadline to file a Proof of Claim. If a deadline is set, you will be sent another notice. A secured creditor retains rights in its collateral regardless of whether that creditor files a Proof of Claim. Filing a Proof of Claim submits the creditor to the jurisdiction of the bankruptcy court, with consequences a lawyer can explain. For example, a secured creditor who files a Proof of Claim may surrender important nonmonetary rights, including the right to a jury trial. **Filing Deadline for a Creditor with a Foreign Address:** The deadline for filing claims will be set in a later court order and will apply to all creditors unless the order provides otherwise. If notice of the order setting the deadline is sent to a creditor at a foreign address, the creditor may file a motion requesting the court to extend the deadline. *Do not include this notice with any filing you make with the court.*
Discharge of Debts	Confirmation of a chapter 11 plan may result in a discharge of debts, which may include all or part of your debt. *See* Bankruptcy Code § 1141 (d). A discharge means that you may never try to collect the debt from the debtor, except as provided in the plan. If you believe that a debt owed to you is not dischargeable under Bankruptcy Code § 1141 (d) (6) (A), you must start a lawsuit by filing a complaint in the bankruptcy clerk's office by the "Deadline to File a Complaint to Determine Dischargeability of Certain Debts" listed on the front side. The bankruptcy clerk's office must receive the complaint and any required filing fee by that deadline.
Bankruptcy Clerk's Office	Any paper that you file in this bankruptcy case should be filed at the bankruptcy clerk's office at the address listed on the front side. You may inspect all papers filed, including the list of the debtor's property and debts and the list of the property claimed as exempt, at the bankruptcy clerk's office.
Creditor with a Foreign Address	Consult a lawyer familiar with United States bankruptcy law if you have any questions regarding your rights in this case.
Refer To Other Side For Important Deadlines and Notices	

(Amended Oct. 17, 2005; Dec. 1, 2007; Dec. 1, 2008; Dec. 1, 2011; Dec. 1, 2012.)

Form 9F (Alt). Chapter 11 Corporation/Partnership Case

B9F ALT (Official Form 9F ALT) (Chapter 11 Corporation/Partnership Case) (12/12)

UNITED STATES BANKRUPTCY COURT ____________ **District of** ____________________

Notice of
Chapter 11 Bankruptcy Case, Meeting of Creditors, & Deadlines

[A chapter 11 bankruptcy case concerning the debtor(s) listed below was filed on ______________(date).]
or [A bankruptcy case concerning the debtor(s) listed below was originally filed under chapter __________ on ______________(date) and was converted to a case under chapter 11 on ____________(date).]

You may be a creditor of the debtor. **This notice lists important deadlines.** You may want to consult an attorney to protect your rights. All documents filed in the case may be inspected at the bankruptcy clerk's office at the address listed below.
NOTE: The staff of the bankruptcy clerk's office cannot give legal advice.

Creditors -- Do not file this notice in connection with any proof of claim you submit to the court.
See Reverse Side for Important Explanations.

Debtor(s) (name(s) and address):	Case Number:
	Last four digits of Social-Security or Individual Taxpayer-ID (ITIN) No(s)./Complete EIN:
All other names used by the Debtor(s) in the last 8 years (include trade names):	Attorney for Debtor(s) (name and address): Telephone number:

Meeting of Creditors

Date: / / Time: ( ) A. M. ( ) P. M. Location:

Deadline to File a Proof of Claim

Proof of Claim must be *received* by the bankruptcy clerk's office by the following deadline:

For all creditors (except a governmental unit): For a governmental unit:

Creditor with a Foreign Address:
A creditor to whom this notice is sent at a foreign address should read the information under "Claims" on the reverse side.

Deadline to File a Complaint to Determine Dischargeability of Certain Debts:

Creditors May Not Take Certain Actions:
In most instances, the filing of the bankruptcy case automatically stays certain collection and other actions against the debtor and the debtor's property. Under certain circumstances, the stay may be limited to 30 days or not exist at all, although the debtor can request the court to extend or impose a stay. If you attempt to collect a debt or take other action in violation of the Bankruptcy Code, you may be penalized. Consult a lawyer to determine your rights in this case.

Address of the Bankruptcy Clerk's Office: **Telephone number:**	**For the Court:** Clerk of the Bankruptcy Court:
Hours Open:	Date:

EXPLANATIONS **B9F ALT (Official Form 9F ALT) (12/12)**

Filing of Chapter 11 Bankruptcy Case	A bankruptcy case under Chapter 11 of the Bankruptcy Code (title 11, United States Code) has been filed in this court by or against the debtor(s) listed on the front side, and an order for relief has been entered. Chapter 11 allows a debtor to reorganize or liquidate pursuant to a plan. A plan is not effective unless confirmed by the court. You may be sent a copy of the plan and a disclosure statement telling you about the plan, and you might have the opportunity to vote on the plan. You will be sent notice of the date of the confirmation hearing, and you may object to confirmation of the plan and attend the confirmation hearing. Unless a trustee is serving, the debtor will remain in possession of the debtor's property and may continue to operate any business.
Legal Advice	The staff of the bankruptcy clerk's office cannot give legal advice. Consult a lawyer to determine your rights in this case.
Creditors Generally May Not Take Certain Actions	Prohibited collection actions are listed in Bankruptcy Code § 362. Common examples of prohibited actions include contacting the debtor by telephone, mail, or otherwise to demand repayment; taking actions to collect money or obtain property from the debtor; repossessing the debtor's property; and starting or continuing lawsuits or foreclosures. Under certain circumstances, the stay may be limited to 30 days or not exist at all, although the debtor can request the court to extend or impose a stay.
Meeting of Creditors	A meeting of creditors is scheduled for the date, time, and location listed on the front side. *The debtor's representative must be present at the meeting to be questioned under oath by the trustee and by creditors.* Creditors are welcome to attend, but are not required to do so. The meeting may be continued and concluded at a later date specified in a notice filed with the court. The court, after notice and a hearing, may order that the United States trustee not convene the meeting if the debtor has filed a plan for which the debtor solicited acceptances before filing the case.
Claims	A Proof of Claim is a signed statement describing a creditor's claim. If a Proof of Claim form is not included with this notice, you can obtain one at any bankruptcy clerk's office. You may look at the schedules that have been or will be filed at the bankruptcy clerk's office. If your claim is scheduled and is *not* listed as disputed, contingent, or unliquidated, it will be allowed in the amount scheduled unless you filed a Proof of Claim or you are sent further notice about the claim. Whether or not your claim is scheduled, you are permitted to file a Proof of Claim. If your claim is not listed at all *or* if your claim is listed as disputed, contingent, or unliquidated, then you must file a Proof of Claim by the "Deadline to File Proof of Claim" listed on the front side, or you might not be paid any money on your claim and may be unable to vote on a plan. A secured creditor retains rights in its collateral regardless of whether that creditor files a Proof of Claim. Filing a Proof of Claim submits the creditor to the jurisdiction of the bankruptcy court, with consequences a lawyer can explain. For example, a secured creditor who files a Proof of Claim may surrender important nonmonetary rights, including the right to a jury trial. **Filing Deadline for a Creditor with a Foreign Address:** The deadlines for filing claims set forth on the front of this notice apply to all creditors. If this notice has been mailed to a creditor at a foreign address, the creditor may file a motion requesting the court to extend the deadline. *Do not include this notice with any filing you make with the court.*
Discharge of Debts	Confirmation of a chapter 11 plan may result in a discharge of debts, which may include all or part of your debt. *See* Bankruptcy Code § 1141 (d). A discharge means that you may never try to collect the debt from the debtor, except as provided in the plan. If you believe that a debt owed to you is not dischargeable under Bankruptcy Code § 1141 (d) (6) (A), you must start a lawsuit by filing a complaint in the bankruptcy clerk's office by the "Deadline to File a Complaint to Determine Dischargeability of Certain Debts" listed on the front side. The bankruptcy clerk's office must receive the complaint and any required filing fee by that deadline.
Bankruptcy Clerk's Office	Any paper that you file in this bankruptcy case should be filed at the bankruptcy clerk's office at the address listed on the front side. You may inspect all papers filed, including the list of the debtor's property and debts and the list of the property claimed as exempt, at the bankruptcy clerk's office.
Creditor with a Foreign Address	Consult a lawyer familiar with United States bankruptcy law if you have any questions regarding your rights in this case.
Refer To Other Side For Important Deadlines and Notices	

(Amended Oct. 17, 2005; Dec. 1, 2007; Dec. 1, 2011; Dec. 1, 2012.)

Form 9G. Chapter 12 Individual or Joint Debtor Family Farmer or Family Fisherman

B9G (Official Form 9G) (Chapter 12 Individual or Joint Debtor Family Farmer or Family Fisherman) (12/12)

UNITED STATES BANKRUPTCY COURT__________________ **District of**__________________

Notice of
Chapter 12 Bankruptcy Case, Meeting of Creditors, & Deadlines

[The debtor(s) listed below filed a chapter 12 bankruptcy case on __________________(date).]
or [A bankruptcy case concerning the debtor(s) listed below was originally filed under chapter______________on __________________ (date) and was converted to a case under chapter 12 on______________(date).]

You may be a creditor of the debtor. **This notice lists important deadlines.** You may want to consult an attorney to protect your rights. All documents filed in the case may be inspected at the bankruptcy clerk's office at the address listed below.
NOTE: The staff of the bankruptcy clerk's office cannot give legal advice.

Creditors -- Do not file this notice in connection with any proof of claim you submit to the court.
See Reverse Side for Important Explanations.

Debtor(s) (name(s) and address):	Case Number:
	Last four digits of Social-Security or Individual Taxpayer-ID (ITIN) No(s)./Complete EIN:
All other names used by the Debtor(s) in the last 8 years (include married, maiden, and trade names):	Bankruptcy Trustee (name and address):
Attorney for Debtor(s) (name and address): Telephone number:	Telephone number:

Meeting of Creditors

Date: / / Time: ( ) A. M. ( ) P. M. Location:

Deadlines:
Papers must be *received* by the bankruptcy clerk's office by the following deadlines:

Deadline to File a Proof of Claim:

For all creditors(except a governmental unit): For a governmental unit:

Creditor with a Foreign Address:
A creditor to whom this notice is sent at a foreign address should read the information under "Claims" on the reverse side.

Deadline to File a Complaint to Determine Dischargeability of Certain Debts:

Deadline to Object to Exemptions:
Thirty (30) days after the *conclusion* of the meeting of creditors.

Filing of Plan, Hearing on Confirmation of Plan
[The debtor has filed a plan. The plan or a summary of the plan is enclosed. The hearing on confirmation will be held:
Date:__________________Time:__________________Location:__________________]
or [The debtor has filed a plan. The plan or a summary of the plan and notice of confirmation hearing will be sent separately.]
or [The debtor has not filed a plan as of this date. You will be sent separate notice of the hearing on confirmation of the plan.]

Creditors May Not Take Certain Actions:
In most instances, the filing of the bankruptcy case automatically stays certain collection and other actions against the debtor, the debtor's property, and certain codebtors. Under certain circumstances, the stay may be limited to 30 days or not exist at all, although the debtor can request the court to extend or impose a stay. If you attempt to collect a debt or take other action in violation of the Bankruptcy Code, you may be penalized. Consult a lawyer to determine your rights in this case.

Address of the Bankruptcy Clerk's Office:	For the Court:
	Clerk of the Bankruptcy Court:
Telephone number:	
Hours Open:	Date:

EXPLANATIONS **B9G (Official Form 9G) (12/12)**

Filing of Chapter 12 Bankruptcy Case	A bankruptcy case under Chapter 12 of the Bankruptcy Code (title 11, United States Code) has been filed in this court by the debtor(s) listed on the front side, and an order for relief has been entered. Chapter 12 allows family farmers and family fishermen to adjust their debts pursuant to a plan. A plan is not effective unless confirmed by the court. You may object to confirmation of the plan and appear at the confirmation hearing. A copy or summary of the plan [is included with this notice] *or* [will be sent to you later], and [the confirmation hearing will be held on the date indicated on the front of this notice] *or* [you will be sent notice of the confirmation hearing]. The debtor will remain in possession of the debtor's property and may continue to operate the debtor's business unless the court orders otherwise.
Legal Advice	The staff of the bankruptcy clerk's office cannot give legal advice. Consult a lawyer to determine your rights in this case.
Creditors Generally May Not Take Certain Actions	Prohibited collection actions against the debtor and certain codebtors are listed in Bankruptcy Code § 362 and § 1201. Common examples of prohibited actions include contacting the debtor by telephone, mail, or otherwise to demand repayment; taking actions to collect money or obtain property from the debtor; repossessing the debtor's property; starting or continuing lawsuits or foreclosures; and garnishing or deducting from the debtor's wages. Under certain circumstances, the stay may be limited in duration or not exist at all, although the debtor may have the right to request the court to extend or impose a stay.
Meeting of Creditors	A meeting of creditors is scheduled for the date, time, and location listed on the front side. *The debtor (both spouses in a joint case) must be present at the meeting to be questioned under oath by the trustee and by creditors.* Creditors are welcome to attend, but are not required to do so. The meeting may be continued and concluded at a later date specified in a notice filed with the court.
Claims	A Proof of Claim is a signed statement describing a creditor's claim. If a Proof of Claim form is not included with this notice, you can obtain one at any bankruptcy clerk's office. A secured creditor retains rights in its collateral regardless of whether that creditor files a Proof of Claim. If you do not file a Proof of Claim by the "Deadline to File a Proof of Claim" listed on the front side, you might not be paid any money on your claim from other assets in the bankruptcy case. To be paid, you must file a Proof of Claim even if your claim is listed in the schedules filed by the debtor. Filing a Proof of Claim submits the creditor to the jurisdiction of the bankruptcy court, with consequences a lawyer can explain. For example, a secured creditor who files a Proof of Claim may surrender important nonmonetary rights, including the right to a jury trial. **Filing Deadline for a Creditor with a Foreign Address:** The deadlines for filing claims set forth on the front of this notice apply to all creditors. If this notice has been mailed to a creditor at a foreign address, the creditor may file a motion requesting the court to extend the deadline. *Do not include this notice with any filing you make with the court.*
Discharge of Debts	The debtor is seeking a discharge of most debts, which may include your debt. A discharge means that you may never try to collect the debt from the debtor. If you believe that a debt owed to you is not dischargeable under Bankruptcy Code § 523 (a) (2), (4), or (6), you must start a lawsuit by filing a complaint in the bankruptcy clerk's office by the "Deadline to File a Complaint to Determine Dischargeability of Certain Debts" listed on the front side. The bankruptcy clerk's office must receive the complaint and any required filing fee by that Deadline.
Exempt Property	The debtor is permitted by law to keep certain property as exempt. Exempt property will not be sold and distributed to creditors, even if the debtor's case is converted to chapter 7. The debtor must file a list of all property claimed as exempt. You may inspect that list at the bankruptcy clerk's office. If you believe that an exemption claimed by the debtor is not authorized by law, you may file an objection to that exemption. The bankruptcy clerk's office must receive the objection by the "Deadline to Object to Exemptions" listed on the front side.
Bankruptcy Clerk's Office	Any paper that you file in this bankruptcy case should be filed at the bankruptcy clerk's office at the address listed on the front side. You may inspect all papers filed, including the list of the debtor's property and debts and the list of the property claimed as exempt, at the bankruptcy clerk's office.
Creditor with a Foreign Address	Consult a lawyer familiar with United States bankruptcy law if you have any questions regarding your rights in this case.
Refer To Other Side For Important Deadlines and Notices	

(Amended Oct. 17, 2005; Oct. 1, 2006; Dec. 1, 2007; Dec. 1, 2011; Dec. 1, 2012.)

Form 9H. Chapter 12 Corporation/Partnership Family Farmer or Family Fisherman

B9H (Official Form 9H) (Chapter 12 Corporation/Partnership Family Farmer or Family Fisherman) (12/12)

UNITED STATES BANKRUPTCY COURT ____________ **District of** ____________

Notice of
Chapter 12 Bankruptcy Case, Meeting of Creditors, & Deadlines

[The debtor [corporation] *or* [partnership] listed below filed a chapter 12 bankruptcy case on ____________ (date).]
or [A bankruptcy case concerning the debtor [corporation] *or* [partnership] listed below was originally filed under chapter ________ on ____________ (date) and was converted to a case under chapter 12 on ____________ (date).]

You may be a creditor of the debtor. **This notice lists important deadlines.** You may want to consult an attorney to protect your rights. All documents filed in the case may be inspected at the bankruptcy clerk's office at the address listed below.
NOTE: The staff of the bankruptcy clerk's office cannot give legal advice.

Creditors -- Do not file this notice in connection with any proof of claim you submit to the court.
See Reverse Side for Important Explanations.

Debtor(s) (name(s) and address):	Case Number:
	Last four digits of Social-Security or Individual Taxpayer-ID (ITIN) No(s)./Complete EIN:
All other names used by the Debtor(s) in the last 8 years (include trade names):	Bankruptcy Trustee (name and address):
Attorney for Debtor(s) (name and address): Telephone number:	Telephone number:

Meeting of Creditors

Date: / / Time: ( ) A. M. ( ) P. M. Location:

Deadlines:

Papers must be *received* by the bankruptcy clerk's office by the following deadlines:

Deadline to File a Proof of Claim:

For all creditors(except a governmental unit): For a governmental unit:

Creditor with a Foreign Address:
A creditor to whom this notice is sent at a foreign address should read the information under "Claims" on the reverse side.

Deadline to File a Complaint to Determine Dischargeability of Certain Debts:

Filing of Plan, Hearing on Confirmation of Plan

[The debtor has filed a plan. The plan or a summary of the plan is enclosed. The hearing on confirmation will be held:
Date:____________ Time:____________ Location:____________]
or [The debtor has filed a plan. The plan or a summary of the plan and notice of confirmation hearing will be sent separately.]
or [The debtor has not filed a plan as of this date. You will be sent separate notice of the hearing on confirmation of the plan.]

Creditors May Not Take Certain Actions:
In most instances, the filing of the bankruptcy case automatically stays certain collection and other actions against the debtor and the debtor's property. Under certain circumstances, the stay may be limited to 30 days or not exist at all, although the debtor can request the court to extend or impose a stay. If you attempt to collect a debt or take other action in violation of the Bankruptcy Code, you may be penalized. Consult a lawyer to determine your rights in this case.

Address of the Bankruptcy Clerk's Office:	**For the Court:**
Telephone number:	Clerk of the Bankruptcy Court:
Hours Open:	Date:

EXPLANATIONS **B9H (Official Form 9H) (12/12)**

Filing of Chapter 12 Bankruptcy Case	A bankruptcy case under Chapter 12 of the Bankruptcy Code (title 11, United States Code) has been filed in this court by the debtor listed on the front side, and an order for relief has been entered. Chapter 12 allows family farmers and family fishermen to adjust their debts pursuant to a plan. A plan is not effective unless confirmed by the court. You may object to confirmation of the plan and appear at the confirmation hearing. A copy or summary of the plan [is included with this notice] *or* [will be sent to you later], and [the confirmation hearing will be held on the date indicated on the front of this notice] *or* [you will be sent notice of the confirmation hearing]. The debtor will remain in possession of the debtor's property and may continue to operate the debtor's business unless the court orders otherwise.
Legal Advice	The staff of the bankruptcy clerk's office cannot give legal advice. Consult a lawyer to determine your rights in this case.
Creditors Generally May Not Take Certain Actions	Prohibited collection actions against the debtor and certain codebtors are listed in Bankruptcy Code § 362 and § 1201. Common examples of prohibited actions include contacting the debtor by telephone, mail, or otherwise to demand repayment; taking actions to collect money or obtain property from the debtor; repossessing the debtor's property; and starting or continuing lawsuits or foreclosures. Under certain circumstances, the stay may be limited in duration or not exist at all, although the debtor may have the right to request the court to extend or impose a stay.
Meeting of Creditors	A meeting of creditors is scheduled for the date, time, and location listed on the front side. *The debtor's representative must be present at the meeting to be questioned under oath by the trustee and by creditors.* Creditors are welcome to attend, but are not required to do so. The meeting may be continued and concluded at a later date specified in a notice filed with the court.
Claims	A Proof of Claim is a signed statement describing a creditor's claim. If a Proof of Claim form is not included with this notice, you can obtain one at any bankruptcy clerk's office. A secured creditor retains rights in its collateral regardless of whether that creditor files a Proof of Claim. If you do not file a Proof of Claim by the "Deadline to File a Proof of Claim" listed on the front side, you might not be paid any money on your claim from other assets in the bankruptcy case. To be paid, you must file a Proof of Claim even if your claim is listed in the schedules filed by the debtor. Filing a Proof of Claim submits the creditor to the jurisdiction of the bankruptcy court, with consequences a lawyer can explain. For example, a secured creditor who files a Proof of Claim may surrender important nonmonetary rights, including the right to a jury trial. **Filing Deadline for a Creditor with a Foreign Address:** The deadlines for filing claims set forth on the front of this notice apply to all creditors. If this notice has been mailed to a creditor at a foreign address, the creditor may file a motion requesting the court to extend the deadline. *Do not include this notice with any filing you make with the court.*
Discharge of Debts	The debtor is seeking a discharge of most debts, which may include your debt. A discharge means that you may never try to collect the debt from the debtor. If you believe that a debt owed to you is not dischargeable under Bankruptcy Code § 523 (a) (2), (4), or (6), you must start a lawsuit by filing a complaint in the bankruptcy clerk's office by the "Deadline to File a Complaint to Determine Dischargeability of Certain Debts" listed on the front side. The bankruptcy clerk's office must receive the complaint and any required filing fee by that Deadline.
Bankruptcy Clerk's Office	Any paper that you file in this bankruptcy case should be filed at the bankruptcy clerk's office at the address listed on the front side. You may inspect all papers filed, including the list of the debtor's property and debts and the list of the property claimed as exempt, at the bankruptcy clerk's office.
Creditor with a Foreign Address	Consult a lawyer familiar with United States bankruptcy law if you have any questions regarding your rights in this case.

Refer To Other Side For Important Deadlines and Notices

(Amended Oct. 17, 2005; Oct. 1, 2006; Dec. 1, 2007; Dec. 1, 2011; Dec. 1, 2012.)

Form 9I. Chapter 13 Case

B9I (Official Form 9I) (Chapter 13 Case) (12/12)

UNITED STATES BANKRUPTCY COURT ______________ **District of** ______________

Notice of
Chapter 13 Bankruptcy Case, Meeting of Creditors, & Deadlines

[The debtor(s) listed below filed a chapter 13 bankruptcy case on ______________ (date).]
or [A bankruptcy case concerning the debtor(s) listed below was originally filed under chapter ______________
on ______________ (date) and was converted to a case under chapter 13 on ______________ (date).]

You may be a creditor of the debtor. **This notice lists important deadlines.** You may want to consult an attorney to protect your rights. All documents filed in the case may be inspected at the bankruptcy clerk's office at the address listed below.
NOTE: The staff of the bankruptcy clerk's office cannot give legal advice.

Creditors -- Do not file this notice in connection with any proof of claim you submit to the court.
See Reverse Side for Important Explanations.

Debtor(s) (name(s) and address):	Case Number:
	Last four digits of Social-Security or Individual Taxpayer-ID (ITIN) No(s)./Complete EIN:
All other names used by the Debtor(s) in the last 8 years (include married, maiden, and trade names):	Bankruptcy Trustee (name and address):
Attorney for Debtor(s) (name and address):	
Telephone number:	Telephone number:

Meeting of Creditors

Date: / / Time: ( ) A. M. ( ) P. M. Location:

Deadlines:

Papers must be *received* by the bankruptcy clerk's office by the following deadlines:

Deadline to File a Proof of Claim:

For all creditors (except a governmental unit):

For a governmental unit (except as otherwise provided in Fed. R. Bankr. P. 3002(c)(1)):

Creditor with a Foreign Address:

A creditor to whom this notice is sent at a foreign address should read the information under "Claims" on the reverse side.

Deadline to Object to Debtor's Discharge or to Challenge Dischargeability of Certain Debts:

Deadline to Object to Exemptions:

Thirty (30) days after the *conclusion* of the meeting of creditors.

Filing of Plan, Hearing on Confirmation of Plan

[The debtor has filed a plan. The plan or a summary of the plan is enclosed. The hearing on confirmation will be held:
Date:______________ Time:______________ Location:______________]
or [The debtor has filed a plan. The plan or a summary of the plan and notice of confirmation hearing will be sent separately.]
or [The debtor has not filed a plan as of this date. You will be sent separate notice of the hearing on confirmation of the plan.]

Creditors May Not Take Certain Actions:

In most instances, the filing of the bankruptcy case automatically stays certain collection and other actions against the debtor, the debtor's property, and certain codebtors. Under certain circumstances, the stay may be limited to 30 days or not exist at all, although the debtor can request the court to extend or impose a stay. If you attempt to collect a debt or take other action in violation of the Bankruptcy Code, you may be penalized. Consult a lawyer to determine your rights in this case.

Address of the Bankruptcy Clerk's Office:	**For the Court:**
	Clerk of the Bankruptcy Court:
Telephone number:	
Hours Open:	Date:

EXPLANATIONS **B9I (Official Form 9I) (12/12)**

Filing of Chapter 13 Bankruptcy Case	A bankruptcy case under Chapter 13 of the Bankruptcy Code (title 11, United States Code) has been filed in this court by the debtor(s) listed on the front side, and an order for relief has been entered. Chapter 13 allows an individual with regular income and debts below a specified amount to adjust debts pursuant to a plan. A plan is not effective unless confirmed by the bankruptcy court. You may object to confirmation of the plan and appear at the confirmation hearing. A copy or summary of the plan [is included with this notice] *or* [will be sent to you later], and [the confirmation hearing will be held on the date indicated on the front of this notice] *or* [you will be sent notice of the confirmation hearing]. The debtor will remain in possession of the debtor's property and may continue to operate the debtor's business, if any, unless the court orders otherwise.
Legal Advice	The staff of the bankruptcy clerk's office cannot give legal advice. Consult a lawyer to determine your rights in this case.
Creditors Generally May Not Take Certain Actions	Prohibited collection actions against the debtor and certain codebtors are listed in Bankruptcy Code § 362 and § 1301. Common examples of prohibited actions include contacting the debtor by telephone, mail, or otherwise to demand repayment; taking actions to collect money or obtain property from the debtor; repossessing the debtor's property; starting or continuing lawsuits or foreclosures; and garnishing or deducting from the debtor's wages. Under certain circumstances, the stay may be limited to 30 days or not exist at all, although the debtor can request the court to exceed or impose a stay.
Meeting of Creditors	A meeting of creditors is scheduled for the date, time, and location listed on the front side. *The debtor (both spouses in a joint case) must be present at the meeting to be questioned under oath by the trustee and by creditors.* Creditors are welcome to attend, but are not required to do so. The meeting may be continued and concluded at a later date specified in a notice filed with the court.
Claims	A Proof of Claim is a signed statement describing a creditor's claim. If a Proof of Claim form is not included with this notice, you can obtain one at any bankruptcy clerk's office. A secured creditor retains rights in its collateral regardless of whether that creditor files a Proof of Claim. If you do not file a Proof of Claim by the "Deadline to File a Proof of Claim" listed on the front side, you might not be paid any money on your claim from other assets in the bankruptcy case. To be paid, you must file a Proof of Claim even if your claim is listed in the schedules filed by the debtor. Filing a Proof of Claim submits the creditor to the jurisdiction of the bankruptcy court, with consequences a lawyer can explain. For example, a secured creditor who files a Proof of Claim may surrender important nonmonetary rights, including the right to a jury trial. **Filing Deadline for a Creditor with a Foreign Address:** The deadlines for filing claims set forth on the front of this notice apply to all creditors. If this notice has been mailed to a creditor at a foreign address, the creditor may file a motion requesting the court to extend the deadline. *Do not include this notice with any filing you make with the court.*
Discharge of Debts	The debtor is seeking a discharge of most debts, which may include your debt. A discharge means that you may never try to collect the debt from the debtor. If you believe that the debtor is not entitled to a discharge under Bankruptcy Code § 1328(f), you must file a motion objecting to discharge in the bankruptcy clerk's office by the "Deadline to Object to Debtor's Discharge or to Challenge the Dischargeability of Certain Debts" listed on the front of this form. If you believe that a debt owed to you is not dischargeable under Bankruptcy Code § 523(a)(2) or (4), you must file a complaint in the bankruptcy clerk's office by the same deadline. The bankruptcy clerk's office must receive the motion or the complaint and any required filing fee by that deadline.
Exempt Property	The debtor is permitted by law to keep certain property as exempt. Exempt property will not be sold and distributed to creditors, even if the debtor's case is converted to chapter 7. The debtor must file a list of all property claimed as exempt. You may inspect that list at the bankruptcy clerk's office. If you believe that an exemption claimed by the debtor is not authorized by law, you may file an objection to that exemption. The bankruptcy clerk's office must receive the objection by the "Deadline to Object to Exemptions" listed on the front side.
Bankruptcy Clerk's Office	Any paper that you file in this bankruptcy case should be filed at the bankruptcy clerk's office at the address listed on the front side. You may inspect all papers filed, including the list of the debtor's property and debts and the list of the property claimed as exempt, at the bankruptcy clerk's office.
Creditor with a Foreign Address	Consult a lawyer familiar with United States bankruptcy law if you have any questions regarding your rights in this case.
Refer To Other Side For Important Deadlines and Notices	

(Amended Oct. 17, 2005; Oct. 1, 2006; Dec. 1, 2007; Dec. 1, 2010; Dec. 1, 2011; Dec. 1, 2012.)

Form 10. Proof of Claim

B 10 (Official Form 10) (12/12)

UNITED STATES BANKRUPTCY COURT		PROOF OF CLAIM
Name of Debtor:	Case Number:	
NOTE: *Do not use this form to make a claim for an administrative expense that arises after the bankruptcy filing. You may file a request for payment of an administrative expense according to 11 U.S.C. § 503.*		
Name of Creditor (the person or other entity to whom the debtor owes money or property):		COURT USE ONLY
Name and address where notices should be sent: Telephone number: email:		❐ Check this box if this claim amends a previously filed claim. **Court Claim Number:**________ *(If known)* Filed on:________
Name and address where payment should be sent (if different from above): Telephone number: email:		❐ Check this box if you are aware that anyone else has filed a proof of claim relating to this claim. Attach copy of statement giving particulars.

1. Amount of Claim as of Date Case Filed: $________________

If all or part of the claim is secured, complete item 4.

If all or part of the claim is entitled to priority, complete item 5.

❐Check this box if the claim includes interest or other charges in addition to the principal amount of the claim. Attach a statement that itemizes interest or charges.

2. Basis for Claim: ________________
(See instruction #2)

3. Last four digits of any number by which creditor identifies debtor:	3a. Debtor may have scheduled account as:	3b. Uniform Claim Identifier (optional):
__ __ __ __	____________ (See instruction #3a)	____________ (See instruction #3b)

4. Secured Claim (See instruction #4)
Check the appropriate box if the claim is secured by a lien on property or a right of setoff, attach required redacted documents, and provide the requested information.

Nature of property or right of setoff: ❐Real Estate ❐Motor Vehicle ❐Other
Describe:

Value of Property: $__________

Annual Interest Rate_____% ❐Fixed or ❐Variable
(when case was filed)

Amount of arrearage and other charges, as of the time case was filed, included in secured claim, if any:

$__________

Basis for perfection: ________________

Amount of Secured Claim: **$**__________

Amount Unsecured: **$**__________

5. Amount of Claim Entitled to Priority under 11 U.S.C. § 507 (a). If any part of the claim falls into one of the following categories, check the box specifying the priority and state the amount.

❐ Domestic support obligations under 11 U.S.C. § 507 (a)(1)(A) or (a)(1)(B).

❐ Wages, salaries, or commissions (up to $11,725*) earned within 180 days before the case was filed or the debtor's business ceased, whichever is earlier – 11 U.S.C. § 507 (a)(4).

❐ Contributions to an employee benefit plan – 11 U.S.C. § 507 (a)(5).

❐ Up to $2,600* of deposits toward purchase, lease, or rental of property or services for personal, family, or household use – 11 U.S.C. § 507 (a)(7).

❐ Taxes or penalties owed to governmental units – 11 U.S.C. § 507 (a)(8).

❐ Other – Specify applicable paragraph of 11 U.S.C. § 507 (a)(__).

Amount entitled to priority:

$__________

**Amounts are subject to adjustment on 4/1/13 and every 3 years thereafter with respect to cases commenced on or after the date of adjustment.*

6. Credits. The amount of all payments on this claim has been credited for the purpose of making this proof of claim. (See instruction #6)

B 10 (Official Form 10) (12/12) 2

7. Documents: Attached are **redacted** copies of any documents that support the claim, such as promissory notes, purchase orders, invoices, itemized statements of running accounts, contracts, judgments, mortgages, security agreements, or, in the case of a claim based on an open-end or revolving consumer credit agreement, a statement providing the information required by FRBP 3001(c)(3)(A). If the claim is secured, box 4 has been completed, and **redacted** copies of documents providing evidence of perfection of a security interest are attached. If the claim is secured by the debtor's principal residence, the Mortgage Proof of Claim Attachment is being filed with this claim. *(See instruction #7, and the definition of "**redacted**".)*

DO NOT SEND ORIGINAL DOCUMENTS. ATTACHED DOCUMENTS MAY BE DESTROYED AFTER SCANNING.

If the documents are not available, please explain:

8. Signature: (See instruction #8)

Check the appropriate box.

❒ I am the creditor. ❒ I am the creditor's authorized agent. ❒ I am the trustee, or the debtor, or their authorized agent. (See Bankruptcy Rule 3004.) ❒ I am a guarantor, surety, indorser, or other codebtor. (See Bankruptcy Rule 3005.)

I declare under penalty of perjury that the information provided in this claim is true and correct to the best of my knowledge, information, and reasonable belief.

Print Name: ____________________
Title: ____________________
Company: ____________________
Address and telephone number (if different from notice address above):
____
____
____
Telephone number: email:

____
(Signature) (Date)

Penalty for presenting fraudulent claim: Fine of up to $500,000 or imprisonment for up to 5 years, or both. 18 U.S.C. §§ 152 and 3571.

INSTRUCTIONS FOR PROOF OF CLAIM FORM

The instructions and definitions below are general explanations of the law. In certain circumstances, such as bankruptcy cases not filed voluntarily by the debtor, exceptions to these general rules may apply.

Items to be completed in Proof of Claim form

Court, Name of Debtor, and Case Number:
Fill in the federal judicial district in which the bankruptcy case was filed (for example, Central District of California), the debtor's full name, and the case number. If the creditor received a notice of the case from the bankruptcy court, all of this information is at the top of the notice.

Creditor's Name and Address:
Fill in the name of the person or entity asserting a claim and the name and address of the person who should receive notices issued during the bankruptcy case. A separate space is provided for the payment address if it differs from the notice address. The creditor has a continuing obligation to keep the court informed of its current address. See Federal Rule of Bankruptcy Procedure (FRBP) 2002(g).

1. Amount of Claim as of Date Case Filed:
State the total amount owed to the creditor on the date of the bankruptcy filing. Follow the instructions concerning whether to complete items 4 and 5. Check the box if interest or other charges are included in the claim.

2. Basis for Claim:
State the type of debt or how it was incurred. Examples include goods sold, money loaned, services performed, personal injury/wrongful death, car loan, mortgage note, and credit card. If the claim is based on delivering health care goods or services, limit the disclosure of the goods or services so as to avoid embarrassment or the disclosure of confidential health care information. You may be required to provide additional disclosure if an interested party objects to the claim.

3. Last Four Digits of Any Number by Which Creditor Identifies Debtor:
State only the last four digits of the debtor's account or other number used by the creditor to identify the debtor.

3a. Debtor May Have Scheduled Account As:
Report a change in the creditor's name, a transferred claim, or any other information that clarifies a difference between this proof of claim and the claim as scheduled by the debtor.

3b. Uniform Claim Identifier:
If you use a uniform claim identifier, you may report it here. A uniform claim identifier is an optional 24-character identifier that certain large creditors use to facilitate electronic payment in chapter 13 cases.

4. Secured Claim:
Check whether the claim is fully or partially secured. Skip this section if the claim is entirely unsecured. (See Definitions.) If the claim is secured, check the box for the nature and value of property that secures the claim, attach copies of lien documentation, and state, as of the date of the bankruptcy filing, the annual interest rate (and whether it is fixed or variable), and the amount past due on the claim.

5. Amount of Claim Entitled to Priority Under 11 U.S.C. § 507 (a).
If any portion of the claim falls into any category shown, check the appropriate box(es) and state the amount entitled to priority. (See Definitions.) A claim may be partly priority and partly non-priority. For example, in some of the categories, the law limits the amount entitled to priority.

6. Credits:
An authorized signature on this proof of claim serves as an acknowledgment that when calculating the amount of the claim, the creditor gave the debtor credit for any payments received toward the debt.

7. Documents:
Attach redacted copies of any documents that show the debt exists and a lien secures the debt. You must also attach copies of documents that evidence perfection of any security interest and documents required by FRBP 3001(c) for claims based on an open-end or revolving consumer credit agreement or secured by a security interest in the debtor's principal residence. You may also attach a summary in addition to the documents themselves. FRBP 3001(c) and (d). If the claim is based on delivering health care goods or services, limit disclosing confidential health care information. Do not send original documents, as attachments may be destroyed after scanning.

8. Date and Signature:
The individual completing this proof of claim must sign and date it. FRBP 9011. If the claim is filed electronically, FRBP 5005(a)(2) authorizes courts to establish local rules specifying what constitutes a signature. If you sign this form, you declare under penalty of perjury that the information provided is true and correct to the best of your knowledge, information, and reasonable belief. Your signature is also a certification that the claim meets the requirements of FRBP 9011(b). Whether the claim is filed electronically or in person, if your name is on the signature line, you are responsible for the declaration. Print the name and title, if any, of the creditor or other person authorized to file this claim. State the filer's address and telephone number if it differs from the address given on the top of the form for purposes of receiving notices. If the claim is filed by an authorized agent, provide both the name of the individual filing the claim and the name of the agent. If the authorized agent is a servicer, identify the corporate servicer as the company. Criminal penalties apply for making a false statement on a proof of claim.

B 10 (Official Form 10) (12/12) 3

DEFINITIONS

Debtor
A debtor is the person, corporation, or other entity that has filed a bankruptcy case.

Creditor
A creditor is a person, corporation, or other entity to whom debtor owes a debt that was incurred before the date of the bankruptcy filing. See 11 U.S.C. §101 (10).

Claim
A claim is the creditor's right to receive payment for a debt owed by the debtor on the date of the bankruptcy filing. See 11 U.S.C. §101 (5). A claim may be secured or unsecured.

Proof of Claim
A proof of claim is a form used by the creditor to indicate the amount of the debt owed by the debtor on the date of the bankruptcy filing. The creditor must file the form with the clerk of the same bankruptcy court in which the bankruptcy case was filed.

Secured Claim Under 11 U.S.C. § 506 (a)
A secured claim is one backed by a lien on property of the debtor. The claim is secured so long as the creditor has the right to be paid from the property prior to other creditors. The amount of the secured claim cannot exceed the value of the property. Any amount owed to the creditor in excess of the value of the property is an unsecured claim. Examples of liens on property include a mortgage on real estate or a security interest in a car. A lien may be voluntarily granted by a debtor or may be obtained through a court proceeding. In some states, a court judgment is a lien.

A claim also may be secured if the creditor owes the debtor money (has a right to setoff).

Unsecured Claim
An unsecured claim is one that does not meet the requirements of a secured claim. A claim may be partly unsecured if the amount of the claim exceeds the value of the property on which the creditor has a lien.

Claim Entitled to Priority Under 11 U.S.C. § 507 (a)
Priority claims are certain categories of unsecured claims that are paid from the available money or property in a bankruptcy case before other unsecured claims.

Redacted
A document has been redacted when the person filing it has masked, edited out, or otherwise deleted, certain information. A creditor must show only the last four digits of any social-security, individual's tax-identification, or financial-account number, only the initials of a minor's name, and only the year of any person's date of birth. If the claim is based on the delivery of health care goods or services, limit the disclosure of the goods or services so as to avoid embarrassment or the disclosure of confidential health care information.

Evidence of Perfection
Evidence of perfection may include a mortgage, lien, certificate of title, financing statement, or other document showing that the lien has been filed or recorded.

INFORMATION

Acknowledgment of Filing of Claim
To receive acknowledgment of your filing, you may either enclose a stamped self-addressed envelope and a copy of this proof of claim or you may access the court's PACER system (www.pacer.psc.uscourts.gov) for a small fee to view your filed proof of claim.

Offers to Purchase a Claim
Certain entities are in the business of purchasing claims for an amount less than the face value of the claims. One or more of these entities may contact the creditor and offer to purchase the claim. Some of the written communications from these entities may easily be confused with official court documentation or communications from the debtor. These entities do not represent the bankruptcy court or the debtor. The creditor has no obligation to sell its claim. However, if the creditor decides to sell its claim, any transfer of such claim is subject to FRBP 3001(e), any applicable provisions of the Bankruptcy Code (11 U.S.C. § 101 *et seq.*), and any applicable orders of the bankruptcy court.

(Amended April 1, 2004; Oct. 17, 2005; April 1, 2007; Dec. 1, 2007; April 1, 2010; Dec. 1, 2011; Dec. 1, 2012; April 1, 2013.)

Form 10A. Proof of Claim, Attachment A

B 10A (Attachment A) (12/11)

Mortgage Proof of Claim Attachment

If you file a claim secured by a security interest in the debtor's principal residence, you must use this form as an attachment to your proof of claim. See Bankruptcy Rule 3001(c)(2).

Name of debtor: ______________________ **Case number:** ______________

Name of creditor: ______________________ **Last four digits** of any number you use to identify the debtor's account: __ __ __ __

Part 1: Statement of Principal and Interest Due as of the Petition Date

Itemize the principal and interest due on the claim as of the petition date (included in the Amount of Claim listed in Item 1 on your Proof of Claim form).

1. **Principal due** (1) $ ________

2. **Interest due**

Interest rate	From mm/dd/yyyy	To mm/dd/yyyy	Amount
____%	________	________	$ ____
____%	________	________	$ ____
____%	________	________	+ $ ____
Total interest due as of the petition date			$ ____

Copy total here ▶ (2) + $ ________

3. **Total principal and interest due** (3) $ ________

Part 2: Statement of Prepetition Fees, Expenses, and Charges

Itemize the fees, expenses, and charges due on the claim as of the petition date (included in the Amount of Claim listed in Item 1 on the Proof of Claim form).

Description	Dates incurred		Amount
1. **Late charges**	________	(1)	$ ________
2. **Non-sufficient funds (NSF) fees**	________	(2)	$ ________
3. **Attorney's fees**	________	(3)	$ ________
4. **Filing fees and court costs**	________	(4)	$ ________
5. **Advertisement costs**	________	(5)	$ ________
6. **Sheriff/auctioneer fees**	________	(6)	$ ________
7. **Title costs**	________	(7)	$ ________
8. **Recording fees**	________	(8)	$ ________
9. **Appraisal/broker's price opinion fees**	________	(9)	$ ________
10. **Property inspection fees**	________	(10)	$ ________
11. **Tax advances (non-escrow)**	________	(11)	$ ________
12. **Insurance advances (non-escrow)**	________	(12)	$ ________
13. **Escrow shortage or deficiency** (Do not include amounts that are part of any installment payment listed in Part 3.)	________	(13)	$ ________
14. **Property preservation expenses. Specify:**________	________	(14)	$ ________
15. **Other. Specify:**________	________	(15)	$ ________
16. **Other. Specify:**________	________	(16)	$ ________
17. **Other. Specify:**________	________	(17)	+ $ ________
18. **Total prepetition fees, expenses, and charges. Add all of the amounts listed above.**		(18)	$ ________

B 10A (Attachment A) (12/11) Page 2

Part 3. Statement of Amount Necessary to Cure Default as of the Petition Date

Does the installment payment amount include an escrow deposit?

❑ No

❑ Yes Attach to the Proof of Claim form an escrow account statement prepared as of the petition date in a form consistent with applicable nonbankruptcy law.

1. **Installment payments due**

   Date last payment received by creditor ____________ mm/dd/yyyy

   Number of installment payments due (1) ____________

2. **Amount of installment payments due**

   _____installments @ $ ____________

   _____installments @ $ ____________

   _____installments @ + $ ____________

   Total installment payments due as of the petition date $ ____________ Copy total here ► (2) $ ____________

3. **Calculation of cure amount**

   Add total prepetition fees, expenses, and charges Copy total from Part 2 here ► + $ ____________

   Subtract total of unapplied funds (funds received but not credited to account) - $ ____________

   Subtract amounts for which debtor is entitled to a refund - $ ____________

   Total amount necessary to cure default as of the petition date (3) $ ____________

   Copy total onto Item 4 of Proof of Claim form

(As added Dec. 1, 2011.)

Form 10S1. Proof of Claim, Supplement 1

B 10S1 (Supplement 1) (12/11)

UNITED STATES BANKRUPTCY COURT

In re ______________________________,
Debtor

Case No. ______________________

Chapter 13

Notice of Mortgage Payment Change

If you file a claim secured by a security interest in the debtor's principal residence provided for under the debtor's plan pursuant to § 1322(b)(5), you must use this form to give notice of any changes in the installment payment amount. File this form as a supplement to your proof of claim at least 21 days before the new payment amount is due. See Bankruptcy Rule 3002.1.

Name of creditor: ______________________________

Court claim no. (if known): ____________________

Last four digits of any number you use to identify the debtor's account: ___ ___ ___ ___

Date of payment change: ______________
Must be at least 21 days after date of this notice
mm/dd/yyyy

New total payment: $ ______________
Principal, interest, and escrow, if any

Part 1: Escrow Account Payment Adjustment

Will there be a change in the debtor's escrow account payment?

❑ No
❑ Yes Attach a copy of the escrow account statement prepared in a form consistent with applicable nonbankruptcy law. Describe the basis for the change. If a statement is not attached, explain why: ______________________________

Current escrow payment: $ ______________ **New escrow payment:** $ ______________

Part 2: Mortgage Payment Adjustment

Will the debtor's principal and interest payment change based on an adjustment to the interest rate in the debtor's variable-rate note?

❑ No
❑ Yes Attach a copy of the rate change notice prepared in a form consistent with applicable nonbankruptcy law. If a notice is not attached, explain why: ______________________________

Current interest rate: ______________% **New interest rate:** ______________%

Current principal and interest payment: $ ______________ **New principal and interest payment:** $ ______________

Part 3: Other Payment Change

Will there be a change in the debtor's mortgage payment for a reason not listed above?

❑ No
❑ Yes Attach a copy of any documents describing the basis for the change, such as a repayment plan or loan modification agreement. (*Court approval may be required before the payment change can take effect.*)

Reason for change: ______________________________

Current mortgage payment: $ ______________ **New mortgage payment:** $ ______________

B 10 (Supplement 1) (12/11) Page 2

Part 4: Sign Here

The person completing this Notice must sign it. Sign and print your name and your title, if any, and state your address and telephone number if different from the notice address listed on the proof of claim to which this Supplement applies.

Check the appropriate box.

❒ I am the creditor. ❒ I am the creditor's authorized agent.
(Attach copy of power of attorney, if any.)

I declare under penalty of perjury that the information provided in this Notice is true and correct to the best of my knowledge, information, and reasonable belief.

✘ ______________________________ Date __________
Signature mm/dd/yyyy

Print: ______________________________ Title ______________
First Name Middle Name Last Name

Company ______________________________

Address ______________________________
Number Street

____
City State ZIP Code

Contact phone ______________ Email ______________

(As added Dec. 1, 2011.)

Form 10S2. Proof of Claim, Supplement 2

B 10S2 (Supplement 2) (12/11)

UNITED STATES BANKRUPTCY COURT

In re ______________________________,
Debtor

Case No. ______________________

Chapter 13

Notice of Postpetition Mortgage Fees, Expenses, and Charges

If you hold a claim secured by a security interest in the debtor's principal residence, you must use this form to give notice of any postpetition fees, expenses, and charges that you assert are recoverable against the debtor or against the debtor's principal residence. File this form as a supplement to your proof of claim. See Bankruptcy Rule 3002.1.

Name of creditor: ______________________________ **Court claim no.** (if known): ____________________

Last four digits of any number you use to identify the debtor's account: ___ ___ ___ ___

Does this notice supplement a prior notice of postpetition fees, expenses, and charges?

❑ No

❑ Yes. Date of the last notice: ______________
mm/dd/yyyy

Part 1: Itemize Postpetition Fees, Expenses, and Charges

Itemize the fees, expenses, and charges incurred on the debtor's mortgage account after the petition was filed. Do not include any escrow account disbursements or any amounts previously itemized in a notice filed in this case or ruled on by the bankruptcy court.

Description	Dates incurred		Amount
1. Late charges	________________	(1)	$ __________
2. Non-sufficient funds (NSF) fees	________________	(2)	$ __________
3. Attorney fees	________________	(3)	$ __________
4. Filing fees and court costs	________________	(4)	$ __________
5. Bankruptcy/Proof of claim fees	________________	(5)	$ __________
6. Appraisal/Broker's price opinion fees	________________	(6)	$ __________
7. Property inspection fees	________________	(7)	$ __________
8. Tax advances (non-escrow)	________________	(8)	$ __________
9. Insurance advances (non-escrow)	________________	(9)	$ __________
10. Property preservation expenses. Specify: __________	________________	(10)	$ __________
11. Other. Specify: __________	________________	(11)	$ __________
12. Other. Specify: __________	________________	(12)	$ __________
13. Other. Specify: __________	________________	(13)	$ __________
14. Other. Specify: __________	________________	(14)	$ __________

The debtor or trustee may challenge whether the fees, expenses, and charges you listed are required to be paid. See 11 U.S.C. § 1322(b)(5) and Bankruptcy Rule 3002.1.

B 10S2 (Supplement 2) (12/11) Page 2

Part 2: Sign Here

The person completing this Notice must sign it. Sign and print your name and your title, if any, and state your address and telephone number if different from the notice address listed on the proof of claim to which this Supplement applies.

Check the appropriate box.

❒ I am the creditor.

❒ I am the creditor's authorized agent. (Attach copy of power of attorney, if any.)

I declare under penalty of perjury that the information provided in this Notice is true and correct to the best of my knowledge, information, and reasonable belief.

✘ ______________________________ Date ____________
Signature mm/dd/yyyy

Print: ______________________________ Title ______________________
First Name Middle Name Last Name

Company ______________________________

Address ______________________________
Number Street
____
City State ZIP Code

Contact phone ______________ Email ______________________

(As added Dec. 1, 2011.)

Form 11A. General Power of Attorney

[Caption as in Form 16B]

GENERAL POWER OF ATTORNEY

To ______________________ of * ______________________, and
______________________ of * ______________________.

The undersigned claimant hereby authorizes you, or any one of you, as attorney in fact for the undersigned and with full power of substitution, to vote on any question that may be lawfully submitted to creditors of the debtor in the above-entitled case; *[if appropriate]* to vote for a trustee of the estate of the debtor and for a committee of creditors; to receive dividends; and in general to perform any act not constituting the practice of law for the undersigned in all matters arising in this case.

Dated: ______________________

Signed: ______________________

By ______________________

as ______________________

Address: ______________________
____

[If executed by an individual] Acknowledged before me on ______________________.

[If executed on behalf of a partnership] Acknowledged before me on ______________________, by ______________________, who says that he [*or* she] is a member of the partnership named above and is authorized to execute this power of attorney in its behalf.

[If executed on behalf of a corporation] Acknowledged before me on ______________________, by ______________________, who says that he [*or* she] is ______________________ of the corporation named above and is authorized to execute this power of attorney in its behalf.

____

____
[Official character.]

* State mailing address.

Form 11B. Special Power of Attorney

[Caption as in Form 16B]

SPECIAL POWER OF ATTORNEY

To ______________________ of * ______________________, and
______________________ of * ______________________.

The undersigned claimant hereby authorizes you, or any one of you, as attorney in fact for the undersigned [*if desired:* and with full power of substitution,] to attend the meeting of creditors of the debtor or any adjournment thereof, and to vote in my behalf on any question that may be lawfully submitted to creditors at such meeting or adjourned meeting, and for a trustee or trustees of the estate of the debtor.

Dated: ______________________

Signed: ______________________

By ______________________

as______________________

Address: ______________________
____

[If executed by an individual] Acknowledged before me on ______________________.

[If executed on behalf of a partnership] Acknowledged before me on ______________________, by ______________________, who says that he [*or* she] is a member of the partnership named above and is authorized to execute this power of attorney in its behalf.

[If executed on behalf of a corporation] Acknowledged before me on ______________________, by ______________________, who says that he [*or* she] is ______________________of the corporation named above and is authorized to execute this power of attorney in its behalf.

____

____
[Official character.]

* State mailing address.

Form 12. Order and Notice for Hearing on Disclosure Statement

[Caption as in Form 16A]

ORDER AND NOTICE FOR HEARING ON DISCLOSURE STATEMENT

To the debtor, its creditors, and other parties in interest:

A disclosure statement and a plan under chapter 11 [*or* chapter 9] of the Bankruptcy Code having been filed by ______________________ on ______________________, IT IS ORDERED and notice is hereby given, that:

1. The hearing to consider the approval of the disclosure statement shall be held at: ______________________, on ______________________, at ______________ o'clock .m.

2. ______________________ is fixed as the last day for filing and serving in accordance with Fed. R. Bankr. P. 3017(a) written objections to the disclosure statement.

3. Within ______________ days after entry of this order, the disclosure statement and plan shall be distributed in accordance with Fed. R. Bankr. P. 3017(a).

4. Requests for copies of the disclosure statement and plan shall be mailed to the debtor in possession [*or* trustee *or* debtor *or* ______________________] at * ______________________.

Dated:______________________

BY THE COURT

____
United States Bankruptcy Judge

* State mailing address

Form 13. Order Approving Disclosure Statement and Fixing Time for Filing Acceptances or Rejections of Plan, Combined with Notice Thereof

[Caption as in Form 16A]

ORDER APPROVING DISCLOSURE STATEMENT AND FIXING TIME FOR FILING ACCEPTANCES OR REJECTIONS OF PLAN, COMBINED WITH NOTICE THEREOF

A disclosure statement under chapter 11 of the Bankruptcy Code having been filed by , on [*if appropriate,* and by , on], referring to a plan under chapter 11 of the Code filed by , on [*if appropriate,* and by , on respectively] [*if appropriate,* as modified by a modification filed on]; and
It having been determined after hearing on notice that the

[Caption as in Form 16A]

ORDER APPROVING DISCLOSURE STATEMENT AND FIXING TIME FOR FILING ACCEPTANCES OR REJECTIONS OF PLAN, COMBINED WITH NOTICE THEREOF

A disclosure statement under chapter 11 of the Bankruptcy Code having been filed by ____________________, on ____________________ [*if appropriate,* and by ____________________, on ____________________], referring to a plan under chapter 11 of the Code filed by ____________________, on ____________________ [*if appropriate,* and by ____________________, on ____________________ respectively] [*if appropriate,* as modified by a modification filed on ____________________]; and

It having been determined after hearing on notice that the disclosure statement [*or* statements] contains[s] adequate information:

IT IS ORDERED, and notice is hereby given, that:

A. The disclosure statement filed by ____________________ dated ____________________ [*if appropriate,* and by ____________________, dated is [are] approved.

B. ____________________ is fixed as the last day for filing written acceptances or rejections of the plan [*or* plans] referred to above.

C. Within ______ days after the entry of this order, the plan [*or* plans] *or* a summary *or* summaries thereof approved by the court, [and *[if appropriate]* a summary approved by the court of its opinion, if any, dated ____________________, approving the disclosure statement [*or* statements]], the disclosure statement [*or* statements], and a ballot conforming to Official Form 14 shall be mailed to creditors, equity security holders, and other parties in interest, and shall be transmitted to the United States trustee, as provided in Fed. R. Bankr. P. 3017(d).

D. If acceptances are filed for more than one plan, preferences among the plans so accepted may be indicated.

E. *[If appropriate]* ____ is fixed for the hearing on confirmation of the plan [*or* plans].

F. *[If appropriate]* ____________________ is fixed as the last day for filing and serving pursuant to Fed. R. Bankr. P. 3020(b)(1) written objections to confirmation of the plan.

Dated:______________________________

BY THE COURT

____
United States Bankruptcy Judge

[If the court directs that a copy of the opinion should be transmitted in lieu of or in addition to the summary thereof, the appropriate change should be made in paragraph C of this order.]

Form 14. Ballot for Accepting or Rejecting a Plan
Form B14 (Official Form 14)
(9/97)

Form 14. BALLOT FOR ACCEPTING OR REJECTING A PLAN

[*Caption as in Form 16A*]

CLASS [ ] BALLOT FOR ACCEPTING OR REJECTING PLAN OF REORGANIZATION

[Proponent] filed a plan of reorganization dated *[Date]* (the "Plan") for the Debtor in this case. The Court has *[conditionally]* approved a disclosure statement with respect to the Plan (the "Disclosure Statement"). The Disclosure Statement provides information to assist you in deciding how to vote your ballot. If you do not have a Disclosure Statement, you may obtain a copy from *[name, address, telephone number and telecopy number of proponent/proponent's attorney.]* Court approval of the disclosure statement does not indicate approval of the Plan by the Court.

You should receive the Disclosure Statement and the Plan before you vote. You may wish to seek legal advice concerning the Plan and your classification and treatment under the Plan. Your *[claim] [equity interest]* had been placed in class [ ] under the Plan. If you hold claims or equity interests in more than one class, you will receive a ballot for each class in which you are entitled to vote.

If your ballot is not received by *[name and address of proponent's attorney or other appropriate address]* on or before *[date]*, and such deadline is not extended, your vote will not count as either and acceptance or rejection of the Plan.

If the Plan is confirmed by the Bankruptcy Court it will be binding on you whether or not you vote.

ACCEPTANCE OR REJECTION OF THE PLAN

[At this point the ballot should provide for voting by the particular class of creditors or equity holders receiving the ballot using one of the following alternatives;]

[If the voter is the holder of a secured, priority, or unsecured nonpriority claim:]

The undersigned, the holder of a Class [ ] claim against the Debtor in the unpaid amount of Dollars ($)

[or, if the voter is the holder of a bond, debenture, or other debt security:]

The undersigned, the holder of a Class [ ] claim against the Debtor, consisting of Dollars ($) principal amount of *[describe bond, debenture, or other debt security]* of the Debtor (For purposes of this Ballot, it is not necessary and you should not adjust the principal amount for any accrued or unmatured interest.)

[or, if the voter is the holder of an equity interest:]

The undersigned, the holder of Class [ ] equity interest in the Debtor, consisting of shares or other interests of *[describe equity interest]* in the Debtor

[In each case, the following language should be included:]

(Check one box only)

[ ] ACCEPTS THE PLAN [ ] REJECTS THE PLAN

Dated: ________________

Print or type name: ______________________________

Signature: ______________________________

Title (if corporation or partnership) ______________

Address: ______________________________

____

RETURN THIS BALLOT TO:

[Name and address of proponent's attorney or other appropriate address]

Form 15. Order Confirming Plan

[Caption as in Form 16A]

ORDER CONFIRMING PLAN

The plan under chapter 11 of the Bankruptcy Code filed by ____________________, on [*if applicable,* as modified by a modification filed on ____________________,] or a summary thereof, having been transmitted to creditors and equity security holders; and

It having been determined after hearing on notice that the requirements for confirmation set forth in 11 U.S.C. § 1129(a) [*or, if appropriate,* 11 U.S.C. § 1129(b)] have been satisfied;

IT IS ORDERED that:

The plan filed by ______________________________, on ____________________, *[If appropriate, include dates and any other pertinent details of modifications to the plan]* is confirmed. *[If the plan provides for an injunction against conduct not otherwise enjoined under the Code, include the information required by Rule3020.]*

A copy of the confirmed plan is attached.

Dated:______________________________

BY THE COURT

____
United States Bankruptcy Judge.

(Amended Dec. 2001.)

Form 16A. Caption (Full)

Official Form 16A (12/07)

Form 16A. CAPTION (FULL)

United States Bankruptcy Court

____________ District Of ____________

In re ______________________________,	)	
[Set forth here all names including married, maiden, and trade names used by debtor within last 8 years.]	)	
Debtor	)	Case No. ______
Address ______________________	)	
______________________	)	Chapter ____
Last four digits of Social-Security or Individual Tax-payer-Identification (ITIN) No(s)., (if any): ______ ______________________________________	)	
Employer's Tax-Identification (EIN) No(s). (if any): ______________________________________	)	

[Designation of Character of Paper]

(Amended Oct. 17, 2005; Dec. 1, 2007.)

Form 16B. Caption (Short Title)

Official Form 16B
12/94

FORM 16B. CAPTION (SHORT TITLE)

(May be used if 11 U.S.C. § 342(c) is not applicable)

United States Bankruptcy Court

_______________ District Of _______________

In re ________________________,
Debtor

Case No. ____________________

Chapter ____________

[Designation of Character of Paper]

Form 16C. Caption of Adversary Proceeding
Official Form 16C
(12/03)

FORM 16C. CAPTION OF COMPLAINT IN ADVERSARY PROCEEDING FILED BY A DEBTOR

[Abrogated]

Form 16D. Caption for use in Adversary Proceeding other than for a Complaint Filed by a Debtor

Official Form 16D
(12/04)

Form 16D. CAPTION FOR USE IN ADVERSARY PROCEEDING

United States Bankruptcy Court

_______________ District Of _______________

In re _______________________________,) Case No. ________________
Debtor)
) Chapter ____________
_______________________________,)
Plaintiff)
)
_______________________________,) Adv. Proc. No. ________________
Defendant

COMPLAINT [*or* other Designation]

[If in a Notice of Appeal (see Form 17) or other notice filed and served by a debtor, this caption must be altered to include the debtor's address and Employer's Tax Identification Number(s) or last four digits of Social Security Number(s) as in Form 16A.]

Form 17. Notice of Appeal Under 28 U.S.C. § 158(a) or (b) from a Judgment, Order, or Decree of a Bankruptcy Court

Official Form 17
(12/02)

[Caption as in Form 16A, 16B, or 16D, as appropriate]

NOTICE OF APPEAL

______________________________, the plaintiff [*or* defendant *or* other party] appeals under 28 U.S.C. § 158(a) or (b) from the judgment, order, or decree of the bankruptcy judge (describe) entered in this adversary proceeding [*or other proceeding, describe type*]on the ________ day of month, year.

The names of all parties to the judgment, order, or decree appealed from and the names, addresses, and telephone numbers of their respective attorneys are as follows:

Dated: ________________

Signed: ____
Attorney for Appellant (or Appellant, if not represented by an Attorney)

Attorney Name: ____________________________________

Address: ____

____

Telephone No: ______________________________________

If a Bankruptcy Appellate Panel Service is authorized to hear this appeal, each party has a right to have the appeal heard by the district court. The appellant may exercise this right only by filing a separate statement of election at the time of the filing of this notice of appeal. Any other party may elect, within the time provided in 28 U.S.C. § 158(c), to have the appeal heard by the district court.

If a child support creditor or its representative is the appellant, and if the child support creditor or its representative files the form specified in § 304(g) of the Bankruptcy Reform Act of 1994, no fee is required.

Form 17A. Notice of Appeal and Statement of Election

Official Form 17A (12/14)

[Caption as in Form 16A, 16B, or 16D, as appropriate]

NOTICE OF APPEAL AND STATEMENT OF ELECTION

Part 1: Identify the appellant(s)

1. Name(s) of appellant(s):
____

2. Position of appellant(s) in the adversary proceeding or bankruptcy case that is the subject of this appeal:

For appeals in an adversary proceeding.
- ❑ Plaintiff
- ❑ Defendant
- ❑ Other (describe) ________________

For appeals in a bankruptcy case and not in an adversary proceeding.
- ❑ Debtor
- ❑ Creditor
- ❑ Trustee
- ❑ Other (describe) ________________

Part 2: Identify the subject of this appeal

1. Describe the judgment, order, or decree appealed from: ________________________

2. State the date on which the judgment, order, or decree was entered: ________________

Part 3: Identify the other parties to the appeal

List the names of all parties to the judgment, order, or decree appealed from and the names, addresses, and telephone numbers of their attorneys (attach additional pages if necessary):

1. Party: ______________ Attorney: ________________________
____
____
____

2. Party: ______________ Attorney: ________________________
____
____
____

Official Form 17A (12/14)

Part 4: Optional election to have appeal heard by District Court (applicable only in certain districts)

If a Bankruptcy Appellate Panel is available in this judicial district, the Bankruptcy Appellate Panel will hear this appeal unless, pursuant to 28 U.S.C. § 158(c)(1), a party elects to have the appeal heard by the United States District Court. If an appellant filing this notice wishes to have the appeal heard by the United States District Court, check below. Do not check the box if the appellant wishes the Bankruptcy Appellate Panel to hear the appeal.

☐ Appellant(s) elect to have the appeal heard by the United States District Court rather than by the Bankruptcy Appellate Panel.

Part 5: Sign below

_______________________________ Date: ___________________

Signature of attorney for appellant(s) (or appellant(s) if not represented by an attorney)

Name, address, and telephone number of attorney (or appellant(s) if not represented by an attorney):

____

____

____

____

Fee waiver notice: If appellant is a child support creditor or its representative and appellant has filed the form specified in § 304(g) of the Bankruptcy Reform Act of 1994, no fee is required.

(As added Dec. 14, 2014.)

Form 17B. Optional Appellee Statement of Election to Proceed in District Court

Official Form 17B (12/14)

[Caption as in Form 16A, 16B, or 16D, as appropriate]

OPTIONAL APPELLEE STATEMENT OF ELECTION TO PROCEED IN DISTRICT COURT

This form should be filed only if all of the following are true:

- this appeal is pending in a district served by a Bankruptcy Appellate Panel,
- the appellant(s) did not elect in the Notice of Appeal to proceed in the District Court rather than in the Bankruptcy Appellate Panel,
- no other appellee has filed a statement of election to proceed in the district court, and
- you elect to proceed in the District Court.

Part 1: Identify the appellee(s) electing to proceed in the District Court

1. Name(s) of appellee(s): ______________________________

2. Position of appellee(s) in the adversary proceeding or bankruptcy case that is the subject of this appeal:

For appeals in an adversary proceeding.

- ❑ Plaintiff
- ❑ Defendant
- ❑ Other (describe) ____________________

For appeals in a bankruptcy case and not in an adversary proceeding.

- ❑ Debtor
- ❑ Creditor
- ❑ Trustee
- ❑ Other (describe) ____________________

Part 2: Election to have this appeal heard by the District Court (applicable only in certain districts)

I (we) elect to have the appeal heard by the United States District Court rather than by the Bankruptcy Appellate Panel.

Part 3: Sign below

____
Signature of attorney for appellee(s) (or appellee(s) if not represented by an attorney)

Date: ______________________________

Name, address, and telephone number of attorney (or appellee(s) if not represented by an attorney):
____
____
____

(As added Dec. 14, 2014.)

Form 17C. Certificate of Compliance With Rule 8015(a)(7)(B) or 8016(d)(2)

Official Form 17C (12/14)

[This certification must be appended to your brief if the length of your brief is calculated by maximum number of words or lines of text rather than number of pages.]

Certificate of Compliance With Rule 8015(a)(7)(B) or 8016(d)(2)

This brief complies with the type-volume limitation of Rule 8015(a)(7)(B) or 8016(d)(2) because:

❑ this brief contains [*state the number of*] words, excluding the parts of the brief exempted by Rule 8015(a)(7)(B)(iii) or 8016(d)(2)(D), or

❑ this brief uses a monospaced typeface having no more than 10½ characters per inch and contains [*state the number of*] lines of text, excluding the parts of the brief exempted by Rule 8015(a)(7)(B)(iii) or 8016(d)(2)(D).

______________________________ Date: ______________________

Signature

Print name of person signing certificate of compliance:

____

(As added Dec. 14, 2014.)

Form 18. Discharge of Debtor

Official Form 18 (12/07)

United States Bankruptcy Court

____________ District Of ____________

In re ______________________________,)
[Set forth here all names including married, maiden, and trade names used by debtor within last 8 years.])
Debtor) Case No. ______

Address ______________________________)

______________________________) Chapter 7

Last four digits of Social-Security or other Individual Taxpayer-Identification No(s). (if any): ________)

______________________________)

Employer's Tax-Identification No(s). (EIN) (if any):)

______________________________)

DISCHARGE OF DEBTOR

It appearing that the debtor is entitled to a discharge, **IT IS ORDERED:** The debtor is granted a discharge under section 727 of title 11, United States Code, (the Bankruptcy Code).

Dated: ______________

BY THE COURT

____
United States Bankruptcy Judge

SEE THE BACK OF THIS ORDER FOR IMPORTANT INFORMATION.

EXPLANATION OF BANKRUPTCY DISCHARGE IN A CHAPTER 7 CASE

This court order grants a discharge to the person named as the debtor. It is not a dismissal of the case and it does not determine how much money, if any, the trustee will pay to creditors.

Collection of Discharged Debts Prohibited

The discharge prohibits any attempt to collect from the debtor a debt that has been discharged. For example, a creditor is not permitted to contact a debtor by mail, phone, or otherwise, to file or continue a lawsuit, to attach wages or other property, or to take any other action to collect a discharged debt from the debtor. *[In a case involving community property:* There are also special rules that protect certain community property owned by the debtor's spouse, even if that spouse did not file a bankruptcy case.] A creditor who violates this order can be required to pay damages and attorney's fees to the debtor.

However, a creditor may have the right to enforce a valid lien, such as a mortgage or security interest, against the debtor's property after the bankruptcy, if that lien was not avoided or eliminated in the bankruptcy case. Also, a debtor may voluntarily pay any debt that has been discharged.

Debts That are Discharged

The chapter 7 discharge order eliminates a debtor's legal obligation to pay a debt that is discharged. Most, but not all, types of debts are discharged if the debt existed on the date the bankruptcy case was filed. (If this case was begun under a different chapter of the Bankruptcy Code and converted to chapter 7, the discharge applies to debts owed when the bankruptcy case was converted.)

Debts that are Not Discharged

Some of the common types of debts which are not discharged in a chapter 7 bankruptcy case are:

a. Debts for most taxes;

b. Debts incurred to pay nondischargeable taxes;

c. Debts that are domestic support obligations;

d. Debts for most student loans;

e. Debts for most fines, penalties, forfeitures, or criminal restitution obligations;

f. Debts for personal injuries or death caused by the debtor's operation of a motor vehicle, vessel, or aircraft while intoxicated;

g. Some debts which were not properly listed by the debtor;

h. Debts that the bankruptcy court specifically has decided or will decide in this bankruptcy case are not discharged;

i. Debts for which the debtor has given up the discharge protections by signing a reaffirmation agreement in compliance with the Bankruptcy Code requirements for reaffirmation of debts; and

j. Debts owed to certain pension, profit sharing, stock bonus, other retirement plans, or to the Thrift Savings Plan for federal employees for certain types of loans from these plans.

This information is only a general summary of the bankruptcy discharge. There are exceptions to these general rules. Because the law is complicated, you may want to consult and attorney to determine the exact effect of the discharge in this case.

(As amended Oct. 17, 2005; Dec. 1, 2007.)

Form 19. Declaration and Signature of Non-Attorney Bankruptcy Petition Preparer (11 U.S.C. § 110)

Official Form 19 (12/07)

United States Bankruptcy Court

____________ District Of ____________

In re ____________________,
Debtor

Case No. ____________

Chapter ____________

DECLARATION AND SIGNATURE OF NON-ATTORNEY BANKRUPTCY PETITION PREPARER (11 U.S.C. § 110)

I declare under penalty of perjury that: (1) I am a bankruptcy petition preparer as defined in 11 U.S.C. § 110; (2) I prepared the accompanying document(s) for compensation and have provided the debtor with a copy of the document(s) and the attached notice as required by 11 U.S.C. §§ 110(b), 110(h), and 342(b); and (3) if rules or guidelines have been promulgated pursuant to 11 U.S.C. § 110(h) setting a maximum fee for services chargeable by bankruptcy petition preparers, I have given the debtor notice of the maximum amount before preparing any document for filing for a debtor or accepting any fee from the debtor, as required by that section.

Accompanying documents:
____
____
____
____
____

Printed or Typed Name and Title, if any, of Bankruptcy Petition Preparer:
____

Social-Security No. of Bankruptcy Petition Preparer (Required by 11 U.S.C. § 110):
____

If the bankruptcy petition preparer is not an individual, state the name, title (if any), address, and social-security number of the officer, principal, responsible person or partner who signs this document.

____

____
Address

X____________________ ____________________
Signature of Bankruptcy Petition Preparer Date

Names and social-security numbers of all other individuals who prepared or assisted in preparing this document, unless the bankruptcy petition preparer is not an individual.:

If more than one person prepared this document, attach additional signed sheets conforming to the appropriate Official Form for each person.

A bankruptcy petition preparer's failure to comply with the provisions of title 11 and the Federal Rules of Bankruptcy Procedure may result in fines or imprisonment or both. 11 U.S.C. § 110; 18 U.S.C. § 156.

NOTICE TO DEBTOR BY NON-ATTORNEY BANKRUPTCY PETITION PREPARER

[Must be filed with any document prepared by a bankruptcy petition preparer.]

I am a bankruptcy petition preparer. I am not an attorney and may not practice law or give legal advice. Before preparing any document for filing as defined in § 110(a)(2) of the Bankruptcy Code or accepting any fees, I am required by law to provide you with this notice concerning bankruptcy petition preparers. Under the law, § 110 of the Bankruptcy Code (11 U.S.C. § 110), I am forbidden to offer you any legal advice, including advice about any of the following:

- whether to file a petition under the Bankruptcy Code (11 U.S.C. § 101 et seq.);
- whether commencing a case under chapter 7, 11, 12, or 13 is appropriate;

- whether your debts will be eliminated or discharged in a case under the Bankruptcy Code;
- whether you will be able to retain your home, car, or other property after commencing a case under the Bankruptcy Code;
- the tax consequences of a case brought under the Bankruptcy Code;
- the dischargeability of tax claims;
- whether you may or should promise to repay debts to a creditor or enter into a reaffirmation agreement with a creditor to reaffirm a debt;
- how to characterize the nature of your interests in property or your debts; or
- bankruptcy procedures and rights.

[The notice may provide additional examples of legal advice that a bankruptcy petition preparer is not authorized to give.]

In addition, under 11 U.S.C. § 110(h), the Supreme Court or the Judicial Conference of the United States may promulgate rules or guidelines setting a maximum allowable fee chargeable by a bankruptcy petition preparer. As required by law, I have notified you of the maximum allowable fee, if any, before preparing any document for filing or accepting any fee from you.

______________________________ ______________________________

Signature of Debtor Date Joint Debtor (if any) Date

[In a joint case, both spouses must sign.]

(Amended Oct. 17, 2005; Dec. 1, 2007.)

Form 20A. Notice of Motion or Objection

Official Form 20A
(12/10)

United States Bankruptcy Court

__________ District Of __________

In re ______________________________,)
[Set forth here all names including married, maiden, and trade names used by debtor within last 8 years.])
Debtor) Case No. ______

Address ____________________)
____________________) Chapter ____

Last four digits of Social-Security or Individual Tax-payer-Identification (ITIN) No(s)., (if any): ______)
____
Employer's Tax-Identification (EIN) No(s). (if any):)
____

NOTICE OF [MOTION TO] [OBJECTION TO]

has filed papers with the court to [relief sought in motion or objection].

Your rights may be affected. You should read these papers carefully and discuss them with your attorney, if you have one in this bankruptcy case. (If you do not have an attorney, you may wish to consult one.)

If you do not want the court to [relief sought in motion or objection], or if you want the court to consider your views on the [motion] [objection], then on or before (date), you or your attorney must:

[File with the court a written request for a hearing { *or, if the court requires a written response* , an answer, explaining your position} at:

{address of the bankruptcy clerk's office}

If you mail your {request} {response} to the court for filing, you must mail it early enough so the court will **receive** it on or before the date stated above.

You must also mail a copy to:

{movant's attorney's name and address}

{names and addresses of others to be served}]

[Attend the hearing scheduled to be held on (date), (year), at a.m./p.m. in Courtroom ____________, United States Bankruptcy Court, {address}.]

[Other steps required to oppose a motion or objection under local rule or court order.]

If you or your attorney do not take these steps, the court may decide that you do not oppose the relief sought in the motion or objection and may enter an order granting that relief.

Date: ____________ Signature: ____________________
Name:
Address:

Form 20B. Notice of Objection to Claim

Official Form 20B
(12/10)

United States Bankruptcy Court

______________ District Of ____________

In re ______________________________,
[Set forth here all names including married, maiden, and trade names used by debtor within last 8 years.]
Debtor

Case No. ______

Address ________________________

____

Chapter ____

Last four digits of Social-Security or Individual Tax-payer-Identification (ITIN) No(s)., (if any): ______

____

Employer's Tax-Identification (EIN) No(s). (if any):

____

NOTICE OF OBJECTION TO CLAIM

has filed an objection to your claim in this bankruptcy case.

Your claim may be reduced, modified, or eliminated. You should read these papers carefully and discuss them with your attorney, if you have one.

If you do not want the court to eliminate or change your claim, then on or before (date), you or your lawyer must:

{If required by local rule or court order.}

[File with the court a written response to the objection, explaining your position, at:

{address of the bankruptcy clerk's office}

If you mail your response to the court for filing, you must mail it early enough so that the court will **receive** it on or before the date stated above.

You must also mail a copy to:

{objector's attorney's name and address}

{names and addresses of others to be served}]

Attend the hearing on the objection, scheduled to be held on (date), (year), at a.m./p.m. in Courtroom ____________________, United States Bankruptcy Court, {address}.

If you or your attorney do not take these steps, the court may decide that you do not oppose the objection to your claim.

Date: ______________

Signature: ____________________
Name:
Address:

Form 21. Statement of Social Security Number

Do not file this form as part of the public case file. This form must be submitted separately and must not be included in the court's public electronic records. Please consult local court procedures for submission requirements.

B21 (Official Form 21) (12/12)

UNITED STATES BANKRUPTCY COURT

In re ______________________________,)
[Set forth here all names including married, maiden, and trade names used by debtor within last 8 years])

Debtor) Case No. __________

Address ______________________________)
______________________________) Chapter __________

Last four digits of Social-Security or Individual Taxpayer-Identification (ITIN) No(s).,(if any):)
______________________________)

Employer Tax-Identification (EIN) No(s).(if any):)
______________________________)

STATEMENT OF SOCIAL-SECURITY NUMBER(S)

*(or other Individual Taxpayer-Identification Number(s) (ITIN(s)))**

1.Name of Debtor (Last, First, Middle): ______________________________
(Check the appropriate box and, if applicable, provide the required information.)

☐ Debtor has a Social-Security Number and it is: __________
(If more than one, state all.)

☐ Debtor does not have a Social-Security Number but has an Individual Taxpayer-Identification Number (ITIN), and it is: __________
(If more than one, state all.)

☐ Debtor does not have either a Social-Security Number or an Individual Taxpayer-Identification Number (ITIN).

2.Name of Joint Debtor (Last, First, Middle): ______________________________
(Check the appropriate box and, if applicable, provide the required information.)

☐ Joint Debtor has a Social-Security Number and it is: __________
(If more than one, state all.)

☐ Joint Debtor does not have a Social-Security Number but has an Individual Taxpayer-Identification Number (ITIN) and it is: __________
(If more than one, state all.)

☐ Joint Debtor does not have either a Social-Security Number or an Individual Taxpayer-Identification Number (ITIN).

I declare under penalty of perjury that the foregoing is true and correct.

X ______________________________ __________
Signature of Debtor Date

X ______________________________ __________
Signature of Joint Debtor Date

____

Joint debtors must provide information for both spouses.
Penalty for making a false statement: Fine of up to $250,000 or up to 5 years imprisonment or both. 18 U.S.C. §§ 152 and 3571.

(As added Dec. 1, 2003; Dec. 1, 2007; Dec. 1, 2012.)

Bankruptcy Form 21

Form 22A. Chapter 7 Statement of Current Monthly Income and Means-Test Calculation

B22A (Official Form 22A) (Chapter 7) (04/13)

In re ______________________
Debtor(s)

Case Number: ______________
(If known)

According to the information required to be entered on this statement (check one box as directed in Part I, III, or VI of this statement):

☐ **The presumption arises.**
☐ **The presumption does not arise.**
☐ **The presumption is temporarily inapplicable.**

CHAPTER 7 STATEMENT OF CURRENT MONTHLY INCOME AND MEANS-TEST CALCULATION

In addition to Schedules I and J, this statement must be completed by every individual chapter 7 debtor. If none of the exclusions in Part I applies, joint debtors may complete one statement only. If any of the exclusions in Part I applies, joint debtors should complete separate statements if they believe this is required by § 707(b)(2)(C).

<table>
<tr><th colspan="2">Part I. MILITARY AND NON-CONSUMER DEBTORS</th></tr>
<tr><td>IA</td><td>Disabled Veterans. If you are a disabled veteran described in the Declaration in this Part IA, (1) check the box at the beginning of the Declaration, (2) check the box for "The presumption does not arise" at the top of this statement, and (3) complete the verification in Part VIII. Do not complete any of the remaining parts of this statement.

☐ Declaration of Disabled Veteran. By checking this box, I declare under penalty of perjury that I am a disabled veteran (as defined in 38 U.S.C. § 3741(1)) whose indebtedness occurred primarily during a period in which I was on active duty (as defined in 10 U.S.C. § 101(d)(1)) or while I was performing a homeland defense activity (as defined in 32 U.S.C. §901(1)).</td></tr>
<tr><td>IB</td><td>Non-consumer Debtors. If your debts are not primarily consumer debts, check the box below and complete the verification in Part VIII. Do not complete any of the remaining parts of this statement.

☐ Declaration of non-consumer debts. By checking this box, I declare that my debts are not primarily consumer debts.</td></tr>
<tr><td>IC</td><td>Reservists and National Guard Members; active duty or homeland defense activity. Members of a reserve component of the Armed Forces and members of the National Guard who were called to active duty (as defined in 10 U.S.C. § 101(d)(1)) after September 11, 2001, for a period of at least 90 days, or who have performed homeland defense activity (as defined in 32 U.S.C. § 901(1)) for a period of at least 90 days, are excluded from all forms of means testing during the time of active duty or homeland defense activity and for 540 days thereafter (the "exclusion period"). If you qualify for this temporary exclusion, (1) check the appropriate boxes and complete any required information in the Declaration of Reservists and National Guard Members below, (2) check the box for "The presumption is temporarily inapplicable" at the top of this statement, and (3) complete the verification in Part VIII. During your exclusion period you are not required to complete the balance of this form, but you must complete the form no later than 14 days after the date on which your exclusion period ends, unless the time for filing a motion raising the means test presumption expires in your case before your exclusion period ends.

☐ Declaration of Reservists and National Guard Members. By checking this box and making the appropriate entries below, I declare that I am eligible for a temporary exclusion from means testing because, as a member of a reserve component of the Armed Forces or the National Guard

a. ☐ I was called to active duty after September 11, 2001, for a period of at least 90 days and
☐ I remain on active duty /or/
☐ I was released from active duty on ______________, which is less than 540 days before this bankruptcy case was filed;

OR

b. ☐ I am performing homeland defense activity for a period of at least 90 days /or/
☐ I performed homeland defense activity for a period of at least 90 days, terminating on ______________, which is less than 540 days before this bankruptcy case was filed.</td></tr>
</table>

B 22A (Official Form 22A) (Chapter 7) (04/13)

<table>
<tr><th colspan="4">Part II. CALCULATION OF MONTHLY INCOME FOR § 707(b)(7) EXCLUSION</th></tr>
<tr><td>2</td><td colspan="3">Marital/filing status. Check the box that applies and complete the balance of this part of this statement as directed.
a. ☐ Unmarried. Complete only Column A ("Debtor's Income") for Lines 3-11.
b. ☐ Married, not filing jointly, with declaration of separate households. By checking this box, debtor declares under penalty of perjury: "My spouse and I are legally separated under applicable non-bankruptcy law or my spouse and I are living apart other than for the purpose of evading the requirements of § 707(b)(2)(A) of the Bankruptcy Code." Complete only Column A ("Debtor's Income") for Lines 3-11.
c. ☐ Married, not filing jointly, without the declaration of separate households set out in Line 2.b above. Complete both Column A ("Debtor's Income") and Column B ("Spouse's Income") for Lines 3-11.
d. ☐ Married, filing jointly. Complete both Column A ("Debtor's Income") and Column B ("Spouse's Income") for Lines 3-11.</td></tr>
<tr><td></td><td>All figures must reflect average monthly income received from all sources, derived during the six calendar months prior to filing the bankruptcy case, ending on the last day of the month before the filing. If the amount of monthly income varied during the six months, you must divide the six-month total by six, and enter the result on the appropriate line.</td><td>Column A
Debtor's Income</td><td>Column B
Spouse's Income</td></tr>
<tr><td>3</td><td>Gross wages, salary, tips, bonuses, overtime, commissions.</td><td>$</td><td>$</td></tr>
<tr><td>4</td><td>Income from the operation of a business, profession or farm. Subtract Line b from Line a and enter the difference in the appropriate column(s) of Line 4. If you operate more than one business, profession or farm, enter aggregate numbers and provide details on an attachment. Do not enter a number less than zero. Do not include any part of the business expenses entered on Line b as a deduction in Part V.
a. | Gross receipts | $
b. | Ordinary and necessary business expenses | $
c. | Business income | Subtract Line b from Line a</td><td>$</td><td>$</td></tr>
<tr><td>5</td><td>Rent and other real property income. Subtract Line b from Line a and enter the difference in the appropriate column(s) of Line 5. Do not enter a number less than zero. Do not include any part of the operating expenses entered on Line b as a deduction in Part V.
a. | Gross receipts | $
b. | Ordinary and necessary operating expenses | $
c. | Rent and other real property income | Subtract Line b from Line a</td><td>$</td><td>$</td></tr>
<tr><td>6</td><td>Interest, dividends and royalties.</td><td>$</td><td>$</td></tr>
<tr><td>7</td><td>Pension and retirement income.</td><td>$</td><td>$</td></tr>
<tr><td>8</td><td>Any amounts paid by another person or entity, on a regular basis, for the household expenses of the debtor or the debtor's dependents, including child support paid for that purpose. Do not include alimony or separate maintenance payments or amounts paid by your spouse if Column B is completed. Each regular payment should be reported in only one column; if a payment is listed in Column A, do not report that payment in Column B.</td><td>$</td><td>$</td></tr>
<tr><td>9</td><td>Unemployment compensation. Enter the amount in the appropriate column(s) of Line 9. However, if you contend that unemployment compensation received by you or your spouse was a benefit under the Social Security Act, do not list the amount of such compensation in Column A or B, but instead state the amount in the space below:
Unemployment compensation claimed to be a benefit under the Social Security Act | Debtor $ ______ | Spouse $ ______</td><td>$</td><td>$</td></tr>
</table>

B 22A (Official Form 22A) (Chapter 7) (04/13)

10	**Income from all other sources.** Specify source and amount. If necessary, list additional sources on a separate page. **Do not include alimony or separate maintenance payments paid by your spouse if Column B is completed, but include all other payments of alimony or separate maintenance.** Do not include any benefits received under the Social Security Act or payments received as a victim of a war crime, crime against humanity, or as a victim of international or domestic terrorism. a. ______ $ b. ______ $ Total and enter on Line 10	$	$
11	**Subtotal of Current Monthly Income for § 707(b)(7).** Add Lines 3 thru 10 in Column A, and, if Column B is completed, add Lines 3 through 10 in Column B. Enter the total(s).	$	$
12	**Total Current Monthly Income for § 707(b)(7).** If Column B has been completed, add Line 11, Column A to Line 11, Column B, and enter the total. If Column B has not been completed, enter the amount from Line 11, Column A.	$	

	Part III. APPLICATION OF § 707(b)(7) EXCLUSION	
13	**Annualized Current Monthly Income for § 707(b)(7).** Multiply the amount from Line 12 by the number 12 and enter the result.	$
14	**Applicable median family income.** Enter the median family income for the applicable state and household size. (This information is available by family size at www.usdoj.gov/ust/ or from the clerk of the bankruptcy court.) a. Enter debtor's state of residence: ______ b. Enter debtor's household size: ______	$
15	**Application of Section 707(b)(7).** Check the applicable box and proceed as directed. ☐ **The amount on Line 13 is less than or equal to the amount on Line 14.** Check the box for "The presumption does not arise" at the top of page 1 of this statement, and complete Part VIII; do not complete Parts IV, V, VI or VII. ☐ **The amount on Line 13 is more than the amount on Line 14.** Complete the remaining parts of this statement.	

Complete Parts IV, V, VI, and VII of this statement only if required. (See Line 15.)

	Part IV. CALCULATION OF CURRENT MONTHLY INCOME FOR § 707(b)(2)	
16	**Enter the amount from Line 12.**	$
17	**Marital adjustment.** If you checked the box at Line 2.c, enter on Line 17 the total of any income listed in Line 11, Column B that was NOT paid on a regular basis for the household expenses of the debtor or the debtor's dependents. Specify in the lines below the basis for excluding the Column B income (such as payment of the spouse's tax liability or the spouse's support of persons other than the debtor or the debtor's dependents) and the amount of income devoted to each purpose. If necessary, list additional adjustments on a separate page. If you did not check box at Line 2.c, enter zero. a. ______ $ b. ______ $ c. ______ $ Total and enter on Line 17.	$
18	**Current monthly income for § 707(b)(2).** Subtract Line 17 from Line 16 and enter the result.	$

B 22A (Official Form 22A) (Chapter 7) (04/13)

Part V. CALCULATION OF DEDUCTIONS FROM INCOME

Subpart A: Deductions under Standards of the Internal Revenue Service (IRS)

19A	**National Standards: food, clothing and other items.** Enter in Line 19A the "Total" amount from IRS National Standards for Food, Clothing and Other Items for the applicable number of persons. (This information is available at www.usdoj.gov/ust/ or from the clerk of the bankruptcy court.) The applicable number of persons is the number that would currently be allowed as exemptions on your federal income tax return, plus the number of any additional dependents whom you support.	$
19B	**National Standards: health care.** Enter in Line a1 below the amount from IRS National Standards for Out-of-Pocket Health Care for persons under 65 years of age, and in Line a2 the IRS National Standards for Out-of-Pocket Health Care for persons 65 years of age or older. (This information is available at www.usdoj.gov/ust/ or from the clerk of the bankruptcy court.) Enter in Line b1 the applicable number of persons who are under 65 years of age, and enter in Line b2 the applicable number of persons who are 65 years of age or older. (The applicable number of persons in each age category is the number in that category that would currently be allowed as exemptions on your federal income tax return, plus the number of any additional dependents whom you support.) Multiply Line a1 by Line b1 to obtain a total amount for persons under 65, and enter the result in Line c1. Multiply Line a2 by Line b2 to obtain a total amount for persons 65 and older, and enter the result in Line c2. Add Lines c1 and c2 to obtain a total health care amount, and enter the result in Line 19B.	$

Persons under 65 years of age			Persons 65 years of age or older		
a1.	Allowance per person		a2.	Allowance per person	
b1.	Number of persons		b2.	Number of persons	
c1.	Subtotal		c2.	Subtotal	

20A	**Local Standards: housing and utilities; non-mortgage expenses.** Enter the amount of the IRS Housing and Utilities Standards; non-mortgage expenses for the applicable county and family size. (This information is available at www.usdoj.gov/ust/ or from the clerk of the bankruptcy court). The applicable family size consists of the number that would currently be allowed as exemptions on your federal income tax return, plus the number of any additional dependents whom you support.	$
20B	**Local Standards: housing and utilities; mortgage/rent expense.** Enter, in Line a below, the amount of the IRS Housing and Utilities Standards; mortgage/rent expense for your county and family size (this information is available at www.usdoj.gov/ust/ or from the clerk of the bankruptcy court) (the applicable family size consists of the number that would currently be allowed as exemptions on your federal income tax return, plus the number of any additional dependents whom you support); enter on Line b the total of the Average Monthly Payments for any debts secured by your home, as stated in Line 42; subtract Line b from Line a and enter the result in Line 20B. **Do not enter an amount less than zero.**	$

a.	IRS Housing and Utilities Standards; mortgage/rental expense	$
b.	Average Monthly Payment for any debts secured by your home, if any, as stated in Line 42	$
c.	Net mortgage/rental expense	Subtract Line b from Line a.

21	**Local Standards: housing and utilities; adjustment.** If you contend that the process set out in Lines 20A and 20B does not accurately compute the allowance to which you are entitled under the IRS Housing and Utilities Standards, enter any additional amount to which you contend you are entitled, and state the basis for your contention in the space below:	$

B 22A (Official Form 22A) (Chapter 7) (04/13)

<table>
<tr><td>22A</td><td>Local Standards: transportation; vehicle operation/public transportation expense. You are entitled to an expense allowance in this category regardless of whether you pay the expenses of operating a vehicle and regardless of whether you use public transportation.

Check the number of vehicles for which you pay the operating expenses or for which the operating expenses are included as a contribution to your household expenses in Line 8.
☐ 0 ☐ 1 ☐ 2 or more.
If you checked 0, enter on Line 22A the "Public Transportation" amount from IRS Local Standards: Transportation. If you checked 1 or 2 or more, enter on Line 22A the "Operating Costs" amount from IRS Local Standards: Transportation for the applicable number of vehicles in the applicable Metropolitan Statistical Area or Census Region. (These amounts are available at www.usdoj.gov/ust/ or from the clerk of the bankruptcy court.)</td><td>$</td></tr>
<tr><td>22B</td><td>Local Standards: transportation; additional public transportation expense. If you pay the operating expenses for a vehicle and also use public transportation, and you contend that you are entitled to an additional deduction for your public transportation expenses, enter on Line 22B the "Public Transportation" amount from IRS Local Standards: Transportation. (This amount is available at www.usdoj.gov/ust/ or from the clerk of the bankruptcy court.)</td><td>$</td></tr>
<tr><td>23</td><td>Local Standards: transportation ownership/lease expense; Vehicle 1. Check the number of vehicles for which you claim an ownership/lease expense. (You may not claim an ownership/lease expense for more than two vehicles.)
☐ 1 ☐ 2 or more.
Enter, in Line a below, the "Ownership Costs" for "One Car" from the IRS Local Standards: Transportation (available at www.usdoj.gov/ust/ or from the clerk of the bankruptcy court); enter in Line b the total of the Average Monthly Payments for any debts secured by Vehicle 1, as stated in Line 42; subtract Line b from Line a and enter the result in Line 23. Do not enter an amount less than zero.
<table><tr><td>a.</td><td>IRS Transportation Standards, Ownership Costs</td><td>$</td></tr><tr><td>b.</td><td>Average Monthly Payment for any debts secured by Vehicle 1, as stated in Line 42</td><td>$</td></tr><tr><td>c.</td><td>Net ownership/lease expense for Vehicle 1</td><td>Subtract Line b from Line a.</td></tr></table></td><td>$</td></tr>
<tr><td>24</td><td>Local Standards: transportation ownership/lease expense; Vehicle 2. Complete this Line only if you checked the "2 or more" Box in Line 23.
Enter, in Line a below, the "Ownership Costs" for "One Car" from the IRS Local Standards: Transportation (available at www.usdoj.gov/ust/ or from the clerk of the bankruptcy court); enter in Line b the total of the Average Monthly Payments for any debts secured by Vehicle 2, as stated in Line 42; subtract Line b from Line a and enter the result in Line 24. Do not enter an amount less than zero.
<table><tr><td>a.</td><td>IRS Transportation Standards, Ownership Costs</td><td>$</td></tr><tr><td>b.</td><td>Average Monthly Payment for any debts secured by Vehicle 2, as stated in Line 42</td><td>$</td></tr><tr><td>c.</td><td>Net ownership/lease expense for Vehicle 2</td><td>Subtract Line b from Line a.</td></tr></table></td><td>$</td></tr>
<tr><td>25</td><td>Other Necessary Expenses: taxes. Enter the total average monthly expense that you actually incur for all federal, state and local taxes, other than real estate and sales taxes, such as income taxes, self-employment taxes, social-security taxes, and Medicare taxes. Do not include real estate or sales taxes.</td><td>$</td></tr>
<tr><td>26</td><td>Other Necessary Expenses: involuntary deductions for employment. Enter the total average monthly payroll deductions that are required for your employment, such as retirement contributions, union dues, and uniform costs. Do not include discretionary amounts, such as voluntary 401(k) contributions.</td><td>$</td></tr>
<tr><td>27</td><td>Other Necessary Expenses: life insurance. Enter total average monthly premiums that you actually pay for term life insurance for yourself. Do not include premiums for insurance on your dependents, for whole life or for any other form of insurance.</td><td>$</td></tr>
<tr><td>28</td><td>Other Necessary Expenses: court-ordered payments. Enter the total monthly amount that you are required to pay pursuant to the order of a court or administrative agency, such as spousal or child support payments. Do not include payments on past due obligations included in Line 44.</td><td>$</td></tr>
</table>

B 22A (Official Form 22A) (Chapter 7) (04/13)

29	**Other Necessary Expenses: education for employment or for a physically or mentally challenged child.** Enter the total average monthly amount that you actually expend for education that is a condition of employment and for education that is required for a physically or mentally challenged dependent child for whom no public education providing similar services is available.	$
30	**Other Necessary Expenses: childcare.** Enter the total average monthly amount that you actually expend on childcare—such as baby-sitting, day care, nursery and preschool. **Do not include other educational payments.**	$
31	**Other Necessary Expenses: health care.** Enter the total average monthly amount that you actually expend on health care that is required for the health and welfare of yourself or your dependents, that is not reimbursed by insurance or paid by a health savings account, and that is in excess of the amount entered in Line 19B. **Do not include payments for health insurance or health savings accounts listed in Line 34.**	$
32	**Other Necessary Expenses: telecommunication services.** Enter the total average monthly amount that you actually pay for telecommunication services other than your basic home telephone and cell phone service—such as pagers, call waiting, caller id, special long distance, or internet service—to the extent necessary for your health and welfare or that of your dependents. **Do not include any amount previously deducted.**	$
33	**Total Expenses Allowed under IRS Standards.** Enter the total of Lines 19 through 32.	$

Subpart B: Additional Living Expense Deductions

Note: Do not include any expenses that you have listed in Lines 19-32

34	**Health Insurance, Disability Insurance, and Health Savings Account Expenses.** List the monthly expenses in the categories set out in lines a-c below that are reasonably necessary for yourself, your spouse, or your dependents. a. Health Insurance $ b. Disability Insurance $ c. Health Savings Account $ Total and enter on Line 34	$
	If you do not actually expend this total amount, state your actual total average monthly expenditures in the space below: $ ________	
35	**Continued contributions to the care of household or family members.** Enter the total average actual monthly expenses that you will continue to pay for the reasonable and necessary care and support of an elderly, chronically ill, or disabled member of your household or member of your immediate family who is unable to pay for such expenses.	$
36	**Protection against family violence.** Enter the total average reasonably necessary monthly expenses that you actually incurred to maintain the safety of your family under the Family Violence Prevention and Services Act or other applicable federal law. The nature of these expenses is required to be kept confidential by the court.	$
37	**Home energy costs.** Enter the total average monthly amount, in excess of the allowance specified by IRS Local Standards for Housing and Utilities, that you actually expend for home energy costs. **You must provide your case trustee with documentation of your actual expenses, and you must demonstrate that the additional amount claimed is reasonable and necessary.**	$
38	**Education expenses for dependent children less than 18.** Enter the total average monthly expenses that you actually incur, not to exceed $156.25* per child, for attendance at a private or public elementary or secondary school by your dependent children less than 18 years of age. **You must provide your case trustee with documentation of your actual expenses, and you must explain why the amount claimed is reasonable and necessary and not already accounted for in the IRS Standards.**	$

**Amount subject to adjustment on 4/01/16, and every three years thereafter with respect to cases commenced on or after the date of adjustment.*

B 22A (Official Form 22A) (Chapter 7) (04/13)

39	**Additional food and clothing expense.** Enter the total average monthly amount by which your food and clothing expenses exceed the combined allowances for food and clothing (apparel and services) in the IRS National Standards, not to exceed 5% of those combined allowances. (This information is available at www.usdoj.gov/ust/ or from the clerk of the bankruptcy court.) **You must demonstrate that the additional amount claimed is reasonable and necessary.**	$
40	**Continued charitable contributions.** Enter the amount that you will continue to contribute in the form of cash or financial instruments to a charitable organization as defined in 26 U.S.C. § 170(c)(1)-(2).	$
41	**Total Additional Expense Deductions under § 707(b).** Enter the total of Lines 34 through 40	$

Subpart C: Deductions for Debt Payment

42 **Future payments on secured claims.** For each of your debts that is secured by an interest in property that you own, list the name of the creditor, identify the property securing the debt, state the Average Monthly Payment, and check whether the payment includes taxes or insurance. The Average Monthly Payment is the total of all amounts scheduled as contractually due to each Secured Creditor in the 60 months following the filing of the bankruptcy case, divided by 60. If necessary, list additional entries on a separate page. Enter the total of the Average Monthly Payments on Line 42.

	Name of Creditor	Property Securing the Debt	Average Monthly Payment	Does payment include taxes or insurance?
a.			$	☐ yes ☐ no
b.			$	☐ yes ☐ no
c.			$	☐ yes ☐ no
			Total: Add Lines a, b and c.	

$

43 **Other payments on secured claims.** If any of debts listed in Line 42 are secured by your primary residence, a motor vehicle, or other property necessary for your support or the support of your dependents, you may include in your deduction 1/60th of any amount (the "cure amount") that you must pay the creditor in addition to the payments listed in Line 42, in order to maintain possession of the property. The cure amount would include any sums in default that must be paid in order to avoid repossession or foreclosure. List and total any such amounts in the following chart. If necessary, list additional entries on a separate page.

	Name of Creditor	Property Securing the Debt	1/60th of the Cure Amount
a.			$
b.			$
c.			$
			Total: Add Lines a, b and c

$

44	**Payments on prepetition priority claims.** Enter the total amount, divided by 60, of all priority claims, such as priority tax, child support and alimony claims, for which you were liable at the time of your bankruptcy filing. **Do not include current obligations, such as those set out in Line 28.**	$

B 22A (Official Form 22A) (Chapter 7) (04/13)

45	**Chapter 13 administrative expenses.** If you are eligible to file a case under chapter 13, complete the following chart, multiply the amount in line a by the amount in line b, and enter the resulting administrative expense. a. Projected average monthly chapter 13 plan payment. — $ b. Current multiplier for your district as determined under schedules issued by the Executive Office for United States Trustees. (This information is available at www.usdoj.gov/ust/ or from the clerk of the bankruptcy court.) — x c. Average monthly administrative expense of chapter 13 case — Total: Multiply Lines a and b	$
46	**Total Deductions for Debt Payment.** Enter the total of Lines 42 through 45.	$
	Subpart D: Total Deductions from Income	
47	**Total of all deductions allowed under § 707(b)(2).** Enter the total of Lines 33, 41, and 46.	$
	Part VI. DETERMINATION OF § 707(b)(2) PRESUMPTION	
48	**Enter the amount from Line 18 (Current monthly income for § 707(b)(2))**	$
49	**Enter the amount from Line 47 (Total of all deductions allowed under § 707(b)(2))**	$
50	**Monthly disposable income under § 707(b)(2).** Subtract Line 49 from Line 48 and enter the result	$
51	**60-month disposable income under § 707(b)(2).** Multiply the amount in Line 50 by the number 60 and enter the result.	$
52	**Initial presumption determination.** Check the applicable box and proceed as directed. ☐ **The amount on Line 51 is less than $7,475*.** Check the box for "The presumption does not arise" at the top of page 1 of this statement, and complete the verification in Part VIII. Do not complete the remainder of Part VI. ☐ **The amount set forth on Line 51 is more than $12,475*.** Check the box for "The presumption arises" at the top of page 1 of this statement, and complete the verification in Part VIII. You may also complete Part VII. Do not complete the remainder of Part VI. ☐ **The amount on Line 51 is at least $7,475*, but not more than $12,475*.** Complete the remainder of Part VI (Lines 53 through 55).	
53	**Enter the amount of your total non-priority unsecured debt**	$
54	**Threshold debt payment amount.** Multiply the amount in Line 53 by the number 0.25 and enter the result.	$
55	**Secondary presumption determination.** Check the applicable box and proceed as directed. ☐ **The amount on Line 51 is less than the amount on Line 54.** Check the box for "The presumption does not arise" at the top of page 1 of this statement, and complete the verification in Part VIII. ☐ **The amount on Line 51 is equal to or greater than the amount on Line 54.** Check the box for "The presumption arises" at the top of page 1 of this statement, and complete the verification in Part VIII. You may also complete Part VII.	
	Part VII: ADDITIONAL EXPENSE CLAIMS	
56	**Other Expenses.** List and describe any monthly expenses, not otherwise stated in this form, that are required for the health and welfare of you and your family and that you contend should be an additional deduction from your current monthly income under § 707(b)(2)(A)(ii)(I). If necessary, list additional sources on a separate page. All figures should reflect your average monthly expense for each item. Total the expenses.	

	Expense Description	Monthly Amount
a.		$
b.		$
c.		$
	Total: Add Lines a, b and c	$

**Amounts are subject to adjustment on 4/01/16, and every three years thereafter with respect to cases commenced on or after the date of adjustment.*

(As added Oct. 17, 2005; Oct. 1, 2006; April 1, 2007; Jan. 1, 2008; Dec. 19, 2008; April 1, 2010; December 1, 2010; April 1, 2013.)

Form 22A-1. Chapter 7 Statement of Current Monthly Income

Fill in this information to identify your case:

Debtor 1 ______________________________
First Name Middle Name Last Name

Debtor 2 ______________________________
(Spouse, if filing) First Name Middle Name Last Name

United States Bankruptcy Court for the: ______________ District of ________

Case number ______________________
(If known)

Check one box only as directed in this form and in Form 22A-1Supp:

❑ 1. There is no presumption of abuse.

❑ 2. The calculation to determine if a presumption of abuse applies will be made under *Chapter 7 Means Test Calculation* (Official Form 22A–2).

❑ 3. The Means Test does not apply now because of qualified military service but it could apply later.

❑ Check if this is an amended filing

OFFICIAL FORM B 22A1

Chapter 7 Statement of Your Current Monthly Income

12/14

Be as complete and accurate as possible. If two married people are filing together, both are equally responsible for being accurate. If more space is needed, attach a separate sheet to this form. Include the line number to which the additional information applies. On the top of any additional pages, write your name and case number (if known). If you believe that you are exempted from a presumption of abuse because you do not have primarily consumer debts or because of qualifying military service, complete and file *Statement of Exemption from Presumption of Abuse Under § 707(b)(2)* (Official Form 22A-1Supp) with this form.

Part 1: Calculate Your Current Monthly Income

1. **What is your marital and filing status?** Check one only.
   - ❑ **Not married.** Fill out Column A, lines 2-11.
   - ❑ **Married and your spouse is filing with you.** Fill out both Columns A and B, lines 2-11.
   - ❑ **Married and your spouse is NOT filing with you. You and your spouse are:**
     - ❑ **Living in the same household and are not legally separated.** Fill out both Columns A and B, lines 2-11.
     - ❑ **Living separately or are legally separated.** Fill out Column A, lines 2-11; do not fill out Column B. By checking this box, you declare under penalty of perjury that you and your spouse are legally separated under nonbankruptcy law that applies or that you and your spouse are living apart for reasons that do not include evading the Means Test requirements. 11 U.S.C. § 707(b)(7)(B).

Fill in the average monthly income that you received from all sources, derived during the 6 full months before you file this bankruptcy case. 11 U.S.C. § 101(10A). For example, if you are filing on September 15, the 6-month period would be March 1 through August 31. If the amount of your monthly income varied during the 6 months, add the income for all 6 months and divide the total by 6. Fill in the result. Do not include any income amount more than once. For example, if both spouses own the same rental property, put the income from that property in one column only. If you have nothing to report for any line, write $0 in the space.

			Column A **Debtor 1**	*Column B* **Debtor 2 or non-filing spouse**
2. **Your gross wages, salary, tips, bonuses, overtime, and commissions** (before all payroll deductions).			$________	$________
3. **Alimony and maintenance payments.** Do not include payments from a spouse if Column B is filled in.			$________	$________
4. **All amounts from any source which are regularly paid for household expenses of you or your dependents, including child support.** Include regular contributions from an unmarried partner, members of your household, your dependents, parents, and roommates. Include regular contributions from a spouse only if Column B is not filled in. Do not include payments you listed on line 3.			$________	$________
5. **Net income from operating a business, profession, or farm**				
Gross receipts (before all deductions)	$________			
Ordinary and necessary operating expenses	– $________			
Net monthly income from a business, profession, or farm	$________	**Copy here➔**	$________	$________
6. **Net income from rental and other real property**				
Gross receipts (before all deductions)	$________			
Ordinary and necessary operating expenses	– $________			
Net monthly income from rental or other real property	$________	**Copy here➔**	$________	$________
7. **Interest, dividends, and royalties**			$________	$________

Debtor 1 ______________________ (First Name / Middle Name / Last Name) Case number (if known) ______________________

	Column A Debtor 1	Column B Debtor 2 or non-filing spouse
8. **Unemployment compensation**	$______	$______
Do not enter the amount if you contend that the amount received was a benefit under the Social Security Act. Instead, list it here:		
For you .... $______		
For your spouse .... $______		
9. **Pension or retirement income.** Do not include any amount received that was a benefit under the Social Security Act.	$______	$______
10. **Income from all other sources not listed above.** Specify the source and amount. Do not include any benefits received under the Social Security Act or payments received as a victim of a war crime, a crime against humanity, or international or domestic terrorism. If necessary, list other sources on a separate page and put the total on line 10c.		
10a. ______________	$______	$______
10b. ______________	$______	$______
10c. Total amounts from separate pages, if any.	+$______	+ $______
11. **Calculate your total current monthly income.** Add lines 2 through 10 for each column. Then add the total for Column A to the total for Column B.	$______ +	$______ = $______ Total current monthly income

Part 2: Determine Whether the Means Test Applies to You

12. **Calculate your current monthly income for the year.** Follow these steps:

12a. Copy your total current monthly income from line 11 .... **Copy line 11 here** → 12a. $______

Multiply by 12 (the number of months in a year). **x 12**

12b. The result is your annual income for this part of the form. 12b. $______

13. **Calculate the median family income that applies to you.** Follow these steps:

Fill in the state in which you live. [ ]

Fill in the number of people in your household. [ ]

Fill in the median family income for your state and size of household. .... 13. $______

To find a list of applicable median income amounts, go online using the link specified in the separate instructions for this form. This list may also be available at the bankruptcy clerk's office.

14. **How do the lines compare?**

14a. ☐ Line 12b is less than or equal to line 13. On the top of page 1, check box 1, *There is no presumption of abuse*. Go to Part 3.

14b. ☐ Line 12b is more than line 13. On the top of page 1, check box 2, *The presumption of abuse is determined by Form 22A-2*. Go to Part 3 and fill out Form 22A–2.

Part 3: Sign Below

By signing here, I declare under penalty of perjury that the information on this statement and in any attachments is true and correct.

✘ ______________________ Signature of Debtor 1

✘ ______________________ Signature of Debtor 2

Date ________ MM / DD / YYYY

Date ________ MM / DD / YYYY

If you checked line 14a, do NOT fill out or file Form 22A–2.

If you checked line 14b, fill out Form 22A–2 and file it with this form.

Official Form B 22A1 Chapter 7 Statement of Your Current Monthly Income page 2

(As added Dec. 14, 2014.)

Form 22A-1 Supp. Statement of Exemption from Presumption of Abuse Under § 707(b)(2)

Fill in this information to identify your case:

Debtor 1 ______ First Name ______ Middle Name ______ Last Name

Debtor 2 (Spouse, if filing) ______ First Name ______ Middle Name ______ Last Name

United States Bankruptcy Court for the: ______ District of ______

Case number (If known) ______

☐ Check if this is an amended filing

OFFICIAL FORM B 22A1 SUPP

Statement of Exemption from Presumption of Abuse Under § 707(b)(2) 12/14

File this supplement together with *Chapter 7 Statement of Your Current Monthly Income* (Official Form 22A-1), if you believe that you are exempted from a presumption of abuse. Be as complete and accurate as possible. If two married people are filing together, and any of the exclusions in this statement applies to only one of you, the other person should complete a separate Form 22A-1 if you believe that this is required by 11 U.S.C. § 707(b)(2)(C).

Part 1: Identify the Kind of Debts You Have

1. **Are your debts primarily consumer debts?** *Consumer debts* are defined in 11 U.S.C. § 101(8) as "incurred by an individual primarily for a personal, family, or household purpose." Make sure that your answer is consistent with the "Nature of Debts" box on page 1 of the *Voluntary Petition* (Official Form 1).

   ☐ No. Go to Form 22A-1; on the top of page 1 of that form, check box 1, *There is no presumption of abuse*, and sign Part 3. Then submit this supplement with the signed Form 22A-1.

   ☐ Yes. Go to Part 2.

Part 2: Determine Whether Military Service Provisions Apply to You

2. **Are you a disabled veteran** (as defined in 38 U.S.C. § 3741(1))?

   ☐ No. Go to line 3.

   ☐ Yes. Did you incur debts mostly while you were on active duty or while you were performing a homeland defense activity? 10 U.S.C. § 101(d)(1); 32 U.S.C. § 901(1).

   ☐ No. Go to line 3.

   ☐ Yes. Go to Form 22A-1; on the top of page 1 of that form, check box 1, *There is no presumption of abuse*, and sign Part 3. Then submit this supplement with the signed Form 22A-1.

3. **Are you or have you been a Reservist or member of the National Guard?**

   ☐ No. Complete Form 22A-1. Do not submit this supplement.

   ☐ Yes. Were you called to active duty or did you perform a homeland defense activity? 10 U.S.C. § 101(d)(1); 32 U.S.C. § 901(1)

   ☐ No. Complete Form 22A-1. Do not submit this supplement.

   ☐ Yes. Check any one of the following categories that applies:

   ☐ **I was called to active duty after September 11, 2001**, for at least 90 days and remain on active duty.

   ☐ **I was called to active duty after September 11, 2001,** for at least 90 days and was released from active duty on ______, which is fewer than 540 days before I file this bankruptcy case.

   ☐ **I am performing a homeland defense activity for at least 90 days.**

   ☐ **I performed a homeland defense activity for at least 90 days,** ending on ______, which is fewer than 540 days before I file this bankruptcy case.

If you checked one of the categories to the left, go to Form 22A-1. On the top of page 1 of Form 22A-1, check box 3, *The Means Test does not apply now*, and sign Part 3. Then submit this supplement with the signed Form 22A-1. You are not required to fill out the rest of Official Form 22A-1 during the exclusion period. The *exclusion period* means the time you are on active duty or are performing a homeland defense activity, and for 540 days afterward. 11 U.S.C. § 707(b)(2)(D)(ii).

If your exclusion period ends before your case is closed, you may have to file an amended form later.

(As added Dec. 14, 2014.)

Form 22A-2. Chapter 7 Means Test Calculation

Fill in this information to identify your case:

Debtor 1 ______ First Name ______ Middle Name ______ Last Name

Debtor 2 (Spouse, if filing) ______ First Name ______ Middle Name ______ Last Name

United States Bankruptcy Court for the: ______ District of ______ (State)

Case number (If known) ______

Check the appropriate box as directed in lines 40 or 42:

According to the calculations required by this Statement:

☐ 1. There is no presumption of abuse.

☐ 2. There is a presumption of abuse.

☐ Check if this is an amended filing

Official Form B 22A2

Chapter 7 Means Test Calculation

12/14

To fill out this form, you will need your completed copy of *Chapter 7 Statement of Your Current Monthly Income* (Official Form 22A-1).

Be as complete and accurate as possible. If two married people are filing together, both are equally responsible for being accurate. If more space is needed, attach a separate sheet to this form. Include the line number to which the additional information applies. On the top of any additional pages, write your name and case number (if known).

Part 1: Determine Your Adjusted Income

1. **Copy your total current monthly income.** .... **Copy line 11 from Official Form 22A-1 here➔** ....1. $______

2. **Did you fill out Column B in Part 1 of Form 22A–1?**

☐ No. Fill in $0 on line 3d.

☐ Yes. Is your spouse filing with you?

☐ No. Go to line 3.

☐ Yes. Fill in $0 on line 3d.

3. **Adjust your current monthly income by subtracting any part of your spouse's income not used to pay for the household expenses of you or your dependents.** Follow these steps:

On line 11, Column B of Form 22A–1, was any amount of the income you reported for your spouse NOT regularly used for the household expenses of you or your dependents?

☐ No. Fill in 0 on line 3d.

☐ Yes. Fill in the information below:

State each purpose for which the income was used For example, the income is used to pay your spouse's tax debt or to support people other than you or your dependents	**Fill in the amount you are subtracting from your spouse's income**
3a. ______	$______
3b. ______	$______
3c. ______	+ $______
3d. **Total.** Add lines 3a, 3b, and 3c.	$______

Copy total here ➔.........3d. — $______

4. **Adjust your current monthly income.** Subtract line 3d from line 1. $______

Debtor 1 ______________________________ Case number (if known)______________
First Name Middle Name Last Name

Part 2: Calculate Your Deductions from Your Income

The Internal Revenue Service (IRS) issues National and Local Standards for certain expense amounts. Use these amounts to answer the questions in lines 6-15. To find the IRS standards, go online using the link specified in the separate instructions for this form. This information may also be available at the bankruptcy clerk's office.

Deduct the expense amounts set out in lines 6-15 regardless of your actual expense. In later parts of the form, you will use some of your actual expenses if they are higher than the standards. Do not deduct any amounts that you subtracted from your spouse's income in line 3 and do not deduct any operating expenses that you subtracted from income in lines 5 and 6 of Form 22A–1.

If your expenses differ from month to month, enter the average expense.

Whenever this part of the form refers to *you*, it means both you and your spouse if Column B of Form 22A–1 is filled in.

5. **The number of people used in determining your deductions from income**

Fill in the number of people who could be claimed as exemptions on your federal income tax return, plus the number of any additional dependents whom you support. This number may be different from the number of people in your household. [ ]

National Standards You must use the IRS National Standards to answer the questions in lines 6-7.

6. **Food, clothing, and other items:** Using the number of people you entered in line 5 and the IRS National Standards, fill in the dollar amount for food, clothing, and other items. $________

7. **Out-of-pocket health care allowance:** Using the number of people you entered in line 5 and the IRS National Standards, fill in the dollar amount for out-of-pocket health care. The number of people is split into two categories—people who are under 65 and people who are 65 or older—because older people have a higher IRS allowance for health care costs. If your actual expenses are higher than this IRS amount, you may deduct the additional amount on line 22.

People who are under 65 years of age

7a. Out-of-pocket health care allowance per person $________

7b. Number of people who are under 65 X______

7c. **Subtotal.** Multiply line 7a by line 7b. $________ **Copy line 7c here➔** ...... $________

People who are 65 years of age or older

7d. Out-of-pocket health care allowance per person $________

7e. Number of people who are 65 or older X______

7f. **Subtotal.** Multiply line 7d by line 7e. $________ **Copy line 7f here➔** ...... + $________

7g. **Total.** Add lines 7c and 7f.. $________ **Copy total here➔** .... 7g. $________

Debtor 1 ______________________________ First Name Middle Name Last Name   Case number (if known) ______________________

Local Standards You must use the IRS Local Standards to answer the questions in lines 8-15.

Based on information from the IRS, the U.S. Trustee Program has divided the IRS Local Standard for housing for bankruptcy purposes into two parts:

- **Housing and utilities – Insurance and operating expenses**
- **Housing and utilities – Mortgage or rent expenses**

To answer the questions in lines 8-9, use the U.S. Trustee Program chart.

To find the chart, go online using the link specified in the separate instructions for this form. This chart may also be available at the bankruptcy clerk's office.

8. **Housing and utilities – Insurance and operating expenses:** Using the number of people you entered in line 5, fill in the dollar amount listed for your county for insurance and operating expenses. $________

9. **Housing and utilities – Mortgage or rent expenses:**

9a. Using the number of people you entered in line 5, fill in the dollar amount listed for your county for mortgage or rent expenses. 9a. $________

9b. Total average monthly payment for all mortgages and other debts secured by your home.

To calculate the total average monthly payment, add all amounts that are contractually due to each secured creditor in the 60 months after you file for bankruptcy. Then divide by 60.

Name of the creditor	Average monthly payment
______________________	$________
______________________	$________
______________________	+ $________

9b. Total average monthly payment $________ Copy line 9b here➔ — $________ Repeat this amount on line 33a.

9c. Net mortgage or rent expense.

Subtract line 9b (*total average monthly payment*) from line 9a (*mortgage or rent expense*). If this amount is less than $0, enter $0. 9c. $________ Copy line 9c here➔ $________

10. **If you claim that the U.S. Trustee Program's division of the IRS Local Standard for housing is incorrect and affects the calculation of your monthly expenses, fill in any additional amount you claim.** $________

Explain why: ______________________________________

11. **Local transportation expenses:** Check the number of vehicles for which you claim an ownership or operating expense.

- ☐ 0. Go to line 14.
- ☐ 1. Go to line 12.
- ☐ 2 or more. Go to line 12.

12. **Vehicle operation expense:** Using the IRS Local Standards and the number of vehicles for which you claim the operating expenses, fill in the *Operating Costs* that apply for your Census region or metropolitan statistical area. $________

Debtor 1 ______________________________ Case number (if known)______________________
First Name Middle Name Last Name

13. **Vehicle ownership or lease expense:** Using the IRS Local Standards, calculate the net ownership or lease expense for each vehicle below. You may not claim the expense if you do not make any loan or lease payments on the vehicle. In addition, you may not claim the expense for more than two vehicles.

Vehicle 1 **Describe Vehicle 1:** ______________________________

13a. Ownership or leasing costs using IRS Local Standard 13a. $________

13b. Average monthly payment for all debts secured by Vehicle 1.
Do not include costs for leased vehicles.

To calculate the average monthly payment here and on line 13e, add all amounts that are contractually due to each secured creditor in the 60 months after you filed for bankruptcy. Then divide by 60.

Name of each creditor for Vehicle 1	Average monthly payment
______________________	$________

Copy 13b here➔ – $________ Repeat this amount on line 33b.

13c. Net Vehicle 1 ownership or lease expense
Subtract line 13b from line 13a. If this amount is less than $0, enter $0. 13c. $________ **Copy net Vehicle 1 expense here.....➔** $________

Vehicle 2 **Describe Vehicle 2:** ______________________________

13d. Ownership or leasing costs using IRS Local Standard 13d. $________

13e. Average monthly payment for all debts secured by Vehicle 2. Do not include costs for leased vehicles.

Name of each creditor for Vehicle 2	Average monthly payment
______________________	$________

Copy 13e here➔ – $________ Repeat this amount on line 33c.

13f. Net Vehicle 2 ownership or lease expense
Subtract line 13e from 13d. If this amount is less than $0, enter $0. 13f. $________ **Copy net Vehicle 2 expense here.....➔** $________

14. **Public transportation expense**: If you claimed 0 vehicles in line 11, using the IRS Local Standards, fill in the *Public Transportation* expense allowance regardless of whether you use public transportation. $________

15. **Additional public transportation expense:** If you claimed 1 or more vehicles in line 11 and if you claim that you may also deduct a public transportation expense, you may fill in what you believe is the appropriate expense, but you may not claim more than the IRS Local Standard for *Public Transportation*. $________

Debtor 1 ______________________________ Case number (if known) ______________
First Name Middle Name Last Name

Other Necessary Expenses In addition to the expense deductions listed above, you are allowed your monthly expenses for the following IRS categories.

16. **Taxes:** The total monthly amount that you will actually owe for federal, state and local taxes, such as income taxes, self-employment taxes, social security taxes, and Medicare taxes. You may include the monthly amount withheld from your pay for these taxes. However, if you expect to receive a tax refund, you must divide the expected refund by 12 and subtract that number from the total monthly amount that is withheld to pay for taxes.
   Do not include real estate, sales, or use taxes. $______

17. **Involuntary deductions:** The total monthly payroll deductions that your job requires, such as retirement contributions, union dues, and uniform costs.
   Do not include amounts that are not required by your job, such as voluntary 401(k) contributions or payroll savings. $______

18. **Life insurance:** The total monthly premiums that you pay for your own term life insurance. If two married people are filing together, include payments that you make for your spouse's term life insurance. Do not include premiums for life insurance on your dependents, for a non-filing spouse's life insurance, or for any form of life insurance other than term. $______

19. **Court-ordered payments:** The total monthly amount that you pay as required by the order of a court or administrative agency, such as spousal or child support payments.
   Do not include payments on past due obligations for spousal or child support. You will list these obligations in line 35. $______

20. **Education:** The total monthly amount that you pay for education that is either required:
   - as a condition for your job, or
   - for your physically or mentally challenged dependent child if no public education is available for similar services. $______

21. **Childcare:** The total monthly amount that you pay for childcare, such as babysitting, daycare, nursery, and preschool.
   Do not include payments for any elementary or secondary school education. $______

22. **Additional health care expenses, excluding insurance costs:** The monthly amount that you pay for health care that is required for the health and welfare of you or your dependents and that is not reimbursed by insurance or paid by a health savings account. Include only the amount that is more than the total entered in line 7.
   Payments for health insurance or health savings accounts should be listed only in line 25. $______

23. **Optional telephones and telephone services:** The total monthly amount that you pay for telecommunication services for you and your dependents, such as pagers, call waiting, caller identification, special long distance, or business cell phone service, to the extent necessary for your health and welfare or that of your dependents or for the production of income, if it is not reimbursed by your employer. + $______
   Do not include payments for basic home telephone, internet and cell phone service. Do not include self-employment expenses, such as those reported on line 5 of Official Form 22A-1, or any amount you previously deducted.

24. **Add all of the expenses allowed under the IRS expense allowances.**
   Add lines 6 through 23. $______

Debtor 1 ______________________________ Case number (if known)______________
First Name Middle Name Last Name

Additional Expense Deductions These are additional deductions allowed by the Means Test.
Note: Do not include any expense allowances listed in lines 6-24.

25. **Health insurance, disability insurance, and health savings account expenses.** The monthly expenses for health insurance, disability insurance, and health savings accounts that are reasonably necessary for yourself, your spouse, or your dependents.

Health insurance $________

Disability insurance $________

Health savings account + $________

Total $________ Copy total here➔ .... $________

Do you actually spend this total amount?

☐ No. How much do you actually spend? $________
☐ Yes

26. **Continued contributions to the care of household or family members.** The actual monthly expenses that you will continue to pay for the reasonable and necessary care and support of an elderly, chronically ill, or disabled member of your household or member of your immediate family who is unable to pay for such expenses. $________

27. **Protection against family violence.** The reasonably necessary monthly expenses that you incur to maintain the safety of you and your family under the Family Violence Prevention and Services Act or other federal laws that apply. $________

By law, the court must keep the nature of these expenses confidential.

28. **Additional home energy costs.** Your home energy costs are included in your non-mortgage housing and utilities allowance on line 8.

If you believe that you have home energy costs that are more than the home energy costs included in the non-mortgage housing and utilities allowance, then fill in the excess amount of home energy costs. $________

You must give your case trustee documentation of your actual expenses, and you must show that the additional amount claimed is reasonable and necessary.

29. **Education expenses for dependent children who are younger than 18.** The monthly expenses (not more than $156.25* per child) that you pay for your dependent children who are younger than 18 years old to attend a private or public elementary or secondary school. $________

You must give your case trustee documentation of your actual expenses, and you must explain why the amount claimed is reasonable and necessary and not already accounted for in lines 6-23.

* Subject to adjustment on 4/01/16, and every 3 years after that for cases begun on or after the date of adjustment.

30. **Additional food and clothing expense.** The monthly amount by which your actual food and clothing expenses are higher than the combined food and clothing allowances in the IRS National Standards. That amount cannot be more than 5% of the food and clothing allowances in the IRS National Standards. $________

To find a chart showing the maximum additional allowance, go online using the link specified in the separate instructions for this form. This chart may also be available at the bankruptcy clerk's office.

You must show that the additional amount claimed is reasonable and necessary.

31. **Continuing charitable contributions.** The amount that you will continue to contribute in the form of cash or financial instruments to a religious or charitable organization. 26 U.S.C. § 170(c)(1)-(2). $________

32. **Add all of the additional expense deductions.** $________
Add lines 25 through 31.

Debtor 1 ______________________ First Name Middle Name Last Name Case number (if known)______________________

Deductions for Debt Payment

33. For debts that are secured by an interest in property that you own, including home mortgages, vehicle loans, and other secured debt, fill in lines 33a through 33g.

To calculate the total average monthly payment, add all amounts that are contractually due to each secured creditor in the 60 months after you file for bankruptcy. Then divide by 60.

	Average monthly payment
Mortgages on your home:	
33a. Copy line 9b here .... →	$________
Loans on your first two vehicles:	
33b. Copy line 13b here. .... →	$________
33c. Copy line 13e here. .... →	$________

	Name of each creditor for other secured debt	Identify property that secures the debt	Does payment include taxes or insurance?	
33d.	________	________	☐ No ☐ Yes	$________
33e.	________	________	☐ No ☐ Yes	$________
33f.	________	________	☐ No ☐ Yes	+ $________

33g. Total average monthly payment. Add lines 33a through 33f. .... $________ Copy total here→ $________

34. Are any debts that you listed in line 33 secured by your primary residence, a vehicle, or other property necessary for your support or the support of your dependents?

☐ No. Go to line 35.

☐ Yes. State any amount that you must pay to a creditor, in addition to the payments listed in line 33, to keep possession of your property (called the *cure amount*). Next, divide by 60 and fill in the information below.

Name of the creditor	Identify property that secures the debt	Total cure amount		Monthly cure amount
________	________	$________	÷ 60 =	$________
________	________	$________	÷ 60 =	$________
________	________	$________	÷ 60 =	+ $________
			Total	$________

Copy total here→ $________

35. Do you owe any priority claims such as a priority tax, child support, or alimony — that are past due as of the filing date of your bankruptcy case? 11 U.S.C. § 507.

☐ No. Go to line 36.

☐ Yes. Fill in the total amount of all of these priority claims. Do not include current or ongoing priority claims, such as those you listed in line 19.

Total amount of all past-due priority claims .... $________ ÷ 60 = $________

Debtor 1 ______________________ First Name Middle Name Last Name Case number (if known) ______________

36. **Are you eligible to file a case under Chapter 13?** 11 U.S.C. § 109(e).
For more information, go online using the link for *Bankruptcy Basics* specified in the separate instructions for this form. *Bankruptcy Basics* may also be available at the bankruptcy clerk's office.

☐ No. Go to line 37.

☐ Yes. Fill in the following information.

Projected monthly plan payment if you were filing under Chapter 13 $________

Current multiplier for your district as stated on the list issued by the Administrative Office of the United States Courts (for districts in Alabama and North Carolina) or by the Executive Office for United States Trustees (for all other districts). x ____

To find a list of district multipliers that includes your district, go online using the link specified in the separate instructions for this form. This list may also be available at the bankruptcy clerk's office.

Average monthly administrative expense if you were filing under Chapter 13 $________ Copy total here→ $________

37. **Add all of the deductions for debt payment.**
Add lines 33g through 36. $________

Total Deductions from Income

38. **Add all of the allowed deductions.**

Copy line 24, *All of the expenses allowed under IRS expense allowances* .... $________

Copy line 32, *All of the additional expense deductions* .... $________

Copy line 37, *All of the deductions for debt payment* .... + $________

Total deductions $________ Copy total here → $________

Part 3: Determine Whether There Is a Presumption of Abuse

39. **Calculate monthly disposable income for 60 months**

39a. Copy line 4, *adjusted current monthly income* ..... $________

39b. Copy line 38, *Total deductions*......... − $________

39c. Monthly disposable income. 11 U.S.C. § 707(b)(2). Subtract line 39b from line 39a. $________ Copy line 39c here→ $________

For the next 60 months (5 years)........................ x 60

39d. **Total**. Multiply line 39c by 60. .... 39d. $________ Copy line 39d here→ $________

40. **Find out whether there is a presumption of abuse.** Check the box that applies:

☐ **The line 39d is less than $7,475*.** On the top of page 1 of this form, check box 1, *There is no presumption of abuse*. Go to Part 5.

☐ **The line 39d is more than $12,475*.** On the top of page 1 of this form, check box 2, *There is a presumption of abuse*. You may fill out Part 4 if you claim special circumstances. Then go to Part 5.

☐ **The line 39d is at least $7,475*, but not more than $12,475*.** Go to line 41.

* Subject to adjustment on 4/01/16, and every 3 years after that for cases filed on or after the date of adjustment.

Debtor 1 ______________________________ Case number (if known) ______________________________
First Name Middle Name Last Name

41. 41a. **Fill in the amount of your total nonpriority unsecured debt.** If you filled out *A Summary of Your Assets and Liabilities and Certain Statistical Information Schedules* (Official Form 6), you may refer to line 5 on that form. 41a. $________

x .25

41b. **25% of your total nonpriority unsecured debt.** 11 U.S.C. § 707(b)(2)(A)(i)(I)
Multiply line 41a by 0.25. $________ Copy here➔ $________

42. **Determine whether the income you have left over after subtracting all allowed deductions is enough to pay 25% of your unsecured, nonpriority debt.**
Check the box that applies:

☐ **Line 39d is less than line 41b.** On the top of page 1 of this form, check box 1, *There is no presumption of abuse.* Go to Part 5.

☐ **Line 39d is equal to or more than line 41b.** On the top of page 1 of this form, check box 2, *There is a presumption of abuse.* You may fill out Part 4 if you claim special circumstances. Then go to Part 5.

Part 4: Give Details About Special Circumstances

43. **Do you have any special circumstances that justify additional expenses or adjustments of current monthly income for which there is no reasonable alternative?** 11 U.S.C. § 707(b)(2)(B).

☐ No. Go to Part 5.

☐ Yes. Fill in the following information. All figures should reflect your average monthly expense or income adjustment for each item. You may include expenses you listed in line 25.

You must give a detailed explanation of the special circumstances that make the expenses or income adjustments necessary and reasonable. You must also give your case trustee documentation of your actual expenses or income adjustments.

Give a detailed explanation of the special circumstances	Average monthly expense or income adjustment
______________________________	$________
______________________________	$________
______________________________	$________
______________________________	$________

Part 5: Sign Below

By signing here, I declare under penalty of perjury that the information on this statement and in any attachments is true and correct.

✘ ______________________________ ✘ ______________________________
Signature of Debtor 1 Signature of Debtor 2

Date ____________ Date ____________
MM / DD / YYYY MM / DD / YYYY

(As added Dec. 14, 2014.)

Form 22B. Statement of Current Monthly Income

Fill in this information to identify your case:

Debtor 1 ______ First Name ______ Middle Name ______ Last Name

Debtor 2 (Spouse, if filing) ______ First Name ______ Middle Name ______ Last Name

United States Bankruptcy Court for the: ______ District of ______

Case number (If known) ______

☐ Check if this is an amended filing

Official Form B 22B

Chapter 11 Statement of Your Current Monthly Income

12/14

You must file this form if you are an individual and are filing for bankruptcy under Chapter 11. If more space is needed, attach a separate sheet to this form. Include the line number to which the additional information applies. On the top of any additional pages, write your name and case number (if known).

Part 1: Calculate Your Average Monthly Income

1. **What is your marital and filing status?** Check one only.

☐ **Not married.** Fill out Column A, lines 2-11.

☐ **Married and your spouse is filing with you.** Fill out both Columns A and B, lines 2-11.

☐ **Married and your spouse is NOT filing with you.** Fill out Column A, lines 2-11.

Fill in the average monthly income that you received from all sources, derived during the 6 full months before you file this bankruptcy case. 11 U.S.C. § 101(10A). For example, if you are filing on September 15, the 6-month period would be March 1 through August 31. If the amount of your monthly income varied during the 6 months, add the income for all 6 months and divide the total by 6. Fill in the result.

Do not include any income amount more than once. For example, if both spouses own the same rental property, put the income from that property in one column only. If you have nothing to report for any line, write $0 in the space.

			Column A Debtor 1	Column B Debtor 2
2. **Your gross wages, salary, tips, bonuses, overtime, and commissions** (before all payroll deductions).			$______	$______
3. **Alimony and maintenance payments.** Do not include payments from a spouse if Column B is filled in.			$______	$______
4. **All amounts from any source which are regularly paid for household expenses of you or your dependents, including child support.** Include regular contributions from an unmarried partner, members of your household, your dependents, parents, and roommates. Include regular contributions from a spouse only if Column B is not filled in. Do not include payments you listed on line 3.			$______	$______
5. **Net income from operating a business, profession, or farm**				
Gross receipts (before all deductions)	$______			
Ordinary and necessary operating expenses	– $______			
Net monthly income from a business, profession, or farm	$______	Copy here→	$______	$______
6. **Net income from rental and other real property**				
Gross receipts (before all deductions)	$______			
Ordinary and necessary operating expenses	– $______			
Net monthly income from rental or other real property	$______	Copy here→	$______	$______

Debtor 1 ______________________________ Case number (if known) ______________________
First Name Middle Name Last Name

	Column A Debtor 1	Column B Debtor 2
7. **Interest, dividends, and royalties**	$________	$________
8. **Unemployment compensation**	$________	$________

Do not enter the amount if you contend that the amount received was a benefit under the Social Security Act. Instead, list it here:..............................

For you .... $________

For your spouse .... $________

9. **Pension or retirement income.** Do not include any amount received that was a benefit under the Social Security Act.	$________	$________

10. **Income from all other sources not listed above.** Specify the source and amount.

Do not include any benefits received under the Social Security Act or payments received as a victim of a war crime, a crime against humanity, or international or domestic terrorism. If necessary, list other sources on a separate page and put the total on line 10c.

10a. ______________________________	$________	$________
10b. ______________________________	$________	$________
10c. Total amounts from separate pages, if any.	+ $________	+ $________

11. **Calculate your total average monthly income.**
Add lines 2 through 10 for each column.
Then add the total for Column A to the total for Column B.

$________ + $________ = $________
Total average monthly income

Part 2: Deduct any applicable marital adjustment

12. **Copy your total average monthly income from line 11.** $________

13. **Calculate the marital adjustment.** Check one:

☐ You are not married. Fill in 0 in line 13d.

☐ You are married and your spouse is filing with you. Fill in 0 in line 13d.

☐ You are married and your spouse is not filing with you.

Fill in the amount of the income listed in line 11, Column B, that was NOT regularly paid for the household expenses of you or your dependents, such as payment of the spouse's tax liability or the spouse's support of someone other than you or your dependents.

In lines 13a-c, specify the basis for excluding this income and the amount of income devoted to each purpose. If necessary, list additional adjustments on a separate page.

If this adjustment does not apply, enter 0 on line 13d.

13a. ______________________________ $________

13b. ______________________________ $________

13c. ______________________________ + $________

13d. Total.............................. $________ Copy here. → 13d. − ________

14. **Your current monthly income.** Subtract line 13d from line 12. 14. $________

Bankruptcy Form 22B

Debtor 1 ______________________________ Case number (if known) ______________
First Name Middle Name Last Name

Part 3: Sign Below

By signing here, under penalty of perjury I declare that the information on this statement and in any attachments is true and correct.

✘ ______________________ ✘ ______________________
Signature of Debtor 1 Signature of Debtor 2

Date __________ Date __________
MM / DD / YYYY MM / DD / YYYY

(As added Oct. 17, 2005; Jan. 1, 2008; Dec. 1, 2010; Dec. 14, 2014.)

Form 22C. Chapter 13 Statement of Current Monthly Income and Calculation of Commitment Period and Disposable Income

B 22C (Official Form 22C) (Chapter 13) (04/13)

In re ______________________
Debtor(s)

Case Number: ______________
(If known)

According to the calculations required by this statement:
☐ **The applicable commitment period is 3 years.**
☐ **The applicable commitment period is 5 years.**
☐ **Disposable income is determined under § 1325(b)(3).**
☐ **Disposable income is not determined under § 1325(b)(3).**
(Check the boxes as directed in Lines 17 and 23 of this statement.)

CHAPTER 13 STATEMENT OF CURRENT MONTHLY INCOME AND CALCULATION OF COMMITMENT PERIOD AND DISPOSABLE INCOME

In addition to Schedules I and J, this statement must be completed by every individual chapter 13 debtor, whether or not filing jointly. Joint debtors may complete one statement only.

	Part I. REPORT OF INCOME		
1	**Marital/filing status.** Check the box that applies and complete the balance of this part of this statement as directed. a. ☐ Unmarried. **Complete only Column A ("Debtor's Income") for Lines 2-10.** b. ☐ Married. **Complete both Column A ("Debtor's Income") and Column B ("Spouse's Income") for Lines 2-10.**		
	All figures must reflect average monthly income received from all sources, derived during the six calendar months prior to filing the bankruptcy case, ending on the last day of the month before the filing. If the amount of monthly income varied during the six months, you must divide the six-month total by six, and enter the result on the appropriate line.	**Column A** **Debtor's Income**	**Column B** **Spouse's Income**
2	**Gross wages, salary, tips, bonuses, overtime, commissions.**	$	$
3	**Income from the operation of a business, profession, or farm.** Subtract Line b from Line a and enter the difference in the appropriate column(s) of Line 3. If you operate more than one business, profession or farm, enter aggregate numbers and provide details on an attachment. Do not enter a number less than zero. **Do not include any part of the business expenses entered on Line b as a deduction in Part IV.** a. Gross receipts — $ b. Ordinary and necessary business expenses — $ c. Business income — Subtract Line b from Line a	$	$
4	**Rent and other real property income.** Subtract Line b from Line a and enter the difference in the appropriate column(s) of Line 4. Do not enter a number less than zero. **Do not include any part of the operating expenses entered on Line b as a deduction in Part IV.** a. Gross receipts — $ b. Ordinary and necessary operating expenses — $ c. Rent and other real property income — Subtract Line b from Line a	$	$
5	**Interest, dividends, and royalties.**	$	$
6	**Pension and retirement income.**	$	$
7	**Any amounts paid by another person or entity, on a regular basis, for the household expenses of the debtor or the debtor's dependents, including child support paid for that purpose.** Do not include alimony or separate maintenance payments or amounts paid by the debtor's spouse. Each regular payment should be reported in only one column; if a payment is listed in Column A, do not report that payment in Column B.	$	$

B 22C (Official Form 22C) (Chapter 13) (04/13)

8	**Unemployment compensation.** Enter the amount in the appropriate column(s) of Line 8. However, if you contend that unemployment compensation received by you or your spouse was a benefit under the Social Security Act, do not list the amount of such compensation in Column A or B, but instead state the amount in the space below: Unemployment compensation claimed to be a benefit under the Social Security Act | Debtor $ ______ | Spouse $ ______	$	$
9	**Income from all other sources.** Specify source and amount. If necessary, list additional sources on a separate page. Total and enter on Line 9. **Do not include alimony or separate maintenance payments paid by your spouse, but include all other payments of alimony or separate maintenance. Do not include** any benefits received under the Social Security Act or payments received as a victim of a war crime, crime against humanity, or as a victim of international or domestic terrorism. a. | | $ b. | | $	$	$
10	**Subtotal.** Add Lines 2 thru 9 in Column A, and, if Column B is completed, add Lines 2 through 9 in Column B. Enter the total(s).	$	$
11	**Total.** If Column B has been completed, add Line 10, Column A to Line 10, Column B, and enter the total. If Column B has not been completed, enter the amount from Line 10, Column A.	$	

	Part II. CALCULATION OF § 1325(b)(4) COMMITMENT PERIOD	
12	**Enter the amount from Line 11.**	$
13	**Marital adjustment.** If you are married, but are not filing jointly with your spouse, AND if you contend that calculation of the commitment period under § 1325(b)(4) does not require inclusion of the income of your spouse, enter on Line 13 the amount of the income listed in Line 10, Column B that was NOT paid on a regular basis for the household expenses of you or your dependents and specify, in the lines below, the basis for excluding this income (such as payment of the spouse's tax liability or the spouse's support of persons other than the debtor or the debtor's dependents) and the amount of income devoted to each purpose. If necessary, list additional adjustments on a separate page. If the conditions for entering this adjustment do not apply, enter zero. a. | | $ b. | | $ c. | | $ Total and enter on Line 13.	$
14	**Subtract Line 13 from Line 12 and enter the result.**	$
15	**Annualized current monthly income for § 1325(b)(4).** Multiply the amount from Line 14 by the number 12 and enter the result.	$
16	**Applicable median family income.** Enter the median family income for applicable state and household size. (This information is available by family size at www.usdoj.gov/ust/ or from the clerk of the bankruptcy court.) a. Enter debtor's state of residence: ______ b. Enter debtor's household size: ______	$
17	**Application of § 1325(b)(4).** Check the applicable box and proceed as directed. ☐ **The amount on Line 15 is less than the amount on Line 16.** Check the box for "The applicable commitment period is 3 years" at the top of page 1 of this statement and continue with this statement. ☐ **The amount on Line 15 is not less than the amount on Line 16.** Check the box for "The applicable commitment period is 5 years" at the top of page 1 of this statement and continue with this statement.	
	Part III. APPLICATION OF § 1325(b)(3) FOR DETERMINING DISPOSABLE INCOME	
18	**Enter the amount from Line 11.**	$

B 22C (Official Form 22C) (Chapter 13) (04/13)

19	**Marital adjustment.** If you are married, but are not filing jointly with your spouse, enter on Line 19 the total of any income listed in Line 10, Column B that was NOT paid on a regular basis for the household expenses of the debtor or the debtor's dependents. Specify in the lines below the basis for excluding the Column B income (such as payment of the spouse's tax liability or the spouse's support of persons other than the debtor or the debtor's dependents) and the amount of income devoted to each purpose. If necessary, list additional adjustments on a separate page. If the conditions for entering this adjustment do not apply, enter zero. a. ____ $ b. ____ $ c. ____ $ Total and enter on Line 19.	$
20	**Current monthly income for § 1325(b)(3).** Subtract Line 19 from Line 18 and enter the result.	$
21	**Annualized current monthly income for § 1325(b)(3).** Multiply the amount from Line 20 by the number 12 and enter the result.	$
22	**Applicable median family income.** Enter the amount from Line 16.	$
23	**Application of § 1325(b)(3).** Check the applicable box and proceed as directed. ☐ **The amount on Line 21 is more than the amount on Line 22.** Check the box for "Disposable income is determined under § 1325(b)(3)" at the top of page 1 of this statement and complete the remaining parts of this statement. ☐ **The amount on Line 21 is not more than the amount on Line 22.** Check the box for "Disposable income is not determined under § 1325(b)(3)" at the top of page 1 of this statement and complete Part VII of this statement. **Do not complete Parts IV, V, or VI.**	
	Part IV. CALCULATION OF DEDUCTIONS FROM INCOME	
	Subpart A: Deductions under Standards of the Internal Revenue Service (IRS)	
24A	**National Standards: food, apparel and services, housekeeping supplies, personal care, and miscellaneous.** Enter in Line 24A the "Total" amount from IRS National Standards for Allowable Living Expenses for the applicable number of persons. (This information is available at www.usdoj.gov/ust/ or from the clerk of the bankruptcy court.) The applicable number of persons is the number that would currently be allowed as exemptions on your federal income tax return, plus the number of any additional dependents whom you support.	$
24B	**National Standards: health care.** Enter in Line a1 below the amount from IRS National Standards for Out-of-Pocket Health Care for persons under 65 years of age, and in Line a2 the IRS National Standards for Out-of-Pocket Health Care for persons 65 years of age or older. (This information is available at www.usdoj.gov/ust/ or from the clerk of the bankruptcy court.) Enter in Line b1 the applicable number of persons who are under 65 years of age, and enter in Line b2 the applicable number of persons who are 65 years of age or older. (The applicable number of persons in each age category is the number in that category that would currently be allowed as exemptions on your federal income tax return, plus the number of any additional dependents whom you support.) Multiply Line a1 by Line b1 to obtain a total amount for persons under 65, and enter the result in Line c1. Multiply Line a2 by Line b2 to obtain a total amount for persons 65 and older, and enter the result in Line c2. Add Lines c1 and c2 to obtain a total health care amount, and enter the result in Line 24B.	$
25A	**Local Standards: housing and utilities; non-mortgage expenses.** Enter the amount of the IRS Housing and Utilities Standards; non-mortgage expenses for the applicable county and family size. (This information is available at www.usdoj.gov/ust/ or from the clerk of the bankruptcy court). The applicable family size consists of the number that would currently be allowed as exemptions on your federal income tax return, plus the number of any additional dependents whom you support.	$

Line 24B worksheet:

Persons under 65 years of age			Persons 65 years of age or older		
a1.	Allowance per person		a2.	Allowance per person	
b1.	Number of persons		b2.	Number of persons	
c1.	Subtotal		c2.	Subtotal	

B 22C (Official Form 22C) (Chapter 13) (04/13)

<table>
<tr><td>25B</td><td>Local Standards: housing and utilities; mortgage/rent expense. Enter, in Line a below, the amount of the IRS Housing and Utilities Standards; mortgage/rent expense for your county and family size (this information is available at www.usdoj.gov/ust/ or from the clerk of the bankruptcy court) (the applicable family size consists of the number that would currently be allowed as exemptions on your federal income tax return, plus the number of any additional dependents whom you support); enter on Line b the total of the Average Monthly Payments for any debts secured by your home, as stated in Line 47; subtract Line b from Line a and enter the result in Line 25B. Do not enter an amount less than zero.
a. | IRS Housing and Utilities Standards; mortgage/rent expense | $
b. | Average Monthly Payment for any debts secured by your home, if any, as stated in Line 47 | $
c. | Net mortgage/rental expense | Subtract Line b from Line a.</td><td>$</td></tr>
<tr><td>26</td><td>Local Standards: housing and utilities; adjustment. If you contend that the process set out in Lines 25A and 25B does not accurately compute the allowance to which you are entitled under the IRS Housing and Utilities Standards, enter any additional amount to which you contend you are entitled, and state the basis for your contention in the space below:
____
____
____________________</td><td>$</td></tr>
<tr><td>27A</td><td>Local Standards: transportation; vehicle operation/public transportation expense. You are entitled to an expense allowance in this category regardless of whether you pay the expenses of operating a vehicle and regardless of whether you use public transportation.
Check the number of vehicles for which you pay the operating expenses or for which the operating expenses are included as a contribution to your household expenses in Line 7. ☐ 0 ☐ 1 ☐ 2 or more.
If you checked 0, enter on Line 27A the "Public Transportation" amount from IRS Local Standards: Transportation. If you checked 1 or 2 or more, enter on Line 27A the "Operating Costs" amount from IRS Local Standards: Transportation for the applicable number of vehicles in the applicable Metropolitan Statistical Area or Census Region. (These amounts are available at www.usdoj.gov/ust/ or from the clerk of the bankruptcy court.)</td><td>$</td></tr>
<tr><td>27B</td><td>Local Standards: transportation; additional public transportation expense. If you pay the operating expenses for a vehicle and also use public transportation, and you contend that you are entitled to an additional deduction for your public transportation expenses, enter on Line 27B the "Public Transportation" amount from IRS Local Standards: Transportation. (This amount is available at www.usdoj.gov/ust/ or from the clerk of the bankruptcy court.)</td><td>$</td></tr>
<tr><td>28</td><td>Local Standards: transportation ownership/lease expense; Vehicle 1. Check the number of vehicles for which you claim an ownership/lease expense. (You may not claim an ownership/lease expense for more than two vehicles.) ☐ 1 ☐ 2 or more.
Enter, in Line a below, the "Ownership Costs" for "One Car" from the IRS Local Standards: Transportation (available at www.usdoj.gov/ust/ or from the clerk of the bankruptcy court); enter in Line b the total of the Average Monthly Payments for any debts secured by Vehicle 1, as stated in Line 47; subtract Line b from Line a and enter the result in Line 28. Do not enter an amount less than zero.
a. | IRS Transportation Standards, Ownership Costs | $
b. | Average Monthly Payment for any debts secured by Vehicle 1, as stated in Line 47 | $
c. | Net ownership/lease expense for Vehicle 1 | Subtract Line b from Line a.</td><td>$</td></tr>
</table>

B 22C (Official Form 22C) (Chapter 13) (04/13)

<table>
<tr><td>29</td><td>Local Standards: transportation ownership/lease expense; Vehicle 2. Complete this Line only if you checked the "2 or more" Box in Line 28.
Enter, in Line a below, the "Ownership Costs" for "One Car" from the IRS Local Standards: Transportation (available at www.usdoj.gov/ust/ or from the clerk of the bankruptcy court); enter in Line b the total of the Average Monthly Payments for any debts secured by Vehicle 2, as stated in Line 47; subtract Line b from Line a and enter the result in Line 29. Do not enter an amount less than zero.
<table>
<tr><td>a.</td><td>IRS Transportation Standards, Ownership Costs</td><td>$</td></tr>
<tr><td>b.</td><td>Average Monthly Payment for any debts secured by Vehicle 2, as stated in Line 47</td><td>$</td></tr>
<tr><td>c.</td><td>Net ownership/lease expense for Vehicle 2</td><td>Subtract Line b from Line a.</td></tr>
</table></td><td>$</td></tr>
<tr><td>30</td><td>Other Necessary Expenses: taxes. Enter the total average monthly expense that you actually incur for all federal, state, and local taxes, other than real estate and sales taxes, such as income taxes, self-employment taxes, social-security taxes, and Medicare taxes. Do not include real estate or sales taxes.</td><td>$</td></tr>
<tr><td>31</td><td>Other Necessary Expenses: involuntary deductions for employment. Enter the total average monthly deductions that are required for your employment, such as mandatory retirement contributions, union dues, and uniform costs. Do not include discretionary amounts, such as voluntary 401(k) contributions.</td><td>$</td></tr>
<tr><td>32</td><td>Other Necessary Expenses: life insurance. Enter total average monthly premiums that you actually pay for term life insurance for yourself. Do not include premiums for insurance on your dependents, for whole life or for any other form of insurance.</td><td>$</td></tr>
<tr><td>33</td><td>Other Necessary Expenses: court-ordered payments. Enter the total monthly amount that you are required to pay pursuant to the order of a court or administrative agency, such as spousal or child support payments. Do not include payments on past due obligations included in Line 49.</td><td>$</td></tr>
<tr><td>34</td><td>Other Necessary Expenses: education for employment or for a physically or mentally challenged child. Enter the total average monthly amount that you actually expend for education that is a condition of employment and for education that is required for a physically or mentally challenged dependent child for whom no public education providing similar services is available.</td><td>$</td></tr>
<tr><td>35</td><td>Other Necessary Expenses: childcare. Enter the total average monthly amount that you actually expend on childcare—such as baby-sitting, day care, nursery and preschool. Do not include other educational payments.</td><td>$</td></tr>
<tr><td>36</td><td>Other Necessary Expenses: health care. Enter the total average monthly amount that you actually expend on health care that is required for the health and welfare of yourself or your dependents, that is not reimbursed by insurance or paid by a health savings account, and that is in excess of the amount entered in Line 24B. Do not include payments for health insurance or health savings accounts listed in Line 39.</td><td>$</td></tr>
<tr><td>37</td><td>Other Necessary Expenses: telecommunication services. Enter the total average monthly amount that you actually pay for telecommunication services other than your basic home telephone and cell phone service—such as pagers, call waiting, caller id, special long distance, or internet service—to the extent necessary for your health and welfare or that of your dependents. Do not include any amount previously deducted.</td><td>$</td></tr>
<tr><td>38</td><td>Total Expenses Allowed under IRS Standards. Enter the total of Lines 24 through 37.</td><td>$</td></tr>
<tr><td colspan="3">Subpart B: Additional Living Expense Deductions
Note: Do not include any expenses that you have listed in Lines 24-37</td></tr>
</table>

B 22C (Official Form 22C) (Chapter 13) (04/13)

39	**Health Insurance, Disability Insurance, and Health Savings Account Expenses.** List the monthly expenses in the categories set out in lines a-c below that are reasonably necessary for yourself, your spouse, or your dependents. a. Health Insurance $ b. Disability Insurance $ c. Health Savings Account $ Total and enter on Line 39	$
	If you do not actually expend this total amount, state your actual total average monthly expenditures in the space below: $ ______	
40	**Continued contributions to the care of household or family members.** Enter the total average actual monthly expenses that you will continue to pay for the reasonable and necessary care and support of an elderly, chronically ill, or disabled member of your household or member of your immediate family who is unable to pay for such expenses. **Do not include payments listed in Line 34.**	$
41	**Protection against family violence.** Enter the total average reasonably necessary monthly expenses that you actually incur to maintain the safety of your family under the Family Violence Prevention and Services Act or other applicable federal law. The nature of these expenses is required to be kept confidential by the court.	$
42	**Home energy costs.** Enter the total average monthly amount, in excess of the allowance specified by IRS Local Standards for Housing and Utilities that you actually expend for home energy costs. **You must provide your case trustee with documentation of your actual expenses, and you must demonstrate that the additional amount claimed is reasonable and necessary.**	$
43	**Education expenses for dependent children under 18.** Enter the total average monthly expenses that you actually incur, not to exceed $156.25 per child, for attendance at a private or public elementary or secondary school by your dependent children less than 18 years of age. **You must provide your case trustee with documentation of your actual expenses, and you must explain why the amount claimed is reasonable and necessary and not already accounted for in the IRS Standards.**	$
44	**Additional food and clothing expense.** Enter the total average monthly amount by which your food and clothing expenses exceed the combined allowances for food and clothing (apparel and services) in the IRS National Standards, not to exceed 5% of those combined allowances. (This information is available at www.usdoj.gov/ust/ or from the clerk of the bankruptcy court.) **You must demonstrate that the additional amount claimed is reasonable and necessary.**	$
45	**Charitable contributions.** Enter the amount reasonably necessary for you to expend each month on charitable contributions in the form of cash or financial instruments to a charitable organization as defined in 26 U.S.C. § 170(c)(1)-(2). **Do not include any amount in excess of 15% of your gross monthly income.**	$
46	**Total Additional Expense Deductions under § 707(b).** Enter the total of Lines 39 through 45.	$

Subpart C: Deductions for Debt Payment

47	**Future payments on secured claims.** For each of your debts that is secured by an interest in property that you own, list the name of the creditor, identify the property securing the debt, state the Average Monthly Payment, and check whether the payment includes taxes or insurance. The Average Monthly Payment is the total of all amounts scheduled as contractually due to each Secured Creditor in the 60 months following the filing of the bankruptcy case, divided by 60. If necessary, list additional entries on a separate page. Enter the total of the Average Monthly Payments on Line 47.	

	Name of Creditor	Property Securing the Debt	Average Monthly Payment	Does payment include taxes or insurance?
a.			$	☐ yes ☐ no
b.			$	☐ yes ☐ no
c.			$	☐ yes ☐ no
			Total: Add Lines a, b, and c	

Line 47 total: $

B 22C (Official Form 22C) (Chapter 13) (04/13)

48	**Other payments on secured claims.** If any of debts listed in Line 47 are secured by your primary residence, a motor vehicle, or other property necessary for your support or the support of your dependents, you may include in your deduction 1/60th of any amount (the "cure amount") that you must pay the creditor in addition to the payments listed in Line 47, in order to maintain possession of the property. The cure amount would include any sums in default that must be paid in order to avoid repossession or foreclosure. List and total any such amounts in the following chart. If necessary, list additional entries on a separate page.	

	Name of Creditor	Property Securing the Debt	1/60th of the Cure Amount
a.			$
b.			$
c.			$
			Total: Add Lines a, b, and c

Line 48 amount: $

49	**Payments on prepetition priority claims.** Enter the total amount, divided by 60, of all priority claims, such as priority tax, child support and alimony claims, for which you were liable at the time of your bankruptcy filing. **Do not include current obligations, such as those set out in Line 33.**	$
50	**Chapter 13 administrative expenses.** Multiply the amount in Line a by the amount in Line b, and enter the resulting administrative expense.	

a.	Projected average monthly chapter 13 plan payment.	$
b.	Current multiplier for your district as determined under schedules issued by the Executive Office for United States Trustees. (This information is available at www.usdoj.gov/ust/ or from the clerk of the bankruptcy court.)	x
c.	Average monthly administrative expense of chapter 13 case	Total: Multiply Lines a and b

Line 50 amount: $

51	**Total Deductions for Debt Payment.** Enter the total of Lines 47 through 50.	$

Subpart D: Total Deductions from Income

52	**Total of all deductions from income.** Enter the total of Lines 38, 46, and 51.	$

Part V. DETERMINATION OF DISPOSABLE INCOME UNDER § 1325(b)(2)

53	**Total current monthly income.** Enter the amount from Line 20.	$
54	**Support income.** Enter the monthly average of any child support payments, foster care payments, or disability payments for a dependent child, reported in Part I, that you received in accordance with applicable nonbankruptcy law, to the extent reasonably necessary to be expended for such child.	$
55	**Qualified retirement deductions.** Enter the monthly total of (a) all amounts withheld by your employer from wages as contributions for qualified retirement plans, as specified in § 541(b)(7) and (b) all required repayments of loans from retirement plans, as specified in § 362(b)(19).	$
56	**Total of all deductions allowed under § 707(b)(2).** Enter the amount from Line 52.	$
57	**Deduction for special circumstances.** If there are special circumstances that justify additional expenses for which there is no reasonable alternative, describe the special circumstances and the resulting expenses in lines a-c below. If necessary, list additional entries on a separate page. Total the expenses and enter the total in Line 57. **You must provide your case trustee with documentation of these expenses and you must provide a detailed explanation of the special circumstances that make such expenses necessary and reasonable.**	

	Nature of special circumstances	Amount of expense
a.		$
b.		$
c.		$
		Total: Add Lines a, b, and c

Line 57 amount: $

B 22C (Official Form 22C) (Chapter 13) (04/13)

58	**Total adjustments to determine disposable income.** Add the amounts on Lines 54, 55, 56, and 57 and enter the result.	$
59	**Monthly Disposable Income Under § 1325(b)(2).** Subtract Line 58 from Line 53 and enter the result.	$

Part VI: ADDITIONAL EXPENSE CLAIMS

60 **Other Expenses.** List and describe any monthly expenses, not otherwise stated in this form, that are required for the health and welfare of you and your family and that you contend should be an additional deduction from your current monthly income under § 707(b)(2)(A)(ii)(I). If necessary, list additional sources on a separate page. All figures should reflect your average monthly expense for each item. Total the expenses.

	Expense Description	Monthly Amount
a.		$
b.		$
c.		$
	Total: Add Lines a, b, and c	$

Part VII: VERIFICATION

61 I declare under penalty of perjury that the information provided in this statement is true and correct. *(If this is a joint case, both debtors must sign.)*

Date: ____________________ Signature: ____________________
(Debtor)

Date: ____________________ Signature: ____________________
(Joint Debtor, if any)

Bankruptcy Form 22C

(As added Oct. 17, 2005; Oct. 1, 2006; April 1, 2007; Jan. 1, 2008; April 1, 2010; April 1, 2013.)

Form 22C-1. Chapter 13 Statement of Current Monthly Income and Calculation of Commitment Period

Fill in this information to identify your case:

Debtor 1 ______ First Name Middle Name Last Name

Debtor 2 (Spouse, if filing) ______ First Name Middle Name Last Name

United States Bankruptcy Court for the: ______ District of ______

Case number (If known) ______

Check as directed in lines 17 and 21:

According to the calculations required by this Statement:

☐ 1. Disposable income is not determined under 11 U.S.C. § 1325(b)(3).

☐ 2. Disposable income is determined under 11 U.S.C. § 1325(b)(3).

☐ 3. The commitment period is 3 years.

☐ 4. The commitment period is 5 years.

☐ Check if this is an amended filing

Official Form B 22C1

Chapter 13 Statement of Your Current Monthly Income and Calculation of Commitment Period

12/14

Be as complete and accurate as possible. If two married people are filing together, both are equally responsible for being accurate. If more space is needed, attach a separate sheet to this form. Include the line number to which the additional information applies. On the top of any additional pages, write your name and case number (if known).

Part 1: Calculate Your Average Monthly Income

1. **What is your marital and filing status?** Check one only.

   ☐ **Not married.** Fill out Column A, lines 2-11.

   ☐ **Married.** Fill out both Columns A and B, lines 2-11.

Fill in the average monthly income that you received from all sources, derived during the 6 full months before you file this bankruptcy case. 11 U.S.C. § 101(10A). For example, if you are filing on September 15, the 6-month period would be March 1 through August 31. If the amount of your monthly income varied during the 6 months, add the income for all 6 months and divide the total by 6. Fill in the result. Do not include any income amount more than once. For example, if both spouses own the same rental property, put the income from that property in one column only. If you have nothing to report for any line, write $0 in the space.

		Column A Debtor 1	Column B Debtor 2 or non-filing spouse
2. **Your gross wages, salary, tips, bonuses, overtime, and commissions** (before all payroll deductions).		$______	$______
3. **Alimony and maintenance payments.** Do not include payments from a spouse if Column B is filled in.		$______	$______
4. **All amounts from any source which are regularly paid for household expenses of you or your dependents, including child support.** Include regular contributions from an unmarried partner, members of your household, your dependents, parents, and roommates. Include regular contributions from a spouse only if Column B is not filled in. Do not include payments you listed on line 3.		$______	$______
5. **Net income from operating a business, profession, or farm**			
Gross receipts (before all deductions)	$______		
Ordinary and necessary operating expenses	− $______		
Net monthly income from a business, profession, or farm	$______ Copy here➔	$______	$______
6. **Net income from rental and other real property**			
Gross receipts (before all deductions)	$______		
Ordinary and necessary operating expenses	− $______		
Net monthly income from rental or other real property	$______ Copy here➔	$______	$______

Debtor 1 ______________________________ Case number (if known) ______________
First Name Middle Name Last Name

	Column A Debtor 1	Column B Debtor 2 or non-filing spouse
7. **Interest, dividends, and royalties**	$________	$________
8. **Unemployment compensation**	$________	$________

Do not enter the amount if you contend that the amount received was a benefit under the Social Security Act. Instead, list it here:

For you .... $________

For your spouse .... $________

9. **Pension or retirement income.** Do not include any amount received that was a benefit under the Social Security Act.	$________	$________

10. **Income from all other sources not listed above.** Specify the source and amount. Do not include any benefits received under the Social Security Act or payments received as a victim of a war crime, a crime against humanity, or international or domestic terrorism. If necessary, list other sources on a separate page and put the total on line 10c.

10a. ______________________________	$________	$________
10b. ______________________________	$________	$________
10c. Total amounts from separate pages, if any.	+ $________	+ $________

11. **Calculate your total average monthly income.** Add lines 2 through 10 for each column. Then add the total for Column A to the total for Column B. $________ + $________ = $________ Total average monthly income

Part 2: Determine How to Measure Your Deductions from Income

12. **Copy your total average monthly income from line 11.** .... $________

13. **Calculate the marital adjustment.** Check one:

☐ You are not married. Fill in 0 in line 13d.

☐ You are married and your spouse is filing with you. Fill in 0 in line 13d.

☐ You are married and your spouse is not filing with you.

Fill in the amount of the income listed in line 11, Column B, that was NOT regularly paid for the household expenses of you or your dependents, such as payment of the spouse's tax liability or the spouse's support of someone other than you or your dependents.

In lines 13a-c, specify the basis for excluding this income and the amount of income devoted to each purpose. If necessary, list additional adjustments on a separate page.

If this adjustment does not apply, enter 0 on line 13d.

13a. ______________________________ $________

13b. ______________________________ $________

13c. ______________________________ + $________

13d. Total .... $________ Copy here. → 13d. − ________

14. **Your current monthly income.** Subtract line 13d from line 12. 14. $________

15. **Calculate your current monthly income for the year.** Follow these steps:

15a. Copy line 14 here → .... 15a. $________

Multiply line 15a by 12 (the number of months in a year). x 12

15b. The result is your current monthly income for the year for this part of the form. 15b. $________

Debtor 1 ______ First Name Middle Name Last Name Case number (if known) ______

16. **Calculate the median family income that applies to you.** Follow these steps:

16a. Fill in the state in which you live. ______

16b. Fill in the number of people in your household. ______

16c. Fill in the median family income for your state and size of household. .... 16c. $______
To find a list of applicable median income amounts, go online using the link specified in the separate instructions for this form. This list may also be available at the bankruptcy clerk's office.

17. **How do the lines compare?**

17a. ☐ Line 15b is less than or equal to line 16c. On the top of page 1 of this form, check box 1, *Disposable income is not determined under 11 U.S.C. § 1325(b)(3)*. **Go to Part 3.** Do NOT fill out *Calculation of Disposable Income* (Official Form 22C–2).

17b. ☐ Line 15b is more than line 16c. On the top of page 1 of this form, check box 2, *Disposable income is determined under 11 U.S.C. § 1325(b)(3)*. **Go to Part 3 and fill out Calculation of Disposable Income (Official Form 22C–2).** On line 39 of that form, copy your current monthly income from line 14 above.

Part 3: Calculate Your Commitment Period Under 11 U.S.C. §1325(b)(4)

18. **Copy your total average monthly income from line 11.** .... 18. $______

19. **Deduct the marital adjustment if it applies.** If you are married, your spouse is not filing with you, and you contend that calculating the commitment period under 11 U.S.C. § 1325(b)(4) allows you to deduct part of your spouse's income, copy the amount from line 13d.
If the marital adjustment does not apply, fill in 0 on line 19a. 19a. – $______

Subtract line 19a from line 18. 19b. $______

20. **Calculate your current monthly income for the year.** Follow these steps:

20a. Copy line 19b.. .... 20a. $______

Multiply by 12 (the number of months in a year). x 12

20b. The result is your current monthly income for the year for this part of the form. 20b. $______

20c. Copy the median family income for your state and size of household from line 16c. .... $______

21. **How do the lines compare?**

☐ Line 20b is less than line 20c. Unless otherwise ordered by the court, on the top of page 1 of this form, check box 3, *The commitment period is 3 years*. Go to Part 4.

☐ Line 20b is more than or equal to line 20c. Unless otherwise ordered by the court, on the top of page 1 of this form, check box 4, *The commitment period is 5 years*. Go to Part 4.

Part 4: Sign Below

By signing here, under penalty of perjury I declare that the information on this statement and in any attachments is true and correct.

✘ ______ Signature of Debtor 1 ✘ ______ Signature of Debtor 2

Date ______ MM / DD / YYYY Date ______ MM / DD / YYYY

If you checked 17a, do NOT fill out or file Form 22C–2.

If you checked 17b, fill out Form 22C–2 and file it with this form. On line 39 of that form, copy your current monthly income from line 14 above.

Official Form B 22C1 **Chapter 13 Statement of Your Current Monthly Income and Calculation of Commitment Period** page 3

(As added Dec. 14, 2014.)

Form 22C-2. Chapter 13 Calculation of Disposable Income

Fill in this information to identify your case:

Debtor 1 ______ First Name ______ Middle Name ______ Last Name

Debtor 2 (Spouse, if filing) ______ First Name ______ Middle Name ______ Last Name

United States Bankruptcy Court for the: ______ District of ______

Case number (If known) ______

☐ Check if this is an amended filing

Official Form B 22C2

Chapter 13 Calculation of Your Disposable Income

12/14

To fill out this form, you will need your completed copy of *Chapter 13 Statement of Your Current Monthly Income and Calculation of Commitment Period* (Official Form 22C–1).

Be as complete and accurate as possible. If two married people are filing together, both are equally responsible for being accurate. If more space is needed, attach a separate sheet to this form. Include the line number to which the additional information applies. On the top of any additional pages, write your name and case number (if known).

Part 1: Calculate Your Deductions from Your Income

The Internal Revenue Service (IRS) issues National and Local Standards for certain expense amounts. Use these amounts to answer the questions in lines 6-15. To find the IRS standards, go online using the link specified in the separate instructions for this form. This information may also be available at the bankruptcy clerk's office.

Deduct the expense amounts set out in lines 6-15 regardless of your actual expense. In later parts of the form, you will use some of your actual expenses if they are higher than the standards. Do not include any operating expenses that you subtracted from income in lines 5 and 6 of Form 22C–1, and do not deduct any amounts that you subtracted from your spouse's income in line 13 of Form 22C–1.

If your expenses differ from month to month, enter the average expense.

Note: Line numbers 1-4 are not used in this form. These numbers apply to information required by a similar form used in chapter 7 cases.

5. **The number of people used in determining your deductions from income**
Fill in the number of people who could be claimed as exemptions on your federal income tax return, plus the number of any additional dependents whom you support. This number may be different from the number of people in your household. ☐

National Standards You must use the IRS National Standards to answer the questions in lines 6-7.

6. **Food, clothing, and other items:** Using the number of people you entered in line 5 and the IRS National Standards, fill in the dollar amount for food, clothing, and other items. $______

7. **Out-of-pocket health care allowance:** Using the number of people you entered in line 5 and the IRS National Standards, fill in the dollar amount for out-of-pocket health care. The number of people is split into two categories–people who are under 65 and people who are 65 or older–because older people have a higher IRS allowance for health care costs. If your actual expenses are higher than this IRS amount, you may deduct the additional amount on line 22.

Debtor 1 ______________________ Case number (if known) ______________________
First Name Middle Name Last Name

People who are under 65 years of age

7a. Out-of-pocket health care allowance per person $________

7b. Number of people who are under 65 X______

7c. Subtotal. Multiply line 7a by line 7b. $________ **Copy line 7c here➔** $________

People who are 65 years of age or older

7d. Out-of-pocket health care allowance per person $________

7e. Number of people who are 65 or older X______

7f. Subtotal. Multiply line 7d by line 7e. $________ **Copy line 7f here➔** + $________

7g. **Total**. Add lines 7c and 7f. .... $________ **Copy total here➔** ....7g. $________

Local Standards You must use the IRS Local Standards to answer the questions in lines 8-15.

Based on information from the IRS, the U.S. Trustee Program has divided the IRS Local Standard for housing for bankruptcy purposes into two parts:

- **Housing and utilities – Insurance and operating expenses**
- **Housing and utilities – Mortgage or rent expenses**

To answer the questions in lines 8-9, use the U.S. Trustee Program chart. To find the chart, go online using the link specified in the separate instructions for this form. This chart may also be available at the bankruptcy clerk's office.

8. **Housing and utilities – Insurance and operating expenses:** Using the number of people you entered in line 5, fill in the dollar amount listed for your county for insurance and operating expenses. $________

9. **Housing and utilities – Mortgage or rent expenses:**

9a. Using the number of people you entered in line 5, fill in the dollar amount listed for your county for mortgage or rent expenses. $________

9b. Total average monthly payment for all mortgages and other debts secured by your home.

To calculate the total average monthly payment, add all amounts that are contractually due to each secured creditor in the 60 months after you file for bankruptcy. Next divide by 60.

Name of the creditor	Average monthly payment
______________________	$________
______________________	$________
______________________	+ $________

9b. Total average monthly payment .... $________ **Copy line 9b here➔** – $________ Repeat this amount on line 33a.

9c. Net mortgage or rent expense.

Subtract line 9b (*total average monthly payment*) from line 9a (*mortgage or rent expense*). If this number is less than $0, enter $0. $________ **Copy 9c here➔** $________

10. **If you claim that the U.S. Trustee Program's division of the IRS Local Standard for housing is incorrect and affects the calculation of your monthly expenses, fill in any additional amount you claim.** $________

Explain why: ____

Debtor 1 ______________________ First Name Middle Name Last Name Case number (if known)______________________

11. **Local transportation expenses:** Check the number of vehicles for which you claim an ownership or operating expense.

☐ 0. Go to line 14.
☐ 1. Go to line 12.
☐ 2 or more. Go to line 12.

12. **Vehicle operation expense:** Using the IRS Local Standards and the number of vehicles for which you claim the operating expenses, fill in the *Operating Costs* that apply for your Census region or metropolitan statistical area. $______

13. **Vehicle ownership or lease expense:** Using the IRS Local Standards, calculate the net ownership or lease expense for each vehicle below. You may not claim the expense if you do not make any loan or lease payments on the vehicle. In addition, you may not claim the expense for more than two vehicles.

Vehicle 1 **Describe Vehicle 1:** ______________________

13a. Ownership or leasing costs using IRS Local Standard 13a. $______

13b. Average monthly payment for all debts secured by Vehicle 1.
Do not include costs for leased vehicles.

To calculate the average monthly payment here and on line 13e, add all amounts that are contractually due to each secured creditor in the 60 months after you file for bankruptcy. Then divide by 60.

Name of each creditor for Vehicle 1	Average monthly payment
______________________	$______

Copy13b here➔ – $______ Repeat this amount on line 33b.

13c. Net Vehicle 1 ownership or lease expense
Subtract line 13b from line 13a. If this number is less than $0, enter $0. 13c. $______ **Copy net Vehicle 1 expense here➔** $______

Vehicle 2 **Describe Vehicle 2:** ______________________

13d. Ownership or leasing costs using IRS Local Standard 13d. $______

13e. Average monthly payment for all debts secured by Vehicle 2.
Do not include costs for leased vehicles.

Name of each creditor for Vehicle 2	Average monthly payment
______________________	$______

Copy here➔ – $______ Repeat this amount on line 33c.

13f. Net Vehicle 2 ownership or lease expense
Subtract line 13e from 13d. If this number is less than $0, enter $0. 13f. $______ **Copy net Vehicle 2 expense here ➔** $______

14. **Public transportation expense**: If you claimed 0 vehicles in line 11, using the IRS Local Standards, fill in the *Public Transportation* expense allowance regardless of whether you use public transportation. $______

15. **Additional public transportation expense:** If you claimed 1 or more vehicles in line 11 and if you claim that you may also deduct a public transportation expense, you may fill in what you believe is the appropriate expense, but you may not claim more than the IRS Local Standard for *Public Transportation*. $______

Debtor 1 ____________________________________ Case number (if known) ____________________
First Name Middle Name Last Name

Other Necessary Expenses In addition to the expense deductions listed above, you are allowed your monthly expenses for the following IRS categories.

16. **Taxes:** The total monthly amount that you actually pay for federal, state and local taxes, such as income taxes, self-employment taxes, social security taxes, and Medicare taxes. You may include the monthly amount withheld from your pay for these taxes. However, if you expect to receive a tax refund, you must divide the expected refund by 12 and subtract that number from the total monthly amount that is withheld to pay for taxes. $______

    Do not include real estate, sales, or use taxes.

17. **Involuntary deductions:** The total monthly payroll deductions that your job requires, such as retirement contributions, union dues, and uniform costs.

    Do not include amounts that are not required by your job, such as voluntary 401(k) contributions or payroll savings. $______

18. **Life insurance:** The total monthly premiums that you pay for your own term life insurance. If two married people are filing together, include payments that you make for your spouse's term life insurance.

    Do not include premiums for life insurance on your dependents, for a non-filing spouse's life insurance, or for any form of life insurance other than term. $______

19. **Court-ordered payments:** The total monthly amount that you pay as required by the order of a court or administrative agency, such as spousal or child support payments. $______

    Do not include payments on past due obligations for spousal or child support. You will list these obligations in line 35.

20. **Education:** The total monthly amount that you pay for education that is either required:
    - as a condition for your job, or
    - for your physically or mentally challenged dependent child if no public education is available for similar services. $______

21. **Childcare:** The total monthly amount that you pay for childcare, such as babysitting, daycare, nursery, and preschool. Do not include payments for any elementary or secondary school education. $______

22. **Additional health care expenses, excluding insurance costs:** The monthly amount that you pay for health care that is required for the health and welfare of you or your dependents and that is not reimbursed by insurance or paid by a health savings account. Include only the amount that is more than the total entered in line 7. $______

    Payments for health insurance or health savings accounts should be listed only in line 25.

23. **Optional telephones and telephone services:** The total monthly amount that you pay for telecommunication services for you and your dependents, such as pagers, call waiting, caller identification, special long distance, or business cell phone service, to the extent necessary for your health and welfare or that of your dependents or for the production of income, if it is not reimbursed by your employer. + $______

    Do not include payments for basic home telephone, internet or cell phone service. Do not include self-employment expenses, such as those reported on line 5 of Form 22C-1, or any amount you previously deducted.

24. **Add all of the expenses allowed under the IRS expense allowances.** Add lines 6 through 23. $______

Additional Expense Deductions These are additional deductions allowed by the Means Test. *Note:* Do not include any expense allowances listed in lines 6-24.

25. **Health insurance, disability insurance, and health savings account expenses.** The monthly expenses for health insurance, disability insurance, and health savings accounts that are reasonably necessary for yourself, your spouse, or your dependents.

    Health insurance $______

    Disability insurance $______

    Health savings account + $______

    Total $______ Copy total here➔ .... $______

    Do you actually spend this total amount?

    ☐ No. How much do you actually spend? $______

    ☐ Yes

26. **Continuing contributions to the care of household or family members.** The actual monthly expenses that you will continue to pay for the reasonable and necessary care and support of an elderly, chronically ill, or disabled member of your household or member of your immediate family who is unable to pay for such expenses. $______

27. **Protection against family violence.** The reasonably necessary monthly expenses that you incur to maintain the safety of you and your family under the Family Violence Prevention and Services Act or other federal laws that apply. $______

    By law, the court must keep the nature of these expenses confidential.

Debtor 1 ______ First Name Middle Name Last Name Case number (if known) ______

28. **Additional home energy costs.** Your home energy costs are included in your non-mortgage housing and utilities allowance on line 8.

If you believe that you have home energy costs that are more than the home energy costs included in the non-mortgage housing and utilities allowance, then fill in the excess amount of home energy costs. $______

You must give your case trustee documentation of your actual expenses, and you must show that the additional amount claimed is reasonable and necessary.

29. **Education expenses for dependent children who are younger than 18.** The monthly expenses (not more than $156.25* per child) that you pay for your dependent children who are younger than 18 years old to attend a private or public elementary or secondary school. $______

You must give your case trustee documentation of your actual expenses, and you must explain why the amount claimed is reasonable and necessary and not already accounted for in lines 6-23.

* Subject to adjustment on 4/01/16, and every 3 years after that for cases begun on or after the date of adjustment.

30. **Additional food and clothing expense.** The monthly amount by which your actual food and clothing expenses are higher than the combined food and clothing allowances in the IRS National Standards. That amount cannot be more than 5% of the food and clothing allowances in the IRS National Standards. $______

To find a chart showing the maximum additional allowance, go online using the link specified in the separate instructions for this form. This chart may also be available at the bankruptcy clerk's office.

You must show that the additional amount claimed is reasonable and necessary.

31. **Continuing charitable contributions.** The amount that you will continue to contribute in the form of cash or financial instruments to a religious or charitable organization. 11 U.S.C. § 548(d)3 and (4). + ______

Do not include any amount more than 15% of your gross monthly income.

32. **Add all of the additional expense deductions.** $______

Add lines 25 through 31.

Deductions for Debt Payment

33. **For debts that are secured by an interest in property that you own, including home mortgages, vehicle loans, and other secured debt, fill in lines 33a through 33g.**

To calculate the total average monthly payment, add all amounts that are contractually due to each secured creditor in the 60 months after you file for bankruptcy. Then divide by 60.

			Average monthly payment
Mortgages on your home			
33a. Copy line 9b here →			$______
Loans on your first two vehicles			
33b. Copy line 13b here. →			$______
33c. Copy line 13e here. →			$______
Name of each creditor for other secured debt	**Identify property that secures the debt**	**Does payment include taxes or insurance?**	
33d. ______	______	☐ No ☐ Yes	$______
33e. ______	______	☐ No ☐ Yes	$______
33f. ______	______	☐ No ☐ Yes	+ $______
33g. Total average monthly payment. Add lines 33a through 33f.			$______

Copy total here → $______

Debtor 1 ______ First Name Middle Name Last Name Case number (if known)______

34. **Are any debts that you listed in line 33 secured by your primary residence, a vehicle, or other property necessary for your support or the support of your dependents?**

☐ No. Go to line 35.
☐ Yes. State any amount that you must pay to a creditor, in addition to the payments listed in line 33, to keep possession of your property (called the *cure amount*). Next, divide by 60 and fill in the information below.

Name of the creditor	Identify property that secures the debt	Total cure amount		Monthly cure amount
______	______	$______	÷ 60 =	$______
______	______	$______	÷ 60 =	$______
______	______	$______	÷ 60 =	+ $______

Total $______ Copy total here➔ $______

35. **Do you owe any priority claims—such as a priority tax, child support, or alimony— that are past due as of the filing date of your bankruptcy case?** 11 U.S.C. § 507.

☐ No. Go to line 36.
☐ Yes. Fill in the total amount of all of these priority claims. Do not include current or ongoing priority claims, such as those you listed in line 19.

Total amount of all past-due priority claims. .... $______ ÷ 60 $______

36. **Projected monthly Chapter 13 plan payment** $______

Current multiplier for your district as stated on the list issued by the Administrative Office of the United States Courts (for districts in Alabama and North Carolina) or by the Executive Office for United States Trustees (for all other districts).

To find a list of district multipliers that includes your district, go online using the link specified in the separate instructions for this form. This list may also be available at the bankruptcy clerk's office. x ______

Average monthly administrative expense $______ Copy total here➔ $______

37. **Add all of the deductions for debt payment.** Add lines 33g through 36. $______

Total Deductions from Income

38. **Add all of the allowed deductions.**

Copy line 24, *All of the expenses allowed under IRS expense allowances*.......... $______

Copy line 32, *All of the additional expense deductions*.......... $______

Copy line 37, *All of the deductions for debt payment*.......... + $______

Total deductions $______ Copy total here ➔ $______

Debtor 1 ______ First Name Middle Name Last Name Case number (if known) ______

Part 2: Determine Your Disposable Income Under 11 U.S.C. § 1325(b)(2)

39. **Copy your total current monthly income from line 14 of Form 22C-1, *Chapter 13 Statement of Your Current Monthly Income and Calculation of Commitment Period.*** .... $______

40. **Fill in any reasonably necessary income you receive for support for dependent children.** The monthly average of any child support payments, foster care payments, or disability payments for a dependent child, reported in Part I of Form 22C-1, that you received in accordance with applicable nonbankruptcy law to the extent reasonably necessary to be expended for such child. $______

41. **Fill in all qualified retirement deductions.** The monthly total of all amounts that your employer withheld from wages as contributions for qualified retirement plans, as specified in 11 U.S.C. § 541(b)(7) plus all required repayments of loans from retirement plans, as specified in 11 U.S.C. § 362(b)(19). $______

42. **Total of all deductions allowed under 11 U.S.C. § 707(b)(2)(A).** Copy line 38 here .... → $______

43. **Deduction for special circumstances.** If special circumstances justify additional expenses and you have no reasonable alternative, describe the special circumstances and their expenses. You must give your case trustee a detailed explanation of the special circumstances and documentation for the expenses.

Describe the special circumstances	Amount of expense
43a. ______	$______
43b. ______	$______
43c. ______	+ $______
43d. **Total**. Add lines 43a through 43c	$______

Copy 43d here → + $______

44. **Total adjustments.** Add lines 40 through 43d. .... → $______ Copy total here → − $______

45. **Calculate your monthly disposable income under § 1325(b)(2).** Subtract line 44 from line 39. $______

Part 3: Change in Income or Expenses

46. **Change in income or expenses.** If the income in Form 22C-1 or the expenses you reported in this form have changed or are virtually certain to change after the date you filed your bankruptcy petition and during the time your case will be open, fill in the information below. For example, if the wages reported increased after you filed your petition, check 22C-1 in the first column, enter line 2 in the second column, explain why the wages increased, fill in when the increase occurred, and fill in the amount of the increase.

Form	Line	Reason for change	Date of change	Increase or decrease?	Amount of change
☐ 22C–1 ☐ 22C–2	___	______	______	☐ Increase ☐ Decrease	$______
☐ 22C–1 ☐ 22C–2	___	______	______	☐ Increase ☐ Decrease	$______
☐ 22C–1 ☐ 22C–2	___	______	______	☐ Increase ☐ Decrease	$______
☐ 22C–1 ☐ 22C–2	___	______	______	☐ Increase ☐ Decrease	$______

Debtor 1 ______ First Name Middle Name Last Name Case number (if known)______

Part 4: **Sign Below**

By signing here, under penalty of perjury you declare that the information on this statement and in any attachments is true and correct.

✘ ______ Signature of Debtor 1

✘ ______ Signature of Debtor 2

Date ______ MM / DD / YYYY

Date ______ MM / DD / YYYY

(As added Dec. 14, 2014.)

Form 23. Debtor's Certification of Completion of Postpetition Instructional Course Concerning Personal Financial Management

B 23 (Official Form 23) (12/13)

UNITED STATES BANKRUPTCY COURT

In re ______________________________, Case No. ________________
Debtor

Chapter __________

DEBTOR'S CERTIFICATION OF COMPLETION OF POSTPETITION INSTRUCTIONAL COURSE CONCERNING PERSONAL FINANCIAL MANAGEMENT

This form should not be filed if an approved provider of a postpetition instructional course concerning personal financial management has already notified the court of the debtor's completion of the course. Otherwise, every individual debtor in a chapter 7 or a chapter 13 case or in a chapter 11 case in which § 1141(d)(3) applies must file this certification. If a joint petition is filed and this certification is required, each spouse must complete and file a separate certification. Complete one of the following statements and file by the deadline stated below:

☐ I, ________________________________, the debtor in the above-styled case, hereby
(Printed Name of Debtor)
certify that on ______________ (Date), I completed an instructional course in personal financial management provided by ________________________________, an approved personal financial
(Name of Provider)
management provider.

Certificate No. (if any):_________________________.

☐ I, ________________________________, the debtor in the above-styled case, hereby
(Printed Name of Debtor)
certify that no personal financial management course is required because of *[Check the appropriate box.]*:

☐ Incapacity or disability, as defined in 11 U.S.C. § 109(h);

☐ Active military duty in a military combat zone; or

☐ Residence in a district in which the United States trustee (or bankruptcy administrator) has determined that the approved instructional courses are not adequate at this time to serve the additional individuals who would otherwise be required to complete such courses.

Signature of Debtor: ______________________________

Date: ___________

Instructions: Use this form only to certify whether you completed a course in personal financial management and only if your course provider has not already notified the court of your completion of the course. (Fed. R. Bankr. P. 1007(b)(7).) Do NOT use this form to file the certificate given to you by your prepetition credit counseling provider and do NOT include with the petition when filing your case.

Filing Deadlines: In a chapter 7 case, file within 60 days of the first date set for the meeting of creditors under § 341 of the Bankruptcy Code. In a chapter 11 or 13 case, file no later than the last payment made by the debtor as required by the plan or the filing of a motion for a discharge under § 1141(d)(5)(B) or § 1328(b) of the Code. (See Fed. R. Bankr. P. 1007(c).)

(As added Oct. 17, 2005; Oct. 1, 2006; Dec. 1, 2007; Dec. 1, 2008; Dec. 1, 2013.)

Form 24. Certification to Court of Appeals By All Parties

Official Form 24 (12/07)

[Caption as described in Fed. R. Bankr. P. 7010 or 9004(b), as applicable.]

CERTIFICATION TO COURT OF APPEALS BY ALL PARTIES

A notice of appeal having been filed in the above-styled matter on ________ *[Date]*, ________________, ________________, and ________________, *[Names of all the appellants and all the appellees, if any]* , who are all the appellants [and all the appellees] hereby certify to the court under 28 U.S.C. § 158(d)(2)(A) that a circumstance specified in 28 U.S.C. § 158(d)(2) exists as stated below.

Leave to appeal in this matter ☐ is ☐ is not required under 28 U.S.C. § 158(a).

[If from a final judgment, order, or decree] This certification arises in an appeal from a final judgment, order, or decree of the United States Bankruptcy Court for the ________ District of ________ entered on ________ *[Date]*.

[If from an interlocutory order or decree] This certification arises in an appeal from an interlocutory order or decree, and the parties hereby request leave to appeal as required by 28 U.S.C. § 158(a).

[The certification shall contain one or more of the following statements, as is appropriate to the circumstances.]

The judgment, order, or decree involves a question of law as to which there is no controlling decision of the court of appeals for this circuit or of the Supreme Court of the United States, or involves a matter of public importance.

Or

The judgment, order, or decree involves a question of law requiring resolution of conflicting decisions.

Or

An immediate appeal from the judgment, order, or decree may materially advance the progress of the case or proceeding in which the appeal is taken.

[The parties may include or attach the information specified in Rule 8001(f)(3)(C).]

Signed: *[If there are more than two signatories, all must sign and provide the information requested below. Attach additional signed sheets if needed.]*

________________	________________
Attorney for Appellant (or Appellant, if not represented by an attorney)	Attorney for Appellant (or Appellant if not represented by an attorney)
________________	________________
Printed Name of Signer	Printed Name of Signer
________________	________________
________________	________________
Address	Address
________________	________________
Telephone No.	Telephone No.
________________	________________
Date	Date

(As added Oct. 17, 2005; Dec. 1, 2007.)

Form 25A. Plan of Reorganization in Small Business Case Under Chapter 11

B25A (Official Form 25A) (12/11)

United States Bankruptcy Court
_________________ District of _____________

In re_________________________, Case No. _____________________
Debtor
Small Business Case under Chapter 11

[NAME OF PROPONENT]'S PLAN OF REORGANIZATION, DATED [INSERT DATE]

ARTICLE I
SUMMARY

This Plan of Reorganization (the "Plan") under chapter 11 of the Bankruptcy Code (the "Code") proposes to pay creditors of [insert the name of the debtor] (the "Debtor") from [specify sources of payment, such as an infusion of capital, loan proceeds, sale of assets, cash flow from operations, or future income].

This Plan provides for _________ classes of secured claims; _____ classes of unsecured claims; and ______ classes of equity security holders. Unsecured creditors holding allowed claims will receive distributions, which the proponent of this Plan has valued at approximately __cents on the dollar. This Plan also provides for the payment of administrative and priority claims [if payment is not in full on the effective date of this Plan with respect to any such claim (to the extent permitted by the Code or the claimant's agreement), identify such claim and briefly summarize the proposed treatment.]

All creditors and equity security holders should refer to Articles III through VI of this Plan for information regarding the precise treatment of their claim. A disclosure statement that provides more detailed information regarding this Plan and the rights of creditors and equity security holders has been circulated with this Plan. **Your rights may be affected. You should read these papers carefully and discuss them with your attorney, if you have one. (If you do not have an attorney, you may wish to consult one.)**

ARTICLE II
CLASSIFICATION OF CLAIMS AND INTERESTS

2.01 Class 1. All allowed claims entitled to priority under § 507 of the Code (except administrative expense claims under § 507(a)(2), ["gap" period claims in an involuntary case under § 507(a)(3),] and priority tax claims under § 507(a)(8)).

2.02 Class 2. The claim of ________________________, to the extent allowed as a secured claim under § 506 of the Code.

[Add other classes of secured creditors, if any. Note: Section 1129(a)(9)(D) of the Code provides that a secured tax claim which would otherwise meet the description of a priority tax claim under § 507(a)(8) of the Code is to be paid in the same manner and over the same period as prescribed in § 507(a)(8).]

2.03 Class 3. All unsecured claims allowed under § 502 of the Code.

[Add other classes of unsecured claims, if any.]

2.04 Class 4 . Equity interests of the Debtor. [If the Debtor is an individual, change this heading to "The interests of the individual Debtor in property of the estate."]

ARTICLE III
TREATMENT OF ADMINISTRATIVE EXPENSE CLAIMS, U.S. TRUSTEES FEES, AND PRIORITY TAX CLAIMS

3.01 Unclassified Claims. Under section §1123(a)(1), administrative expense claims, ["gap" period claims in an involuntary case allowed under § 502(f) of the Code,] and priority tax claims are not in classes.

3.02 Administrative Expense Claims. Each holder of an administrative expense claim allowed under § 503 of the Code [, and a "gap" claim in an involuntary case allowed under § 502(f) of the Code,] will be paid in full on the effective date of this Plan (as defined in Article VII), in cash, or upon such other terms as may be agreed upon by the holder of the claim and the Debtor.

3.03 Priority Tax Claims. Each holder of a priority tax claim will be paid [specify terms of treatment consistent with § 1129(a)(9)(C) of the Code].

3.04 United States Trustee Fees. All fees required to be paid by 28 U.S.C. §1930(a)(6) (U.S. Trustee Fees) will accrue and be timely paid until the case is closed, dismissed, or converted to another chapter of the Code. Any U.S. Trustee Fees owed on or before the effective date of this Plan will be paid on the effective date.

ARTICLE IV
TREATMENT OF CLAIMS AND INTERESTS UNDER THE PLAN

4.01 Claims and interests shall be treated as follows under this Plan:

Class	Impairment	Treatment
Class 1 - Priority Claims	[State whether impaired or unimpaired.]	[Insert treatment of priority claims in this Class, including the form, amount and timing of distribution, if any. For example: "Class 1 is unimpaired by this Plan, and each holder of a Class 1 Priority Claim will be paid in full, in cash, upon the later of the effective date of this Plan as defined in Article VII, or the date on which such claim is allowed by a final non-appealable order. Except: ________."]
Class 2 – Secured Claim of [Insert name of secured creditor.]	[State whether impaired or unimpaired.]	[Insert treatment of secured claim in this Class, including the form, amount and timing of distribution, if any.] [Add class[es] of secured claims if applicable]
Class 3 - General Unsecured Creditors	[State whether impaired or unimpaired.]	[Insert treatment of unsecured creditors in this Class, including the form, amount and timing of distribution, if any.] [Add administrative convenience class if applicable]
Class 4 - Equity Security Holders of the Debtor	[State whether impaired or unimpaired.]	[Insert treatment of equity security holders in this Class, including the form, amount and timing of distribution, if any.]

ARTICLE V
ALLOWANCE AND DISALLOWANCE OF CLAIMS

5.01 Disputed Claim. A disputed claim is a claim that has not been allowed or disallowed [by a final non-appealable order], and as to which either: (i) a proof of claim has been filed or deemed filed, and the Debtor or another party in interest has filed an objection; or (ii) no proof of claim has been filed, and the Debtor has scheduled such claim as disputed, contingent, or unliquidated.

5.02 Delay of Distribution on a Disputed Claim. No distribution will be made on account of a disputed claim unless such claim is allowed [by a final non-appealable order].

5.03 Settlement of Disputed Claims. The Debtor will have the power and authority to settle and compromise a disputed claim with court approval and compliance with Rule 9019 of the Federal Rules of Bankruptcy Procedure.

ARTICLE VI
PROVISIONS FOR EXECUTORY CONTRACTS AND UNEXPIRED LEASES

6.01 Assumed Executory Contracts and Unexpired Leases.

(a) The Debtor assumes the following executory contracts and/or unexpired leases effective upon the [Insert "effective date of this Plan as provided in Article VII," "the date of the entry of the order confirming this Plan," or other applicable date]:

[List assumed executory contracts and/or unexpired leases.]

(b) The Debtor will be conclusively deemed to have rejected all executory contracts and/or unexpired leases not expressly assumed under section 6.01(a) above, or before the date of the order confirming this Plan, upon the [Insert "effective date of this Plan," "the date of the entry of the order confirming this Plan," or other applicable date]. A proof of a claim arising from the rejection of an executory contract or unexpired lease under this section must be filed no later than __________ (___) days after the date of the order confirming this Plan.

ARTICLE VII
MEANS FOR IMPLEMENTATION OF THE PLAN

[Insert here provisions regarding how the plan will be implemented as required under §1123(a)(5) of the Code. For example, provisions may include those that set out how the plan will be funded, as well as who will be serving as directors, officers or voting trustees of the reorganized debtor.]

ARTICLE VIII
GENERAL PROVISIONS

8.01 Definitions and Rules of Construction. The definitions and rules of construction set forth in §§ 101 and 102 of the Code shall apply when terms defined or construed in the Code are used in this Plan, and they are supplemented by the following definitions: [Insert additional definitions if necessary].

8.02 Effective Date of Plan. The effective date of this Plan is the first business day following the date that is fourteen days after the entry of the order of confirmation. If, however, a stay of the confirmation order is in effect on that date, the effective date will be the first business day after the date on which the stay of the confirmation order expires or is otherwise terminated.

8.03 Severability. If any provision in this Plan is determined to be unenforceable, the determination will in no way limit or affect the enforceability and operative effect of any other provision of this Plan.

8.04 Binding Effect. The rights and obligations of any entity named or referred to in this Plan will be binding upon, and will inure to the benefit of the successors or assigns of such entity.

8.05 Captions. The headings contained in this Plan are for convenience of reference only and do not affect the meaning or interpretation of this Plan.

[8.06 Controlling Effect. Unless a rule of law or procedure is supplied by federal law (including the Code or the Federal Rules of Bankruptcy Procedure), the laws of the State of ___________ govern this Plan and any agreements, documents, and instruments executed in connection with this Plan, except as otherwise provided in this Plan.]

[8.07 Corporate Governance. [If the Debtor is a corporation include provisions required by § 1123(a)(6) of the Code.]]

ARTICLE IX
DISCHARGE

[If the Debtor is not entitled to discharge under 11 U.S.C. § 1141(d)(3) change this heading to **"NO DISCHARGE OF DEBTOR."**]

9.01. **[Option 1 – If Debtor is an individual and § 1141(d)(3) is not applicable]**
Discharge. Confirmation of this Plan does not discharge any debt provided for in this Plan until the court grants a discharge on completion of all payments under this Plan, or as otherwise provided in § 1141(d)(5) of the Code. The Debtor will not be discharged from any debt excepted from discharge under § 523 of the Code, except as provided in Rule 4007(c) of the Federal Rules of Bankruptcy Procedure.

[Option 2 -- If the Debtor is a partnership and section 1141(d)(3) of the Code is not applicable]
Discharge. On the confirmation date of this Plan, the debtor will be discharged from any debt that arose before confirmation of this Plan, subject to the occurrence of the effective date, to the extent specified in § 1141(d)(1)(A) of the Code. The Debtor will not be discharged from any debt imposed by this Plan.

[Option 3 -- If the Debtor is a corporation and § 1141(d)(3) is not applicable]

Discharge. On the confirmation date of this Plan, the debtor will be discharged from any debt that arose before confirmation of this Plan, subject to the occurrence of the effective date, to the extent specified in § 1141(d)(1)(A) of the Code, except that the Debtor will not be discharged of any debt: (i) imposed by this Plan; (ii) of a kind specified in § 1141(d)(6)(A) if a timely complaint was filed in accordance with Rule 4007(c) of the Federal Rules of Bankruptcy Procedure; or (iii) of a kind specified in § 1141(d)(6)(B).

[Option 4 – If § 1141(d)(3) is applicable]

No Discharge. In accordance with § 1141(d)(3) of the Code, the Debtor will not receive any discharge of debt in this bankruptcy case.

ARTICLE X
OTHER PROVISIONS

[Insert other provisions, as applicable.]

Respectfully submitted,

By:______________________________
The Plan Proponent

By:______________________________
Attorney for the Plan Proponent

Form 25A, Instructions (12/08)

Instructions for Small Business Plan of Reorganization Form

BACKGROUND AND GENERAL INSTRUCTIONS

1. This small business chapter 11 plan of reorganization form is promulgated pursuant to § 433 of the Bankruptcy Abuse Prevention and Consumer Protection Act of 2005. It may be used in cases where the debtor (whether an individual or an artificial entity) is a small business debtor under § 101(51D) of the Code. This form is intended to be used in conjunction with the small business chapter 11 disclosure statement form (Official Form 25B). Because the type of debtor and the details of the proposed plan will vary from case to case, this form is intended to provide an illustrative format, rather than a specific prescription for the language or content of a plan in any particular case.
2. Some language in this form appears in brackets. The bracketed language sometimes instructs the plan's proponent to provide certain information and sometimes provides optional or alternative language that should be used when and where appropriate. Proponents should make the necessary insertions and/or delete inapplicable language.

SPECIFIC INSTRUCTIONS

SUMMARY

3. The first article should provide a summary of the debtor's proposed plan. It should describe the manner in which the plan will be consummated and the source of funds for payments to be made under the plan. These sources might include an infusion of capital, loan proceeds, sale of assets, cash flow from operations, or future income. The summary should also describe the treatment of the various classes of claimants under the plan.

CLASSIFICATION OF CLAIMS AND INTERESTS

4. The second article describes each class of claimants that will receive a distribution under the plan. The first class consists of claimants entitled to priority pursuant to § 507 of the Code other than those entitled to priority under § 507(a)(2), (3), or (8). The next class or group of classes consists of creditor(s) with allowed secured claims. Secured creditors are usually classified individually, with each secured creditor being placed in its own separate class. Classes of secured creditors should be added as necessary. Next, unsecured claimants, not entitled to priority, should be classified. The proponent may, to the extent allowed by law, create additional classes of unsecured claims, including an administrative convenience class pursuant to §

1122(b) of the Code. The last class comprises the holders of equity interests in the debtor.

TREATMENT OF ADMINISTRATIVE EXPENSE CLAIMS, U.S. TRUSTEES FEES, AND PRIORITY TAX CLAIMS

5. The treatment of certain claims, such as administrative expense claims, allowed under § 503 of the Code, and priority tax claims, allowed under §507(a)(8) of the Code, is statutorily specified. These claims are not, therefore, placed into classes. Their treatment is described in the third Article.

TREATMENT OF CLAIMS AND INTERESTS UNDER THE PLAN

6. The fourth article specifies the treatment accorded the various classes of claims and interests provided for under the plan.
7. Priority claimants other than those allowed under §§ 503 and 507(a)(8) must be classified and paid in full under the plan unless the claimant agrees otherwise.
8. Each secured creditor is generally placed in its own class, with a particular treatment specified for that class. Section 1129(a)(9)(D) of the Code provides that a secured tax claim which would otherwise meet the description of a priority tax claim under § 507(a)(8) of the Code is to be paid in the same manner and over the same period as prescribed in § 507(a)(8).
9. The plan should describe the treatment of the general unsecured claims. An administrative convenience class may be created pursuant to § 1122(b) of the Code, and other classes of unsecured claims may be created to the extent permitted by applicable law.
10. Finally, the plan should describe the treatment of equity interests.

ALLOWANCE AND DISALLOWANCE OF CLAIMS

11. The fifth article addresses the treatment of disputed claims. A "disputed claim" is a claim that has not been allowed or disallowed. No distribution will be made on account of a disputed claim unless such claim is allowed. The debtor will have the power and authority to settle and compromise a disputed claim with court approval and compliance with Rule 9019.

PROVISIONS FOR EXECUTORY CONTRACTS AND UNEXPIRED LEASES

12. The sixth article deals with executory contracts and unexpired leases. The plan proponent should list all executory contracts and unexpired leases that it has already assumed, or which it intends to assume under the plan. All other executory contracts will be deemed rejected.

GENERAL PROVISIONS

13. The seventh article provides certain general provisions. Definitions from the Code are incorporated by reference, and any other definitions required by the plan should be listed in section 7.01 of the plan. If a governing law clause is desired, it should be included here, and if the debtor is a corporation, provisions required by §1123(a)(6) of the Code should be included.

DISCHARGE

14. The eighth article describes the effect of discharge under the plan. When and whether the debtor is entitled to a discharge will depend, among other things, upon whether the debtor is an individual, partnership, or corporation, and whether the debtor is continuing in business after consummation of the plan. The proponent should choose the appropriate language from the options provided.

OTHER PROVISIONS

15. To the extent that other provisions, not provided in the plan, are desired, they should be placed in the ninth article.

(As added Dec. 1, 2008; Dec. 1, 2011.)

Form 25B. Disclosure Statement in Small Business Case Under Chapter 11

Official Form 25B (12/08)

United States Bankruptcy Court
_______________ District of _______________

In re____________________, Case No. _______________
Debtor

Small Business Case under Chapter 11

[NAME OF PLAN PROPONENT]'S DISCLOSURE STATEMENT, DATED [INSERT DATE]

Table of Contents

[Insert when text is finalized]

I. INTRODUCTION

This is the disclosure statement (the "Disclosure Statement") in the small business chapter 11 case of _____________ (the "Debtor"). This Disclosure Statement contains information about the Debtor and describes the [insert name of plan] (the "Plan") filed by [the Debtor] on [insert date]. A full copy of the Plan is attached to this Disclosure Statement as Exhibit A. ***Your rights may be affected. You should read the Plan and this Disclosure Statement carefully and discuss them with your attorney. If you do not have an attorney, you may wish to consult one.***

The proposed distributions under the Plan are discussed at pages __-__ of this Disclosure Statement. [General unsecured creditors are classified in Class __, and will receive a distribution of ___ % of their allowed claims, to be distributed as follows _________.]

A. Purpose of This Document

This Disclosure Statement describes:

- The Debtor and significant events during the bankruptcy case,
- How the Plan proposes to treat claims or equity interests of the type you hold (*i.e.*, what you will receive on your claim or equity interest if the plan is confirmed),
- Who can vote on or object to the Plan,
- What factors the Bankruptcy Court (the "Court") will consider when deciding whether to confirm the Plan,
- Why [the Proponent] believes the Plan is feasible, and how the treatment of your claim or equity interest under the Plan compares to what you would receive on your claim or equity interest in liquidation, and
- The effect of confirmation of the Plan.

Be sure to read the Plan as well as the Disclosure Statement. This Disclosure Statement describes the Plan, but it is the Plan itself that will, if confirmed, establish your rights.

B. Deadlines for Voting and Objecting; Date of Plan Confirmation Hearing

The Court has not yet confirmed the Plan described in this Disclosure Statement. This section describes the procedures pursuant to which the Plan will or will not be confirmed.

1. *Time and Place of the Hearing to [Finally Approve This Disclosure Statement and] Confirm the Plan*

The hearing at which the Court will determine whether to [finally approve this Disclosure Statement and] confirm the Plan will take place on [insert date], at [insert time], in Courtroom ____, at the [Insert Courthouse Name, and Full Court Address, City, State, Zip Code].

2. *Deadline For Voting to Accept or Reject the Plan*

If you are entitled to vote to accept or reject the plan, vote on the enclosed ballot and return the ballot in the enclosed envelope to [insert address]. See section IV.A. below for a discussion of voting eligibility requirements.

Your ballot must be received by [insert date] or it will not be counted.

3. *Deadline For Objecting to the [Adequacy of Disclosure and] Confirmation of the Plan*

Objections to [this Disclosure Statement or to] the confirmation of the Plan must be filed with the Court and served upon [insert entities] by [insert date].

4. *Identity of Person to Contact for More Information*

If you want additional information about the Plan, you should contact [insert name and address of representative of plan proponent].

C. Disclaimer

The Court has [conditionally] approved this Disclosure Statement as containing adequate information to enable parties affected by the Plan to make an informed judgment about its terms. The Court has not yet determined whether the Plan meets the legal requirements for confirmation, and the fact that the Court has approved this Disclosure Statement does not constitute an endorsement of the Plan by the Court, or a recommendation that it be accepted. [The Court's approval of this Disclosure Statement is subject to final approval at the hearing on confirmation of the Plan. Objections to the adequacy of this Disclosure Statement may be filed until ______.]

II. BACKGROUND

A. Description and History of the Debtor's Business

The Debtor is a [corporation, partnership, etc.]. Since [insert year operations commenced], the Debtor has been in the business of _________. [Describe the Debtor's business].

B. Insiders of the Debtor

[Insert a detailed list of the names of Debtor's insiders as defined in §101(31) of the United States Bankruptcy Code (the "Code") and their relationship to the Debtor. For each insider, list all compensation paid by the Debtor or its affiliates to that person or entity during the two years prior to the commencement of the Debtor's bankruptcy case, as well as compensation paid during the pendency of this chapter 11 case.]

C. **Management of the Debtor Before and During the Bankruptcy**

During the two years prior to the date on which the bankruptcy petition was filed, the officers, directors, managers or other persons in control of the Debtor (collectively the "Managers") were [List the Managers of the Debtor prior to the petition date].

The Managers of the Debtor during the Debtor's chapter 11 case have been: [List Managers of the Debtor during the Debtor's chapter 11 case.]

After the effective date of the order confirming the Plan, the directors, officers, and voting trustees of the Debtor, any affiliate of the Debtor participating in a joint Plan with the Debtor, or successor of the Debtor under the Plan (collectively the "Post Confirmation Managers"), will be: [List Post Confirmation Managers of the Debtor.] The responsibilities and compensation of these Post Confirmation Managers are described in section __ of this Disclosure Statement.

D. **Events Leading to Chapter 11 Filing**

[Describe the events that led to the commencement of the Debtor's bankruptcy case.]

E. **Significant Events During the Bankruptcy Case**

[Describe significant events during the Debtor's bankruptcy case:

- Describe any asset sales outside the ordinary course of business, debtor in possession financing, or cash collateral orders.
- Identify the professionals approved by the court.
- Describe any adversary proceedings that have been filed or other significant litigation that has occurred (including contested claim disallowance proceedings), and any other significant legal or administrative proceedings that are pending or have been pending during the case in a forum other than the Court.
- Describe any steps taken to improve operations and profitability of the Debtor.
- Describe other events as appropriate.]

F. **Projected Recovery of Avoidable Transfers [Choose the option that applies]**

[Option 1 – If the Debtor does not intend to pursue avoidance actions]

The Debtor does not intend to pursue preference, fraudulent conveyance, or other avoidance actions.

[Option 2 – If the Debtor intends to pursue avoidance actions]

The Debtor estimates that up to $__________ may be realized from the recovery of fraudulent, preferential or other avoidable transfers. While the results of litigation cannot be predicted with certainty and it is possible that other causes of action may be identified, the following is a summary of the preference, fraudulent conveyance and other avoidance actions filed or expected to be filed in this case:

Transaction	Defendant	Amount Claimed

[Option 3 – If the Debtor does not yet know whether it intends to pursue avoidance actions]

The Debtor has not yet completed its investigation with regard to prepetition transactions. If you received a payment or other transfer within 90 days of the bankruptcy, or other transfer avoidable under the Code, the Debtor may seek to avoid such transfer.

G. **Claims Objections**

Except to the extent that a claim is already allowed pursuant to a final non-appealable order, the Debtor reserves the right to object to claims. Therefore, even if your claim is allowed for voting purposes, you may not be entitled to a distribution if an objection to your claim is later upheld. The procedures for resolving disputed claims are set forth in Article V of the Plan.

H. **Current and Historical Financial Conditions**

The identity and fair market value of the estate's assets are listed in Exhibit B. [Identify source and basis of valuation.]

The Debtor's most recent financial statements [if any] issued before bankruptcy, each of which was filed with the Court, are set forth in Exhibit C.

[The most recent post-petition operating report filed since the commencement of the Debtor's bankruptcy case are set forth in Exhibit D.] [A summary of the Debtor's periodic operating reports filed since the commencement of the Debtor's bankruptcy case is set forth in Exhibit D.]

III. SUMMARY OF THE PLAN OF REORGANIZATION AND TREATMENT OF CLAIMS AND EQUITY INTERESTS

A. What is the Purpose of the Plan of Reorganization?

As required by the Code, the Plan places claims and equity interests in various classes and describes the treatment each class will receive. The Plan also states whether each class of claims or equity interests is impaired or unimpaired. If the Plan is confirmed, your recovery will be limited to the amount provided by the Plan.

B. Unclassified Claims

Certain types of claims are automatically entitled to specific treatment under the Code. They are not considered impaired, and holders of such claims do not vote on the Plan. They may, however, object if, in their view, their treatment under the Plan does not comply with that required by the Code. As such, the Plan Proponent has *not* placed the following claims in any class:

1. *Administrative Expenses*

Administrative expenses are costs or expenses of administering the Debtor's chapter 11 case which are allowed under § 507(a)(2) of the Code. Administrative expenses also include the value of any goods sold to the Debtor in the ordinary course of business and received within 20 days before the date of the bankruptcy petition. The Code requires that all administrative expenses be paid on the effective date of the Plan, unless a particular claimant agrees to a different treatment.

The following chart lists the Debtor's estimated administrative expenses, and their proposed treatment under the Plan:

Type	Estimated Amount Owed	Proposed Treatment
Expenses Arising in the Ordinary Course of Business After the		Paid in full on the effective date of the Plan, or according to terms of obligation if later

Petition Date		
The Value of Goods Received in the Ordinary Course of Business Within 20 Days Before the Petition Date		Paid in full on the effective date of the Plan, or according to terms of obligation if later
Professional Fees, as approved by the Court.		Paid in full on the effective date of the Plan, or according to separate written agreement, or according to court order if such fees have not been approved by the Court on the effective date of the Plan
Clerk's Office Fees		Paid in full on the effective date of the Plan
Other administrative expenses		Paid in full on the effective date of the Plan or according to separate written agreement
Office of the U.S. Trustee Fees		Paid in full on the effective date of the Plan
TOTAL		

2. *Priority Tax Claims*

Priority tax claims are unsecured income, employment, and other taxes described by § 507(a)(8) of the Code. Unless the holder of such a § 507(a)(8) priority tax claim agrees otherwise, it must receive the present value of such claim, in regular installments paid over a period not exceeding 5 years from the order of relief.

The following chart lists the Debtor's estimated § 507(a)(8) priority tax claims and their proposed treatment under the Plan:

Description (name and type of tax)	Estimated Amount Owed	Date of Assessment	Treatment
			Pmt interval = [Monthly] payment = Begin date = End date = Interest Rate % = Total Payout Amount = $
			Pmt interval = [Monthly] payment = Begin date =

Description (name and type of tax)	Estimated Amount Owed	Date of Assessment	Treatment
			End date = Interest Rate % = Total Payout Amount = $

C. **Classes of Claims and Equity Interests**

The following are the classes set forth in the Plan, and the proposed treatment that they will receive under the Plan:

1. *Classes of Secured Claims*

Allowed Secured Claims are claims secured by property of the Debtor's bankruptcy estate (or that are subject to setoff) to the extent allowed as secured claims under § 506 of the Code. If the value of the collateral or setoffs securing the creditor's claim is less than the amount of the creditor's allowed claim, the deficiency will [be classified as a general unsecured claim].

The following chart lists all classes containing Debtor's secured prepetition claims and their proposed treatment under the Plan:

Class #	Description	Insider? (Yes or No)	Impairment	Treatment
	Secured claim of: Name = Collateral description = Allowed Secured Amount = $________ Priority of lien = Principal owed = $________ Pre-pet. arrearage = $________ Total claim = $________		[State whether impaired or unimpaired]	[Monthly] Pmt = Pmts Begin = Pmts End = [Balloon pmt] = Interest rate % = Treatment of Lien = [Additional payment required to cure defaults] =

	Secured claim of: Name = Collateral description = Allowed Secured Amount = $________ Priority of lien = Principal owed = $________ Pre-pet. arrearage = $________ Total claim = $________		[State whether impaired or unimpaired]	Monthly Pmt = Pmts Begin = Pmts End = [Balloon pmt] = Interest rate % = Treatment of Lien = [Additional payment required to cure defaults] =

2. *Classes of Priority Unsecured Claims*

Certain priority claims that are referred to in §§ 507(a)(1), (4), (5), (6), and (7) of the Code are required to be placed in classes. The Code requires that each holder of such a claim receive cash on the effective date of the Plan equal to the allowed amount of such claim. However, a class of holders of such claims may vote to accept different treatment.

The following chart lists all classes containing claims under §§ 507(a)(1), (4), (5), (6), and (a)(7) of the Code and their proposed treatment under the Plan:

Class #	Description	Impairment	Treatment
	Priority unsecured claim pursuant to Section [insert] Total amt of claims = $	[State whether impaired or unimpaired]	
	Priority unsecured claim pursuant to Section [insert] Total amt of claims = $	[State whether impaired or unimpaired]	

3. *Class[es]of General Unsecured Claims*

General unsecured claims are not secured by property of the estate and are not entitled to priority under § 507(a) of the Code. [Insert description of §1122(b) convenience class if applicable.]

The following chart identifies the Plan's proposed treatment of Class[es] __ through __, which contain general unsecured claims against the Debtor:

Class #	Description	Impairment	Treatment
	[1122(b) Convenience Class]	[State whether impaired or unimpaired]	[Insert proposed treatment, such as "Paid in full in cash on effective date of the Plan or when due under contract or applicable nonbankruptcy law"]
	General Unsecured Class	[State whether impaired or unimpaired]	Monthly Pmt = Pmts Begin = Pmts End = [Balloon pmt] = Interest rate % from [date] = Estimated percent of claim paid =

4. *Class[es] of Equity Interest Holders*

Equity interest holders are parties who hold an ownership interest (*i.e.*, equity interest) in the Debtor. In a corporation, entities holding preferred or common stock are equity interest holders. In a partnership, equity interest holders include both general and limited partners. In a limited liability company ("LLC"), the equity interest holders are the members. Finally, with respect to an individual who is a debtor, the Debtor is the equity interest holder.

The following chart sets forth the Plan's proposed treatment of the class[es] of equity interest holders: [There may be more than one class of equity interests in, for example, a partnership case, or a case where the prepetition debtor had issued multiple classes of stock.]

Class #	Description	Impairment	Treatment
	Equity interest holders	[State whether impaired or unimpaired]	

D. **Means of Implementing the Plan**

1. *Source of Payments*

Payments and distributions under the Plan will be funded by the following:

[Describe the source of funds for payments under the Plan.]

2. *Post-confirmation Management*

The Post-Confirmation Managers of the Debtor, and their compensation, shall be as follows:

Name	Affiliations	Insider (yes or no)?	Position	Compensation

E. **Risk Factors**

The proposed Plan has the following risks:

[List all risk factors that might affect the Debtor's ability to make payments and other distributions required under the Plan.]

F. **Executory Contracts and Unexpired Leases**

The Plan, in Exhibit 5.1, lists all executory contracts and unexpired leases that the Debtor will assume under the Plan. Assumption means that the Debtor has elected to continue to perform the obligations under such contracts and unexpired leases, and to cure defaults of the type that must be cured under the Code, if any. Exhibit 5.1 also lists how the Debtor will cure and compensate the other party to such contract or lease for any such defaults.

If you object to the assumption of your unexpired lease or executory contract, the proposed cure of any defaults, or the adequacy of assurance of performance, you must file and serve your objection to the Plan within the deadline for objecting to the confirmation of the Plan, unless the Court has set an earlier time.

All executory contracts and unexpired leases that are not listed in Exhibit 5.1 will be rejected under the Plan. Consult your adviser or attorney for more specific information about particular contracts or leases.

If you object to the rejection of your contract or lease, you must file and serve your objection to the Plan within the deadline for objecting to the confirmation of the Plan.

[***The Deadline for Filing a Proof of Claim Based on a Claim Arising from the Rejection of a Lease or Contract Is _______.*** Any claim based on the rejection of a contract or lease will be barred if the proof of claim is not timely filed, unless the Court orders otherwise.]

G. **Tax Consequences of Plan**

Creditors and Equity Interest Holders Concerned with How the Plan May Affect Their Tax Liability Should Consult with Their Own Accountants, Attorneys, And/Or Advisors.

The following are the anticipated tax consequences of the Plan: [List the following general consequences as a minimum: (1)Tax consequences to the Debtor of the Plan; (2) General tax consequences on creditors of any discharge, and the general tax consequences of receipt of plan consideration after confirmation.]

IV. CONFIRMATION REQUIREMENTS AND PROCEDURES

To be confirmable, the Plan must meet the requirements listed in §§ 1129(a) or (b) of the Code. These include the requirements that: the Plan must be proposed in good faith; at least one impaired class of claims must accept the plan, without counting votes of insiders; the Plan must distribute to each creditor and equity interest holder at least as much as the creditor or equity interest holder would receive in a chapter 7 liquidation case, unless the creditor or equity interest holder votes to accept the Plan; and the Plan must be feasible. These requirements are not the only requirements listed in § 1129, and they are not the only requirements for confirmation.

A. Who May Vote or Object

Any party in interest may object to the confirmation of the Plan if the party believes that the requirements for confirmation are not met.

Many parties in interest, however, are not entitled to vote to accept or reject the Plan. A creditor or equity interest holder has a right to vote for or against the Plan only if that creditor or equity interest holder has a claim or equity interest that is both (1) allowed or allowed for voting purposes and (2) impaired.

In this case, the Plan Proponent believes that classes ______ are impaired and that holders of claims in each of these classes are therefore entitled to vote to accept or reject the Plan. The Plan Proponent believes that classes ______ are unimpaired and that holders of claims in each of these classes, therefore, do not have the right to vote to accept or reject the Plan.

1. *What Is an Allowed Claim or an Allowed Equity Interest?*

Only a creditor or equity interest holder with an allowed claim or an allowed equity interest has the right to vote on the Plan. Generally, a claim or equity interest is allowed if either (1) the Debtor has scheduled the claim on the Debtor's schedules, unless the claim has been scheduled as disputed, contingent, or unliquidated, or (2) the creditor has filed a proof of claim or equity interest, unless an objection has been filed to such proof of claim or equity interest. When a claim or equity interest is not allowed, the creditor or equity interest holder holding the claim or equity interest cannot vote unless the Court, after notice and hearing, either overrules the objection or allows the claim or equity interest for voting purposes pursuant to Rule 3018(a) of the Federal Rules of Bankruptcy Procedure.

The deadline for filing a proof of claim in this case was _____.
[If applicable – The deadline for filing objections to claims is______.]

2. *What Is an Impaired Claim or Impaired Equity Interest?*

As noted above, the holder of an allowed claim or equity interest has the right to vote only if it is in a class that is *impaired* under the Plan. As provided in § 1124 of the Code, a class is considered impaired if the Plan alters the legal, equitable, or contractual rights of the members of that class.

3. *Who is **Not** Entitled to Vote*

The holders of the following five types of claims and equity interests are *not* entitled to vote:

- holders of claims and equity interests that have been disallowed by an order of the Court;
- holders of other claims or equity interests that are not "allowed claims" or "allowed equity interests" (as discussed above), unless they have been "allowed" for voting purposes.
- holders of claims or equity interests in unimpaired classes;
- holders of claims entitled to priority pursuant to §§ 507(a)(2), (a)(3), and (a)(8) of the Code; and
- holders of claims or equity interests in classes that do not receive or retain any value under the Plan;
- administrative expenses.

Even If You Are Not Entitled to Vote on the Plan, You Have a Right to Object to the Confirmation of the Plan [and to the Adequacy of the Disclosure Statement].

4. *Who Can Vote in More Than One Class*

A creditor whose claim has been allowed in part as a secured claim and in part as an unsecured claim, or who otherwise hold claims in multiple classes, is entitled to accept or reject a Plan in each capacity, and should cast one ballot for each claim.

B. **Votes Necessary to Confirm the Plan**

If impaired classes exist, the Court cannot confirm the Plan unless (1) at least one impaired class of creditors has accepted the Plan without counting the votes of any insiders within that class, and (2) all impaired classes have voted to accept the Plan, unless the Plan is eligible to be confirmed by "cram down" on non-accepting classes, as discussed later in Section [B.2.].

1. *Votes Necessary for a Class to Accept the Plan*

A class of claims accepts the Plan if both of the following occur: (1) the holders of more than one-half (1/2) of the allowed claims in the class, who vote, cast their votes to accept the Plan, and (2) the holders of at least two-thirds (2/3) in dollar amount of the allowed claims in the class, who vote, cast their votes to accept the Plan.

A class of equity interests accepts the Plan if the holders of at least two-thirds (2/3) in amount of the allowed equity interests in the class, who vote, cast their votes to accept the Plan.

2. *Treatment of Nonaccepting Classes*

Even if one or more impaired classes reject the Plan, the Court may nonetheless confirm the Plan if the nonaccepting classes are treated in the manner prescribed by § 1129(b) of the Code. A plan that binds nonaccepting classes is commonly referred to as a "cram down" plan. The Code allows the Plan to bind nonaccepting classes of claims or equity interests if it meets all the requirements for consensual confirmation except the voting requirements of § 1129(a)(8) of the Code, does not "discriminate unfairly," and is "fair and equitable" toward each impaired class that has not voted to accept the Plan.

You should consult your own attorney if a "cramdown" confirmation will affect your claim or equity interest, as the variations on this general rule are numerous and complex.

C. **Liquidation Analysis**

To confirm the Plan, the Court must find that all creditors and equity interest holders who do not accept the Plan will receive at least as much under the Plan as such claim and equity interest holders would receive in a chapter 7 liquidation. A liquidation analysis is attached to this Disclosure Statement as Exhibit E.

D. **Feasibility**

The Court must find that confirmation of the Plan is not likely to be followed by the liquidation, or the need for further financial reorganization, of the Debtor or any successor to the Debtor, unless such liquidation or reorganization is proposed in the Plan.

1. *Ability to Initially Fund Plan*

The Plan Proponent believes that the Debtor will have enough cash on hand on the effective date of the Plan to pay all the claims and expenses that are entitled to be paid on that date. Tables showing the amount of cash on hand on the effective date of the Plan, and the sources of that cash are attached to this disclosure statement as Exhibit F.

2. *Ability to Make Future Plan Payments And Operate Without Further Reorganization*

The Plan Proponent must also show that it will have enough cash over the life of the Plan to make the required Plan payments.

The Plan Proponent has provided projected financial information. Those projections are listed in Exhibit G.

The Plan Proponent's financial projections show that the Debtor will have an aggregate annual average cash flow, after paying operating expenses and post-confirmation taxes, of $. The final Plan payment is expected to be paid on _____.

[Summarize the numerical projections, and highlight any assumptions that are not in accord with past experience. Explain why such assumptions should now be made.]

You Should Consult with Your Accountant or other Financial Advisor If You Have Any Questions Pertaining to These Projections.

V. EFFECT OF CONFIRMATION OF PLAN

A. **DISCHARGE OF DEBTOR** [If the Debtor is not entitled to discharge pursuant to 11 U.S.C. § 1141(d)(3) change this heading to "**NO DISCHARGE OF DEBTOR**."]

[Option 1 – If Debtor is an individual and § 1141(d)(3) is not applicable]
Discharge. Confirmation of the Plan does not discharge any debt provided for in the Plan until the court grants a discharge on completion of all payments under the Plan, or as otherwise provided in § 1141(d)(5) of the Code. Debtor will not be discharged from any debt excepted from discharge under § 523 of the Code, except as provided in Rule 4007(c) of the Federal Rules of Bankruptcy Procedure.

[Option 2 -- If the Debtor is a partnership and § 1141(d)(3) of the Code is not applicable]
Discharge. On the effective date of the Plan, the Debtor shall be discharged from any debt that arose before confirmation of the Plan, subject to the occurrence of the effective date, to the extent specified in § 1141(d)(1)(A) of the Code. However, the Debtor shall not be discharged from any debt imposed by the Plan. After the effective date of the Plan your claims against the Debtor will be limited to the debts imposed by the Plan.

[Option 3 -- If the Debtor is a corporation and § 1141(d)(3) is not applicable]
Discharge. On the effective date of the Plan, the Debtor shall be discharged from any debt that arose before confirmation of the Plan, subject to the occurrence of the effective date, to

the extent specified in § 1141(d)(1)(A) of the Code, except that the Debtor shall not be discharged of any debt (i) imposed by the Plan, (ii) of a kind specified in § 1141(d)(6)(A) if a timely complaint was filed in accordance with Rule 4007(c) of the Federal Rules of Bankruptcy Procedure, or (iii) of a kind specified in § 1141(d)(6)(B). After the effective date of the Plan your claims against the Debtor will be limited to the debts described in clauses (i) through (iii) of the preceding sentence.

[Option 4 – If § 1141(d)(3) is applicable]

No Discharge. In accordance with § 1141(d)(3) of the Code, the Debtor will not receive any discharge of debt in this bankruptcy case.

B. Modification of Plan

The Plan Proponent may modify the Plan at any time before confirmation of the Plan. However, the Court may require a new disclosure statement and/or revoting on the Plan.

[If the Debtor is not an individual, add the following: "The Plan Proponent may also seek to modify the Plan at any time after confirmation only if (1) the Plan has not been substantially consummated *and* (2) the Court authorizes the proposed modifications after notice and a hearing."]

[If the Debtor is an individual, add the following: "Upon request of the Debtor, the United States trustee, or the holder of an allowed unsecured claim, the Plan may be modified at any time after confirmation of the Plan but before the completion of payments under the Plan, to (1) increase or reduce the amount of payments under the Plan on claims of a particular class, (2) extend or reduce the time period for such payments, or (3) alter the amount of distribution to a creditor whose claim is provided for by the Plan to the extent necessary to take account of any payment of the claim made other than under the Plan."]

C. Final Decree

Once the estate has been fully administered, as provided in Rule 3022 of the Federal Rules of Bankruptcy Procedure, the Plan Proponent, or such other party as the Court shall designate in the Plan Confirmation Order, shall file a motion with the Court to obtain a final decree to close the case. Alternatively, the Court may enter such a final decree on its own motion.

VI. OTHER PLAN PROVISIONS

[Insert other provisions here, as necessary and appropriate.]

Official Form 25B (12/08) – Cont. 18

[Signature of the Plan Proponent]

[Signature of the Attorney for the Plan Proponent]

EXHIBITS

Exhibit A – Copy of Proposed Plan of Reorganization

Official Form 25B (12/08) – Cont. 21

Exhibit B – Identity and Value of Material Assets of Debtor

Exhibit C – Prepetition Financial Statements
(to be taken from those filed with the court)

Exhibit D – [Most Recently Filed Postpetition Operating Report][Summary of Postpetition Operating Reports]

Exhibit E – Liquidation Analysis

Plan Proponent's Estimated Liquidation Value of Assets

Assets	
a. Cash on hand	$
b. Accounts receivable	$
c. Inventory	$
d. Office furniture & equipment	$
e. Machinery & equipment	$
f. Automobiles	$
g. Building & Land	$
h. Customer list	$
i. Investment property (such as stocks, bonds or other financial assets)	$
j. Lawsuits or other claims against third-parties	$
k. Other intangibles (such as avoiding powers actions)	$
Total Assets at Liquidation Value	$
Less: Secured creditors' recoveries	$
Less: Chapter 7 trustee fees and expenses	$
Less: Chapter 11 administrative expenses	$
Less: Priority claims, excluding administrative expense claims	$
[Less: Debtor's claimed exemptions]	$
(1) Balance for unsecured claims	$
(2) Total dollar amount of unsecured claims	$
Percentage of Claims Which Unsecured Creditors Would Receive Or Retain in a Chapter 7 Liquidation:	$
Percentage of Claims Which Unsecured Creditors Will Receive or Retain under the Plan:	____% [Divide (1) by (2)]
	____%

Exhibit F – Cash on hand on the effective date of the Plan

Cash on hand on effective date of the Plan:	$
Less –	
Amount of administrative expenses payable on effective date of the Plan	-
Amount of statutory costs and charges	-
Amount of cure payments for executory contracts	-
Other Plan Payments due on effective date of the Plan	-
Balance after paying these amounts..............	$

The sources of the cash Debtor will have on hand by the effective date of the Plan are estimated as follows:

$	Cash in Debtor's bank account now
+	Additional cash Debtor will accumulate from net earnings between now and effective date of the Plan [state the basis for such projections]
+	Borrowing [separately state terms of repayment]
+	Capital Contributions
+	Other
$	Total [This number should match "cash on hand" figure noted above

Exhibit G – Projections of Cash Flow and Earnings for Post-Confirmation Period

Form 25B, Instructions (12/08)

Instructions for Form Disclosure Statement

BACKGROUND AND GENERAL INSTRUCTIONS

1. This small business chapter 11 disclosure statement form is promulgated pursuant to § 433 of the Bankruptcy Abuse Prevention and Consumer Protection Act of 2005. This form may be used in cases where the debtor (whether an individual or an artificial entity) is a small business debtor within the meaning of § 101(51D) of the Code. This form provides a format for disseminating to parties in interest information about the plan of reorganization in a debtor's small business chapter 11 case, so that those parties can make reasonably informed judgments whether to accept, reject or object to the plan. Because the relevant legal requirements for and effects of a plan's confirmation may vary depending on the nature of the debtor, and because the details of any proposed reorganization necessarily vary, this form is intended to provide a format for disclosure, rather than a specific prescription for the language or content of a disclosure statement in any particular case. The form highlights the factual and legal disclosures required by § 1125 of the Code in connection with the plan's confirmation. It is not intended to restrict the plan's proponent from providing additional information where that would be useful.

2. Proponents are encouraged to present material information in as clear a fashion as possible, including, where feasible, in an accompanying executive summary, approved by the court, that highlights particular creditors' or interest holders' voting status and treatment under the plan.

3. Some language in this form appears in brackets. The bracketed language sometimes instructs the plan's proponent to provide certain information, and sometimes provides optional or alternative language that should be used when and where appropriate. Proponents should make the necessary insertions and/or delete inapplicable language.

SPECIFIC INSTRUCTIONS

INTRODUCTORY SECTION

4. The introductory section describes the purpose of the disclosure statement, provides procedural information regarding confirmation of the plan, including where to obtain additional information, indicates whether particular claimants or interest holders will be entitled to vote on the plan, and details the procedures and deadlines for filing objections to confirmation of the plan. A copy of the plan should be attached to the debtor's disclosure statement as

Exhibit A. Where the proposed distribution to unsecured creditors and other classes can be succinctly summarized, describe that distribution in the second introductory paragraph.

5. In some cases, the court will approve the debtor's disclosure statement prior to solicitation of acceptance or rejection of the plan. See Rule 3017. In other cases, the court may conditionally approve the disclosure statement, and combine the hearing on the adequacy of disclosure and the hearing on confirmation of the plan into one hearing. See Rule 3017.1. Use the bracketed language as appropriate in subsections I.B. and I.C.

BACKGROUND SECTION

6. The second part of disclosure statement provides a history of the debtor's business, both before and during the debtor's bankruptcy case. In this section, the plan proponent should describe the debtor's business, the events that led to the filing of the debtor's bankruptcy petition, and the key events in the debtor's bankruptcy case, and identify the people who managed the debtor during the case and who will manage the debtor after the plan is confirmed. The proponent should disclose its intentions with regard to, and the status of, avoidance actions. If the debtor or proponent intends to bring an avoidance action against a particular creditor or equity interest holder, the disclosure statement should disclose this fact so that the creditor or equity interest holder can use that information to determine the value of its claim or interest when considering whether to accept or reject the plan. If the debtor or plan proponent is uncertain as to what avoidance actions might be brought, that fact should be disclosed as well, so that claimants and equity interest holders can take that information into account, as well, when considering whether to accept or reject the plan.

7. A schedule of the debtor's material assets, along with the basis for their valuation should be attached to the debtor's disclosure statement as Exhibit B. Under § 1116 of the Code, the debtor must also file its most recent prepetition financial statements with the petition. These financial statements should be attached to the debtor's disclosure statement as Exhibit C.

8. Sections 434 and 435 of the Bankruptcy Abuse Prevention and Consumer Protection Act of 2005, and § 308 of the Code require the debtor to file periodic operating reports with the court. The most recent such reports, or a summary of the filed reports, should be attached to the debtor's disclosure statement as Exhibit D.

SUMMARY OF PLAN

9. The third part of the disclosure statement describes the treatment of various creditors and equity interest holders who will receive distributions under the plan. Because the treatment of certain claims, such as administrative expense claims, allowed under § 503 of the Code, and priority tax claims, allowed under §507(a)(8) of the Code, is statutorily specified, these claims are not placed into classes. Secured creditors are generally each placed in their own class, with the particular treatment specified for that class. Section 1129(a)(9)(D) of the Code provides that a secured tax claim which would otherwise meet the description of a priority tax claim under § 507(a)(8) of the Code is to be paid in the same manner and over the same period as prescribed in § 507(a)(8) of the Code. While it is not required, the proponent may, where applicable, wish to classify claims under § 507(a)(9) and (10) of the Code. Finally, the disclosure statement should describe the treatment of the general unsecured claimants and equity interest holders. An administrative convenience class may be created pursuant to § 1122(b) of the Code, and other classes of unsecured claims may be created to the extent permitted by applicable case law. Also, while the suggested language of the form contemplates that plan distributions will be in the form of monthly payments, other forms of consideration are permitted and this section of the disclosure statement should be modified to describe clearly the form(s), methods and timing of payments to be made under the particular plan.

10. The disclosure statement should also detail the sources of funds for payments to be made under the plan. These should include the sources of funds for payments to be made on the effective date of the plan (detailed in Exhibit F), and the source of payments that will be made over the life of the plan. The description should be supported by projections about the income and profitability of the debtor. The plan proponent must also fully describe post-confirmation management, as required by § 1129(a)(5) of the Code. The disclosure statement should also describe any risk factors that might influence the debtor's ability to complete the payments or affect the value of the distributions provided for under the plan. Also, the disclosure statement should list any material executory contracts that will be assumed pursuant to the plan, as well as any material contracts that will be rejected. To the extent possible, the tax consequences of the plan should also be summarized.

CONFIRMATION REQUIREMENTS AND PROCEDURES SECTION

11. The fourth part of the disclosure statement sets forth the procedures and requirements for confirmation. In this regard, the disclosure statement should inform creditors and equity interest holders of (1) which class they are in, (2) whether they are entitled to vote, and (3) the amount of their claim allowed for voting purposes. This may be accomplished in the disclosure statement itself or, as noted above, in a summary statement, approved by the court, and sent to

the parties in interest along with the disclosure statement. A liquidation analysis of the debtor should be attached to the disclosure statement as Exhibit E. As noted above, the sources of funds for payments to be made on the effective date of the plan should be detailed in Exhibit F, and projections about the profitability and cash flow of the debtor's business after confirmation should be attached to the disclosure statement as Exhibit G.

EFFECT OF PLAN CONFIRMATION

12. The fifth part of the disclosure statement describes the effect of plan confirmation. The language used here should be chosen with care, as the effect of confirmation differs depending on whether the debtor is an individual, partnership, or corporation, and on whether the debtor will continue in business post-confirmation or will, instead, be liquidated.

13. If the plan provides that, after its confirmation, property of the estate will vest in and be distributed by someone other than the debtor, the disclosure statement should identify any such property and the person in whom the property will vest.

OTHER PROVISIONS

14. Other provisions may be added in Part VI as desired and appropriate.

(As added Dec. 1, 2008.)

Form 25C. Small Business Monthly Operating Report

Official Form 25C (12/08)

United States Bankruptcy Court

_______________ District of _______________

In re_____________________________,
Debtor

Case No. _______________

Small Business Case under Chapter 11

SMALL BUSINESS MONTHLY OPERATING REPORT

Month: _______________ **Date Filed:** _______________

Line of Business: _______________ **NAICS Code:** _______________

IN ACCORDANCE WITH TITLE 28, SECTION 1746, OF THE UNITED STATES CODE, I DECLARE UNDER PENALTY OF PERJURY THAT I HAVE EXAMINED THE FOLLOWING SMALL BUSINESS MONTHLY OPERATING REPORT AND THE ACCOMPANYING ATTACHMENTS AND, TO THE BEST OF MY KNOWLEDGE, THESE DOCUMENTS ARE TRUE, CORRECT AND COMPLETE.

RESPONSIBLE PARTY:

____
ORIGINAL SIGNATURE OF RESPONSIBLE PARTY

____
PRINTED NAME OF RESPONSIBLE PARTY

QUESTIONNAIRE: (All questions to be answered on behalf of the debtor.)	**YES**	**NO**
1. IS THE BUSINESS STILL OPERATING?	☐	☐
2. HAVE YOU PAID ALL YOUR BILLS ON TIME THIS MONTH?	☐	☐
3. DID YOU PAY YOUR EMPLOYEES ON TIME?	☐	☐
4. HAVE YOU DEPOSITED ALL THE RECEIPTS FOR YOUR BUSINESS INTO THE DIP ACCOUNT THIS MONTH?	☐	☐
5. HAVE YOU FILED ALL OF YOUR TAX RETURNS AND PAID ALL OF YOUR TAXES THIS MONTH?	☐	☐
6. HAVE YOU TIMELY FILED ALL OTHER REQUIRED GOVERNMENT FILINGS?	☐	☐
7. HAVE YOU PAID ALL OF YOUR INSURANCE PREMIUMS THIS MONTH?	☐	☐
8. DO YOU PLAN TO CONTINUE TO OPERATE THE BUSINESS NEXT MONTH?	☐	☐
9. ARE YOU CURRENT ON YOUR QUARTERLY FEE PAYMENT TO THE U.S. TRUSTEE?	☐	☐
10. HAVE YOU PAID ANYTHING TO YOUR ATTORNEY OR OTHER PROFESSIONALS THIS MONTH?	☐	☐
11. DID YOU HAVE ANY UNUSUAL OR SIGNIFICANT UNANTICIPATED EXPENSES THIS MONTH?	☐	☐
12. HAS THE BUSINESS SOLD ANY GOODS OR PROVIDED SERVICES OR TRANSFERRED ANY ASSETS TO ANY BUSINESS RELATED TO THE DIP IN ANY WAY?	☐	☐

Official Form 25C (12/08) – Cont. 2

13. DO YOU HAVE ANY BANK ACCOUNTS OPEN OTHER THAN THE DIP ACCOUNT?	☐	☐
14. HAVE YOU SOLD ANY ASSETS OTHER THAN INVENTORY THIS MONTH?	☐	☐
15. DID ANY INSURANCE COMPANY CANCEL YOUR POLICY THIS MONTH?	☐	☐
16. HAVE YOU BORROWED MONEY FROM ANYONE THIS MONTH?	☐	☐
17. HAVE YOU PAID ANY BILLS YOU OWED BEFORE YOU FILED BANKRUPTCY?	☐	☐

TAXES

DO YOU HAVE ANY PAST DUE TAX RETURNS OR PAST DUE POST-PETITION TAX OBLIGATIONS?	☐	☐

IF YES, PLEASE PROVIDE A WRITTEN EXPLANATION INCLUDING WHEN SUCH RETURNS WILL BE FILED, OR WHEN SUCH PAYMENTS WILL BE MADE AND THE SOURCE OF THE FUNDS FOR THE PAYMENT.

(Exhibit A)

INCOME

PLEASE SEPARATELY LIST ALL OF THE INCOME YOU RECEIVED FOR THE MONTH. THE LIST SHOULD INCLUDE ALL INCOME FROM CASH AND CREDIT TRANSACTIONS. (THE U.S. TRUSTEE MAY WAIVE THIS REQUIREMENT.)

TOTAL INCOME ____________

(Exhibit B)

EXPENSES

PLEASE SEPARATELY LIST ALL EXPENSES PAID BY CASH OR BY CHECK FROM YOUR BANK ACCOUNTS THIS MONTH. INCLUDE THE DATE PAID, WHO WAS PAID THE MONEY, THE PURPOSE AND THE AMOUNT. (THE U.S. TRUSTEE MAY WAIVE THIS REQUIREMENT.)

TOTAL EXPENSES ____________

(Exhibit C)

CASH PROFIT

INCOME FOR THE MONTH (TOTAL FROM EXHIBIT B) ____________

EXPENSES FOR THE MONTH (TOTAL FROM EXHIBIT C) ____________

(Subtract Line C from Line B) **CASH PROFIT FOR THE MONTH** ____________

Official Form 25C (12/08) – Cont. 3

UNPAID BILLS

PLEASE ATTACH A LIST OF ALL DEBTS (INCLUDING TAXES) WHICH YOU HAVE INCURRED SINCE THE DATE YOU FILED BANKRUPTCY BUT HAVE NOT PAID. THE LIST MUST INCLUDE THE DATE THE DEBT WAS INCURRED, WHO IS OWED THE MONEY, THE PURPOSE OF THE DEBT AND WHEN THE DEBT IS DUE. (THE U.S. TRUSTEE MAY WAIVE THIS REQUIREMENT.)

TOTAL PAYABLES ________

(Exhibit D)

MONEY OWED TO YOU

PLEASE ATTACH A LIST OF ALL AMOUNTS OWED TO YOU BY YOUR CUSTOMERS FOR WORK YOU HAVE DONE OR THE MERCHANDISE YOU HAVE SOLD. YOU SHOULD INCLUDE WHO OWES YOU MONEY, HOW MUCH IS OWED AND WHEN IS PAYMENT DUE. (THE U.S. TRUSTEE MAY WAIVE THIS REQUIREMENT.)

TOTAL RECEIVABLES ________

(Exhibit E)

BANKING INFORMATION

PLEASE ATTACH A COPY OF YOUR LATEST BANK STATEMENT FOR EVERY ACCOUNT YOU HAVE AS OF THE DATE OF THIS FINANCIAL REPORT OR HAD DURING THE PERIOD COVERED BY THIS REPORT.

(Exhibit F)

EMPLOYEES

NUMBER OF EMPLOYEES WHEN THE CASE WAS FILED? ________

NUMBER OF EMPLOYEES AS OF THE DATE OF THIS MONTHLY REPORT? ________

PROFESSIONAL FEES

BANKRUPTCY RELATED:

PROFESSIONAL FEES RELATING TO THE BANKRUPTCY CASE PAID DURING THIS REPORTING PERIOD? ________

TOTAL PROFESSIONAL FEES RELATING TO THE BANKRUPTCY CASE PAID SINCE THE FILING OF THE CASE? ________

NON-BANKRUPTCY RELATED:

PROFESSIONAL FEES PAID NOT RELATING TO THE BANKRUPTCY CASE DURING THIS REPORTING PERIOD?

Official Form 25C (12/08) – Cont. 4

TOTAL PROFESSIONAL FEES PAID NOT RELATING TO THE BANKRUPTCY CASE PAID DURING THIS REPORTING PERIOD? __________

PROJECTIONS

COMPARE YOUR ACTUAL INCOME AND EXPENSES TO THE PROJECTIONS FOR THE FIRST 180 DAYS OF YOUR CASE PROVIDED AT THE INITIAL DEBTOR INTERVIEW.

	Projected	Actual	Difference
INCOME			
EXPENSES			
CASH PROFIT			

TOTAL PROJECTED INCOME FOR THE NEXT MONTH:

TOTAL PROJECTED EXPENSES FOR THE NEXT MONTH:

TOTAL PROJECTED CASH PROFIT FOR THE NEXT MONTH:

ADDITIONAL INFORMATION

PLEASE ATTACH ALL FINANCIAL REPORTS INCLUDING AN INCOME STATEMENT AND BALANCE SHEET WHICH YOU PREPARE INTERNALLY.

(As added Dec. 1, 2008.)

Form 26. Periodic Report Regarding Value, Operations and Profitability of Entities in Which the Debtor's Estate Holds a Substantial or Controlling Interest

Official Form 26 (12/08)

United States Bankruptcy Court
_______________ District of _____________

In re___________________, Case No. __________________

Debtor Chapter 11

PERIODIC REPORT REGARDING VALUE, OPERATIONS AND PROFITABILITY OF ENTITIES IN WHICH THE ESTATE OF [NAME OF DEBTOR] HOLDS A SUBSTANTIAL OR CONTROLLING INTEREST

This is the report as of _________on the value, operations and profitability of those entities in which the estate holds a substantial or controlling interest, as required by Bankruptcy Rule 2015.3. The estate of [Name of Debtor] holds a substantial or controlling interest in the following entities:

Name of Entity	Interest of the Estate	Tab #

This periodic report (the "Periodic Report") contains separate reports ("Entity Reports") on the value, operations, and profitability of each entity listed above.

Each Entity Report shall consist of three exhibits. Exhibit A contains a valuation estimate for the entity as of a date not more than two years prior to the date of this report. It also contains a description of the valuation method used. Exhibit B contains a balance sheet, a statement of income (loss), a statement of cash flows, and a statement of changes in shareholders' or partners' equity (deficit) for the period covered by the Entity Report, along with summarized footnotes. Exhibit C contains a description of the entity's business operations.

THIS REPORT MUST BE SIGNED BY A REPRESENTATIVE OF THE TRUSTEE OR DEBTOR IN POSSESSION.

The undersigned, having reviewed the above listing of entities in which the estate of [Debtor] holds a substantial or controlling interest, and being familiar with the Debtor's financial affairs, verifies under the penalty of perjury that the listing is complete, accurate and truthful to the best of his/her knowledge.

Official Form 26 (12/08) – Cont. 2

Date: ___________

____
Signature of Authorized Individual

____
Name of Authorized Individual

____
Title of Authorized Individual

[If the Debtor is an individual or in a joint case]

Signature(s) of Debtor(s) (Individual/Joint)

____
Signature of Debtor

____
Signature of Joint Debtor

Exhibit A

Valuation Estimate for [Name of Entity]

[Provide a statement of the entity's value and the value of the estate's interest in the entity, including a description of the basis for the valuation, the date of the valuation and the valuation method used. This valuation must be no more than two years old. Indicate the source of this information.]

Exhibit B

Financial Statements for [Insert Name of Entity]

Exhibit B-1
Balance Sheet for [Name of Entity]
As of [date]

[Provide a balance sheet dated as of the end of the most recent six-month period of the current fiscal year and as of the end of the preceding fiscal year. Indicate the source of this information.]

Exhibit B-2
Statement of Income (Loss) for [Name of Entity]
Period ending [date]

[Provide a statement of income (loss) for the following periods:

(i) For the initial report:
a. the period between the end of the preceding fiscal year and the end of the most recent six-month period of the current fiscal year; and
b. the prior fiscal year.
(ii) For subsequent reports, since the closing date of the last report.

Indicate the source of this information.]

Official Form 26 (12/08) – Cont. 7

Exhibit B-3
Statement of Cash Flows for [Name of Entity]
For the period ending [date]

[Provide a statement of changes in cash flows for the following periods:

(i) For the initial report:
a. the period between the end of the preceding fiscal year and the end of the most recent six-month period of the current fiscal year; and
b. the prior fiscal year.
(ii) For subsequent reports, since the closing date of the last report.

Indicate the source of this information.]

Exhibit B-4
Statement of Changes in Shareholders'/Partners' Equity (Deficit) for [Name of Entity]
period ending [date]

[Provide a statement of changes in shareholders'/partners equity (deficit) for the following periods:

(i) For the initial report:
a. the period between the end of the preceding fiscal year and the end of the most recent six-month period of the current fiscal year; and
b. the prior fiscal year.
(ii) For subsequent reports, since the closing date of the last report.

Indicate the source of this information.]

Exhibit C
Description of Operations for [name of entity]

[Describe the nature and extent of the estate's interest in the entity.

Describe the business conducted and intended to be conducted by the entity, focusing on the entity's dominant business segment(s). Indicate the source of this information.]

Form 26, Instructions (12/08)

Instructions for Periodic Report Concerning Related Entities

General Instructions

1. This form periodic report ("Periodic Report") on value, profitability, and operations of entities in which the estate holds a substantial or controlling interest (the "Form") implements § 419 of the Bankruptcy Abuse Prevention and Consumer Protection Act of 2005, Pub. L. No. 19-8, 119 Stat. 23 (April 20, 2005)("BAPCPA"). This Form should be used when required by Fed. R. Bankr. P. 2015.3, with such variations as may be approved by the court pursuant to subdivisions (d) and (e) of that rule.

2. In a chapter 11 case, the trustee or debtor in possession shall file Periodic Reports of the value, operations, and profitability of each entity that is not also a debtor in a case under title 11, and in which the estate holds a substantial or controlling interest. The reports shall be prepared as prescribed by this Form, and shall be based upon the most recent information reasonably available to the trustee or debtor in possession.

3. Rule 2015.3 provides that, where the estate controls or owns at least a 20 percent interest of an entity, the estate's interest is presumed to be substantial or controlling. Where the estate controls or owns less than a 20 percent interest, the rule presumes that the estate's interest is not substantial or controlling. The question of substantial or controlling interest is, however, a factual one to be decided in each case.

4. The first Periodic Report required by subdivision (a) of Rule 2015.3 shall be filed no later than five days before the first date set for the meeting of creditors under § 341 of the Code. Subsequent Periodic Reports shall be filed no less frequently than every six months thereafter, until a plan of reorganization becomes effective or the case is closed, dismissed, or converted. Copies of the Periodic Report shall be served on the U.S. Trustee, any committee appointed under § 1102 of the Code, and any other party in interest that has filed a request therefor.

5. The source of the information contained in each Periodic Report shall be indicated.

Specific Instructions

6. Each entity subject to the reporting requirement of Rule 2015.3 shall be listed in the table contained on the first page of the form. Reports for each such entity shall be placed behind separate tabs, and each such report shall consist of three exhibits. Exhibit A shall provide valuation information; Exhibit B shall provide financial statements; and Exhibit C shall provide a description of operations.

Instructions for Exhibit A – Valuation

7. Provide a statement of the entity's value and the value of the estate's interest in the entity, including a description of the basis for the valuation, the date of the valuation, the valuation method used and the source or preparer of the information. This valuation must be no more than two years old.

Instructions for Exhibit B – Financial Statements and Profitability

8. The financial statements may be unaudited. The financial statements should be prepared in accordance with generally accepted accounting principles in the United States ("USGAAP"); deviations, if any from USGAAP, shall be disclosed. Indicate the source or preparer of the information.

9. Exhibit B shall include the following financial statements, and shall indicate the source of the information presented:

(a) A balance sheet dated as of the end of the most recent six-month period of the current fiscal year and as of the end of the preceding fiscal year.

(b) A statement of income (loss) for the following periods:
(i) For the initial report:
a. the period between the end of the preceding fiscal year and the end of the most recent six-month period of the current fiscal year; and
b. the prior fiscal year.
(ii) For subsequent reports, since the closing date of the last report.

(c) A statement of changes in cash flows for the following periods:
(i) For the initial report:
a. the period between the end of the preceding fiscal year and the end of the most recent six-month period of the current fiscal year; and
b. the prior fiscal year.
(ii) For subsequent reports, since the closing date of the last report.

(d) A statement of changes in shareholders'/partners' equity (deficit) for the following periods:
(i) For the initial report:
a. the period between the end of the preceding fiscal year and the end of the most recent six-month period of the current fiscal year; and
b. the prior fiscal year.
(ii) For subsequent reports, since the closing date of the last report.

10. The balance sheet contained in Exhibit B-1 may include only major captions with the exception of inventories. Data as to raw materials, work in process, and finished goods inventories should be included either on the face of the balance sheet or in the notes to

the financial statements, if applicable. Where any major balance sheet caption is less than 10% of total assets, the caption may be combined with others. An illustrative example of such a balance sheet is set forth below:

XYZ Company
Balance Sheet
As of________

Assets	Year to date	Prior Fiscal Year
Cash and cash items	________	________
Marketable securities	________	________
Accounts and notes receivable (non-affiliates), net of allowances	________	________
Accounts due from affiliates	________	________
Inventories		
Raw materials	________	________
Work in Process	________	________
Finished goods	________	________
Long-term contract costs	________	________
Supplies	________	________
LIFO reserve	________	________
Total inventories	________	________
Prepaid expenses	________	________
Other current assets	________	________
Total current assets	________	________
Securities of affiliates	________	________
Indebtedness of affiliates (non-current)	________	________
Other investments	________	________
Property, plant and equipment, net of accumulated depreciation and amortization	________	________
Intangible assets	________	________
Other assets	________	________
Total Assets	________	________

Liabilities and Shareholders'/Partners' Equity	Year to date	Prior Fiscal Year
Accounts and notes payable (non-affiliates)	________	________
Payables to affiliates	________	________
Other current liabilities	________	________
Total current liabilities	________	________

Bonds, mortgages, and other long-term debt, including capitalized leases	______	______
Indebtedness to affiliates (non-current)	______	______
Other liabilities	______	______
Commitments and contingencies	______	______
Deferred credits	______	______
Minority interests in consolidated subsidiaries	______	______
Preferred stock subject to mandatory redemption or whose redemption is outside the control of the issuer	______	______
Total liabilities	______	______
Shareholders' equity	______	______
Total liabilities and shareholders'/partners' equity	______	______

11. The statement of income (loss) contained in Exhibit B-2 should also include major captions. When any major statement of income (loss) caption is less than 15% of net income (loss) for the most recent fiscal year, the caption may be combined with others. Notwithstanding these tests, *de minimis* amounts need not be shown separately. An illustrative example of such a statement of income (loss) is set forth below:

XYZ Company
Statement of income (loss)
For the periods ending________

	Year to date	Prior Fiscal Year
Net sales and gross revenues	______	______
Costs and expenses applicable to sales and revenues	______	______
Gross profit	______	______
Selling, general, and administrative expenses	______	______
Provision for doubtful accounts	______	______
Other general expenses	______	______
Operating income (loss)	______	______
Non-operating income (loss)	______	______
Interest and amortization of debt discount	______	______
Non-operating expenses	______	______
Income or loss before income tax expense	______	______
Income tax expense	______	______
Minority interest in income of consolidated subsidiaries	______	______
Equity in earnings of unconsolidated subsidiaries		

and 50 per cent or less owned persons		
Income or loss from continuing operations		
Discontinued operations		
Income or loss before extraordinary items and cumulative effects of changes in accounting principles		
Extraordinary items, net of tax		
Cumulative effects of changes in accounting principles		
Net income (loss)		
Earnings per share data		

12. The statement of cash flows in Exhibit B-3 may be abbreviated, starting with a single figure of funds provided by operations and showing other changes individually only when they exceed 10% of the average of funds provided by operations for the most recent fiscal year. Notwithstanding this test, *de minimis* amounts need not be shown separately. An illustrative example of such a statement of cash flows is set forth below:

XYZ Company
Statement of cash flows
For the periods ending________

	Year to date	Prior Fiscal Year
Net cash provided (used) by operating activities		
Cash flows from investing activities		
Capital expenditures		
Sale of ___________		
Other (describe)		
Net cash provided (used) in investing activities		
Cash flows provided (used) by financing activities		
Net borrowings under line-of-credit		
Principal payments under capital leases		
Proceeds from issuance of long-term debt		
Proceeds from sale of stock		
Dividends paid/Partner Distributions		
Net cash provided (used) in financing activities		
Net increase (decrease) in cash and cash equivalents		
Cash and cash equivalents		

Beginning of period	______	______
End of period	______	______

13. Subject to paragraph 11 above, an illustrative example of such a statement of changes in shareholders'/partners' equity in Exhibit B-4 is set forth below:

XYZ Company
Statement of changes in shareholders'/partners' equity (deficit)
For the periods ending

	Year to date	Prior Fiscal Year
Balance, beginning of period	______	______
Comprehensive net income		
Net income	______	______
Other comprehensive income, net of tax	______	______
Unrealized gains (losses) on securities	______	______
Foreign translation adjustments	______	______
Minimum pension liability adjustment	______	______
Issuance of stock	______	______
Dividends paid	______	______
Balance, end of period	______	______

14. The financial information in the financial statements shall include disclosures either on the face of the statements or in accompanying footnotes sufficient to make the information not misleading. Disclosures should encompass, but not be limited to, for example, accounting principles and practices; estimates inherent in the preparation of financial statements; status of long-term contracts; capitalization including significant borrowings or modification of existing financing arrangements; and the reporting entity resulting from business combinations or dispositions. Where material contingencies exist, disclosure of such matters shall be provided.

15. If appropriate, the statement of income (loss) should show earnings (loss) per share and dividends declared per share applicable to common stock. The basis of the earnings per share computation should be stated together with the number of shares used in the computation.

16. In addition to the financial statements required above, entities in the development stage should provide the cumulative financial statements (condensed to the same degree as allowed above) and disclosures required by Statement of Financial Accounting Standards No. 7, "Accounting and Reporting by Development Stage Enterprises," to the date of the latest balance sheet presented.

Instructions for Exhibit C – Description of Operations

17. The description of operations contained in Exhibit C of this Form should describe the nature and extent of the estate's interest in the entity, as well as the business conducted by and intended to be conducted by the entity, focusing on the entity's dominant business segment(s) including, but not limited to the following as applicable:

- Principal product produced or services rendered and methods of distribution
- Description of the status of a new product or segment if a public announcement has been made or information publicly disseminated
- Sources and availability of raw materials
- Any significant patents, trademarks, licenses, franchises, and concessions held
- Seasonality of the business
- Dependence upon a single customer or a few customers
- Dollar amount of backlog orders believed to be firm
- Exposure to renegotiation or redetermination or termination of significant contracts
- Competitive conditions facing the entity
- Description of properties owned
- Significant legal proceedings
- Material purchase commitments
- Identified trends events or uncertainties that are likely to have a material impact on the entity's short-term liquidity, net sales, or income from continuing operations

18. The source preparer of the information should be indicated.

(As added Dec. 1, 2008.)

Form 27. Reaffirmation Agreement Cover Sheet

B 27 (Official Form 27) (12/13)

UNITED STATES BANKRUPTCY COURT

In re ______________________________,
Debtor

Case No. ____________________
Chapter ____

REAFFIRMATION AGREEMENT COVER SHEET

This form must be completed in its entirety and filed, with the reaffirmation agreement attached, within the time set under Rule 4008. It may be filed by any party to the reaffirmation agreement.

1. Creditor's Name:______________________________

2. Amount of the debt subject to this reaffirmation agreement:
$__________ on the date of bankruptcy $__________ to be paid under reaffirmation agreement

3. Annual percentage rate of interest: ______% prior to bankruptcy
______% under reaffirmation agreement (___ Fixed Rate ___ Adjustable Rate)

4. Repayment terms (if fixed rate): $______ per month for _______ months

5. Collateral, if any, securing the debt: Current market value: $_________
Description: ______________________________

6. Does the creditor assert that the debt is nondischargeable? ___Yes ___ No
(If yes, attach a declaration setting forth the nature of the debt and basis for the contention that the debt is nondischargeable.)

Debtor's Schedule I and J Entries		**Debtor's Income and Expenses as Stated on Reaffirmation Agreement**	
7A. Total monthly income from Schedule I, line 12	$_______	7B. Monthly income from all sources after payroll deductions	$_______
8A. Total monthly expenses from Schedule J, line 22	$_______	8B. Monthly expenses	$_______
9A. Total monthly payments on reaffirmed debts not listed on Schedule J	$_______	9B. Total monthly payments on reaffirmed debts not included in monthly expenses	$_______
		10B. Net monthly income (Subtract sum of lines 8B and 9B from line 7B. If total is less than zero, put the number in brackets.)	$_______

11. Explain with specificity any difference between the income amounts (7A and 7B):

12. Explain with specificity any difference between the expense amounts (8A and 8B):

If line 11 or12 is completed, the undersigned debtor, and joint debtor if applicable, certifies that any explanation contained on those lines is true and correct.

____________________	____________________
Signature of Debtor (only required if line 11 or 12 is completed)	Signature of Joint Debtor (if applicable, and only required if line 11 or 12 is completed)

Other Information

☐ Check this box if the total on line 10B is less than zero. If that number is less than zero, a presumption of undue hardship arises (unless the creditor is a credit union) and you must explain with specificity the sources of funds available to the Debtor to make the monthly payments on the reaffirmed debt:

Was debtor represented by counsel during the course of negotiating this reaffirmation agreement?
_____Yes _______No

If debtor was represented by counsel during the course of negotiating this reaffirmation agreement, has counsel executed a certification (affidavit or declaration) in support of the reaffirmation agreement?
_____Yes _______No

FILER'S CERTIFICATION

I hereby certify that the attached agreement is a true and correct copy of the reaffirmation agreement between the parties identified on this Reaffirmation Agreement Cover Sheet.

____
Signature

____
Print/Type Name & Signer's Relation to Case

(As added Dec. 1, 2009; Dec. 1, 2013.)

Bankruptcy Procedural Forms

PROCEDURAL FORMS

A substantial number of procedural forms, which are not designated as official, have been developed by the Administrative Office of the United States Courts and published in Part II, "Procedural Forms and Instructions," of the Bankruptcy Forms Manual. Due to the volume and unofficial status of the forms, the forms have been omitted from this publication. However, these forms are published in Collier on Bankruptcy. The forms are also available on the Administrative Office of the United States Courts website at http://www.uscourts.gov/bkforms/bankruptcy_forms.html#procedure.

Bankruptcy Process in France

FEDERAL RULES OF APPELLATE PROCEDURE

I. APPLICABILITY OF RULES

I. APPLICABILITY OF RULES

Rule 1. Scope of Rules; Definition; Title

(a) Scope of Rules. (1) These rules govern procedure in the United States courts of appeals.

(2) When these rules provide for filing a motion or other document in the district court, the procedure must comply with the practice of the district court.

(b) Definition. In these rules, 'state' includes the District of Columbia and any United States commonwealth or territory.

(c) Title. These rules are to be known as the Federal Rules of Appellate Procedure.

(Amended April 30, 1979, effective Aug. 1, 1979; amended Dec. 1, 1989; Dec. 1, 1994; Dec. 1, 1998; Dec. 1, 2002; Dec. 1, 2010.)

Rule 2. Suspension of Rules

On its own or a party's motion, a court of appeals may—to expedite its decision or for other good cause—suspend any provision of these rules in a particular case and order proceedings as it directs, except as otherwise provided in Rule 26(b).

(Amended Dec. 1, 1998.)

II. APPEAL FROM A JUDGMENT OR ORDER OF A DISTRICT COURT

Rule 3. Appeal as of Right—How Taken

(a) Filing the Notice of Appeal. (1) An appeal permitted by law as of right from a district court to a court of appeals may be taken only by filing a notice of appeal with the district clerk within the time allowed by Rule 4. At the time of filing, the appellant must furnish the clerk with enough copies of the notice to enable the clerk to comply with Rule 3(d).

(2) An appellant's failure to take any step other than the timely filing of a notice of appeal does not affect the validity of the appeal, but is ground only for the court of appeals to act as it considers appropriate, including dismissing the appeal.

(3) An appeal from a judgment by a magistrate judge in a civil case is taken in the same way as an appeal from any other district court judgment.

(4) An appeal by permission under 28 U.S.C. § 1292(b) or an appeal in a bankruptcy case may be taken only in the manner prescribed by Rules 5 and 6, respectively.

(b) Joint or Consolidated Appeals. (1) When two or more parties are entitled to appeal from a district-court judgment or order, and their interests make joinder practicable, they may file a joint notice of appeal. They may then proceed on appeal as a single appellant.

(2) When the parties have filed separate timely notices of appeal, the appeals may be joined or consolidated by the court of appeals.

(c) Contents of the Notice of Appeal. (1) The notice of appeal must:

(A) specify the party or parties taking the appeal by naming each one in the caption or body of the notice, but an attorney representing more than one party may describe those parties with such terms as "all plaintiffs," "the defendants," "the plaintiffs A, B, et al.," or "all defendants except X";

(B) designate the judgment, order, or part thereof being appealed; and

(C) name the court to which the appeal is taken.

(2) A pro se notice of appeal is considered filed on behalf of the signer and the signer's spouse and minor children (if they are parties), unless the notice clearly indicates otherwise.

(3) In a class action, whether or not the class has been certified, the notice of appeal is sufficient if it names one person qualified to bring the appeal as representative of the class.

(4) An appeal must not be dismissed for informality of form or title of the notice of appeal, or for failure to name a party whose intent to appeal is otherwise clear from the notice.

(5) Form 1 in the Appendix of Forms is a suggested form of a notice of appeal.

(d) Serving the Notice of Appeal. (1) The district clerk must serve notice of the filing of a notice of appeal by mailing a copy to each party's counsel of record — excluding the appellant's — or, if a party is proceeding pro se, to the party's last known address. When a defendant in a criminal case appeals, the clerk must also serve a copy of the notice of appeal on the defendant, either by personal service or by mail addressed to the defendant. The clerk must promptly send a copy of the notice of appeal and of the docket entries — and any later docket entries — to the clerk of the court of appeals named in the notice. The district clerk must note, on each copy, the date when the notice of appeal was filed.

(2) If an inmate confined in an institution files a notice of appeal in the manner provided by Rule 4(c), the district clerk must also note the date when the clerk docketed the notice.

(3) The district clerk's failure to serve notice does not affect the validity of the appeal. The clerk must note on the docket the names of the parties to whom the clerk mails copies, with the date of mailing. Service is sufficient despite the death of a party or the party's counsel.

(e) Payment of Fees. Upon filing a notice of appeal, the appellant must pay the district clerk all required fees. The district clerk receives the appellate docket fee on behalf of the court of appeals.

(Amended April 30, 1979, effective Aug. 1, 1979; amended July 1, 1986; Dec. 1, 1989; Dec. 1, 1993; Dec. 1, 1994; Dec. 1, 1998.)

Rule 3.1. Appeal from a Judgment of a Magistrate Judge in a Civil Case [Abrogated Dec. 1, 1998]

Rule 4. Appeal as of Right—When Taken

(a) Appeal in a Civil Case.

(1) *Time for Filing a Notice of Appeal.*

(A) In a civil case, except as provided in Rules 4(a)(1)(B), 4(a)(4), and 4(c), the notice of appeal required by Rule 3 must be filed with the district clerk within 30 days after entry of the judgment or order appealed from.

(B) The notice of appeal may be filed by any party within 60 days after entry of the judgment or order appealed from if one of the parties is:

(i) the United States;

(ii) a United States agency;

(iii) a United States officer or employee sued in an official capacity; or

(iv) a current or former United States officer or employee sued in an individual capacity for an act or omission occurring in connection with duties performed on the United States' behalf—including all instances in which the United States represents that person when the judgment or order is entered or files the appeal for that person.

(C) An appeal from an order granting or denying an application for a writ of error *coram nobis* is an appeal in a civil case for purposes of Rule 4(a).

(2) *Filing Before Entry of Judgment.* A notice of appeal filed after the court announces a decision or order — but before the entry of the judgment or

order — is treated as filed on the date of and after the entry.

(3) *Multiple Appeals.* If one party timely files a notice of appeal, any other party may file a notice of appeal within 14 days after the date when the first notice was filed, or within the time otherwise prescribed by this Rule 4(a), whichever period ends later.

(4) *Effect of a Motion on a Notice of Appeal.* (A) If a party timely files in the district court any of the following motions under the Federal Rules of Civil Procedure, the time to file an appeal runs for all parties from the entry of the order disposing of the last such remaining motion:

(i) for judgment under Rule 50(b);

(ii) to amend or make additional factual findings under Rule 52(b), whether or not granting the motion would alter the judgment;

(iii) for attorney's fees under Rule 54 if the district court extends the time to appeal under Rule 58;

(iv) to alter or amend the judgment under Rule 59;

(v) for a new trial under Rule 59; or

(vi) for relief under Rule 60 if the motion is filed no later than 28 days after the judgment is entered.

(B)(i) If a party files a notice of appeal after the court announces or enters a judgment — but before it disposes of any motion listed in Rule 4(a)(4)(A) — the notice becomes effective to appeal a judgment or order, in whole or in part, when the order disposing of the last such remaining motion is entered.

(ii) A party intending to challenge an order disposing of any motion listed in Rule 4(a)(4)(A), or a judgment's alteration or amendment upon such a motion, must file a notice of appeal, or an amended notice of appeal — in compliance with Rule 3(c) — within the time prescribed by this Rule measured from the entry of the order disposing of the last such remaining motion.

(iii) No additional fee is required to file an amended notice.

(5) *Motion for Extension of Time.* (A) The district court may extend the time to file a notice of appeal if:

(i) a party so moves no later than 30 days after the time prescribed by this Rule 4(a) expires; and

(ii) regardless of whether its motion is filed before or during the 30 days after the time prescribed by this Rule 4(a) expires, that party shows excusable neglect or good cause.

(B) A motion filed before the expiration of the time prescribed in Rule 4(a)(1) or (3) may be ex parte unless the court requires otherwise. If the motion is filed after the expiration of the prescribed time, notice must be given to the other parties in accordance with local rules.

(C) No extension under this Rule 4(a)(5) may exceed 30 days after the prescribed time or 14 days after the date when the order granting the motion is entered, whichever is later.

(6) *Reopening the Time to File an Appeal.* The district court may reopen the time to file an appeal for a period of 14 days after the date when its order to reopen is entered, but only if all the following conditions are satisfied:

(A) the court finds that the moving party did not receive notice under Federal Rule of Civil Procedure 77(d) of the entry of the judgment or order sought to be appealed within 21 days after entry;

(B) the motion is filed within 180 days after the judgment or order is entered or within 14 days after the moving party receives notice under Federal Rule of Civil Procedure 77(d) of the entry, whichever is earlier; and

(C) the court finds that no party would be prejudiced.

(7) *Entry Defined.* (A) A judgment or order is entered for purposes of this Rule 4(a):

(i) if Federal Rule of Civil Procedure 58(a) does not require a separate document, when the judgment or order is entered in the civil docket under Federal Rule of Civil Procedure 79(a); or

(ii) if Federal Rule of Civil Procedure 58(a) requires a separate document, when the judgment or order is entered in the civil docket under Federal Rule of Civil Procedure 79(a) and when the earlier of these events occurs:

- the judgment or order is set forth on a separate document, or
- 150 days have run from entry of the judgment or order in the civil docket under Federal Rule of Civil Procedure 79(a).

(B) A failure to set forth a judgment or order on a separate document when required by Federal Rule of Civil Procedure 58(a) does not affect the validity of an appeal from that judgment or order.

(b) Appeal in a Criminal Case. (1) *Time for Filing a Notice of Appeal.* (A) In a criminal case, a defendant's notice of appeal must be filed in the district court within 14 days after the later of:

(i) the entry of either the judgment or the order being appealed; or

(ii) the filing of the government's notice of appeal.

(B) When the government is entitled to appeal, its notice of appeal must be filed in the district court within 30 days after the later of:

(i) the entry of the judgment or order being appealed; or

(ii) the filing of a notice of appeal by any defendant.

(2) *Filing Before Entry of Judgment.* A notice of appeal filed after the court announces a decision, sentence, or order — but before the entry of the judgment or order — is treated as filed on the date of and after the entry.

(3) *Effect of a Motion on a Notice of Appeal.*

(A) If a defendant timely makes any of the following motions under the Federal Rules of Criminal Procedure, the notice of appeal from a judgment of conviction must be filed within 14 days after the entry of the order disposing of the last such remaining motion, or within 14 days after the entry of the judgment of conviction, whichever period ends later. This provision applies to a timely motion:

(i) for judgment of acquittal under Rule 29;

(ii) for a new trial under Rule 33, but if based on newly discovered evidence, only if the motion is made no later than 14 days after the entry of the judgment; or

(iii) for arrest of judgment under Rule 34.

(B) A notice of appeal filed after the court announces a decision, sentence, or order — but before it disposes of any of the motions referred to in Rule 4(b)(3)(A) — becomes effective upon the later of the following:

(i) the entry of the order disposing of the last such remaining motion; or

(ii) the entry of the judgment of conviction.

(C) A valid notice of appeal is effective — without amendment — to appeal from an order disposing of any of the motions referred to in Rule 4(b)(3)(A).

(4) *Motion for Extension of Time.* Upon a finding of excusable neglect or good cause, the district court may — before or after the time has expired, with or without motion and notice — extend the time to file a notice of appeal for a period not to exceed 30 days from the expiration of the time otherwise prescribed by this Rule 4(b).

(5) *Jurisdiction.* The filing of a notice of appeal under this Rule 4(b) does not divest a district court of jurisdiction to correct a sentence under Federal Rule of Criminal Procedure 35(a), nor does the filing of a motion under 35(a) affect the validity of a notice of appeal filed before entry of the order disposing of the motion. The filing of a motion under Federal Rule of Criminal Procedure 35(a) does not suspend the time for filing a notice of appeal from a judgment of conviction.

(6) *Entry Defined.* A judgment or order is entered for purposes of this Rule 4(b) when it is entered on the criminal docket.

(c) Appeal by an Inmate Confined in an Institution. (1) If an inmate confined in an institution files a notice of appeal in either a civil or a criminal case, the notice is timely if it is deposited in the institution's internal mail system on or before the last day for filing. If an institution has a system designed for legal mail, the inmate must use that system to receive the benefit of this rule. Timely filing may be shown by a declaration in compliance with 28 U.S.C. § 1746 or by a notarized statement, either of which must set forth the date of deposit and state that first-class postage has been prepaid.

(2) If an inmate files the first notice of appeal in a civil case under this Rule 4(c), the 14-day period provided in Rule 4(a)(3) for another party to file a notice of appeal runs from the date when the district court dockets the first notice.

(3) When a defendant in a criminal case files a notice of appeal under this Rule 4(c), the 30-day period for the government to file its notice of appeal runs from the entry of the judgment or order appealed from or from the district court's docketing of the defendant's notice of appeal, whichever is later.

(d) Mistaken Filing in the Court of Appeals. If a notice of appeal in either a civil or a criminal case is mistakenly filed in the court of appeals, the clerk of that court must note on the notice the date when it was received and send it to the district clerk. The notice is then considered filed in the district court on the date so noted.

(Amended April 30, 1979, effective Aug. 1, 1979; amended Nov. 18, 1988, P. L. 100-690, Title VII, Subtitle C, § 7111, 102 Stat. 4419; Dec. 1, 1991; Dec. 1, 1993; Dec. 1, 1995; Dec. 1, 1998; Dec. 1, 2002; Dec. 1, 2005; Dec. 1, 2009; Dec. 1, 2010; Dec. 1, 2011.)

Rule 5. Appeal by Permission

(a) Petition for Permission to Appeal. (1) To request permission to appeal when an appeal is within the court of appeals' discretion, a party must file a petition for permission to appeal. The petition must be filed with the circuit clerk with proof of service on all other parties to the district-court action.

(2) The petition must be filed within the time specified by the statute or rule authorizing the appeal or, if no such time is specified, within the time provided by Rule 4(a) for filing a notice of appeal.

(3) If a party cannot petition for appeal unless the district court first enters an order granting permission to do so or stating that the necessary conditions are met, the district court may amend its order, either on its own or in response to a party's motion, to include the required permission or statement. In that event, the time to petition runs from entry of the amended order.

(b) Contents of the Petition; Answer or Cross-Petition; Oral Argument. (1) The petition must include the following:

(A) the facts necessary to understand the question presented;

(B) the question itself;

(C) the relief sought;

(D) the reasons why the appeal should be allowed and is authorized by a statute or rule; and

(E) an attached copy of:

(i) the order, decree, or judgment complained of and any related opinion or memorandum, and

(ii) any order stating the district court's permission to appeal or finding that the necessary conditions are met.

(2) A party may file an answer in opposition or a cross-petition within 10 days after the petition is served.

(3) The petition and answer will be submitted without oral argument unless the court of appeals orders otherwise.

(c) Form of Papers; Number of Copies. All papers must conform to Rule 32(c)(2). Except by the court's permission, a paper must not exceed 20 pages, exclusive of the disclosure statement, the proof of service, and the accompanying documents required by Rule 5(b)(1)(E). An original and 3 copies must be filed unless the court requires a different number by local rule or by order in a particular case.

(d) Grant of Permission; Fees; Cost Bond; Filing the Record. (1) Within 14 days after the entry of the order granting permission to appeal, the appellant must:

(A) pay the district clerk all required fees; and

(B) file a cost bond if required under Rule 7.

(2) A notice of appeal need not be filed. The date when the order granting permission to appeal is entered serves as the date of the notice of appeal for calculating time under these rules.

(3) The district clerk must notify the circuit clerk once the petitioner has paid the fees. Upon receiving this notice, the circuit clerk must enter the appeal on the docket. The record must be forwarded and filed in accordance with Rules 11 and 12(c).

(Amended April 30, 1979, effective Aug. 1, 1979; amended Dec. 1, 1994; Dec. 1, 1998; Dec. 1, 2002; Dec. 1, 2009.)

Rule 5.1. Appeal by Leave under 28 U.S.C. § 636(c)(5) [Abrogated Dec. 1, 1998]

Rule 6. Appeal in a Bankruptcy Case

(a) Appeal From a Judgment, Order, or Decree of a District Court Exercising Original Jurisdiction in a Bankruptcy Case. An appeal to a court of appeals from a final judgment, order, or decree of a district court exercising jurisdiction under 28 U.S.C. § 1334 is taken as any other civil appeal under these rules.

(b) Appeal From a Judgment, Order, or Decree of a District Court or Bankruptcy Appellate Panel Exercising Appellate Jurisdiction in a Bankruptcy Case.

(1) *(1) Applicability of Other Rules.* These rules apply to an appeal to a court of appeals under 28 U.S.C. § 158(d)(1) from a final judgment, order, or decree of a district court or bankruptcy appellate panel exercising appellate jurisdiction under 28 U.S.C. § 158(a) or (b), but with these qualifications:

(A) Rules 4(a)(4), 4(b), 9, 10, 11, 12(c), 13–20, 22–23, and 24(b) do not apply;

(B) the reference in Rule 3(c) to "Form 1 in the Appendix of Forms" must be read as a reference to Form 5;

(C) when the appeal is from a bankruptcy appellate panel, "district court," as used in any applicable rule, means "appellate panel"; and

(D) in Rule 12.1, "district court" includes a bankruptcy court or bankruptcy appellate panel.

(2) *Additional Rules.* In addition to the rules made applicable by Rule 6(b)(1), the following rules apply:

(A) Motion for rehearing.

(i) If a timely motion for rehearing under Bankruptcy Rule 8022 is filed, the time to appeal for all parties runs from the entry of the order disposing of the motion. A notice of appeal filed after the district court or bankruptcy appellate panel announces or enters a judgment, order, or decree—but before disposition of the motion for rehearing—becomes effective when the order disposing of the motion for rehearing is entered.

(ii) If a party intends to challenge the order disposing of the motion—or the alteration or amendment of a judgment, order, or decree upon the motion—then the party, in compliance with Rules 3(c) and 6(b)(1)(B), must file a notice of appeal or amended notice of appeal. The notice or amended notice must be filed within the time prescribed by Rule 4—excluding Rules 4(a)(4) and 4(b)—measured from the entry of the order disposing of the motion.

(iii) No additional fee is required to file an amended notice.

(B) The record on appeal.

(i) Within 14 days after filing the notice of appeal, the appellant must file with the clerk possessing the record assembled in accordance with Bankruptcy Rule 8009—and serve on the appellee—a statement of the issues to be presented on appeal and a designation of the record to be certified and made available to the circuit clerk.

(ii) An appellee who believes that other parts of the record are necessary must, within 14 days after being served with the appellant's designation, file with the clerk and serve on the appellant a designation of additional parts to be included.

(iii) The record on appeal consists of:

- the redesignated record as provided above;
- the proceedings in the district court or bankruptcy appellate panel; and
- a certified copy of the docket entries prepared by the clerk under Rule 3(d).

(C) Making the record available.

(i) When the record is complete, the district clerk or bankruptcy-appellate-panel clerk must number the documents constituting the record and promptly make it available to the circuit clerk. If the clerk makes the record available in paper form, the clerk will not send documents of unusual bulk or weight, physical exhibits other than documents, or other parts of the record designated for omission by local rule of the court of appeals, unless directed to do so by a party or the circuit clerk. If unusually bulky or heavy exhibits are to be made available in paper form, a party must arrange with the clerks in advance for their transportation and receipt.

(ii) All parties must do whatever else is necessary to enable the clerk to assemble the record and make it available. When the record is made available in paper form, the court of appeals may provide by rule or order that a certified copy of the docket entries be made available in place of the redesignated record. But any party may request at any time during the pendency of the appeal that the redesignated record be made available.

(D) Filing the record. When the district clerk or bankruptcy-appellate-panel clerk has made the record available, the circuit clerk must note that fact on the docket. The date noted on the docket serves as the filing date of the record. The circuit clerk must immediately notify all parties of the filing date.

(c) Direct Review by Permission Under 28 U.S.C. § 158(d)(2).

(1) *Applicability of Other Rules.* These rules apply to a direct appeal by permission under 28 U.S.C. § 158(d)(2), but with these qualifications:

(A) Rules 3–4, 5(a)(3), 6(a), 6(b), 8(a), 8(c), 9–12, 13–20, 22–23, and 24(b) do not apply;

(B) as used in any applicable rule, "district court" or "district clerk" includes—to the extent appropriate—a bankruptcy court or bankruptcy appellate panel or its clerk; and

(C) the reference to "Rules 11 and 12(c)" in Rule 5(d)(3) must be read as a reference to Rules 6(c)(2)(B) and (C).

(2) *Additional Rules.* In addition, the following rules apply:

(A) The record on appeal. Bankruptcy Rule 8009 governs the record on appeal.

(B) Making the record available. Bankruptcy Rule 8010 governs completing the record and making it available.

(C) Stays pending appeal. Bankruptcy Rule 8007 applies to stays pending appeal.

(D) Duties of the circuit clerk. When the bankruptcy clerk has made the record available, the circuit clerk must note that fact on the docket. The date noted on the docket serves as the filing date of the record. The circuit clerk must immediately notify all parties of the filing date.

(E) Filing a representation statement. Unless the court of appeals designates another time, within 14 days after entry of the order granting permission to appeal, the attorney who sought permission must file a statement with the circuit clerk naming the parties that the attorney represents on appeal.

(Amended April 30, 1979, effective Aug. 1, 1979; amended Dec. 1, 1989; Dec. 1, 1993; Dec. 1, 1998; Dec. 1, 2009; April 25, 2014, eff. Dec. 1, 2014.)

Rule 7. Bond for Costs on Appeal in a Civil Case

In a civil case, the district court may require an appellant to file a bond or provide other security in any form and amount necessary to ensure payment of costs on appeal. Rule 8(b) applies to a surety on a bond given under this rule.

(Amended April 30, 1979, effective Aug. 1, 1979; amended Dec. 1, 1998.)

Rule 8. Stay or Injunction Pending Appeal

(a) Motion for Stay. (1) *Initial Motion in the District Court.* A party must ordinarily move first in the district court for the following relief:

(A) a stay of the judgment or order of a district court pending appeal;

(B) approval of a supersedeas bond; or

(C) an order suspending, modifying, restoring, or granting an injunction while an appeal is pending.

(2) *Motion in the Court of Appeals; Conditions on Relief.* A motion for the relief mentioned in Rule 8(a)(1) may be made to the court of appeals or to one of its judges.

(A) The motion must:

(i) show that moving first in the district court would be impracticable; or

(ii) state that, a motion having been made, the district court denied the motion or failed to afford the relief requested and state any reasons given by the district court for its action.

(B) The motion must also include:

(i) the reasons for granting the relief requested and the facts relied on;

(ii) originals or copies of affidavits or other sworn statements supporting facts subject to dispute; and

(iii) relevant parts of the record.

(C) The moving party must give reasonable notice of the motion to all parties.

(D) A motion under this Rule 8(a)(2) must be filed with the circuit clerk and normally will be considered by a panel of the court. But in an exceptional case in which time requirements make that procedure impracticable, the motion may be made to and considered by a single judge.

(E) The court may condition relief on a party's filing a bond or other appropriate security in the district court.

(b) Proceeding Against a Surety. If a party gives security in the form of a bond or stipulation or other undertaking with one or more sureties, each surety submits to the jurisdiction of the district court and irrevocably appoints the district clerk as the surety's agent on whom any papers affecting the surety's liability on the bond or undertaking may be served. On motion, a surety's liability may be enforced in the district court without the necessity of an independent action. The motion and any notice that the district court prescribes may be served on the district clerk, who must promptly mail a copy to each surety whose address is known.

(c) Stay in a Criminal Case. Rule 38 of the Federal Rules of Criminal Procedure governs a stay in a criminal case.

(Amended July 1, 1986; Dec. 1, 1995; Dec. 1, 1998.)

Rule 9. Release in a Criminal Case

(a) Release Before Judgment of Conviction. (1) The district court must state in writing, or orally on the record, the reasons for an order regarding the release or detention of a defendant in a criminal case. A party appealing from the order must file with the court of appeals a copy of the district court's order and the court's statement of reasons as soon as practicable after filing the notice of appeal. An appellant who questions the factual basis for the district court's order must file a transcript of the release proceedings or an explanation of why a transcript was not obtained.

(2) After reasonable notice to the appellee, the court of appeals must promptly determine the appeal on the basis of the papers, affidavits, and parts

of the record that the parties present or the court requires. Unless the court so orders, briefs need not be filed.

(3) The court of appeals or one of its judges may order the defendant's release pending the disposition of the appeal.

(b) Release After Judgment of Conviction. A party entitled to do so may obtain review of a district-court order regarding release after a judgment of conviction by filing a notice of appeal from that order in the district court, or by filing a motion in the court of appeals if the party has already filed a notice of appeal from the judgment of conviction. Both the order and the review are subject to Rule 9(a). The papers filed by the party seeking review must include a copy of the judgment of conviction.

(c) Criteria for Release. The court must make its decision regarding release in accordance with the applicable provisions of 18 U.S.C. §§ 3142, 3143, and 3145(c).

(As amended April 24, 1972, effective Oct. 1, 1972; amended Oct. 12, 1984, P. L. 98-473, Title II, Ch I, § 210, 98 Stat. 1987; Dec. 1, 1994; Dec. 1, 1998.)

Rule 10. The Record on Appeal

(a) Composition of the Record on Appeal. The following items constitute the record on appeal:

(1) the original papers and exhibits filed in the district court;

(2) the transcript of proceedings, if any; and

(3) a certified copy of the docket entries prepared by the district clerk.

(b) The Transcript of Proceedings. (1) *Appellant's Duty to Order.* Within 14 days after filing the notice of appeal or entry of an order disposing of the last timely remaining motion of a type specified in Rule 4(a)(4)(A), whichever is later, the appellant must do either of the following:

(A) order from the reporter a transcript of such parts of the proceedings not already on file as the appellant considers necessary, subject to a local rule of the court of appeals and with the following qualifications:

(i) the order must be in writing;

(ii) if the cost of the transcript is to be paid by the United States under the Criminal Justice Act, the order must so state; and

(iii) the appellant must, within the same period, file a copy of the order with the district clerk; or

(B) file a certificate stating that no transcript will be ordered.

(2) *Unsupported Finding or Conclusion.* If the appellant intends to urge on appeal that a finding or conclusion is unsupported by the evidence or is contrary to the evidence, the appellant must include in the record a transcript of all evidence relevant to that finding or conclusion.

(3) *Partial Transcript.* Unless the entire transcript is ordered:

(A) the appellant must—within the 14 days provided in Rule 10(b)(1)—file a statement of the issues that the appellant intends to present on the appeal and must serve on the appellee a copy of both the order or certificate and the statement;

(B) if the appellee considers it necessary to have a transcript of other parts of the proceedings, the appellee must, within 14 days after the service of the order or certificate and the statement of the issues, file and serve on the appellant a designation of additional parts to be ordered; and

(C) unless within 14 days after service of that designation the appellant has ordered all such parts, and has so notified the appellee, the appellee may within the following 14 days either order the parts or move in the district court for an order requiring the appellant to do so.

(4) *Payment.* At the time of ordering, a party must make satisfactory arrangements with the reporter for paying the cost of the transcript.

(c) Statement of the Evidence When the Proceedings Were Not Recorded or When a Transcript Is Unavailable. If the transcript of a hearing or trial is unavailable, the appellant may prepare a statement of the evidence or proceedings from the best available means, including the appellant's recollection. The statement must be served on the appellee, who may serve objections or proposed amendments within 14 days after being served. The statement and any objections or proposed amendments must then be submitted to the district court for settlement and approval. As settled and approved, the statement must be included by the district clerk in the record on appeal.

(d) Agreed Statement as the Record on Appeal. In place of the record on appeal as defined in Rule 10(a), the parties may prepare, sign, and submit to the district court a statement of the case showing how the issues presented by the appeal arose and were decided in the district court. The statement must set forth only those facts averred and proved or sought to be proved that are essential to the court's resolution of the issues. If the statement is truthful, it — together with any additions that the district court may consider necessary to a full presentation of the issues on appeal — must be approved by the district court and must then be certified to the court of appeals as the record on appeal. The district clerk must then send it to the circuit clerk within the time provided by Rule 11. A copy of the agreed statement may be filed in place of the appendix required by Rule 30.

(e) Correction or Modification of the Record. (1) If any difference arises about whether the record truly discloses what occurred in the district court, the difference must be submitted to and settled by that court and the record conformed accordingly.

(2) If anything material to either party is omitted from or misstated in the record by error or accident, the omission or misstatement may be corrected and a supplemental record may be certified and forwarded:

(A) on stipulation of the parties;

(B) by the district court before or after the record has been forwarded; or

(C) by the court of appeals.

(3) All other questions as to the form and content of the record must be presented to the court of appeals.

(Amended April 30, 1979, effective Aug. 1, 1979; amended July 1, 1986; Dec. 1, 1991; Dec. 1, 1993; Dec. 1, 1995; Dec. 1, 1998; Dec. 1, 2009.)

Rule 11. Forwarding the Record

(a) Appellant's Duty. An appellant filing a notice of appeal must comply with Rule 10(b) and must do whatever else is necessary to enable the clerk to assemble and forward the record. If there are multiple appeals from a judgment or order, the clerk must forward a single record.

(b) Duties of Reporter and District Clerk. (1) *Reporter's Duty to Prepare and File a Transcript.* The reporter must prepare and file a transcript as follows:

(A) Upon receiving an order for a transcript, the reporter must enter at the foot of the order the date of its receipt and the expected completion date and send a copy, so endorsed, to the circuit clerk.

(B) If the transcript cannot be completed within 30 days of the reporter's receipt of the order, the reporter may request the circuit clerk to grant additional time to complete it. The clerk must note on the docket the action taken and notify the parties.

(C) When a transcript is complete, the reporter must file it with the district clerk and notify the circuit clerk of the filing.

(D) If the reporter fails to file the transcript on time, the circuit clerk must notify the district judge and do whatever else the court of appeals directs.

(2) *District Clerk's Duty to Forward.* When the record is complete, the district clerk must number the documents constituting the record and send them promptly to the circuit clerk together with a list of the documents correspondingly numbered and reasonably identified. Unless directed to do so by a party or the circuit clerk, the district clerk will not send to the court of appeals documents of unusual bulk or weight, physical exhibits other than documents, or other parts of the record designated for omission by local rule of the court of appeals. If the exhibits are unusually bulky or heavy, a party must arrange with the clerks in advance for their transportation and receipt.

(c) Retaining the Record Temporarily in the District Court for Use in Preparing the Appeal. The parties may stipulate, or the district court on motion may order, that the district clerk retain the record temporarily for the parties to use in preparing the papers on appeal. In that event the district clerk must certify to the circuit clerk that the record on appeal is complete. Upon receipt of the appellee's brief, or earlier if the court orders or the parties agree, the appellant must request the district clerk to forward the record.

(d) [Abrogated]

(e) Retaining the Record by Court Order. (1) The court of appeals may, by order or local rule, provide that a certified copy of the docket entries be forwarded instead of the entire record. But a party may at any time during the appeal request that designated parts of the record be forwarded.

(2) The district court may order the record or some part of it retained if the court needs it while the appeal is pending, subject, however, to call by the court of appeals.

(3) If part or all of the record is ordered retained, the district clerk must send to the court of appeals a copy of the order and the docket entries together with the parts of the original record allowed by the district court and copies of any parts of the record designated by the parties.

(f) Retaining Parts of the Record in the District Court by Stipulation of the Parties. The parties may agree by written stipulation filed in the district court that designated parts of the record be retained in the district court subject to call by the court of appeals or request by a party. The parts of the record so designated remain a part of the record on appeal.

(g) Record for a Preliminary Motion in the Court of Appeals. If, before the record is forwarded, a party makes any of the following motions in the court of appeals:

- for dismissal;
- for release;
- for a stay pending appeal;
- for additional security on the bond on appeal or on a supersedeas bond; or
- for any other intermediate order —

the district clerk must send the court of appeals any parts of the record designated by any party.

(Amended April 30, 1979, effective Aug. 1, 1979; amended July 1, 1986; Dec. 1, 1998.)

Rule 12. Docketing the Appeal; Filing a Representation Statement; Filing the Record

(a) Docketing the Appeal. Upon receiving the copy of the notice of appeal and the docket entries from the district clerk under Rule 3(d), the circuit clerk must docket the appeal under the title of the district-court action and must identify the appellant, adding the appellant's name if necessary.

(b) Filing a Representation Statement. Unless the court of appeals designates another time, the attorney who filed the notice of appeal must, within 14 days after filing the notice, file a statement with the circuit clerk naming the parties that the attorney represents on appeal.

(c) Filing the Record, Partial Record, or Certificate. Upon receiving the record, partial record, or district clerk's certificate as provided in Rule 11, the circuit clerk must file it and immediately notify all parties of the filing date.

(Amended April 30, 1979, effective Aug. 1, 1979; amended July 1, 1986; Dec. 1, 1993; Dec. 1, 1998;

Dec. 1, 2009.)

Rule 12.1. Remand After an Indicative Ruling by the District Court on a Motion for Relief That Is Barred by a Pending Appeal

(a) Notice to the Court of Appeals. If a timely motion is made in the district court for relief that it lacks authority to grant because of an appeal that has been docketed and is pending, the movant must promptly notify the circuit clerk if the district court states either that it would grant the motion or that the motion raises a substantial issue.

(b) Remand After an Indicative Ruling. If the district court states that it would grant the motion or that the motion raises a substantial issue, the court of appeals may remand for further proceedings but retains jurisdiction unless it expressly dismisses the appeal. If the court of appeals remands but retains jurisdiction, the parties must promptly notify the circuit clerk when the district court has decided the motion on remand.

(As added Dec. 1, 2009.)

III. APPEALS FROM THE UNITED STATES TAX COURT

Rule 13. Appeals from the Tax Court

(a) Appeal as of Right. (1) *How Obtained; Time for Filing a Notice of Appeal.* (A) An appeal as of right from the United States Tax Court is commenced by filing a notice of appeal with the Tax Court clerk within 90 days after the entry of the Tax Court's decision. At the time of filing, the appellant must furnish the clerk with enough copies of the notice to enable the clerk to comply with Rule 3(d). If one party files a timely notice of appeal, any other party may file a notice of appeal within 120 days after the Tax Court's decision is entered.

(B) If, under Tax Court rules, a party makes a timely motion to vacate or revise the Tax Court's decision, the time to file a notice of appeal runs from the entry of the order disposing of the motion or from the entry of a new decision, whichever is later.

(2) *Notice of Appeal; How Filed.* The notice of appeal may be filed either at the Tax Court clerk's office in the District of Columbia or by mail addressed to the clerk. If sent by mail the notice is considered filed on the postmark date, subject to § 7502 of the Internal Revenue Code, as amended, and the applicable regulations.

(3) *Contents of the Notice of Appeal; Service; Effect of Filing and Service.* Rule 3 prescribes the contents of a notice of appeal, the manner of service, and the effect of its filing and service. Form 2 in the Appendix of Forms is a suggested form of a notice of appeal.

(4) *The Record on Appeal; Forwarding; Filing.* (A) Except as otherwise provided under Tax Court rules for the transcript of proceedings, the appeal is governed by the parts of Rules 10, 11, and 12 regarding the record on appeal from a district court, the time and manner of forwarding and filing, and the docketing in the court of appeals.

(B) If an appeal is taken to more than one court of appeals, the original record must be sent to the court named in the first notice of appeal filed. In an appeal to any other court of appeals, the appellant must apply to that other court to make provision for the record.

(b) Appeal by Permission. An appeal by permission is governed by Rule 5.

(Amended April 30, 1979, effective Aug. 1, 1979; Dec. 1, 1994; Dec. 1, 1998; Dec. 1, 2013.)

Rule 14. Applicability of Other Rules to Appeals from the Tax Court

All provisions of these rules, except Rules 4, 6–9, 15–20, and 22–23, apply to appeals from the Tax Court. References in any applicable rule (other than Rule 24(a)) to the district court and district clerk are to be read as referring to the Tax Court and its clerk.

(Amended Dec. 1, 1998; Dec. 1, 2013.)

IV. REVIEW OR ENFORCEMENT OF AN ORDER OF AN ADMINISTRATIVE AGENCY, BOARD, COMMISSION, OR OFFICER

Rule 15. Review or Enforcement of an Agency Order—How Obtained; Intervention

(a) Petition for Review; Joint Petition. (1) Review of an agency order is commenced by filing, within the time prescribed by law, a petition for review with the clerk of a court of appeals authorized to review the agency order. If their interests make joinder practicable, two or more persons may join in a petition to the same court to review the same order.

(2) The petition must:

(A) name each party seeking review either in the caption or the body of the petition — using such terms as "et al.," "petitioners," or "respondents" does not effectively name the parties;

(B) name the agency as a respondent (even though not named in the petition, the United States is a respondent if required by statute); and

(C) specify the order or part thereof to be reviewed.

(3) Form 3 in the Appendix of Forms is a suggested form of a petition for review.

(4) In this rule "agency" includes an agency, board, commission, or officer; "petition for review" includes a petition to enjoin, suspend, modify, or otherwise review, or a notice of appeal, whichever form is indicated by the applicable statute.

(b) Application or Cross-Application to Enforce an Order; Answer; Default. (1) An application to enforce an agency order must be filed with the clerk of a court of appeals authorized to enforce the order. If a petition is filed to review an agency order that the court may enforce, a party opposing the petition may file a cross-application for enforcement.

(2) Within 21 days after the application for enforcement is filed, the respondent must serve on the applicant an answer to the application and file it with the clerk. If the respondent fails to answer in time, the court will enter judgment for the relief requested.

(3) The application must contain a concise statement of the proceedings in which the order was entered, the facts upon which venue is based, and the relief requested.

(c) Service of the Petition or Application. The circuit clerk must serve a copy of the petition for review, or an application or cross-application to enforce an agency order, on each respondent as prescribed by Rule 3(d), unless a different manner of service is prescribed by statute. At the time of filing, the petitioner must:

(1) serve, or have served, a copy on each party admitted to participate in the agency proceedings, except for the respondents;

(2) file with the clerk a list of those so served; and

(3) give the clerk enough copies of the petition or application to serve each respondent.

(d) Intervention. Unless a statute provides another method, a person who wants to intervene in a proceeding under this rule must file a motion for leave to intervene with the circuit clerk and serve a copy on all parties. The motion — or other notice of intervention authorized by statute — must be filed within 30 days after the petition for review is filed and must contain a concise statement of the interest of the moving party and the grounds for intervention.

(e) Payment of Fees. When filing any separate or joint petition for review in a court of appeals, the petitioner must pay the circuit clerk all required fees.

(Amended Dec. 1, 1998; Dec. 1, 2009.)

Rule 15.1. Briefs and Oral Argument in a National Labor Relations Board Proceeding

In either an enforcement or a review proceeding, a party adverse to the National Labor Relations Board proceeds first on briefing and at oral argument, unless the court orders otherwise.

(Added July 1, 1986; amended Dec. 1, 1998.)

Rule 16. The Record on Review or Enforcement

(a) Composition of the Record. The record on review or enforcement of an agency order consists of:

(1) the order involved;

(2) any findings or report on which it is based; and

(3) the pleadings, evidence, and other parts of the proceedings before the agency.

(b) Omissions From or Misstatements in the Record. The parties may at any time, by stipulation, supply any omission from the record or correct a misstatement, or the court may so direct. If necessary, the court may direct that a supplemental record be prepared and filed.

(Amended Dec. 1, 1998.)

Rule 17. Filing the Record

(a) Agency to File; Time for Filing; Notice of Filing. The agency must file the record with the circuit clerk within 40 days after being served with a petition for review, unless the statute authorizing review provides otherwise, or within 40 days after it files an application for enforcement unless the respondent fails to answer or the court orders otherwise. The court may shorten or extend the time to file the record. The clerk must notify all parties of the date when the record is filed.

(b) Filing—What Constitutes. (1) The agency must file:

(A) the original or a certified copy of the entire record or parts designated by the parties; or

(B) a certified list adequately describing all documents, transcripts of testimony, exhibits, and other material constituting the record, or describing those parts designated by the parties.

(2) The parties may stipulate in writing that no record or certified list be filed. The date when the stipulation is filed with the circuit clerk is treated as the date when the record is filed.

(3) The agency must retain any portion of the record not filed with the clerk. All parts of the record retained by the agency are a part of the record on review for all purposes and, if the court or a party so requests, must be sent to the court regardless of any prior stipulation.

(Amended Dec. 1, 1998.)

Rule 18. Stay Pending Review

(a) Motion for a Stay. (1) *Initial Motion Before the Agency.* A petitioner must ordinarily move first before the agency for a stay pending review of its decision or order.

(2) *Motion in the Court of Appeals.* A motion for a stay may be made to the court of appeals or one of its judges.

(A) The motion must:

(i) show that moving first before the agency would be impracticable; or

(ii) state that, a motion having been made, the agency denied the motion or failed to afford the relief requested and state any reasons given by the agency for its action.

(B) The motion must also include:

(i) the reasons for granting the relief requested and the facts relied on;

(ii) originals or copies of affidavits or other sworn statements supporting facts subject to dispute; and

(iii) relevant parts of the record.

(C) The moving party must give reasonable notice of the motion to all parties.

(D) The motion must be filed with the circuit clerk and normally will be considered by a panel of the court. But in an exceptional case in which time requirements make that procedure impracticable, the motion may be made to and considered by a single judge.

(b) Bond. The court may condition relief on the filing of a bond or other appropriate security.

(Amended Dec. 1, 1998.)

Rule 19. Settlement of a Judgment Enforcing an Agency Order in Part

When the court files an opinion directing entry of judgment enforcing the agency's order in part, the agency must within 14 days file with the clerk and serve on each other party a proposed judgment conforming to the opinion. A party who disagrees with the agency's proposed judgment must within 10 days file with the clerk and serve the agency with a proposed judgment that the party believes conforms to the opinion. The court will settle the judgment and direct entry without further hearing or argument.

(Amended July 1, 1986; Dec. 1, 1998; Dec. 1, 2009.)

Rule 20. Applicability of Rules to the Review or Enforcement of an Agency Order

All provisions of these rules, except Rules 3–14 and 22–23, apply to the review or enforcement of an agency order. In these rules, "appellant" includes a petitioner or applicant, and "appellee" includes a respondent.

(Amended Dec. 1, 1998.)

V. EXTRAORDINARY WRITS

Rule 21. Writs of Mandamus and Prohibition, and Other Extraordinary Writs

(a) Mandamus or Prohibition to a Court: Petition, Filing, Service, and Docketing. (1) A party petitioning for a writ of mandamus or prohibition directed to a court must file a petition with the circuit clerk with proof of service on all parties to the proceeding in the trial court. The party must also provide a copy to the trial-court judge. All parties to the proceeding in the trial court other than the petitioner are respondents for all purposes.

(2) (A) The petition must be titled "In re [name of petitioner]."

(B) The petition must state:

(i) the relief sought;

(ii) the issues presented;

(iii) the facts necessary to understand the issue presented by the petition; and

(iv) the reasons why the writ should issue.

(C) The petition must include a copy of any order or opinion or parts of the record that may be essential to understand the matters set forth in the petition.

(3) Upon receiving the prescribed docket fee, the clerk must docket the petition and submit it to the court.

(b) Denial; Order Directing Answer; Briefs; Precedence. (1) The court may deny the petition without an answer. Otherwise, it must order the respondent, if any, to answer within a fixed time.

(2) The clerk must serve the order to respond on all persons directed to respond.

(3) Two or more respondents may answer jointly.

(4) The court of appeals may invite or order the trial-court judge to address the petition or may invite an amicus curiae to do so. The trial-court judge may request permission to address the petition but may not do so unless invited or ordered to do so by the court of appeals.

(5) If briefing or oral argument is required, the clerk must advise the parties, and when appropriate, the trial-court judge or amicus curiae.

(6) The proceeding must be given preference over ordinary civil cases.

(7) The circuit clerk must send a copy of the final disposition to the trial-court judge.

(c) Other Extraordinary Writs. An application for an extraordinary writ other than one provided for in Rule 21(a) must be made by filing a petition with the circuit clerk with proof of service on the respondents. Proceedings on the application must conform, so far as is practicable, to the procedures prescribed in Rule 21(a) and (b).

(d) Form of Papers; Number of Copies. All papers must conform to Rule 32(c)(2). Except by the court's permission, a paper must not exceed 30 pages, exclusive of the disclosure statement, the proof of service, and the accompanying documents required by Rule 21(a)(2)(C). An original and 3 copies must be filed unless the court requires the filing of a different number by local rule or by order in a particular case.

(Amended Dec. 1, 1994; Dec. 1, 1996; Dec. 1, 1998; Dec. 1, 2002.)

VI. HABEAS CORPUS; PROCEEDINGS IN FORMA PAUPERIS

Rule 22. Habeas corpus and Section 2255 Proceedings

(a) Application for the Original Writ. An application for a writ of habeas corpus must be made to the appropriate district court. If made to a circuit judge, the application must be transferred to the appropriate district court. If a district court denies an application made or transferred to it, renewal of the application before a circuit judge is not permitted. The applicant may, under 28 U.S.C. § 2253, appeal to the court of appeals from the district court's order denying the application.

(b) Certificate of Appealability. (1) In a habeas corpus proceeding in which the detention complained of arises from process issued by a state court, or in a 28 U.S.C. § 2255 proceeding, the applicant cannot take an appeal unless a circuit justice or a circuit or district judge issues a certificate of appealability under 28 U.S.C. § 2253(c). If an applicant files a notice of appeal, the district clerk must send to the court of appeals the certificate (if any) and the statement described in Rule 11(a) of the Rules Governing Proceedings Under 28 U.S.C. § 2254 or § 2255 (if any), along with the notice of appeal and the file of the district-court proceedings. If the district judge has denied the certificate, the applicant may request a circuit judge to issue it.

(2) A request addressed to the court of appeals may be considered by a circuit judge or judges, as the court prescribes. If no express request for a certificate is filed, the notice of appeal constitutes a request addressed to the judges of the court of appeals.

(3) A certificate of appealability is not required when a state or its representative or the United States or its representative appeals.

(As amended April 24, 1996, P. L. 104-132, Title I, § 103, 110 Stat. 1218; Dec. 1, 1998; Dec. 1, 2009.)

Rule 23. Custody or Release of a Prisoner in a Habeas Corpus Proceeding

(a) Transfer of Custody Pending Review. Pending review of a decision in a habeas corpus proceeding commenced before a court, justice, or judge of the United States for the release of a prisoner, the person having custody of the prisoner must not transfer custody to another unless a transfer is directed in accordance with this rule. When, upon application, a custodian shows the need for a transfer, the court, justice, or judge rendering the decision under review may authorize the transfer and substitute the successor custodian as a party.

(b) Detention or Release Pending Review of Decision Not to Release. While a decision not to release a prisoner is under review, the court or judge rendering the decision, or the court of appeals, or the Supreme Court, or a judge or justice of either court, may order that the prisoner be:

(1) detained in the custody from which release is sought;

(2) detained in other appropriate custody; or

(3) released on personal recognizance, with or without surety.

(c) Release Pending Review of Decision Ordering Release. While a decision ordering the release of a prisoner is under review, the prisoner must — unless the court or judge rendering the decision, or the court of appeals, or the Supreme Court, or a judge or justice of either court orders otherwise — be released on personal recognizance, with or without surety.

(d) Modification of the Initial Order on Custody. An initial order governing the prisoner's custody or release, including any recognizance or surety, continues in effect pending review unless for special reasons shown to the court of appeals or the Supreme Court, or to a judge or justice of either court, the order is modified or an independent order regarding custody, release, or surety is issued.

(Amended July 1, 1986; Dec. 1, 1998)

Rule 24. Proceeding in Forma Pauperis

(a) Leave to Proceed in Forma Pauperis. (1) *Motion in the District Court.* Except as stated in Rule 24(a)(3), a party to a district-court action who desires to appeal in forma pauperis must file a motion in the district court. The party must attach an affidavit that:

(A) shows in the detail prescribed by Form 4 of the Appendix of Forms the party's inability to pay or to give security for fees and costs;

(B) claims an entitlement to redress; and

(C) states the issues that the party intends to present on appeal.

(2) *Action on the Motion.* If the district court grants the motion, the party may proceed on appeal without prepaying or giving security for fees and costs, unless a statute provides otherwise. If the district court denies the motion, it must state its reasons in writing.

(3) *Prior Approval.* A party who was permitted to proceed in forma pauperis in the district-court action, or who was determined to be financially unable to obtain an adequate defense in a criminal case, may proceed on appeal in forma pauperis without further authorization, unless:

(A) the district court — before or after the notice of appeal is filed — certifies that the appeal is not taken in good faith or finds that the party is not otherwise entitled to proceed in forma pauperis and states in writing its reasons for the certification or finding; or

(B) a statute provides otherwise.

(4) *Notice of District Court's Denial.* The district clerk must immediately notify the parties and the court of appeals when the district court does any of the following:

(A) denies a motion to proceed on appeal in forma pauperis;

(B) certifies that the appeal is not taken in good faith; or

(C) finds that the party is not otherwise entitled to proceed in forma pauperis.

(5) *Motion in the Court of Appeals.* A party may file a motion to proceed on appeal in forma pauperis in the court of appeals within 30 days after service of the notice prescribed in Rule 24(a)(4). The motion must include a copy of the affidavit filed in the district court and the district court's statement of reasons for its action. If no affidavit was filed in the district court, the party must include the affidavit prescribed by Rule 24(a)(1).

(b) Leave to Proceed in Forma Pauperis on Appeal from the United States Tax Court or on Appeal or Review of an Administrative-Agency Proceeding. A party may file in the court of appeals a motion for leave to proceed on appeal in forma pauperis with an affidavit prescribed by Rule 24(a)(1):

(1) in an appeal from the United States Tax Court; and

(2) when an appeal or review of a proceeding before an administrative agency, board, commission,

or officer proceeds directly in the court of appeals.

(c) Leave to Use Original Record. A party allowed to proceed on appeal in forma pauperis may request that the appeal be heard on the original record without reproducing any part.

(Amended April 30, 1979, effective Aug. 1, 1979; amended July 1, 1986; Dec. 1, 1998; Dec. 1, 2002; Dec. 1, 2013.)

VII. GENERAL PROVISIONS

Rule 25. Filing and Service

(a) Filing. (1) *Filing with the Clerk.* A paper required or permitted to be filed in a court of appeals must be filed with the clerk.

(2) *Filing: Method and Timeliness.* (A) *In general.* Filing may be accomplished by mail addressed to the clerk, but filing is not timely unless the clerk receives the papers within the time fixed for filing.

(B) *A brief or appendix.* A brief or appendix is timely filed, however, if on or before the last day for filing, it is:

(i) mailed to the clerk by First-Class Mail, or other class of mail that is at least as expeditious, postage prepaid; or

(ii) dispatched to a third-party commercial carrier for delivery to the clerk within 3 days.

(C) *Inmate filing.* A paper filed by an inmate confined in an institution is timely if deposited in the institution's internal mailing system on or before the last day for filing. If an institution has a system designed for legal mail, the inmate must use that system to receive the benefit of this rule. Timely filing may be shown by a declaration in compliance with 28 U.S.C. § 1746 or by a notarized statement, either of which must set forth the date of deposit and state that first-class postage has been prepaid.

(D) *Electronic filing.* A court of appeals may by local rule permit or require papers to be filed, signed, or verified by electronic means that are consistent with technical standards, if any, that the Judicial Conference of the United States establishes. A local rule may require filing by electronic means only if reasonable exceptions are allowed. A paper filed by electronic means in compliance with a local rule constitutes a written paper for the purpose of applying these rules.

(3) *Filing a Motion with a Judge.* If a motion requests relief that may be granted by a single judge, the judge may permit the motion to be filed with the judge; the judge must note the filing date on the motion and give it to the clerk.

(4) *Clerk's Refusal of Documents.* The clerk must not refuse to accept for filing any paper presented for that purpose solely because it is not presented in proper form as required by these rules or by any local rule or practice.

(5) *Privacy Protection.* An appeal in a case whose privacy protection was governed by Federal Rule of Bankruptcy Procedure 9037, Federal Rule of Civil Procedure 5.2, or Federal Rule of Criminal Procedure 49.1 is governed by the same rule on appeal. In all other proceedings, privacy protection is governed by Federal Rule of Civil Procedure 5.2, except that Federal Rule of Criminal Procedure 49.1 governs when an extraordinary writ is sought in a criminal case.

(b) Service of All Papers Required. Unless a rule requires service by the clerk, a party must, at or before the time of filing a paper, serve a copy on the other parties to the appeal or review. Service on a party represented by counsel must be made on the party's counsel.

(c) Manner of Service. (1) Service may be any of the following:

(A) personal, including delivery to a responsible person at the office of counsel;

(B) by mail;

(C) by third-party commercial carrier for delivery within 3 days; or

(D) by electronic means, if the party being served consents in writing.

(2) If authorized by local rule, a party may use the court's transmission equipment to make electronic service under Rule 25(c)(1)(D).

(3) When reasonable considering such factors as the immediacy of the relief sought, distance, and cost, service on a party must be by a manner at least as expeditious as the manner used to file the paper with the court.

(4) Service by mail or by commercial carrier is complete on mailing or delivery to the carrier. Service by electronic means is complete on transmission, unless the party making service is notified that the paper was not received by the party served.

(d) Proof of Service. (1) A paper presented for filing must contain either of the following:

(A) an acknowledgment of service by the person served; or

(B) proof of service consisting of a statement by the person who made service certifying:

(i) the date and manner of service;

(ii) the names of the persons served; and

(iii) their mail or electronic addresses, facsimile numbers, or the addresses of the places of delivery, as appropriate for the manner of service.

(2) When a brief or appendix is filed by mailing or dispatch in accordance with Rule 25(a)(2)(B), the proof of service must also state the date and manner by which the document was mailed or dispatched to the clerk.

(3) Proof of service may appear on or be affixed to the papers filed.

(e) Number of Copies. When these rules require the filing or furnishing of a number of copies, a court may require a different number by local rule or by order in a particular case.

(Amended July 1, 1986; Dec. 1, 1991; Dec. 1, 1993; Dec. 1, 1994; Dec. 1, 1996; Dec. 1, 1998; Dec. 1, 2002; Dec. 1, 2006; Dec. 1, 2007; Dec. 1, 2009.)

Rule 26. Computing and Extending Time

(a) Computing Time. The following rules apply in computing any time period specified in these rules, in any local rule or court order, or in any statute that does not specify a method of computing time.

(1) *Period Stated in Days or a Longer Unit.* When the period is stated in days or a longer unit of time:

(A) exclude the day of the event that triggers the period;

(B) count every day, including intermediate Saturdays, Sundays, and legal holidays; and

(C) include the last day of the period, but if the last day is a Saturday, Sunday, or legal holiday, the period continues to run until the end of the next day that is not a Saturday, Sunday, or legal holiday.

(2) *Period Stated in Hours.* When the period is stated in hours:

(A) begin counting immediately on the occurrence of the event that triggers the period;

(B) count every hour, including hours during intermediate Saturdays, Sundays, and legal holidays; and

(C) if the period would end on a Saturday, Sunday, or legal holiday, the period continues to run until the same time on the next day that is not a Saturday, Sunday, or legal holiday.

(3) *Inaccessibility of the Clerk's Office.* Unless the court orders otherwise, if the clerk's office is inaccessible:

(A) on the last day for filing under Rule 26(a)(1), then the time for filing is extended to the first accessible day that is not a Saturday, Sunday, or legal holiday; or

(B) during the last hour for filing under Rule 26(a)(2), then the time for filing is extended to the same time on the first accessible day that is not a Saturday, Sunday, or legal holiday.

(4) *"Last Day" Defined.* Unless a different time is set by a statute, local rule, or court order, the last day ends:

(A) for electronic filing in the district court, at midnight in the court's time zone;

(B) for electronic filing in the court of appeals, at midnight in the time zone of the circuit clerk's principal office;

(C) for filing under Rules 4(c)(1), 25(a)(2)(B), and 25(a)(2)(C)—and filing by mail under Rule 13(b)—at the latest time for the method chosen for delivery to the post office, third-party commercial carrier, or prison mailing system; and

(D) for filing by other means, when the clerk's office is scheduled to close.

(5) *"Next Day" Defined.* The "next day" is determined by continuing to count forward when the period is measured after an event and backward when measured before an event.

(6) *"Legal Holiday" Defined.* "Legal holiday" means:

(A) the day set aside by statute for observing New Year's Day, Martin Luther King Jr.'s Birthday, Washington's Birthday, Memorial Day, Independence Day, Labor Day, Columbus Day, Veterans' Day, Thanksgiving Day, or Christmas Day;

(B) any day declared a holiday by the President or Congress; and

(C) for periods that are measured after an event, any other day declared a holiday by the state where either of the following is located: the district court that rendered the challenged judgment or order, or the circuit clerk's principal office.

(b) Extending Time. For good cause, the court may extend the time prescribed by these rules or by its order to perform any act, or may permit an act to be done after that time expires. But the court may not extend the time to file:

(1) a notice of appeal (except as authorized in Rule 4) or a petition for permission to appeal; or

(2) a notice of appeal from or a petition to enjoin, set aside, suspend, modify, enforce, or otherwise review an order of an administrative agency, board, commission, or officer of the United States, unless specifically authorized by law.

(c) Additional Time after Service. When a party may or must act within a specified time after service, 3 days are added after the period would otherwise expire under Rule 26(a), unless the paper is delivered on the date of service stated in the proof of service. For purposes of this Rule 26(c), a paper that is served electronically is not treated as delivered on the date of service stated in the proof of service.

(Amended March 1, 1971, effective July 1, 1971; amended July 1, 1986; Dec. 1, 1989; Dec. 1, 1991; Dec. 1, 1996; Dec. 1, 1998; Dec. 1, 2002; Dec. 1, 2005; Dec. 1, 2009.)

Rule 26.1. Corporate Disclosure Statement

(a) Who Must File. Any nongovernmental corporate party to a proceeding in a court of appeals must file a statement that identifies any parent corporation and any publicly held corporation that owns 10% or more of its stock or states that there is no such corporation.

(b) Time for Filing; Supplemental Filing. A party must file the Rule 26.1(a) statement with the principal brief or upon filing a motion, response, petition, or answer in the court of appeals, whichever occurs first, unless a local rule requires earlier filing. Even if the statement has already been filed, the party's principal brief must include the statement before the table of contents. A party must supplement its statement whenever the information that must be disclosed under Rule 26.1(a) changes.

(c) Number of Copies. If the Rule 26.1(a) statement is filed before the principal brief, or if a supplemental statement is filed, the party must file an original and 3 copies unless the court requires a different number by local rule or by order in a particular case.

(Added Dec. 1, 1989; amended Dec. 1, 1991; Dec. 1, 1994; Dec. 1, 1998; Dec. 1, 2002.)

Rule 27. Motions

(a) In General. (1) *Application for Relief.* An application for an order or other relief is made by motion unless these rules prescribe another form. A motion must be in writing unless the court permits otherwise.

(2) *Contents of a Motion.* (A) *Grounds and relief sought.* A motion must state with particularity the grounds for the motion, the relief sought, and the legal argument necessary to support it.

(B) *Accompanying documents.* (i) Any affidavit or other paper necessary to support a motion must be served and filed with the motion.

(ii) An affidavit must contain only factual information, not legal argument.

(iii) A motion seeking substantive relief must include a copy of the trial court's opinion or agency's decision as a separate exhibit.

(C) *Documents barred or not required.* (i) A separate brief supporting or responding to a motion must not be filed.

(ii) A notice of motion is not required.

(iii) A proposed order is not required.

(3) *Response.* (A) *Time to file.* Any party may file a response to a motion; Rule 27(a)(2) governs its contents. The response must be filed within 10 days after service of the motion unless the court shortens or extends the time. A motion authorized by Rules 8, 9, 18, or 41 may be granted before the 10-day period runs only if the court gives reasonable notice to the parties that it intends to act sooner.

(B) *Request for affirmative relief.* A response may include a motion for affirmative relief. The time to respond to the new motion, and to reply to that response, are governed by Rule 27(a)(3)(A) and (a)(4). The title of the response must alert the court to the request for relief.

(4) *Reply to Response.* Any reply to a response must be filed within 7 days after service of the response. A reply must not present matters that do not relate to the response.

(b) Disposition of a Motion for a Procedural Order. The court may act on a motion for a procedural order—including a motion under Rule 26(b)—at any time without awaiting a response, and may, by rule or by order in a particular case, authorize its clerk to act on specified types of procedural motions. A party adversely affected by the court's, or the clerk's, action may file a motion to reconsider, vacate, or modify that action. Timely opposition filed after the motion is granted in whole or in part does not constitute a request to reconsider, vacate, or modify the disposition; a motion requesting that relief must be filed.

(c) Power of a Single Judge to Entertain a Motion. A circuit judge may act alone on any motion, but may not dismiss or otherwise determine an appeal or other proceeding. A court of appeals may provide by rule or by order in a particular case that only the court may act on any motion or class of motions. The court may review the action of a single judge.

(d) Form of Papers; Page Limits; and Number of Copies. (1) *Format.* (A) *Reproduction.* A motion, response, or reply may be reproduced by any process that yields a clear black image on light paper. The paper must be opaque and unglazed. Only one side of the paper may be used.

(B) *Cover.* A cover is not required, but there must be a caption that includes the case number, the name of the court, the title of the case, and a brief descriptive title indicating the purpose of the motion and identifying the party or parties for whom it is filed. If a cover is used, it must be white.

(C) *Binding.* The document must be bound in any manner that is secure, does not obscure the text, and permits the document to lie reasonably flat when open.

(D) *Paper size, line spacing, and margins.* The document must be on 8½ by 11 inch paper. The text must be double-spaced, but quotations more than two lines long may be indented and single-spaced. Headings and footnotes may be single-spaced. Margins must be at least one inch on all four sides. Page numbers may be placed in the margins, but no text may appear there.

(E) *Typeface and type styles.* The document must comply with the typeface requirements of Rule 32(a)(5) and the type-style requirements of Rule 32(a)(6).

(2) *Page Limits.* A motion or a response to a motion must not exceed 20 pages, exclusive of the corporate disclosure statement and accompanying documents authorized by Rule 27(a)(2)(B), unless the court permits or directs otherwise. A reply to a response must not exceed 10 pages.

(3) *Number of Copies.* An original and 3 copies must be filed unless the court requires a different number by local rule or by order in a particular case.

(e) Oral Argument. A motion will be decided without oral argument unless the court orders otherwise.

(Amended April 30, 1979, effective Aug. 1, 1979; amended Dec. 1, 1989; Dec. 1, 1994; Dec. 1, 1998; Dec. 1, 2002; Dec. 1, 2005; Dec. 1, 2009.)

Rule 28. Briefs

(a) Appellant's Brief. The appellant's brief must contain, under appropriate headings and in the order indicated:

(1) a corporate disclosure statement if required by Rule 26.1;

(2) a table of contents, with page references;

(3) a table of authorities — cases (alphabetically arranged), statutes, and other authorities — with references to the pages of the brief where they are cited;

(4) a jurisdictional statement, including:

(A) the basis for the district court's or agency's subject-matter jurisdiction, with citations to applicable statutory provisions and stating relevant facts establishing jurisdiction;

(B) the basis for the court of appeals' jurisdiction, with citations to applicable statutory provisions and stating relevant facts establishing jurisdiction;

(C) the filing dates establishing the timeliness of the appeal or petition for review; and

(D) an assertion that the appeal is from a final order or judgment that disposes of all parties' claims, or information establishing the court of appeals' jurisdiction on some other basis;

(5) a statement of the issues presented for review;

(6) a concise statement of the case setting out the facts relevant to the issues submitted for review, describing the relevant procedural history, and identifying the rulings presented for review, with appropriate references to the record (see Rule 28(e));

(7) a summary of the argument, which must contain a succinct, clear, and accurate statement of the arguments made in the body of the brief, and which must not merely repeat the argument headings;

(8) the argument, which must contain:

(A) appellant's contentions and the reasons for them, with citations to the authorities and parts of the record on which the appellant relies; and

(B) or each issue, a concise statement of the applicable standard of review (which may appear in the discussion of the issue or under a separate heading placed before the discussion of the issues);

(9) a short conclusion stating the precise relief sought; and

(10) the certificate of compliance, if required by Rule 32(a)(7).

(b) Appellee's Brief. The appellee's brief must conform to the requirements of Rule 28(a)(1)–(8) and (10), except that none of the following need appear unless the appellee is dissatisfied with the appellant's statement:

(1) the jurisdictional statement;

(2) the statement of the issues;

(3) the statement of the case; and

(4) the statement of the standard of review.

(c) Reply Brief. The appellant may file a brief in reply to the appellee's brief. Unless the court permits, no further briefs may be filed. A reply brief must contain a table of contents, with page references, and a table of authorities—cases (alphabetically arranged), statutes, and other authorities—with references to the pages of the reply brief where they are cited.

(d) References to Parties. In briefs and at oral argument, counsel should minimize use of the terms "appellant" and "appellee." To make briefs clear, counsel should use the parties' actual names or the designations used in the lower court or agency proceeding, or such descriptive terms as "the employee," "the injured person," "the taxpayer," "the ship," "the stevedore."

(e) References to the Record. References to the parts of the record contained in the appendix filed with the appellant's brief must be to the pages of the appendix. If the appendix is prepared after the briefs are filed, a party referring to the record must follow one of the methods detailed in Rule 30(c). If the original record is used under Rule 30(f) and is not consecutively paginated, or if the brief refers to an unreproduced part of the record, any reference must be to the page of the original document. For example:

- Answer p. 7;
- Motion for Judgment p. 2;
- Transcript p. 231.

Only clear abbreviations may be used. A party referring to evidence whose admissibility is in controversy must cite the pages of the appendix or of the transcript at which the evidence was identified, offered, and received or rejected.

(f) Reproduction of Statutes, Rules, Regulations, etc. If the court's determination of the issues presented requires the study of statutes, rules, regulations, etc., the relevant parts must be set out in the brief or in an addendum at the end, or may be supplied to the court in pamphlet form.

(g) [Reserved]

(h) [Reserved]

(i) Briefs in a Case Involving Multiple Appellants or Appellees. In a case involving more than one appellant or appellee, including consolidated cases, any number of appellants or appellees may join in a brief, and any party may adopt by reference a part of another's brief. Parties may also join in reply briefs.

(j) Citation of Supplemental Authorities. If pertinent and significant authorities come to a party's attention after the party's brief has been filed — or after oral argument but before decision — a party may promptly advise the circuit clerk by letter, with a copy to all other parties, setting forth the citations. The letter must state the reasons for the supplemental citations, referring either to the page of the brief or to a point argued orally. The body of the letter must not exceed 350 words. Any response must be made promptly and must be similarly limited.

(Amended April 30, 1979, effective Aug. 1, 1979; amended July 1, 1986; Dec. 1, 1989; Dec. 1, 1991; Dec. 1, 1993; Dec. 1, 1994; Dec. 1, 1998; Dec. 1, 2002; Dec. 1, 2005; Dec. 1, 2013.)

Rule 28.1. Cross-Appeals

(a) Applicability. This rule applies to a case in which a cross-appeal is filed. Rules 28(a)–(c), 31(a)(1), 32(a)(2), and 32(a)(7)(A)–(B) do not apply to such a case, except as otherwise provided in this rule.

(b) Designation of Appellant. The party who files a notice of appeal first is the appellant for the purposes of this rule and Rules 30 and 34. If notices are filed on the same day, the plaintiff in the proceeding below is the appellant. These designations may be modified by the parties' agreement or by court order.

(c) Briefs. In a case involving a cross-appeal:

(1) *Appellant's Principal Brief.* The appellant must file a principal brief in the appeal. That brief

must comply with Rule 28(a).

(2) *Appellee's Principal and Response Brief.* The appellee must file a principal brief in the cross-appeal and must, in the same brief, respond to the principal brief in the appeal. That appellee's brief must comply with Rule 28(a), except that the brief need not include a statement of the case unless the appellee is dissatisfied with the appellant's statement.

(3) *Appellant's Response and Reply Brief.* The appellant must file a brief that responds to the principal brief in the cross-appeal and may, in the same brief, reply to the response in the appeal. That brief must comply with Rule 28(a)(2)–(8) and (10), except that none of the following need appear unless the appellant is dissatisfied with the appellee's statement in the cross-appeal:

(A) the jurisdictional statement;

(B) the statement of the issues;

(C) the statement of the case; and

(D) the statement of the standard of review.

(4) *Appellee's Reply Brief.* The appellee may file a brief in reply to the response in the cross-appeal. That brief must comply with Rule 28(a)(2)–(3) and (10) and must be limited to the issues presented by the cross-appeal.

(5) *No Further Briefs.* Unless the court permits, no further briefs may be filed in a case involving a cross-appeal.

(d) Cover. Except for filings by unrepresented parties, the cover of the appellant's principal brief must be blue; the appellee's principal and response brief, red; the appellant's response and reply brief, yellow; the appellee's reply brief, gray; an intervenor's or amicus curiae's brief, green; and any supplemental brief, tan. The front cover of a brief must contain the information required by Rule 32(a)(2).

(e) Length. (1) *Page Limitation.* Unless it complies with Rule 28.1(e)(2) and (3), the appellant's principal brief must not exceed 30 pages; the appellee's principal and response brief, 35 pages; the appellant's response and reply brief, 30 pages; and the appellee's reply brief, 15 pages.

(2) *Type-Volume Limitation.* (A) The appellant's principal brief or the appellant's response and reply brief is acceptable if:

(i) it contains no more than 14,000 words; or

(ii) it uses a monospaced face and contains no more than 1,300 lines of text.

(B) The appellee's principal and response brief is acceptable if:

(i) it contains no more than 16,500 words; or

(ii) it uses a monospaced face and contains no more than 1,500 lines of text.

(C) The appellee's reply brief is acceptable if it contains no more than half of the type volume specified in Rule 28.1(e)(2)(A).

(3) *Certificate of Compliance.* A brief submitted under Rule 28.1(e)(2) must comply with Rule 32(a)(7)(C).

(f) Time to Serve and File a Brief. Briefs must be served and filed as follows:

(1) the appellant's principal brief, within 40 days after the record is filed;

(2) the appellee's principal and response brief, within 30 days after the appellant's principal brief is served;

(3) the appellant's response and reply brief, within 30 days after the appellee's principal and response brief is served; and

(4) the appellee's reply brief, within 14 days after the appellant's response and reply brief is served, but at least 7 days before argument unless the court, for good cause, allows a later filing.

(As added April 25, 2005, eff. Dec. 1, 2005; amended Dec. 1, 2009; Dec. 1, 2013.)

Rule 29. Brief of an Amicus Curiae

(a) When Permitted. The United States or its officer or agency or a state may file an amicus-curiae brief without the consent of the parties or leave of court. Any other amicus curiae may file a brief only by leave of court or if the brief states that all parties have consented to its filing.

(b) Motion for Leave to File. The motion must be accompanied by the proposed brief and state:

(1) the movant's interest; and

(2) the reason why an amicus brief is desirable and why the matters asserted are relevant to the disposition of the case.

(c) Contents and Form. An amicus brief must comply with Rule 32. In addition to the requirements of Rule 32, the cover must identify the party or parties supported and indicate whether the brief supports affirmance or reversal. An amicus brief need not comply with Rule 28, but must include the following:

(1) if the amicus curiae is a corporation, a disclosure statement like that required of parties by Rule 26.1;

(2) a table of contents, with page references;

(3) a table of authorities — cases (alphabetically arranged), statutes, and other authorities — with references to the pages of the brief where they are cited;

(4) a concise statement of the identity of the amicus curiae, its interest in the case, and the source of its authority to file;

(5) unless the amicus curiae is one listed in the first sentence of Rule 29(a), a statement that indicates whether:

(A) a party's counsel authored the brief in whole or in part;

(B) a party or a party's counsel contributed money that was intended to fund preparing or submitting the brief; and

(C) a person — other than the amicus curiae, its members, or its counsel — contributed money that was intended to fund preparing or submitting the brief and, if so, identifies each such person;

(6) an argument, which may be preceded by a summary and which need not include a statement of

the applicable standard of review; and

(7) a certificate of compliance, if required by Rule 32(a)(7).

(d) Length. Except by the court's permission, an amicus brief may be no more than one-half the maximum length authorized by these rules for a party's principal brief. If the court grants a party permission to file a longer brief, that extension does not affect the length of an amicus brief.

(e) Time for Filing. An amicus curiae must file its brief, accompanied by a motion for filing when necessary, no later than 7 days after the principal brief of the party being supported is filed. An amicus curiae that does not support either party must file its brief no later than 7 days after the appellant's or petitioner's principal brief is filed. A court may grant leave for later filing, specifying the time within which an opposing party may answer.

(f) Reply Brief. Except by the court's permission, an amicus curiae may not file a reply brief.

(g) Oral Argument. An amicus curiae may participate in oral argument only with the court's permission.

(Amended Dec. 1, 1998; Dec. 1, 2010.)

Rule 30. Appendix to the Briefs

(a) Appellant's Responsibility. (1) *Contents of the Appendix.* The appellant must prepare and file an appendix to the briefs containing:

(A) the relevant docket entries in the proceeding below;

(B) the relevant portions of the pleadings, charge, findings, or opinion;

(C) the judgment, order, or decision in question; and

(D) other parts of the record to which the parties wish to direct the court's attention.

(2) *Excluded Material.* Memoranda of law in the district court should not be included in the appendix unless they have independent relevance. Parts of the record may be relied on by the court or the parties even though not included in the appendix.

(3) *Time to File; Number of Copies.* Unless filing is deferred under Rule 30(c), the appellant must file 10 copies of the appendix with the brief and must serve one copy on counsel for each party separately represented. An unrepresented party proceeding in forma pauperis must file 4 legible copies with the clerk, and one copy must be served on counsel for each separately represented party. The court may by local rule or by order in a particular case require the filing or service of a different number.

(b) All Parties' Responsibilities. (1) *Determining the Contents of the Appendix.* The parties are encouraged to agree on the contents of the appendix. In the absence of an agreement, the appellant must, within 14 days after the record is filed, serve on the appellee a designation of the parts of the record the appellant intends to include in the appendix and a statement of the issues the appellant intends to present for review. The appellee may, within 14 days after receiving the designation, serve on the appellant a designation of additional parts to which it wishes to direct the court's attention. The appellant must include the designated parts in the appendix. The parties must not engage in unnecessary designation of parts of the record, because the entire record is available to the court. This paragraph applies also to a cross-appellant and a cross-appellee.

(2) *Costs of Appendix.* Unless the parties agree otherwise, the appellant must pay the cost of the appendix. If the appellant considers parts of the record designated by the appellee to be unnecessary, the appellant may advise the appellee, who must then advance the cost of including those parts. The cost of the appendix is a taxable cost. But if any party causes unnecessary parts of the record to be included in the appendix, the court may impose the cost of those parts on that party. Each circuit must, by local rule, provide for sanctions against attorneys who unreasonably and vexatiously increase litigation costs by including unnecessary material in the appendix.

(c) Deferred Appendix. (1) *Deferral Until After Briefs Are Filed.* The court may provide by rule for classes of cases or by order in a particular case that preparation of the appendix may be deferred until after the briefs have been filed and that the appendix may be filed 21 days after the appellee's brief is served. Even though the filing of the appendix may be deferred, Rule 30(b) applies; except that a party must designate the parts of the record it wants included in the appendix when it serves its brief, and need not include a statement of the issues presented.

(2) *References to the Record.* (A) If the deferred appendix is used, the parties may cite in their briefs the pertinent pages of the record. When the appendix is prepared, the record pages cited in the briefs must be indicated by inserting record page numbers, in brackets, at places in the appendix where those pages of the record appear.

(B) A party who wants to refer directly to pages of the appendix may serve and file copies of the brief within the time required by Rule 31(a), containing appropriate references to pertinent pages of the record. In that event, within 14 days after the appendix is filed, the party must serve and file copies of the brief, containing references to the pages of the appendix in place of or in addition to the references to the pertinent pages of the record. Except for the correction of typographical errors, no other changes may be made to the brief.

(d) Format of the Appendix. The appendix must begin with a table of contents identifying the page at which each part begins. The relevant docket entries must follow the table of contents. Other parts of the record must follow chronologically. When pages from the transcript of proceedings are placed in the appendix, the transcript page numbers must be shown in brackets immediately before the included pages. Omissions in the text of papers or of the transcript must be indicated by asterisks. Immaterial formal matters (captions, subscriptions, acknowledgments, etc.) should be omitted.

(e) Reproduction of Exhibits. Exhibits designated for inclusion in the appendix may be reproduced in a separate volume, or volumes, suitably indexed. Four copies must be filed with the appendix, and one copy must be served on counsel for each separately represented party. If a transcript of a proceeding before an administrative agency, board, commission, or officer was used in a district-court action and has been designated for inclusion in the appendix, the transcript must be placed in the appendix as an exhibit.

(f) Appeal on the Original Record Without an Appendix. The court may, either by rule for all cases or classes of cases or by order in a particular case, dispense with the appendix and permit an appeal to proceed on the original record with any copies of the record, or relevant parts, that the court may order the parties to file.

(Amended March 30, 1970, effective July 1, 1970; amended July 1, 1986; Dec. 1, 1991; Dec. 1, 1994; Dec. 1, 1998; Dec. 1, 2009.)

Rule 31. Serving and Filing Briefs

(a) Time to Serve and File a Brief. (1) The appellant must serve and file a brief within 40 days after the record is filed. The appellee must serve and file a brief within 30 days after the appellant's brief is served. The appellant may serve and file a reply brief within 14 days after service of the appellee's brief but a reply brief must be filed at least 7 days before argument, unless the court, for good cause, allows a later filing.

(2) A court of appeals that routinely considers cases on the merits promptly after the briefs are filed may shorten the time to serve and file briefs, either by local rule or by order in a particular case.

(b) Number of Copies. Twenty-five copies of each brief must be filed with the clerk and 2 copies must be served on each unrepresented party and on counsel for each separately represented party. An unrepresented party proceeding in forma pauperis must file 4 legible copies with the clerk, and one copy must be served on each unrepresented party and on counsel for each separately represented party. The court may by local rule or by order in a particular case require the filing or service of a different number.

(c) Consequence of Failure to File. If an appellant fails to file a brief within the time provided by this rule, or within an extended time, an appellee may move to dismiss the appeal. An appellee who fails to file a brief will not be heard at oral argument unless the court grants permission.

(Amended March 30, 1970, effective July 1, 1970; amended July 1, 1986; Dec. 1, 1994; Dec. 1, 1998; Dec. 1, 2002; Dec. 1, 2009.)

Rule 32. Form of Briefs, Appendices, and Other Papers

(a) Form of a Brief. (1) *Reproduction.* (A) A brief may be reproduced by any process that yields a clear black image on light paper. The paper must be opaque and unglazed. Only one side of the paper may be used.

(B) Text must be reproduced with a clarity that equals or exceeds the output of a laser printer.

(C) Photographs, illustrations, and tables may be reproduced by any method that results in a good copy of the original; a glossy finish is acceptable if the original is glossy.

(2) *Cover.* Except for filings by unrepresented parties, the cover of the appellant's brief must be blue; the appellee's, red; an intervenor's or amicus curiae's, green; and any reply brief, gray; and any supplemental brief, tan. The front cover of a brief must contain:

(A) the number of the case centered at the top;

(B) the name of the court;

(C) the title of the case (see Rule 12(a));

(D) the nature of the proceeding (e.g., Appeal, Petition for Review) and the name of the court, agency, or board below;

(E) the title of the brief, identifying the party or parties for whom the brief is filed; and

(F) the name, office address, and telephone number of counsel representing the party for whom the brief is filed.

(3) *Binding.* The brief must be bound in any manner that is secure, does not obscure the text, and permits the brief to lie reasonably flat when open.

(4) *Paper Size, Line Spacing, and Margins.* The brief must be on 8½ by 11 inch paper. The text must be double-spaced, but quotations more than two lines long may be indented and single-spaced. Headings and footnotes may be single-spaced. Margins must be at least one inch on all four sides. Page numbers may be placed in the margins, but no text may appear there.

(5) *Typeface.* Either a proportionally spaced or a monospaced face may be used.

(A) A proportionally spaced face must include serifs, but sans-serif type may be used in headings and captions. A proportionally spaced face must be 14-point or larger.

(B) A monospaced face may not contain more than 10½ characters per inch.

(6) *Type Styles.* A brief must be set in a plain, roman style, although italics or boldface may be used for emphasis. Case names must be italicized or underlined.

(7) *Length.* (A) *Page limitation.* A principal brief may not exceed 30 pages, or a reply brief 15 pages, unless it complies with Rule 32(a)(7)(B) and (C).

(B) *Type-volume limitation.* (i) A principal brief is acceptable if:

- it contains no more than 14,000 words; or
- it uses a monospaced face and contains no more than 1,300 lines of text.

(ii) A reply brief is acceptable if it contains no more than half of the type volume specified in Rule 32(a)(7)(B)(i).

(iii) Headings, footnotes, and quotations count toward the word and line limitations. The corporate disclosure statement, table of contents, table of citations, statement with respect to oral argument, any addendum containing statutes, rules or regulations, and any certificates of counsel do not count toward the limitation.

(C) *Certificate of compliance.* (i) A brief submitted under Rules 28.1(e)(2) or 32(a)(7)(B) must include a certificate by the attorney, or an unrepresented party, that the brief complies with the type-volume limitation. The person preparing the certificate may rely on the word or line count of the word-processing system used to prepare the brief. The certificate must state either:

- the number of words in the brief; or
- the number of lines of monospaced type in the brief.

(ii) Form 6 in the Appendix of Forms is a suggested form of a certificate of compliance. Use of Form 6 must be regarded as sufficient to meet the requirements of Rules 28.1(e)(3) and 32(a)(7)(C)(i).

(b) Form of an Appendix. An appendix must comply with Rule 32(a)(1), (2), (3), and (4), with the following exceptions:

(1) The cover of a separately bound appendix must be white.

(2) An appendix may include a legible photocopy of any document found in the record or of a printed judicial or agency decision.

(3) When necessary to facilitate inclusion of odd-sized documents such as technical drawings, an appendix may be a size other than 8½ by 11 inches, and need not lie reasonably flat when opened.

(c) Form of Other Papers. (1) *Motion.* The form of a motion is governed by Rule 27(d).

(2) *Other Papers.* Any other paper, including a petition for panel rehearing and a petition for hearing or rehearing en banc, and any response to such a petition, must be reproduced in the manner prescribed by Rule 32(a), with the following exceptions:

(A) A cover is not necessary if the caption and signature page of the paper together contain the information required by Rule 32(a)(2). If a cover is used, it must be white.

(B) Rule 32(a)(7) does not apply.

(d) Signature. Every brief, motion, or other paper filed with the court must be signed by the party filing the paper or, if the party is represented, by one of the party's attorneys.

(e) Local Variation. Every court of appeals must accept documents that comply with the form requirements of this rule. By local rule or order in a particular case a court of appeals may accept documents that do not meet all of the form requirements of this rule.

(Amended Dec. 1, 1998; Dec. 1, 2002; Dec. 1, 2005.)

Rule 32.1. Citing Judicial Dispositions

(a) Citation Permitted. A court may not prohibit or restrict the citation of federal judicial opinions, orders, judgments, or other written dispositions that have been:

(i) designated as "unpublished," "not for publication," "non-precedential," "not precedent," or the like; and

(ii) issued on or after January 1, 2007.

(b) Copies Required. If a party cites a federal judicial opinion, order, judgment, or other written disposition that is not available in a publicly accessible electronic database, the party must file and serve a copy of that opinion, order, judgment, or disposition with the brief or other paper in which it is cited.

(As added Dec. 1, 2006.)

Rule 33. Appeal Conferences

The court may direct the attorneys — and, when appropriate, the parties — to participate in one or more conferences to address any matter that may aid in disposing of the proceedings, including simplifying the issues and discussing settlement. A judge or other person designated by the court may preside over the conference, which may be conducted in person or by telephone. Before a settlement conference, the attorneys must consult with their clients and obtain as much authority as feasible to settle the case. The court may, as a result of the conference, enter an order controlling the course of the proceedings or implementing any settlement agreement.

(Amended Dec. 1, 1994; Dec. 1, 1998.)

Rule 34. Oral Argument

(a) In General. (1) *Party's Statement.* Any party may file, or a court may require by local rule, a statement explaining why oral argument should, or need not, be permitted.

(2) *Standards.* Oral argument must be allowed in every case unless a panel of three judges who have examined the briefs and record unanimously agrees that oral argument is unnecessary for any of the following reasons:

(A) the appeal is frivolous;

(B) the dispositive issue or issues have been authoritatively decided; or

(C) the facts and legal arguments are adequately presented in the briefs and record, and the decisional process would not be significantly aided by oral argument.

(b) Notice of Argument; Postponement. The clerk must advise all parties whether oral argument will be scheduled, and, if so, the date, time, and place for it, and the time allowed for each side. A motion to postpone the argument or to allow longer argument must be filed reasonably in advance of the hearing date.

(c) Order and Contents of Argument. The appellant opens and concludes the argument. Counsel must not read at length from briefs, records, or authorities.

(d) Cross-Appeals and Separate Appeals. If there is a cross-appeal, Rule 28.1(b) determines which party is the appellant and which is the appellee for purposes of oral argument. Unless the court directs otherwise, a cross-appeal or separate appeal must be argued when the initial appeal is argued. Separate parties should avoid duplicative argument.

(e) Nonappearance of a Party. If the appellee fails to appear for argument, the court must hear appellant's argument. If the appellant fails to appear for argument, the court may hear the appellee's argument. If neither party appears, the case will be decided on the briefs, unless the court orders otherwise.

(f) Submission on Briefs. The parties may agree to submit a case for decision on the briefs, but the court may direct that the case be argued.

(g) Use of Physical Exhibits at Argument; Removal. Counsel intending to use physical exhibits other than documents at the argument must arrange to place them in the courtroom on the day of the argument before the court convenes. After the argument, counsel must remove the exhibits from the courtroom, unless the court directs otherwise. The clerk may destroy or dispose of the exhibits if counsel does not reclaim them within a reasonable time after the clerk gives notice to remove them.

(Amended April 30, 1979, effective Aug. 1, 1979; amended July 1, 1986; Dec. 1, 1991; Dec. 1, 1993; Dec. 1, 1998; Dec. 1, 2005.)

Rule 35. En Banc Determination

(a) When Hearing or Rehearing En Banc May Be Ordered. A majority of the circuit judges who are in regular active service and who are not disqualified may order that an appeal or other proceeding be heard or reheard by the court of appeals en banc. An en banc hearing or rehearing is not favored and ordinarily will not be ordered unless:

(1) en banc consideration is necessary to secure or maintain uniformity of the court's decisions; or

(2) the proceeding involves a question of exceptional importance.

(b) Petition for Hearing or Rehearing En Banc. A party may petition for a hearing or rehearing en banc.

(1) The petition must begin with a statement that either:

(A) the panel decision conflicts with a decision of the United States Supreme Court or of the court to which the petition is addressed (with citation to the conflicting case or cases) and consideration by the full court is therefore necessary to secure and maintain uniformity of the court's decisions; or

(B) the proceeding involves one or more questions of exceptional importance, each of which must be concisely stated; for example, a petition may assert that a proceeding presents a question of exceptional importance if it involves an issue on which the panel decision conflicts with the authoritative decisions of other United States Courts of Appeals that have addressed the issue.

(2) Except by the court's permission, a petition for an en banc hearing or rehearing must not exceed 15 pages, excluding material not counted under Rule 32.

(3) For purposes of the page limit in Rule 35(b)(2), if a party files both a petition for panel rehearing and a petition for rehearing en banc, they are considered a single document even if they are filed separately, unless separate filing is required by local rule.

(c) Time for Petition for Hearing or Rehearing En Banc. A petition that an appeal be heard initially en banc must be filed by the date when the appellee's brief is due. A petition for a rehearing en banc must be filed within the time prescribed by Rule 40 for filing a petition for rehearing.

(d) Number of Copies. The number of copies to be filed must be prescribed by local rule and may be altered by order in a particular case.

(e) Response. No response may be filed to a petition for an en banc consideration unless the court orders a response.

(f) Call for a Vote. A vote need not be taken to determine whether the case will be heard or reheard en banc unless a judge calls for a vote.

(Amended Aug. 1, 1979; Dec. 1, 1994; Dec. 1, 1998, April 25, 2005, eff. Dec. 1, 2005.)

Rule 36. Entry of Judgment; Notice

(a) Entry. A judgment is entered when it is noted on the docket. The clerk must prepare, sign, and enter the judgment:

(1) after receiving the court's opinion — but if settlement of the judgment's form is required, after final settlement; or

(2) if a judgment is rendered without an opinion, as the court instructs.

(b) Notice. On the date when judgment is entered, the clerk must serve on all parties a copy of the opinion — or the judgment, if no opinion was written — and a notice of the date when the judgment was entered.

(Amended Dec. 1, 1998; Dec. 1, 2002.)

Rule 37. Interest on Judgment

(a) When the Court Affirms. Unless the law provides otherwise, if a money judgment in a civil case is affirmed, whatever interest is allowed by law is payable from the date when the district court's judgment was entered.

(b) When the Court Reverses. If the court modifies or reverses a judgment with a direction that a money judgment be entered in the district court, the mandate must contain instructions about the allowance of interest.

(Amended Dec. 1, 1998.)

Rule 38. Frivolous Appeal—Damages and Costs

If a court of appeals determines that an appeal is frivolous, it may, after a separately filed motion or notice from the court and reasonable opportunity to respond, award just damages and single or double costs to the appellee.

(Amended Dec. 1, 1994; Dec. 1, 1998.)

Rule 39. Costs

(a) Against Whom Assessed. The following rules apply unless the law provides or the court orders otherwise:

(1) if an appeal is dismissed, costs are taxed against the appellant, unless the parties agree otherwise;

(2) if a judgment is affirmed, costs are taxed against the appellant;

(3) if a judgment is reversed, costs are taxed against the appellee;

(4) if a judgment is affirmed in part, reversed in part, modified, or vacated, costs are taxed only as the court orders.

(b) Costs For and Against the United States. Costs for or against the United States, its agency, or officer will be assessed under Rule 39(a) only if authorized by law.

(c) Costs of Copies. Each court of appeals must, by local rule, fix the maximum rate for taxing the cost of producing necessary copies of a brief or appendix, or copies of records authorized by Rule 30(f). The rate must not exceed that generally charged for such work in the area where the clerk's office is located and should encourage economical methods of copying.

(d) Bill of Costs: Objections; Insertion in Mandate. (1) A party who wants costs taxed must — within 14 days after entry of judgment — file with the circuit clerk, with proof of service, an itemized and verified bill of costs.

(2) Objections must be filed within 14 days after service of the bill of costs, unless the court extends the time.

(3) The clerk must prepare and certify an itemized statement of costs for insertion in the mandate, but issuance of the mandate must not be delayed for taxing costs. If the mandate issues before costs are finally determined, the district clerk must — upon the circuit clerk's request — add the statement of costs, or any amendment of it, to the mandate.

(e) Costs on Appeal Taxable in the District Court. The following costs on appeal are taxable in the district court for the benefit of the party entitled to costs under this rule:

(1) the preparation and transmission of the record;

(2) the reporter's transcript, if needed to determine the appeal;

(3) premiums paid for a supersedeas bond or other bond to preserve rights pending appeal; and

(4) the fee for filing the notice of appeal.

(Amended April 30, 1979, effective Aug. 1, 1979; amended July 1, 1986; Dec. 1, 1998; Dec. 1, 2009.)

Rule 40. Petition for Panel Rehearing

(a) Time to File; Contents; Answer; Action by the Court if Granted. (1) *Time.* Unless the time is shortened or extended by order or local rule, a petition for panel rehearing may be filed within 14 days after entry of judgment. But in a civil case, unless an order shortens or extends the time, the petition may be filed by any party within 45 days after entry of judgment if one of the parties is:

(A) the United States;

(B) a United States agency;

(C) a United States officer or employee sued in an official capacity; or

(D) a current or former United States officer or employee sued in an individual capacity for an act or omission occurring in connection with duties performed on the United States' behalf—including all instances in which the United States represents that person when the court of appeals' judgment is entered or files the petition for that person.

(2) *Contents.* The petition must state with particularity each point of law or fact that the petitioner believes the court has overlooked or misapprehended and must argue in support of the petition. Oral argument is not permitted.

(3) *Answer.* Unless the court requests, no answer to a petition for panel rehearing is permitted. But ordinarily rehearing will not be granted in the absence of such a request.

(4) *Action by the Court.* If a petition for panel rehearing is granted, the court may do any of the following:

(A) make a final disposition of the case without reargument;

(B) restore the case to the calendar for reargument or resubmission; or

(C) issue any other appropriate order.

(b) Form of Petition; Length. The petition must comply in form with Rule 32. Copies must be served and filed as Rule 31 prescribes. Unless the court permits or a local rule provides otherwise, a petition for panel rehearing must not exceed 15 pages.

(Amended Aug. 1, 1979; Dec. 1, 1994; Dec. 1, 1998; Dec. 1, 2011.)

Rule 41. Mandate: Contents; Issuance and Effective Date; Stay

(a) Contents. Unless the court directs that a formal mandate issue, the mandate consists of a certified copy of the judgment, a copy of the court's opinion, if any, and any direction about costs.

(b) When Issued. The court's mandate must issue 7 days after the time to file a petition for rehearing expires, or 7 days after entry of an order denying a timely petition for panel rehearing, petition for rehearing en banc, or motion for stay of mandate, whichever is later. The court may shorten or extend the time.

(c) Effective Date. The mandate is effective when issued.

(d) Staying the Mandate. (1) *On Petition for Rehearing or Motion.* The timely filing of a petition for panel rehearing, petition for rehearing en banc, or motion for stay of mandate, stays the mandate until disposition of the petition or motion, unless the court orders otherwise.

(2) *Pending Petition for Certiorari.* (A) A party may move to stay the mandate pending the filing of a petition for a writ of certiorari in the Supreme Court. The motion must be served on all parties and must show that the certiorari petition would present a substantial question and that there is good cause for a stay.

(B) The stay must not exceed 90 days, unless the period is extended for good cause or unless the party who obtained the stay files a petition for the writ and so notifies the circuit clerk in writing within the period of the stay. In that case, the stay continues until the Supreme Court's final disposition.

(C) The court may require a bond or other security as a condition to granting or continuing a stay of the mandate.

(D) The court of appeals must issue the mandate immediately when a copy of a Supreme Court order denying the petition for writ of certiorari is filed.

(Amended Dec. 1, 1994; Dec. 1, 1998; Dec. 1, 2002; Dec. 1, 2009.)

Rule 42. Voluntary Dismissal

(a) Dismissal in the District Court. Before an appeal has been docketed by the circuit clerk, the district court may dismiss the appeal on the filing of a stipulation signed by all parties or on the appellant's motion with notice to all parties.

(b) Dismissal in the Court of Appeals. The circuit clerk may dismiss a docketed appeal if the parties file a signed dismissal agreement specifying how costs are to be paid and pay any fees that are due. But no mandate or other process may issue without a court order. An appeal may be dismissed on the appellant's motion on terms agreed to by the parties or fixed by the court.

(Amended Dec. 1, 1998.)

Rule 43. Substitution of Parties

(a) Death of a Party. (1) *After Notice of Appeal Is Filed.* If a party dies after a notice of appeal has been filed or while a proceeding is pending in the court of appeals, the decedent's personal representative may be substituted as a party on motion filed with the circuit clerk by the representative or by any party. A party's motion must be served on the representative in accordance with Rule 25. If the decedent has no representative, any party may suggest the death on the record, and the court of appeals may then direct appropriate proceedings.

(2) *Before Notice of Appeal Is Filed — Potential Appellant.* If a party entitled to appeal dies before filing a notice of appeal, the decedent's personal representative — or, if there is no personal representative, the decedent's attorney of record — may file a notice of appeal within the time prescribed by these rules. After the notice of appeal is filed, substitution must be in accordance with Rule 43(a)(1).

(3) *Before Notice of Appeal Is Filed — Potential Appellee.* If a party against whom an appeal may be taken dies after entry of a judgment or order in the district court, but before a notice of appeal is filed, an appellant may proceed as if the death had not occurred. After the notice of appeal is filed, substitution must be in accordance with Rule 43(a)(1).

(b) Substitution for a Reason Other Than Death. If a party needs to be substituted for any reason other than death, the procedure prescribed in Rule 43(a) applies.

(c) Public Officer: Identification; Substitution. (1) *Identification of Party.* A public officer who is a party to an appeal or other proceeding in an official capacity may be described as a party by the public officer's official title rather than by name. But the court may require the public officer's name to be added.

(2) *Automatic Substitution of Officeholder.* When a public officer who is a party to an appeal or other proceeding in an official capacity dies, resigns, or otherwise ceases to hold office, the action does not abate. The public officer's successor is automatically substituted as a party. Proceedings following the substitution are to be in the name of the substituted party, but any misnomer that does not affect the substantial rights of the parties may be disregarded. An order of substitution may be entered at any time, but failure to enter an order does not affect the substitution.

(Amended July 1, 1986; Dec. 1, 1998.)

Rule 44. Case Involving a Constitutional Question When the United States Is Not a Party

(a) Constitutional Challenge to Federal Statute. If a party questions the constitutionality of an Act of Congress in a proceeding in which the United States or its agency, officer, or employee is not a party in an official capacity, the questioning party must give written notice to the circuit clerk immediately upon the filing of the record or as soon as the question is raised in the court of appeals. The clerk must then certify that fact to the Attorney General.

(b) Constitutional Challenge to State Statute. If a party questions the constitutionality of a statute of a State in a proceeding in which that State or its agency, officer, or employee is not a party in an official capacity, the questioning party must give written notice to the circuit clerk immediately upon the filing of the record or as soon as the question is raised in the court of appeals. The clerk must then certify that fact to the attorney general of the State.

(Amended Dec. 1, 1998; Dec. 1, 2002.)

Rule 45. Clerk's Duties

(a) General Provisions. (1) *Qualifications.* The circuit clerk must take the oath and post any bond required by law. Neither the clerk nor any deputy clerk may practice as an attorney or counselor in any court while in office.

(2) *When Court Is Open.* The court of appeals is always open for filing any paper, issuing and returning process, making a motion, and entering an order. The clerk's office with the clerk or a deputy in attendance must be open during business hours on all days except Saturdays, Sundays, and legal holidays. A court may provide by local rule or by order that the clerk's office be open for specified hours on Saturdays or on legal holidays other than New Year's Day, Martin Luther King, Jr.'s Birthday, Washington's Birthday, Memorial Day, Independence Day, Labor Day, Columbus Day, Veterans' Day, Thanksgiving Day, and Christmas Day.

(b) Records. (1) *The Docket.* The circuit clerk must maintain a docket and an index of all docketed cases in the manner prescribed by the Director of the Administrative Office of the United States Courts. The clerk must record all papers filed with the clerk and all process, orders, and judgments.

(2) *Calendar.* Under the court's direction, the clerk must prepare a calendar of cases awaiting argument. In placing cases on the calendar for argument, the clerk must give preference to appeals in criminal cases and to other proceedings and appeals entitled to preference by law.

(3) *Other Records.* The clerk must keep other books and records required by the Director of the Administrative Office of the United States Courts, with the approval of the Judicial Conference of the United States, or by the court.

(c) Notice of an Order or Judgment. Upon the entry of an order or judgment, the circuit clerk must immediately serve a notice of entry on each party, with a copy of any opinion, and must note the date of service on the docket. Service on a party represented by counsel must be made on counsel.

(d) Custody of Records and Papers. The circuit clerk has custody of the court's records and papers. Unless the court orders or instructs otherwise, the clerk must not permit an original record or paper to be taken from the clerk's office. Upon disposition of the case, original papers constituting the record on appeal or review must be returned to the court or agency from which they were received. The clerk must preserve a copy of any brief, appendix, or other paper that has been filed.

(Amended March 1, 1971, effective July 1, 1971; amended July 1, 1986; Dec. 1, 1998; Dec. 1, 2002; Dec. 1, 2005.)

Rule 46. Attorneys

(a) Admission to the Bar. (1) *Eligibility.* An attorney is eligible for admission to the bar of a court of appeals if that attorney is of good moral and professional character and is admitted to practice before the Supreme Court of the United States, the highest court of a state, another United States court of appeals, or a United States district court (including the district courts for Guam, the Northern Mariana Islands, and the Virgin Islands).

(2) *Application.* An applicant must file an application for admission, on a form approved by the court that contains the applicant's personal statement showing eligibility for membership. The applicant must subscribe to the following oath or affirmation:

"I, ________, do solemnly swear [or affirm] that I will conduct myself as an attorney and counselor of this court, uprightly and according to law; and that I will support the Constitution of the United States."

(3) *Admission Procedures.* On written or oral motion of a member of the court's bar, the court will act on the application. An applicant may be admitted by oral motion in open court. But, unless the court orders otherwise, an applicant need not appear before the court to be admitted. Upon admission, an applicant must pay the clerk the fee prescribed by local rule or court order.

(b) Suspension or Disbarment. (1) *Standard.* A member of the court's bar is subject to suspension or disbarment by the court if the member:

(A) has been suspended or disbarred from practice in any other court; or

(B) is guilty of conduct unbecoming a member of the court's bar.

(2) *Procedure.* The member must be given an opportunity to show good cause, within the time prescribed by the court, why the member should not be suspended or disbarred.

(3) *Order.* The court must enter an appropriate order after the member responds and a hearing is held, if requested, or after the time prescribed for a response expires, if no response is made.

(c) Discipline. A court of appeals may discipline an attorney who practices before it for conduct unbecoming a member of the bar or for failure to comply with any court rule. First, however, the court must afford the attorney reasonable notice, an opportunity to show cause to the contrary, and, if requested, a hearing.

(Amended July 1, 1986; Dec. 1, 1998.)

Rule 47. Local Rules by Courts of Appeals

(a) Local Rules. (1) Each court of appeals acting by a majority of its judges in regular active service may, after giving appropriate public notice and opportunity for comment, make and amend rules governing its practice. A generally applicable direction to parties or lawyers regarding practice before a court must be in a local rule rather than an internal operating procedure or standing order. A local rule must be consistent with — but not duplicative of — Acts of Congress and rules adopted under 28 U.S.C. § 2072 and must conform to any uniform numbering system prescribed by the Judicial Conference of the United States. Each circuit clerk must send the Administrative Office of the United States Courts a copy of each local rule and internal operating procedure when it is promulgated or amended.

(2) A local rule imposing a requirement of form must not be enforced in a manner that causes a party to lose rights because of a nonwillful failure to comply with the requirement.

(b) Procedure When There Is No Controlling Law. A court of appeals may regulate practice in a particular case in any manner consistent with federal law, these rules, and local rules of the circuit. No sanction or other disadvantage may be imposed for noncompliance with any requirement not in federal law, federal rules, or the local circuit rules unless the alleged violator has been furnished in the particular case with actual notice of the requirement.

(Amended Dec. 1, 1995; Dec. 1, 1998.)

Rule 48. Masters

(a) Appointment; Powers. A court of appeals may appoint a special master to hold hearings, if necessary, and to recommend factual findings and disposition in matters ancillary to proceedings in the court. Unless the order referring a matter to a master specifies or limits the master's powers, those powers include, but are not limited to, the following:

(1) regulating all aspects of a hearing;

(2) taking all appropriate action for the efficient performance of the master's duties under the order;

(3) requiring the production of evidence on all matters embraced in the reference; and

(4) administering oaths and examining witnesses and parties.

(b) Compensation. If the master is not a judge or court employee, the court must determine the master's compensation and whether the cost is to be charged to any party.

(Amended Dec. 1, 1994; Dec. 1, 1998.)

APPENDICES

APPENDIX OF FORMS

Form No. 1. —Notice of Appeal to a Court of Appeals from a Judgment or Order of a District Court.

United States District Court for the ______
District of ________
File Number ________

A.B., Plaintiff)
)
v.) Notice of Appeal
)
C.D., Defendant)

Notice is hereby given that (here name all parties taking the appeal), (plaintiffs) (defendants) in the above named case,* hereby appeal to the United States Court of Appeals for the ________ Circuit (from the final judgment) (from an order (describing it)) entered in this action on the ______ day of ______ 20, ____.

(s) ____________________
Attorney for ____________________
Address ____________________

* See Rule 3(c) for permissible ways of identifying appellants.

(Amended Dec. 1, 1993; Dec. 1, 2003.)

Form No. 2. —Notice of Appeal to a Court of Appeals From a Decision of the Tax Court.

UNITED STATES TAX COURT
Washington, D.C.

A.B., Petitioner)
)
v.) Docket No. ______
)
Commissioner of)
Internal Revenue,
Respondent

Notice of Appeal

Notice is hereby given that (here name all parties taking the appeal),* hereby appeal to the United States Court of Appeals for the ________ Circuit from (that part of) the decision of this court entered in the above captioned proceeding on the ______ day of ______, 20 ____ (relating to ______).

(s) ____________________
Counsel for____________________
Address: ____________________

* See Rule 3(c) for permissible ways of identifying appellants.

(Amended Dec. 1, 1993; Dec. 1, 2003.)

Form No. 3. —Petition for Review of Order of an Agency, Board, Commission or Officer

United States Court of Appeals for the ______ Circuit

A.B., Petitioner)
)
)
) Petition for Review
)
)
XYZ Commission, Respondent)

(here name all parties bringing the petition) * hereby petition the court for review of the Order of the XYZ Commission (describe the order) entered on ______, 20 ____ .

[(s)] ____________________
Attorney for Petitioners

Address: ______________________________

* See Rule 15.
(Amended Dec. 1, 1993; Dec. 1, 2003.)

Form No. 4. Affidavit Accompanying Motion for Permission to Appeal In Forma Pauperis

UNITED STATES DISTRICT COURT
for the
<______________> DISTRICT OF <______________>

<Name(s) of plaintiff(s)>,	)	
	)	
Plaintiff(s)	)	
	)	
v.	)	
	)	Case No. <Number>
<Name(s) of defendant(s)>,	)	
	)	
Defendant(s)	)	
	)	

AFFIDAVIT ACCOMPANYING MOTION
FOR PERMISSION TO APPEAL IN FORMA PAUPERIS

Affidavit in Support of Motion	**Instructions**
I swear or affirm under penalty of perjury that, because of my poverty, I cannot prepay the docket fees of my appeal or post a bond for them. I believe I am entitled to redress. I swear or affirm under penalty of perjury under United States laws that my answers on this form are true and correct. (28 U.S.C. § 1746; 18 U.S.C. § 1621.)	Complete all questions in this application and then sign it. Do not leave any blanks: if the answer to a question is "0," "none," or "not applicable (N/A)," write in that response. If you need more space to answer a question or to explain your answer, attach a separate sheet of paper identified with your name, your case's docket number, and the question number.
Signed: ____________________	Date: ____________________

My issues on appeal are:

1. *For both you and your spouse estimate the average amount of money received from each of the following sources during the past 12 months. Adjust any amount that was received weekly, biweekly, quarterly, semiannually, or annually to show the monthly rate. Use gross amounts, that is, amounts before any deductions for taxes or otherwise.*

Income source	Average monthly amount during the past 12 months		Amount expected next month	
	You	Spouse	You	Spouse
Employment	$	$	$	$
Self-employment	$	$	$	$
Income from real property (such as rental income)	$	$	$	$
Interest and dividends	$	$	$	$
Gifts	$	$	$	$
Alimony	$	$	$	$
Child support	$	$	$	$
Retirement (such as social security, pensions, annuities, insurance)	$	$	$	$
Disability (such as social security, insurance payments)	$	$	$	$
Unemployment payments	$	$	$	$
Public-assistance (such as welfare)	$	$	$	$
Other (specify):	$	$	$	$
Total monthly income:	**$**	**$**	**$**	**$**

2. *List your employment history for the past two years, most recent employer first. (Gross monthly pay is before taxes or other deductions.)*

Employer	Address	Dates of employment	Gross monthly pay
			$
			$
			$

3. *List your spouse's employment history for the past two years, most recent employer first. (Gross monthly pay is before taxes or other deductions.)*

Employer	Address	Dates of employment	Gross monthly pay
			$
			$
			$

4. *How much cash do you and your spouse have? $________*

Below, state any money you or your spouse have in bank accounts or in any other financial institution.

Financial Institution	Type of Account	Amount you have	Amount your spouse has
		$	$
		$	$
		$	$

If you are a prisoner seeking to appeal a judgment in a civil action or proceeding, you must attach a statement certified by the appropriate institutional officer showing all receipts, expenditures, and balances during the last six months in your institutional accounts. If you have multiple accounts, perhaps because you have been in multiple institutions, attach one certified statement of each account.

5. *List the assets, and their values, which you own or your spouse owns. Do not list clothing and ordinary household furnishings.*

Home	Other real estate	Motor vehicle #1
(Value) $	(Value) $	(Value) $
		Make and year:
		Model:
		Registration #:

Motor vehicle #2	Other assets	Other assets
(Value) $	(Value) $	(Value) $
Make and year:		
Model:		
Registration #:		

6. *State every person, business, or organization owing you or your spouse money, and the amount owed.*

Person owing you or your spouse money	Amount owed to you	Amount owed to your spouse
	$	$
	$	$
	$	$
	$	$

7. *State the persons who rely on you or your spouse for support.*

Name [or, if under 18, initials only]	Relationship	Age

8. *Estimate the average monthly expenses of you and your family. Show separately the amounts paid by your spouse. Adjust any payments that are made weekly, biweekly, quarterly, semiannually, or annually to show the monthly rate.*

	You	Your Spouse
Rent or home-mortgage payment (include lot rented for mobile home) Are real estate taxes included? [ ] Yes [ ] No Is property insurance included? [ ] Yes [ ] No	$	$

Utilities (electricity, heating fuel, water, sewer, and telephone)	$	$
Home maintenance (repairs and upkeep)	$	$
Food	$	$
Clothing	$	$
Laundry and dry-cleaning	$	$
Medical and dental expenses	$	$
Transportation (not including motor vehicle payments)	$	$
Recreation, entertainment, newspapers, magazines, etc.	$	$
Insurance (not deducted from wages or included in mortgage payments)		
Homeowner's or renter's:	$	$
Life:	$	$
Health:	$	$
Motor vehicle:	$	$
Other:	$	$
Taxes (not deducted from wages or included in mortgage payments) (specify):	$	$
Installment payments		
Motor Vehicle:	$	$
Credit card (name):	$	$
Department store (name):	$	$
Other:	$	$
Alimony, maintenance, and support paid to others	$	$
Regular expenses for operation of business, profession, or farm (attach detailed statement)	$	$
Other (specify):	$	$
Total monthly expenses:	**$**	**$**

9. *Do you expect any major changes to your monthly income or expenses or in your assets or liabilities during the next 12 months?*

[ ] Yes [ ] No If yes, describe on an attached sheet.

10. *Have you spent — or will you be spending — any money for expenses or attorney fees in connection with this lawsuit?* [ ] Yes [ ] No

If yes, how much? $ ___________

11. *Provide any other information that will help explain why you cannot pay the docket fees for your appeal.*

12. *State the city and state of your legal residence.*

Your daytime phone number: (___) ___________

Your age: _______ *Your years of schooling*: _______

Last four digits of your social-security number: _____

(Amended Dec. 1, 1998; Dec. 1, 2010; Dec. 1, 2013.)

Form No. 5. Notice of Appeal to a Court of Appeals from a Judgment or Order of a District Court or a Bankruptcy Appellate Panel

United States District Court for the

____

District of

____

In re

______________,
Debtor,

__________________, File No. ______
Plaintiff
v.

__________________,
Defendant

Notice of Appeal to the United States Court of Appeals for the

______________Circuit.

___________, the plaintiff [or defendant or other party] appeals to the United States Court of Appeals for the ___________ Circuit from the final judgment [or order or decree] of the district court for the district of _________ [or bankruptcy appellate panel of the _________ circuit], entered in this case on _______, 20___ [here describe the judgment, order, or decree] ______________.

The parties to the judgment [or order or decree] appealed from and the names and addresses of their respective attorneys are as follows:

Dated ___________
Signed ___________
Attorney for Appellant
Address: ___________
____

(Added Dec. 1, 1989; Dec. 1, 2003.)

Form No. 6. Certificate of Compliance With Rule 32(a)

Certificate of Compliance With Type-Volume Limitation, Typeface Requirements, and Type Style Requirements

1. This brief complies with the type-volume limitation of Fed. R. App. P. 32(a)(7)(B) because:

[ ] this brief contains [*state the number of*] words, excluding the parts of the brief exempted by Fed. R. App. P. 32(a)(7)(B)(iii), *or*

[ ] this brief uses a monospaced typeface and contains [*state the number of*] lines of text, excluding the parts of the brief exempted by Fed. R. App. P. 32(a)(7)(B)(iii).

2. This brief complies with the typeface requirements of Fed. R. App. P. 32(a)(5) and the type style

Appellate Procedure Form No. 5

requirements of Fed. R. App. P. 32(a)(6) because:

[ ] this brief has been prepared in a proportionally spaced typeface using [*state name and version of word processing program*] in [*state font size and name of type style*], *or*

[ ] this brief has been prepared in a monospaced typeface using [*state name and version of word processing program] with [state number of characters per inch and name of type style].*

(s)_________________________

Attorney for______________________

Dated:____________________

(Added December 1, 2002.)

Appellate Procedure
Form No. 6

RULES OF THE SUPREME COURT OF THE UNITED STATES

PART I. THE COURT

PART I. THE COURT

Rule 1. Clerk

1. The Clerk receives documents for filing with the Court and has authority to reject any submitted filing that does not comply with these Rules.

2. The Clerk maintains the Court's records and will not permit any of them to be removed from the Court building except as authorized by the Court. Any document filed with the Clerk and made a part of the Court's records may not thereafter be withdrawn from the official Court files. After the conclusion of proceedings in this Court, original records and documents transmitted to this Court by any other court will be returned to the court from which they were received.

3. Unless the Court or the Chief Justice orders otherwise, the Clerk's office is open from 9 a.m. to 5 p.m., Monday through Friday, except on federal legal holidays listed in 5 U.S.C. § 6103.

Rule 2. Library

1. The Court's library is available for use by appropriate personnel of this Court, members of the Bar of this Court, Members of Congress and their legal staffs, and attorneys for the United States and for federal departments and agencies.

2. The library's hours are governed by regulations made by the Librarian with the approval of the Chief Justice or the Court.

3. Library books may not be removed from the Court building, except by a Justice or a member of a Justice's staff.

Rule 3. Term

The Court holds a continuous annual Term commencing on the first Monday in October and ending on the day before the first Monday in October of the following year. See 28 U.S.C. § 2. At the end of each Term, all cases pending on the docket are continued to the next Term.

Rule 4. Sessions and Quorum

1. Open sessions of the Court are held beginning at 10 a.m. on the first Monday in October of each

year, and thereafter as announced by the Court. Unless it orders otherwise, the Court sits to hear arguments from 10 a.m. until noon and from 1 p.m. until 3 p.m.

2. Six Members of the Court constitute a quorum. See 28 U.S.C. § 1. In the absence of a quorum on any day appointed for holding a session of the Court, the Justices attending—or if no Justice is present, the Clerk or a Deputy Clerk—may announce that the Court will not meet until there is a quorum.

3. When appropriate, the Court will direct the Clerk or the Marshal to announce recesses.

PART II. ATTORNEYS AND COUNSELORS

Rule 5. Admission to the Bar

1. To qualify for admission to the Bar of this Court, an applicant must have been admitted to practice in the highest court of a State, Commonwealth, Territory or Possession, or the District of Columbia for a period of at least three years immediately before the date of application; must not have been the subject of any adverse disciplinary action pronounced or in effect during that 3-year period; and must appear to the Court to be of good moral and professional character.

2. Each applicant shall file with the Clerk (1) a certificate from the presiding judge, clerk, or other authorized official of that court evidencing the applicant's admission to practice there and the applicant's current good standing, and (2) a completely executed copy of the form approved by this Court and furnished by the Clerk containing (a) the applicant's personal statement, and (b) the statement of two sponsors endorsing the correctness of the applicant's statement, stating that the applicant possesses all the qualifications required for admission, and affirming that the applicant is of good moral and professional character. Both sponsors must be members of the Bar of this Court who personally know, but are not related to, the applicant.

3. If the documents submitted demonstrate that the applicant possesses the necessary qualifications, and if the applicant has signed the oath or affirmation and paid the required fee, the Clerk will notify the applicant of acceptance by the Court as a member of the Bar and issue a certificate of admission. An applicant who so wishes may be admitted in open court on oral motion by a member of the Bar of this Court, provided that all other requirements for admission have been satisfied.

4. Each applicant shall sign the following oath or affirmation: I, ________, do solemnly swear (or affirm) that as an attorney and as a counselor of this Court, I will conduct myself uprightly and according to law, and that I will support the Constitution of the United States.

5. The fee for admission to the Bar and a certificate bearing the seal of the Court is $200, payable to the United States Supreme Court. The Marshal will deposit such fees in a separate fund to be disbursed by the Marshal at the direction of the Chief Justice for the costs of admissions, for the benefit of the Court and its Bar, and for related purposes.

6. The fee for a duplicate certificate of admission to the Bar bearing the seal of the Court is $15, and the fee for a certificate of good standing is $10, payable to the United States Supreme Court. The proceeds will be maintained by the Marshal as provided in paragraph 5 of this Rule.

Rule 6. Argument *Pro Hac Vice*

1. An attorney not admitted to practice in the highest court of a State, Commonwealth, Territory or Possession, or the District of Columbia for the requisite three years, but otherwise eligible for admission to practice in this Court under Rule 5.1, may be permitted to argue *pro hac vice*.

2. An attorney qualified to practice in the courts of a foreign state may be permitted to argue *pro hac vice*.

3. Oral argument *pro hac vice* is allowed only on motion of the counsel of record for the party on whose behalf leave is requested. The motion shall state concisely the qualifications of the attorney who is to argue *pro hac vice*. It shall be filed with the Clerk, in the form required by Rule 21, no later than the date on which the respondent's or appellee's brief on the merits is due to be filed, and it shall be accompanied by proof of service as required by Rule 29.

Rule 7. Prohibition Against Practice

No employee of this Court shall practice as an attorney or counselor in any court or before any agency of government while employed by the Court; nor shall any person after leaving such employment participate in any professional capacity in any case pending before this Court or in any case being considered for filing in this Court, until two years have elapsed after separation; nor shall a former employee ever participate in any professional capacity in any case that was pending in this Court during the employee's tenure.

Rule 8. Disbarment and Disciplinary Action

1. Whenever a member of the Bar of this Court has been disbarred or suspended from practice in any court of record, or has engaged in conduct unbecoming a member of the Bar of this Court, the Court will enter an order suspending that member from practice before this Court and affording the member an opportunity to show cause, within 40 days, why a disbarment order should not be entered. Upon response, or if no response is timely filed, the Court will enter an appropriate order.

2. After reasonable notice and an opportunity to show cause why disciplinary action should not be taken, and after a hearing if material facts are in

dispute, the Court may take any appropriate disciplinary action against any attorney who is admitted to practice before it for conduct unbecoming a member of the Bar or for failure to comply with these Rules or any Rule or order of the Court.

Rule 9. Appearance of Counsel

1. An attorney seeking to file a document in this Court in a representative capacity must first be admitted to practice before this Court as provided in Rule 5, except that admission to the Bar of this Court is not required for an attorney appointed under the Criminal Justice Act of 1964, see 18 U. S. C. § 3006A(d)(6), or under any other applicable federal statute. The attorney whose name, address, and telephone number appear on the cover of a document presented for filing is considered counsel of record, and a separate notice of appearance need not be filed. If the name of more than one attorney is shown on the cover of the document, the attorney who is counsel of record shall be clearly identified. See Rule 34.1(f).

2. An attorney representing a party who will not be filing a document shall enter a separate notice of appearance as counsel of record indicating the name of the party represented. A separate notice of appearance shall also be entered whenever an attorney is substituted as counsel of record in a particular case.

PART III. JURISDICTION ON WRIT OF CERTIORARI

Rule 10. Considerations Governing Review on Certiorari

Review on a writ of certiorari is not a matter of right, but of judicial discretion. A petition for a writ of certiorari will be granted only for compelling reasons. The following, although neither controlling nor fully measuring the Court's discretion, indicate the character of the reasons the Court considers:

(a) a United States court of appeals has entered a decision in conflict with the decision of another United States court of appeals on the same important matter; has decided an important federal question in a way that conflicts with a decision by a state court of last resort; or has so far departed from the accepted and usual course of judicial proceedings, or sanctioned such a departure by a lower court, as to call for an exercise of this Court's supervisory power;

(b) a state court of last resort has decided an important federal question in a way that conflicts with the decision of another state court of last resort or of a United States court of appeals;

(c) a state court or a United States court of appeals has decided an important question of federal law that has not been, but should be, settled by this Court, or has decided an important federal question in a way that conflicts with relevant decisions of this Court.

A petition for a writ of certiorari is rarely granted when the asserted error consists of erroneous factual findings or the misapplication of a properly stated rule of law.

Rule 11. Certiorari to a United States Court of Appeals Before Judgment

A petition for a writ of certiorari to review a case pending in a United States court of appeals, before judgment is entered in that court, will be granted only upon a showing that the case is of such imperative public importance as to justify deviation from normal appellate practice and to require immediate determination in this Court. See 28 U.S.C. § 2101(e).

Rule 12. Review on Certiorari: How Sought; Parties

1. Except as provided in paragraph 2 of this Rule, the petitioner shall file 40 copies of a petition for a writ of certiorari, prepared as required by Rule 33.1, and shall pay the Rule 38(a) docket fee.

2. A petitioner proceeding *in forma pauperis* under Rule 39 shall file an original and 10 copies of a petition for a writ of certiorari prepared as required by Rule 33.2, together with an original and 10 copies of the motion for leave to proceed *in forma pauperis*. A copy of the motion shall precede and be attached to each copy of the petition. An inmate confined in an institution, if proceeding *in forma pauperis* and not represented by counsel, need file only an original petition and motion.

3. Whether prepared under Rule 33.1 or Rule 33.2, the petition shall comply in all respects with Rule 14 and shall be submitted with proof of service as required by Rule 29. The case then will be placed on the docket. It is the petitioner's duty to notify all respondents promptly, on a form supplied by the Clerk, of the date of filing, the date the case was placed on the docket, and the docket number of the case. The notice shall be served as required by Rule 29.

4. Parties interested jointly, severally, or otherwise in a judgment may petition separately for a writ of certiorari; or any two or more may join in a petition. A party not shown on the petition as joined therein at the time the petition is filed may not later join in that petition. When two or more judgments are sought to be reviewed on a writ of certiorari to the same court and involve identical or closely related questions, a single petition for a writ of certiorari covering all the judgments suffices. A petition for a writ of certiorari may not be joined with any other pleading, except that any motion for leave to proceed *in forma pauperis* shall be attached.

5. No more than 30 days after a case has been placed on the docket, a respondent seeking to file a conditional cross-petition (*i.e.*, a cross-petition that otherwise would be untimely) shall file, with proof of service as required by Rule 29, 40 copies of the cross-petition prepared as required by Rule 33.1,

except that a cross-petitioner proceeding *in forma pauperis* under Rule 39 shall comply with Rule 12.2. The cross-petition shall comply in all respects with this Rule and Rule 14, except that material already reproduced in the appendix to the opening petition need not be reproduced again. A cross-petitioning respondent shall pay the Rule 38(a) docket fee or submit a motion for leave to proceed *in forma pauperis*. The cover of the cross-petition shall clearly that it is a conditional cross-petition. The cross-petition then will be placed on the docket, subject to the provisions of Rule 13.4. It is the cross-petitioner's duty to notify all cross-respondents promptly, on a form supplied by the Clerk, of the date of filing, the date the cross-petition was placed on the docket, and the docket number of the cross-petition. The notice shall be served as required by Rule 29. A cross-petition for a writ of certiorari may not be joined with any other pleading, except that any motion for leave to proceed *in forma pauperis* shall be attached. The time to file a conditional cross-petition will not be extended.

6. All parties to the proceeding in the court whose judgment is sought to be reviewed are deemed parties entitled to file documents in this Court, unless the petitioner notifies the Clerk of this Court in writing of the petitioner's belief that one or more of the parties below have no interest in the outcome of the petition. A copy of such notice shall be served as required by Rule 29 on all parties to the proceeding below. A party noted as no longer interested may remain a party by notifying the Clerk promptly, with service on the other parties, of an intention to remain a party. All parties other than the petitioner are considered respondents, but any respondent who supports the position of a petitioner shall meet the petitioner's time schedule for filing documents, with the following exception: A response of a party aligned with petitioner below who supports granting the petition shall be filed within 30 days after the case is placed on the docket, and that time will not be extended. Counsel for such respondent shall ensure that counsel of record for all parties receive notice of its intention to file a brief in support within 20 days after the case is placed on the docket. A respondent not aligned with petitioner below who supports granting the petition, or a respondent aligned with petitioner below who takes the position that the petition should be denied, is not subject to the notice requirement and may file a response within the time otherwise provided by Rule 15.3. Parties who file no document will not qualify for any relief from this Court.

7. The clerk of the court having possession of the record shall keep it until notified by the Clerk of this Court to certify and transmit it. In any document filed with this Court, a party may cite or quote from the record, even if it has not been transmitted to this Court. When requested by the Clerk of this Court to certify and transmit the record, or any part of it, the clerk of the court having possession of the record shall number the documents to be certified and shall transmit therewith a numbered list specifically identifying each document transmitted. If the record, or stipulated portions, have been printed for the use of the court below, that printed record, plus the proceedings in the court below, may be certified as the record unless one of the parties or the Clerk of this Court requests otherwise. The record may consist of certified copies, but if the lower court is of the view that original documents of any kind should be seen by this Court, that court may provide by order for the transport, safekeeping, and return of such originals.

Rule 13. Review on Certiorari: Time for Petitioning

1. Unless otherwise provided by law, a petition for a writ of certiorari to review a judgment in any case, civil or criminal, entered by a state court of last resort or a United States court of appeals (including the United States Court of Appeals for the Armed Forces) is timely when it is filed with the Clerk of this Court within 90 days after entry of the judgment. A petition for a writ of certiorari seeking review of a judgment of a lower state court that is subject to discretionary review by the state court of last resort is timely when it is filed with the Clerk within 90 days after entry of the order denying discretionary review.

2. The Clerk will not file any petition for a writ of certiorari that is jurisdictionally out of time. See, *e.g.*, 28 U.S.C. § 2101(c).

3. The time to file a petition for a writ of certiorari runs from the date of entry of the judgment or order sought to be reviewed, and not from the issuance date of the mandate (or its equivalent under local practice). But if a petition for rehearing is timely filed in the lower court by any party, or if the lower court appropriately entertains an untimely petition for rehearing or *sua sponte* considers rehearing, the time to file the petition for a writ of certiorari for all parties (whether or not they requested rehearing or joined in the petition for rehearing) runs from the date of the denial of rehearing or, if rehearing is granted, the subsequent entry of judgment.

4. A cross-petition for a writ of certiorari is timely when it is filed with the Clerk as provided in paragraphs 1, 3, and 5 of this Rule, or in Rule 12.5. However, a conditional cross-petition (which except for Rule 12.5 would be untimely) will not be granted unless another party's timely petition for a writ of certiorari is granted.

5. For good cause, a Justice may extend the time to file a petition for a writ of certiorari for a period not exceeding 60 days. An application to extend the time to file shall set out the basis for jurisdiction in this Court, identify the judgment sought to be reviewed, include a copy of the opinion and any order respecting rehearing, and set out specific reasons why an extension of time is justified. The application

must be filed with the Clerk at least 10 days before the date the petition is due, except in extraordinary circumstances. The application must clearly identify each party for whom an extension is being sought, as any extension that might be granted would apply solely to the party or parties named in the application. For the time and manner of presenting the application, see Rules 21, 22, 30, and 33.2. An application to extend the time to file a petition for a writ of certiorari is not favored.

Rule 14. Content of a Petition for a Writ of Certiorari

1. A petition for a writ of certiorari shall contain, in the order indicated:

(a) The questions presented for review, expressed concisely in relation to the circumstances of the case, without unnecessary detail. The questions should be short and should not be argumentative or repetitive. If the petitioner or respondent is under a death sentence that may be affected by the disposition of the petition, the notation "capital case" shall precede the questions presented. The questions shall be set out on the first page following the cover, and no other information may appear on that page. The statement of any question presented is deemed to comprise every subsidiary question fairly included therein. Only the questions set out in the petition, or fairly included therein, will be considered by the Court.

(b) A list of all parties to the proceeding in the court whose judgment is sought to be reviewed (unless the caption of the case contains the names of all the parties), and a corporate disclosure statement as required by Rule 29.6.

(c) If the petition prepared under Rule 33.1 exceeds 1,500 words or exceeds five pages if prepared under Rule 33.2, a table of contents and a table of cited authorities. The table of contents shall include the items contained in the appendix.

(d) Citations of the official and unofficial reports of the opinions and orders entered in the case by courts or administrative agencies.

(e) A concise statement of the basis for jurisdiction in this Court, showing:

(i) the date the judgment or order sought to be reviewed was entered (and, if applicable, a statement that the petition is filed under this Court's Rule 11);

(ii) the date of any order respecting rehearing, and the date and terms of any order granting an extension of time to file the petition for a writ of certiorari;

(iii) express reliance on Rule 12.5, when a cross-petition for a writ of certiorari is filed under that Rule, and the date of docketing of the petition for a writ of certiorari in connection with which the cross-petition is filed;

(iv) the statutory provision believed to confer on this Court jurisdiction to review on a writ of certiorari the judgment or order in question; and

(v) if applicable, a statement that the notifications required by Rule 29.4(b) or (c) have been made.

(f) The constitutional provisions, treaties, statutes, ordinances, and regulations involved in the case, set out verbatim with appropriate citation. If the provisions involved are lengthy, their citation alone suffices at this point, and their pertinent text shall be set out in the appendix referred to in subparagraph 1(i).

(g) A concise statement of the case setting out the facts material to consideration of the questions presented, and also containing the following:

(i) If review of a state-court judgment is sought, specification of the stage in the proceedings, both in the court of first instance and in the appellate courts, when the federal questions sought to be reviewed were raised; the method or manner of raising them and the way in which they were passed on by those courts; and pertinent quotations of specific portions of the record or summary thereof, with specific reference to the places in the record where the matter appears (*e. g.*, court opinion, ruling on exception, portion of court's charge and exception thereto, assignment of error), so as to show that the federal question was timely and properly raised and that this Court has jurisdiction to review the judgment on a writ of certiorari. When the portions of the record relied on under this subparagraph are voluminous, they shall be included in the appendix referred to in subparagraph 1(I).

(ii) If review of a judgment of a United States court of appeals is sought, the basis for federal jurisdiction in the court of first instance.

(h) A direct and concise argument amplifying the reasons relied on for allowance of the writ. See Rule 10.

(i) An appendix containing, in the order indicated:

(i) the opinions, orders, findings of fact, and conclusions of law, whether written or orally given and transcribed, entered in conjunction with the judgment sought to be reviewed;

(ii) any other relevant opinions, orders, findings of fact, and conclusions of law entered in the case by courts or administrative agencies, and, if reference thereto is necessary to ascertain the grounds of the judgment, of those in companion cases (each document shall include the caption showing the name of the issuing court or agency, the title and number of the case, and the date of entry);

(iii) any order on rehearing, including the caption showing the name of the issuing court, the title and number of the case, and the date of entry;

(iv) the judgment sought to be reviewed if the date of its entry is different from the date of the opinion or order required in sub-subparagraph (i) of this subparagraph;

(v) material required by subparagraphs 1(f) or 1(g)(i); and

(vi) any other material the petitioner believes essential to understand the petition.

If the material required by this subparagraph is voluminous, it may be presented in a separate volume or volumes with appropriate covers.

2. All contentions in support of a petition for a writ of certiorari shall be set out in the body of the petition, as provided in subparagraph 1(h) of this Rule. No separate brief in support of a petition for a writ of certiorari may be filed, and the Clerk will not file any petition for a writ of certiorari to which any supporting brief is annexed or appended.

3. A petition for a writ of certiorari should be stated briefly and in plain terms and may not exceed the word or page limitations specified in Rule 33.

4. The failure of a petitioner to present with accuracy, brevity, and clarity whatever is essential to ready and adequate understanding of the points requiring consideration is sufficient reason for the Court to deny a petition.

5. If the Clerk determines that a petition submitted timely and in good faith is in a form that does not comply with this Rule or with Rule 33 or Rule 34, the Clerk will return it with a letter indicating the deficiency. A corrected petition submitted in accordance with Rule 29.2 no more than 60 days after the date of the Clerk's letter will be deemed timely.

Rule 15. Briefs in Opposition; Reply Briefs; Supplemental Briefs

1. A brief in opposition to a petition for a writ of certiorari may be filed by the respondent in any case, but is not mandatory except in a capital case, see Rule 14.1(a), or when ordered by the Court.

2. A brief in opposition should be stated briefly and in plain terms and may not exceed the word or page limitations specified in Rule 33. In addition to presenting other arguments for denying the petition, the brief in opposition should address any perceived misstatement of fact or law in the petition that bears on what issues properly would be before the Court if certiorari were granted. Counsel are admonished that they have an obligation to the Court to point out in the brief in opposition, and not later, any perceived misstatement made in the petition. Any objection to consideration of a question presented based on what occurred in the proceedings below, if the objection does not go to jurisdiction, may be deemed waived unless called to the Court's attention in the brief in opposition.

3. Any brief in opposition shall be filed within 30 days after the case is placed on the docket, unless the time is extended by the Court or a Justice, or by the Clerk under Rule 30.4. Forty copies shall be filed, except that a respondent proceeding *in forma pauperis* under Rule 39, including an inmate of an institution, shall file the number of copies required for a petition by such a person under Rule 12.2, together with a motion for leave to proceed *in forma pauperis*, a copy of which shall precede and be attached to each copy of the brief in opposition. If the petitioner is proceeding *in forma pauperis*, the respondent shall prepare its brief in opposition, if any, as required by Rule 33.2, and shall file an original and 10 copies of that brief. Whether prepared under Rule 33.1 or Rule 33.2, the brief in opposition shall comply with the requirements of Rule 24 governing a respondent's brief, except that no summary of the argument is required. A brief in opposition may not be joined with any other pleading, except that any motion for leave to proceed *in forma pauperis* shall be attached. The brief in opposition shall be served as required by Rule 29.

4. No motion by a respondent to dismiss a petition for a writ of certiorari may be filed. Any objections to the jurisdiction of the Court to grant a petition for a writ of certiorari shall be included in the brief in opposition.

5. The Clerk will distribute the petition to the Court for its consideration upon receiving an express waiver of the right to file a brief in opposition, or, if no waiver or brief in opposition is filed, upon the expiration of the time allowed for filing. If a brief in opposition is timely filed, the Clerk will distribute the petition, brief in opposition, and any reply brief to the Court for its consideration no less than 14 days after the brief in opposition is filed, unless the petitioner expressly waives the 14-day waiting period.

6. Any petitioner may file a reply brief addressed to new points raised in the brief in opposition, but distribution and consideration by the Court under paragraph 5 of this Rule will not be deferred pending its receipt. Forty copies shall be filed, except that petitioner proceeding *in forma pauperis* under Rule 39, including an inmate of an institution, shall file the number of copies required for a petition by such a person under Rule 12.2. The reply brief shall be served as required by Rule 29.

7. If a cross-petition for a writ of certiorari has been docketed, distribution of both petitions will be deferred until the cross-petition is due for distribution under this Rule.

8. Any party may file a supplemental brief at any time while a petition for a writ of certiorari is pending, calling attention to new cases, new legislation, or other intervening matter not available at the time of the party's last filing. A supplemental brief shall be restricted to new matter and shall follow, insofar as applicable, the form for a brief in opposition prescribed by this Rule. Forty copies shall be filed, except that a party proceeding *in forma pauperis* under Rule 39, including an inmate of an institution, shall file the number of copies required for a petition by such a person under Rule 12.2. The supplemental brief shall be served as required by Rule 29.

Rule 16. Disposition of a Petition for a Writ of Certiorari

1. After considering the documents distributed under Rule 15, the Court will enter an appropriate order. The order may be a summary disposition on the merits.

2. Whenever the Court grants a petition for a writ of certiorari, the Clerk will prepare, sign, and

enter an order to that effect and will notify forthwith counsel of record and the court whose judgment is to be reviewed. The case then will be scheduled for briefing and oral argument. If the record has not previously been filed in this Court, the Clerk will request the clerk of the court having possession of the record to certify and transmit it. A formal writ will not issue unless specially directed.

3. Whenever the Court denies a petition for a writ of certiorari, the Clerk will prepare, sign, and enter an order to that effect and will notify forthwith counsel of record and the court whose judgment was sought to be reviewed. The order of denial will not be suspended pending disposition of a petition for rehearing except by order of the Court or a Justice.

PART IV. OTHER JURISDICTION

Rule 17. Procedure in an Original Action

1. This Rule applies only to an action invoking the Court's original jurisdiction under Article III of the Constitution of the United States. See also 28 U.S.C. § 1251 and U. S. Const., Amdt. 11. A petition for an extraordinary writ in aid of the Court's appellate jurisdiction shall be filed as provided in Rule 20.

2. The form of pleadings and motions prescribed by the Federal Rules of Civil Procedure is followed. In other respects, those Rules and the Federal Rules of Evidence may be taken as guides.

3. The initial pleading shall be preceded by a motion for leave to file, and may be accompanied by a brief in support of the motion. Forty copies of each document shall be filed, with proof of service. Service shall be as required by Rule 29, except that when an adverse party is a State, service shall be made on both the Governor and the Attorney General of that State.

4. The case will be placed on the docket when the motion for leave to file and the initial pleading are filed with the Clerk. The Rule 38(a) docket fee shall be paid at that time.

5. No more than 60 days after receiving the motion for leave to file and the initial pleading, an adverse party shall file 40 copies of any brief in opposition to the motion, with proof of service as required by Rule 29. The Clerk will distribute the filed documents to the Court for its consideration upon receiving an express waiver of the right to file a brief in opposition, or, if no waiver or brief is filed, upon the expiration of the time allowed for filing. If a brief in opposition is timely filed, the Clerk will distribute the filed documents to the Court for its consideration no less than 10 days after the brief in opposition is filed. A reply brief may be filed, but consideration of the case will not be deferred pending its receipt. The Court thereafter may grant or deny the motion, set it for oral argument, direct that additional documents be filed, or require that other proceedings be conducted.

6. A summons issued out of this Court shall be served on the defendant 60 days before the return day specified therein. If the defendant does not respond by the return day, the plaintiff may proceed *ex parte*.

7. Process against a State issued out of this Court shall be served on both the Governor and the Attorney General of that State.

Rule 18. Appeal from a United States District Court

1. When a direct appeal from a decision of a United States district court is authorized by law, the appeal is commenced by filing a notice of appeal with the clerk of the district court within the time provided by law after entry of the judgment sought to be reviewed. The time to file may not be extended. The notice of appeal shall specify the parties taking the appeal, designate the judgment, or part thereof, appealed from and the date of its entry, and specify the statute or statutes under which the appeal is taken. A copy of the notice of appeal shall be served on all parties to the proceeding as required by Rule 29, and proof of service shall be filed in the district court together with the notice of appeal.

2. All parties to the proceeding in the district court are deemed parties entitled to file documents in this Court, but a party having no interest in the outcome of the appeal may so notify the Clerk of this Court and shall serve a copy of the notice on all other parties. Parties interested jointly, severally, or otherwise in the judgment may appeal separately, or any two or more may join in an appeal. When two or more judgments involving identical or closely related questions are sought to be reviewed on appeal from the same court, a notice of appeal for each judgment shall be filed with the clerk of the district court, but a single jurisdictional statement covering all the judgments suffices. Parties who file no document will not qualify for any relief from this Court.

3. No more than 60 days after filing the notice of appeal in the district court, the appellant shall file 40 copies of a jurisdictional statement and shall pay the Rule 38 docket fee, except that an appellant proceeding *in forma pauperis* under Rule 39, including an inmate of an institution, shall file the number of copies required for a petition by such a person under Rule 12.2, together with a motion for leave to proceed *in forma pauperis*, a copy of which shall precede and be attached to each copy of the jurisdictional statement. The jurisdictional statement shall follow, insofar as applicable, the form for a petition for a writ of certiorari prescribed by Rule 14, and shall be served as required by Rule 29. The case will then be placed on the docket. It is the appellant's duty to notify all appellees promptly, on a form supplied by the Clerk, of the date of filing, the date the case was placed on the docket, and the docket number of the case. The notice shall be served as required by Rule 29. The appendix shall include a

copy of the notice of appeal showing the date it was filed in the district court. For good cause, a Justice may extend the time to file a jurisdictional statement for a period not exceeding 60 days. An application to extend the time to file a jurisdictional statement shall set out the basis for jurisdiction in this Court; identify the judgment sought to be reviewed; include a copy of the opinion, any order respecting rehearing, and the notice of appeal; and set out specific reasons why an extension of time is justified. For the time and manner of presenting the application, see Rules 21, 22, and 30. An application to extend the time to file a jurisdictional statement is not favored.

4. No more than 30 days after a case has been placed on the docket, an appellee seeking to file a conditional cross-appeal (*i. e.*, a cross-appeal that otherwise would be untimely) shall file, with proof of service as required by Rule 29, a jurisdictional statement that complies in all respects (including number of copies filed) with paragraph 3 of this Rule, except that material already reproduced in the appendix to the opening jurisdictional statement need not be reproduced again. A cross-appealing appellee shall pay the Rule 38 docket fee or submit a motion for leave to proceed *in forma pauperis*. The cover of the cross-appeal shall indicate clearly that it is a conditional cross-appeal. The cross-appeal then will be placed on the docket. It is the cross-appellant's duty to notify all cross-appellees promptly, on a form supplied by the Clerk, of the date of filing, the date the cross-appeal was placed on the docket, and the docket number of the cross- appeal. The notice shall be served as required by Rule 29. A cross-appeal may not be joined with any other pleading, except that any motion for leave to proceed *in forma pauperis* shall be attached. The time to file a cross-appeal will not be extended.

5. After a notice of appeal has been filed in the district court, but before the case is placed on this Court's docket, the parties may dismiss the appeal by stipulation filed in the district court, or the district court may dismiss the appeal on the appellant's motion, with notice to all parties. If a notice of appeal has been filed, but the case has not been placed on this Court's docket within the time prescribed for docketing, the district court may dismiss the appeal on the appellee's motion, with notice to all parties, and may make any just order with respect to costs. If the district court has denied the appellee's motion to dismiss the appeal, the appellee may move this Court to docket and dismiss the appeal by filing an original and 10 copies of a motion presented in conformity with Rules 21 and 33.2. The motion shall be accompanied by proof of service as required by Rule 29, and by a certificate from the clerk of the district court, certifying that a notice of appeal was filed and that the appellee's motion to dismiss was denied. The appellant may not thereafter file a jurisdictional statement without special leave of the Court, and the Court may allow costs against the appellant.

6. Within 30 days after the case is placed on this Court's docket, the appellee may file a motion to dismiss, to affirm, or in the alternative to affirm or dismiss. Forty copies of the motion shall be filed, except that an appellee proceeding *in forma pauperis* under Rule 39, including an inmate of an institution, shall file the number of copies required for a petition by such a person under Rule 12.2, together with a motion for leave to proceed *in forma pauperis*, a copy of which shall precede and be attached to each copy of the motion to dismiss, to affirm, or in the alternative to affirm or dismiss. The motion shall follow, insofar as applicable, the form for a brief in opposition prescribed by Rule 15, and shall comply in all respects with Rule 21.

7. The Clerk will distribute the jurisdictional statement to the Court for its consideration upon receiving an express waiver of the right to file a motion to dismiss or to affirm or, if no waiver or motion is filed, upon the expiration of the time allowed for filing. If a motion to dismiss or to affirm is timely filed, the Clerk will distribute the jurisdictional statement, motion, and any brief opposing the motion to the Court for its consideration no less than 14 days after the motion is filed, unless the appellant expressly waives the 14-day waiting period.

8. Any appellant may file a brief opposing a motion to dismiss or to affirm, but distribution and consideration by the Court under paragraph 7 of this Rule will not be deferred pending its receipt. Forty copies shall be filed, except that an appellant proceeding *in forma pauperis* under Rule 39, including an inmate of an institution, shall file the number of copies required for a petition by such a person under Rule 12.2. The brief shall be served as required by Rule 29.

9. If a cross-appeal has been docketed, distribution of both jurisdictional statements will be deferred until the cross-appeal is due for distribution under this Rule.

10. Any party may file a supplemental brief at any time while a jurisdictional statement is pending, calling attention to new cases, new legislation, or other intervening matter not available at the time of the party's last filing. A supplemental brief shall be restricted to new matter and shall follow, insofar as applicable, the form for a brief in opposition prescribed by Rule 15. Forty copies shall be filed, except that a party proceeding *in forma pauperis* under Rule 39, including an inmate of an institution, shall file the number of copies required for a petition by such a person under Rule 12.2. The supplemental brief shall be served as required by Rule 29.

11. The clerk of the district court shall retain possession of the record until notified by the Clerk of this Court to certify and transmit it. See Rule 12.7.

12. After considering the documents distributed under this Rule, the Court may dispose summarily of the appeal on the merits, note probable jurisdiction, or postpone consideration of jurisdiction until a

hearing of the case on the merits. If not disposed of summarily, the case stands for briefing and oral argument on the merits. If consideration of jurisdiction is postponed, counsel, at the outset of their briefs and at oral argument, shall address the question of jurisdiction. If the record has not previously been filed in this Court, the Clerk of this Court will request the clerk of the court in possession of the record to certify and transmit it.

13. If the Clerk determines that a jurisdictional statement submitted timely and in good faith is in a form that does not comply with this Rule or with Rule 33 or Rule 34, the Clerk will return it with a letter indicating the deficiency. If a corrected jurisdictional statement is submitted in accordance with Rule 29.2 no more than 60 days after the date of the Clerk's letter it will be deemed timely.

Rule 19. Procedure on a Certified Question

1. A United States court of appeals may certify to this Court a question or proposition of law on which it seeks instruction for the proper decision of a case. The certificate shall contain a statement of the nature of the case and the facts on which the question or proposition of law arises. Only questions or propositions of law may be certified, and they shall be stated separately and with precision. The certificate shall be prepared as required by Rule 33.2 and shall be signed by the clerk of the court of appeals.

2. When a question is certified by a United States court of appeals, this Court, on its own motion or that of a party, may consider and decide the entire matter in controversy. See 28 U.S.C. § 1254(2).

3. When a question is certified, the Clerk will notify the parties and docket the case. Counsel shall then enter their appearances. After docketing, the Clerk will submit the certificate to the Court for a preliminary examination to determine whether the case should be briefed, set for argument, or dismissed. No brief may be filed until the preliminary examination of the certificate is completed.

4. If the Court orders the case briefed or set for argument, the parties will be notified and permitted to file briefs. The Clerk of this Court then will request the clerk of the court in possession of the record to certify and transmit it. Any portion of the record to which the parties wish to direct the Court's particular attention should be printed in a joint appendix, prepared in conformity with Rule 26 by the appellant or petitioner in the court of appeals, but the fact that any part of the record has not been printed does not prevent the parties or the Court from relying on it.

5. A brief on the merits in a case involving a certified question shall comply with Rules 24, 25, and 33.1, except that the brief for the party who is the appellant or petitioner below shall be filed within 45 days of the order requiring briefs or setting the case for argument.

Rule 20. Procedure on a Petition for an Extraordinary Writ

1. Issuance by the Court of an extraordinary writ authorized by 28 U.S.C. § 1651(a) is not a matter of right, but of discretion sparingly exercised. To justify the granting of any such writ, the petition must show that the writ will be in aid of the Court's appellate jurisdiction, that exceptional circumstances warrant the exercise of the Court's discretionary powers, and that adequate relief cannot be obtained in any other form or from any other court.

2. A petition seeking a writ authorized by 28 U.S.C. § 1651(a), § 2241, or § 2254(a) shall be prepared in all respects as required by Rules 33 and 34. The petition shall be captioned "*In re* [name of petitioner]" and shall follow, insofar as applicable, the form of a petition for a writ of certiorari prescribed by Rule 14. All contentions in support of the petition shall be included in the petition. The case will be placed on the docket when 40 copies of the petition are filed with the Clerk and the docket fee is paid, except that a petitioner proceeding *in forma pauperis* under Rule 39, including an inmate of an institution, shall file the number of copies required for a petition by such a person under Rule 12.2, together with a motion for leave to proceed *in forma pauperis*, a copy of which shall precede and be attached to each copy of the petition. The petition shall be served as required by Rule 29 (subject to subparagraph 4(b) of this Rule).

3. (a) A petition seeking a writ of prohibition, a writ of mandamus, or both in the alternative shall state the name and office or function of every person against whom relief is sought and shall set out with particularity why the relief sought is not available in any other court. A copy of the judgment with respect to which the writ is sought, including any related opinion, shall be appended to the petition together with any other document essential to understanding the petition.

(b) The petition shall be served on every party to the proceeding with respect to which relief is sought. Within 30 days after the petition is placed on the docket, a party shall file 40 copies of any brief or briefs in opposition thereto, which shall comply fully with Rule 15. If a party named as a respondent does not wish to respond to the petition, that party may so advise the Clerk and all other parties by letter. All persons served are deemed respondents for all purposes in the proceedings in this Court.

4. (a) A petition seeking a writ of habeas corpus shall comply with the requirements of 28 U.S.C. §§ 2241 and 2242, and in particular with the provision in the last paragraph of § 2242, which requires a statement of the "reasons for not making application to the district court of the district in which the applicant is held." If the relief sought is from the judgment of a state court, the petition shall set out specifically how and where the petitioner has exhausted available remedies in the state courts or otherwise comes within the provisions of 28 U.S.C.

§ 2254(b). To justify the granting of a writ of habeas corpus, the petitioner must show that exceptional circumstances warrant the exercise of the Court's discretionary powers, and that adequate relief cannot be obtained in any other form or from any other court. This writ is rarely granted.

(b) Habeas corpus proceedings, except in capital cases, are *ex parte*, unless the Court requires the respondent to show cause why the petition for a writ of habeas corpus should not be granted. A response, if ordered, or in a capital case, shall comply fully with Rule 15. Neither the denial of the petition, without more, nor an order of transfer to a district court under the authority of 28 U.S.C. § 2241(b), is an adjudication on the merits, and therefore does not preclude further application to another court for the relief sought.

5. The Clerk will distribute the documents to the Court for its consideration when a brief in opposition under subparagraph 3(b) of this Rule has been filed, when a response under subparagraph 4(b) has been ordered and filed, when the time to file has expired, or when the right to file has been expressly waived.

6. If the Court orders the case set for argument, the Clerk will notify the parties whether additional briefs are required, when they shall be filed, and, if the case involves a petition for a common-law writ of certiorari, that the parties shall prepare a joint appendix in accordance with Rule 26.

PART V. MOTIONS AND APPLICATIONS

Rule 21. Motions to the Court

1. Every motion to the Court shall clearly state its purpose and the facts on which it is based and may present legal argument in support thereof. No separate brief may be filed. A motion should be concise and shall comply with any applicable page limits. Non-dispositive motions and applications in cases in which certiorari has been granted, probable jurisdiction noted, or consideration of jurisdiction postponed shall state the position on the disposition of the motion or application of the other party or parties to the case. Rule 22 governs an application addressed to a single Justice.

2. (a) A motion in any action within the Court's original jurisdiction shall comply with Rule 17.3.

(b) A motion to dismiss as moot (or a suggestion of mootness), a motion for leave to file a brief as *amicus curiae*, and any motion the granting of which would dispose of the entire case or would affect the final judgment to be entered (other than a motion to docket and dismiss under Rule 18.5 or a motion for voluntary dismissal under Rule 46) shall be prepared as required by Rule 33.1, and 40 copies shall be filed, except that a movant proceeding *in forma pauperis* under Rule 39, including an inmate of an institution, shall file a motion prepared as required by Rule 33.2, and shall file the number of copies required for a petition by such a person under Rule 12.2. The motion shall be served as required by Rule 29.

(c) Any other motion to the Court shall be prepared as required by Rule 33.2; the moving party shall file an original and 10 copies. The Court subsequently may order the moving party to prepare the motion as required by Rule 33.1; in that event, the party shall file 40 copies.

3. A motion to the Court shall be filed with the Clerk and shall be accompanied by proof of service as required by Rule 29. No motion may be presented in open Court, other than a motion for admission to the Bar, except when the proceeding to which it refers is being argued. Oral argument on a motion will not be permitted unless the Court so directs.

4. Any response to a motion shall be filed as promptly as possible considering the nature of the relief sought and any asserted need for emergency action, and, in any event, within 10 days of receipt, unless the Court or a Justice, or the Clerk under Rule 30.4, orders otherwise. A response to a motion prepared as required by Rule 33.1, except a response to a motion for leave to file an *amicus curiae* brief (see Rule 37.5), shall be prepared in the same manner if time permits. In an appropriate case, the Court may act on a motion without waiting for a response.

Rule 22. Applications to Individual Justices

1. An application addressed to an individual Justice shall be filed with the Clerk, who will transmit it promptly to the Justice concerned if an individual Justice has authority to grant the sought relief.

2. The original and two copies of any application addressed to an individual Justice shall be prepared as required by Rule 33.2, and shall be accompanied by proof of service as required by Rule 29.

3. An application shall be addressed to the Justice allotted to the Circuit from which the case arises. An application arising from the United States Court of Appeals for the Armed Forces shall be addressed to the Chief Justice. When the Circuit Justice is unavailable for any reason, the application addressed to that Justice will be distributed to the Justice then available who is next junior to the Circuit Justice; the turn of the Chief Justice follows that of the most junior Justice.

4. A Justice denying an application will note the denial thereon. Thereafter, unless action thereon is restricted by law to the Circuit Justice or is untimely under Rule 30.2, the party making an application, except in the case of an application for an extension of time, may renew it to any other Justice, subject to the provisions of this Rule. Except when the denial is without prejudice, a renewed application is not favored. Renewed application is made by a letter to the Clerk, designating the Justice to whom the application is to be directed, and accompanied by 10 copies of the original application and proof of service

as required by Rule 29.

5. A Justice to whom an application for a stay or for bail is submitted may refer it to the Court for determination.

6. The Clerk will advise all parties concerned, by appropriately speedy means, of the disposition made of an application.

Rule 23. Stays

1. A stay may be granted by a Justice as permitted by law.

2. A party to a judgment sought to be reviewed may present to a Justice an application to stay the enforcement of that judgment. See 28 U.S.C. § 2101(f).

3. An application for a stay shall set out with particularity why the relief sought is not available from any other court or judge. Except in the most extraordinary circumstances, an application for a stay will not be entertained unless the relief requested was first sought in the appropriate court or courts below or from a judge or judges thereof. An application for a stay shall identify the judgment sought to be reviewed and have appended thereto a copy of the order and opinion, if any, and a copy of the order, if any, of the court or judge below denying the relief sought, and shall set out specific reasons why a stay is justified. The form and content of an application for a stay are governed by Rules 22 and 33.2.

4. A judge, court, or Justice granting an application for a stay pending review by this Court may condition the stay on the filing of a supersedeas bond having an approved surety or sureties. The bond will be conditioned on the satisfaction of the judgment in full, together with any costs, interest, and damages for delay that may be awarded. If a part of the judgment sought to be reviewed has already been satisfied, or is otherwise secured, the bond may be conditioned on the satisfaction of the part of the judgment not otherwise secured or satisfied, together with costs, interest, and damages.

PART VI. BRIEFS ON THE MERITS AND ORAL ARGUMENT

Rule 24. Briefs on the Merits: In General

1. A brief on the merits for a petitioner or an appellant shall comply in all respects with Rules 33.1 and 34 and shall contain in the order here indicated:

(a) The questions presented for review under Rule 14.1(a). The questions shall be set out on the first page following the cover, and no other information may appear on that page. The phrasing of the questions presented need not be identical with that in the petition for a writ of certiorari or the jurisdictional statement, but the brief may not raise additional questions or change the substance of the questions already presented in those documents. At its option, however, the Court may consider a plain error not among the questions presented but evident from the record and otherwise within its jurisdiction to decide.

(b) A list of all parties to the proceeding in the court whose judgment is under review (unless the caption of the case in this Court contains the names of all parties). Any amended corporate disclosure statement as required by Rule 29.6 shall be placed here.

(c) If the brief exceeds 1,500 words, a table of contents and a table of cited authorities.

(d) Citations of the official and unofficial reports of the opinions and orders entered in the case by courts and administrative agencies.

(e) A concise statement of the basis for jurisdiction in this Court, including the statutory provisions and time factors on which jurisdiction rests.

(f) The constitutional provisions, treaties, statutes, ordinances, and regulations involved in the case, set out verbatim with appropriate citation. If the provisions involved are lengthy, their citation alone suffices at this point, and their pertinent text, if not already set out in the petition for a writ of certiorari, jurisdictional statement, or an appendix to either document, shall be set out in an appendix to the brief.

(g) A concise statement of the case, setting out the facts material to the consideration of the questions presented, with appropriate references to the joint appendix, *e. g.*, App. 12, or to the record, *e. g.*, Record 12.

(h) A summary of the argument, suitably paragraphed. The summary should be a clear and concise condensation of the argument made in the body of the brief; mere repetition of the headings under which the argument is arranged is not sufficient.

(i) The argument, exhibiting clearly the points of fact and of law presented and citing the authorities and statutes relied on.

(j) A conclusion specifying with particularity the relief the party seeks.

2. A brief on the merits for a respondent or an appellee shall conform to the foregoing requirements, except that items required by subparagraphs 1(a), (b), (d), (e), (f), and (g) of this Rule need not be included unless the respondent or appellee is dissatisfied with their presentation by the opposing party.

3. A brief on the merits may not exceed the word limitations specified in Rule 33.1(g). An appendix to a brief may include only relevant material, and counsel are cautioned not to include in an appendix arguments or citations that properly belong in the body of the brief.

4. A reply brief shall conform to those portions of this Rule applicable to the brief for a respondent or an appellee, but, if appropriately divided by topical headings, need not contain a summary of the argument.

5. A reference to the joint appendix or to the record set out in any brief shall indicate the appro-

priate page number. If the reference is to an exhibit, the page numbers at which the exhibit appears, at which it was offered in evidence, and at which it was ruled on by the judge shall be indicated, *e. g.*, Pl. Exh. 14, Record 199, 2134.

6. A brief shall be concise, logically arranged with proper headings, and free of irrelevant, immaterial, or scandalous matter. The Court may disregard or strike a brief that does not comply with this paragraph.

Rule 25. Briefs on the Merits: Number of Copies and Time to File

1. The petitioner or appellant shall file 40 copies of the brief on the merits within 45 days of the order granting the writ of certiorari, noting probable jurisdiction, or postponing consideration of jurisdiction. Any respondent or appellee who supports the petitioner or appellant shall meet the petitioner's or appellant's time schedule for filing documents.

2. The respondent or appellee shall file 40 copies of the brief on the merits within 30 days after the brief for the petitioner or appellant is filed.

3. The petitioner or appellant shall file 40 copies of the reply brief, if any, within 30 days after the brief for the respondent or appellee is filed, but any reply brief must actually be received by the Clerk not later than 2 p.m. one week before the date of oral argument. Any respondent or appellee supporting the petitioner or appellant may file a reply brief.

4. If cross-petitions or cross-appeals have been consolidated for argument, the Clerk, upon request of the parties, may designate one of the parties to file an initial brief and reply brief as provided in paragraphs 1 and 3 of this Rule (as if the party were petitioner or appellant), and may designate the other party to file an initial brief as provided in paragraph 2 of this Rule and, to the extent appropriate, a supplemental brief following the submission of the reply brief. In such a case, the Clerk may establish the time for the submission of the briefs and alter the otherwise applicable word limits. Except as approved by the Court or a Justice, the total number of words permitted for the briefs of the parties cumulatively shall not exceed the maximum that would have been allowed in the absence of an order under this paragraph.

5. The time periods stated in paragraphs 1, 2, and 3 of this Rule may be extended as provided in Rule 30. An application to extend the time to file a brief on the merits is not favored. If a case is advanced for hearing, the time to file briefs on the merits may be abridged as circumstances require pursuant to an order of the Court on its own motion or that of a party.

6. A party wishing to present late authorities, newly enacted legislation, or other intervening matter that was not available in time to be included in a brief may file 40 copies of a supplemental brief, restricted to such new matter and otherwise presented in conformity with these Rules, up to the time the case is called for oral argument or by leave of the Court thereafter.

7. After a case has been argued or submitted, the Clerk will not file any brief, except that of a party filed by leave of the Court.

8. The Clerk will not file any brief that is not accompanied by proof of service as required by Rule 29.

9. An electronic version of every brief on the merits shall be transmitted to the Clerk of Court and to opposing counsel of record at the time the brief is filed in accordance with guidelines established by the Clerk. The electronic transmission requirement is in addition to the requirement that booklet-format briefs be timely filed.

Rule 26. Joint Appendix

1. Unless the Clerk has allowed the parties to use the deferred method described in paragraph 4 of this Rule, the petitioner or appellant, within 45 days after entry of the order granting the writ of certiorari, noting probable jurisdiction, or postponing consideration of jurisdiction, shall file 40 copies of a joint appendix, prepared as required by Rule 33.1. The joint appendix shall contain: (1) the relevant docket entries in all the courts below; (2) any relevant pleadings, jury instructions, findings, conclusions, or opinions; (3) the judgment, order, or decision under review; and (4) any other parts of the record that the parties particularly wish to bring to the Court's attention. Any of the foregoing items already reproduced in a petition for a writ of certiorari, jurisdictional statement, brief in opposition to a petition for a writ of certiorari, motion to dismiss or affirm, or any appendix to the foregoing, that was prepared as required by Rule 33.1, need not be reproduced again in the joint appendix. The petitioner or appellant shall serve three copies of the joint appendix on each of the other parties to the proceeding as required by Rule 29.

2. The parties are encouraged to agree on the contents of the joint appendix. In the absence of agreement, the petitioner or appellant, within 10 days after entry of the order granting the writ of certiorari, noting probable jurisdiction, or postponing consideration of jurisdiction, shall serve on the respondent or appellee a designation of parts of the record to be included in the joint appendix. Within 10 days after receiving the designation, a respondent or appellee who considers the parts of the record so designated insufficient shall serve on the petitioner or appellant a designation of additional parts to be included in the joint appendix, and the petitioner or appellant shall include the parts so designated. If the Court has permitted the respondent or appellee to proceed *in forma pauperis*, the petitioner or appellant may seek by motion to be excused from printing portions of the record the petitioner or appellant considers unnecessary. In making these designations, counsel should include only those materials the Court should examine;

unnecessary designations should be avoided. The record is on file with the Clerk and available to the Justices, and counsel may refer in briefs and in oral argument to relevant portions of the record not included in the joint appendix.

3. When the joint appendix is filed, the petitioner or appellant immediately shall file with the Clerk a statement of the cost of printing 50 copies and shall serve a copy of the statement on each of the other parties as required by Rule 29. Unless the parties agree otherwise, the cost of producing the joint appendix shall be paid initially by the petitioner or appellant; but a petitioner or appellant who considers that parts of the record designated by the respondent or appellee are unnecessary for the determination of the issues presented may so advise the respondent or appellee, who then shall advance the cost of printing the additional parts, unless the Court or a Justice otherwise fixes the initial allocation of the costs. The cost of printing the joint appendix is taxed as a cost in the case, but if a party unnecessarily causes matter to be included in the joint appendix or prints excessive copies, the Court may impose these costs on that party.

4. (a) On the parties' request, the Clerk may allow preparation of the joint appendix to be deferred until after the briefs have been filed. In that event, the petitioner or appellant shall file the joint appendix no more than 14 days after receiving the brief for the respondent or appellee. The provisions of paragraphs 1, 2, and 3 of this Rule shall be followed, except that the designations referred to therein shall be made by each party when that party's brief is served. Deferral of the joint appendix is not favored.

(b) If the deferred method is used, the briefs on the merits may refer to the pages of the record. In that event, the joint appendix shall include in brackets on each page thereof the page number of the record where that material may be found. A party wishing to refer directly to the pages of the joint appendix may serve and file copies of its brief prepared as required by Rule 33.2 within the time provided by Rule 25, with appropriate references to the pages of the record. In that event, within 10 days after the joint appendix is filed, copies of the brief prepared as required by Rule 33.1 containing references to the pages of the joint appendix in place of, or in addition to, the initial references to the pages of the record, shall be served and filed. No other change may be made in the brief as initially served and filed, except that typographical errors may be corrected.

5. The joint appendix shall be prefaced by a table of contents showing the parts of the record that it contains, in the order in which the parts are set out, with references to the pages of the joint appendix at which each part begins. The relevant docket entries shall be set out after the table of contents, followed by the other parts of the record in chronological order. When testimony contained in the reporter's transcript of proceedings is set out in the joint appendix, the page of the transcript at which the testimony appears shall be indicated in brackets immediately before the statement that is set out. Omissions in the transcript or in any other document printed in the joint appendix shall be indicated by asterisks. Immaterial formal matters (*e. g.*, captions, subscriptions, acknowledgments) shall be omitted. A question and its answer may be contained in a single paragraph.

6. Two lines must appear at the bottom of the cover of the joint appendix: (1) The first line must indicate the date the petition for the writ of certiorari was filed or the date the appeal was docketed; (2) the second line must indicate the date certiorari was granted or the date jurisdiction of the appeal was noted or postponed.

7. Exhibits designated for inclusion in the joint appendix may be contained in a separate volume or volumes suitably indexed. The transcript of a proceeding before an administrative agency, board, commission, or officer used in an action in a district court or court of appeals is regarded as an exhibit for the purposes of this paragraph.

8. The Court, on its own motion or that of a party, may dispense with the requirement of a joint appendix and may permit a case to be heard on the original record (with such copies of the record, or relevant parts thereof, as the Court may require) or on the appendix used in the court below, if it conforms to the requirements of this Rule.

9. For good cause, the time limits specified in this Rule may be shortened or extended by the Court or a Justice, or by the Clerk under Rule 30.4.

Rule 27. Calendar

1. From time to time, the Clerk will prepare a calendar of cases ready for argument. A case ordinarily will not be called for argument less than two weeks after the brief on the merits for the respondent or appellee is due.

2. The Clerk will advise counsel when they are required to appear for oral argument and will publish a hearing list in advance of each argument session for the convenience of counsel and the information of the public.

3. The Court, on its own motion or that of a party, may order that two or more cases involving the same or related questions be argued together as one case or on such other terms as the Court may prescribe.

Rule 28. Oral Argument

1. Oral argument should emphasize and clarify the written arguments in the briefs on the merits. Counsel should assume that all Justices have read the briefs before oral argument. Oral argument read from a prepared text is not favored.

2. The petitioner or appellant shall open and may conclude the argument. A cross-writ of certiorari or cross-appeal will be argued with the initial writ of certiorari or appeal as one case in the time allowed

for that one case, and the Court will advise the parties who shall open and close.

3. Unless the Court directs otherwise, each side is allowed one-half hour for argument. Counsel is not required to use all the allotted time. Any request for additional time to argue shall be presented by motion under Rule 21 in time to be considered at a scheduled Conference prior to the date of oral argument and no later than 7 days after the respondent's or appellee's brief on the merits is filed, and shall set out specifically and concisely why the case cannot be presented within the half-hour limitation. Additional time is rarely accorded.

4. Only one attorney will be heard for each side, except by leave of the Court on motion filed in time to be considered at a scheduled Conference prior to the date of oral argument and no later than 7 days after the respondent's or appellee's brief on the merits is filed. Any request for divided argument shall be presented by motion under Rule 21 and shall set out specifically and concisely why more than one attorney should be allowed to argue. Divided argument is not favored.

5. Regardless of the number of counsel participating in oral argument, counsel making the opening argument shall present the case fairly and completely and not reserve points of substance for rebuttal.

6. Oral argument will not be allowed on behalf of any party for whom a brief has not been filed.

7. By leave of the Court, and subject to paragraph 4 of this Rule, counsel for an *amicus curiae* whose brief has been filed as provided in Rule 37 may argue orally on the side of a party, with the consent of that party. In the absence of consent, counsel for an *amicus curiae* may seek leave of the Court to argue orally by a motion setting out specifically and concisely why oral argument would provide assistance to the Court not otherwise available. Such a motion will be granted only in the most extraordinary circumstances.

8. Oral arguments may be presented only by members of the Bar of this Court. Attorneys who are not members of the Bar of this Court may make a motion to argue *pro hac vice* under the provisions of Rule 6.

PART VII. PRACTICE AND PROCEDURE

Rule 29. Filing and Service of Documents; Special Notifications; Corporate Disclosure Statement

1. Any document required or permitted to be presented to the Court or to a Justice shall be filed with the Clerk.

2. A document is timely filed if it is received by the Clerk within the time specified for filing; or if it is sent to the Clerk through the United States Postal Service by first-class mail (including express or priority mail), postage prepaid, and bears a postmark, other than a commercial postage meter label, showing that the document was mailed on or before the last day for filing; or if it is delivered on or before the last day for filing to a third-party commercial carrier for delivery to the Clerk within 3 calendar days. If submitted by an inmate confined in an institution, a document is timely filed if it is deposited in the institution's internal mail system on or before the last day for filing and is accompanied by a notarized statement or declaration in compliance with 28 U.S.C. § 1746 setting out the date of deposit and stating that first-class postage has been prepaid. If the postmark is missing or not legible, or if the third-party commercial carrier does not provide the date the document was received by the carrier, the Clerk will require the person who sent the document to submit a notarized statement or declaration in compliance with 28 U.S.C. § 1746 setting out the details of the filing and stating that the filing took place on a particular date within the permitted time.

3. Any document required by these Rules to be served may be served personally, by mail, or by third-party commercial carrier for delivery within 3 calendar days on each party to the proceeding at or before the time of filing. If the document has been prepared as required by Rule 33.1, three copies shall be served on each other party separately represented in the proceeding. If the document has been prepared as required by Rule 33.2, service of a single copy on each other separately represented party suffices. If personal service is made, it shall consist of delivery at the office of the counsel of record, either to counsel or to an employee therein. If service is by mail or third-party commercial carrier, it shall consist of depositing the document with the United States Postal Service, with no less than first-class postage prepaid, or delivery to the carrier for delivery within 3 calendar days, addressed to counsel of record at the proper address. When a party is not represented by counsel, service shall be made on the party, personally, by mail, or by commercial carrier. Ordinarily, service on a party must be by a manner at least as expeditious as the manner used to file the document with the Court. An electronic version of the document shall also be transmitted to all other parties at the time of filing or reasonably contemporaneous therewith, unless the party filing the document is proceeding *pro se* and *in forma pauperis* or the electronic service address of the party being served is unknown and not identifiable through reasonable efforts.

4. (a) If the United States or any federal department, office, agency, officer, or employee is a party to be served, service shall be made on the Solicitor General of the United States, Room 5614, Department of Justice, 950 Pennsylvania Ave., N. W., Washington, DC 20530-0001. When an agency of the United States that is a party is authorized by law to appear before this Court on its own behalf, or when

an officer or employee of the United States is a party, the agency, officer, or employee shall be served in addition to the Solicitor General.

(b) In any proceeding in this Court in which the constitutionality of an Act of Congress is drawn into question, and neither the United States nor any federal department, office, agency, officer, or employee is a party, the initial document filed in this Court shall recite that 28 U.S.C. § 2403(a) may apply and shall be served on the Solicitor General of the United States, Room 5614, Department of Justice, 950 Pennsylvania Ave., N. W., Washington, DC 20530-0001. In such a proceeding from any court of the United States, as defined by 28 U.S.C. § 451, the initial document also shall state whether that court, pursuant to 28 U.S.C. § 2403(a), certified to the Attorney General the fact that the constitutionality of an Act of Congress was drawn into question. See Rule 14.1(e)(v).

(c) In any proceeding in this Court in which the constitutionality of any statute of a State is drawn into question, and neither the State nor any agency, officer, or employee thereof is a party, the initial document filed in this Court shall recite that 28 U.S.C. § 2403(b) may apply and shall be served on the Attorney General of that State. In such a proceeding from any court of the United States, as defined by 28 U.S.C. § 451, the initial document also shall state whether that court, pursuant to 28 U.S.C. § 2403(b), certified to the State Attorney General the fact that the constitutionality of a statute of that State was drawn into question. See Rule 14.1(e)(v).

5. Proof of service, when required by these Rules, shall accompany the document when it is presented to the Clerk for filing and shall be separate from it. Proof of service shall contain, or be accompanied by, a statement that all parties required to be served have been served, together with a list of the names, addresses, and telephone numbers of counsel indicating the name of the party or parties each counsel represents. It is not necessary that service on each party required to be served be made in the same manner or evidenced by the same proof. Proof of service may consist of any one of the following:

(a) an acknowledgment of service, signed by counsel of record for the party served, and bearing the address and telephone number of such counsel;

(b) a certificate of service, reciting the facts and circumstances of service in compliance with the appropriate paragraph or paragraphs of this Rule, and signed by a member of the Bar of this Court representing the party on whose behalf service is made or by an attorney appointed to represent that party under the Criminal Justice Act of 1964, see 18 U.S.C. § 3006A(d)(6), or under any other applicable federal statute; or

(c) a notarized affidavit or declaration in compliance with 28 U.S.C. § 1746, reciting the facts and circumstances of service in accordance with the appropriate paragraph or paragraphs of this Rule, whenever service is made by any person not a member of the Bar of this Court and not an attorney appointed to represent a party under the Criminal Justice Act of 1964, see 18 U.S.C. § 3006A(d)(6), or under any other applicable federal statute.

6. Every document, except a joint appendix or amicus curiae brief, filed by or on behalf of a nongovernmental corporation shall contain a corporate disclosure statement identifying the parent corporations and listing any publicly held company that owns 10% or more of the corporation's stock. If there is no parent or publicly held company owning 10% or more of the corporation's stock, a notation to this effect shall be included in the document. If a statement has been included in a document filed earlier in the case, reference may be made to the earlier document (except when the earlier statement appeared in a document prepared under Rule 33.2), and only amendments to the statement to make it current need be included in the document being filed. In addition, whenever there is a material change in the identity of the parent corporation or publicly held companies that own 10% or more of the corporation's stock, counsel shall promptly inform the Clerk by letter and include, within that letter, any amendment needed to make the statement current.

Rule 30. Computation and Extension of Time

1. In the computation of any period of time prescribed or allowed by these Rules, by order of the Court, or by an applicable statute, the day of the act, event, or default from which the designated period begins to run is not included. The last day of the period shall be included, unless it is a Saturday, Sunday, federal legal holiday listed in 5 U.S.C. § 6103, or day on which the Court building is closed by order of the Court or the Chief Justice, in which event the period shall extend until the end of the next day that is not a Saturday, Sunday, federal legal holiday, or day on which the Court building is closed.

2. Whenever a Justice or the Clerk is empowered by law or these Rules to extend the time to file any document, an application seeking an extension shall be filed within the period sought to be extended. An application to extend the time to file a petition for a writ of certiorari or to file a jurisdictional statement must be filed at least 10 days before the specified final filing date as computed under these Rules; if filed less than 10 days before the final filing date, such application will not be granted except in the most extraordinary circumstances.

3. An application to extend the time to file a petition for a writ of certiorari, to file a jurisdictional statement, to file a reply brief on the merits, or to file a petition for rehearing of any judgment or decision of the Court on the merits shall be made to an individual Justice and presented and served on all other parties as provided by Rule 22. Once denied, such an application may not be renewed.

4. An application to extend the time to file any document or paper other than those specified in paragraph 3 of this Rule may be presented in the form of a letter to the Clerk setting out specific reasons why an extension of time is justified. The letter shall be served on all other parties as required by Rule 29. The application may be acted on by the Clerk in the first instance, and any party aggrieved by the Clerk's action may request that the application be submitted to a Justice or to the Court. The Clerk will report action under this paragraph to the Court as instructed.

Rule 31. Translations

Whenever any record to be transmitted to this Court contains material written in a foreign language without a translation made under the authority of the lower court, or admitted to be correct, the clerk of the court transmitting the record shall advise the Clerk of this Court immediately so that this Court may order that a translation be supplied and, if necessary, printed as part of the joint appendix.

Rule 32. Models, Diagrams, Exhibits, and Lodgings

1. Models, diagrams, and exhibits of material forming part of the evidence taken in a case and brought to this Court for its inspection shall be placed in the custody of the Clerk at least two weeks before the case is to be heard or submitted.

2. All models, diagrams, exhibits, and other items placed in the custody of the Clerk shall be removed by the parties no more than 40 days after the case is decided. If this is not done, the Clerk will notify counsel to remove the articles forthwith. If they are not removed within a reasonable time thereafter, the Clerk will destroy them or dispose of them in any other appropriate way.

3. Any party or *amicus curiae* desiring to lodge non-record material with the Clerk must set out in a letter, served on all parties, a description of the material proposed for lodging and the reasons why the non-record material may properly be considered by the Court. The material proposed for lodging may not be submitted until and unless requested by the Clerk.

Rule 33. Document Preparation: Booklet Format; 8½- by 11-Inch Paper Format

1. *Booklet Format:*

(a) Except for a document expressly permitted by these Rules to be submitted on 8½-by 11-inch paper, see, *e. g.*, Rules 21, 22, and 39, every document filed with the Court shall be prepared in a 6⅛-by 9¼-inch booklet format using a standard typesetting process (*e. g.*, hot metal, photocomposition, or computer typesetting) to produce text printed in typographic (as opposed to typewriter) characters. The process used must produce a clear, black image on white paper. The text must be reproduced with a clarity that equals or exceeds the output of a laser printer.

(b) The text of every booklet-format document, including any appendix thereto, shall be typeset in a Century family (*e. g.*, Century Expanded, New Century Schoolbook, or Century Schoolbook) 12-point type with 2-point or more leading between lines. Quotations in excess of 50 words shall be indented. The typeface of footnotes shall be 10-point type with 2-point or more leading between lines. The text of the document must appear on both sides of the page.

(c) Every booklet-format document shall be produced on paper that is opaque, unglazed, and not less than 60 pounds in weight, and shall have margins of at least three-fourths of an inch on all sides. The text field, including footnotes, may not exceed 4⅛ by 7⅛ inches. The document shall be bound firmly in at least two places along the left margin (saddle stitch or perfect binding preferred) so as to permit easy opening, and no part of the text should be obscured by the binding. Spiral, plastic, metal, or string bindings may not be used. Copies of patent documents, except opinions, may be duplicated in such size as is necessary in a separate appendix.

(d) Every booklet-format document shall comply with the word limits shown on the chart in subparagraph 1(g) of this Rule. The word limits do not include the questions presented, the list of parties and the corporate disclosure statement, the table of contents, the table of cited authorities, the listing of counsel at the end of the document, or any appendix. The word limits include footnotes. Verbatim quotations required under Rule 14.1(f) and Rule 24.1(f), if set out in the text of a brief rather than in the appendix, are also excluded. For good cause, the Court or a Justice may grant leave to file a document in excess of the word limits, but application for such leave is not favored. An application to exceed word limits shall comply with Rule 22 and must be received by the Clerk at least 15 days before the filing date of the document in question, except in the most extraordinary circumstances.

(e) Every booklet-format document shall have a suitable cover consisting of 65-pound weight paper in the color indicated on the chart in subparagraph 1(g) of this Rule. If a separate appendix to any document is filed, the color of its cover shall be the same as that of the cover of the document it supports. The Clerk will furnish a color chart upon request. Counsel shall ensure that there is adequate contrast between the printing and the color of the cover. A document filed by the United States, or by any other federal party represented by the Solicitor General, shall have a gray cover. A joint appendix, answer to a bill of complaint, motion for leave to intervene, and any other document not listed in subparagraph 1(g) of this Rule shall have a tan cover.

(f) Forty copies of a booklet-format document shall be filed.

(g) Word limits and cover colors for booklet-format

documents are as follows:

	Type of Document	Word Limits	Color of Cover
(i)	Petition for a Writ of Certiorari (Rule 14); Motion for Leave to File a Bill of Complaint and Brief in Support (Rule 17.3); Jurisdictional Statement (Rule 18.3); Petition for an Extraordinary Writ (Rule 20.2)	9,000	white
(ii)	Brief in Opposition (Rule 15.3); Brief in Opposition to Motion for Leave to File an Original Action (Rule 17.5); Motion to Dismiss or Affirm (Rule 18.6); Brief in Opposition to Mandamus or Prohibition (Rule 20.3(b)); Response to a Petition for Habeas Corpus (Rule 20.4); Respondent's Brief in Support of Certiorari (Rule 12.6)	9,000	orange
(iii)	Reply to Brief in Opposition (Rules 15.6 and 17.5); Brief Opposing a Motion to Dismiss or Affirm (Rule 18.8)	3,000	tan
(iv)	Supplemental Brief (Rules 15.8, 17, 18.10, and 25.5)	3,000	tan
(v)	Brief on the Merits for Petitioner or Appellant (Rule 24); Exceptions by Plaintiff to Report of Special Master (Rule 17)	15,000	light blue
(vi)	Brief on the Merits for Respondent or Appellee (Rule 24.2); Brief on the Merits for Respondent or Appellee Supporting Petitioner or Appellant (Rule 12.6); Exceptions by Party Other Than Plaintiff to Report of Special Master (Rule 17)	15,000	light red
(vii)	Reply Brief on the Merits (Rule 24.4)	6,000	yellow
(viii)	Reply to Plaintiff's Exceptions to Report of Special Master (Rule 17)	15,000	orange
(ix)	Reply to Exceptions by Party Other Than Plaintiff to Report of Special Master (Rule 17)	15,000	yellow
(x)	Brief for an *Amicus Curiae* at the Petition Stage or pertaining to a Motion for Leave to file a Bill of Complaint (Rule 37.2)	6,000	cream
(xi)	Brief for an *Amicus Curiae* in Support of the Plaintiff, Petitioner, or Appellant, or in Support of Neither Party, on the Merits or in an Original Action at the Exceptions Stage (Rule 37.3)	9,000	light green
(xii)	Brief for an *Amicus Curiae* in Support of the Defendant, Respondent, or Appellee, on the Merits or in an Original Action at the Exceptions Stage (Rule 37.3)	9,000	dark green
(xiii)	Petition for Rehearing (Rule 44)	3,000	tan

(h) A document prepared under Rule 33.1 must be accompanied by a certificate signed by the attorney, the unrepresented party, or the preparer of the document stating that the brief complies with the word limitations. The person preparing the certificate may rely on the word count of the word-processing system used to prepare the document. The word-processing system must be set to include footnotes in the word count. The certificate must state the number of words in the document. The certificate shall accompany the document when it is presented to the Clerk for filing and shall be separate from it. If the certificate is signed by a person other than a member of the Bar of this Court, the counsel of record, or the unrepresented party, it must contain a notarized affidavit or declaration in compliance with 28 U. S. C. § 1746.

2. *8½- by 11-Inch Paper Format:*

(a) The text of every document, including any appendix thereto, expressly permitted by these Rules to be presented to the Court on 8½- by 11-inch paper shall appear double spaced, except for indented quotations, which shall be single spaced, on opaque, unglazed, white paper. The document shall be stapled or bound at the upper left-hand corner. Copies, if required, shall be produced on the same type of paper and shall be legible. The original of any such document (except a motion to dismiss or affirm under Rule 18.6) shall be signed by the party proceeding *pro se* or by counsel of record who must be a member of the Bar of this Court or an attorney appointed under the Criminal Justice Act of 1964, see 18 U.S.C. § 3006A(d)(6), or under any other applicable federal statute. Subparagraph 1(g) of this Rule does not apply to documents prepared under this paragraph.

(b) Page limits for documents presented on 8½-by 11-inch paper are: 40 pages for a petition for a writ of certiorari, jurisdictional statement, petition for an extraordinary writ, brief in opposition, or motion to dismiss or affirm; and 15 pages for a reply to a brief in opposition, brief opposing a motion to dismiss or affirm, supplemental brief, or petition for rehearing. The exclusions specified in subparagraph 1(d) of this Rule apply.

Rule 34. Document Preparation: General Requirements

Every document, whether prepared under Rule 33.1 or Rule 33.2, shall comply with the following provisions:

1. Each document shall bear on its cover, in the order indicated, from the top of the page:

(a) the docket number of the case or, if there is none, a space for one;

(b) the name of this Court;

(c) the caption of the case as appropriate in this Court;

(d) the nature of the proceeding and the name of the court from which the action is brought (*e.g.*, "On Petition for Writ of Certiorari to the United States Court of Appeals for the Fifth Circuit"; or, for a merits brief, "On Writ of Certiorari to the United States Court of Appeals for the Fifth Circuit");

(e) the title of the document (*e.g.*, "Petition for Writ of Certiorari," "Brief for Respondent," "Joint Appendix");

(f) the name of the attorney who is counsel of record for the party concerned (who must be a member of the Bar of this Court except as provided in Rule 9.1) and on whom service is to be made, with a notation directly thereunder identifying the attorney as counsel of record and setting out counsel's office address, e-mail address, and telephone number. Only one counsel of record may be noted on a single document, except that counsel of record for each party must be listed on the cover of a joint appendix. The names of other members of the Bar of this Court or of the bar of the highest court of State acting as counsel, and, if desired, their addresses, may be added, but counsel of record shall be clearly identified. Names of persons other than attorneys admitted to a state bar may not be listed, unless the party is appearing *pro se,* in which case the party's name, address, and telephone number shall appear.

(g) The foregoing shall be displayed in an appropriate typographical manner and, except for identification of counsel, may not be set in type smaller than standard 11-point, if the document is prepared as required by Rule 33.1.

2. Every document (other than a joint appendix), that excees 1,500 words when prepared under Rule 33.1, or that exceeds five pages when prepared under Rule 33.2, shall contain a table of contents and a table of cited authorities (*i. e.*, cases alphabetically arranged, constitutional provisions, statutes, treatises, and other materials) with references to the pages in the document where such authorities are cited.

3. The body of every document shall bear at its close the name of counsel of record and such other counsel, identified on the cover of the document in conformity with subparagraph 1(g) of this Rule, as may be desired.

4. Every appendix to a document must be preceded by a table of contents that provides a description of each document in the appendix.

5. All references to a provision of federal statutory law should ordinarily be cited to the United States Code, if the provision has been codified therein. In the event the provision has not been classified to the United States Code, citation should be to the Statutes at Large. Additional or alternative citations should be provided only if there is a particular reason why those citations are relevant or necessary to the argument.

Rule 35. Death, Substitution, and Revivor; Public Officers

1. If a party dies after the filing of a petition for a writ of certiorari, or after the filing of a notice of appeal, the authorized representative of the deceased party may appear and, on motion, be substituted as a party. If the representative does not voluntarily become a party, any other party may suggest the death on the record and, on motion, seek an order requiring the representative to become a party within a designated time. If the representative then fails to become a party, the party so moving, if a respondent or appellee, is entitled to have the petition for a writ of certiorari or the appeal dismissed, and if a petitioner or appellant, is entitled to proceed as in any other case of nonappearance by a respondent or appellee. If the substitution of a representative of the deceased is not made within six months after the death of the party, the case shall abate.

2. Whenever a case cannot be revived in the court whose judgment is sought to be reviewed, because the deceased party's authorized representative is not subject to that court's jurisdiction, proceedings will be conducted as this Court may direct.

3. When a public officer who is a party to a proceeding in this Court in an official capacity dies, resigns, or otherwise ceases to hold office, the action does not abate and any successor in office is automatically substituted as a party. The parties shall notify the Clerk in writing of any such successions. Proceedings following the substitution shall be in the name of the substituted party, but any misnomer

not affecting substantial rights of the parties will be disregarded.

4. A public officer who is a party to a proceeding in this Court in an official capacity may be described as a party by the officer's official title rather than by name, but the Court may require the name to be added.

Rule 36. Custody of Prisoners in Habeas Corpus Proceedings

1. Pending review in this Court of a decision in a habeas corpus proceeding commenced before a court, Justice, or judge of the United States, the person having custody of the prisoner may not transfer custody to another person unless the transfer is authorized under this Rule.

2. Upon application by a custodian, the court, Justice, or judge who entered the decision under review may authorize transfer and the substitution of a successor custodian as a party.

3. (a) Pending review of a decision failing or refusing to release a prisoner, the prisoner may be detained in the custody from which release is sought or in other appropriate custody or may be enlarged on personal recognizance or bail, as may appear appropriate to the court, Justice, or judge who entered the decision, or to the court of appeals, this Court, or a judge or Justice of either court.

(b) Pending review of a decision ordering release, the prisoner shall be enlarged on personal recognizance or bail, unless the court, Justice, or judge who entered the decision, or the court of appeals, this Court, or a judge or Justice of either court, orders otherwise.

4. An initial order respecting the custody or enlargement of the prisoner, and any recognizance or surety taken, shall continue in effect pending review in the court of appeals and in this Court unless for reasons shown to the court of appeals, this Court, or a judge or Justice of either court, the order is modified or an independent order respecting custody, enlargement, or surety is entered.

Rule 37. Brief for an *Amicus Curiae*

1. An *amicus curiae* brief that brings to the attention of the Court relevant matter not already brought to its attention by the parties may be of considerable help to the Court. An *amicus curiae* brief that does not serve this purpose burdens the Court, and its filing is not favored. An *amicus curiae* brief may be filed only by an attorney admitted to practice before this Court as provided in Rule 5.

2. (a) An *amicus curiae* brief submitted before the Court's consideration of a petition for a writ of certiorari, motion for leave to file a bill of complaint, jurisdictional statement, or petition for an extraordinary writ may be filed if accompanied by the written consent of all parties, or if the Court grants leave to file under subparagraph 2(b) of this Rule. An *amicus curiae* brief in support of a petitioner or appellant shall be filed within 30 days after the case is placed on the docket or a response is called for by the Court, whichever is later, and that time will not be extended. An *amicus curiae* brief in support of a motion of a plaintiff for leave to file a bill of complaint in an original action shall be filed within 60 days after the case is placed on the docket, and that time will not be extended. An *amicus curiae* brief in support of a respondent, an appellee, or a defendant shall be submitted within the time allowed for filing a brief in opposition or a motion to dismiss or affirm. An *amicus curiae* filing a brief under this subparagraph shall ensure that the counsel of record for all parties receive notice of its intention to file an *amicus curiae* brief at least 10 days prior to the due date for the *amicus curiae* brief, unless the *amicus curiae* brief is filed earlier than 10 days before the due date. Only one signatory to any *amicus curiae* brief filed jointly by more than one *amicus curiae* must timely notify the parties of its intent to file that brief. The *amicus curiae* brief shall indicate that counsel of record received timely notice of the intent to file the brief under this Rule and shall specify whether consent was granted, and its cover shall identify the party supported. Only one signatory to an *amicus curiae* brief filed jointly by more than one *amicus curiae* must obtain consent of the parties to file that brief. A petitioner or respondent may submit to the Clerk a letter granting blanket consent to *amicus curiae* briefs, stating that the party consents to the filing of *amicus curiae* briefs in support of either or of neither party. The Clerk will note all notices of blanket consent on the docket.

(b) When a party to the case has withheld consent, a motion for leave to file an *amicus curiae* brief before the Court's consideration of a petition for a writ of certiorari, motion for leave to file a bill of complaint, jurisdictional statement, or petition for an extraordinary writ may be presented to the Court. The motion, prepared as required by Rule 33.1 and as one document with the brief sought to be filed, shall be submitted within the time allowed for filing an *amicus curiae* brief, and shall indicate the party or parties who have withheld consent and state the nature of the movant's interest. Such a motion is not favored.

3. (a) An *amicus curiae* brief in a case before the Court for oral argument may be filed if accompanied by the written consent of all parties, or if the Court grants leave to file under subparagraph 3(b) of this Rule. The brief shall be submitted within 7 days after the brief for the party supported is filed, or if in support of neither party, within 7 days after the time allowed for filing the petitioner's or appellant's brief. Motions to extend the time for filing an *amicus curiae* brief will not be entertained. The 10-day notice requirement of subparagraph 2(a) of this Rule does not apply to an *amicus curiae* brief in a case before the Court for oral argument. An electronic version of every *amicus curiae* brief in a case before the Court for oral argument shall be transmitted to the Clerk of Court and to counsel for the parties at

the time the brief is filed in accordance with guidelines established by the Clerk. The electronic transmission requirement is in addition to the requirement that booklet-format briefs be timely filed. The *amicus curiae* brief shall specify whether consent was granted, and its cover shall identify the party supported or indicate whether it suggests affirmance or reversal. The Clerk will not file a reply brief for an *amicus curiae*, or a brief for an *amicus curiae* in support of, or in opposition to, a petition for rehearing. Only one signatory to an *amicus curiae* brief filed jointly by more than one *amicus curiae* must obtain consent of the parties to file that brief. A petitioner or respondent may submit to the Clerk a letter granting blanket consent to *amicus curiae* briefs, stating that the party consents to the filing of *amicus curiae* briefs in support of either or of neither party. The Clerk will note all notices of blanket consent on the docket.

(b) When a party to a case before the Court for oral argument has withheld consent, a motion for leave to file an *amicus curiae* brief may be presented to the Court. The motion, prepared as required by Rule 33.1 and as one document with the brief sought to be filed, shall be submitted within the time allowed for filing an *amicus curiae* brief, and shall indicate the party or parties who have withheld consent and state the nature of the movant's interest.

4. No motion for leave to file an *amicus curiae* brief is necessary if the brief is presented on behalf of the United States by the Solicitor General; on behalf of any agency of the United States allowed by law to appear before this Court when submitted by the agency's authorized legal representative; on behalf of a State, Commonwealth, Territory, or Possession when submitted by its Attorney General; or on behalf of a city, county, town, or similar entity when submitted by its authorized law officer.

5. A brief or motion filed under this Rule shall be accompanied by proof of service as required by Rule 29, and shall comply with the applicable provisions of Rules 21, 24, and 33.1 (except that it suffices to set out in the brief the interest of the *amicus curiae*, the summary of the argument, the argument, and the conclusion). A motion for leave to file may not exceed 1,500 words. A party served with the motion may file an objection thereto, stating concisely the reasons for withholding consent; the objection shall be prepared as required by Rule 33.2.

6. Except for briefs presented on behalf of *amicus curiae* listed in Rule 37.4, a brief filed under this Rule shall indicate whether counsel for a party authored the brief in whole or in part and whether such counsel or a party made a monetary contribution intended to fund the preparation or submission of the brief, and shall identify every person other than the *amicus curiae*, its members, or its counsel, who made such a monetary contribution. The disclosure shall be made in the first footnote on the first page of text.

Rule 38. Fees

Under 28 U.S.C. § 1911, the fees charged by the Clerk are:

(a) for docketing a case on a petition for a writ of certiorari or on appeal or for docketing any other proceeding, except a certified question or a motion to docket and dismiss an appeal under Rule 18.5, $300;

(b) for filing a petition for rehearing or a motion for leave to file a petition for rehearing, $200;

(c) for reproducing and certifying any record or paper, $1 per page; and for comparing with the original thereof any photographic reproduction of any record or paper, when furnished by the person requesting its certification, $.50 per page;

(d) for a certificate bearing the seal of the Court, $10; and

(e) for a check paid to the Court, Clerk, or Marshal that is returned for lack of funds, $35.

Rule 39. Proceedings *In Forma Pauperis*

1. A party seeking to proceed *in forma pauperis* shall file a motion for leave to do so, together with the party's notarized affidavit or declaration (in compliance with 28 U.S.C. § 1746) in the form prescribed by the Federal Rules of Appellate Procedure, Form 4. The motion shall state whether leave to proceed *in forma pauperis* was sought in any other court and, if so, whether leave was granted. If the court below appointed counsel for an indigent party, no affidavit or declaration is required, but the motion shall cite the provision of law under which counsel was appointed, or a copy of the order of appointment shall be appended to the motion.

2. If leave to proceed *in forma pauperis* is sought for the purpose of filing a document, the motion, and an affidavit or declaration if required, shall be filed together with that document and shall comply in every respect with Rule 21. As provided in that Rule, it suffices to file an original and 10 copies, unless the party is an inmate confined in an institution and is not represented by counsel, in which case the original, alone, suffices. A copy of the motion, and affidavit or declaration if required, shall precede and be attached to each copy of the accompanying document.

3. Except when these Rules expressly provide that a document shall be prepared as required by Rule 33.1, every document presented by a party proceeding under this Rule shall be prepared as required by Rule 33.2 (unless such preparation is impossible). Every document shall be legible. While making due allowance for any case presented under this Rule by a person appearing *pro se*, the Clerk will not file any document if it does not comply with the substance of these Rules or is jurisdictionally out of time.

4. When the documents required by paragraphs 1 and 2 of this Rule are presented to the Clerk, accompanied by proof of service as required by Rule 29, they will be placed on the docket without the payment of a docket fee or any other fee.

5. The respondent or appellee in a case filed *in forma pauperis* shall respond in the same manner and within the same time as in any other case of the same nature, except that the filing of an original and 10 copies of a response prepared as required by Rule 33.2, with proof of service as required by Rule 29, suffices. The respondent or appellee may challenge the grounds for the motion for leave to proceed *in forma pauperis* in a separate document or in the response itself.

6. Whenever the Court appoints counsel for an indigent party in a case set for oral argument, the briefs on the merits submitted by that counsel, unless otherwise requested, shall be prepared under the Clerk's supervision. The Clerk also will reimburse appointed counsel for any necessary travel expenses to Washington, D. C., and return in connection with the argument.

7. In a case in which certiorari has been granted, probable jurisdiction noted, or consideration of jurisdiction postponed, this Court may appoint counsel to represent a party financially unable to afford an attorney to the extent authorized by the Criminal Justice Act of 1964, 18 U.S.C. § 3006A, or by any other applicable federal statute.

8. If satisfied that a petition for a writ of certiorari, jurisdictional statement, or petition for an extraordinary writ is frivolous or malicious, the Court may deny leave to proceed *in forma pauperis*.

Rule 40. Veterans, Seamen, and Military Cases

1. A veteran suing under any provision of law exempting veterans from the payment of fees or court costs, may proceed without prepayment of fees or costs or furnishing security therefor and may file a motion for leave to proceed on papers prepared as required by Rule 33.2. The motion shall ask leave to proceed as a veteran and be accompanied by an affidavit or declaration setting out the moving party's veteran status. A copy of the motion shall precede and be attached to each copy of the petition for a writ of certiorari or other substantive document filed by the veteran.

2. A seaman suing under 28 U. S. C. § 1916 may proceed without prepayment of fees or costs or furnishing security therefor and may file a motion for leave to proceed on papers prepared as required by Rule 33.2. The motion shall ask leave to proceed as a seaman and be accompanied by an affidavit or declaration setting out the moving party's seaman status. A copy of the motion shall precede and be attached to each copy of the petition for a writ of certiorari or other substantive document filed by the seaman.

3. An accused person petitioning for a writ of certiorari to review a decision of the United States Court of Appeals for the Armed Forces under 28 U.S.C. § 1259 may proceed without prepayment of fees or costs or furnishing security therefor and without filing an affidavit of indigency, but is not entitled to proceed on papers prepared as required by Rule 33.2, except as authorized by the Court on separate motion under Rule 39.

PART VIII. DISPOSITION OF CASES

Rule 41. Opinions of the Court

Opinions of the Court will be released by the Clerk immediately upon their announcement from the bench, or as the Court otherwise directs. Thereafter, the Clerk will cause the opinions to be issued in slip form, and the Reporter of Decisions will prepare them for publication in the preliminary prints and bound volumes of the United States Reports.

Rule 42. Interest and Damages

1. If a judgment for money in a civil case is affirmed, any interest allowed by law is payable from the date the judgment under review was entered. If a judgment is modified or reversed with a direction that a judgment for money be entered below, the courts below may award interest to the extent permitted by law. Interest in cases arising in a state court is allowed at the same rate that similar judgments bear interest in the courts of the State in which judgment is directed to be entered. Interest in cases arising in a court of the United States is allowed at the interest rate authorized by law.

2. When a petition for a writ of certiorari, an appeal, or an application for other relief is frivolous, the Court may award the respondent or appellee just damages, and single or double costs under Rule 43. Damages or costs may be awarded against the petitioner, appellant, or applicant, against the party's counsel, or against both party and counsel.

Rule 43. Costs

1. If the Court affirms a judgment, the petitioner or appellant shall pay costs unless the Court otherwise orders.

2. If the Court reverses or vacates a judgment, the respondent or appellee shall pay costs unless the Court otherwise orders.

3. The Clerk's fees and the cost of printing the joint appendix are the only taxable items in this Court. The cost of the transcript of the record from the court below is also a taxable item, but shall be taxable in that court as costs in the case. The expenses of printing briefs, motions, petitions, or jurisdictional statements are not taxable.

4. In a case involving a certified question, costs are equally divided unless the Court otherwise orders, except that if the Court decides the whole matter in controversy, as permitted by Rule 19.2, costs are allowed as provided in paragraphs 1 and 2 of this Rule.

5. To the extent permitted by 28 U.S.C. § 2412, costs under this Rule are allowed for or against the

United States or an officer or agent thereof, unless expressly waived or unless the Court otherwise orders.

6. When costs are allowed in this Court, the Clerk will insert an itemization of the costs in the body of the mandate or judgment sent to the court below. The prevailing side may not submit a bill of costs.

7. In extraordinary circumstances the Court may adjudge double costs.

Rule 44. Rehearing

1. Any petition for the rehearing of any judgment or decision of the Court on the merits shall be filed within 25 days after entry of the judgment or decision, unless the Court or a Justice shortens or extends the time. The petitioner shall file 40 copies of the rehearing petition and shall pay the filing fee prescribed by Rule 38(b), except that a petitioner proceeding *in forma pauperis* under Rule 39, including an inmate of an institution, shall file the number of copies required for a petition by such a person under Rule 12.2. The petition shall state its grounds briefly and distinctly and shall be served as required by Rule 29. The petition shall be presented together with certification of counsel (or of a party unrepresented by counsel) that it is presented in good faith and not for delay; one copy of the certificate shall bear the signature of counsel (or of a party unrepresented by counsel). A copy of the certificate shall follow and be attached to each copy of the petition. A petition for rehearing is not subject to oral argument and will not be granted except by a majority of the Court, at the instance of a Justice who concurred in the judgment or decision.

2. Any petition for the rehearing of an order denying a petition for a writ of certiorari or extraordinary writ shall be filed within 25 days after the date of the order of denial and shall comply with all the form and filing requirements of paragraph 1 of this Rule, including the payment of the filing fee if required, but its grounds shall be limited to intervening circumstances of a substantial or controlling effect or to other substantial grounds not previously presented. The time for filing a petition for the rehearing of an order denying a petition for a writ of certiorari or extraordinary writ will not be extended. The petition shall be presented together with certification of counsel (or of a party unrepresented by counsel) that it is restricted to the grounds specified in this paragraph and that it is presented in good faith and not for delay; one copy of the certificate shall bear the signature of counsel (or of a party unrepresented by counsel). The certificate shall be bound with each copy of the petition. The Clerk will not file a petition without a certificate. The petition is not subject to oral argument.

3. The Clerk will not file any response to a petition for rehearing unless the Court requests a response. In the absence of extraordinary circumstances, the Court will not grant a petition for rehearing without first requesting a response.

4. The Clerk will not file consecutive petitions and petitions that are out of time under this Rule.

5. The Clerk will not file any brief for an *amicus curiae* in support of, or in opposition to, a petition for rehearing.

6. If the Clerk determines that a petition for rehearing submitted timely and in good faith is in a form that does not comply with this Rule or with Rule 33 or Rule 34, the Clerk will return it with a letter indicating the deficiency. A corrected petition for rehearing submitted in accordance with Rule 29.2 no more than 15 days after the date of the Clerk's letter will be deemed timely.

Rule 45. Process; Mandates

1. All process of this Court issues in the name of the President of the United States.

2. In a case on review from a state court, the mandate issues 25 days after entry of the judgment, unless the Court or a Justice shortens or extends the time, or unless the parties stipulate that it issue sooner. The filing of a petition for rehearing stays the mandate until disposition of the petition, unless the Court orders otherwise. If the petition is denied, the mandate issues forthwith.

3. In a case on review from any court of the United States, as defined by 28 U.S.C. § 451, a formal mandate does not issue unless specially directed; instead, the Clerk of this Court will send the clerk of the lower court a copy of the opinion or order of this Court and a certified copy of the judgment. The certified copy of the judgment, prepared and signed by this Court's Clerk, will provide for costs if any are awarded. In all other respects, the provisions of paragraph 2 of this Rule apply.

Rule 46. Dismissing Cases

1. At any stage of the proceedings, whenever all parties file with the Clerk an agreement in writing that a case be dismissed, specifying the terms for payment of costs, and pay to the Clerk any fees then due, the Clerk, without further reference to the Court, will enter an order of dismissal.

2. (a) A petitioner or appellant may file a motion to dismiss the case, with proof of service as required by Rule 29, tendering to the Clerk any fees due and costs payable. No more than 15 days after service thereof, an adverse party may file an objection, limited to the amount of damages and costs in this Court alleged to be payable or to showing that the moving party does not represent all petitioners or appellants. The Clerk will not file any objection not so limited.

(b) When the objection asserts that the moving party does not represent all the petitioners or appellants, the party moving for dismissal may file a reply within 10 days, after which time the matter will be submitted to the Court for its determination.

(c) If no objection is filed—or if upon objection going only to the amount of damages and costs in this Court, the party moving for dismissal tenders the additional damages and costs in full within 10 days of the demand therefor—the Clerk, without further reference to the Court, will enter an order of dismissal. If, after objection as to the amount of damages and costs in this Court, the moving party does not respond by a tender within 10 days, the Clerk will report the matter to the Court for its determination.

3. No mandate or other process will issue on a dismissal under this Rule without an order of the Court.

PART IX. DEFINITIONS AND EFFECTIVE DATE

Rule 47. Reference to "State Court" and "State Law"

The term "state court," when used in these Rules, includes the District of Columbia Court of Appeals, the Supreme Court of the Commonwealth of Puerto Rico, the courts of the Northern Mariana Islands, the local courts of Guam, and the Supreme Court of the Virgin Islands. References in these Rules to the statutes of a State include the statutes of the District of Columbia, the Commonwealth of Puerto Rico, the Commonwealth of the Northern Mariana Islands, the Territory of Guam, and the Territory of the Virgin Islands.

Rule 48. Effective Date of Rules

1. These Rules, adopted April 19, 2013, will be effective July 1, 2013.

2. The Rules govern all proceedings after their effective date except to the extent that, in the opinion of the Court, their application to a pending matter would not be feasible or would work an injustice, in which event the former procedure applies.

Index to Federal Rules of Court

A

C

F

Index

Index

Index

Index

J

S

U

Notes

Notes